ADVERTISING RESEARCH: THEORY AND PRACTICE

ADVERTISING RESEARCH: THEORY AND PRACTICE

Joel J. Davis
School of Communication
College of Professional Studies and Fine Arts
San Diego State University

Prentice Hall, Upper Saddle River, NJ 07458

Acquisitions Editor: David Borkowsky
Assistant Editor: John Larkin
Editorial Assistant: Theresa Festa
Editor-in-Chief: James Boyd
Director of Development: Steve Deitmer
Marketing Manager: John Chillingworth
Production Editor: Aileen Mason
Production Coordinator: Renee Pelletier
Managing Editor: Valerie Q. Lentz
Manufacturing Buyer: Kenneth J. Clinton
Manufacturing Supervisor: Arnold Vila
Manufacturing Manager: Vincent Scelta
Senior Designer: Ann France
Design Director: Patricia Wosczyk
Cover Design: Bruce Kenselaar
Composition: Maryland Composition Company, Inc.

Copyright © 1997 by Prentice-Hall, Inc.
A Simon & Schuster Company
Upper Saddle River, New Jersey 07458

Library of Congress Cataloging-in-Publication Data
Davis, Joel J.
     Advertising research : theory and practice/Joel J. Davis.
       p. cm.
     Includes bibliographical references and index.
     ISBN 0-13-221813-5
     1. Advertising—Research.   2. Advertising—Research—United States. I. Title.
     HF5814.D38 1997
     659.1′072—dc21   96-45163
                                              CIP

Prentice-Hall International (UK) Limited, London
Prentice-Hall of Australia Pty. Limited, Sydney
Prentice-Hall Canada, Inc., Toronto
Prentice-Hall Hispanoamericana, S.A., Mexico
Prentice-Hall of India Private Limited, New Delhi
Prentice-Hall of Japan, Inc., Tokyo
Simon & Schuster Asia Pte. Ltd., Singapore
Editora Prentice-Hall do Brasil, Ltda., Rio de Janeiro

Printed in the United States of America

10 9 8 7 6 5 4 3 2

With love,
To Danna, who makes each day a new and wonderful experience.
To Kyle and McKenna, who make me smile and who make life a joy.
To Rebecca Emily (the boo-boo dog), who makes us all laugh.

Brief
Contents

Contents

Preface

Many students enter my research class believing the following:

- Learning about research is useless and unnecessary unless you want to be a researcher.
- Research is the same as number crunching; research and statistics are one and the same.
- Research is the antithesis of creative.

Over the course of the semester I try to show my students that each of these statements is, in fact, false. This text is my attempt to convince you of the same.

Advertising Research Touches Everyone in the Advertising Business

As an advertising professional, you will encounter and use research in one of two ways. If you decide to become a research specialist, you will be responsible for the planning, execution, analysis, and presentation of research findings. It will be your job to provide the information others need to make the best advertising and marketing related decisions. However, if you decide to take a position in a different department of an agency, such as account management, media, or creative, you will be a research user. You will use the information gathered by others to help you make better decisions and to help you do your job more efficiently and successfully.

In short, regardless of the type of position you take in the advertising industry, you will either be a user or a creator of research. *Advertising Research: Theory and Practice* will help you in both capacities. This text will teach you how to use and design research. You will also learn how to evaluate the soundness of the information gathered by research and how to evaluate the appropriateness of various research techniques for different informational needs. Most important, you will learn that better advertising decision making occurs when you are able to support your professional judgment with research insights.

Research is not the esoteric function of an agency research department. It is a vital, ongoing activity used by successful advertisers to outsmart, outmaneuver, and surpass their competition.

Research Is Not the Same As Number Crunching

It is important for you to understand that not all research is numeric. Focus groups and similar forms of research do not even use numbers to summarize the research findings.

Other types of research are numeric. Quantitative research entails numeric manipulation, calculations, and the application of statistical techniques. However, these are only the tools that one uses to find out what the numbers mean and imply for the decisions that need to be made.

Research, therefore, is not number crunching, nor is it the rote and unthinking application of sets of principles or directives. Computers can quickly do the math. However, computers cannot tell us what the numbers mean nor what their implications are for the decisions that must be made. Thinking, insightful people are needed to bring meaning to the numbers and words collected in a research project. As a consequence, successful advertising researchers *are not* necessarily those who are good at math. Successful advertising researchers *are* those individuals who are good at thinking, finding patterns, and explaining what a finding *means* as opposed to what it *says*.

Advertising Research: Theory and Practice emphasizes the interpretation of research. The text tries to show you how analysis, especially numeric analysis, leads to insights and better decisions. It views numeric analyses as a means to the discovery of insights, rather than an end in themselves.

The Best Research Is Creative Research

Advertising Research: Theory and Practice comes from the perspective that the planning, conduct, analysis, and presentation of research is, indeed, a creative process. As you read the text, you will see that it takes a great deal of creativity to clearly identify a research problem, design the most appropriate research study, create the most useful questionnaire or interview guide, and analyze and present the findings in a way that maximizes the usefulness of those findings.

It is easy to design bad research. It is easy to present research findings that decision makers ignore because the findings are viewed as simplistic or irrelevant. Creative research is much more difficult to design, interpret, and present, but the findings and insights provided by creative research are welcomed by advertising decision makers.

Advertising Research: Theory and Practice provides you with the knowledge and skills that you need to be a creative research end-user or creator. Each chapter includes numerous examples of the creative side of research.

READING THE TEXT

Every attempt has been made to make the information in *Advertising Research: Theory and Practice* useful and understandable. Nevertheless, some content is by its very nature difficult to understand. With this in mind, it is recommended that you begin the study of each chapter at the *end* of the chapter. Read the review questions before you read the chapter. This will help you identify key terms and concepts. Then read the application exercises. This will help you understand the type of real-world situations to which the chapter content is applicable. Then read the chapter. Finally, answer the review questions and any application exercises that you are assigned. Your postreading performance on the review questions and application exercises will help you understand what you have successfully learned and what ideas and concepts you need to review.

TO THE INSTRUCTOR

The advertising business is in a state of transition. Advertisers are faced with an increasingly diverse consumer population in which international and cultural challenges are more and more commonplace. Media decisions, once simple, are becoming increasingly complex as media options increase at an astonishing pace. Consumers, advertising's predominant target, are becoming more sophisticated, more questioning, and more resistant to advertising's influence. New products, supported by advertising, are entering the marketplace at an astonishing pace. In each of these areas, advertisers are increasingly turning to research to help them identify options and make decisions.

Advertising Research: Theory and Practice is designed to provide your students with the knowledge and skills necessary to be successful advertising professionals in the new advertising business. *Advertising Research: Theory and Practice* accomplishes this task by distinguishing itself from other advertising research texts in four important ways: breadth, depth, integration, and discussion of current issues.

The text's breadth can be seen in the table of contents. *Advertising Research: Theory and Practice* is the only advertising research text to provide *detailed* discussions of

- The analysis of qualitative data
- The analysis of quantitative data using inferential statistics
- Advertising content analysis
- Perceptual mapping
- Advertising spending analysis
- Q-sort methodology
- Concept and benefit testing
- Copy testing from a legal perspective
- Computer-assisted data analysis

The text's depth of discussion can be seen in every chapter. The chapters that address experimentation, sampling, qualitative research, consumer segmentation, communication research, and copy testing, for example, provide detailed discussions accompanied by illustrative examples to help the student acquire a thorough understanding of the content. The depth of discussion is also evident in the explanations of secondary source information. *Advertising Research: Theory and Practice,* for example, provides step-by-step explanations for interpreting and applying syndicated target audience information, media expenditures, and media audience measures.

Great effort has been made to integrate key topics throughout the text. Most research texts address the issues of research planning, analysis, and presentation in separate chapters. Once addressed, these topics are rarely referred to again. Similar to these texts, *Advertising Research: Theory and Practice* provides independent chapter coverage of these topics. However, unlike other advertising research texts, *Advertising Research: Theory and Practice* reviews and revisits these issues within the context of specific research applications, such as perceptual mapping, segmentation, and communication testing.

Finally, every attempt has been made to address current issues. *Advertising Research: Theory and Practice,* for example, addresses the use of the Internet and World Wide Web for secondary research and the issue of interactive and Internet audience measurement.

Fostering Student Learning

Advertising Research: Theory and Practice has been written and structured with the goals of improving student learning and facilitating the application of learned material to new situations. Some of the features of the text that help achieve these goals are

- A clear and direct writing style that makes complex concepts accessible and understandable.
- Extensive use of advertising-related examples that support and extend the discussion in ways that clarify rather than confuse.
- Chapter introductions that clearly explain the topic addressed and identify chapter learning objectives.
- Chapter organization that moves the student from broader to more specific levels of discussion.
- Clear and concise chapter summaries.
- Chapter review questions that help students assess their acquisition of key concepts and ideas.
- Extensive chapter application exercises that help students extend their knowledge by responding to challenging, thought-provoking, "real-world" problems.
- Extensive chapter references that direct the student to additional sources of related information.

Text Organization

Advertising Research: Theory and Practice is divided into eight parts. This organization of the text, coupled with its breadth of coverage, provides a great deal of instructor flexibility. Chapter assignments can be sequenced to reflect course priorities and prior student course work.

The discussion in Parts 1 to 4 applies to all types of advertising research. The sixteen chapters presented there provide a foundation for understanding advertising research planning, research design, qualitative and quantitative research, data analysis, and data presentation.

Part 1 contains four chapters that provide an introduction to the context and conduct of advertising research. Chapter 1 provides a broad overview of how advertisers use research, the types of advertising-related questions typically addressed by research, and the types of individuals who participate in the research process. Chapter 2 describes the major steps and considerations related to the planning, conduct, and analysis of advertising research. Chapter 3 raises issues related to ethical considerations in the conduct of advertising research. These ethical considerations are addressed later in the text in the context of specific research techniques in Parts 5 to 8. Chapter 4 addresses research reporting with particular emphasis on the written and oral presentation of findings and conclusions.

Part 2 expands the information presented in the preceding chapters. Chapter 5 introduces the student to secondary research through discussion of traditional and electronic sources of information including the World Wide Web. This information is organized by advertising-related questions (for example, "How can I learn more about my target consumer?"), rather than the traditional organization by type of source (for example, printed materials, periodicals, etc.). This organization helps students focus on the use of information as opposed to the source of information. Chapter 6 provides a detailed discussion of primary advertising research options, with a particular focus on the types of qualitative and quantitative research techniques commonly used by advertising researchers, the most common types of survey research methods, and the types of errors that may occur in survey research. Chapters 7 and 8 provide a comprehensive discussion of experimentation and sampling, respectively.

Part 3 focuses on qualitative research. Chapter 9 discusses the planning and conduct of qualitative research and presents an extensive discussion of the goals and application of qualitative research, qualitative interviewing, and qualitative research techniques. Chapter 10 discusses the planning for and conduct of one of the most common forms of qualitative research, focus groups. This chapter leads the student through the steps and considerations required to conduct useful, insightful focus groups. Chapter 11 presents guidelines and techniques for the analysis of qualitative research data.

Part 4 focuses on the conduct and analysis of quantitative research. Chapters 12 (Measurement), 13 (Question Development), and 14 (Questionnaire Design) focus on tasks that need to be accomplished prior to the conduct of research. Chapters 15 (Descriptive Approaches) and 16 (Inferential Statistics) discuss data analysis. The discussion in all chapters is supported by extensive advertising-related examples designed to help students acquire information and understand how the learned information is critical to the decision-making process.

Parts 5 to 8 discuss specific research techniques and the application of these techniques to different types of advertising-related decisions. Each of the four sections addresses a different type of advertising informational need.

Part 5 addresses issues related to the competition and the competitive environment. Chapter 17 (Advertising Content Analysis) explains why content analysis is an important tool, presents a step-by-step guide to conducting content analysis, and shows how advertisers can learn more about their competition (and thus make better strategic decisions) when content analysis is used. Chapter 18 addresses perceptual mapping. This chapter illustrates the importance of perceptual mapping as a research tool, presents a step-by-step guide to conducting perceptual mapping research, and explains why advertisers can make better strategic and creative decisions when perceptual mapping data is available.

Part 6 presents two different research techniques designed to foster an improved understanding of the target consumer. Chapter 19 (Segmentation) discusses the reasons marketers and advertisers segment markets, the criteria that can be used to define consumer segments, and the most common forms of syndicated segmentation research. It also explains how to plan and conduct proprietary segmentation research and how to evaluate and select segments for communications targeting. Chapter 20 discusses Q-sort methodology within the content of target audience analysis. This chapter explains the nature and use of Q-methodology, presents the steps and considerations involved

in a Q-methodology study, and shows how insights obtained via this technique can lead to improved understanding of consumer perceptions and attitudes.

Part 7 addresses creative and product development, screening, and evaluation. Chapter 21 addresses concept and benefit testing. This chapter helps students understand what a concept is and how it differs from an advertisement and the steps involved in concept test planning, administration, and analysis. Students will also learn how to prepare written concepts for use in concept tests and how to develop a concept test questionnaire. Chapters 22 and 23 discuss advertising testing. Chapter 22 discusses the role, options, and use of communication testing, while Chapter 23 discusses the role of, options for, and use of copy testing. Chapter 23 also addresses copy testing from a legal perspective and shows students the critical role of research design and questionnaire construction when responding to advertiser or legal challenges.

Part 8 discusses media research. Chapter 24 provides a comprehensive discussion of audience measures for television, radio, newspaper, magazines, outdoor, Yellow Pages, and the World Wide Web. Chapter 25 provides an in-depth introduction to LNA/Mediawatch™ Multi-Media Service and provides clear, step-by-step procedures for using this data to better understand budgeting, product category dynamics, and the actions of specific brands within a product category.

The text is supplemented by two appendices. Appendix A, which discusses computer-assisted data analysis, will help your students in two ways. First, it provides clear, easy-to-follow instructions for using computers (specifically SPSS) for data analysis. Second, and perhaps more important, Appendix A uses SPSS as a framework to show students the steps underlying the process of data preparation and analysis. Here, the sequence of events a researcher might follow and the types of analyses a researcher might conduct are made explicit. Thus, when your students have completed reading Appendix A, they will better understand how a researcher approaches the task of finding meaning in data. Appendix B presents a comprehensive set of statistical tables.

Instructor's Manual

A detailed Instructor's Manual has been developed to accompany *Advertising Research: Theory and Practice*. The manual contains chapter summaries, suggestions for lecture emphasis, detailed chapter outlines/lecture notes, suggested answers to application exercises, and overhead transparency masters. Please contact your Prentice Hall representative to obtain a copy of the Instructor's Manual or other support materials.

Acknowledgments

There are two reasons why I have been looking forward to writing the acknowledgments for *Advertising Research: Theory and Practice*. First, the acknowledgments provide me with the opportunity to thank those who have made an important contribution to this text. Second, the acknowledgments are the last thing that I need to write. After this, the text is done.

Several people made important, although indirect, contributions to *Advertising Research: Theory and Practice*. William Barclay, my first supervisor at Foote Cone & Belding taught me that superior research is that which is well-planned, ethically conducted, and maximally useful to those who need the information. Bill was a role model for what all researchers should strive to be, and his influence lingers to today, many years after we worked together. Richard Grant and John Breen, Account Managers at D'Arcy Masius Benton & Bowles and Greg Wagner, a D'Arcy Creative Director, helped me to see what research looks like from the account management and creative perspective. All three quite ably identified the characteristics of research that worked and the characteristics of research that didn't work.

Two colleagues at San Diego State, Glen Broom and David Dozier, also indirectly contributed to the text. Glen and David's classes are excellent examples of how theory and practice go hand in hand, each perspective providing important direction for the planning, conduct, analysis, and presentation of research. A great deal of their approach is reflected in this text. My students at San Diego State also merit acknowledgment. Never at a loss for words, their comments and feedback to earlier drafts of the text helped to increase the text's clarity and student-friendliness.

Many individuals spent a considerable time reading draft copies of the manuscript. These reviewers provided a great deal of positive feedback, which was appreciated. However, perhaps more important, reviewers were never hesitant to provide a good reason why a particular section should be "substantially rewritten," "significantly edited," or even "shredded." The text is much better for their insightful comments. The reviewers of *Advertising Research: Theory and Practice* were Gerald Cavallo, Fairfield University; Dennis J. Ganahl, Drake University; Charles Gulas, Wright State University; Randall W. Hines, East Tennessee State University; Wei-Na Lee, University of Texas at Austin; James Ogden, Kutztown University; Paula M. Poindexter, University of Texas at Austin; Peter A. Schneider, Seton Hall University; Peter Turk, University of Akron.

Beyond acknowledging the assistance of academic reviewers, I would be remiss if I did not acknowledge the truly invaluable assistance and support of my family. My

two children, Kyle and McKenna, helped with the charts and tables and actually read early drafts of the manuscript. Their comments were interesting, insightful, and useful. After an especially long day, it was always good to hear one of them comment, "But Dad, can't you make this any more interesting?" Well, I've tried. My wife, Danna Givot, was in every sense a contributing editor. Danna read every word and provided invaluable suggestions for improving the text's clarity. In addition, Danna drew on her experience as an advertising Account Supervisor to provide numerous examples of how theory actually does get translated into practice. Many of the text's strengths are direct responses to her contributions.

David Borkowsky and Theresa Festa at Prentice Hall deserve recognition. Together, they made the development and writing of *Advertising Research: Theory and Practice* a painless and even fun experience. Finally, I would be remiss if I failed to acknowledge the important contribution of copyeditor Barbara Pomfret. Somehow Barbara always managed to figure out what I meant to say, and then say it a little bit more clearly. Thanks to all.

THE NATURE OF ADVERTISING RESEARCH

Research plays a critical role in advertising decision making. It provides information that helps individuals at the agency and client better understand their product and target audience, the marketing environment, and the effectiveness of the product's advertising and media placement. Research helps inform advertisers' judgment so that they can identify their range of options and evaluate the strengths and weaknesses of each option.

After reading this chapter, you will be able to

■ Understand the types of research advertising agencies use to help them
  make better advertising and marketing-related decisions.

■ Identify the individuals and companies who participate in the design,
  conduct, and analysis of advertising research.

Every day, in every advertising agency around the world, account executives, creatives, media planners, and researchers make decisions related to some aspect of their client's business. Many of these decisions directly relate to the traditional role of the advertising agency: preparing and executing communication and promotional plans for their client's company, products, or services. Other decisions flow from the agency's role as the client's marketing partner and relate to marketing aspects of the product or service, such as product naming, packaging, and distribution. In both cases agency decision makers have two choices: they can rely entirely on their professional judgment to make the decision, or they can use research to reach a more informed decision. In general, the more important the decision and the more significant the impact of the decision on the agency's or client's business, the greater the likelihood that research will be conducted and used as part of the decision-making process.

THE CONTRIBUTION OF RESEARCH TO COMMUNICATIONS PLANNING

Advertising agencies typically take a systematic approach to advertising planning and development. As shown in Figure 1.1, each step in the advertising planning and development process provides a foundation for future decisions and may provide feedback for the decisions made in prior steps. One important component of this systematic approach is research. Agency personnel have more confidence in the decisions reached at each step when their decisions are supported by research.

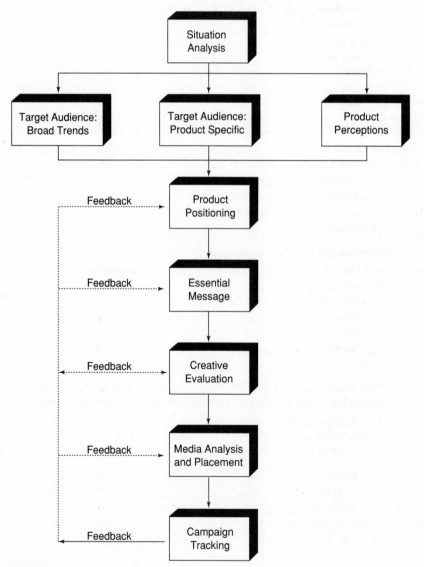

FIGURE 1.1
The advertising planning process.

Situation Analysis

The advertising planning process begins with an examination of the marketplace. The outcome of this examination, commonly called a *situation analysis*, summarizes the brand's current circumstances and identifies factors that might affect future marketing and advertising success. A situation analysis helps the client and agency better understand the forces shaping the marketplace and how these forces may affect their own and their competitors' brands. Advertisers rely on research to answer the following types of questions raised in a situation analysis:

- What are industry trends? To what extent do these trends affect the sales of the product? Are these trends likely to continue or shift? In what ways can the product capitalize on these trends?
- What is the competitive environment? Who are the category leaders? What brands are *currently* our primary and secondary competition? With what brands do we *want* to compete?
- What are our competitors' current positionings? How successful have these positionings been?
- What are our competitors' sales trends and shifts in positioning or advertising strategy?

An executive summary from a situation analysis of the disposable camera category is shown in Figure 1.2 (pages 4–5).[1] Note how research information provides important details about current category trends in a way that helps the agency identify problems faced by the brand and opportunities on which the brand can capitalize.

Target Audience Analysis

An understanding of the marketplace involves more than a study and analysis of sales trends, brand activities, and positionings. An additional analysis, commonly called *target audience analysis*, involves an in-depth exploration of the characteristics of current and potential consumers for a product or service. There are two dimensions of target audience analysis, both of which are better understood when research is utilized. One dimension relates to *general consumer trends* that might have an impact on the brand's positioning and advertising. Questions often answered by research in this area include, for example:

- What changes in consumer lifestyles have accelerated or slowed over the past five years? How might these trends affect perceptions and use of the product?
- What changes in consumer attitudes, beliefs, and priorities have accelerated or slowed over the past five years? How might changes in these trends affect perceptions and use of the product?

The effect of this type of analysis on advertisers' behaviors can be seen in the recent emphasis given to products' environmentally related attributes and benefits. During the early 1990s a growing number of advertisers began to stress the environmental characteristics of their products and their own corporate contributions to environmental improvement. This emphasis on environmental friendliness likely reflected the ad-

---

[1] The data are adopted from Laura Luro, "Single-Use Cameras Snap the Photo Industry Awake," *Advertising Age* 65 (September 28, 1994): 28. The agency is fictitious.

DHS   **Internal Memorandum**

348 E. Randolph
Albany, NY

To: James Montgomery   Fr: Richard Rosen
                                           Date: April 5, 1994

                    Re: Situation Analysis of Disposable Camera Category

Jimmy, attached you'll find our situation analysis of the disposable camera category. This cover memo summarizes our findings.

Background

Disposable (also known as single-use) cameras were introduced in 1987 by Fuji Photo Film. Fuji introduced a basic, no-frills camera that contained a single roll of 35mm film. When the film was used the film and camera were sent for developing. The developed pictures, but not the camera, were returned to the consumer.

Units are commonly priced under $13 (which typically includes the cost of film processing).

Brands and Sales Trends

The disposable camera category is dominated by Kodak which has a 72% share of market (according to industry sources). Fuji and Konica USA are the two remaining name brands in the category with shares of 16% and 9%, respectively. Polaroid has recently introduced products into the category, but its share is estimated to be less than 3%.

Approximately 3 million units were sold in the first full year of availability (estimates by the Photo Marketing Association). Since that time growth has rapidly accelerated. It is estimated that nearly 22 million units were sold in 1992.

Category Trends

Projections for category growth appear optimistic. It is estimated that nearly 40 million units will be sold in 1994. Beyond historical growth trends, an additional reason for optimism that the category will continue to grow is the camera's low penetration. Levels of usage in the United States (about 4% of all film sales) are well below that of other countries such as Japan, where disposable cameras account for about 15% of all film sales.

Category growth is also stimulated by numerous line extensions. These include: built-in flash, telephoto or wide angle lens and waterproof for underwater uses. Two recent innovations illustrate the dynamic nature of the category.

(continued)

- Packaging—Kodak has introduced a five-pack wedding set where camera cardboard covers are "dressed" in bells and lace. This is likely in response to the growing trend of placing disposable cameras on guest tables for their personal use at the wedding.

- Technology—Polaroid has introduced the Talking Sidekick disposable camera which comes in four expressions: "Say cheese," "It's picture time," "You look marvelous," and "Right, left, back, forward, just right."

Advertising

Advertising spending in the category has declined slightly from 1992 (approximately $75 million) to 1993 (approximately $66 million). Advertising spending follows brand share (Kodak's share of spending is 83%, Fuji's share is 14%, and Konica USA's share is 3%). However, it is important to note that the decline in category advertising spending reflects cuts by Kodak, both Fuji and Konica USA increased their spending between 1992 and 1993. Finally, Polaroid is expected to support the introduction and marketing of the Talking Sidekick with significant advertising dollars.

Category Dynamics and Outlook

We believe that there is significant sales potential in this category. Category sales continue to accelerate in spite of the fact that both penetration and awareness (estimated to be less than 50%) are low. Thus, there is an opportunity through advertising to effectively position our brand. However, category dynamics must be considered as part of the product development and introduction process. These include:

- increasing market fragmentation and segmentation

- constant technological and/or packaging innovations

- current category dominance by Kodak

- increasing competitiveness from current secondary brands (Fuji, Konica USA, and Polaroid)

FIGURE 1.2
Executive summary from a situation analysis of the disposable camera category.

vertisers' beliefs that (1) consumers' concern with environmental quality was increasing and (2) consumers were willing to act on these concerns when making specific brand purchase decisions, favoring brands and companies perceived to be more environmentally friendly. A research-based target audience analysis that may have encouraged an advertiser to develop environmental product advertising is shown in Figure 1.3 (pages 6–7).[2]

The second dimension of target audience analysis specifically focuses on the client's product or service. Here, questions addressed by research include:

- What segments of consumers exist?
- Within each segment, what are the characteristics of the consumers in terms of demographics, psychographics, and lifestyle?
- What are our opportunities within each segment based on their purchase patterns, brand trial, and brand loyalty?

---

[2] The data in this memo are based on Joel J. Davis, "Consumer Response to Corporate Environmental Advertising," *Journal of Consumer Marketing* 11 (1994): 25–37; Riley E. Dunlap and Rik Scarce, "Environmental Problems and Protection," *Public Opinion Quarterly* 55 (1991): 651–72. The agency and client are fictitious.

SsAs Advertising, Inc.
Chicago Office   **Inter-office Memo**

To: Roberta Harris
From: James Doolan
Date: August 23, 1991
Re: Opportunities for Aramverco Advertising

Roberta, I believe that an opportunity exists to affect product sales by communicating to consumers Aramverco's current environmentally sensitive behaviors and the positive environmental characteristics of several of its products. Note that since Aramverco is already engaged in a significant number of environmentally beneficial activities *and* that many of its products already have attributes that are environmentally sensitive, this campaign would entail new message strategies rather than an actual change in corporate behaviors or product formulations.

Consumer Concern With Environmental Quality

Recent survey data reveal a significant increase in concern about environmental trends and environmental quality. Overall, the proportion of the public which express concern about environmental quality has risen dramatically over the past ten years. Cambridge Reports notes that nearly 25% of the population now believe that the environment is one of the two *most important* problems facing the country. (This compares with less than 2% of the population just five years ago.)

Consumers' concern with the environment is more than a general fear; it is seen as a threat to human well-being. Roper reports that nearly two-thirds of the population now considers the threat posed to the environment as "very serious." (This compares to about 40% of consumers five years ago.) A majority of the public now sees environmental quality as deteriorating and likely to continue to deteriorate in a number of specific areas such as air and water quality. Garbage and garbage disposal problems are also of high concern.

Rationale for Corporate Environmental Advertising Campaign

The Roper Organization reports that 84% of adults feel that corporations should be "doing more" to help the environment. Similarly, Gallup reports that 83% of adults believe that business and industry are "not worried enough" about the environment and environmental problems. It is important to note that consumers say that they are acting on these beliefs. Consumers say that they are rewarding (through their purchase behaviors) those companies which they perceive to be sufficiently concerned about the environment. The Michael Peters Group reports that over three-quarters of consumers state that their product purchase decisions are at least in part influenced by a company's overall image or reputation on environmental issues.

Given the apparent relationship between consumers' perceptions of corporate environmental "citizenship" and purchase behaviors it might make sense to begin communicating the broad range of corporate environmental behaviors supported by Aramverco such as donations to wildlife and environmental groups, corporate recycling efforts and sponsorship of elementary school environmental awareness programs. I believe that the positive perceptions fostered by these activities can have a "halo effect" and help influence purchase decisions in favor of our client's products.

(continued)

Rationale for Product Environmental Advertising Campaign

Beyond consumers' consideration of a corporation's environmental citizenship, product decisions are also increasingly being influenced by perceptions of a product's environmental "friendliness." Over the past several years the Gallop and Roper organizations report that environmental considerations are exerting greater influence on which specific products are purchased. Eighty-two percent of consumers now report buying products made of recycled materials whenever possible. Moreover, consumers say that they are willing to pay more for products that are good for the environment. About two-thirds of consumers, according to a survey by Yankelovich Skelly White, say that they would be willing to pay as much as 10% more per week for grocery items if they could be sure that those items would not harm the environment.

Of course, there is a difference between saying and doing. But, I think that the strength of the attitudes should at least encourage us to test some environmental product messages.

Roberta, I hope this provides some "food for thought." Let's discuss at your convenience.

FIGURE 1.3
Analysis of consumer attitudes toward the environment.

A target audience analysis identifies different segments of consumers and the characteristics of each segment. Once segments have been identified, the agency and client then use research to better understand how different segments of consumers perceive the advertiser's and competitor's brands. This knowledge helps an advertiser determine whether it is best to reinforce attitudes toward the brand within one segment of the population or change current attitudes toward the brand within a different segment. Here, research helps to answer the following types of questions:

- What are current perceptions of the brand? Are these perceptions in the brand's best interest?
- How do brand perceptions differ among users and nonusers? What is the source or basis of these perceptions? How firmly held are these perceptions?
- What benefits does the target audience seek from products in this category? To what extent is our brand seen as delivering these benefits?
- Are there benefits that our brand offers that other brands do not? Are these benefits currently important to the target? Can these benefits be potentially important to the target? Can these benefits *be made* important to the target?

Research also helps an advertiser understand how the consumer *interacts* with brands and products. Research can, for example, help an advertiser understand whether the decision to purchase the product is more rational or emotional, whether or not a great deal of thought or consideration underlies brand selection, and the extent to which consumers perceive the choice of a particular brand as making a statement about themselves. These types of research-based insights provide direction for strategic and creative development, especially for the selection of essential message and creative tone.

Creative Development

An analysis of the marketplace, consumer, and product leads to a determination of the brand's *positioning*—a descriptive statement of the agency's and client's view of the marketplace niche that they believe the brand can most successfully fill.

A clear, concise, research-justified positioning is the foundation for successful advertising. It is, however, the task of the agency creative department to translate the positioning into compelling and motivating advertising. An initial step in the creative development process is the identification of the *essential message*—the advertising's communication goal. Once the essential message is identified and agreed on, research often plays an important role in the evaluation and selection of the creative itself.

Advertising agencies rarely approach a client with a single "take-it-or-leave-it" execution or campaign. Typically, a range of creative executions and campaign ideas are explored and presented to the client for feedback and evaluation. Given the importance of selecting the strongest execution or campaign from among those presented, research is often conducted to evaluate each of the proposed advertisements *from the consumers' perspective*. This type of research, *communication testing* or *copy development research*, is conducted in the early stages of creative development and is designed to identify the strengths and weaknesses of a proposed advertisement prior to production.[3] The results of a communication test helps the agency better understand how to revise an advertisement so that the finished ad maximizes strengths and minimizes weaknesses. Communication testing is typically conducted by the advertising agency. After an advertisement has been selected (and often produced), a second form of creative research, *copy testing*, is often conducted to help advertisers make a "go–no go" decision about the advertisement.[4] Copy testing can be conducted by the agency or by a specialized third-party research company. The following example illustrates how communication contributed to the development of the AT&T "You Will" campaign.

> AT&T sought to create an advertising campaign that would: (1) update AT&T's image, (2) introduce America to the information superhighway and (3) improve the positioning of AT&T among 18 to 34 year olds. AT&T hoped to accomplish these goals through advertising that communicated a hopefulness about the future impact of the superhighway and AT&T's role in the world. Two alternative creative approaches were tested. One approach used Robin Williams as the spokesperson while the other used humor in the context of the "You Will" campaign theme. Both approaches were tested on a wide range of measures such as potential impact on company image, communication playback, diagnostics (such as likes and dislikes, innovativeness), commercial recall and potential impact on behaviors. Research showed that the "You Will" campaign was seen as more innovative, easier to understand and had better recall. The "You Will" campaign was selected for airing.[5]

Media Analysis and Placement

As seen, research addresses a broad range of issues during advertising planning and creative development. The use of research to reach an informed judgment tends to increase the likelihood that appropriate insights into the marketplace will be drawn and that the strongest of the proposed executional alternatives will be selected. However, advertising that is not placed where the target has a high likelihood to see or hear it has little chance of affecting and motivating the target. Unseen or unheard advertising can-

---

[3] PACT, "Positioning Advertising Copy Testing: A Consensus of Leading American Advertising Agencies," *Journal of Advertising* 11 (1982): 3–29.

[4] Ibid., 8.

[5] Chad Rubel, "Three Firms Show That Good Research Makes Good Ads," *Marketing News* (March 13, 1995): 18.

not work. Thus, one important form of advertising research, *media research*, helps media planners answer questions such as:

- How much are competitors spending on their advertising? How do these levels of spending affect budget recommendations?
- Where, if anywhere, should the advertising be concentrated? Should equal emphasis be given to all areas of the country or should the focus and concentration of spending be in specific geographic areas?
- What media should be used? What media overall, and specific programming within media, has the greatest likelihood to reach the specific target audience?
- When and how should advertising be scheduled?

Campaign Tracking

Once the creative has been produced and aired, research is often used to assess the validity of decisions reached. This type of *tracking research* collects information that can be used to assess the impact of decisions on the brand and to determine how future strategic, creative, and media approaches can be improved. Here, research addresses questions such as:

- To what extent did we accomplish our communication objectives?
- To what extent did we accomplish the desired attitudinal changes in the target audience?
- To what extent did the media plan deliver desired levels of exposure?

The following example illustrates how tracking research plays an important role in decisions related to how and where a brand is advertised.

> Master Lock spends more than 50% of its total advertising budget for one commercial exposure during the Super Bowl because Master Lock's research shows that this commercial placement generates very high levels of awareness. Tracking studies show that over 96% of those who bought a padlock in the past year were aware of the Master Lock brand. And much of this awareness is attributed to the Super Bowl ad. Ad effectiveness research shows that Master Lock's commercials shown during the Super Bowl generate about twice the recall of its commercials which appear during prime time.[6]

THE CONTRIBUTION OF RESEARCH TO OTHER AGENCY FUNCTIONS

Major advertising agencies are their client's marketing partner. A client relies on the advertising agency's judgment and expertise in areas beyond the advertising and promotion of products and services, most often in areas that will have some impact on what might eventually be said or shown in the advertising. As a consequence, agencies often work with their clients in conducting research related to the following:

- *Product names*—What should the new product be named? What names should we consider for product line extensions?
- *Product packaging*—What should the new product's packaging look like? What changes, if any, should we make to the current package? What should the packaging of line extensions look like?

---

[6] Joe Mandese, "Getting Key Ad Exposure," *Advertising Age* 63 (January 20, 1992): 60.

- *Product characteristics*—What changes, if any, in terms of product formulation and characteristics, are warranted given the current competitive set and consumer perceptions and desires?

- *Product distribution*—What types of distribution strategies are in the best interest of the brand?

- *Sales trends and analysis*—How have changes in marketing and advertising programs affected product marketplace performance?

WHO CONDUCTS RESEARCH?

Having seen how research is used, it is now important to see who is involved in the design, conduct, analysis, and presentation of research. Various types of individuals and organizations contribute to the collection and analysis of research information. These individuals and organizations can be distinguished on the basis of their ultimate involvement in research-based decisions.

Information Users

Individuals at the agency and the client have the ultimate responsibility for brand- and advertising-related decisions and, as a consequence, are the ultimate end users of the research. These individuals are involved in all stages of the research project, from problem definition and research design through analysis and implications of research results.

Two types of individuals are typically involved in the research process on the client side: brand managers and research specialists. Brand managers are responsible for the marketing and advertising of a particular brand. These individuals, in conjunction with others at their company, use research to help them make decisions related to the product itself (e.g., product formulation, pricing, distribution), product marketing and advertising, and the product's current and potential consumers. Most clients also have an internal research department. Individuals in this department are responsible for coordinating, gathering, analyzing, and disseminating information on all aspects of the marketing activities for one or more of the company's brands and products. The client's research department is involved with a broad range of product and consumer research, the development of advertising campaigns, and the tracking of advertising effectiveness.

Individuals in all agency departments use research to help them make better decisions. In most full-service agencies, research is conducted and analyzed by an internal research department. Smaller agencies may use their account or media personnel as their internal researchers or they may hire research consultants on an as-needed basis. In both cases, agency researchers, the counterparts of the client's research department, serve two main functions:

1. They respond to the ongoing informational needs of agency account management, media, and creative departments by planning, conducting, and analyzing original research as well as by examining and analyzing research conducted by other companies.

2. They work closely with the client's research department to make certain that pertinent research conducted by the client is disseminated, with a point of view, to the appropriate agency personnel.

In addition to client-specific research, advertising agency research departments may also conduct research designed to foster a better understanding of consumers or current "hot topics" in advertising and media planning. These research studies, for example, may track changes in consumer attitudes, as in the ongoing DDB Needham Life Style Study, or investigate how consumers use advertising in various media to form brand attitudes, as in a recent Ketchum Communications study.[7] Some agencies conduct research to help improve the advertising planning process. The FCB Grid is the result of this type of agency-initiated research.[8]

Many advertising agencies have established a presence on the World Wide Web. In addition to agency news and descriptions, several agencies use their web site to conduct and disseminate the results of agency initiated research. The Techsetter site of the BBDO advertising agency presents the results of agency research surveys, for example

- football and movie viewing habits
- interactive TV
- online habits and online purchasing
- video games
- sports, athletes, and the media

The address for the Techsetter homepage is http://www.techsetter.com.

Research Suppliers

No matter how brilliant or experienced a client or agency researcher is, there are still times when assistance is needed in the design or execution of a specific research project. In these cases, a client or agency may turn to a *custom research supplier*. Individuals who work at these companies are research specialists hired on a project-by-project basis. These specialists may assist in any phase of research: the conceptualization of the research problem, research design and methodology, data analysis, and data interpretation. Other custom research suppliers specialize in particular areas of research (for example, testing and evaluation of the advertising creative, product posi-

---

[7] For further information on the DDB Needham research see William Wells, John Burnett, and Sandra Moriarty, *Advertising: Principles and Practice* (Englewood Cliffs, NJ: Prentice Hall 1995), 201–5; Joseph M. Winski, "Who We Are, How We Live, What We Think," *Advertising Age* 63 (January 20, 1992): 16–18. For further information on the Ketchum research see Melanie Wells, "Purposeful Grazing in Ad Land," *Brandweek* 35 (April 11, 1994): 18.

[8] The FCB Grid made a major contribution to how advertisers determine the most appropriate message and creative tone for a brand or product. The FCB Grid, developed by the Foote, Cone & Belding advertising agency, illustrated how consumers approach different product categories with different mind-sets. The Grid assigns products and product categories to one of four categories, each category representing a dimension of cognition and involvement. The cognitive dimension is divided into thinking and feeling, while the involvement dimension is divided into high and low involvement. Life insurance, for example, is a thinking-high involvement product, while a popsicle is a feeling-low involvement product. See Richard Vaughn, "How Advertising Works: A Planning Model Revisited," *Journal of Advertising Research* 26 (February/March 1986): 57–66.

tioning, product naming, package design) and in different types of research (for example, focus groups, research among minorities and children, brainstorming, and new product development). This type of research assistance is typically *proprietary*, that is, a single client pays the custom research supplier and only that client receives the results of the research.

A cousin of the custom research supplier is the *syndicated research firm*. These firms provide expertise in a particular area, but, rather than perform proprietary customized research and consultation, they collect and sell the same information to all companies that pay the subscription fee. Advertising agencies are generally interested in four types of syndicated information: media ratings, target audience media usage and demographics, advertising expenditures, and consumer trends.

Media usage is monitored by several different companies. Publishers' statements regarding newspaper and magazine circulation are audited and verified by the Audit Bureau of Circulation (ABC). The A. C. Nielsen Company provides local and national television ratings. Radio usage is measured by Arbitron and RADAR (Radio's All-Dimension Audience Research), while Yellow Pages usage is provided by the National Yellow Pages Monitor (NYPM).

Simmons Market Research Bureau (SMRB) and Mediamark Research Inc. (MRI) cross-tabulate demographics and media usage by product usage behavior. These syndicated studies describe product users (for example, all diaper purchasers or purchasers of Huggies) in terms of age, household size, income, education, marital status, occupation, race, home ownership, television viewing, radio listening, newspaper and magazine readership, outdoor advertising exposure, and Yellow Pages usage. This information helps agencies better understand the characteristics of individuals who use specific products and brands and how to select media that most efficiently reach these individuals.

Advertising expenditures, the amount of money companies spend on advertising for their specific products and services, is provided in reports compiled by Leading National Advertisers. Each quarterly report estimates how much advertising support was given to each advertised product overall and in each of the ten monitored media (magazines, Sunday supplements, newspapers, network television, spot television, syndicated television, network radio, national spot radio, cable television, and outdoor advertising). Information on advertising expenditures helps the agency track competitive activity and determine optimal advertising budgets.

The Roper and Gallup organizations, as well as others such as the Cambridge Group, conduct ongoing syndicated studies of consumer behaviors and attitudes. These companies periodically ask a representative sample of consumers a series of questions. They analyze the results and send the analysis and conclusions to subscribers. Subscriptions to these services provide a cost-effective way for agencies to keep abreast of consumer trends.

Field Services

The actual collection of data is typically performed by *field services*, data collection specialists who collect data on a subcontract basis for agency and client research departments and custom and syndicated research companies. Field services perform this

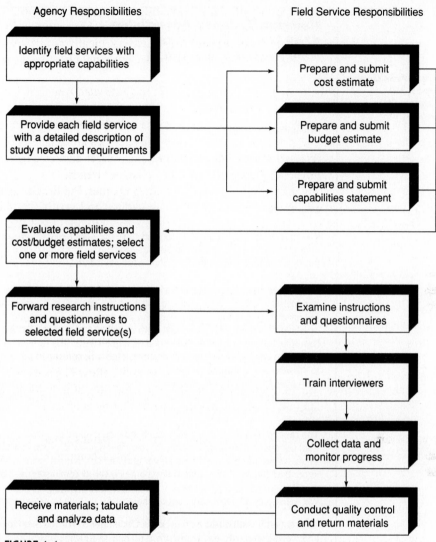

Agency Responsibilities

Field Service Responsibilities

Identify field services with appropriate capabilities

Provide each field service with a detailed description of study needs and requirements

Prepare and submit cost estimate

Prepare and submit budget estimate

Prepare and submit capabilities statement

Evaluate capabilities and cost/budget estimates; select one or more field services

Forward research instructions and questionnaires to selected field service(s)

Examine instructions and questionnaires

Train interviewers

Collect data and monitor progress

Receive materials; tabulate and analyze data

Conduct quality control and return materials

FIGURE 1.4
How a field service works with the agency research department.

function because it is not economically feasible for the agencies, clients, and most research companies to perform this research function. The sequence of events by which field services are hired and collect data is shown in Figure 1.4. The most important step in the process is the letter of specification written by the agency, which details the study needs and requirements. Based on this information, field services will estimate the cost to perform a research study. An example of the specification "bid letter" is shown in Figure 1.5 (page 14).[9]

[9] This is a prototype letter. The agency and field service are fictitious.

**Harrison T. Jones Advertising
1362 Middle Trace Road
New Rochelle, NY 10032**

**H. Jones, President
R. Harper, VP
T. Blakeley, VP
M. Murphy, VP**

November 23, 1996

Professional Field Tests of America
654 Center Street
New York, NY 10151

Dear Cindy:

We once again have a need to conduct mall-intercept research. Because I know that you have facilities in our desired cities, I thought I'd give you the opportunity to bid on the job. Specifications follow.

We will need 180 completed interviews. Ninety interviews will need to be completed in Dallas; 90 in Chicago. Within each city half of the interviews will need to be conducted with men who are aged 35 to 54, who are employed full-time, who personally earn over $30,000 a year and who have played golf at least once in the past eight weeks. The remaining half of the interviews will need to be conducted among women aged 25 to 49, who are employed full-time outside the home and who personally earn over $30,000 a year. Additionally, these women must have played golf at least once in the past twelve weeks. Each of these groups represents about 1%–2% of the adult population.

The research consists of showing each individual an ad on video and then conducting an approximately 20 minute interview to probe reactions. Thus, we will need a video tape player and monitor, a quiet room in which to conduct the interview and a trained interviewer to administer the interview.

We will supply all necessary support materials (i.e., videos, questionnaires).

The research should begin on or about December 3. We will need to have the interviews completed and in our office no later than December 17.

Thanks for consideration on this project. Please call if you have any questions or need any clarification.

Sincerely,

Harrison Jones

FIGURE 1.5
Research "bid" letter.

Support Services

Field services, research companies, and agency/client research departments can use a number of firms that provide specialized forms of support and service. The major types of support and service companies are involved in data processing (editing, coding, computer data entry, and tabulation) and sample generation (names, addresses, and phone numbers of individuals that satisfy specific research needs).

Summary

Advertising agencies and their clients use primary and secondary research to better identify the range of marketing and advertising options and to evaluate the strengths and weaknesses of each option.

Research is used throughout the advertising planning and development process to help the agency better understand the marketplace (situation analysis), the target consumer (target audience analysis), and the relationship between the consumer and the product. These insights lead to the creation of the product's positioning and essential message. Once these are determined, research helps identify the strongest of the creative execution alternatives (copy or communications research), helps assess the effectiveness of produced commercials (copy research) and assists in the identification and scheduling of media (media research). Research is also used to evaluate the success of decisions reached earlier in the planning process (tracking research) and to provide feedback for the identification of any necessary changes.

Research helps agencies and clients make better decisions with regard to the marketing aspects of the product or service. It can be used to make decisions related to product naming, packaging, and characteristics and to provide insights into product distribution and sales trends.

Agencies and clients are the ultimate end users of information provided by research and, as a consequence, are generally involved in all aspects of the research process. Agencies and clients may draw on a vast number of additional companies and individuals to assist in or compliment their own research efforts, for example, custom research suppliers, research specialists, syndicated research firms, field services and data tabulation, and sample generation companies.

Review Questions

1. What is the primary function of marketing and advertising research?
2. What is a *situation analysis*? What types of questions does a situation analysis address?
3. What is *target audience analysis*? What types of questions does each type of target audience analysis address?
4. Why is it important to understand the relationship between the target audience and brand or product perceptions? What types of questions does research address to help agency personnel understand this relationship?
5. What is *communication testing* or *copy development research*? What types of questions does this research address?

6. What is *media research*? What types of questions does this research address?

7. What is *tracking research*? What types of questions does this research address?

8. What is the role and function of the agency research department? Compare this role to the role of the client research department.

9. What are *custom research suppliers*? What are some of their areas of specialization?

10. What is the difference between *proprietary* and *syndicated* research?

11. What is a *field service*? What functions does it provide?

12. Referring to Figure 1.5, what are the important components of a specification "bid" letter?

13. How does an agency research department work with field services?

Application Exercises

1. Examine recent issues of *Advertising Age, Adweek, Branding,* or other related advertising industry publications. Find an instance of research being used to better understand: (a) the competitive marketplace, (b) current or potential consumers, (c) the strengths and weaknesses of advertising creative, and (d) media usage or placement. For each instance (a–d), discuss the nature of the research conducted and how the research was used to inform decision making. Provide a full reference to each article.

2. Researchers have identified a number of demographic, lifestyle, and attitudinal trends. These include: population aging, women having children later in life, reductions in "disposable time," a quest for "quality" and "value" in product purchases, a general dissatisfaction with "quality of life," an increasingly pessimistic outlook toward the future, fewer meals eaten as a family, and a rise in both the use of convenience foods and cooking from scratch. Select one of these trends or another of your choosing. Then, select a food or health and beauty aid product category (such as toothpaste and shampoo) and write a memo (similar to that shown in Figure 1.3) that (a) describes the consumer trend and (b) draws implications for the advertising of the product you chose. Be certain to use research to explain your trend and justify your conclusions. (Note: *American Demographics* is an excellent source for identifying consumer trends.)

3. Your client, Computer Wizards of America, comes to your agency and says that they have just developed a new product, CompWiz. CompWiz is a computer teaching aid designed for children aged three to five. CompWiz teaches basic spelling and mathematical skills. The target purchaser is any adult who buys presents for children aged three to five. You have been asked to develop the advertising for this product. Write a memo to Jan Bride, President of Computer Wizards of America, describing the types of research that you recommend be conducted as part of the advertising development process. Remember, Jan is not a "research-sophisticate" so be clear in describing why each step is necessary and what she will learn once each step of research is complete.[10]

4. *The Green Book: The International Directory of Marketing Research Houses and Services* is a comprehensive listing of custom, specialized, and syndicated research companies as well as field services. If your library has a copy of *The Green Book* use it to identify (a) three field service companies that have mall-intercept facilities in Chicago, (b) two companies that specialize in research with children, and (c) two companies that

---

[10] This company is fictitious.

specialize in the testing of advertising creative. Provide the name, address, and telephone number for each identified field service.

5. Select an advertisement. Assume that you need to test this ad to determine how well it communicates its intended message and motivates the reader to try the product. You decide to conduct the research among 200 target-audience consumers using mall-intercept interviews in Chicago, Atlanta, and Denver. Write a letter soliciting "bids" for this reseach project. (You will need to speculate as to the demographics of the target audience for your selected ad.) Make certain that your letter addresses all of the issues illustrated in Figure 1.5.

2

THE PROCESS OF ADVERTISING RESEARCH

Chapter 1 discussed how research contributes to the marketing and advertising deci-sion-making process. However, not all research contributes equally well. Research that succeeds in providing useful information for decision making is research that is conducted in a systematic manner. The planning, conduct, and analysis of the research follows a predetermined sequence of events, and options are identified, evaluated, and selected at each stage in the sequence.

After reading this chapter, you will be able to

■ Understand the sequence of steps underlying useful, successful advertising research.

■ Describe the events and decisions that occur at each step in the research process.

Advertising research is a continuous process. Information and insights acquired from one research project often lead to the identification of ways additional research can be beneficial to the client and agency. In addition, one research study can provide insights into procedures for improving future research. Within this context of ongoing research, specific information needs are satisfied by specific research projects.

The design and conduct of a successful advertising research project passes through three broad stages (Figure 2.1, page 20):

• *Preliminary discussions and agreements*—Involve identification of a communications or marketing problem or opportunity, justification for the research itself, and specifica-tion of informational needs.

• *Planning and data collection*—Operationalizes agreements reached in the prior stage. As a result, activities carried out in this stage relate to the planning and conduct of the research. During this stage, decisions are reached with regard to the most appropriate

type of research to use, study cost and timing, determination of how and from whom (or where) the data will be obtained, and questionnaire and other material preparation. At the end of this stage the research is initiated and data is collected.

- *Application*—Involves activities carried out after the data is collected. Data is analyzed, results are reported, and decisions are made based on implications drawn from the data.

This chapter provides an overview of the characteristics of each step in the research process and, where appropriate, notes where more detailed information relevant to that step is presented later in the text.

PRELIMINARY DISCUSSIONS AND AGREEMENTS

The end product of this first broad stage of the research process is a *problem statement* that contains three elements: (1) a description of the problem or opportunity facing the agency or client that is motivating the research, (2) an explanation as to why research is appropriate for providing the information needed to solve the problem or capitalize on the opportunity, and (3) a statement of specific information that is needed to determine the best way to resolve the problem or capitalize on the opportunity. Each of these components of the problem statement is developed in the sequence shown in Figure 2.1.

Problem Definition

Problem definition is the first and most important step in the research process. Decisions reached later in the research planning process, such as the types of information needed and the best manner in which to obtain this information, are all affected by how the problem motivating the research is initially formulated. Unless the research problem is properly defined and focused on the *real* problem facing the agency or client, the information produced by the research is unlikely to have any value to decision makers.[1] It is critical, therefore, that the description of the problem motivating the research be clear, concise, and properly focused.

There are three general types of advertising-related problems and informational needs. Each requires a slightly different type of problem definition.

The first type of problem statement relates to the *selection of alternatives and evaluation of alternative actions.* Some problems arise when an advertiser or client is faced with evaluating the relative "goodness" of alternative choices or courses of action. In these situations, the problem definition clearly lists each alternative action under consideration, the reasons for the actions, and the decisions to be reached based on the research findings, for example:

> The Creative Department has written three alternative executions for the new Toyota campaign. These executions are labeled "Fast Car," "Value," and "Still The Best." Only one execution will be produced. We need to conduct research in order to determine the single execution that should be selected and taken forward into production.

> The company is considering changing the design of the product's package. The existing package places the deodorant within a cardboard container while the proposed new pack-

---

[1] S. Jones, "Problem-Definition in Marketing Research," *Psychology & Marketing* 3 (Summer 1985): 83–92.

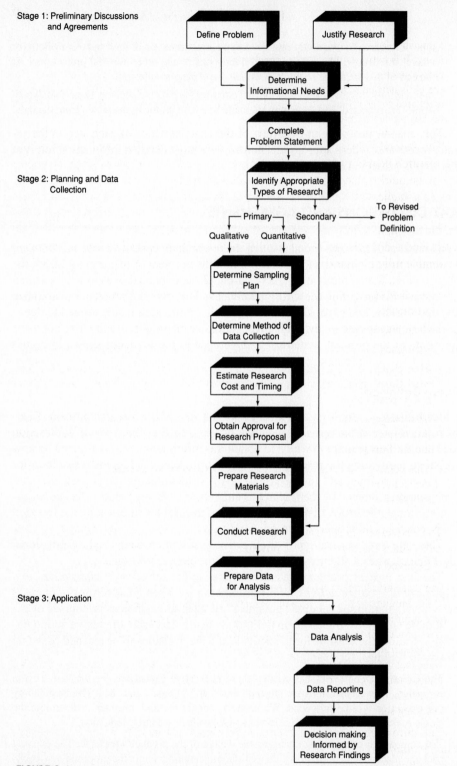

Stage 1: Preliminary Discussions
and Agreements

Define Problem

Justify Research

Determine
Informational Needs

Complete
Problem Statement

Stage 2: Planning and Data
Collection

Identify Appropriate
Types of Research

Primary   Secondary   To Revised
                                    Problem
                                    Definition

Qualitative   Quantitative

Determine Sampling
Plan

Determine Method of
Data Collection

Estimate Research
Cost and Timing

Obtain Approval for
Research Proposal

Prepare Research
Materials

Conduct Research

Prepare Data
for Analysis

Stage 3: Application

Data Analysis

Data Reporting

Decision making
Informed by
Research Findings

FIGURE 2.1
The research process.

aging shrink wraps the product so that it can stand on the shelf without additional packaging. It is believed that this new packaging will have greater consumer appeal, will increase positive perceptions of the product and will improve levels of purchase intent. Research is needed to help us understand the effect of this design change in these areas as compared to the effect and impact of the current packaging so that a decision on product packaging can be made.

The second type of problem statement relates to *problems and opportunities.* Some research begins with the feeling or knowledge that there is a problem or opportunity in the marketplace. In this case, the statement of the research problem typically begins as a vague statement of beliefs or information needs, for example: "Our sales are down. It's the advertising's fault. Find out what's going on. Fast!" In these situations, the problem definition arises out of a series of questions designed to focus on the problem and reduce the ambiguity of the initial problem statement. The questions in this example might include:

- On what basis are you calculating sales trends? Are you calculating sales based on dollar amounts, units sold, or some other criterion?
- What time periods are you using to determine the sales trend?
- What leads you to believe that the advertising is the root cause of observed sales trends?
- What changes, if any, have been made in your advertising program over the indicated time period? Have there been any shifts in strategy, creative approach, or media spending?
- What changes, if any, have been made in your marketing program over the indicated time period? Have there been any changes in, for example, pricing, product formulation, or distribution?
- What competitive activities have occurred in the indicated time period that might have affected your sales? Have there been any shifts in competitive advertising or marketing activities?

The answers to these questions provide the basis for writing a problem definition that clearly states the reasons why a problem or opportunity is believed to exist and the reasons believed to be the cause of the problem or opportunity, for example:

Our sales in calendar year 1995 (as measured in units sold) are down 15 percent versus 1994. Monitoring of our own and competitive activities in the marketplace do not reveal any significant changes in marketplace factors that might affect our sales, for example, new product introductions, pricing, distribution, changes in advertising strategy, or changes in advertising spending. As a consequence, we believe that it is reasonable to assume that the underlying cause of sales declines are consumer-related. Research is needed to determine which consumer factors, such as product awareness and perceptions, product satisfaction, advertising awareness and advertising impact, may be responsible for the declining sales trend.

The third type of problem statement responds to a need to broaden *knowledge and understanding* of the consumer, product, or marketing environment. Problem definitions falling into this group reflect the agency's or client's need for information that will make them better, smarter marketers or advertisers. Problem statements that re-

spond to this type of information need to explicitly address the types of information *really* needed, why this information is needed, and how the information collected by the research will be used, for example:

> The client has initiated their 1995–1996 strategic planning process. One important part of their strategic planning process is an examination of consumer attitudinal and lifestyle trends that may have an impact on the identification and evaluation of strategic alternatives. The client is interested in consumer trends that may have an impact on the proposed repositioning of their All Natural Potato Chip line of products. Research is therefore recommended to explore and determine the potential effects of the following consumer trends for the repositioning: attitudes toward healthy eating, attitudes toward snack foods, attitudes and perceptions of "health"-positioned products (especially in the snack food category), behavioral changes in diet with particular emphasis on the consumption of snack foods, behavioral acceptance and rejection of "health"-positioned products (especially in the snack food category).

Justifying the Need for Research

Problem definitions are a result of the difference between what is known and what needs to be known to reduce uncertainty and increase confidence in decisions reached. However, it is not true that the decisions can be reached only with the assistance of research. When faced with the selection of one of three creative executions, for example, judgment alone can be used to select the one that should be produced. The question, then, is when should judgment alone be used and when should judgment be supported by research?

The appropriateness of research can be evaluated through a cost-value analysis. In general, the justification for research increases when

- the value of the information obtained (in terms of assisting in the decision-making process) exceeds the cost to acquire the information, or
- the cost implications of making the wrong decision increases.

Specifying Informational Needs

The final step in completing the problem statement requires the specification of informational needs, that is, identifying the information that responds to the problem definition and best helps the decision maker evaluate the strengths and weaknesses of various decision options and courses of action. The specification of informational needs is extremely important. Specified informational needs become the focus and core of the research questionnaire or interview.

The specification of informational needs is also important from another perspective. Prior to additional research planning, it is extremely important that those who initiate the request for research agree with the statement of information needs. If this agreement is not obtained in advance of the research, a researcher runs the risk of conducting research that is seen as incomplete or unresponsive to the agency's or client's needs. Consider the Toyota problem definition presented earlier. While this statement clearly defines the problem, it is vague as to what information will be used to evaluate

the executions and to select the "winning" execution. The specification of informational needs for this problem definition might read:

> The commercials will be evaluated in four areas: communication of the main idea, reactions to main message communication (believability, uniqueness, and relevance), effect on product perceptions (competitive value, styling, performance, and handling), and reactions to the execution (likeability, uniqueness, relevance).

This statement of informational needs gives management the opportunity to agree or disagree that the criteria listed are an appropriate basis for commercial evaluation and selection.

The Complete Problem Statement

The end result of this initial stage in the research process is a well-defined and focused problem statement that contains three elements: a problem definition, a justification for the research, and the specification of informational needs. An example of a complete problem statement follows.

> The agency is unsure which of two product benefits to emphasize in the new advertising campaign. Alternative benefits are "unsurpassed cleaning ability" and "environmental safety." Benefit research is needed to help identify the one product benefit that should be the focus of the new advertising campaign. The research will evaluate each benefit in terms of communication, believability, uniqueness and personal relevance; purchase interest and purchase intent; and anticipated product purchase frequency, reasons for purchase intent, and frequency of purchase. Primary, proprietary research is needed to provide this information as the required information is unavailable from any other source. Research is a justified response to this problem given the importance of the decision to be made. The benefit selected will become the focus of the upcoming $5 MM advertising campaign. Basing this decision purely on judgment severely limits confidence that the proper decision has been made and, as a result, the maximum return on advertising investment has been realized.

PLANNING AND DATA COLLECTION

Activities conducted in this middle stage of the research process relate to the actual planning and conduct of the research. The specific activities conducted in this phase are (1) identify the appropriate type of research, (2) address sampling and data collection issues, (3) set the research budget and timing, (4) prepare, distribute, and obtain approval of the research proposal, (5) prepare the questionnaire and other support materials, (6) conduct the research, and (7) prepare the data for analysis. The sequence and interrelationship of these events are shown in Figure 2.1.

Identify the Appropriate Type of Research

Secondary or Primary Research The problem definition and identified informational needs determine the approach and types of information that will be collected in the research. As discussed in Chapter 1, you have two options in selecting the most ap-

propriate approach to collecting the information that satisfies the problem's informational needs: secondary research and primary research.

Secondary research examines data gathered for a research need other than the current one that already exists in printed or electronic form.[2] Sources of secondary research information include internal agency or client records, government agencies, trade associations, information brokers, marketing and advertising research companies, specialized and general interest books, magazines, and academic journals. (Secondary research is discussed in greater detail in Chapter 5.) *Primary research* involves the collection of original, often proprietary, data specifically collected for the identified problem and generally entails some form of target audience interviewing or observation. (Primary research is discussed in greater detail in Chapters 6 and 7.) The selection of primary versus secondary research is determined by the specific problem addressed by the research and the types of information required for decision making.

Some research informational needs can be thoroughly satisfied by secondary research, for example, levels of competitive advertising spending and consumer demographic trends. Information on advertising spending is available through syndicated sources, while ample data on demographic trends have been gathered by governmental agencies and analyzed by general interest and specialized magazines, journals, and books. Some research informational needs can only be satisfied by primary research, for example, the identification of the strongest of three creative approaches or reactions to a specific new product concept. No information likely exists anywhere that will satisfy this type of unique informational need. Finally, some problem statements are best addressed by a combination of secondary and primary research. In these cases, an analysis of secondary information is performed first, for example a general analysis of consumer demographic and lifestyle trends. Insights from this analysis are then used to refine the original problem statement, for example, specific trends can be isolated and then quantitatively explored in primary research to determine the applicability and effects of these trends on the client's product, service, or communications program.

Different events occur following the selection of a primary or secondary research approach to data collection. As shown in Figure 2.1, when secondary research is conducted, there are no intervening steps between the selection of this approach and the collection of the secondary information (although, infrequently, a research proposal is prepared for secondary research projects). However, before primary research can be conducted a number of additional steps must take place.

Qualitative Versus Quantitative Research Once primary research is selected as the most appropriate means for obtaining the desired information, you must then determine the primary research approach that provides the type of information that best meets informational needs and provides desired insights. You have two options: qualitative research and quantitative research.

Qualitative research primarily uses open-ended, probing questions (that is, questions without a prespecified set of answers) to encourage consumers to discuss and share their thoughts and feelings on a particular subject. As a result, qualitative research is most appropriate when one needs

---

[2] René Y. Darmon, Michel Larouche, and K. Lee McGown, *Marketing Research In Canada* (Scarborough, Ontario, Canada: Gage Educational Publishing Company, 1989), 120.

- background information in a particular area when little is already known;
- information to assist in problem formulation or the development of research hypotheses;
- a thorough understanding of the underlying relationship between consumers' feelings, attitudes, and beliefs and their behaviors, *especially* when information on this relationship cannot be obtained through direct, structured, primarily closed-ended questioning.

Common forms of qualitative research include in-depth individual interviews and focus groups. (Qualitative research is discussed in greater detail in Chapters 9 through 11.)

Quantitative research is best used when generalizability to a larger population is important, when the determination of statistically reliable, quantifiable differences between groups is important, and when statistical analysis of the data is required. Quantitative research encompasses three types of research techniques: observation, physiological measurement, and survey research.

- *Observation research*—The recording of objects, events, situations, or people's behaviors. Observations can take place in either a natural or contrived situation where the presence of the observer may or may not be known.
- *Physiological research*—Entails the direct measurement of an individual's physical responses to stimuli such as an advertisement. Physiological research measures voluntary (such as eye movements) and involuntary responses (such as brain waves and galvanic skin response).
- *Survey research*—The most common form of quantitative research. It is the systematic collection of information from respondents through the use of questionnaires. Surveys are most commonly administered over the telephone, through the mail, or in person-to-person interviews. Electronic interactive surveys may also take place.

(Quantitative research is discussed in greater detail in Chapters 12 through 16.)

Qualitative and quantitative research have the same relationship to each other as do secondary and primary research. Qualitative research can be the sole response to an informational need, or it can be used to acquire insights that contribute to a refinement of the problem statement as a precursor to quantitative research. Consider the need for your local metropolitan transit line to increase ridership. They decide that one means to accomplish this goal is to commit funds to an advertising campaign. But they do not know what idea should serve as the core communication of this campaign. Consumer insights are clearly needed. In cases such as these, qualitative research is an appropriate first step:

Prior to a quantitative survey of the target audience you conduct a series of focus groups where, among other things, you ask participants to describe their commuting and other transportation habits and to explain why they have adapted these habits. One respondent says: "I don't care if I'm trapped in traffic for an hour or two. I love the freedom my car gives me. There's just so much freedom when I drive myself." This remark is important because you did not consider "freedom" as one of the areas that would be explored in the quantitative phase of the research. When the focus groups are completed, "freedom" and other issues not previously considered are used to refine the problem statement for the next phase of (quantitative) research.[3]

---

[3] Adopted from Glen M. Broom and David M. Dozier, *Using Research in Public Relations* (New York: Prentice-Hall, 1990), 147.

Sampling and Data Collection

Sampling The sampling plan specifies how study participants will be selected. You have two sampling options: probability sampling and nonprobability sampling.

A *probability sample* is a sample in which each individual or household comprising the universe from which the sample is drawn has a known chance or probability of being selected for inclusion in the research. The selection of specific individuals from this universe is done purely by chance, for example, through the use of a table of random numbers. When probability sampling is used, selection of individuals for survey participation continues until the required number of individuals has been selected and interviewed. The primary advantage of probability sampling lies in the ability to generalize findings to the population from which the sample was drawn. Probability samples, for example, are often used in national opinion polls because of the important need to generalize the findings to the total population.

A *nonprobability sample* is a sample of individuals who are not selected strictly by chance from the universe of all individuals, but rather are selected in some less random, often more purposeful way. Here, the selection of individuals for study participation can be conducted on the basis of convenience or judgment.

The sampling option selected is determined by a number of factors: the objectives of the research, the research budget, urgency in knowing the results of the research, and the need for generalizability to larger or broader populations. The vast majority of research conducted by advertising agencies uses nonprobability sampling primarily because the procedures associated with probability sampling make them too expensive and time consuming for most advertising-related research needs. (Sampling techniques and sampling options are discussed in Chapter 8.)

Selection of Data Collection Method Once the sampling plan is chosen, you then determine the specific method by which identified respondents will be interviewed. There are four primary approaches to respondent interviewing: in-person face to face, by telephone, through printed mail surveys, or through mediated electronic media (for instance, through electronic bulletin boards or by sending them a computer disk onto which they record their responses). Qualitative research almost always utilizes some form of in-person face-to-face interview. Quantitative research may use any data collection format. Each approach, in the context of quantitative research, is associated with a unique set of advantages and disadvantages (see Chapter 6). The data collection method selected will be determined by the types and sensitivity of information required, the complexity of the questionnaire, the research budget, and timing constraints.

Determine the Research Budget and Timing

Cost and timing estimates can be determined before or after the prior steps in the research design process. In the best of all cases, cost and timing estimates follow the prior steps. First identify the most appropriate way to meet informational needs and then determine the cost and amount of time necessary to plan the research, collect and analyze the data, and then present the findings and implications. In this case, budget and timing estimates can be accomplished through the Program Evaluation and Review Technique (PERT):

1. Prepare a list of all activities that need to be completed from the time the study is approved until the results are presented.
2. Arrange listed items in time sequence, paying particular attention to tasks that need to be addressed or completed simultaneously.
3. Determine the amount of time needed to complete each item.
4. Determine the longest "path"—the maximum amount of time required to complete all tasks. This is the amount of time required for the complete research study.
5. Determine the estimated cost of each listed task. Add individual task costs together to determine the total research budget.

Time and money, however, are limited commodities in the advertising business and, as a consequence, cost and timing estimates may precede decisions related to sampling and data collection. You may be told "You have $2,000 and ten days to get me what I need to know." In such cases, you must decide whether appropriate, useful, valid research can be performed within the time and budget constraints (in which case you then revise prior decisions and continue the research planning process) or whether research conducted within the imposed constraints is likely to be worse than no research at all. The latter conclusion should lead to the decision not to conduct the proposed research, but to instead find alternative ways to meet informational needs.

Prepare, Distribute, and Obtain Approval of Research Proposal

The decisions reached in the prior steps are summarized in a written proposal and presented to management and other end users of the research. The research proposal consists of several parts.

- *Executive summary*—A brief synopsis of the key points from each of the more detailed sections in the proposal.
- *Background*—A brief statement of the situational factors and informational needs that led to the decision to conduct the research plus a discussion of any factors that may have influenced subsequent decisions in the research process, for example, budget or time constraints.
- *Problem statement*—A full problem statement containing a detailed, focused description of the problem(s) motivating the research, a rationale for why research is the recommended approach (as opposed to the sole use of judgment), and a description of the specific types of information the research will provide.
- *Research methodology*—A clear, nontechnical description of the research design explaining how the research will be conducted. The data collection method, types of data to be collected, measurement instruments, and analytical procedures should all be discussed.
- *Cost*—A statement of the funds allocated to the research and a detailed breakdown of how this money will be spent.
- *Timing*—A statement of how long the research will take from the time of final approval and a breakdown of the amount of time needed for key components of the research.
- *Appendices*—Any statistical or other detailed information necessary for a complete understanding of the research. The material in this section is typically of a technical nature and is of interest either to those in management who need more detailed information or to those individuals who need to completely understand the research but did not participate in the discussions that led to the research.

The research proposal, therefore, is a very important document. It provides one last opportunity for management to contribute their thoughts to the research process, a set of expectations for what management is paying for and the information they will receive, a record of decisions reached and agreed on, and a permanent record to assist those who need to understand and/or replicate the research in the future.

Prepare Research Materials

Once the primary research project is approved, the creation of all necessary research materials begins. The questionnaire or interview guide is created and any necessary directions are written for research companies assisting in the research, such as field services or tabulation houses. If the research requires stimulus materials such as storyboards, animatics, or product concepts, these are also developed at this time.

Conduct the Research

The next to last step in this stage of the research process is data collection. The appropriate sources are consulted and written documents are obtained in secondary research. Interviews or other forms of observation take place in primary research.

Prepare Information for Analysis

Raw, unorganized information is hard to work with. Thus, the final step in this stage of the research process is to organize and prepare the data so that it can be analyzed in the application stage. The way in which raw information is organized depends on its source and characteristics.

Secondary information is organized in much the same way that you organize information for a term paper or similar report. The information obtained from personal and written sources is read, categories of information are developed, and then related information is grouped together into the appropriate categories. Qualitative information is organized in a similar manner. Here, however, the sources of the information are the verbal and written records of the interviews with the individuals participating in the research. Primary, quantitative information is typically edited and translated into a computer data file prior to analysis. *Editing* involves examining the responses recorded on the questionnaires for omissions, appropriateness, and consistency. The editing process is important, therefore, because it increases the quality of the data. The personal computer and user-friendly statistical programs have greatly increased the ease with which computer data analysis can take place. However, before a computer can be used, the codes representing each individual's responses to the survey questions must be input and stored in a data file.

APPLICATION

This final stage of the research process focuses on what has been learned and the implications of this learning for decision making. The specific activities conducted in this stage are: (1) data analysis, (2) presentation of findings, and (3) application of the findings to decision making. The sequence and interrelationships of these activities is shown in Figure 2.1.

Data Analysis

Raw data is useless; only data that has been thoroughly analyzed is of any value to decision makers. Thus, one of the major roles of the researcher is to examine, organize, and if appropriate, statistically test the data so that meaningful conclusions and insights can be drawn. The specific types of analytical procedures carried out are determined by the type of data collected.

The analysis of secondary and qualitative information generally requires synthesis. Analysis of these types of data is similar to the process of putting together a jigsaw puzzle *without* knowing what the finished puzzle will look like. In both cases, individual pieces (of the puzzle or information) need to be pieced together to determine important patterns and trends so that, eventually, the "big picture" is revealed and understood. Quantitative data analysis generally involves data manipulation, summarization, and statistical testing. Analysis may involve descriptive statistics such as percents and frequencies or inferential statistics such as correlation, tests of mean differences, and chi-square.

Present the Results

Next, findings and conclusions drawn from data analysis are presented to management. This presentation can be oral, written, or both (an oral presentation followed by a written report).

Regardless of the way in which results are communicated, the report must be management-oriented. Many research reports are written from the researcher's perspective. These reports are a complicated and often convoluted description of research methodology and highly technical descriptions of the statistical techniques that were used as part of data analysis. Table after table is presented without organization or interpretation. In these circumstances the needs of management are not met. A report written from the management perspective, clearly and concisely answers management's most basic questions: "What does this information mean?" "What do I know now that I didn't know before?" and "What have I learned so that I can better evaluate my decision alternatives?" (Chapter 4 contains a detailed discussion of how to present research results.)

Decision Making

The last and one of the most important steps in the research process is using the findings to influence decision making. If you present your findings to management and receive the response "That's nice. Thanks," you can be assured that you have made an error somewhere in the research planning process and that you have wasted the agency's time, personnel resources, and money. The research process should end with a management response of "The research has certainly helped us to better understand the strengths and weaknesses of each of our options. Let's use these findings to evaluate each option one more time before we reach our decision." If you receive this response, you deserve congratulations. You have designed and presented an important, valuable piece of research.

Summary

The goal of research is to provide information that helps individuals at the advertising agency and at the client make better informed, more successful decisions. The likelihood of accomplishing this goal is increased when the research is planned and conducted in a systematic manner.

A systematic approach to research consists of following a number of steps nested within three broad stages of planning.

- The first stage, *preliminary discussions and agreements*, lays the foundation for the research by culminating in a problem statement. This statement, the result of three planning steps, describes the problem or opportunity facing the agency or client that is motivating the research, explains why research is appropriate for providing the information needed to solve the problem or capitalize on the opportunity, and explicitly identifies specific management informational needs.

- Activities carried out in the second stage of research planning, *planning and data collection*, relate to the planning and conduct of the research. These activities entail identifying the appropriate type of research; addressing sampling and data collection issues; setting the research budget and timing; preparing, distributing, and obtaining approval of the research proposal; preparing the questionnaire and other support materials; conducting the research; and preparing the data for analysis.

- The final stage of the research process, *application*, focuses on what has been learned and the implications of this learning for decision making. The specific activities conducted in this stage are data analysis, presentation of the findings, and application of the findings to decision making.

Review Questions

1. What is the ultimate purpose of advertising research?

2. What are the names of the three main stages of advertising research?

3. What is the end product of the first main stage of research? What specific steps lead to the development of this product?

4. What are the names and characteristics of the three main types of problems faced by advertising agencies?

5. What are the characteristics of a well-written problem definition?

6. What procedures can be used to improve the quality of a problem definition?

7. In what types of situations is there a high justification to conduct research pertinent to a specific problem definition?

8. What is the third and final component of the problem statement? What is the role of this component?

9. What seven steps comprise the second main stage of the research process?

10. What is the difference between *primary* and *secondary* research? In what situations is each type of research most appropriate?

11. What is the difference between *qualitative* and *quantitative* research? In what situations is each type of research most appropriate?

12. What is the difference between *probability* and *nonprobability* sampling? In what situations is each type of sampling most appropriate?

13. What are the four major methods for collecting data in a quantitative research study?

14. What is the function of the *research proposal*?

15. What are the major components of the research proposal? What is the function of each component?

16. What are the three steps in the final stage of the research process? What events occur in each step?

17. What do we mean when we say *research should be presented from the management perspective?*

Application Exercises[4]

1. Read each of the following problem statements. Using the criteria presented earlier in the chapter, decide if the statement is acceptable as written. If the statement is not acceptably written, (a) identify the problem or problems with the statement, (b) list the types of questions you would ask to clarify the problem statement, and (c) rewrite the statement to make it acceptably written (speculating as to the types of answers you would receive to your questions).

   Account Management has identified three potential ways in which we can position our product: extra gentle, extra cleaning ability, and better value. We need research to identify the best positioning.

   It's time to develop 1996 advertising. But we haven't done research for a long time. We don't know how individuals who use our competitor's products perceive our product. We need to do research to understand what our perceived strengths and weaknesses are among this group so that we can address any perceived weaknesses in the new advertising.

   We have received mixed reactions to our advertising. We need to conduct research to determine the strengths and weaknesses of our advertising among our important target of influential opinion-leaders. Based on their reactions, modifications to the advertising will be implemented.

   The client's new consultant has encouraged us to show the product for longer periods of time in the television advertising. He said that this would make for more effective advertising. We need to develop some new advertising with longer product shots and then get our target audience's reactions to this advertising. Then we'll know if the consultant is right.

2. Tom's Lo-Cost Save-More Pharmacies, located in middle- to small-sized towns throughout the western United States, has hired your agency to develop their new $3 million advertising campaign. Tom's Pharmacies had tremendous growth throughout the early 1990s but growth has slowed over the past several years. Advertising spending has remained consistent at about $3 million. Sales last year were flat. Unfortunately, the company does not have a good understanding of why this slowing has occurred. They do, however, see the new advertising campaign as *the* way to reverse this trend.

   Think about the discussion of primary and secondary research and the differences between qualitative and quantitative information. Think about how each of these

---

[4] The companies in exercises two, four, and five are fictitious.

approaches can be used independently or in sequence. Then, write a memo to William Masterly, the CEO of Tom's Pharmacies, describing the research that you recommend be conducted prior to the development of the advertising creative. Your recommendation can consist of a single piece of research or a sequence of related research steps, each step being informed by the prior steps. Be certain to fully explain how each step or steps of recommended research will contribute to the creative development process *and* provide a justification for your selection of information type (primary or secondary) and research approach (qualitative or quantitative) at each stage of research. Your recommendation should reflect your best thinking, and as a consequence, you should not be concerned at this point with budget or timing.

3. Use trade magazines such as *Advertising Age*, *Ad Week*, or *Branding* to find two instances of how research helped to solve an advertising or marketing problem. For each instance, first determine whether primary or secondary research was used. Next, if primary research was used determine (a) if qualitative or quantitative methods were selected and (b) if a probability or nonprobability sampling was used. Finally, comment on the appropriateness of the approach taken. Provide a full reference to each cited instance.

4. Twister's Pizza is a local chain of pizza restaurants specializing in unique pizzas, such as oven-roasted Middle Eastern vegetarian pizza and Parisian sourdough. Sales, after an initial peak soon after opening, have dropped steadily over the past several months. The drop in sales coincided with the termination of the Twister's television campaign.

   The agency is pleased that Twister's has observed the simultaneous occurrence of these two events and is ready to begin a new wave of advertising. The same commercials used in the initial wave of advertising will be used in the new wave. The agency and Twister's believe that this new wave of advertising should reverse the steadily declining sales trend.

   You, a leading consultant, have been hired by Twister's to provide an independent point of view. Do you support the decision to begin airing the new campaign without any research? If so, support your recommendation. If you do not support the decision, specifically describe the unmet information need(s) that you think research should address and then, for each information need, specify (a) why you think collecting information to meet that need is important and (b) the approach you would take to collect the information.

5. There is a crisis on the agency's new account. The creative team is scheduled to go into production in two weeks but the client, Mary Roberts, has changed her mind as to which commercial should be produced. Mary now says that "the consumer should decide." No commercial will be approved for production prior to examination of the findings from consumer research. She says, "I don't care about the specifics, do some good research and then we'll decide."

   Time is of the essence. You and your assistant begin planning the research. It will be tight, but it can be done if the two of you spend all your time on research planning and data analysis. Late that night, after the research design is formulated, your assistant says, "What a day. And tomorrow will be a long one, too. Mary's the lucky one. She'll be out of the fire for a while. She'll be up at the corporate offices until the day after tomorrow." Your assistant pauses and then says, "You know what this means. We can't get to Mary for two days. So, we'll just have to skip her approval on the research proposal prior to starting the research. Let's get everything going and we'll get her approval when she gets back. After all, she left the details up to us."

   What is your response to your assistant? Do you agree or disagree? Why?

CHAPTER

3

THE ETHICS OF ADVERTISING RESEARCH

Ethics: principles of morality; values that guide the behavior of individuals or groups.

The advertising community forgives most honest mistakes. What it does not forgive, and what you must absolutely, completely avoid are ethical lapses in judgment or action. You must conduct yourself and your research in ways that meet the highest ethical standards. When your actions do not meet these standards you hurt yourself, your agency, the advertising profession, and potentially, the consumer.

After reading this chapter, you will be able to

■ Understand how to maintain high ethical principles in the planning, conduct, analysis, and presentation of advertising research.

Ethical or moral principles are important. They implicitly and explicitly influence our thinking as we evaluate the relative "goodness" of alternative courses of action, and they guide our explanations when we are asked to justify our behaviors. Three moral principles that, to a greater or lesser extent, guide our daily behavior are also applicable to the conduct, analysis, and application of advertising research.[1]

The first principle is that of *autonomy*, often referred to as the principle of self-determination or respect for the values and decisions of other people. The principle of

---

[1] This discussion is based on Tom. L. Beauchamp, Ruth R. Faden, R. Jay Wallace, Jr., LeRoy Walters, eds., *Ethical Issues in Social Science Research* (Baltimore, MD: The Johns Hopkins University Press, 1982), 18–19. These issues are also discussed by George M. Zinkhan and Sandra J. Milberg, "Deception in Survey Research: A Cross-Cultural, Managerial Perspective," *Advances in Consumer Research* 22 (1995): 763–67.

autonomy states that as long as others' decisions and actions are not harmful then the reasons for the actions must be respected and the actions themselves not interfered with. The second principle is that of *nonmaleficence*, which states that it is wrong to intentionally inflict harm on another person. Nonmaleficence is often discussed in the same context as the third principle, beneficence. *Beneficence* states that one has a positive obligation to remove existing harms and to confer benefits on others.

Most would agree that these principles are important and should be adhered to in an absolute sense in the conduct of business in general and in the conduct of research in particular. However, in terms of their actual application, research conducted among business professionals indicates that in a business context these ethical principles are not perceived and applied in absolutist terms.[2] Instead, they are most frequently interpreted and applied in *relative* shades of right and wrong as each unique situation is believed to dictate. The application of what is known as situational ethics, as opposed to the application of an absolute code of moral principles, appears to be the preferred mode of operation among U. S. businesspeople.[3]

In response to this phenomenon, several marketing and research organizations have developed codes of ethics.[4] These codes, designed to provide the research profession with *stability and consistency* in the ethical decision making of its members across *all* research situations, specifies in *absolute* terms the conditions of a researcher's interactions with others involved in the research process, specifically

- the individuals who supply information on attitudes, beliefs, and behaviors,
- management who uses the information,
- research suppliers who provide consultation and who help collect information, and
- society as a whole, which is often affected by decisions based on the information.

The remainder of this chapter explores how the ethical principles of autonomy, nonmaleficence, and beneficence govern an advertising researcher's relationships with these four groups of individuals (see Figure 3.1). This exploration and discussion reflects the principles expressed in the codes of ethics of the following organizations: The Council of American Survey Research Organizations (CASRO), The American Marketing Association (AMA), and The Professional Marketing Research Society (PMRS).

---

[2] C. B. Pratt, "PRSA Members' Perceptions of Public Relations Ethics," *Public Relations Review* 17 (1991): 145–59; D. J. Fritzsche, "An Examination of Marketing Ethics: Role of the Decision Maker, Consequences of the Decision, Management Position and Sex of the Respondent," *Journal of Macromarketing* 8 (1988): 29–39; D. J. Fritzsche and H. Becker, "Ethical Behavior of Marketing Managers," *Journal of Business Ethics* 2 (1983): 291–99; D. M. Krugman and O. C. Ferrell, "The Organizational Ethics of Advertising: Corporate and Agency Views," *Journal of Advertising* 10 (1981): 21–30, 48; O. C. Ferrell and K. M. Weaver, "Ethical Beliefs of Marketing Managers," *Journal of Marketing* 42 (1978): 69–73.

[3] D. J. Fritzsche, "A Model of Decision-Making Incorporating Ethical Values," *Journal of Business Ethics* 10 (1991): 841–52; T. M. Jones, "Ethical Decision-Making by Individuals in Organizations: An Issue Contingent Model," *The Academy of Management Review* 16 (1991): 366–95; Fritzsche, "An Examination of Marketing Ethics," 29–39.

[4] This view of the role of codes of ethics is taken from S. D. Beets, "Personal Morals and Professional Ethics: A Review and an Empirical Examination of Public Accounting," *Business and Professional Ethics Journal* 10 (1991): 63–84.

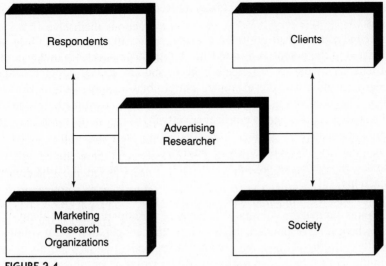

FIGURE 3.1
The professional relationships of advertising researchers.

ETHICS AND INDIVIDUAL RESPONDENTS

The ethical principles of autonomy and nonmaleficence apply to the interactions of researchers and respondents, the individuals who provide the raw information for the vast majority of primary research studies. These principles are reflected in a set of guidelines designed to protect the rights and well-being of respondents as follows:

- A respondent's decision whether or not to participate in a research study should be an informed decision.
- A respondent's decision to withdraw from participation in a research study may not be infringed in any way.
- A respondent may not be mistreated in any way.
- Deception should be minimal, cause no harm, and be justifiable by the research design and information needs.
- A respondent has an absolute right to confidentiality.
- A respondent has an absolute right to privacy.

An Informed Decision

There are several aspects of an informed decision. First, all aspects of the interview or research task must be thoroughly explained to potential respondents so that they can make an informed decision whether or not to participate in the research study. Respondents should be appraised of (1) what they will have to do to participate (for example: answer questions, some perhaps of a personal nature, taste products, watch advertising, etc.), (2) how long the interview will take, and (3) what will be done with the data. Ethical standards require that statements or assurances given to a respondent in

these areas must not only be factually correct but must not be misleading or ambiguous.[5]

A second aspect of an informed decision relates to the purpose of the research communicated to the potential respondent. A respondent can only make an informed decision whether or not to participate if he or she has a clear understanding of the study's purpose and goals. For example, it might bias a study of political advertising to say that "I am conducting some research to determine how people respond to positive and negative approaches to political advertising." The study's purpose can, however, be communicated by saying "I am conducting some research to determine how people respond to different types of advertising." The respondent then has the option to decide whether or not he or she wants to see some advertising and share his or her reactions.

A third aspect of informed choice relates to the voluntary nature of participation. CASRO points out that the voluntary character of participation should always be stated explicitly whenever a respondent might believe that cooperation is not voluntary.

Finally, informed choice requires that a respondent understand his or her long-term commitment to the research project. It is a violation of ethical standards not to forewarn respondents of the possibility that further contact and/or follow-up interviewing is a part of the study's design.

Withdrawing From Participation

During the course of an interview a respondent may change his or her mind with regard to willingness to continue participation in the research study. This may occur for any number of reasons: the respondent has lost interest, is confused, doesn't like the interviewer, or the interview is running too long. Given the investment of time (and as a consequence, money) in the partially completed interview, interviewers have an understandable reluctance to terminate the interview. However, regardless of the reason why, a respondent always has the right to end the interview at any time *without* the need to explain why. It is unethical to design or conduct a research study in a way that prevents a respondent from exercising his or her right to withdraw or refuse to answer at *any stage* during the interview. Any request of the respondent to end the interview must be granted. PMRS goes on to point out that if the respondent so requests, as part of withdrawing from the interview, any information already collected must be deleted from the data base or destroyed.

Mistreatment

There are several ways in which research participants can be mistreated. The conduct of ethical research requires that the following types of situations be avoided:

- Frequent, repeated attempts to conduct the interview or attempts to conduct the interview at the researcher's convenience (for example, phone calls during the supper hour).

---

[5] It is important to point out that adherence to these standards does not compromise the integrity of a research study. "Full disclosure" in these areas does not appear to negatively affect respondents' willingness to participate in research, willingness to answer specific questions, or the quality or information they provide. See, for example, E. Singer, "Informed Consent: Consequences for Response Rate and Response Quality in Social Surveys," *American Sociological Review* (April 1978): 144–62; E. Singer and M. R. Frankel, "Informed Consent Procedures in Telephone Interviews," *American Sociological Review* (June 1982): 416–27.

- Overly long surveys that are not accurately described as such. It is unethical to recruit respondents by misrepresenting the length of the interview. A researcher has an obligation to provide a reasonably accurate estimate of the interview length.
- Asking personal questions for "information's sake."

Deception

Most marketing research relies on respondent naïveté. Researchers generally agree that a full and detailed explanation of study goals and approach have a strong potential to bias the respondent. As a consequence, the vast majority of advertising research incorporates some deception. The extent of deception varies across studies, from vagueness in presenting the topic of the research to outright falsification (for example, offering the choice of nonexistent products in order to conduct a concept test, sparing the expense of actually manufacturing the items under consideration).[6] While there is no consensus as to where to draw the line, it is generally agreed that the approach discussed earlier under "informed consent" is appropriate. It is generally considered ethical to tell the respondent nothing but the truth, but not necessarily the whole truth (with the strong caveat that the deception does not result in any harm to the respondent).[7]

Right to Confidentiality

Respondents' expectations that their responses will be treated confidentially is absolute unless they are explicitly informed that confidentiality will not be maintained and a written waiver is signed. Except in this latter case, any violation of confidentiality, no matter how minor you perceive that violation, is a severe breach of ethical research standards. CASRO addresses this point in great detail:

> Researchers have the "responsibility to protect the identities of respondents and to insure that individuals and their responses cannot be related . . . This principle of confidentiality includes the following specific applications: (a) restricting the company's own personnel from the use, or discussion, of respondent-identifiable data beyond legitimate internal research purposes, (b) accepting the responsibility for seeing that subcontractors . . . as well as . . . consultants are aware of and agree to the principle of respondent confidentiality and (c) denying requested access to respondent-identifiable opinion or fact (in questionnaires or other survey documents) on the part of the client, sponsor or any other organization."[8]

Right to Privacy

Closely related to confidentiality is privacy. Respondents must be informed of any data collection methods that might violate their expectation of privacy. Electronic equipment, such as taping, recording, photographing and one-way viewing rooms may be used after explicitly informing respondents.

---

[6] Sidney Hollander, Jr., "Ethics in Marketing Research," *Handbook of Marketing Research*, ed. Robert Ferber (New York, NY: McGraw-Hill Book Company, 1974), Section 1, 117.

[7] Ibid.

[8] Council of American Survey Research Organizations, "Code of Standards for Survey Research" (February 1981).

A Special Consideration: Research With Children

A great deal of advertising is directed toward children, and as a consequence, a great deal of research is conducted with children. The guidelines for ethical behavior discussed earlier in this section apply to both children and adults. But, the way in which each guideline is applied differs for children and adults. How, for example, do you obtain informed consent from a child or make certain that the child understands that he or she may stop participation at any time (after all, they can't tell their schoolteacher they don't want to do their class work)? Clearly, special care and provisions must be made to protect the interests of child participants as illustrated in the following guidelines:

- *The child's rights supersede the investigator's rights.* The rights of children research participants are greater than a researcher's need for information. In the conduct of research, a research design must primarily be evaluated in terms of how well the rights and needs of the child are protected.
- *There may be absolutely no physical or psychological harm.*
- *There must be informed written consent of the child's primary caretaker.* Informed consent requires that the caretaker be given accurate information on the professional training and competence of the researcher, the purpose and operation of the research, the nature of any deception involved in the research, and how the information collected by the research will be used.
- *There may be no coercion to participate.* The rights of parents and children to decline participation must be respected. Parents should be given the explicit opportunity to refuse participation. The child should also be given the right to refuse participation. No counter arguments, incentives, or coercion should be used in an effort to change the child's mind.
- *No diagnostic or other information on the child's participation should be offered.* An advertising researcher is not a clinical psychologist or child development specialist. As a consequence, he or she should not offer interpretations of the child's behavior based on the child's responses to the research stimuli. Comments such as the following are clearly inappropriate.

  "Out of all the advertising we showed Jerry, he most liked advertising for new guns and soldiers. He was *really* smiling as those guns were shown. He really seems to be into violence."

- *Principles apply even if the child or his family is paid for participation.* Payment in money or gifts does not annul any of the prior principles.

RESPONSIBILITIES TO CLIENTS

Every advertising research study has a client. The client may be internal (that is, other departments within the advertising agency such as Account Management or Creative) or external (that is, the company that employs the agency). Your dealings with both types of clients requires adherence to the principles of nonmaleficence and beneficence as reflected in the following four guidelines:

- Research recommendations will be appropriate. Recommend research when it is the best means for satisfying the client's marketing or communications problem and infor-

mational needs. When research is recommended, use only those techniques that most efficiently gather the required information.

- All information gathered throughout the research process will be treated in a confidential and proprietary manner.
- All findings will be presented in a straightforward and nonmisleading manner.
- Clients will be kept informed of all changes or departures from methodology, cost, or timing as initially presented in the research proposal.

Appropriate Research

Most researchers love to do research. They enjoy the challenge of identifying problems and developing creative ways to find information that helps solve these problems. As a consequence, there is a tendency for researchers to recommend research. Ethical standards, however, require that recommendations to conduct research be supportable by valid arguments (see the Justifying the Need for Research step in the research planning process, Chapter 2, page 22). Research should only be recommended when it has a high likelihood of providing valid, useful information that contributes to the decision-making process *and* when the economic consequences of making a wrong decision outweigh the cost of conducting the research.

A second aspect of appropriateness relates to research methodology. Clients are rarely sophisticated researchers and therefore rely on your expertise to recommend the methodology that has the greatest potential for collecting reliable, useful information in a timely and cost-efficient manner. You must make certain that your recommendations meet these criteria. If, for example, four focus groups are sufficient, it is unfair to the client and unethical on your part to recommend eight or twelve groups. If a convenience sample of 200 respondents can provide the required information it is unfair and unethical to recommend a national probability sample of 1,000 individuals.

The difficulty in recommending research methodology, however, lies in the fact that each research project has its own unique history, context, and informational needs. Methodological solutions to advertising research needs are seldom "off the shelf." As a consequence, any particular research problem can be addressed by several approaches. Advertising creative, for example, can be tested in preliminary or finished form via a qualitative or quantitative approach. Therefore, one sign of ethical professionalism is, whenever appropriate, you should develop several reasonable approaches to a particular problem and then discuss the relative advantages of each with the client. Express a point of view on which approach you consider to be the most appropriate. A client may not always agree with your recommendation, but you have acted ethically in (we assume) fairly presenting the strengths and weaknesses of viable alternatives.

Confidential and Proprietary

Maintaining the confidentiality of information and treating information in a proprietary manner are extremely important. Requirements of confidentiality apply to all information learned as part of the research process, that is, information acquired through conversations with the client and other involved individuals, information acquired through examination of the client's written documents, and information collected by the research project itself. All client-provided information and information generated as a

result of the examination of this information remain the proprietary property of the client and should never be revealed without the client's permission. Professional codes of ethics are unambiguous on these points:

> Research organizations will hold confidential all information which they obtain about a client's general business operations and about matters connected with research projects which they conduct for a client. (CASRO)[9]

> For research findings obtained by the agency which are the property of the client, the research organization may make no public release or revelation of the findings without express prior approval from the client. (CASRO)[10]

Presentation of Findings

The presentation of data and findings must be straightforward and not misleading. The failure to completely report all relevant data is a violation of ethical standards; it is deceptive and untruthful. Additionally, beyond ethical considerations, it is dangerous from a business perspective. This practice prevents the ultimate goal of the research from being realized (specifically, a clear and objective application of the findings to the decisions that initially motivated the research) and greatly increases the probability of the wrong decision being reached. Incomplete reporting generally takes one of two forms.

One form of misleading data presentation occurs when there is a failure to include all information necessary to evaluate presented data and findings. Data and findings can only be fairly evaluated and applied to the decision-making process when all pertinent information is available for examination. When presenting data, therefore, partial or summary presentations without accompanying detail should be avoided. The following example illustrates this principle:

> Two finished commercials are tested. It is decided that the commercial that has the most positive effect on purchase intent will receive the greater amount of airing in the commercial rotation. The following table is presented. Statistical tests reveal that average purchase intent is not statistically different between the two commercials, but the percent showing strong purchase intent is significantly higher for Commercial A versus Commercial B.

	Commercial A	*Commercial B*
Average purchase intent	3.0	2.8
Percent of respondents "Strongly agreeing" that they were likely to purchase the product after seeing the commercial	30%	15%

Based on this presentation of the findings, the researcher recommended that Commercial A be given greater media weight than Commercial B.

Unfortunately, this may be the wrong decision.

The researcher did not specify the level at which statistical significance was found, and as a consequence, it is impossible to evaluate the confidence one should have in drawing the conclusion that Commercial A is better than Commercial B in the level of "strong"

---

[9] Ibid.
[10] Ibid.

purchase intent generated. Additionally, the full pattern of response to the commercial was not presented. In reality, the commercials had very different effects on purchase intent as shown by the complete data table:

Purchase Intent	*Commercial A*	*Commercial B*
Strongly agree	30%	15%
Slightly agree	15	40
Neither agree or disagree	10	0
Slightly disagree	15	45
Strongly disagree	30	0

The incomplete reporting of the full findings on this measure masked the real and important differences in the pattern of response to the two commercials. Commercial A tended to polarize the sample. As many people "strongly agreed" that they were interested in the product as "strongly disagreed." No individual who saw Commercial B had a strong negative reaction. Additionally, in terms *of total* agreement, more people who saw Commercial A (55 percent versus 45 percent) agreed that they were interested in purchasing the product.

A second form of misleading data reporting occurs when impressions left by the presentation of the data are not, in reality, justified by the data itself. This often occurs, for example, when inappropriate scales are used on tables or charts. The graph in Figure 3.2 displays levels of advertising awareness during the past year. Note how the use of small increments between scale points and the use of perspective and shading makes a visual statement of growth in awareness not justified by the actual data.

Project Changes

Many research projects are executed as planned. The study's methodological approach works well to collect the desired information, and cost and timing estimates are accu-

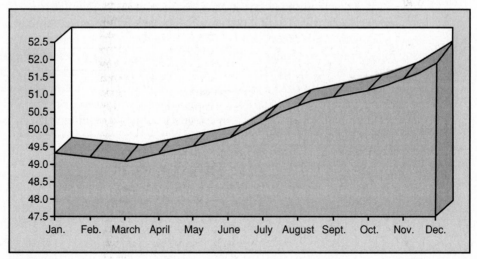

FIGURE 3.2
Example of misleading data presentation.

rate. Some projects, however, can encounter problems once they are in the field. These problems can be related to unforeseen difficulty with contacting and recruiting target respondents, the questionnaire taking longer to administer than indicated in the pilot tests, or the field service being unable to collect the data as quickly as indicated in the bid letter.

None of these types of problems are particularly disastrous for a research study. However, what is disastrous (and unethical) is responding to research-related problems and altering study design, cost or timing *without* informing the client. It is unethical (as well as unprofessional) to make any changes in research design without client consultation. Moreover, the client must be promptly informed of the cost or timing implications of any changes to the research study.

RESPONSIBILITIES TO MARKETING RESEARCH ORGANIZATIONS

Chapter 1 discussed the manner by which custom research organizations and field services provide invaluable assistance to advertising researchers. Unfortunately, researchers have not always treated these organizations in an ethical manner.[11] Common practices that violate the principles of nonmaleficence and beneficence and, as a consequence, which you should avoid in your interactions with these organizations, include

- issuing calls for bids or proposals when a supplier has already been selected;
- using the proposal process to obtain free advice;
- making false promises to obtain lower costs.

Preselection

As an advertising researcher you interact with a great number of research companies. You will find that companies vary in their responsiveness to your particular needs and requirements. You will also find that some companies will be enjoyable and stimulating to work with, while others will not. When presented with the choice of which company to select for a particular project, there is nothing wrong in selecting a company that in the past has demonstrated high levels of professionalism and expertise and with which you have established a good working relationship. It is unethical, however, to predetermine prior to the bid process which company will receive the project but then issue a call for bids and proposals only to satisfy corporate requirements.

Free Advice

Researchers and research companies deal with ideas; their products are their original thoughts, insights, and expertise. As a result, we strongly caution you against soliciting detailed proposals in order to "pick the brains" of those with expertise in cases where you have no intention to award the project to one of the companies that has submitted a proposal. Further, we caution you against stealing the recommendations and

---

[11] Michel Laroche, K. L. McGowan, and Joyce Rainville, "How Ethical are Professional Marketing Researchers?" *Business Forum* (Winter 1986): 20–25.

techniques submitted as part of the proposal process without appropriate compensation. Proper, ethical procedures for soliciting bids and proposals require the following:

- A company should be informed that its proposal is one of several being solicited.
- Technical ideas and methodological recommendations must be treated confidentially. No technique or recommendation can be taken from one proposal for use by another organization without prior permission.
- All unaccepted proposals remain the property of the originating organization unless appropriate payment has been made.

False Promises

An unethical practice closely related to "free advice" is making false promises to reduce the cost of conducting a research study. It is unethical to falsely say to a research supplier, "If you give us a break on the cost of this research, I know that I can throw a lot of business your way later in the year."

RESPONSIBILITIES TO SOCIETY

It is my responsibility, as a researcher, to listen for the voice of the people and make it heard. Research serves its highest purpose when it speaks for the citizen or the consumer, when it brings the wants and wishes and ideas of people to light, not for manipulation or exploitation, but for translation into needed products and laws and services.[12]

This pledge should be your guiding principle for every project you initiate and for every project for which you report results. Additionally, adherence to the principles of nonmaleficence and beneficence requires the following:

- Data and findings reported for public use should be complete.
- Data and findings reported for public use should be nonmisleading and properly interpreted.
- Data reported for public use will be based on sound, objective research judgment.
- Research will not be used as a guise for marketing or sales efforts.

Complete Data and Findings

One ethical responsibility to clients is the full and complete reporting of data and findings. This responsibility is equally important when preparing data for public use. A researcher who withholds negative or damaging information from public release of the research is no different than the manufacturer who fails to disclose potentially damaging information about a product. Both mislead through deception, misinformation, and failure to fully disclose.

Proper Interpretation

Misleading reporting of research findings occurs when "the research is presented in such a manner that the intended audience will draw a conclusion that is not justified by

---

[12] Portion of the pledge of the New York Chapter of the American Marketing Association.

the results."[13] Misleading data presentation occurs most frequently in two cases: when one uses inappropriate frames of reference and when the data is manipulated or placed in a context in order to support an advocacy position.

Inappropriate frames of reference commonly occur when percent change is reported. Consider the following:

> (From a radio report): The demographics of Plainville are certainly changing. It's not the town it once was, that's for certain. Over the past two years the ethnic composition of Plainville has shown phenomenal increases. The percent of African-Americans in town has increased nearly 400 percent while the number of Hispanics has increased nearly 700 percent. And these trends show no sign of slowing.

> Trends in advertising awareness are very positive. Our major competitor, the Jones Company, has shown no growth in awareness over the past year while awareness of our advertising (the Harris Company) has tripled.

The radio report is clearly alarmist. It leaves the impression that African-Americans and Hispanics are taking over the town. A much different impression would have been left if it were reported that the percentage of the total population accounted for by African-Americans rose from 0.5 percent to 2 percent while the percentage accounted for by Hispanics rose from 0.2 percent to 1.4 percent. Similarly, a quite different impression of the trends in advertising awareness would have been reached from a full presentation of the data, specifically, that awareness of Jones advertising is stable at 93 percent, while awareness of Harris' advertising rose from 3 percent to 6 percent.

The use of research to support an advocacy position commonly occurs in the presentation of advertising claims. Consider the following:

> The Smith Company conducts research to evaluate consumers' preference for brands of shampoo. They find that

> - 15 percent of consumers prefer Swell Shampoo;
> - 5 percent prefer any of the other three leading brands;
> - 80 percent have no preference and rate all brands the same.

> Based on this research, the Smith Company advertises that "Among those with a preference, Swell Shampoo is preferred over all other leading brands by an astonishing three to one."

The claim is factually correct, but nevertheless represents an unethical use of the research findings. The advertising claim leaves an impression (Swell is overwhelmingly preferred) not justified by the actual findings (that is, that 80 percent of the sample felt that there were no differences between any of the brands).

Sound, Objective Research

Advertising or marketing research that is not conducted in a sound manner tarnishes the entire research industry and has the potential to harm the public. This type of research, which is typically conducted in a way that will maximize the likelihood of obtaining the desired result, is unethical and should be avoided at all costs. This type of research occurs, for example, when there is nonscientific and biased selection of samples. This may involve, for example, conducting preference research among those who

---

[13] Donald S. Tull and Del I. Hawkins, *Marketing Research, 5th Edition* (New York, NY: Macmillan Publishing Company, 1990), 726.

are already favorable toward you or conducting research in markets that do not represent normal or ordinary market conditions.

Research Is Not a Guise

In recent years there has been a rise in the number of mailings and telephone calls that use research as a pretext for accomplishing nonresearch objectives such as sales, fund solicitation, or the creation of a data base. A respondent will interpret a lead-in of "I'm taking a survey and am interested in your opinions" as an indication that the goal is the collection of information. Using this type of approach for other reasons is not only deceptive and a clear violation of ethical standards, it is also illegal.

Summary

As a member of the advertising profession you have the responsibility to act ethically and, to the absolute best of your ability, to adhere to the ethical principles of autonomy, nonmaleficence, and beneficence as you interact with four groups of individuals: research respondents, your internal and external clients, research support companies, and the public. Ethical standards and behaviors that you should follow in your professional relationships with each of these groups are summarized below.

Research Respondents:	The decision to participate must be an informed decision.
	The decision to terminate participation cannot be infringed on.
	There must be no mistreatment.
	Deceptions must cause no harm and be justifiable given research design and informational needs.
	There is an absolute right to confidentiality and privacy.
Research Clients:	Methodological recommendations will be appropriate.
	All information is confidential and proprietary.
	Findings will be presented honestly in a nonmisleading manner.
	Notification will be made of all changes in study parameters.
Research Companies:	No false calls for proposals.
	No use of the proposal process to obtain free advice.
	No false promises.
Society:	Data and findings will be complete.
	Data and findings will not be misleading and will be properly interpreted.
	Data will be based on sound, objective research judgment.
	Research should not be used as a pretext for sales, fundraising, or data base creation efforts.

Review Questions

1. Define the ethical principles of autonomy, nonmaleficence, and beneficence.
2. What are the four groups with which advertising researchers have professional relationships?
3. What six guidelines describe how a researcher should interact with study respondents?

4. What do we mean when we say, "Participation in a research study must be the result of an informed decision"?

5. Under what circumstances may a respondent decide that he or she no longer wishes to participate in the research study?

6. How can you plan a research study to minimize or eliminate respondent mistreatment?

7. Are all deceptive practices unethical? Which specific deceptive practices are clearly unethical?

8. What is meant by, "A respondent has an absolute right to confidentiality and privacy"?

9. What guidelines govern a researcher's interactions with his or her internal and external clients?

10. How can a researcher make certain that appropriate approaches to the research problem are selected?

11. What is meant by, "A client has an absolute right to confidentiality and privacy"?

12. What guidelines are important to keep in mind when presenting data to one's client?

13. What is the ethical way to handle changes in research design, cost, or timing once the study is approved?

14. What ethical guidelines govern a researcher's interactions with marketing research organizations? Briefly describe each of these principles.

15. What ethical guidelines govern a researcher's responsibilities to society? Briefly describe each of these principles.

Application Exercises

1. Each of the situations described next represents a type of practice that some researchers have engaged in or have approved.[14] Read each hypothetical situation and then discuss the ethical implications of the actions described in each situation.

   a. The Harris Corporation is the parent company of Pizza-to-Go, a chain of franchised Pizza Restaurants. Melvin Harris asks you to conduct a survey of their franchisees. You and Melvin agree that, in order to obtain the most honest answers, strict confidentiality of respondents and their responses must be maintained. You then prepare the questionnaires for mailing. In order to know who has responded to the first mailing (so that a second mailing can be sent to nonresponders) you place an identification code on the questionnaires. After the study is complete you present the results to Melvin. One question on the survey asked each franchisee to rate the leadership ability of Melvin Harris. Twenty-five percent of the sample rated Melvin Harris' leadership ability "excellent." Melvin asks for the names of those who provided the "excellent" rating in order to give them a more substantial Christmas bonus.

   b. You conduct personal interviews with target audience women in a mall. As part of the interview, each woman tries and comments on your client's shampoo. At the end of the interview you give each woman a free bottle of the shampoo as a "thanks for participating gift." You do not tell each woman that they will be called back in a week to be reinterviewed after they have used the product at home.

---

[14] These cases are based on the research of Larouche et al., "How Ethical Are Marketing Researchers?"

c. You have constructed a 30-minute telephone interview. During the first week of interviewing potential respondents were told of the interview length. Unfortunately, fewer individuals than anticipated have agreed to be interviewed. You change the introduction to the survey to say: "This is an important survey. It will take a relatively short amount of time."

d. You are interviewing a number of doctors on their drug prescribing behaviors. A number of doctors say that they will participate only if you send them the results of the study. You agree to send them the results, even though you have no intention of doing so.

e. You are conducting a series of focus groups. You explain that the client and other interested parties are seated behind the one-way mirror and that the responses will be tape-recorded. You do not mention that the groups are being filmed from behind the mirror.

f. You are in a bind. You have been asked to design a research study in an area in which you do not have a great deal of expertise. You decide to solicit a number of proposals from customized research companies, take the best ideas from each, and then rebid the job and award the job to the lowest bidder.

g. Your client has decided that telemarketing has the potential to be a successful way to market his product, an expensive but very well-made and effective water purifier. He says that this product is really only useful to those households that drink more than two gallons of water per day. He does not wish to take advantage by selling the product to those who really do not have the need. (He wants to feel good about each sale.) So, he needs to identify just the right people. Your client asks you to evaluate the telemarketing script that he has written:

> Hello. My name is _____ and I am calling from WaterCo. Inc. I'm taking just a brief survey of Escalipho residents to determine their satisfaction with the municipal drinking water. Can you please tell me . . .

1. Your age (FILL IN) _____
2. The number of people in your household (FILL IN) _____
3. Are you currently satisfied with the quality of the tap water used for drinking in your household?
   YES _____ NO _____
4. Do you currently have an in-tap water purification system?
   YES _____ NO _____
5. Does your family drink, on average, at least two gallons of water per day?
   YES _____ NO _____

IF "NO" TO QUESTION 3 AND "YES" TO QUESTION 5, ARRANGE A TIME FOR AN IN-HOME DEMONSTRATION.

h. The executives of the GIBA Company are very difficult to reach by telephone. However, this is the way that you must reach them to successfully conduct your research. In order to get past each executive's secretary you say, "I have been referred to (name of executive) to discuss an important, but personal matter."

i. You have noticed that many people are hanging up before the end of a complex 15-minute interview. You offer those who wish to hang up $5 for completing the interview. You offer no money to those who do not state a desire to terminate.

j. You need to obtain copies of competitive advertising and (hopefully) media plans. You call your competitors and ask for the information under the guise of a student working on a class assignment.

2. Review the guidelines that govern the nature of a researcher's interactions with respondents. Prepare a "Bill of Rights" that can be shown to respondents prior to their participation in a research study.

3. Richard Fedman has just joined the SSDR Advertising Agency as an Associate Research Director. Richard will supervise research on the Tico Fast Food account.[15] Richard's prior position was a Research Supervisor at another agency where he worked on the Mexicale Foods Account, a competitor of Tico Fast Food. Think about each of the following situations in which Richard might find himself. What course of action would you suggest Richard take in each situation?

   a. In a meeting with Tico's management, Todd Kilgore, a Senior Vice President of Development, says that Tico needs to begin to capitalize on consumers' desire to eat healthy. He suggests that Richard plan and conduct a research study to determine the appeal of health-positioned Mexican fast food. Richard knows the answer without doing the research. He conducted the exact same study for Mexicale prior to leaving the company. He knows that consumers are very interested in this type of product, and that based on the research, Mexicale is planning on revising their menu. Should Richard share this knowledge with Todd?

   b. Richard learned a unique and accurate way to identify consumers' taste preferences while working on the Mexicale account. Tico now wants to conduct taste tests of their products. Should Richard describe and recommend this methodology to Tico?

   c. Richard is a very creative researcher. While working at his prior agency he developed a method for obtaining very meaningful insights into consumers' reactions to advertising. One of SSDR's clients is about to conduct this type of research. Should Richard share this new methodology with SSDR's clients?

4. Each of the hypothetical situations described next relate to the ethics of data presentation. Read each hypothetical situation and then determine if the relevant chart shown in Figure 3.3 satisfies or violates ethical standards for data presentation. Be certain to explain the basis of your decision.

   a. The AABB Agency conducts a quarterly research study to measure awareness levels of one of their client's advertising. The percent of individuals from among the total sample who say that they are aware of the advertising is as follows:

Quarter	1994	1995
Q1 (Jan. to March)	14%	15%
Q2 (April to June)	10	16
Q3 (July to Sept.)	7	14
Q4 (Oct. to Dec.)	5	12

   An agency researcher takes this data and computes the percent change in each 1995 quarter compared to the same quarter in 1994. For example, awareness in Q1 1995 is 107 percent of the same quarter in 1994 (calculated as 15 ÷ 14). The researcher takes this data and prepares Chart A in Figure 3.3.

---

[15] The individuals, companies, and situation described in this exercise are fictitious.

Chart A

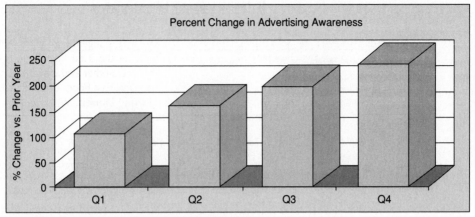

Chart B

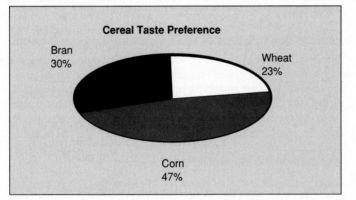

Chart C

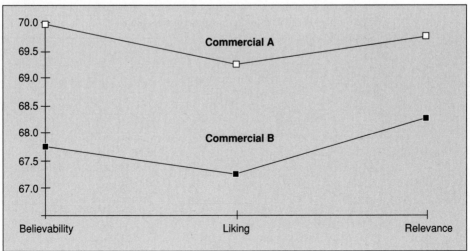

FIGURE 3.3 Approaches to data presentation.

b. The client research team conducts a survey to determine the cereal taste preferences of adults aged 25 to 39. They obtain the following results:

Product	Percent of Sample
Prefer Wheat	10%
Prefer Corn	16
Prefer Bran	11
No preference	63

The research team re-percents to obtain preferences among those who express a preference. Chart B in Figure 3.3 is prepared to communicate this finding.

c. Two commercials are tested. Three key measures of the test are believability, liking, and relevance. The percent of individuals providing a positive rating (for example, agreeing that the commercial is believable) for each measure for each commercial is shown as Chart C in Figure 3.3.

5. Examine consumer-oriented publications such as *USA Today*, *Time*, and *Newsweek* or more demographically focused publications such as *Gentleman's Quarterly*, *Redbook*, or *Sassy*. Find a discussion of survey results. Evaluate whether the results and conclusions presented in the article meet the standards of ethical data presentation.

6. You are hired as the Research Director for a national wild animal conservancy. The conservancy wants to put pressure on congress to preserve more land as animal preserves. You conduct research among the members of the conservancy and find that 93 percent of the members support the increased preservation of land for animal preserves. These individuals agreed with the statement: "The increased preservation of natural lands is an important goal for the United States." The conservancy wants to send a letter to all members of congress announcing the results of this study. The introduction of the letter would report the following:

We've worked for more natural preserves. We know that this is important. And so do the American people. Over 90 percent of Americans agree that increasing the preservation of land is an important national goal.

The remainder of the letter discusses the conservancy but not the research. Would you approve of this use and communication of the results?[15]

CHAPTER

4 | REPORTING RESEARCH

The presentation of research findings and implications is an extremely important step in the overall research process. An excellent presentation gives decision makers the information and insights they need to evaluate alternative courses of action and to better understand the consumer and the marketplace. A poor research presentation greatly diminishes the usefulness of the research. After all, a decision maker cannot decide how to use the results if he or she cannot understand what the results are or what they infer. Advertising researchers must therefore strive for excellence not only in research design and analysis, but also in the presentation of research findings. This chapter discusses the presentation of advertising research.

After reading this chapter you will be able to

■ Identify the characteristics of good research report writing.

■ Use tables and charts to improve communication.

■ Structure and present research findings and implications in written and oral formats.

THE CHARACTERISTICS OF GOOD RESEARCH REPORT WRITING

An excellent research report successfully communicates a research project's goals, objectives, methodology, key findings, and implications. Excellence in the oral and written presentation of research can be achieved if your report is clear, concise, complete, correct, and coherent.[1]

Clarity and Conciseness

Clarity and *conciseness* are important attributes of a well-prepared research report. A report must clearly communicate the project's methodology, findings, implications,

---

[1] For an extended discussion of these issues see Ray E. Barfield and Sylvia S. Titus, *Business Communication* (Hauppauge, NY: Barron's Education Series, Inc., 1992). The discussion in this section is based on this source.

and recommendations in a way that is immediately understandable by the report's target audience. Clarity permits the audience to focus on what has been discovered and the implications of these discoveries. Conciseness in reporting saves the audience time and energy. A research report's audience often consists of busy professionals who appreciate receiving information in the fewest possible words. The clarity and conciseness of a research report are improved when you

- *Eliminate unnecessary words.* Many reports take ten or twelve words to say what could be said in one or two words. For example,

eliminate...	*in favor of...*
it is important to note that...	importantly
due to the fact that...	because
for the purpose of...	to
in view of the foregoing analysis	therefore
a supplemental review of the data...	additional analyses

- *Use common words and simple phrasing.* Researchers often think that a formal oral or written report means that formal, stiff language must be used. This is not true. You can keep your report clear and concise by avoiding popular "buzzwords" and phrases (for example, parameter, interface, prioritize, strategize, conceptualize, and scenario). In addition, you can improve clarity and conciseness by directly saying what you mean. For example,

eliminate...	*in favor of...*
as previously alluded to...	earlier
in accordance with the preponderance of the analytical results...	the results indicate
a factor which exerts a significant influence...	an influential factor
the format that we will adhere to in...	we will present the data
terms of data presentation will be...	as follows

- *Minimize the use of technical jargon and use vocabulary that matches that of the reader or listener.* Technical jargon plays an important role in intradiscipline communication. It helps individuals who share a common outlook and training quickly communicate with each other. Jargon and technical terminology, however, hinder communication when they are used with audiences who do not have the appropriate training and expertise.

   Most individuals in the research report's audience are not trained researchers and, as a consequence, jargon and highly technical terms should be avoided. Terms such as chi-square distribution, correlation coefficient, and significance level are often unfamiliar and confusing to nonresearchers at the agency and the client. Leave the technical jargon for the appendices. This does not mean, however, that the concepts underlying technical terminology are inappropriate for a research report. Rather, it is the concept that should be explained and used rather than the technical terminology. For example,

instead of...	*say...*
the chi-square contingency table...	a cross-tabulation
correlation coefficient...	relationship between
level of statistical significance...	certainty

Finally, in those cases where the use of technical terminology cannot be avoided, the technical term should be clearly explained at the point where it is introduced into the report.

- *Avoid run-on sentences*. Run-on sentences tend to bore the reader and make it quite difficult to discern the meaning or implications of the information contained in the sentence. For example:

> There are many unresolved questions regarding the use of humor in advertising, in general, and within the context of Xerox advertising in particular, and as a consequence the client has requested research designed to help us more thoroughly understand the effect of humor on television commercial main message communication and brand perceptions within the context of Xerox advertising.

This sentence should be broken down into a series of shorter sentences, presenting just the most important information. For example:

> The agency is currently using humor in Xerox advertising but is unsure how it affects the target audience. No Xerox-specific research has been performed and other research investigating the effects of humor in advertising has shown conflicting results. Research is needed to determine the effect of humor in Xerox television commercials on message communication and Xerox brand perceptions.

- *Use the active versus passive voice*. Communication in the active voice adds interest, brevity, and clarity to the research report, as illustrated in the following pairs of sentences:

Passive	*Active*
In the course of my analysis it became apparent that...	The analysis shows...
There were three reasons for this trend in response.	The response trend occurred for three reasons.
The option of checking as many or as few of the choices on the checklist was given to each respondent.	Respondents could check as many or as few checklist items as they desired.

Clarity and conciseness are also improved through the physical organization and presentation of the oral or written report. You can use informative section labels to summarize key findings and bullet points to isolate and highlight key points.

Completeness

A complete report provides details at a sufficient depth of understandability. You can evaluate the breadth and depth of reported information by objectively reading your report and then asking yourself: "Can my audience fully understand the research findings and *independently* evaluate the appropriateness of conclusions and recommendations?" If the answer is "yes," then your report is likely complete.

Correctness

Correctness in content, style, and form is vital to every report. Correctness has three aspects: information content, grammar, and spelling. The information presented must be

without error. Tables and charts must be double-checked for accuracy, columns must total to the appropriate number, and table and chart labels must be correct. Errors in any aspect of data presentation, no matter how insignificant in the "big picture," typically lead to a reduction in the audience's view of the overall research project's and researcher's credibility. After all, if the researcher cannot get the details correct in the presentation of the research findings, how can anyone be sure that the design, conduct, and analysis of the research was handled properly?

Correctness in the use of language, grammar, and spelling is also extremely important. Incorrect grammar and spelling get in the way of clear, direct communication of research results. Moreover, grammatical and spelling errors lessen the audience's view of the researcher's competence and professionalism.

Coherence

Coherence refers to the smooth flow of thoughts in the presentation of findings. A research report is coherent when

- there are smooth transitions between thoughts,
- related pieces of information are grouped and presented together,
- topics are logically arranged and follow each other in an intuitively reasonable way, and
- a clear, explicit presentation of findings serves as the direct basis for conclusions, implications, and recommendations.

PREPARING AND USING TABLES AND CHARTS

Written and oral research reports typically consist of both narrative and graphics. Recommendations for improving the narrative portion of the report were presented in the prior section. This section explains the proper use of four types of graphics: numeric tables, line charts, bar charts, and pie charts. Tables and charts are important parts of the research report because they

- help to focus the audience's attention on specific aspects of the data,
- facilitate the communication of data findings and trends, and
- add visual interest.

We begin by discussing the characteristics and use of numeric tables and different types of charts.[2] This is followed by considerations that guide the use of all graphic materials.

Numeric Tables

Numeric tables are most appropriate for providing exact figures on a single topic or multiple related topics. Table 4.1, for example, displays consumers' product purchase intent after viewing one of three commercials. The data shown is for the total sample.

---

[2] The physical generation of tables and charts is facilitated through the use of any of several personal computer programs. Two of the more popular graphics programs are Harvard Graphics and Microsoft Excel.

TABLE 4.1 Purchase Intent After Commercial Viewing (Total Sample)			
Purchase Intent Scale	*Commercial A* *(Base = 140)*	*Commercial B* *(Base = 140)*	*Commercial C* *(Base = 140)*
Extremely likely	50.0%	14.2%	7.8%
Slightly likely	21.6	14.2	44.2
Slightly unlikely	14.2	50.0	26.4
Extremely unlikely	14.2	21.6	21.6
Total	100.0%	100.0%	100.0%

The creation of a simple table of this type is straightforward and the table itself illustrates important elements of a well-constructed table:

- the table is identified by number
- a descriptive title appears on the top of the table
- columns are clearly labeled
- the number of respondents in each group is shown
- numbers are rounded to a reasonable level of precision
- decimal points are aligned
- columns add to the appropriate total

Table preparation is more complex when multiple groups of data are presented in the same table. These circumstances require the need to organize the table so that it is easy for the audience to visually see the desired data trends and relationships. Imagine, for example, that you wanted to present the purchase intent of men and women as well as that of the overall sample after viewing the three commercials. This would result in a table with nine columns (three commercials with three columns per commercial: total sample, men and women). The organization of the columns within the table would vary in accordance with the points you wanted to make and where you wanted to focus the audience's attention. Table 4.2A (page 56) focuses on the three commercials noting reactions *within* each commercial. This organization makes it easy to compare men's versus women's reactions to the same commercial. The organization of the data in Table 4.2B (page 56) reflects the opposite focus. Here, the focus is on reactions to each commercial *within* each group of respondents. This organization makes it easy to see which of the three commercials was preferred by men and which was preferred by women.

Bar Charts   Bar charts are a common graphical method of presenting research findings. Bar graphs are appropriate whenever the goal is to show a comparison of quantities or amounts at different points in time or the relative size or amount of several groups compared at the same point in time. Figure 4.1 (page 57) presents data regarding the marital status of a study sample. Bar Chart A lists the categories on the bottom of the graph in the order the categories were asked in the survey question. The vertical axis represents the percentage of the sample (and is labeled as such) and the height of each bar represents the percentage of respondents in each category (as indicated on the chart). Note also that the chart is given an informative title and the total number of respondents is noted on the bottom of the chart.

TABLE 4.2A Purchase Intent After Commercial Viewing (Gender Within Commercial)

Purchase Intent Scale	Commercial A			Commercial B			Commercial C		
	Overall (Base = 140)	*Men (Base = 70)*	*Women (Base = 70)*	*Overall (Base = 140*	*Men (Base = 70)*	*Women (Base = 70)*	*Overall (Base = 140)*	*Men (Base = 70)*	*Women (Base = 70)*
Extremely likely	50.0%	50.0%	50.0%	14.2%	7.1%	21.4%	7.8%	1.4%	14.4%
Slightly likely	21.6	24.3	18.6	14.2	11.4	17.1	44.2	44.2	44.2
Slightly unlikely	14.2	18.6	10.0	50.0	52.9	47.1	26.4	25.8	27.0
Extremely unlikely	14.2	7.1	21.4	21.6	28.6	14.4	21.6	28.6	14.4
Total	100.0%	100.0%	100.0%	100.0%	100.0%	100.0%	100.0%	100.0%	100.0%

TABLE 4.2B Purchase Intent After Commercial Viewing (Commercial Within Gender)

Purchase Intent Scale	Total Sample			Men			Women		
	Com. A (Base = 140)	*Com. B (Base = 140)*	*Com. C (Base = 140)*	*Com. A (Base = 70*	*Com. B (Base = 70)*	*Com. C (Base = 70)*	*Com. A (Base = 70)*	*Com. B (Base = 70)*	*Com. C (Base = 70)*
Extremely likely	50.0%	14.2%	7.8%	50.0%	7.1%	1.4%	50.0%	21.4%	14.4%
Slightly likely	21.6	14.2	44.2	24.3	11.4	44.2	18.6	17.1	44.2
Slightly unlikely	14.2	50.0	26.4	18.6	52.9	25.8	10.0	47.1	27.0
Extremely unlikely	14.2	21.6	21.6	7.1	28.6	28.6	21.4	14.4	14.4
Total	100.0%	100.0%	100.0%	100.0%	100.0%	100.0%	100.0%	100.0%	100.0%

Bar charts are flexible both in terms of their physical format and the way in which the categories are presented. In terms of physical format, the relative positions of response categories and percentages can be reversed so that the bars move horizontally; the longer the bar the greater the percentage of responses represented by the bar. Additionally, in terms of the way in which categories are presented, you might decide that a presentation of categories in the order they appeared on the questionnaire does not communicate the desired insight, deciding instead to order the categories from lowest to highest or vice versa to provide an immediate view of the relative sizes of each group. Bar Chart B (Figure 4.1) reorders the marital status groups to reflect relative group size.

Pie Charts   Pie charts are another option for the display of data. Pie charts are appropriate whenever you need to visually represent a share or segment of the whole, for example, a proportion or a percentage. The pie represents 100 percent of the total and each segment represents a share of the total. Figure 4.2 (page 58) illustrates two types of pie charts. Pie Chart A, unexploded, shows the distribution of marital status in the study sample. Aside from size, each segment receives equal emphasis in terms of attracting atten-

Bar Chart A

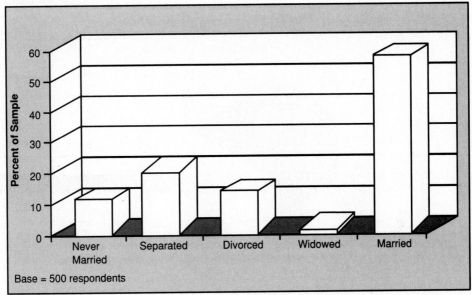

Bar Chart B

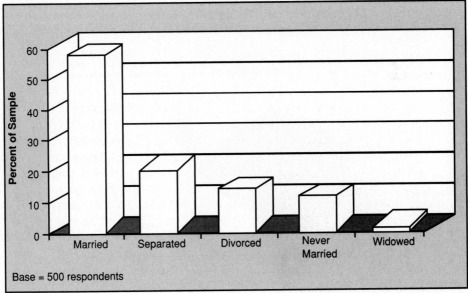

FIGURE 4.1
Bar charts.

Chart A

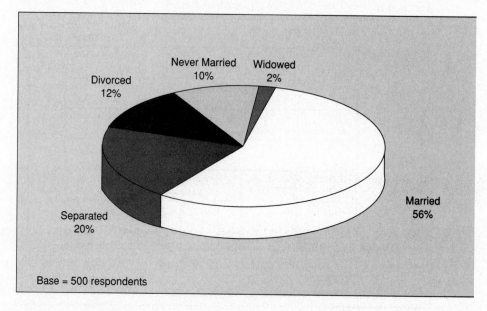

Chart B

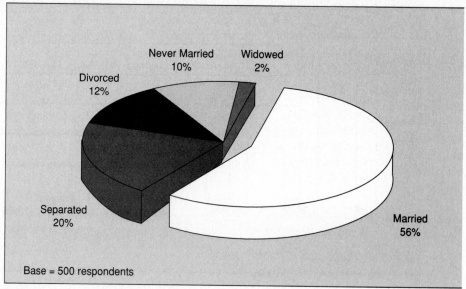

FIGURE 4.2
Unexploded and exploded pie charts.

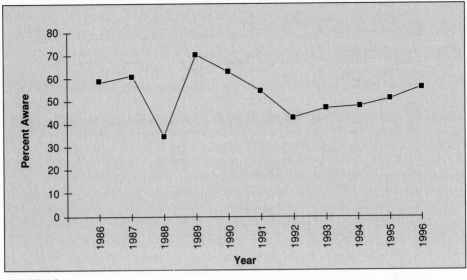

FIGURE 4.3
Line chart.

tion. Pie Chart B, exploded, isolates one segment for greater emphasis. The exploded segment is the one on which you want to focus the audience's attention. In this example, the "never married" section of Chart B has been exploded. Note that in both versions of the pie chart each section of the pie is differentially shaded and labeled with the name of the segment and the percentage of the total represented by the segment. Finally, as with bar charts, each pie chart is given an informative title, number, and name, and the total number of respondents represented in the chart is shown beneath the pie.

Line Charts   Line charts are appropriate for displaying data trends, especially trends over time (Figure 4.3). It is important that the chart be given an appropriate number and title and that both axes and all lines be appropriately labeled.

Except in well-justified and specialized circumstances, we do not recommend the use of multiple line graphs where the two vertical axes represent different measures and each line is read against a different axis. This type of line chart (Figure 4.4, page 60) is often very difficult to explain to and be understood by the report's audience. It is difficult in this chart, for example, to tell if 1995 awareness is 41 percent or 62 percent.

Using Tables and Charts Effectively

Tables and charts should add to, not detract from, your oral and written research report. To maximize the effective use of these tables and charts, keep the following in mind:[3]

1. Be certain that the table or chart is an improvement over the narrative presentation of the same information. A table or chart that does not improve clarity is probably not needed.

[3] Charles B. Smith, *A Guide to Business Research* (Chicago, IL: Nelson-Hall, 1981), 135–36; Michael C. Thomsett, *The Little Black Book of Business Reports* (New York: AMACOM, 1988), 69–70.

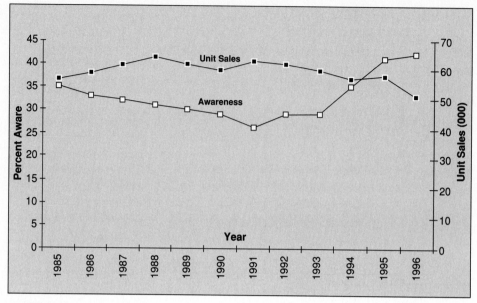

FIGURE 4.4
Line chart with multiple data.

2. Keep tables and graphs simple. They should not present more information than your audience can quickly understand. The line chart shown in Figure 4.4 is an example of a chart that is too complex. When it is necessary to present complex information (for example, the relationship between multiple measures) side-by-side graphs in which conclusions are provided on the graph itself work well.

3. Be consistent when using charts. Do not use a pie chart and a bar chart to present the same type of data. For example, if you first present subgroup analyses via a bar chart then use the bar chart format for similar data throughout the report or presentation.

4. Make certain that the table or chart is well integrated with the narrative. A *collection* of tables placed at the end of a report tends to decrease comprehension when (and if) it is referred to by making the reader jump from one part of the report to another. It is much better to interweave text, tables, and charts. This can be done by placing narrative, tables, and charts on the same page and referring to these items in the narrative. This also prevents tables and charts from being taken out of context.

5. Use tables and charts to *present* the data. Use narrative to *interpret* the data. Merely describing or reiterating what can readily be seen in the table or graph is boring, wastes time, and insults the audience's intelligence. The narrative should point out the significance of the information the table or chart contains and how this information provides a foundation for later conclusions and recommendations.

Finally, remember the guidelines for the ethical presentation of data discussed in Chapter 3. You must make very certain that charts and tables clearly, and without deception, communicate appropriate trends and conclusions.

THE WRITTEN RESEARCH REPORT

The content and organization of a written research report varies as a function of the report's audience and topic. However, most reports will contain the following elements:

- title page
- table of contents and list of illustrations/figures
- executive summary
- background
- description of the methodology
- findings
- conclusions and limitations
- recommendations and next steps
- appendices

The remainder of this section discusses each of these components of the research report as well as the cover letter that accompanies the report when it is distributed to the agency and client.[4]

Title Page

The title page is the report's first or cover page. While the physical format of title pages varies among advertising agencies, most title pages contain the same core set of information, specifically

- the title of the study
- the date or period of the study
- the date the report was prepared
- the account for which the study was conducted
- internal agency job or control number
- the names of the principal agency researchers involved in the planning, conduct, and analysis of the research
- any restrictions related to distribution or confidentiality

Table of Contents and List of Illustrations/Figures

All but the shortest research reports require a table of contents. The table of contents should list the page numbers of major sections and subsections as well as items placed in the report appendix. The table of contents is typically followed by a listing of illustrations and figures appearing in the main body of the report. The format of the table of contents and list of illustrations should reflect their purpose—to help the reader obtain an overview of the report contents and flow.

---

[4] The materials shown in this section are fictitious and are for illustrative purposes only.

Executive Summary

The executive summary is the most important part of the research report. It contains a clear and concise *summary* of the information presented in more detail later in the report. An executive summary presents information related to

- *Study background and purpose*—Why the study was done and how the information is to be used.
- *Methodology*—How the information was collected.
- *Main findings*—What was learned.
- *Conclusions (with any appropriate limitations) and recommendations*—A summary of learning and a point of view regarding what should be done now that the research is complete.

The executive summary should be written so that it stands alone. It is common for the executive summary to be the only part of the full research report that is read and for it to be reproduced and distributed by itself without the full report attached. Thus, it is vitally important that the executive summary provide enough information to permit anyone who reads only this portion of the full report to understand what was learned and the basis for conclusions and recommendations. A sample executive summary is shown in Figure 4.5 (pages 64–65).

Background

The background section of the research report provides a context for approaching and using the information gathered by the research. It presents the background, research objectives, and justification for the research project in greater detail than that presented in the executive summary. Additionally, the introduction places this information within the broader context of why the research was conducted, that is, the marketing or advertising related problem that the research addresses. This broader context is important for two reasons. First, it permits the report to refer to similar or related research, thus placing the current research in an historical perspective. Second, it provides a record for individuals reading the report in the future to understand the reasons for the research.

Methodology

This section of the report *summarizes* the methodology used to collect the research information. The major purpose of this section is to give the reader the information that he or she needs to understand how the study was planned and conducted and, as a consequence, to decide how much confidence to have in the findings and implications of the research. For the reader to have confidence in the research report, the methodology section should describe the type of research used, the research design (with justifications), method of data collection, sampling, sample size, sample selection, and any special data analysis techniques used. Remember, however, that the purpose of this section is a methodological summary. Technical details of the research should be placed in the appendix.

Findings

The findings section constitutes the major portion of the research report and it is here that the audience is exposed to the research results, particularly those results that relate

to the questions motivating the research and raised in the research proposal. A well-prepared findings section does the following:

- *It organizes the findings around core topics.* For example, a report of a test of advertising creative may organize the findings around the following topics: reactions to the message, reactions to the execution, changes in brand attitudes, and purchase intent. A topic-based organization of the findings helps the audience completely understand the findings in one area prior to the introduction of other areas.[5]

- *It presents the findings in a logical order.* There are several ways to logically organize findings:

problem-solution	qualitative-quantitative
simple to complex	general to specific
specific to general	order of importance
cause-effect	effect-cause

    The researcher's task is to first understand the interrelationships of the findings and the characteristics of the audience and to then select the sequencing approach that is most likely to increase the audience's understanding of the findings.

- *It presents only those findings that are important.* A research study collects a great deal of information. After an examination of all of the findings, the researcher must decide which of the findings provide important insights and which are merely interesting. The former should be in the findings section of the research report. The latter should be placed in the appendix.

- *It presents all findings needed to support forthcoming conclusions and recommendations.* Conclusions and recommendations are more likely to be believed and accepted if their basis in fact (the research results) is direct and explicit.

Conclusions and Limitations

This section draws conclusions from the findings presented in the prior section. Thus, while the findings section presents what was learned, the conclusions section represents the analysis of the trends in the data. In other words, the findings section tells what we found while the conclusions sections tells us what the findings mean.

Conclusions should be modified by study limitations. A discussion of limitations addresses the extent to which findings and conclusions can be completely accepted without qualification. Remember, that balance in a discussion of limitations is important. Key limitations must certainly be noted. However, be very careful not to under-

---

[5] The presentation of results by topic area often requires the integration of findings from questions appearing in different parts of the questionnaire. As a result, we recommend against the use of the question and answer format for the presentation of the research results. The question and answer format occurs when the results are presented question by question, that is, the results of question 1 are presented, followed by the results of question 2, question 3, etc. We believe that the question and answer format should be avoided for several reasons. First, questions are sequenced in a questionnaire to facilitate the interview process. They are placed in a particular order so that the most insightful, meaningful information can be collected from a respondent. Questionnaire order is not in any way influenced by the reasonableness of presentation order in a research report. Thus, presenting findings question by question typically has no underlying rationale. Second, and perhaps more importantly, even if the question sequence does lend itself to the presentation sequence, this approach typically prevents the audience from seeing the "big picture." The focus on question by question results makes it very difficult to discern overall trends and the interrelationships between survey questions.

Background

The Abraxis Corporation has a long history of supporting civic and educational programs. Annual donations average about $1,500,000 per year.

The Green Lizard Foundation approached Abraxis in March 1995. The Green Lizard Foundation is a nonprofit foundation that designs environmental awareness workbooks and study guides for children in grades three through six. Educators' comments indicate that these books and guides are extremely well done. Distribution is limited, however, due to a lack of funding. The Green Lizard Foundation asked Abraxis to donate $250,000 to underwrite the printing and duplication of these workbooks and study guides to all schools in Crest County. The Green Lizard Foundation noted that in return for this sponsorship, Abraxis could place a full page ad on the back cover of each workbook and study guide. No restrictions were placed on ad content or form.

The Abraxis Executive Board met in June 1995 and conditionally approved the donation. The condition on the donation reflected the Board's concern regarding parental response. The Board felt that there might be a backlash among parents. There was some concern that parents might view the donation and advertising as a "backdoor" and unethical way to advertise to young children. As a result, the Board requested that SDET&I (the Abraxis advertising agency) determine parents' reactions to the corporate sponsorship and back page advertising prior to final approval of the donation.

The donation will be approved if there is an absence of negative parental response.

Research Purpose

Research was conducted to determine parents' reactions to Abraxis corporate sponsorship of Green Lizard environmental awareness workbooks and study guides. Specifically, the research was designed to answer the following questions:

1. Does Abraxis corporate sponsorship, as communicated in proposed back page advertising, affect parents' perceptions of Abraxis? If perceptions are affected, how are changes in perceptions related to the form and content of the advertising?

2. Does Abraxis corporate sponsorship, as communicated in the proposed back page advertising, affect parents' likelihood to permit their children to purchase Abraxis video games? If the likelihood is affected, how is it related to the form and content of the advertising?

Methodology

A list of all parents with a child in grades three through six was obtained from all local school districts in Crest County. These lists were then combined to form a master list for each grade level. Random selection procedures were used to control for single-versus dual-parent households and for households with multiple children. Three hundred individuals from each grade level list were then randomly selected. Of these three hundred individuals at each grade level, half were randomly assigned to the "Advertising" group and half were randomly assigned to the "Sponsorship" group.

Every individual in each group received a copy of the appropriate grade level Green Lizard Foundation workbook. The workbook was sent through the mail by a local marketing research company. Abraxis was not identified as the sponsor of the research. The "Advertising" group received a workbook with an Abraxis ad on the back page. The "Sponsorship" group received a workbook with a back page that merely mentioned the Abraxis sponsorship.

The ad on the back page of the "Advertising" group's workbook was very simple and consisted of inverted white type on a bright blue background. Several Abraxis games were shown in the corners of the ad. The copy read: "We at Abraxis are pleased that you like our games. And we know that you enjoy playing them. But, there is a time for everything. So, watch how long you play. If you're playing too long, turn it off. Get some air. Do some of the projects in this book. Get involved. We'll all be better off." The back page of the "Sponsorship" group's workbook was printed in the same type and read "Abraxis is proud to be a corporate sponsor of the Green Lizard Foundation." No games were shown on this page.

(continued)

A questionnaire was included with each workbook along with a stamped envelope addressed to the research company. The questionnaire was the same for both groups and probed reactions to the workbook, perceptions of Abraxis, and likelihood to permit the child to purchase Abraxis video games.

Completed, usable questionnaires were returned by 1,053 individuals (87.8%). This high rate of return was consistent across each group and grade level.

Findings

Attitudes Toward Abraxis

Parents were asked to rate Abraxis with regard to 15 corporate characteristics. These characteristics fell into three broad groups:
- Corporate citizenship: Perceptions of Abraxis as being a good caring corporation
- Corporate ethics: Perceptions of Abraxis as being an ethical, responsible corporation
- Corporate motivation: Perceptions of Abraxis as being motivated by ideals rather than profit

The overall average rating of Abraxis in each of these areas differed across the "Advertising" and "Sponsorship" groups. Respondents in the "Advertising" group gave Abraxis generally neutral ratings in each area. Respondents in the "Sponsorship" group were significantly more positive (see Table 1).

Table 1. Ratings of Abraxis

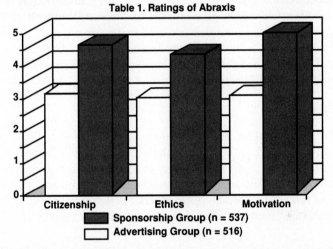

■ Sponsorship Group (n = 537)
□ Advertising Group (n = 516)

Table 1 shows the ratings of the total sample. Individual analyses by grade level were also conducted. The trend within each grade level was identical. Corporate perceptions were more positive among those in the "Sponsorship" group.

Purchase Intent

Parents were also asked to rate how likely they would be to let their children purchase Abraxis video games. There were no differences in this measure across the two groups, either for the total sample or within grade level. Parents' inclination to let their children purchase an Abraxis video game was generally neutral regardless of the type of ad they were shown. The average for the "Advertising" group was 3.1 (on a scale of 1, low, to 5, high) while the average for the "Sponsorship" group was 3.3.

Conclusions

The message presented to the "Sponsorship" group appears to be the stronger of the two messages. While neither message affected parents' inclination to let their children purchase an Abraxis video game, the sponsorship message created much more positive parental perceptions of Abraxis.

Recommendations
Based on the research findings we recommend that
- The Abraxis Board make the donation to the Green Lizard Foundation, and
- Abraxis not place the advertising message on the back page of each workbook, but instead use the message shown to those individuals in the "Sponsorship" group.

FIGURE 4.5
Sample executive summary.

mine the legitimacy of the research and its findings (unless such an undersell is truly warranted).

Recommendations and Next Steps

Conclusions are a researcher's synthesis of what the research uncovered. They represent a researcher's deductions drawn from an examination of the pattern of research findings. Recommendations are a researcher's opinions as to what steps should be taken based on the findings and conclusions. Research reports without recommendations appear incomplete and lack closure. Thus we recommend that all research reports contain recommendations for action and next steps.

Appendices

The appendices to the full research report contain material that is too complex, too detailed, or otherwise inappropriate for the findings and methodology sections of the report (for example, the questionnaire used in the survey, findings that are not relevant to the discussion in the findings section, sampling detail, etc.). Appendices are very important. They provide a place to present important supporting information without interrupting the flow of the main report.

Cover Letter

The cover letter directs the report to the appropriate individuals at the agency and client. Because a research report should not be sent to its audience without some explanation, the cover letter briefly places the research in the context of the broader decision-making problem and summarizes the specific problem or informational needs to which the research responds. A cover letter directed to the client typically uses business style while internal agency distribution typically utilizes memo style.

THE ORAL RESEARCH REPORT

With few exceptions, every research project should be reported in written form. In addition, many researchers also prefer to report the results as an oral presentation that supplements (not replaces) the written report. There are several reasons for making an oral presentation:

- It ensures that appropriate individuals have been exposed to the research findings, recommendations, and conclusions. There is no guarantee that an individual will in fact read the written report.
- It provides an opportunity to clarify any questions or problems associated with the written report.
- It provides an opportunity to expand on and extend discussions not addressed in the written report.

Many of the guidelines and recommendations presented for written reports also hold true for oral reports. The oral report must be clear, concise, complete, coherent, and correct. Numeric tables and especially charts provide an excellent means for de-

scribing and communicating findings, conclusions, and recommendations. The content and areas discussed are generally equivalent. However, the differences between oral and written communication require some departure from the specific characteristics of written reports discussed earlier.

An oral report requires a "road map" to enable the audience to follow the presentation. This "road map" needs to take what the audience has just seen and heard and explicitly relate it to what they are about to see and hear. This can be done through the use of periodic summaries and transitions, for example:

> In sum, we have just seen the three predominant perceptions of the product. Consumers feel the product is too expensive, too hard to locate, and not very dependable. Now let's look at how each of these attitudes affect product purchase.

Audiovisual materials are the medium for the presentation. The vast majority of verbal points are forgotten soon after the presentation ends. A successful presentation uses extensive visual aids to focus the audience on key points and the increase the likelihood that important points will be remembered. The most common forms of presentation visual aids are flip charts, overhead transparencies, and slides.

- A flip chart is a large pad of paper mounted on an easel. Each page is completed in advance of the presentation and the presenter flips the pages to move from one topic to another.
- Overhead transparencies are clear or colored pieces of transparent plastic film that are projected on a screen by an overhead projector.
- Slides are typically 35 mm slide film.

In addition to these presentation media, computer-facilitated presentations are increasingly being used. Popular personal computer programs such as Persuasion, Applause, and Powerpoint help develop visually impressive, professional presentations without the need for extensive computer expertise.

The specific presentation medium selected reflects the formality of the presentation and the size of the audience. Slides tend to be the most formal presentation medium and the medium used for large groups. The use of overhead transparencies is also good for large groups but tends to be a more informal presentation medium then using slides. Flip charts are an informal presentation medium typically used with smaller audiences.

Tables, charts and their interpretation must appear simultaneously. As noted earlier, numeric tables and charts should never be presented without interpretation. A written report provides interpretation by integrating tables and charts with the narrative. Interpretation in oral presentations is accomplished by providing an interpretive headline on the same page as the table or graph.

Text, tables, and charts must be created for visual impact and processing. Effective visuals are simple and make it easier for the audience to understand the presentation. Thus, in preparing visuals try to

- use a readable, consistent, appropriately large typeface.
- avoid full sentences and limit text to a few phrases per page.
- use color for emphasis.
- use pictures or charts whenever possible.

Rehearsal is a critical component of success. You can never, ever rehearse too much.

Preparation and checking is crucial. Prior to the presentation make certain that you have checked the room and equipment. Make certain that all equipment is in working order. Chairs should be arranged and visual aids should be placed where they will be accessible during the presentation.

The Researcher As Presenter

Presenter skills greatly affect the success of any presentation. As you think about your role as a presenter remember the following:[6]

Pace your presentation for the audience, not yourself. Do not be afraid to deviate from your initial presentation plan. Instead, adapt your pace and material to meet audience needs. If it is clear that the audience understands your point, you may want to eliminate overheads that provide further explanation. If your audience appears to be befuddled, slow down and provide more explanation than initially planned.

Encourage participation but do not lose control of the presentation. If your presentation is really interesting, your audience will want to discuss the findings and implications. If your presentation is really dull and uninsightful, your audience may be distracted and discussion may gravitate to other issues. It is your responsibility as the presenter to control the discussion and to make certain that the presentation does not get off track. You must step in if side or other discussions get out of hand.

Show respect for your audience. Do not talk down to your audience or try to show them how smart you are. (They should be able to figure the latter out from the content and style of your presentation.) You demonstrate respect for your audience by

- beginning and staying positive. Do not begin, for example, by apologizing for the length of the presentation. Receive both positive and negative feedback in a professional manner.
- being prepared and knowing your material. The easiest way to show a lack of respect for your audience is to waste their time.

Be aware of nonverbal signals. Your audience will react to what you say, how you say it, *and* the nonverbal signals sent as part of the oral communication process. You can improve the nonverbal signals you send by doing the following:

- *Maintain eye contact with your audience.* Do not talk to the screen or overhead projector.
- *Talk to the entire audience.* Do not talk just to senior management or those on one side of the room.
- *Maintain good body language.* Stand straight and comfortably. Do not cross your arms. Do not distract the audience with jangling keys or coins, waving pointers, etc.
- *Dress appropriately.* Select clothing that is comfortable and appropriate for the level of formality of the presentation setting.

---

[6] This section is based on Thomas Leech, *How to Prepare, Stage and Deliver Winning Presentations* (New York: American Management Association, 1982), 226–49.

COMMUNICATING RESEARCH FINDINGS IN LETTERS AND MEMOS

The oral presentation of research findings and the written research report are events that occur at a single point in time. However, because the use of research in advertising decision making is an ongoing process, it is to be expected that clients or others at the agency will make requests for specific research information after the presentation or issuance of the research report. It is not uncommon, for example, for a researcher to receive the following types of requests:

- The latest copy test showed how well the last two proposed commercials for Mountain Dew performed. How did these commercials compare to executions we tested earlier in the year?

- What is the latest sales data from Baltimore?

- Has advertising awareness increased or decreased since we started the new media schedule? What does the latest research show?

When responding to these types of requests we recommend that you remember two things. First, always ask *why* the information is needed and *how* the information will be used. Individuals requesting information may not always precisely identify (or even know about) the information that they *really* need. Asking why the information is needed and how it will be used helps you to identify the most appropriate and relevant information for the problem at hand. Second, many responses to requests such as these are made by telephone. However, given the potential for misinterpretation of information communicated orally, we recommend that responses for research information also be communicated by memo (if the request is internal) or letter (if the request comes from outside the agency).

The written communication of specific research findings by letter or memo should satisfy the characteristics of good writing discussed earlier in this chapter. In addition, this form of communication should *not* simply provide the requested information without providing context or interpretation. The following communication is not acceptable.

John—

The copy test results you requested are

"Feelings" (tested 1/6/95) had purchase intent of 12.
"Good Times" (tested 1/21/95) had purchase intent of 17.

The communication of research results by letter or memo should contain five elements. Inclusion of these elements greatly reduces the potential for misunderstanding or misuse of the research data. These elements are

- A brief statement of the background, addressing who requested the information, why the information was requested, and how the information will be used.

- A brief description of the source of the data and, if the data is primary data, how the data was collected.

- The data itself.

Memo

To: Bob Daniels
From: Jim Scott
Date: April 11, 1996
Re: Copy testing of prior Mountain Dew creative

Bob, you requested information on the recall scores of Mountain Dew commercials tested since January 1995.

Background

The agency has tested six Mountain Dew commercials since January. All commercials were tested using day after recall. A commercial's recall score represents the percent of individuals in the program target audience who provide evidence for claimed recall. Attached is a brief description of the methodology.

You mentioned that the commercial recall scores are to be used in the annual brand review. As such, I think that it is important that you address two aspects of the data: the trend in scores since January 1995 and the relationship of our commercial recall scores to the overall soft drink norm.

Mountain Dew Recall Scores

The chart shows the recall scores for the six Mountain Dew commercials tested since January.

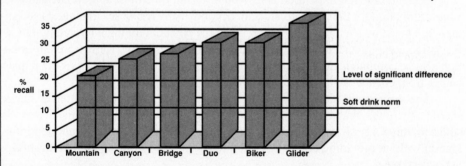

The use of the bar chart makes it easy to see two important trends in the data: (1) the trend in recall scores has steadily improved since January and (2) *all* commercials tested are statistically above the norm for the soft drink category (the level of confidence is 95% or greater).

Additional Information

Bob, as we discussed, we also have test information on purchase intent and commercial diagnostics. I think that this information should also be included in the annual brand review. I'll pull this information together for you and send it to you later this week.

FIGURE 4.6
Communication of research findings via memo.

- An interpretation of what the data means and how it might be appropriately applied to the problem at hand.
- Suggestions (if appropriate) for additional data relevant to the problem.

An example of this form of communication is shown in Figure 4.6.[7]

---

[7] This memo is fictitious.

Summary

The results and implications of advertising research are presented in oral and written form. Effective presentation is a critical final step in the research process. Research that is well-designed, conducted, and analyzed, but poorly presented, is generally research that fails to contribute to the decision-making process.

The written and the oral presentation of findings and implications can be improved when attention is given to the narrative and graphic portions of the report. The narrative portion of the report is improved as one increases clarity, conciseness, completeness, correctness, and coherency. The graphic portion of the report is improved when one prepares and uses the appropriate form of a numeric table, bar, pie or line chart.

A written report generally consists of nine elements: (1) title page, (2) table of contents and list of illustrations/figures, (3) executive summary, (4) background, (5) methodology, (6) findings, (7) conclusions and limitations, (8) recommendations and next steps and (9) appendices. While each of these sections is important, the executive summary is the most important. Reports are accompanied by a cover letter when distributed to the agency and client.

An oral report contains the same nine elements. However, an oral report generally requires greater use of explanatory transitions, more visual aids, and a need for explicit interpretation of tables and charts.

The communication of research findings via letter or memo should satisfy the characteristics of good research writing (clear, concise, etc.). Letters and memos, in addition, should contain the following components: (1) a brief background statement, (2) source of the data, (3) data, (4) interpretation, and (5) suggestions for additional data, if appropriate.

Review Questions

1. What are the five characteristics of effective business communication?
2. List and provide examples of five ways to increase a research report's clarity and conciseness.
3. How can you tell if a research report is complete?
4. Why is it important to make certain that all information in the research report is correct?
5. How can you tell if a research report is coherent?
6. When should numeric tables be used?
7. What are the seven characteristics of a well-created numeric table?
8. When should bar charts be used?
9. Describe a researcher's options for the creation of bar charts.
10. When should pie charts be used?
11. What are the five criteria for determining the appropriateness of tables and charts?
12. What are the components of the written research report?
13. What are the typical elements of a title page?

14. What are the components of an executive summary? What content does each component address?

15. What information is presented in the research report's introduction?

16. What information is contained in the research report's methodology section?

17. What are the characteristics of a well-prepared findings section?

18. What are special considerations for the oral research report?

19. What are special considerations for the communication of research findings via letter or memo?

Application Exercises

1. Read and then revise each of the following paragraphs to improve clarity, conciseness, correctness and coherency.

Every respondent who participated in the study was exposed to one and only one of the three test commercials. The commercials were named "Going Home," "Heart," and "Fathers Day". Respondents saw the commercial that they were assigned to view and then completed a fifteen minute self-administered questionnaire. It was believed by the research staff that a self-administered questionnaire was the best venue for data collection. Each commercial lasted 30 seconds. When the self-administered questionnaire was completed a trained interviewer checked the respondent's responses for accuracy and completeness. It was then decided by the interviewer whether clarification was needed or if the respondent could be excused.

Each interviewed respondent was requested to provide their perceptions of the quality and value of Vita Corporation's shampoos and conditioners so that this recent data could be compared with data from the prior year in order to determine the trend, if any, and the significance of the trend, if any, in changes in the nature of consumers' perceptions of the Corporation's shampoos and conditioners.

A set of seven semantic differential scales were used to obtain consumers' ratings of their perceptions of the believability, and trustworthiness of Star Gel toothpaste advertising. A semantic differential scale is a bipolar scale, that is, it is a rating scale that has opposite words on both ends of the scale, for example, one scale might have the words "believable" and "unbelievable" on the ends, as we did with one of the scales in this research study. A respondent places a check somewhere between the two words and then we translate this check into a numeric rating. First let me tell you what happened when we took an average of the three believability and four trustworthiness scales. Consumers feel that Star Gel advertising is pretty believable (it was given an average rating of five out of seven) and really pretty trustworthy (it was given an average rating of 6.2 out of seven).

Consumers in the advertising target audience were assessed with regard to their affective and cognitive responses to the advertising. Affective responses represent subjective, nonrational, and emotional responses while cognitive responses, for the purposes of this study, were defined as logical, rational responses without an overlay of affect. Respondents' scores on the total set of scales was calculated and then a series of subtest scores were calculated in order to develop a respondent profile. This profile then let us determine the breadth and depth of affective and cognitive response to the advertising.

The decision whether or not to purchase the product appears to be generally related to

three factors. First, there is the factor of advertising awareness. While we cannot postulate a causal relationship, we can state with a high degree of certainty that individuals who are more aware of the advertising tend to be more likely to purchase the product. Keep in mind that all the three factors are all important. The second, middle factor, relates to disposable income. One is more likely to purchase the product when he or she has more disposable income. This is important, and reasonable. Third, but also important, is the factor of geography. Consumers in urban areas versus suburban and rural areas are more likely to purchase the product.

2. Select an article from either the *Journal of Advertising Research* or the *Journal of Advertising* in which you feel the clarity, conciseness, correctness, and coherency of the methodology or results section could be improved. Revise and improve the writing.

3. Select an article from either the *Journal of Advertising Research* or the *Journal of Advertising* in which you feel the visual presentation of the findings could be improved. Revise and improve the visual aspects of the data presentation.

4. The following table presents consumers' awareness of various soda brand advertising over the past five years.[8] The figures represent the percent of consumers who say that they have seen a particular brand's advertising within the past 30 days. Columns do not add to 100 percent because of multiple mentions.

Brand	*1991*	*1992*	*1993*	*1994*	*1995*
Coke Classic	75.5%	73.2%	66.5%	78.5%	81.2%
Pepsi Regular	63.5	66.2	68.5	70.2	72.1
Diet Coke	85.2	50.1	44.9	50.2	65.8
Dr. Pepper	25.5	32.8	35.9	33.5	40.2
7 Up	59.5	44.0	65.2	50.9	47.4

Use a bar, line, or pie chart to

- Demonstrate the trends in advertising awareness for each brand for the period 1991 to 1995.

- Illustrate the changes in relative awareness in the years 1991 and 1995.

Explain your choice of charts.

---

[8] Data are fictitious and for illustrative purposes only.

5

SECONDARY RESEARCH

Advertising research is conducted to help advertisers make better decisions. As discussed in Chapter 2, advertisers can use either primary or secondary research to make an informed decision. Primary research collects original information through projects specifically designed to satisfy a current informational need. Secondary research information, which can be in either printed or electronic form, is information that has been previously gathered by others for purposes other than the specific project at hand. This chapter focuses on secondary research. (Chapter 6 discusses primary research.)

After reading this chapter, you will be able to

■ Identify the characteristics of secondary research information and the difference between secondary information and secondary sources.

■ Explain the uses of secondary research information.

■ Describe the advantages and limitations of secondary research information.

■ Evaluate the appropriateness and acceptability of secondary research information.

■ Describe the types of advertising questions commonly answered by secondary information and the specific sources that provide the relevant information to answer these questions.

Secondary research information is information that has been collected and analyzed by others for a purpose *other* than specifically responding to a current informational need. This contrasts with primary research that is conducted by (or on behalf of) an information user to *specifically satisfy* that individual's informational need. Secondary research is therefore distinguished from primary research on the basis of two criteria:

  • *The individual responsible for planning and conducting the research.* In primary research, the project's researcher is responsible for problem definition, sample design,

data collection, data analysis, and the presentation of results. The involvement of a secondary researcher begins after these tasks have been completed. A secondary researcher does not have any control over what information was collected, the method by which the information was collected, or the procedures used to initially analyze the data.

- *The circumstances under which the research was conducted.* In primary research, research design and questionnaire content are developed to specifically satisfy the *original* end users' informational needs. Thus, data coding, organization, and analysis reflect the needs of the individuals who initially requested the research. A researcher using secondary research information must *adapt and translate* the data from its original use to the secondary researcher's new (and often different) needs.

The United States census illustrates how a research study and the information it gathers can either be primary or secondary depending on the circumstances under which the research was *initially* planned, conducted, and utilized. The census is conducted on behalf of the federal government to help it make decisions related to, among other things, state representation in the House of Representatives and the apportionment of federal funds. In this context, the census is primary research. The initial end users of the information provide direction in the design and conduct of research to make certain that the collected information meets their specific informational needs. An advertiser or marketer, however, could examine census information to better understand shifts in demography so that he or she could identify opportunities for new products or line extensions. In this latter context, census information is being used as secondary research. The advertiser is adapting data collected by others to respond to his or her own informational needs, which are different from the needs that initially motivated the collection of information.[1]

SECONDARY INFORMATION VERSUS SECONDARY SOURCES

It is important to distinguish the concepts of "primary and secondary information" from "primary and secondary sources."[2] As just discussed, the terms primary and secondary information refer to (1) the individual or organization *initially* responsible for the research and (2) the circumstances under which the research was initially conducted. The United States census is primary information when used by the Federal Government; the census is secondary information when used by other parties. Primary and secondary *sources* refer to the involvement of the information's source in the conduct of the research. A primary source is the individual or organization that originated the information; a secondary source is the individual or organization that provides the information after obtaining it from the original source. The United States government, for example, is a primary source for census data while a newspaper or magazine that reprints and/or interprets selected portions of the census is a secondary source.

The distinction between primary and secondary sources is important because, from an information user's perspective, the two sources are not interchangeable or

---

[1] This example illustrates one additional characteristic of secondary research information. The terms "secondary research" or "secondary information" do not imply that the data is of minor value or inferior quality. "Secondary" simply refers to the circumstances of data collection and use. Census data, for example, is equally valid and important when used both as primary and secondary research information.

[2] This section is adapted from René Y. Darmon, Michel Larouche, and K. Lee McGown, *Marketing Research in Canada* (Scarborough, Ontario, Canada: Gage Educational Publishing Company, 1989), 120–21.

equally acceptable. Following are three important reasons why one should, whenever possible, obtain information from its primary source:

- *Completeness*—A primary source is more complete because it presents the full set of findings in an unabridged form. Bias can occur whenever a secondary source selects and presents portions of the data in an abridged form.

- *Accuracy*—Primary sources are considered to be more accurate than secondary sources because of the potential for secondary sources to misinterpret the information or to present the information in a biased or misleading manner. Additionally, secondary sources often omit important footnotes or key textual elements (which were presented by the primary source), thereby changing the meaning and interpretation of the data.

- *Quality assessment*—Primary sources will generally describe the methodology through which the data was collected. An examination of this methodology lets a researcher evaluate information quality. Detailed methodological descriptions are typically not provided by secondary sources.

THE USES OF SECONDARY RESEARCH

Secondary research contributes to advertising and marketing decision making in three ways. Information obtained from secondary research can

- directly answer an advertiser's or marketer's informational needs,
- provide important insights prior to the conduct of primary research,
- contribute to questionnaire development.

Directly Answer Informational Needs

In some instances, information obtained from secondary research can completely satisfy and resolve an advertiser's or marketer's informational needs thereby eliminating the need for *any* primary research. This can be accomplished in one of two ways.

First, secondary information can provide required information without the need for further analysis or manipulation. A media planner, for example, might wish to identify cities in which there is an above average concentration of 18- to 34-year olds who have an annual income under $30,000. This information could be obtained from a source such as the *Lifestyle Market Analyst*[3] (see Figure 5.1 and the discussion on page 92) or through market analyses conducted by the A. C. Nielsen Company (see pages 96–97). No manipulation of the data is required.

Similarly, an advertiser might wish to understand population growth or decline in the country's largest metropolitan areas or among specific demographic groups. This information could be obtained directly from the U.S. census as reported in the *Statistical Abstract of the United States*.

---

[3] *Lifestyle Market Analyst* (Wilmette, IL: Standard Rate and Data Service), annual.

➤

FIGURE 5.1
Excerpt from *Lifestyle Market Analysis.*
Source: Reprinted from the 1996 edition of *The Lifestyle Market Analyst,* published by Standard Rate and Data Service with data supplied by The Polk Company.

18-34 Years Old, Income Under $30,000

▨ : Denotes DMAs ranked 1 - 10

Designated Market Areas	Segment Rank	House-holds	%	Index	Designated Market Areas	Segment Rank	House-holds	%	Index
Abilene-Sweetwater, TX	52	17,942	16.6	133	Denver, CO	66	174,791	15.9	127
Ada-Ardmore, OK	74	11,320	15.8	126	Des Moines-Ames, IA	128	51,109	13.9	111
Albany, GA	54	22,044	16.5	132	Detroit, MI	197	178,379	10.1	81
Albany-Schenectady-Troy, NY	196	52,808	10.2	82	Dothan, AL	89	15,602	15.4	123
Albuquerque-Santa Fe, NM	43	89,043	16.9	135	Duluth-Superior, MN-WI	153	23,063	13.1	105
Alexandria, LA	5	18,768	21.5	172	El Paso, TX	10	49,523	20.2	162
Alpena, MI	181	1,970	11.8	94					
Amarillo, TX	46	28,734	16.8	134	Elmira, NY	171	11,793	12.3	98
Anchorage, AK	88	18,896	15.4	123	Erie, PA	161	19,997	12.8	102
Anniston, AL	63	7,191	16.2	130	Eugene, OR	41	35,030	17.1	137
					Eureka, CA	19	10,547	18.4	147
Atlanta, GA	136	206,327	13.6	109	Evansville, IN	147	36,452	13.3	106
Augusta, GA	117	30,861	14.4	115	Fairbanks, AK	7	6,633	21.3	170
Austin, TX	4	87,853	22.5	180	Fargo-Valley City, ND	28	38,513	17.6	141
Bakersfield, CA	78	25,193	15.7	126	Flint-Saginaw-Bay City, MI	127	64,385	13.9	111
Baltimore, MD	205	89,596	9.1	73	Florence-Myrtle Beach, SC	99	25,990	15.2	122
Bangor, ME	124	18,042	14.0	112	Ft. Myers-Naples, FL	206	25,561	8.6	69
Baton Rouge, LA	23	46,268	17.8	142					
Beaumont-Port Arthur, TX	156	21,544	13.0	104	Ft. Smith, AR	55	32,407	16.4	131
Bend, OR	169	4,229	12.4	99	Ft. Wayne, IN	176	28,519	12.0	96
Billings, MT	106	13,413	15.0	120	Fresno-Visalia, CA	40	80,414	17.1	137
					Gainesville, FL	1	25,614	26.8	214
Biloxi-Gulfport, MS	24	19,253	17.8	142	Glendive, MT	115	598	14.6	117
Binghamton, NY	182	16,367	11.7	94	Grand Junction-Montrose, CO	111	8,980	14.9	119
Birmingham, AL	143	71,337	13.4	107	Grand Rap-Kalamazoo-B Creek, MI	145	86,068	13.3	106
Bluefield-Beckley-Oak Hill, WV	140	18,614	13.5	108	Great Falls, MT	47	11,033	16.8	134
Boise, ID	73	26,953	15.8	126	Green Bay-Appleton, WI	178	47,034	11.9	95
Boston, MA	207	179,207	8.4	67	Greensboro-H Point-W-Salem, NC	146	73,335	13.3	106
Bowling Green, KY	38	9,231	17.2	138					
Buffalo, NY	185	73,527	11.3	90	Greenville-New Bern-Wash, NC	11	46,960	20.2	162
Burlington-Plattsburgh, NY-VT	131	40,040	13.8	110	Greenville-Spartanburg-Asheville-Anderson, NC-SC	160	87,651	12.8	102
Butte, MT	17	9,792	18.9	151	Greenwood-Greenville, MS	50	13,314	16.7	134
					Harlingen-Wes-Brown-McAllen, TX	33	36,345	17.4	139
Casper-Riverton, WY	60	7,946	16.4	131	Harrisburg-Lan-Lebanon-York, PA	199	58,267	9.9	79
Cedar Rapids-Waterloo & Dubuque, IA	102	46,566	15.1	121	Harrisonburg, VA-WV	93	6,263	15.3	122
Champaign & Springfield-Decatur, IL	87	54,002	15.4	123	Hartford & New Haven, CT	210	69,500	7.4	59
Charleston, SC	27	41,527	17.6	141	Hattiesburg-Laurel, MS	16	17,489	18.9	151
Charleston-Huntington, WV	103	72,808	15.0	120	Helena, MT	92	3,079	15.4	123
Charlotte, NC	159	101,070	12.8	102	Honolulu, HI	193	40,735	10.7	86
Charlottesville, VA	9	9,251	20.5	164					
Chattanooga, TN	134	43,594	13.7	110	Houston, TX	64	246,085	16.0	128
Cheyenne-Scottsblf-String, WY-NE	42	8,328	17.0	136	Huntsville-Decatur, Florence, AL	123	41,757	14.0	112
Chicago, IL	202	294,004	9.4	75	Idaho Falls-Pocatello, ID	37	18,112	17.2	138
					Indianapolis, IN	151	121,984	13.1	105
Chico-Redding, CA	68	27,434	15.9	127	Jackson, MS	71	46,846	15.8	126
Cincinnati, OH	168	97,323	12.4	99	Jackson, TN	126	9,087	14.0	112
Clarksburg-Weston, WV	141	14,250	13.5	108	Jacksonville-Brunswick, FL-GA	95	73,734	15.2	122
Cleveland, OH	189	162,147	11.0	88	Johnstown-Altoona, PA	144	39,231	13.4	107
Colorado Springs-Pueblo, CO	29	43,223	17.5	140	Jonesboro, AR	81	12,101	15.6	125
Columbia, SC	77	47,451	15.7	126	Joplin-Pittsburg, MO-KS	101	21,441	15.2	122
Columbia-Jefferson City, MO	21	24,825	18.2	146					
Columbus, GA	13	36,715	19.8	158	Kansas City, MO	137	105,243	13.6	109
Columbus, OH	108	106,980	14.9	119	Knoxville, TN	97	63,840	15.2	122
Columbus -Tupelo-West Point, MS	56	28,151	16.4	131	La Crosse-Eau Claire, WI	100	25,071	15.2	122
					Lafayette, IN	3	11,355	24.0	192
Corpus Christi, TX	51	28,805	16.6	133	Lafayette, LA	14	38,237	19.2	154
Dallas-Ft. Worth, TX	86	281,424	15.4	123	Lake Charles, LA	82	12,023	15.6	125
Davenport-Rock Island- Mol, IL-IA	155	39,390	13.0	104	Lansing, MI	84	36,480	15.5	124
Dayton, OH	173	62,140	12.1	97					

Segment Profiles

Second, secondary information that cannot answer an informational need in its original form can often satisfy that need if it is manipulated, that is, reanalyzed or combined with other secondary research information. Here, the manipulated or combined secondary data provides a perspective or insight beyond that contained in each original information source.

Manipulation of secondary data might occur when an informational need requires categories different than those used in the secondary data. An advertiser might request demographic trends in the following age groups: under 17, 17–30, 31–49, 50–60, 61–75, and 76 and older. Because these are nonstandard age groupings, a researcher would have to create them by combining data from smaller age groupings. Data manipulation might also occur when the secondary research contains the appropriate data but the data is in a form different than that required to meet the advertiser's or marketer's informational need. An advertiser, might wish to determine the *percentage change* in the competitor's advertising expenditures over the prior five years. However, because secondary sources typically report advertising expenditures in terms of dollars, dollar expenditures would need to be changed to percentages in order to respond to the advertiser's request.

Data manipulation can also entail the combination of data from several secondary information sources. The need to combine data might occur when a client needs to determine the relationship between category sales and category advertising expenditures. Category sales would be obtained from one source (for example, industry analysts or trade publications) while advertising expenditures would be obtained from another source (for example, *LNA/MediaWatch Multi-Media Service*,[4] see pages 100–101). Similarly, a client might request a market by market analysis of the relationship between his or her brand's advertising spending and brand sales. The agency, in response to this request, would obtain information on media expenditures by market from the agency media department and information on brand sales by market from the client. This information would then be analyzed to determine the relationship between the two variables of interest.

Finally, it is important to note that secondary information can provide complete answers to both narrow and broad questions. The prior examples were narrowly focused questions reflecting relatively small and distinct informational needs. There are times, however, when an informational need is only satisfied by a *synthesis* of information from multiple secondary information sources. This latter type of secondary research might address questions such as: "How have the marketing and promotional strategies of Crest and Colgate toothpastes changed over the past five years?" or "Is there a market for products specifically positioned as 'better for the environment'?" A useful and insightful answer to this type of broader, more complex question requires that the researcher conduct a thorough search of the available secondary information, synthesize the findings from various sources and then provide a point of view on the meaning and implications of the findings. A report of secondary findings *without* accompanying analysis and interpretation fails to completely satisfy an informational need and provides an incomplete basis for subsequent decision making.[5]

---

[4] *LNA/MediaWatch Multi-Media Service* (New York, NY: Leading National Advertisers), quarterly.

[5] For further discussion of the integration of secondary information see David W. Stewart and Michael A. Kamins, *Secondary Research: Information Sources and Methods* (Newbury Park, CA; SAGE Publications, 1993), 128–37.

Provide Important Insights Prior to Primary Research

Secondary research information can help to clarify, redefine, or refocus a planned primary research study. Stewart and Kamins, in this regard, point out that "An examination of secondary sources provides insights into what is and is not known, the limitations of previous research, the shortcomings of methodologies employed and the generalizability of earlier conclusions."[6] As a result, an examination of relevant secondary research conducted early in the planning process can strengthen subsequent primary research in several ways. Secondary research information can

- answer some of the questions originally addressed in the primary research study, making the exploration of these areas unnecessary;
- provide insights that lead to unforeseen, additional areas to explore in the primary research study. Conversely, secondary research may provide insights that discourage the planned exploration of certain areas in primary research;
- cause a change in research hypotheses, resulting in changes in research design or questionnaire content.

These contributions of secondary research to the planning and conduct of primary research are illustrated in the case described in Figure 5.2 (page 80).

Contribute to Questionnaire Development

Secondary research can contribute to improved questionnaire design in two ways. First, secondary research can alert a researcher to problems that might be encountered in the planned primary research, resulting in changes to the form of the questionnaire. A researcher, for example, might have decided to use a number of open-ended questions to probe consumers' attitudes. However, a review of prior research on the same topic might indicate that this type of question works poorly because consumers are unable to verbalize their attitudes. As a consequence, closed-ended versus the originally planned open-ended questions would be used.

Second, secondary research can provide examples of ways to probe and explore specific areas addressed in primary research. A researcher can examine secondary sources to identify specific measures that prior researchers have used. The most relevant and reliable measures can then be modified for use in the planned research study. A researcher who wishes to probe reactions to advertising could save a great deal of time and effort by using measures developed by other researchers rather than starting from scratch.

ADVANTAGES OF SECONDARY RESEARCH

Secondary research, versus primary research, is typically more efficient in terms of money and time. In general, it is typically much less expensive to use secondary research information than to conduct primary research to collect comparable information. This is almost always true, even when the secondary information must be purchased. Additionally, beyond the absolute cost of obtaining the information, secondary

---

[6] Ibid., 132.

The Tri-Quad Cities Regional Blood Bank is planning to conduct research to determine (1) the reasons individuals do or do not donate blood, (2) the demographic characteristics of individuals who do and do not donate blood, (3) the appeal of various activities designed to motivate blood donation, and (4) the response to messages designed to reduce the fear of blood donation. The sample for the research will consist of 1,000 randomly selected individuals. Interviews will be conducted over the telephone.[a]

A search of secondary information was conducted prior to questionnaire completion. The information obtained from this search resulted in many substantive changes to the questionnaire and the research study, as follows.

Reasons for Blood Donation

Tri-Cities' original list of reasons why people do and do not donate blood was revised and expanded. The original list reflected the hypothesis that the only barrier to donation was fear of physical pain and the key motivator for donation was a sense of community responsibility. The original list exclusively focused on these two areas. Prior research, however, indicated that while donors were distinguished from nondonors in terms of "fear of pain from donating," these two groups could also be distinguished in terms of anticipated physical response to the donation process, fear of AIDS, self-satisfaction, and self-esteem. Items measuring attitudes in these areas were added to the questionnaire.[b]

Demographic Characteristics

Tri-Cities believed that gender and marital status were the major correlates of blood donors, with those donating blood more likely to be male and married. Prior research verified this belief. However, the research also indicated that education, residential proximity to a donation center, number of children, and other family members' receipt of a transfusion also strongly distinguished donors from nondonors.[c] As a result, demographic questions in these areas were added to the questionnaire.

Activities

Brainstorming sessions at Tri-Cities uncovered several innovative approaches to blood donation activities. A description of each of these activities was included in the questionnaire to assess consumer appeal. Several days after the brainstorming session, a review of newspaper articles was conducted. Several articles were uncovered that described activities tried by other blood banks (for example, "Singles Night at the Blood Bank"). Descriptions of these additional activities were added to the questionnaire.

Messages and Appeals

Given Tri-Cities initial hypothesis regarding barriers to blood donation, it is not surprising that the blood bank believed that an advertising message designed to reduce fear would have a positive impact. Three versions of such an appeal were written and included on the questionnaire to determine the strengths and weaknesses of each. Prior research, however, had already explored the effects of various appeals on intent to donate blood. This research found that individuals who heard a message emphasizing moral reasons for donating indicated a greater intention to donate versus those individuals who were exposed to a message aimed at reducing fear or a message that combined fear reduction with a moral appeal.[d] Tri-Cities delayed the research until they could develop and include versions of a moral appeal in the questionnaire.

FIGURE 5.2

Contribution of secondary research to the conduct of primary research.

[a] Tri-Quad Cities Regional Blood Bank is fictitious. References b-d are real.

[b] Melanie Giles and Ed Cairns, "Blood Donation and Ajzen's Theory of Planned Behaviour: An Examination of Perceived Behavioural Control," *British Journal of Social Psychology* 34 (1995): 173–88; Nabil Ibrahim and Mary F. Mobley, "Recruitment and Retention of Blood Donors: A Strategic Linkage Approach," *Health Care Management Review* 18 (1993): 67–73.

[c] Ibraham and Mobley, "Recruitment and Retention."

[d] Joseph Ferrari and Michael R. Leippe, "Noncompliance with Persuasive Appeals for a Prosocial, Altruistic Act: Blood Donating," *Journal of Applied Social Psychology* 22 (1992): 83–101.

information saves money by helping a researcher focus on real and meaningful gaps in knowledge.

Secondary research saves time because of differences in the rate of information acquisition. It may only take a week, for example, to determine a competitors' marketing strategies via an analysis of secondary sources. An analysis of the competitors' marketing strategies via primary research might take several months, if such research could be successfully accomplished at all. As a consequence, when insights (particularly quantitative insights) are needed quickly, the only practical alternative is to consult secondary sources. Moreover, "if stringent budget and time constraints are imposed on primary research, secondary research may provide higher quality data then could be obtained with a new research project."[7]

Finally, there are circumstances in which secondary research is the only type of available information. It would be time and cost prohibitive, for example, for a single advertiser or marketer to conduct research similar to the U.S. census or to monitor advertising expenditures of all national advertisers. Additionally, secondary information is the only type of information that can be used when historical data is required.

LIMITATIONS OF SECONDARY RESEARCH

In spite of the advantages of secondary research information, the use of this type of information poses dangers to the uninformed or uncritical user. Users of secondary research must clearly understand the limitations of secondary information with regard to four criteria: availability, relevance, accuracy, and sufficiency.

Availability

Secondary information cannot be used in some instances simply because it is not available. There may be a lack of secondary information because of

- the uniqueness and specificity of the informational need (for example, determining consumers' responses to advertising concepts or obtaining taste test preferences to alternative product formulations), or
- the proprietary nature of the desired information (for example, consumers' responses to competitors' new line extensions).

Informational needs must be met by primary data whenever secondary information is unavailable.

Relevance

Secondary research best satisfies an advertiser's informational need when it is relevant. The extent to which secondary research information is relevant in a particular circumstance is determined by the correspondence between the advertiser's informational needs and the characteristics of the secondary information in terms of

- units of measurement
- units of analysis
- timeliness of data collection

---

[7] Ibid., 5.

The relevance of secondary information increases when there is a high correspondence between the units of measurement utilized in the secondary research and the advertiser's or marketer's desired units of measurement. An example would be an automobile manufacturer who wishes to track competitors' monthly advertising expenditures. Secondary information that reports dollars spent per month displays an exact correspondence and would therefore be very relevant. Secondary sources that report spending in terms of other units, such as advertising dollars per auto sold or advertising dollars as a percent of gross margin would be less relevant.

The relevance of secondary information also increases when there is a high correspondence between how an advertiser or marketer defines the unit of analysis and how the unit of analysis is defined by the secondary information source. An advertiser may be interested in identifying the average amount of children's cereal purchased per month in households with children aged five to ten. Secondary information that exactly corresponds to this definition would be more relevant than secondary information with different units of analysis, for example, research that uses a different

- category definition (i.e., all cereal purchases versus just children's cereal),
- time period (i.e., per week, every three months), or
- target definition (i.e., households with any child under the age of 12).

Finally, the relevance of secondary information increases with its recency. Most informational needs require current data. Thus, the relevance and usefulness of a secondary information source generally declines as the data it reports become older.

Accuracy

Users of secondary research information should always evaluate the accuracy of the data prior to its application to the decision-making process. The accuracy of secondary research information can be evaluated by asking a series of six questions. Only the secondary information that passes scrutiny through the entire question and examination sequence should be used for decision making.[8] The questions to be considered during the evaluation of secondary information accuracy are as follows:

1. *What was the purpose of the research?* Research conducted to provide objective insights into a particular phenomenon (for example, public opinion polls conducted by news organizations) tend to more useful and accurate than research conducted by advocacy groups to promote or support a particular position. Thus, prior to using a particular secondary source of information, a researcher should determine why the research was conducted and whether the information collected is objective or self-serving.

2. *Was the methodology appropriate and unbiased?* Research conducted for the appropriate purpose can still be inaccurate or misleading if an improper methodology was used to collect the data. It is important to determine the extent to which the research was conducted in a methodologically sound manner. A researcher must examine and assess the appropriateness of the sample and sampling procedures, question formats and data analysis procedures. Problems in any of these areas greatly reduce secondary data accuracy and usefulness.

---

[8] Ibid., 17–32.

3. *Who planned the research, collected the data and analyzed the findings?* The collection of accurate data requires both a sound methodology and the proper implementation of that methodology. Thus, the technical expertise of the individual or organization that actually collected the data must be examined and evaluated. Data collected by individuals or research companies with national reputations tend to be more reliable and accurate than data conducted by parties with lesser research expertise.

4. *Has the data been analyzed and presented properly?* Data can either intentionally or unintentionally be reported in a misleading manner. A user of secondary data must evaluate the data to assess its accuracy in presentation prior to applying the data to satisfy the current informational need. Only data that has been analyzed and reported properly and without bias should be used for decision making.

5. *Is the information consistent with other information?* The accuracy of any particular piece of secondary information can be evaluated in terms of its consistency with secondary information from other independent sources. Data consistency across data sources tends to indicate greater data accuracy.

6. *Has the data been reported by the original source?* The potential for data inaccuracy increases the further one moves from the original source. As a result, whenever possible one should examine original data or original reports should be examined rather than interpretations of the data by a second- or third-party.

Sufficiency

Secondary data may be available, relevant, and accurate but still may not sufficiently satisfy identified informational needs. A shampoo manufacturer might wish to identify best selling shampoos and the brand share of these shampoos among men aged 25 to 54 and women aged 25 to 49. While secondary information might be able to supply overall brand share it may not be able (and is thus insufficient) to report brand shares among these specific gender and age groups. When secondary data is insufficient an advertiser or marketer may either conduct primary research or make decisions based on available but incomplete data.

SOURCES OF SECONDARY INFORMATION

As the examples in the prior section illustrate, some secondary data come from within the client or advertising agency. These *internal sources* of secondary data may be located within the client's finance, marketing, sales, research, and product development departments or within any of the departments within the advertising agency. Advertising agencies and clients generally use internal sources of secondary data to address informational needs in the areas of product development, market tracking, new product development, advertising design, and strategic planning.

External sources of secondary data come from outside the client or agency. The primary sources of external secondary data are books, periodicals, newspapers, trade and nonprofit associations, government agencies, and private business.[9] Information

[9] This chapter focuses on secondary information that appears in either printed or electronic form. However, it is important to point out that individual human beings can also be valuable sources of secondary information. A secondary researcher should always consider consulting experts and authorities who are likely to be knowledgeable on the topic of interest.

from these sources is typically used to answer informational needs in four broad areas: marketing, advertising, the consumer, and the media. In the following sections we identify the specific sources of secondary information that marketers and advertisers use to satisfy their informational needs in each of these areas.[10]

MARKETING ISSUES

Advertisers' and marketers' marketing-related questions and informational needs typically relate to the following:

- *The broader context in which marketing activities will take place.* Questions in this area relate to economic and socioeconomic trends and developments on the national level.
- *The dynamics of the category in which their product is sold and advertised.* Common questions include: How can I learn more about the characteristics and trends within a specific product category? What segments of the category are growing or declining? What recent product innovations have occurred? What are the dominant brands and how have brand shares changed over the past several years? What factors have affected category sales?
- *Competitive activities within this category.* Common questions include: How can I learn more about the activities of specific companies? What are the marketing strategies of competitive brands? How have individual brand's marketing strategies changed over the past several years?

A broad range of secondary resources are available to address informational needs in each of these areas.

The Broader Context for Marketing Activities

The primary sources for national economic and socioeconomic information are federal governmental agencies. Information gathered by these agencies is available in regularly printed reports or interactively via CD-ROM, machine readable tapes, or the World Wide Web. Frequently referenced government reports include the following:

- *Survey of Current Business*—This monthly journal synthesizes the Bureau of Economic Analysis' estimates and analyses. Two levels of data are reported. National data provide a quantitative view of the production, distribution, and use of the nation's output and estimate the country's tangible wealth. Regional data provide estimates, analyses, and projections of personal income, population, and employment. The *Survey of Current*

---

[10] We present and discuss specific sources of information. However, by necessity, only a small portion of available resources and sources are mentioned. Thus, in addition to the appropriate sources noted in this chapter, a secondary researcher will want to consult one or more directories of business information sources. These directories provide extensive references to business, marketing, and advertising information sources. Some of the more popular directories are Lawrence Rasie, *Directory of Business Information* (New York, NY: John Wiley, 1995); Hiram Barksdale and Jack L. Goldstucker, *Marketing Information: A Professional Reference Guide* (Atlanta, GA: Georgia State University Business Press, 1995); *Encyclopedia of Business Information Sources* (Detroit, MI: Gale Research Co., 1994); John Ganly, *Data Sources for Business and Market Analysis* (Metuchen, NJ: The Scarcrow Press, 1994); Ruth A. Pagell and Michael Halperin, *International Business Information: How to Find It, How to Use It* (Phoenix, AZ: Oryx, 1994); Sara Ball, *The Directory of International Sources of Business Information* (London: Pitman Publishing, 1990).

Business also includes the "Business Situation," a review of current economic estimates, trends, and developments.

- *Business Conditions Digest*—A monthly publication of the Department of Commerce, *Business Conditions Digest* contains seventy indicators of business trends. Each issue contains two parts: (1) "cyclical indicators," which reports cyclical indicators for various economic areas, composite indices of economic activity and indices of diffusion and rates of change and (2) "other important economic measures," which include data on the labor force, employment and unemployment, government involvement in business activities, wages, productivity, national income, and international business.

- *Vital Statistics Report*—A monthly publication of the Department of Health and Human Services, *Vital Statistics Report* provides information on births, deaths, marriages, and a variety of health-related statistics.

- *Economic Indicators*—Published by the Council of Economic Advisors, *Economic Indicators* reports current and trend data related to personal consumption expenditures, gross national product, and national economic trends. The Council of Economic Advisors also prepares a review of economic policy and forecasts economic developments. This review is incorporated into the annual *Economic Report of the President.*

Additional governmental reports of economic or socioeconomic trends can be located in the *American Statistics Index: A Comprehensive Guide and Index to the Statistical Publications of the U.S. Government.*[11]

As noted earlier, business and economic data can be obtained interactively using a CD-ROM or the World Wide Web. One of the easiest ways to access economic and socioeconomic data from the federal government is through STAT-USA/INTERNET on the World Wide Web. STAT-USA/INTERNET, nicknamed "The One-Stop Source for Business and Economic Data," currently contains over 300,000 reports, statistical series, press releases, and statistical information from over 50 federal agencies. New reports are added weekly. Some of the data bases contained in STAT-USA/INTERNET that are of particular interest to marketers and advertisers are

- *The National Trade Data Bank (NTDB)*—The NTDB offers an abundance of export and trade related information, including export opportunities by industry, country, and product; how-to-market guides; demographic, political, and socioeconomic conditions in hundreds of countries.

- *The National Economic, Social and Environmental Data Bank (NESE-DB)*—The NESE-DB offers extensive information on socioeconomic programs and trends in the United States today. The NESE-DB provides in-depth coverage of economic trends, education, health issues, criminal justice, and the environment.

- *The Economic Bulletin Board (EBB)*—The EBB is a source for economic and general business press releases, statistical series, and economic information files. It provides information on late-breaking business developments and in-depth analyses of markets, products, and economic trends.

- *Bureau of Economic Analysis (BEA)*—This source provides access to BEA's news releases, the Survey of Current Business, and detailed data files from BEA's national, regional, and international economic accounts. Included are the national income and product accounts, including the gross domestic product (GDP), composite indices of

---

[11] *American Statistics Index: A Comprehensive Guide and Index to the Statistical Publications of the U.S. Government* (Washington, DC: Congressional Information Service), monthly.

leading indicators, personal income for states and local areas, and the U.S. balance of payments.

The STAT-USA/INTERNET data base is searchable through natural language inquiries. Thus, one can access the STAT-USA/INTERNET inquiry site and type "tell me all about the sales of automobiles in Japan" or "what is the trend on consumer expenditures for major appliances." The STAT-USA/INTERNET inquiry processor will then interpret the inquiry and provide the names of relevant documents, which can then be obtained by clicking on the document title.[12] The address for the STAT-USA/INTERNET home page is http://www.stat-usa.gov.

A second source of economic data is Inforum at the University of Maryland. Inforum contains several hundred thousand economic time series reports produced by the federal government. These reports are organized in a way that lets an individual quickly locate, examine, download, and perform additional analyses on relevant data including, national income and product accounts, labor statistics, price indices, and current business indicators. The address of Inforum is http://info.umd.edu:86/Educational Resources/AcademicResourcesByTopic/EconomicResources/EconData/.www/econdata.html.

Category Dynamics and Competitive Activities

Periodicals and Newspapers   Periodicals provide a great deal of information on category dynamics and competitive activities. The type, complexity, and orientation of the provided information depends on whether the information is presented in a journal, magazine, or newspaper.

Journals predominantly publish articles that have passed the scrutiny of the peer review process. Articles within a particular journal tend to relate to a single topic or area of inquiry. Journal articles can be either theoretical or methodological in orientation, but in both cases most journal articles are scholarly in approach and generally assume that the reader has some familiarity with the subject area.

Some journals tend to publish noncategory specific papers on business and marketing issues. As a result, the secondary researcher must independently determine how to apply a paper's insights to the category of interest. The most commonly referenced journals of this type are *Journal of Marketing, Journal of Marketing Research, Journal of Business Research, Journal of Business, Journal of Consumer Marketing, Journal of Direct Marketing*, and *Journal of Public Policy and Marketing*. Other business and marketing-oriented journals specifically focus on individual product categories. They can be located by examining the serial holdings of your local public or university library.

Magazines and newspapers generally publish articles without peer review. The editorial content of mass market consumer and business magazines and newspapers tends to address major category developments and competitive activities without as-

---

[12] STAT-USA/INTERNET is an important source of government economic and socioeconomic information. However, it is important to note that there are many additional World Wide Web and Internet sites where government information can be examined and obtained. See, for example, Max Lent, *Government Online* (New York, NY: Harper Perennial, 1995); Bruce Maxwell, *How to Access the Federal Government on the Internet* (Washington, DC: Congressional Quarterly, 1995); J. Levin, ed., *The Federal Internet Source* (Washington, DC: National Journal, Inc., 1994).

suming a great deal of prior knowledge on the part of the reader. The magazines and newspapers that are commonly used to satisfy informational needs in these areas include *Barron's, Business Week, Forbes, Fortune, Harvard Business Review, The New York Times, The Wall Street Journal*, and *Investor's Daily*. Many of these and related journals have established their own World Wide Web sites that permit searchable access to current and past articles.[13]

Trade magazines are magazines whose editorial content narrowly focuses on a specific product or industry. As a result, trade magazines are best suited for satisfying marketing related informational needs that require in-depth analysis of a narrowly defined area. Advertising and marketing trade magazines, such as *Advertising Age, Adweek, Brandweek*, and *Mediaweek*, keep advertisers and marketers abreast of competitors' advertising and marketing strategies.

Beyond advertising and marketing trade magazines, most advertisers and marketers will also read the trade magazines that cover their specific product or service. Trade magazines exist for almost every product and service category and can be located by referring to *Business Publications Rates and Data*, published by Standard Rate and Data Service. An individual involved with the marketing and advertising of banks, financial institutions, or financial products might read some of the following trade magazines: *American Banker, Bank Marketing Magazine, Bank News, The Bankers Magazine, Banking Week, Savings & Community Banker*, and *United States Banker*.[14]

Supermarket Business and *Progressive Grocer*, two important trade magazines for the food industry, illustrate the quality of insight and information communicated by market-specific trade magazines. *Supermarket Business* conducts an "Annual Consumer Expenditure Survey." This survey reports data on total food expenditures, retail

---

[13] The World Wide Web address for individual magazines can be obtained by typing the magazine's name into a search engine such as Yahoo or InfoSeek or by visiting the business journals homepage at http://www.businessjournals.com.

[14] Relevant articles in journals, magazines, and newspapers are most easily located through electronic data bases. At present, there are more than 4,500 databases available from over 600 data base providers. Some data bases can be searched without charge at public and university libraries while other data bases can only be accessed on a fee basis over a modem. However, regardless of how the data base is accessed, search procedures tend to be generally consistent across data bases. A user types in a key word or key words, subject, or author and the data base retrieves and provides references to relevant articles. In many instances, article references are accompanied by an abstract. Some of the more common data bases used by advertisers and marketers include *PTS MARS (Predicasts' Marketing and Advertising Reference Service)*—MARS contains over 370,000 citations and is described as follows: MARS is a multi-industry advertising and marketing data base with citations, abstracts, and full-text records on a wide variety of consumer products and services taken from journals and trade publication literature. It covers advertising agency strategies, sales strategies, promotional campaigns, advertising slogans, spokespeople, and target market research. It is widely used to locate market size/share information; monitor product or service introductions; evaluate markets for existing products or services; and research the advertising and marketing strategies of competitors. The abstracts and full-text citations are obtained from more than 140 publications that fall into the following categories: advertising trade publications, consumer-oriented trade publications, business methods journals, market research studies, advertising-related articles from newspapers and newsletters; *Newsbank Full Text*—A compilation of full text articles from over 100 newspapers, newswires, and the Congressional Record; *Wilson Business Abstracts*—An index to articles and book reviews in basic business journals and magazines as well as the Wall Street Journal; *Nexis*—A full-text news and business-related information service containing over 2,400 full-text sources; *DataTimes*—A service covering over 5,000 full-text sources such as newswires, regional, national, and international newspapers and magazines; *NewsNet*—A source for information contained in industry-specific newsletters; *Expanded Academic Index*—An index to articles in over 900 scholarly and general interest periodicals focusing on topics in the social sciences, humanities, and nontechnical general science areas; *PsycLit*—An index, with abstracts, to the world's serial and book literature in psychology and related disciplines.

sales by type of food product, retail food sales by state, and the specific outlets at which consumers spend their food dollars (i.e., restaurants, supermarkets, convenience stores, etc.). *Progressive Grocer* presents an annual "Guide to Product Usage." This report, which uses data from SAMI/Burke and Simmons Market Research Bureau, provides an in-depth analysis of food purchase and consumption patterns. The analysis in *Progressive Grocer* describes for individual product categories: the demographics of all product purchasers and heavy product purchasers, brand loyalty (i.e., the percentage of consumers who are exclusive single brand users), and estimated product daily usage.

Trade and Nonprofit Associations   Similar to trade magazines, trade associations are an excellent source of information on trends and developments in narrowly defined areas of interest. A trade association is a voluntary organization whose members are individuals and companies involved in the same type of business, industry, or activity. As a benefit to their members, trade associations often conduct research or prepare position papers on factors influencing their area of business, category growth patterns, factors and trends affecting the category, etc. The names and addresses of trade organizations can be found in the *Encyclopedia of Associations*.[15]

Private Business   Brokerage and investment services are excellent sources of information on category and company activities. These organizations produce thousands of in-depth reports that identify and analyze trends within specific product categories and that describe and evaluate the activities and outlook for specific companies. Given the volume of reports produced, the challenge for the secondary researcher is determining which specific brokerage or investment company produced the relevant report. Fortunately, two organizations facilitate this process.

The Wall Street Transcript Corporation publishes *The Wall Street Transcript (TWST)*. Each 70-page issue of *TWST* presents detailed information on over 300 companies, organized in the following sections:

- "Broker Reports" reprints lengthy excerpts of current brokerage publications.
- "Wall Street Roundup" reprints highlights of additional brokerage reports.
- "Corporate Reports on File" prints paid news releases from the companies themselves, including news of interim earnings, joint-venture announcements, corporate expansions, and other developments.
- "Speeches and Interviews" reprints recent speeches made by corporate executives and interviews with analysts and money managers.
- "Forum" provides space for analysts to comment on specific industries and investments. This section contains transcripts of analysts' round table discussions of a specific industry's outlook, trends, and leading companies.

Investext is a comprehensive and powerful guide to analysts' reports. This online service provides the complete text of more than 150,000 investment reports generated by nearly every major Wall Street broker, investment house, and regional bro-

---

[15] *Encyclopedia of Associations* (Detroit, MI: Gale Research Service), annual.

kers from across the country. In addition to brokerage reports, Investext also contains the complete text of speeches made before the NYSSA (New York Society of Security Analysts). Investext is available thorough a number of on-line providers, such as DIALOG, LEXIS, and NewsNet.

Beyond these collections of analysts' reports, two companies provide resources in book form. Standard & Poor's offers the following:

- *Standard & Poor's Corporate Records* provides historical and current corporate information including company history, officers, product information, and recent corporate news. Updates to the core volume are printed semimonthly.

- *Standard & Poor's Statistical Service* provides historical and current business and economic information organized within the following sections: banking and finance, production and labor, indices (e.g., commodities producer, consumer price, cost of living), income and trade, building and building materials, electric power and fuels, metals, transportation, textiles, chemicals, paper and agricultural products.

- *Standard & Poor's Industry Surveys* are concise and highly detailed analyses for over thirty industries and product sectors. Each industry specific report presents information related to market and brand sales trends, brand share and brand developments, consumer trends and purchase patterns and long-term category prospects.

Gale Research Inc.'s *Market Share Reporter*[16] covers 2,000 product and service categories in all industries. Each table in the *Market Share Reporter* lists the brand shares of the major companies competing in a particular product or service category. Company ranking reflects factors relevant to the product category. Car rental companies, for example, are ranked on the basis of system wide revenue, number of locations, and number of vehicles. The source of each ranking is noted so that a researcher can locate and examine the originating document for additional information.

Government Agencies   In addition to regional and national economic data, the federal government also provides information on specific retail, wholesale, and service industries. The *Census of the Retail Trade* provides information about sales, payroll, employees, number of establishments, sales by merchandise lines, etc., arranged by Standard Industrial Classification (SIC) codes. Units of analysis are states, counties, and other geographic areas such as Primary Metropolitan Statistical Areas (PMSAs), Consolidated Metropolitan Statistical Areas (CMSAs), and Metropolitan Statistical Areas (MSAs). Current survey data is reported in *Monthly Retail Sales and Inventories*. The *Census of Service Industries* provides payroll, employment, and sales information about retail service providers such as hotels, beauty parlors, laundries, etc. Information is reported by state, Standard Metropolitan Statistical Area (SMSA), county, and city. Current data is reported in *Monthly Selected Services Receipts* and *Service Annual Survey*. The *Census of Wholesale Trade* provides information about sales, number of establishments, payrolls, warehouse space, expenses, etc. arranged by SIC code. Information is reported by state, SMSA and county. Current data is reported in *Monthly Wholesale Trade: Sales and Inventories*.

---

[16] Arsen Darnay and Marlita Reddy, *Market Share Reporter* (Detroit, MI: Gale Research Service, 1994).

ADVERTISING PLANNING

Advertisers are continually looking for methods and techniques that they can use to make their advertising more attention-getting, creative, and persuasive. Secondary research often assists in the creative development process by helping advertisers answer questions pertaining to the following:

- *Advertising effectiveness*—How can I make my advertising more effective? What specific strategic or executional considerations are important in the development of my advertising campaign?

- *Competitive advertising activity*—To what extent, and with what success, have others used messages and approaches similar to those that I am considering? What are the advertising strategies of competitive brands? How have competitive brands' advertising strategies changed over the past several years?

- *Advertising practice*—To what extent have my competitors participated in practices that have been found to be misleading or deceptive? Will I have any legal problems with my own planned advertising?

- *Target audience*—How can I learn about individuals who use specific types of products or specific brands? How can I successfully advertise to the these people?

Advertising Effectiveness

Academic and advertising trade magazines are the primary source for information and insights related to advertising effectiveness. Two academic journals *(Journal of Advertising Research, Journal of Advertising)* specialize in the publication of papers that explore the factors that mediate and/or influence attention, communication, persuasiveness, and affective response. Other journals that publish (but do not specialize in) papers related to advertising effectiveness and impact are *Journalism and Mass Communication Quarterly, Advances in Consumer Research, Journal of Consumer Research, Journal of Marketing, Journal of Marketing Research*, and *Psychology & Marketing.*

Advertising trade magazines, such as *Advertising Age* and *Adweek*, often provide commentary or analysis of specific executions and advertising campaigns. Although the information in these magazines typically reflects opinion rather than research findings, the authors nevertheless provide meaningful insights and make an important contribution to the process of creative development.

Competitive Advertising

The periodical sources that describe competitors' marketing strategies also provide a great deal of information about the advertising strategies of various companies. As a result, *Barron's, Business Week, Forbes, Fortune, Harvard Business Review, The New York Times, The Wall Street Journal, Investor's Daily, Advertising Age, Adweek, Brandweek*, and *Mediaweek* are important sources of information on the advertising strategies of various companies.

Two nonperiodical sources also provide important information on competitive advertising strategies:

- *Adtrack* is an on-line data base that presents every advertisement of a quarter page or larger from 150 major consumer and business publications. The information reported

by *Adtrack* is quite comprehensive; it represents over 98 percent of the advertising revenue in major magazine categories. Adtrack provides a quick and easy method to identify and examine the content, style, approach, and placement of individual brand advertising. Additionally, the data base is organized so that a "reverse" analysis can be conducted. Here, rather than examining the advertising of specific brands, one can examine all the advertising that displays specific characteristics, such as a specific sales message, use of coupon or spokesperson, etc. Adtrack is available through several on-line vendors.

- Corporate annual reports provide a different set of insights into corporate advertising and marketing strategies. These reports often discuss the content and success of the prior year's advertising campaigns and plans for the upcoming year.

Finally, Adnews On-line Daily electronically provides advertising and marketing information on a daily basis. (The home page of Adnews On-line Daily can be reached at http://www.io.org/~adnews.) Adnews articles are designed to provide insights into "significant happenings" in the marketing, advertising, and media communities. Importantly, archived articles can be searched by using keywords. A search for the keyword "beer," for example, uncovered 51 articles including: beer by mail, brewers hike prices, brewer expanding in U.S. and Molson Dry is 'animated' in point of purchase (POP).

Advertising Practice

There are two main sources of information for guidance on the legal aspects of advertising practice: LEXIS and the Advertising Law Internet Site.

LEXIS is a major on-line source of legal information. The service contains forty-five specialized libraries covering all major fields of law. Each library contains archives of federal and state case law, current federal and state regulations and statutes, references to articles in legal journals and, where available, annotated case citations. LEXIS is an excellent place to begin the exploration of any legal issues related to advertising practice or message content.

The Advertising Law Internet Site is maintained by Lewis Rose, a partner in the law firm of Arent Fox Kinter Plotkin & Kahn. The site provides access to a broad range of information including:

- *Advertising practice*—Reprints of the Federal Trade Commission (FTC) policy statements on deception.

- *Advertising law*—Numerous articles relating to advertising law and practice, for example, endorsements, testimonials, demonstrations.

- *Better Business Bureau decisions*—Reviews and analyses of major decisions reached by the National Advertising Division of the Council of Better Business Bureaus, Inc.

- *FTC guidelines and enforcement policy statements*—Statements related to FTC regulation of specific advertising practices such as food advertising, environmental claims, and the use of the term "free."

The Advertising Law Internet Site is continually updated to reflect developments in advertising law and regulation. The site's home page can be reached at http://www.webcom.com/~lewrose/home.html.

Target Audience Characteristics

A prerequisite to the development of effective advertising is an understanding of the advertising's target audience. Advertisers can draw from several sources to foster this understanding.

Periodicals often publish reports on the attitudes and behaviors of groups of individuals. Trade journals relevant to the product category provide analyses and discussions of the needs and desires of groups of individuals defined in terms of category or brand usage.

Books are also a useful source of information on target audience characteristics. The *Lifestyle Market Analyst*, for example, provides information on target audiences defined in terms of geography, demographics, or lifestyle. This book is arranged into three sections:

- The first section is arranged *geographically* and presents a two-page profile of each Area of Dominant Influence (ADI) in the United States (see Figure 5.3). The first page describes the ADI in terms of occupation, education, ethnicity, age, marital and family status, income, and credit card usage. Classifications are described in terms of absolute percents and in terms of an index that compares characteristics within the ADI to national levels. The second page reports consumer participation in fifty-seven lifestyle activities grouped into five broad categories: the "Good Life," high tech, sports/leisure, outdoor, and domestic. Again, absolute percentages and indices are reported. The information presented in this section helps an advertiser better understand geographically-defined target audience characteristics.

- The second section is arranged by *lifestyle activity*. This two page profile follows the same format as the pages in the first section, only here descriptors relate to individuals who participate in a specific lifestyle activity. This data is very useful for fostering an understanding of lifestyle-defined target audiences.

- The third section is organized by *household characteristics*. The format is identical to that used in the prior sections, only here descriptors relate to individuals with specific demographic characteristics. This data is very useful for fostering an understanding of demographically-defined target audiences.

Other books focus on advertising and marketing to *specific* demographic or attitudinal groups. These books typically identify salient group characteristics, place these characteristics in an historical context, predict future group trends, discuss and evaluate prior marketing and advertising efforts directed toward the group, and present recommendations for future advertising and marketing efforts. The most current books of this type can be located in *Books in Print*.[17]

---

[17] Representative examples of these types of books include the following: Rena Bartos, *Marketing to Women Around the World* (New York, NY: McGraw-Hill, 1989); Robert Boutilier, *Targeting Families: Marketing to and Through the New Family Structures* (Ithaca, NY: American Demographics Books, 1993); Walter Coddington, *Environmental Marketing: Positive Strategies for Reaching the Green Consumer* (New York, NY: McGraw-Hill, 1993); Janice Leeming, *Segmenting the Women's Market: Using Niche Marketing to Understand and Meet the Diverse Needs of Today's Most Dynamic Consumer Market* (Chicago, IL: Probus Publishing Co., 1994); Paula Mergenhagen, *Marketing Transitions: Marketing to Consumers During Life Stages* (Ithaca, NY: American Demographics Books, 1994); Robert Michman, *Lifestyle Market Segmentation* (New York, NY: Praeger, 1991); Marcia Mogelonsky, *Everybody Eats: Supermarket Consumers in the 1990s* (Ithaca, NY: American Demographics Books, 1995); Carol Morgan, *Segmenting the Mature Market: Identifying, Targeting and Reaching America's Diverse Booming Senior Markets* (Chicago, IL: Probus Publishing Co., 1993); Marlene Rossman, *Multicultural Marketing: Selling to a Diverse America* (New York, NY: American Marketing Association, 1994).

Lifestyles
Base Index US = 100

Fargo-Valley City, ND

The Top Ten Lifestyles Ranked by Index

Hunting/Shooting	201	**Casino Gambling**	133
Recreational Vehicles	154	**Crafts**	129
Fishing Frequently	150	**Grandchildren**	126
Vegetable Gardening	146	**Automotive Work**	125
Needlework/Knitting	136	**Sewing**	125

Home Life	Households	%	Index	Rank
Avid Book Reading	81,183	37.1	98	91
Bible/Devotional Reading	46,609	21.3	120	97
Flower Gardening	85,122	38.9	116	33
Grandchildren	59,082	27.0	126	27
Home Furnishing/Decorating	41,576	19.0	98	99
House Plants	85,341	39.0	115	14
Own a Cat	52,995	24.2	95	170
Own a Dog	66,303	30.3	91	190
Subscribe to Cable TV	130,200	59.5	94	163
Vegetable Gardening	74,619	34.1	146	13

Good Life				
Attend Cultural/Arts Events	24,727	11.3	78	115
Fashion Clothing	24,946	11.4	83	153
Fine Art/Antiques	19,038	8.7	84	168
Foreign Travel	16,849	7.7	53	165
Frequent Flyer	40,045	18.3	91	54
Gourmet Cooking/Fine Food	22,539	10.3	61	189
Travel in USA	72,868	33.3	92	102
Wines	13,348	6.1	53	174

Investing Money				
Casino Gambling	29,760	13.6	133	29
Entering Sweepstakes	36,762	16.8	119	43
Money Making Opportunities	21,882	10.0	95	122
Real Estate Investments	8,972	4.1	66	187
Stock/Bond Investments	26,915	12.3	82	138

Sports, Fitness & Health				
Bicycling Frequently	46,172	21.1	122	33
Dieting/Weight Control	45,953	21.0	100	98
Golf	50,767	23.2	120	30
Health/Natural Foods	26,040	11.9	82	182
Physical Fitness/Exercise	64,553	29.5	85	160
Running/Jogging	18,162	8.3	72	176
Snow Skiing Frequently	15,755	7.2	95	75
Tennis Frequently	7,221	3.3	52	189
Walking for Health	85,997	39.3	111	17
Watching Sports on TV	83,153	38.0	101	84

Great Outdoors	Households	%	Index	Rank
Boating/Sailing	22,539	10.3	94	92
Camping/Hiking	52,518	24.0	114	73
Fishing Frequently	74,619	34.1	150	47
Hunting/Shooting	65,428	29.9	201	27
Motorcycles	17,725	8.1	121	58
Recreational Vehicles	26,259	12.0	154	38
Wildlife/Environmental	33,699	15.4	94	132

Hobbies & Interests				
Automotive Work	40,263	18.4	125	20
Buy Pre-Recorded Videos	30,416	13.9	93	146
Career-Oriented Activities	15,536	7.1	78	153
Coin/Stamp Collecting	17,287	7.9	107	51
Collectibles/Collections	27,791	12.7	111	32
Crafts	75,713	34.6	129	6
Current Affairs/Politics	31,948	14.6	90	137
Home Workshop	57,769	26.4	117	20
Military Veteran in Household	53,174	24.3	96	159
Needlework/Knitting	53,174	24.3	136	10
Our Nation's Heritage	8,753	4.0	83	198
Self-Improvement	37,638	17.2	94	135
Sewing	54,049	24.7	125	43
Supports Health Charities	36,106	16.5	92	83

High Tech Activities				
Electronics	17,506	8.0	82	165
Home Video Games	22,320	10.2	88	184
Listen to Records/Tapes/CDs	94,094	43.0	92	146
Own a CD Player	74,400	34.0	77	167
Personal/Home Computers	57,113	26.1	80	145
Photography	39,826	18.2	99	67
Science Fiction	13,348	6.1	70	200
Science/New Technology	12,129	6.0	70	174

Mean Number of Interests		12.4		103

FIGURE 5.3

Geographically defined target audience from the *Lifestyle Market Analysis*.

Source: Reprinted from the 1996 edition of the *Lifestyle Market Analyst*, published by Standard Rate and Data Service with data supplied by The Polk Company.

Finally, two research companies, Simmons Market Research Bureau (SMRB) and Mediamark Research Inc. (MRI), syndicate extensive information on the demographics and media usage of individuals who are in particular product categories or who use specific brands. The data from both sources reflects the outcomes of extensive interviews conducted with a nationally representative and generalizable sample of approximately 20,000 adults aged 18 and over.

SMRB and MRI publish the results of their research in a set of printed volumes, each of which contains reports for a specific product category.[18] Within each product category there are detailed reports for the specific brands and products measured by SMRB or MRI. SMRB data for the shampoo category, for example, identifies the demographics and media habits of category and brand user groups defined in terms of

- consumption level (all users, heavy users)
- form of consumption (bottle, tube)
- type of hair (color treated/permed, damaged, dandruff, dry, oily, normal)
- specific brand used (Breck, Clairol Condition, Finesse, Flex, Head & Shoulders, Ivory, Johnson's Baby Shampoo, Nexxus, Pert Plus, Salon Selectives, Suave, Vidal Sassoon, White Rain)
- manufacturer (Clairol, Johnson's, Neutrogena, Prell, Revlon, Suave, Vidal Sassoon)

The use of SMRB and MRI data for target audience analysis is discussed in greater detail in Chapter 19.

CONSUMER TRENDS AND ATTITUDES

All advertisers and marketers need to understand *current* consumer demographics, attitudes, and behaviors. This understanding provides the basis for the development of targeted advertising campaigns. Successful advertisers also develop an understanding of *trends* in consumer attitudes and behaviors. An understanding of important trends lets an advertiser anticipate marketplace and consumer developments and become a proactive leader versus a defensive follower. Advertisers use secondary information to answer the following types of consumer-related questions:

- *Demographics*—What are current demographic trends? How have population demographics changed over the past several years? What are the implications of these trends for marketing and advertising?
- *Expenditures*—What is the general pattern of consumer expenditures across various product categories? How do expenditure patterns vary across different demographic groups?
- *Attitudes*—What are current trends in consumer attitudes? How are attitudes and trends affected by demographic or lifestyle characteristics?

Consumer Demographics

The best source for information on demographic trends is the U.S. Government's Bureau of the Census. The 1990 Census of Population and Housing was last conducted in

---

[18] Simmons and MRI data can also be accessed via CD-ROM or on-line.

FIGURE 5.4
Bureau of the Census home page.

April 1, 1990 and will be retaken in the year 2000. The census asks detailed questions on a broad range of areas related to population and housing characteristics, (i.e., personal and household demographics, migration, child care, education, income, housing, and home ownership). This information is analyzed (and at times supplemented by additional surveys) and is presented in both printed and electronic formats. One excellent printed source of census and other federal data is the annual *Statistical Abstract of the United States*. In addition to printed reports, census and related data can be acquired and manipulated interactively using a CD-ROM or the World Wide Web.

The Bureau of the Census' World Wide Web site greatly facilitates the examination of information collected by the census bureau.[19] The census bureau home page (see Figure 5.4) provides access to the broad range of information collected by the census bureau as well as connections to relevant individuals and related agencies. Advertisers and marketers can use the census bureau's inquiry processor to obtain census information on areas defined at the state, county, or city level. An inquiry about Bakersfied, CA, for example, generated a list of over 150 reports.

Working with original census data can, at times, be frustrating and time consuming. Fortunately, several private research companies have organized, reformatted, and supplemented census data bases to help marketers and advertisers better understand demographic trends and the implications of these trends for planning and decision making. These companies are described in more detail in Chapter 19.

Finally, *American Demographics* magazine provides a valuable alternative to individual examination of census and related demographic information. *American Demographics,* written for individuals in marketing, research, advertising, and corporate

---

[19] The Bureau of the Census home page can be reached at http://www.census.gov.

planning, is a magazine that focuses its editorial coverage on regional and national consumer trends, lifestyles, media preferences, and purchasing behavior. Articles in *American Demographics* are always concise and insightful. They provide excellent direction for applying demographic analyses to marketing and advertising planning.

Consumer Expenditures

The Consumer Expenditure Survey, conducted by the census bureau on behalf of the Bureau of Labor Statistics, provides important insights into how consumers spend their money. The Consumer Expenditure Survey tracks the types of products and services on which consumers spend their money and the amount of money spent on each type of product or service. Data is collected via an interview survey (which addresses non-recurring "big ticket" expenditures such as houses, cars, major appliances, and stable but recurring expenditures such as insurance premiums, rent and utility payments) and diary (in which smaller, recurring expenses are recorded for items such as food, drugs, personal care products, etc.). Data from the Consumer Expenditure Survey can be obtained from written reports prepared by the Bureau of Labor Statistics or interactively via CD-ROM or the World Wide Web.

An additional source of data from the Consumer Expenditure Survey is *The Official Guide to Household Spending.*[20] This book organizes Consumer Expenditure Survey data into key categories (food and alcoholic beverages, shelter and utilities, household operations and furnishings, apparel, transportation, health care, entertainment, personal care, financial products, and gifts) and then reports spending by age group, income group, household type, and household size for key products within the category. An example report, showing food expenditures within various age groups, is shown in Figure 5.5.

The Consumer Expenditure Survey provides a great deal of information, however, many marketers and advertisers require even more detailed information on their specific product or service category and brand purchase behavior (which is not monitored by the Consumer Expenditure Survey.) This type of data can be obtained from several private companies.

Two companies offer data that reflects continuous market monitoring. Consumer expenditures and brand sales in specific product categories can be obtained from information collected and syndicated by Sales Areas-Marketing, Inc. (SAMI/Burke), Nielsen, and Information Resources Incorporated (IRI). SAMI and Nielsen use audits to collect their data on product sales.

- SAMI/Burke monitors 425 food and related product categories in forty-two markets. SAMI estimates category sales, brand share, and brand sales by tracking product movement from the warehouse to the retail outlet. Subscribers receive monthly reports.

- Nielsen monitors product movement at the retail outlet. Sales data are obtained by auditing sample stores throughout the United States. Current inventory is subtracted from inventory received since the last audit to determine the amount of product sold. In addition to estimates of category and brand sales, Nielsen's audits also track retail and wholesale prices, gross margins, percentage of stores stocking a particular item, special manufacturer's deals or promotions, and local brand advertising.

---

[20] Margaret Ambry, *The Official Guide to Household Spending* (Ithaca, New York: New Strategist, 1993).

Average expenditures

(average annual expenditures on food and alcoholic beverages, by age of reference person)

	all cu's	under 25	25 to 34	35 to 44	45 to 54	55 to 64	65 to 74	75+
Number of consumer units								
(in thousands, add 000)	*97,918*	*7,422*	*20,184*	*21,777*	*15,276*	*12,558*	*11,935*	*8,767*
Average number of persons per cu	*2.6*	*1.8*	*2.8*	*3.3*	*3.0*	*2.3*	*1.9*	*1.5*
Average total before-tax income	*$33,901.00*	*$14,319.00*	*$34,032.00*	*$41,871.00*	*$48,413.00*	*$38,285.00*	*$22,723.00*	*$16,247.00*
Total average annual expenditures	*$29,614.06*	*$16,745.50*	*$29,279.72*	*$36,445.57*	*$38,137.49*	*$31,944.55*	*$22,563.75*	*$15,781.68*
Food, average annual expenditures	*$4,271.37*	*$2,527.57*	*$4,271.73*	*$5,404.63*	*$5,183.87*	*$4,216.93*	*$3,466.44*	*$2,547.63*
Alcoholic beverages, average								
annual expenditures	*$296.75*	*$251.63*	*$370.02*	*$354.06*	*$359.80*	*$260.32*	*$216.52*	*$80.57*
FOOD AT HOME	**$2,650.89**	**$1.409.92**	**$2,529.44**	**$3,324.28**	**$3,146.62**	**$2,638.52**	**$2,364.48**	**$1,863.65**
Cereals and bakery products	**404.50**	**224.78**	**381.73**	**521.56**	**462.04**	**381.12**	**369.77**	**301.47**
Cereals and cereal products	145.23	84.65	148.34	192.23	165.21	123.84	122.12	101.61
Flour	6.34	2.78	7.68	6.83	6.64	6.67	5.73	4.65
Prepared flour mixes	14.21	7.93	12.95	18.84	16.30	12.15	15.00	9.38
Ready-to-eat and cooked cereal	87.16	50.48	91.58	112.60	94.22	76.22	72.44	68.67
Rice	14.85	8.24	14.70	22.96	18.25	11.17	11.31	5.37
Pasta, cornmeal, and other								
cereal products	22.66	15.23	21.43	31.00	29.80	17.62	17.63	13.53
Bakery products	259.27	140.13	233.39	329.33	296.83	257.28	247.65	199.85
Bread	75.32	41.84	68.63	88.37	86.23	77.83	73.45	66.26
Crackers and cookies	63.25	35.59	56.74	80.53	70.96	58.58	64.52	50.56
Cookies	39.83	22.50	36.44	53.00	45.77	35.71	38.82	27.06
Crackers	23.41	13.10	20.30	27.54	25.19	22.86	25.70	23.50
Frozen and refrigerated bakery products	19.48	9.88	20.03	25.73	20.70	18.14	16.18	15.05
Other bakery products	101.23	52.81	87.98	134.70	118.94	102.73	93.50	67.98
Biscuits and rolls	33.29	12.71	27.95	46.01	38.81	34.35	32.90	20.87
Cakes and cupcakes	28.68	20.08	24.84	38.46	34.92	27.85	22.81	19.54
Bread and cracker products	4.08	2.14	4.25	5.80	5.06	3.40	3.00	1.89
Sweetrolls, coffee cakes, doughnuts	23.60	12.57	20.51	27.04	28.85	27.86	22.54	17.63
Pies, tarts, turnovers	11.58	5.31	10.43	17.39	11.30	9.26	12.25	8.05
Meats, poultry, fish and eggs	**708.68**	**356.40**	**661.88**	**878.90**	**889.35**	**728.87**	**611.36**	**484.87**
Beef	228.37	117.80	217.30	296.14	280.88	221.38	192.94	148.27
Ground beef	86.35	55.09	85.97	113.50	100.75	75.14	75.56	53.41
Roast	41.01	23.80	35.79	42.77	54.60	44.87	43.67	30.42
Steak	82.72	29.55	78.56	116.94	105.28	82.02	56.40	50.81
Other beef	18.29	9.35	16.99	22.94	20.25	19.35	17.31	13.62
Pork	144.23	69.18	129.39	175.32	174.77	153.88	133.48	122.08
Bacon	21.06	9.05	19.90	24.41	23.55	22.07	20.57	20.09
Pork chops	34.62	23.58	32.25	43.68	43.52	31.95	27.07	19.29
Ham	38.26	12.02	32.28	41.40	55.72	44.30	38.29	27.11
Sausage	20.68	10.34	17.55	23.92	24.05	23.35	19.66	20.14
Other pork	29.61	14.21	24.40	41.90	27.94	32.21	27.90	25.46
Other meats	102.25	49.79	94.58	125.90	133.46	100.84	87.32	74.53
Frankfurters	23.43	9.57	23.86	30.83	28.73	20.75	20.41	14.66
Lunch meats (cold cuts)	69.40	33.96	63.24	85.40	88.48	69.44	60.84	52.70

FIGURE 5.5
Excerpt from *The Official Guide to Household Spending.*
Source: New Strategist Publications, Ithaca, NY. Reprinted with permission.

Nielsen and IRI also monitor product sales through the collection of supermarket scanner data. The data from a national sample of grocery stores are collected as items are scanned and are then aggregated to form weekly reports of category and brand sales.

Other companies use diary panels to obtain estimates of product usage and consumer expenditures. A diary panel is a large, nationally representative group of consumers who keep a diary of their product and brand purchases and product usage. At the end of a specified period, typically a month, the diary is submitted to the supervis-

ing research company. The research company then determines which products were purchased, in what quantities those products were purchased, and how those products were used. Two companies provide diary panel data. Each company collects a different type of data and, as a consequence, provides different insights into category and brand usage.

- National Purchase Diary, Inc. (NPD) is probably the largest provider of diary panel data. The core NPD panel consists of 13,000 nationally representative individuals. Panel members record their purchases in fifty basic consumer product categories. The data are analyzed to provide an understanding of sales and share trends by brand as well as brand switching and brand loyalty.

- The Market Research Corporation of America (MRCA) conducts a menu census of 4,000 nationally representative households. Thus, MRCA differs from NPD and IRI in that product usage, rather than product purchase, is tracked. Each household in the MRCA panel examines the products used for each meal during a two-week period and notes whether a particular item was used as a basic dish, an ingredient, or an additive; how the item was prepared; who was present at the meal; how leftovers were used; etc.

Consumer Attitudes

Large Scale Syndicated Surveys Many private companies conduct research to track consumer's attitudes, interests, opinions, and behaviors. Two syndicated research studies are the Yankelovich *Monitor* and *Roper Reports*. The Yankelovich *Monitor* is an annual survey that tracks more than sixty social and economic trends and their effects on consumers' behaviors. *Roper Reports*, issued ten times per year, also tracks changes in attitudes and behaviors, although the focus of each *Roper Reports* tends to be more narrowly focused versus the Yankelovich *Monitor*. The *Monitor* and *Roper Reports* provide important insights on two levels. Firstly, they provide an accurate portrait of current consumer attitudes. Secondly, historical data lets an advertiser or marketer see trends in attitudes, thus allowing them to proactively anticipate changes in consumer behaviors rather than defensively react to changes after they occur.

Information from *Roper Reports*, as well as other Roper Center surveys, are available on-line through POLL (Public Opinion Online). This extensive data base (accessible directly or through on-line services such as DIALOG) permits researchers to search for survey questions that address a specific topic and then obtain the responses to each identified question for the total sample and for specific demographic groups. In addition, researchers can use the data base to identify a specific demographic group's responses to questions asked on the same topic, but in different surveys.

The *Monitor* and *Roper Reports* provide a great deal of useful information. However, their high subscription costs place them out of the reach of many smaller marketers and advertisers. Fortunately, several magazines, books, and nonprofit centers provide lower cost (but not lower quality) alternatives to these sources.

Nonprofit Centers Survey data collected by nonprofit research centers are alternatives to survey data provided by for profit businesses. The two most heavily utilized centers are the National Opinion Research Center (NORC) and the Survey Research Center (SRC).

NORC, located at the University of Chicago, has conducted its "General Social Survey" annually since 1972. The core of the survey is a set of questions that is asked every year. These questions provide a basis for the examination of attitudinal trends among specific demographic and attitudinal groups. The core set of questions is supplemented each year by sets of questions that focus on special study topics. These questions provide in-depth insights into issues of contemporary importance. The results of the NORC survey are available from NORC in both printed and machine readable formats. Additionally, *An American Profile: Opinions and Behavior*[21] presents a summary of responses to core NORC questions asked between 1972 and 1989.

SRC is part of the Institute for Social Research at the University of Michigan. The SRC conducts several major annual surveys. The "Surveys of Consumer Attitudes and Behavior" has been conducted for over 50 years. This study, similar to many SRC studies, combines opinion and attitudinal questions with questions that address consumer, social, and political behavior. One particular SRC study, "Monitoring the Future: A Continuing Study of the Lifestyles and Values of Youth," is particularly relevant for those marketers and advertisers who wish to see what the nation's youth are currently thinking, from where they have come, and to where they might be heading. Question areas relate to academic performance, college and career plans, health, drug use, employment, income, leisure time, social/lifestyle activities, personal satisfaction, family and social relationships, political and social concerns, and quality of life. The data presented in each annual report represent the results of approximately 16,000 surveys conducted at a representative sample of United States high schools.

Periodicals and Books   Several periodicals developed by survey organizations provide timely information on trends in consumer attitudes. The *Gallup Poll Monthly* presents results from the over 100 annual surveys conducted by the Gallup Organization. Each issue of the *Gallup Poll Monthly* focuses on three to four topics with the following information provided for each topic: a narrative summary, sample characteristics, question wording, and question response (often cross-tabulated by key demographics).[22] The Roper Center publishes a bimonthly newsletter entitled *Public Perspective* that presents brief summaries of dozens of surveys on a broad range of topics.

Two independent periodicals, *Public Opinion* and *Public Opinion Quarterly*, are also excellent sources of information on consumer attitudes. The editorial content of *Public Opinion* focuses on the results of public opinion surveys and the implications of survey results. A very important feature of each issue of *Public Opinion* is "Opinion Roundup," which compares survey results from different polls on the same topic. *Public Opinion Quarterly* is more academic in orientation. *Public Opinion Quarterly* publishes papers on survey methodology, independent surveys of public opinion, and syntheses of opinion polls on a particular topic.

Finally, an invaluable reference tool is the *American Public Opinion Index*.[23] The index examines thousands of public opinion surveys conducted by over forty national

---

[21] Floris Wood, ed., *An American Profile: Opinions and Behavior* (Detroit, MI: Gale Research Service, 1990).

[22] Although less timely than the *Gallup Poll Monthly*, the *Gallup Poll: Public Opinion* is an annual compilation of Gallup Poll results. The format of this book is similar to the *Gallup Poll Monthly*, although the results and discussions are somewhat more abbreviated. An extensive index makes it easy to locate questions related to a specific topic. Within a topic, questions are arranged chronologically and, for each question, responses are summarized with respect to important demographics.

[23] *American Public Opinion Index* (Louisville, KY: Opinion Research Service), annual.

survey and market research organizations and then organizes individual survey questions into a master index. The index is arranged by broad topic and then by specific questions within a topic. Once a relevant survey question has been identified, information on the organization responsible for the survey, date and mode of data collection, and sample characteristics can be obtained from a second section of the index. The index, however, does not provide survey results; these must be obtained directly from the survey's source.

MEDIA

Advertising agencies strive to place, with maximum cost efficiency, their client's advertising in those media most appropriate to the advertising's target audience. Agency media planners try to accomplish this by relying on secondary research that provides information related to the following:

- *Advertising expenditures*—Agencies use secondary information to place their client's budgets in a competitive context and to evaluate budget alternatives. Common questions addressed by secondary research are: What are my competitors' advertising budgets? In what media are they placing their advertising? What are my competitors' trends in media expenditures?

- *Media cost*—Media cost is a key component of media planning. Secondary research helps answer the question: What is the cost of placing advertising in specific advertising vehicles?

- *Audience measurement*—Media efficiency is evaluated in terms of cost and audience delivery. Secondary information helps answer the question: What are the audience estimates for various media vehicles?

Advertising Expenditures   Advertisers need to know their competitors' level of advertising spending for several reasons. First, an advertiser's understanding of the competitors' advertising expenditures provides a sound and objective basis for evaluating the most appropriate budget for his or her own brand. The data permit an advertiser to examine the appropriateness of various budget options in light of levels of competitive spending and the competitive environment. Second, competitive spending estimates provide insights into marketplace activities and advertisers' brand strategies and priorities. The data indicate the extent to which competitive advertisers have maintained or shifted support for different products and brands, thus providing direction for determining budget allocation among an advertiser's brands. Third, information on competitive expenditures, when reported by advertising medium, provides insights into competitive advertisers' media strategies, that is, the extent to which they utilize specific media to promote and advertise their brands. This information can help an advertiser identify those media in which his or her brand will or will not be competing with the competition for the consumers' attention.

The primary source of competitive advertising expenditures is the LNA/MediaWatch Multi-Media Service (commonly referred to as Leading National Advertisers or LNA).[24] LNA estimates advertising expenditures by brand, parent company, and

---

[24] Chapter 25 presents a more detailed discussion of the characteristics and uses of the *LNA/Mediawatch Multi-Media Service* for competitive analysis and budget determination.

product category for ten media: magazines, Sunday magazines, newspapers, outdoor, network television, spot television, syndicated television, cable TV networks, network radio, and national spot radio.

LNA issues quarterly and annual reports in three different formats, each of which has its own specific strength. The *Company/Brand $* format facilitates the examination of advertising expenditures by parent company. This volume reports advertising expenditures by company name and then by brand expenditures within each company. The *Class/Brand $* summary organizes expenditures by industry grouping and then by company and brand within each grouping. This data format facilitates the examination of advertising expenditures within a defined product category. The *Ad $ Summary* provides an overview of brand advertising spending and levels of competitive brand expenditures. This volume summarizes individual brand advertising expenditures and presents rankings of the top advertisers in each of the ten monitored media as well as each of the product category subclassifications. Advertising agencies and others in need of these types of estimates have the option of purchasing LNA information in several formats: interactive on-line, CD-ROM, or in bound volumes. Trade magazines such as *Advertising Age, Adweek, Mediaweek, Brandweek*, and *Marketing News* are excellent sources of information on the advertising industry and an individual company's brand specific marketing and advertising activities. In addition to providing current information in these areas, *Advertising Age* and *Adweek* help advertisers better understand competitive pressures by providing estimates of advertising expenditures.

Every September, a special issue of *Advertising Age* identifies the 100 largest advertisers and then reports their expenditures in total and by media category. The issue also presents a list of the top twenty-five advertisers within each advertising medium. *Advertising Age* rankings often differ from those of LNA because of differences in the sources of spending estimates. *Advertising Age* supplements LNA data with data acquired from the advertisers themselves as well as their own independent estimates of advertisers' direct mail, and promotion spending as well as spending in other categories not monitored by LNA.

The *Adweek Client/Brand Directory*, issued annually, reports advertising expenditures for about 6,000 brands with at least $250,000 in spending. *Adweek's* estimates often differ from those of LNA because *Adweek's* data are obtained through a survey of the advertisers themselves. The *Adweek Client/Brand Directory* is published in six regional editions as well as a single national edition. Each geographic edition presents an alphabetical listing of brands. Each listing contains the name and address of the company, total brand media expenditures, key account personnel, the name of the brand's advertising agency and, if relevant, the name of the brand's parent company. The national edition provides a separate list of the 200 largest multibrand advertisers ranked by total brand advertising expenditures.

Media Cost   Advertisers need to know the cost to place their advertising in different media vehicles. This information is used to evaluate alternative methods of allocating the budget among the types of media and to evaluate the relative cost and efficiency of different media vehicles. One option for obtaining this information is to contact each potential media outlet (for example, a magazine or television station) and request a listing of their current rates. This process, however, can be quite time consuming. A sec-

ond and often preferred option is to refer to the information complied by Standard Rate & Data Service.

Standard Rate & Data Service provides the current advertising rates for thousands of television and radio stations, newspapers, magazines, and other advertising media. This information is presented in the following series of volumes that present the costs of advertising in "traditional" advertising media:

- *Network Television and Radio Rates and Data*
- *Spot Television Rates and Data*
- *Spot Radio Rates and Data*
- *Spot Radio Small Markets*
- *Consumer Magazine and Agri-Media Rates and Data*
- *Business Publications Rates and Data*
- *Community Publication Rates and Data*
- *Newspaper Rates and Data*

Data presented in these volumes are updated monthly with the exception of *Spot Radio Small Markets* and *Community Publications*, which are published semiannually.

Standard Rate & Data Service also has publications that address advertising rates in "nontraditional" or "alternative" advertising media. *Card Deck Rates and Data* presents rates for direct mail card decks, newspaper inserts, and other cooperative advertising. *Advertising Options Plus* covers a broad range of "out-of-home" media such as billboards, in-store advertising, mall and airport posters, taxi tops/sides, and bus shelters. *Direct Mail List Rates and Data* describes mailing list availability and cost. The volume contains two sections. The consumer directory organizes lists according to household characteristic while the business section organizes lists by type of business. Entries in both sections follow the same format. Each entry notes the source of the list, the characteristics of the names contained in the list, the geographic area covered, and the cost per thousand names. *Direct Mail List Rates and Data* is published monthly, *Card Deck Rates and Data* is published semiannually and *Advertising Options Plus* is published annually.

Audience Measurement Advertising agency media planners and buyers have two related tasks. They must place the advertising where the target audience has the greatest potential to see it and they must accomplish this placement with a high degree of cost efficiency. They accomplish these tasks by using information that describes various media vehicles' audience size, characteristics, and cost for advertising placement.

- Television and radio program audience measurement is expressed in terms of a share or rating. The A.C. Nielsen Company is the sole provider of television share and rating data. National ratings are collected through the people meter while local ratings are collected through personal diaries or a combination of diaries and meters.

- National radio ratings are collected by RADAR using a telephone interview-recall methodology. Local ratings are collected by Arbitron.

- Magazine audiences are evaluated in two ways: (1) circulation information is used to determine the extent to which a particular magazine's circulation base matches an advertiser's target audience, and (2) readership information is used to determine target audience incidence and concentration within a magazine's readership. Standard Rate &

Data Service provides relevant information for the former case, Simmons Market Research Bureau and Mediamark Research Inc. provide relevant information for the latter case.

- Newspaper and Yellow Pages audience sizes are measured in terms of circulation (provided by the newspaper or Yellow Pages publisher or by an independent audit bureau). Yellow Pages audience size is also evaluated in terms of "ratings"—a Yellow Pages directory's share of usage. The National Yellow Pages Monitor is the organization that collects Yellow Pages ratings.

Chapter 24 discusses these methods of audience measurement in greater detail.

Summary

Secondary research information is information that has been collected and analyzed by others for a purpose *other* than specifically responding to a current informational need. This contrasts with primary research that is conducted by (or on behalf of) an information user to *specifically satisfy* that individual's informational need. Secondary research is therefore distinguished from primary research on the basis of two criteria: (1) the individual responsible for planning and conducting the research and (2) the circumstances under which the research was conducted. Secondary research contributes to advertising and marketing decision making in three ways. Information obtained from secondary research can directly answer an advertiser's or marketer's informational needs, provide important insights prior to the conduct of primary research, and/or contribute to questionnaire development.

Secondary research has two advantages over comparable primary research. Secondary research tends to be more efficient in terms of time and money. Secondary research has several potential limitations. These limitations relate to information availability, relevance, accuracy, and sufficiency.

Secondary research information can come from internal and external sources. Internal sources of secondary data may be located within the client's finance, marketing, sales, research, and product development departments or within any of the departments within the advertising agency. Advertising agencies and clients generally use internal sources of secondary data to address informational needs in the areas of product development, market tracking, new product development, advertising design, and strategic planning. External sources are those outside the client or agency. Information from these sources is typically used to answer informational needs in four broad areas: marketing, advertising, the consumer, and media.

A great diversity of specific external sources exist to answer questions and informational needs in the areas of marketing, advertising, the consumer, and media. The primary sources of external secondary data are books, periodicals, newspapers, trade and nonprofit associations, government agencies, and private business.

Review Questions

1. What criteria differentiate primary from secondary research?
2. What is the difference between *secondary information* and *secondary sources?*

3. What are the three reasons why a primary source is preferred over a secondary source?

4. What are three important ways that secondary research information contributes to advertising and marketing decision making?

5. Should a researcher ever reanalyze, combine, or manipulate information from secondary sources? Why?

6. How can secondary research contribute to the planning and conduct of primary research?

7. What are the two main advantages of secondary research over primary research?

8. What are four potential limitations of secondary research?

9. What specific criteria can be used to determine the relevancy of secondary research information?

10. How can the accuracy of secondary research information be evaluated?

11. What is the difference between *internal* and *external* sources of secondary research information?

12. How do the following publications contribute to marketing-related decisions: *Survey of Current Business, Business Conditions Digest, Vital Statistics Report*, and *Economic Indicators?*

13. What are the primary differences between journals, consumer magazines, and trade magazines? How does each contribute to marketing-related decisions?

14. How do *The Wall Street Transcript* and *Investext* contribute to marketing-related decisions?

15. What secondary sources can an advertiser use to answer questions related to advertising effectiveness?

16. What is *Adtrack*? How is it best utilized?

17. What is the *Lifestyle Market Analyst?* How is it best utilized?

18. What are an advertisers' or marketers' options for obtaining census information?

19. What options do advertisers or marketers have for obtaining information related to consumer expenditures and brand purchase behaviors? What are the relative advantages and disadvantages of each option?

20. What options do advertisers or marketers have for obtaining information on consumers' attitudes and opinions? What are the relative advantages and disadvantages of each option?

21. What is *LNA/MediaWatch Multi-Media Service* (LNA)? How do advertisers use the information provided by LNA?

22. How do advertisers determine the cost of advertising placement?

Application Exercises

1. Select two of the following product categories. For each selected category provide twenty-five references to specific secondary sources that you would use to help you better understand category and brand sales trends, brand share, competitive marketing or advertising activities, and category-specific consumer attitudes and purchase behaviors. For each individual source provide a complete reference and a brief description of why you believe the source is relevant. Use a range of types of sources. There

can be no more than ten references from any particular type of source (i.e., periodical, book, journal, trade association, etc.) Potential product categories are

- coffee
- pain relievers
- ice cream
- dog food
- audio speakers
- toothpaste
- home computers
- mouthwash
- on-line computer services
- domestic beer
- wine coolers
- mineral waters

2. Each of the following questions can be answered through a review of secondary research. Select two questions. For each selected question (a) write a one to two paragraph answer to the question and (b) provide at least ten references to the sources that you used to answer the question.

   - Is there a relationship between commercial liking and commercial persuasiveness? That is, are consumers more likely to be persuaded in situations where they like a commercial versus situations where they do not like the commercial?
   - Does the amount of competitive clutter affect commercial and message recall?
   - When a celebrity spokesperson is used in a commercial, do perceptions of the spokesperson affect product perceptions?
   - How persuasive are negative political commercials?
   - How is commercial length related to commercial recall and commercial persuasiveness?
   - How does the program context for a television commercial affect commercial recall, viewer reactions to the commercial and commercial persuasiveness?

3. Each of the following statements address a common advertising-related stereotype or generalization. Select two statements. Use relevant secondary information to determine the truth of each selected statement. For each selected statement (a) write a one to two paragraph response that presents your point of view on the truth or falseness of the statement and (b) provide at least five references to the sources that you used to answer the question.

   - Exposure to children's advertising (by children) makes children more materialistic.
   - There is more sex in advertising today than there was ten or twenty years ago.
   - The vast majority of ads which stress a product's "environmental benefits" are deceptive.
   - Advertising perpetuates unfavorable racial, ethnic, and gender stereotypes.

4. You are developing a questionnaire to explore consumers' reactions to advertising. Provide three examples (with sources) from secondary research of approaches that have been used to measure (a) commercial recall, (b) attitudes toward an advertised product, (c) attitudes toward the advertising, and (d) commercial persuasiveness.

5. Find two articles in trade magazines that discuss category trends and developments. Evaluate the tone and content of each article for objectivity and bias. Would you use these articles as a source of information? Why or why not?

6. Identify six articles that discuss U. S. demographic trends. Read each article and then identify areas in which the articles agree and areas in which they disagree. What trends do the majority of the articles agree on? What trends do the articles disagree upon? Present a plan for reconciling disagreements among the articles.

CHAPTER

6

PRIMARY RESEARCH

Chapter 5 discussed how secondary research, the collection and analysis of existing information, can satisfy a broad range of advertisers' informational needs. There are times, however, when secondary research is an inappropriate response to an informational need, for example, when secondary information is unavailable, unreliable, or too costly. In these cases primary research, the collection of original information, is required.

There are two types of primary research, qualitative and quantitative. Qualitative research collects detailed, in-depth information on consumers' attitudes, beliefs, and motivations. It then attempts to explain the relationship between these characteristics and consumers' preferences and behaviors. Quantitative research collects statistically reliable, projectable numerical information that attempts to describe, explain, and predict consumers' attitudes and behaviors. This chapter introduces you to both forms of primary research.

After reading this chapter, you will be able to

■ Understand the appropriate uses of qualitative and quantitative research.

■ Describe the types of qualitative and quantitative research techniques commonly used by advertising researchers, noting the relative strengths and weaknesses of each.

■ Describe the most common types of survey research methods, noting the relative strengths and weaknesses of each.

■ Identify the types of errors that may occur in survey research and the techniques used for minimizing their occurrence.

Primary research collects original, typically proprietary, information to meet an advertiser's or marketer's informational needs. Primary research is used when secondary research is either nonexistent, unreliable, or too costly. In these circumstances, advertisers may select either qualitative or quantitative research to collect the information required to satisfy their informational needs. This chapter begins by discussing

the most common forms of qualitative and quantitative research, noting the relative strengths and weaknesses of each.

QUALITATIVE AND QUANTITATIVE RESEARCH

Qualitative and quantitative research provide complementary types of information. Qualitative research provides in-depth, nonnumerical information while quantitative research provides broader numerical information that is statistically reliable and projectable. Neither approach is intrinsically better than the other. Each approach is simply more or less appropriate given a specific circumstance or informational need.

Qualitative Research

Qualitative research (the focus of Chapters 9–11) is most appropriate when informational needs require in-depth or directional information, for example, when an advertiser needs

- to acquire background information in a particular area when little is already known.
- information to assist in problem formulation or the development of research hypotheses.
- a thorough understanding of the underlying relationship between consumers' feelings, attitudes, and beliefs and their behaviors *especially* when information on this relationship cannot be obtained through direct, structured, primarily closed questioning.
- to pretest a questionnaire or refine a research design.
- to listen to consumers express their ideas in their own words.

The most common forms of qualitative research are personal interviews and focus groups.

A *personal interview* (also known as one-on-one or depth interview) is a free-flowing yet structured conversation between a trained qualitative interviewer and a single respondent. This interview typically lasts between 30 and 60 minutes and is designed to elicit a great deal of detailed information from each individual participating in the study. Given the time and expense associated with personal interviews, sample sizes in studies using this form of data collection are generally quite low, typically involving between five and fifteen individuals.

Personal interviews are most appropriate for situations in which *extensive, detailed* probing of attitudes, behaviors, motivations, and needs is required or when

- the subject matter of the interview is likely to be seen as highly confidential (for example, family or personal finances, business practices), emotionally charged (for example, sexual behaviors) or embarrassing (for example, personal hygiene products).
- antitrust restrictions prohibit group discussion (for example, it is illegal to convene a group of CEOs from the same industry to discuss business practices and approaches to product pricing).
- group pressure or the presence of others is likely to alter or discourage honesty in response.

• there is a need to acquire a detailed or step-by-step understanding of complicated behaviors or decision-making patterns (for example, the process underlying the evaluation
and selection of a new automobile).

Focus groups and *minigroups* are an alternative to personal interviews. Focus
groups and minigroups each last about one and one-half to two hours and in both cases
a moderator moves the discussion through desired topic areas. The primary difference
between focus groups and minigroups lies is in the number of participants. Focus
groups generally consist of between eight and twelve individuals, all of whom participate in the group discussion at the same time. Minigroups are smaller, generally consisting of between three and six individuals.

The flexibility of focus groups and minigroups makes them a common approach
to meeting a wide variety of marketer and advertiser informational needs, particularly
in the areas of new product idea generation, product positioning and product perceptions, creative evaluation, product and package screening, and explorations of consumers' attitudes, beliefs, needs, and motivations. Moreover, the interactive nature of
focus groups and minigroups, in which one participant's comments can spark thoughts
and discussion in other participants, often provides information and insights unavailable through personal interviews.

Quantitative Research

Quantitative research encompasses three types of research techniques: observation,
physiological measurement, and survey research.

• *Observation research*—The recording of objects, events, situations, or people's behaviors. Observations can take place in either a natural or contrived situation where the
presence of the observer may or may not be known.
• *Physiological research*—The direct measurement of an individual's physical responses
to stimuli such as an advertisement. Physiological research measures both voluntary
(such as eye movements) and involuntary responses (such as brain waves and galvanic
skin response).
• *Survey research*—The most common form of quantitative research, is the systematic
collection of information from respondents through the use of questionnaires. Surveys
are most commonly administered over the telephone, through the mail, or in person to
person interviews. Electronic interactive surveys may also be used.

All three approaches to quantitative research share a core set of characteristics.
First, each approach is numeric. Descriptive statistics (see Chapter 15) are used to describe the findings in terms of percents, frequencies, averages, etc. Second, collected
data can be examined through the use of statistical techniques (see Chapter 16). Third,
if planned and conducted properly, each approach provides data that is representative
of and generalizable to the population from which the sample participating in the research is drawn (see Chapter 8).

Relative Advantages and Disadvantages of Qualitative
and Quantitative Research

The strengths and weaknesses of qualitative and quantitative research complement
each other. Qualitative research provides an opportunity to "get close to the data;" to

see and hear respondents express their thoughts in their own words. This provides an opportunity to draw insights and explanations from the respondents themselves, rather than having to predetermine areas of response or study importance. Qualitative research also provides the time and opportunity to probe into consumers' attitudes, beliefs, motivations, and perceptions in order to better understand *why* they act as they do.

Quantitative research provides the best means for understanding populations of individuals and for describing this understanding in terms of numerical descriptors. The proper use of sampling procedures in quantitative research (see Chapter 8) helps to ensure that the findings observed in the quantitative research can confidently be generalized to the population from which the sample was drawn. Additionally, proper sampling plus the larger sample sizes used in quantitative research provide the basis for numerical and statistical descriptions. Finally, the data collected by quantitative research can be analyzed through descriptive and inferential statistical procedures, providing additional insights into population attitudes, perceptions, and behaviors.

Chapters 9 through 11 present a detailed discussion of the major types of qualitative research, methods of qualitative data collection, and the analysis and presentation of qualitative research findings. The remainder of this chapter focuses on quantitative research techniques.

OBSERVATION RESEARCH

Observation research involves the collection of information through the recording of objects, events, situations, or people's behaviors. The observation of events and situations is straightforward. A researcher identifies specific informational needs and then conducts observations to collect data pertinent to those needs, for example:

- Ford may wish to determine the extent to which their prime time television ads for Aerostar are subject to competitive clutter. Observation is one means of addressing this informational need. A researcher would determine the appropriate sample (perhaps a week's worth of prime-time advertising on the four major networks) and would then observe all the advertising, recording (among other things) the total number of car ads, the amount of time between car ads, and the number of car ads occurring within a specified amount of time of the Aerostar ads.

- The brand manager of a cake mix may have received a number of complaints about product quality. He may believe that the fault lies in how product users are preparing the mix rather than the directions printed on the package. In order to determine if this is in fact the cause of the problem, he invites target audience women to a test facility and observes how they prepare the cake. Detailed recordings of these women's behaviors are made on observation forms.

- A researcher wishes to determine how viewers' attention to a television program affects attention to television commercials. The researcher observes and quantifies the amount of time viewers spend with "eyes on screen" for different types of programs and commercials.[1]

---

[1] For discussions and examples of actual examples of this type of research see Dean M. Krugman, Glen Y. Cameron, and Candace M. White, "Visual Attention to Programming and Commercials: The Use of In-Home Observations," *Journal of Advertising* 24 (1995): 1–12.

These examples demonstrate that observations may be made of inanimate and animate (human) objects. The observation of inanimate objects is straightforward once the appropriate sample has been identified. The observation of people's behaviors presents a more complex situation. Observation in this context deals with overt behaviors and, as a consequence, is only appropriate when the desired data is in fact accessible to observation. Observation may be an appropriate technique for determining *how* consumers use a particular product but it is an inappropriate technique for determining *why* they use that product or how they feel about it. Similarly, observation may be an appropriate technique for determining how individuals watch television and commercials but it is not an appropriate technique for determining the extent to which consumers are persuaded by the advertising. Informational needs that require an understanding of motives, attitudes, and beliefs cannot be satisfied through observation research.

Care must be taken when considering the use of observation research, for even when the target behaviors are observable, observation research may still not be appropriate. The high cost and extended timing required to conduct observation research makes it appropriate *only* for quantifying behaviors felt to be inadequately described through verbal reports or for those behaviors which people can not or will not communicate. For example:

- Imagine a toy manufacturer with a new advertising campaign directed toward children aged 4–8. Given the relatively low verbal sophistication of children in this age group, showing the children the advertising and then interviewing them is likely to be unsuccessful. An alternative approach might be to show the children the advertising in a room containing the advertised and other toys and then observe if and how the children play with the toys.

- An advertiser may want to determine how influential children are in the cereal purchase decision. It might be expected (given socially desirable responses) that parents' verbal descriptions would attribute little influence on the children. However, observations of parent-child interactions at home and at the grocery store are likely to provide a different perspective.[2]

Dimensions of Observation Research

Observation research, as shown in Figure 6.1 (page 112), can be characterized in terms of three dimensions: the type of situation in which the observation takes place (natural or contrived), observer obtrusiveness (open versus disguised), and the form of data recording (unstructured versus structured).

Situation: Natural Versus Contrived   *Natural observation* of individuals, situations, objects, or events takes place without interference or interaction from the observer, for example,

- counting the number and types of individuals who frequent a particular fast food restaurant and then recording the total amount and types of food orders placed by these individuals.

---

[2] The observation of parents and children shopping together is, in fact, a common area of observation research. See Langbourne Rust, "Observations: Parents and Children Shopping Together," *Journal of Advertising Research* 33 (July/August) 1995: 65–70; Langbourne Rust, "Observations: How to Reach Children in Stores," *Journal of Advertising Research* 33 (November/December 1993): 67–72.

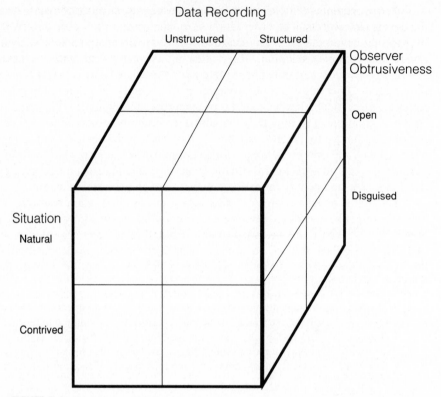

FIGURE 6.1
Dimensions of observation research.

- observing the behaviors of bank tellers as they serve their customers.
- observing the label-reading behaviors of consumers purchasing certain types of canned foods.
- recording the time shoppers spend reading various point-of-purchase displays.

These are natural observations because the researcher plays no role and exerts no influence in the behavior of interest. The behaviors are observed as they occur naturally.

Natural observation of objects (such as competitive advertising) is appropriate whenever the object is easily accessible and observable in its real world setting. Natural observation of events, situations, and individuals is appropriate when the target observations are repetitive, frequent, and occur within a reasonably short time frame. The observation of store clerks or the behaviors of shoppers in busy supermarkets are situations appropriate for natural observation. When target occurrences or behaviors are not repetitive and frequent the extended amount of time (and associated cost) required for data collection have great potential to outweigh the value of any collected information. As a consequence, contrived observation is typically used when these conditions are not met.

Contrived observation records target behaviors or events in the context of an artificial situation. This situation may be a laboratory or a "real world" setting in which the researcher takes an active role in prompting the target behavior. Contrived obser-

vation environments permit a researcher to speed up the data gathering process by initiating the observational situation rather than waiting for it to occur naturally. Additionally, contrived situations permit a researcher to control extraneous variables that might have an impact on what is being observed. Examples of contrived observation are

- *Mystery shopper research*—Here, rather than waiting for a customer to approach a sales clerk, the researcher plays the role of consumer and then observes how he or she is treated by the target employee.
- Commercial test facilities—Here, consumers in a public place are asked to participate in product taste tests or product preparation trials. However, rather than observing their reactions and behaviors in the natural setting of their homes, they are observed in the test facility.

Observer Obtrusiveness: Open Versus Disguised   The second characteristic of observation research relates to the extent to which the presence of an observer is known to the *individuals* under observation. *Open observation* occurs when the presence of the observer is known and explicit while *disguised observation* hides the presence of the observer from the person being observed. (Observer obtrusiveness is obviously not a consideration when observing inanimate objects.)

Researchers have demonstrated that the known presence of an observer has great potential for altering the behaviors of the person being observed. Moreover, the potential for deviation from true or real behaviors increases with the obtrusiveness of the observer. Imagine a car manufacturer who wishes to observe the behaviors of individuals in his showrooms.[3] The behaviors of these individuals would likely change if they knew that they were being watched. Thus, as a consequence of the potential bias introduced by the known presence of an observer (as occurs in open observation), most field advertising and marketing research use disguised observation.[4]

Data Recording: Structured Versus Unstructured   Observations can be recorded in either a structured or unstructured manner. An observer recording data in a *structured manner* knows in advance the types of information and behaviors that are to be observed. Data pertinent to these areas are recorded on a checklist or observation form while all other information and behaviors are ignored. An observer recording data in an *unstructured manner* records his or her impressions of the observed behaviors in verbal form, typically a narrative. There are no restrictions on the types of behaviors observed, although it is expected that preidentified target behaviors will be specifically noted. Figures 6.2 (page 114) and 6.3 (page 115) present hypothetical examples of

---

[3] This example is based on actual research. See Kim Folz, "New Species For Study: Consumers in Action," *New York Times* (December 18, 1989): A1.

[4] It should be noted that natural and disguised observation pose a dilemma for the advertising researcher, particularly in the areas of participants' right to privacy, self-determination, and informed consent. On the one hand, information collected under these circumstances is often the "best," least biased information relative to the behavior under study. On the other hand, the disguised or unobtrusive observation of individuals without their consent violates one of the core principles of research ethics, that is, participation in research should always be the result of an informed consent. Given this situation, we believe that respondents' rights outweigh advertisers' need for observational information and recommend that alternative means to disguised observation be used. For a discussion of these issues see Paul D. Reynolds, *Ethical Dilemmas and Social Science Research* (San Francisco: Jossey-Bass, 1979), 180–225.

Date _____ Time _____

Observer _____ Location _____

Respondent Characteristics

1. Male [ ]   Female [ ]

2. Caucasian [ ]   Black [ ]   Asian [ ]   Other/DK [ ]

3. Alone [ ]   With other adult [ ]   With teens/children [ ]

Reading of POP 1: Large Display Near Entrance

Main display read **before** salesperson contact - Yes [ ]   No [ ]. IF YES...

a. Amount of time reading _____

b. Read alone [ ]   With other adult [ ]   With teens/children [ ]

c. Involvement/interest in reading (rate 1 to 10 from 'very little involvement' to 'great involvement') _____

d. Physical reactions Yes [ ]   No [ ]. IF YES...

   Smile [ ] Laugh [ ] Headshake - approval [ ] Headshake - disapproval [ ] Confusion [ ]

e. Asked salesperson about content - Yes [ ]   No [ ]. IF YES...

      Content asked about _____

Take-away materials taken or examined **before** salesperson contact - Yes [ ]   No [ ]. IF YES...

f. Amount of time reading take-away materials _____

g. Interest in reading (rate 1 to 10 from 'very little involvement' to 'great involvement') _____

h. Physical reactions Yes [ ]   No [ ]. IF YES...

   Smile [ ] Laugh [ ] Headshake - approval [ ] Headshake - disapproval [ ] Confusion [ ]

i. Asked salesperson about content - Yes [ ]   No [ ]. IF YES...

      Content asked about _____

Main display read after salesperson contact - Yes [ ]   No [ ]. IF YES...

j. Amount of time reading _____

k. Read alone [ ]   With other adult [ ]   With teens/children [ ]

l. Involvement/interest in reading (rate 1 to 10 from 'very little involvement' to 'great involvement') _____

m. Physical reactions Yes [ ]   No [ ]. IF YES...

   Smile [ ] Laugh [ ] Headshake - approval [ ] Headshake - disapproval [ ] Confusion [ ]

n. Asked salesperson about content - Yes [ ]   No [ ]. IF YES...

      Content asked about _____

Take-away materials taken or examined before salesperson contact - Yes [ ]   No [ ]. IF YES...

o. Amount of time reading take-away materials _____

p. Interest in reading (rate 1 to 10 from 'very little involvement' to 'great involvement') _____

q. Physical reactions Yes [ ]   No [ ]. IF YES...

   Smile [ ] Laugh [ ] Headshake - approval [ ] Headshake - disapproval [ ] Confusion [ ]

r. Asked salesperson about content - Yes [ ]   No [ ]. IF YES...

      Content asked about _____

(Observation form would continue in a similar manner for remaining three point of purchase displays.)

FIGURE 6.2 Observation form for a structured observation.

The observed individual is a Caucasian male who appears to be between the ages of 40 and 50. He is well dressed in a suit and tie. He entered the dealership alone.

The observee spent the first few minutes after entering the dealership walking from car to car inside the dealership. He stopped at three cars, the 4-door Stanza, the Quest Van, and the 2-door Sentra. Each car's driver's side door was opened, the interior examined, and the list price read. No car was physically entered.

Prior to contact with a salesperson, the observee stopped in front of POP1. Approximately eleven seconds elapsed from the time he appeared to begin to read to the time he walked away. Overall, it appeared that he had a negative reaction to this display. As he read, he grimaced and shook his head in disbelief. He did not appear to mention the content of this display to his salesperson nor did he remove any of the take-away materials.

Salesperson contact was made very soon after the observee walked away from POP1. After discussion, car examination, and a test drive, the observee returned to the showroom. Here, he was left alone by the salesperson.

The observee returned to POP1. This time his reactions appeared to be much more positive. He smiled and nodded his head in an approving way. One minute and fifty-five seconds were spent reading the display. A take-away brochure was taken from the display, quickly looked at (but not read in any detail), and immediately placed in his pocket. The observee left without reading any other POP displays.

FIGURE 6.3
Results of an unstructured observation.

structured and unstructured observations of new car buyers, paying particular attention to the extent to which potential purchasers read various point-of-purchase materials.

Structured and unstructured observations have complementary strengths and weaknesses. Structured observations require more time in advance of the observation (in order to create the observation form) and data collection and analysis are much more efficient than unstructured observations. Unstructured, versus structured, observations provide greater opportunity for discoveries in the field because the observer is not restricted to a predetermined set of behaviors. However, all data must be coded (a time consuming process) prior to input and analysis.

Summary

Observation research is appropriate when informational needs are satisfied through an understanding of *what* is occurring. Observation research provides this information through the recording and analysis of observed objects, situations, events, and overt behaviors. The research can be conducted in a natural or contrived situation, in an open or disguised manner, using a structured or unstructured observation technique. Observation research is inappropriate when informational needs require an understanding of *why* events are occurring or when comparable information can be reliably obtained through verbal reports.

PHYSIOLOGICAL RESEARCH

Physiological research, the second form of quantitative research, measures an individual's voluntary and involuntary responses to stimuli such as advertisements or packages. The most commonly measured voluntary response is eye tracking while the most commonly measured involuntary responses are brain waves, galvanic skin response and voice pitch.

Eye Tracking

The fusion of computer and video technology makes it possible to record the movements of an individual's eye as he or she watches a television commercial or reads an advertisement or product package. Eye tracking research reveals three aspects of how the stimulus is processed:

- the elements of the stimulus looked at by a viewer,
- the order that different elements were viewed, noting the overall pattern of examination, and
- the amount of time spent viewing each element.

Eye tracking research procedures are relatively unobtrusive and permit the respondent to act in a natural manner. A respondent is seated in a chair and initial calibration of the eye tracking apparatus is conducted. The respondent is then presented with a stimulus. While he or she reads or views the stimulus the eye tracking device transmits an undetectable beam of filtered light to his or her eyes. The reflection of this light from the eye to the tracking apparatus identifies the visual focal point, indicating where the respondent is looking. Data recording is continuous and information on where the respondent looked, for how long, and in what order is stored in the computer. The final step prints out the findings in tabular form as well as a superimposition over the visual stimulus. The superimposition provides a "road map" of how the print stimulus was read.

Similar to observation techniques, eye tracking makes explicit a respondent's observable behaviors. It can tell an advertiser what a respondent did as he or she read or watched a stimulus, but it cannot tell *why* he or she acted in a particular way nor can the eye tracking alone predict how well an advertisement will perform in the marketplace. For this reason, eye tracking research is almost always accompanied by additional questioning designed to place the eye tracking data in a broader context. Eye tracking research for a new package, for example, may also probe recall of specific elements, aesthetic appeal, likes and dislikes, and purchase intent.

Eye tracking research is a widely accepted means of testing product packaging, advertising and other consumer-directed visual materials. The combination of eye movement data coupled with diagnostic information provides a sound, insightful basis for understanding consumer response to a particular stimulus. The use of eye tracking research for advertising testing is discussed in greater detail in Chapter 23.

Galvanic Skin Response   The psychogalvanic reflex, an essential component of the lie detector test, occurs when the autonomic nervous system produces perspiration in

response to a change in emotions or level of stress. Because this response is (typically) beyond an individual's conscious control there is little chance that responses can be willfully distorted. Two research companies specialize in this form of physiological research: Walt Wesley Associates and Inner Response.

Galvanic skin response research wires an individual to the psychogalvanometer, shows him or her a stimulus (such as a print or television ad) and then measures emotional responses at various points of exposure. The pattern of responses indicates the physiological changes that occurred during stimulus presentation. The limitation of this approach, however, is that while the presence and degree of response is made explicit, the direction of the emotion cannot be identified. A psychogalvanometer can not distinguish a positive from a negative emotional response. Thus, similar to eye tracking research, galganic skin response research is almost always accompanied by additional diagnostic questions to increase its usefulness.

At this time, researchers continue to explore the relationship between psychogalvanic skin response to a stimulus and subsequent attitudinal and behavioral change. However, until these linkages are made more explicit, galvanic skin response will likely continue to be accepted only by a relatively small number of marketers and advertisers.[5]

Brain-Wave Analysis The human brain is divided into two hemispheres. For most people, the left hemisphere is primarily responsible for logical, rational, analytical thought while the right hemisphere is primarily responsible for nonverbal, affective, emotional thoughts. Both hemispheres produce brain waves. The intensity of emitted waves indicates a hemisphere's level of involvement and activity. High intensity waves from one hemisphere but not the other indicates that the active hemisphere is more involved in the current task or activity.

Researchers, particularly those at the Neuro-Communication Research Laboratories and Advanced Neurotechnologies Inc., have applied these brain characteristics to advertising and marketing problems. These researchers believe that by monitoring brain wave activity during exposure to a stimulus, such as a television commercial, one can then infer the manner by which the commercial is being processed, the respondent's level of interest, and the effect the commercial will have on the respondent.

Advances in technology make the recording of brain waves relatively easy and there is little disagreement that the waves represent something. Disagreements over what this "something" represents makes this form of research quite controversial. Proponents argue that the technique provides insights into the very core of consumer response. Detractors argue that while data is produced, there is little empirical guidance for understanding how specific patterns affect or relate to key measures of commercial effectiveness, such as brand recall and purchase intent. As a consequence, this type of

---

[5] Recently, LaBarbera and Tucciarone have argued that the merits of galvanic skin response should be reconsidered and that there is, in fact, excellent predictive validity. See Priscilla A. LaBarbera and Joel D. Tucciarone, "GSR Reconsidered: A Behavior-Based Approach to Evaluating and Improving the Sales Potency of Advertising," *Journal of Advertising Research* 35 (September/October 1995): 33–53. For a conceptual discussion of this technique see Richard Bagozzi, "The Role of Psychopsysiology in Consumer Research," In Thomas S. Robertson and Harold H. Kassarjian, eds., *Handbook of Consumer Behavior* (Englewood Cliffs, NJ: Prentice-Hall, 1991).

research is unlikely to gain wide acceptance until the relationship between brain patterns and attitudinal or behavioral consumer response is made more explicit.[6]

Voice Pitch Analysis   Imagine showing an individual a television advertisement. After the ad is seen, you ask the viewer questions about likes and dislikes, believability, etc. You record both what the respondent says and how he or she verbalizes the responses. Traditional data analysis techniques are used to examine the values of the responses, voice pitch analysis is used to analyze the sound characteristics of the responses.

Voice pitch analysis is an observational technique that examines changes in the relative vibration frequency of an individual's voice. Changes in voice pitch to specific questions are interpreted to indicate changes in the respondent's level of emotion or stress. Two individuals, for example, might both "agree" that a commercial is believable. Proponents of voice pitch analysis claim that this analysis can distinguish between an individual who "agrees" but is relatively uncommitted from an individual whose "agreement" signals an emotional commitment.

Voice pitch analysis has not yet attained widespread acceptance in advertising research. At this stage in its development, voice pitch analysis suffers from a number of measurement instrument difficulties as well as a lack of an empirical and theoretical foundation.

Summary

Physiological research measures voluntary and involuntary responses to stimuli such as advertisements and product packages. Physiological measurement of voluntary responses, such as eye movement, when used in conjunction with traditional survey techniques, has the potential to provide valuable insights into consumer response. Many marketers and advertisers utilize this form of primary research during advertising, product development, and package development. Physiological measurement of involuntary responses to stimuli, such as galganic skin response, brain wave patterns, and voice pitch have met with less acceptance in the advertising and marketing community due to the lack of empirical and theoretical links between observed reactions and attitudinal and behavioral change.[7]

SURVEY RESEARCH

Survey research is the systematic collection of information (typically via a questionnaire) from respondents in order to better understand and/or predict some aspect of

---

[6] For additional information on this research technique see S. Weinstein, R. Drozdenko, and C. Weinstein, "Advertising Evaluation Using Brain-Wave Measures," *Journal of Advertising Research* 24 (April/May 1984): 67–70; W. A. Katz, "A Critique of Split-Brain Theory," *Journal of Advertising Research* 23 (April/May 1983): 63–66; S. Weinstein, "A Review of Brain Hemisphere Research," *Journal of Advertising Research* 22 (June/July 1982): 59–63; F. Hansen, Hemispheral Lateralization: Implications for Understanding Consumer Behavior," *Journal of Consumer Research* 8 (June 1981): 23–36.

[7] Reviews and analyses of the role of physiological measures in advertising and consumer research have been presented by J. T. Cacioppo and R. E. Pety, "Physiological Responses and Advertising Effects," *Psychology and Marketing* (Summer 1985); M. J. Ryan, "Achieving Correspondence Among Cognitive Processes and Physiological Measures," In A. A. Mitchell ed., *Advances in Consumer Research IX* (Provo, UT: Association for Consumer Research, 1982).

their attitudes or behaviors.[8] The conduct of survey research entails many steps: sampling, question development, questionnaire design, study administration, data analysis, and data interpretation. Each of these issues are addressed in separate chapters in the text. This chapter focuses on the methods used to collect survey information, considerations in the selection of survey research procedures, and the problems of error in the conduct of surveys.

Methods of Collecting Survey Information

Surveys can be classified according to their method of data collection. Advertising and marketing researchers typically utilize one of four data collection methods: personal interviews, telephone interviews, mail surveys, or interactive computer. Each approach has its own set of strengths and weaknesses and, as a consequence, the appropriateness of each method for a particular research study must be evaluated in terms of which approach has the greatest likelihood of providing the most accurate information in the shortest period of time at the lowest cost.

Personal Interviews   *Personal interviews* occur when an interviewer administers a survey to a respondent in a face-to-face setting. There are two types of personal interviews: intercept and prerecruited.

An intercept interview recruits respondents "on the spot," for example, as an individual is walking through a shopping mall, grocery store, airport, or train station. All intercept interviews are generally conducted in the same way regardless of the specific location. A trained interviewer approaches an individual as he or she is walking (through a mall, grocery store, airport, or train station), as follows:

> The interviewer is provided with a description of who should be approached, for example, he or she may be told to approach all women who appear to be between the ages of 18–49. The interviewer approaches individuals who meet the general target description, identifies him- or herself as a marketing researcher and then asks a number of more detailed questions to make certain that the intercepted individual possesses the characteristics of the research study's sample. Respondents who qualify are invited to participate in the survey, which typically takes place in the research company's offices (if the intercept is in a mall) or in a private setting.

Shopping mall intercept interviews are probably the most common setting for intercept interviews. Given the popularity of this setting, many marketing research companies have established permanent shopping mall research facilities. The large number of facilities in shopping malls located in diverse geographic and socioeconomic areas permits researchers to reach a wide range of respondents with great efficiency.

---

[8] For recent examples of the use of survey research to satisfy marketing and advertising informational needs see Jane Hodges, "Magazines Find Out What Men Want," *Advertising Age* (September 25, 1995): 6; Kevin Goldman, "Ads Featuring a Company's Chief Executive Score Poorly in Consumer Survey," *Wall Street Journal* (March 17, 1995): B6; June B. Kim, "Brand Loyalty Wavers," *Advertising Age* (January 23, 1994): 32; Laurie Hays, "Too Many Computer Names Confuse Too Many Buyers," *Wall Street Journal* (June 29, 1994): B1; Kevin Goldman, "Green Campaigns Don't Always Pay Off," *Wall Street Journal* (April 1, 1994): B8; Kevin Goldman, "Nike Print Ads Stumble Badly in Survey," *Wall Street Journal* (May 10, 1994): B8; Stuart Elliot, "Parents' Fears About Toy Marketing," *New York Times* (December 4, 1993): C19; Carole Sugarman, "Gender Gap in Food Habits," *Washington Post* (July 27, 1993): WH16; Stephen Barnett, "What Shoppers Want," *Progressive Grocer* 71 (October 1992): 73–80.

Other personal interviewing situations require that potential respondents be pre-screened and prerecruited. This typically happens when the interview is to be conducted in a respondent's home, at his or her place of business, or when the target definition identifies individuals who comprise a relatively low proportion of the total population. Individuals in these cases are initially contacted first by mail or telephone at which time arrangements for a personal interview are made.

Personal interviews, versus other forms of survey techniques, generally provide the highest level of data quality due to personal administration of the survey by a trained interviewer and the face-to-face contact between the interviewer and interviewee. In addition to data quality, personal interviews have several advantages over other data collection techniques:

- They work extremely well when the questionnaire is very long and/or complex.
- They permit the use of visual stimuli, such as the viewing of television commercials.
- They permit the interviewer to make very certain that the respondent understands individual survey questions or complicated instructions.

The primary disadvantage of personal interviews is their high cost and large amount of time required to complete them. It is both expensive and time consuming to train interviewers, conduct personalized interviews, to prerecruit respondents (when necessary), and travel to the interview location. Moreover, in terms of sample characteristics, it is very difficult to obtain a true random sample. The selection of true random samples for survey research utilizing personal interviews are often time and cost prohibitive. As a result, generalizations to the broader population are often a problem (see Chapter 8).

Telephone Interviews   *Telephone interviews* entail the administration of a survey questionnaire via telephone. This type of survey research technique is typically conducted by a team of trained interviewers telephoning from a central location. Telephone interviewing has increased in popularity in recent years, primarily due to the increase in costs associated with personal interviewing and the decline in long-distance telephone rates.

Telephone interviews, similar to personal interviews, provide an opportunity for an interviewer to explain complicated instructions and questions, although explanations in these areas do tend to be more difficult over the telephone versus a personal setting. Beyond this similarity, telephone interviews present a different set of relative strengths and weaknesses versus personal interviews. On the positive side, telephone interviews

- especially those that are assisted by CATI (Computer Assisted Telephone Interviewing), are able to administer interviews with very complex skip patterns. This is because the computer automatically calls up the next appropriate question based on the respondent's current answer.
- have lower marginal costs because individuals in the sample frame can be contacted several times very inexpensively if they are not available during the first contact.
- can more efficiently obtain a true random sample, increasing the generalizability and representativeness of the results.

On the other hand, telephone interviews have several limitations versus other forms of interviewing.

- Questionnaire length must be relatively short. It is very difficult to keep respondents on the telephone for an extended period of time.
- Question complexity must be relatively simple. Complex or detailed questions and scales are difficult for respondents to remember and answer accurately.
- It is difficult to collect sensitive data such as income. Individuals are often unwilling to give this information to strangers.
- Refusal rates are high. Many individuals do not like to be disturbed at home.
- It is extremely difficult to use visual stimuli, for example, having a respondent view a television commercial. (Stimuli can be mailed after the first contact, viewed by a respondent, and then discussed in a second telephone interview. However, as discussed in the next section, there are significant cost and methodological problems with this procedure.)

Care must be taken when selecting the sample for a telephone survey. A researcher providing or purchasing a list of names and telephone numbers must make very certain that the list is comprehensive and without bias. When lists are not available, or are inappropriate, random digit dialing may be used (see Figure 6.4, page 122).[9]

Mail Surveys   *Mail surveys* entail mailing each potential respondent a package containing a cover letter, the survey questionnaire, instructions for completion and return, and a stamped envelope addressed to the research company conducting the research. An incentive, such as a money or a small gift, may or may not be included in the package. Mail surveys thus differ from personal and telephone interviews because there is no personal interaction between the respondent and the interviewer. Respondents simply fill out and return the questionnaire at their convenience.

Mail surveys may be conducted in one of two ways. First, mailings to a selected sample of the population can be conducted. Similar to telephone surveys, the list of names and addresses can be generated internally or purchased. Second, a mail panel can be used. A mail panel is a continuing group of individuals that have agreed to participate in survey research studies. Panels are created and maintained by a independent marketing research organizations such as Market Facts, National Family Opinion, and the National Panel Diary (NPD) Group. Panel sizes, which range from 100,000 indi-

---

[9] The list procedure is often favored because it tends to create an unbiased sample. However, this technique also generates a sample that contains a relatively high number of disconnected numbers, business and government numbers, and nonexistant numbers. Thus, it is recommended that when this technique is used the initial sample of telephone numbers be at least five times as large as the desired final sample size. The plus one technique tends to be more efficient in that there are typically fewer nonexistent numbers. This reflects the fact that numbers very close to currently existing numbers are also likely to have been assigned by the telephone company. Care must be taken to make certain that the telephone directory used represents the current state of the market, that is, that no new banks of numbers have been assigned since publication. If this is not the case, then the plus one procedure can introduce significant bias into the sample because it will be impossible to sample the banks not represented in the directory. [For a more detailed discussion of random digit sampling techniques see Glen M. Broom and David M. Dozier, *Using Research in Public Relations* (Englewood Cliffs, NJ: Prentice Hall, 1990): 363–68.] A table of random numbers can be found in Appendix B, Table B.1.

Procedure 1: Random Assignment of Suffixes to Selected Prefixes

Step 1: Identify prefixes assigned by telephone company to geographic areas of interest, for example:

545, 546, 765, 766, 767, 769, 772, 776

Step 2: Number prefixes

1. 545	4. 766	7. 772
2. 546	5. 767	8. 776
3. 765	6. 769	

Step 3: Using a table of random numbers, randomly select a prefix.

Step 4: Using a table of random numbers, randomly select a four-number suffix.

Step 5: Combine prefix and suffix to create a telephone number:

Prefix: 772   Suffix: 7642   Telephone Number 772-7642

Step 6: Return to Step 3 and continue until the required number of telephone numbers has been generated.

Procedure 2: Plus One

Step 1: Using a table of random numbers or other sampling method (such as systematic sampling), select a telephone number from the appropriate telephone directory.

Step 2: Add one to the suffix to create the telephone number to be contacted, for example:

Original number:	545–7765
Add 1	+ 1
New number	545–7766

FIGURE 6.4
Procedures for random digit dialing.

viduals to over 1 million, provide several advantages over mailings to the general population:

- Response rates tend to be significantly higher. Panel members have agreed to in advance to answer questionnaires mailed to them.
- Cost efficiencies tend to be greater. Higher levels of response lower the per interview cost.
- The selection of individuals with certain demographic or product usage characteristics can often be made without prescreening. This information has already been collected on all panel members by the marketing research company.
- Prescreening of low-incidence respondents can be efficiently conducted. A post card with screening characteristics can be mailed to a large segment of the panel. Those with the appropriate characteristics are then mailed the main questionnaire.

Regardless of the form of the mail survey, this type of survey research has several strengths and weaknesses versus personal and telephone interviews. Strengths of mail surveys include

- *Cost efficiency*—The cost per completed interview of properly designed mail surveys can be considerably lower than comparable personal or telephone interviews.
- *Respondent convenience*—Respondents may be more willing to participate because they can complete the questionnaire at their convenience.

Weaknesses of mail surveys include

- *Low response rate*—Respondents may not complete or return the questionnaire, causing problems with the integrity of data (see next section on the effects of nonresponse bias).
- *Limited questionnaire length and complexity*—In theory, one can develop mail questionnaires of extreme length and complexity. However, response rate drops as questionnaire length and complexity increase.
- *Extended timing*—Response is mediated by mail delivery and thus data collection takes much longer than other methods.

Finally, the impersonal noninteractive nature of a mail survey is both a strength and a weakness. The impersonal nature often motivates respondents to provide more accurate data on personal feelings and sensitive subjects. However, respondents do not have the opportunity to clarify areas of confusion nor is there any external check that the questionnaire is being completed properly.

Electronic Interactive   *Electronic interactive* surveys are a blending of personal and mail interviews. The level of sophistication of an electronic interactive survey is dependent on the medium used. *Computer* interactive surveys use a freestanding microcomputer or a survey on computer disk (mailed to the respondent). In both cases, the computer program is fully interactive with the respondent. The program administers the survey questions, checks the appropriateness and adequacy of responses, and skips where necessary to questions next in sequence (as in a personal or telephone interview). However, the overall administration of the survey requires only the presence of the respondent (as in mail surveys). This type of survey can be quite complex and sophisticated. *Two-way cable* interactive surveys tend to be much simpler. Here, a relatively straightforward questionnaire is sent via cable to the respondent's home. The respondent uses a keyboard and decoder attached to a television set to respond to the questionnaire.[10] Electronic interactive interviewing is increasing in popularity due to the rise in the cost of personal interviews and the decline in the costs of computer programming and hardware.

Criteria for Selecting a Data Collection Method

The prior section discussed the relative strengths and weaknesses of different methods of data collection. Implicit in this discussion were the criteria that should be considered when evaluating the options for a particular research study. This section specifically discusses these criteria.

Eight factors should be considered when determining which survey method is the best for a particular research study. These factors are:

- cost
- timing requirements
- sample, interview, and administrative control
- sample characteristics

---

[10] René Y. Darmon, Michel Larouche, and K. Lee McGown, *Marketing Research in Canada* (Scarborough, Ontario, Canada: Gage Educational Publishing Company, 1989): 154.

- accuracy
- complexity of the topic and questionnaire
- interview length
- response rate

Cost   Cost is an extremely important consideration in the conduct of survey research. The cost of any particular research study reflects questionnaire length, required response rate, geographic coverage, and sample characteristics. However, when faced with comparable parameters in these areas, personal interviews (particularly those conducted in the respondent's home or place of business) tend to be considerably more expensive than the other methods of data collection. Tuchfarber and Klecka, for example, found that a telephone survey utilizing random digit dialing cost about one-quarter of the cost of comparable personal interviews.[11] Similarly, A. C. Nielsen found that the cost for conducting telephone interviews was about half the cost of personal interviews.[12]

Study cost is the initial starting point in evaluating the suitability of alternative data collection methods. It is not the final or sole consideration. While, it is clearly the researcher's duty to collect information in a cost-effective manner, the information must be reliable and valid. Selecting the *absolute* least expensive method of data collection is *always* inappropriate when, relative to other methods, there is a significant sacrifice in data quality. The inexpensive collection of unreliable data is no bargain.

Timing Requirements   Survey research methods differ in their speed of data collection. Telephone surveys generally require the least amount of time to collect required data for two reasons: all training and coordination can be performed at a central facility and teams of interviewers can work simultaneously. As a result, study timing can be shortened simply by adding more interviewers.

Mail surveys tend to take the longest amount of time. Questionnaires must be put into the mail, processed and delivered by the post office, completed by respondents at their convenience, placed back into the mail, then processed and returned by the post office. Beyond the amount of time required for this initial mailing and return, additional time is often required for reminders, additional contacts, and follow-up mailings.

Personal and electronic interviews are almost always slower than telephone surveys for comparable sample sizes. Personal and electronic interviews are either faster or slower than mail interviews depending on sample size. When the sample is small, personal and electronic interviews tend to be faster than mail. However, as sample size increases, timing advantages begin to favor mail surveys. Increases in sample size tend to dramatically lengthen the amount of time for personal and electronic interviews. (Additional interviewers and computers can always be added, but the increase in cost associated with these additions make these types of modifications very uneconomical after a certain point.)

---

[11] A. J. Tuchfarber and W. R. Klecka, *Random Digit Dialing: Lowering the Cost of Victimization Surveys* (Washington, D. C.: The Police Foundation, 1976).

[12] Reported in E. Telser, "Data Exorcises Bias in Phone vs. Personal Interview Debate, But If You Can't Do It Right, Don't do It At All," *Marketing News* (September 10, 1976): 6.

Sample, Interview, and Administrative Control   *Sample control* refers to the extent to which a researcher can control *who* responds to the survey questionnaire. Obviously, it is important that the individual who meets the sample definition is the person who responds to the survey. The four methods of data collection differ in their ability to make certain that the target respondent is in fact the individual who participates in the research and provides the answers to the survey questions. Personal and telephone interviews provide the greatest degree of sample control. The personal contact and immediate nature of personal and telephone interviews help to ensure that the target respondent is the one providing responses to the survey questions. Mail and interactive interviews provide considerably less control. There is no assurance that the person to whom the questionnaire is directed is in fact the person who completes the questionnaire.

Interview control refers to the extent of control a researcher has over the circumstances in which a respondent provides his or her answers to the survey. Similar to sample control, personal and telephone interviews provide the greatest degree of interview control. An interviewer can make certain that the respondent participates in all required activities (i.e., listening to or reading a product description) and appropriately responds to the information requests of each survey question in the sequence dictated by the questionnaire. Additionally, the immediate nature of personal and telephone interviews permit an interviewer to address ambiguities or errors in response at the time they occur. Electronic interactive data collection techniques provide a relatively lower degree of interviewer control. The computer can be programmed to question inappropriate responses and to lead the respondent through the proper interview sequence. There is no assurance when using this technique that the respondent has read all necessary material before proceeding to a set of questions. Mail surveys provide the least amount of interview control. There is no assurance that the respondent will read necessary materials, answer the questions in the proper sequence, or correct errors in response.

Administrative control refers to the degree to which a researcher is able to monitor interviewer quality. (This aspect of control does not apply to mail surveys because there is no interviewer.) Telephone and interactive survey methods provide the highest degree of administrative control. Supervisors at the telephone facility can monitor the quality of each telephone interviewer and immediately correct any problems with interviewer tone, style, or questionnaire administration. The computer program administering the interactive interview (assuming that is properly written) guarantees that the survey will be conducted in an identical manner time after time. Personal interviews, particularly those conducted in the field, provide the least amount of administrative control. A researcher cannot possibly monitor each personal interview. Thus, while interviewer training is important in all survey methods, given the lack of administrative control it is most critically important in personal interviews.

Sample Characteristics   Personal interviews and telephone surveys appear to be generally insensitive to demographic and socioeconomic differences in the sample population. Participation rates among subsamples interviewed in these ways are generally equivalent. Mail surveys are more sensitive to demographic and socioeconomic differences in the sample population. In the context of mail surveys:

- Race and ethnicity can play a role in study participation. Krysan found that while response rates for a white sample were equivalent between mail and personal interviews,

the response rate for African-Americans was significantly lower for the mail versus personal interview.[13]

- Education appears to play an important role in study participation. Numerous researchers have found that response rate is higher among better educated individuals.[14]

- Socioeconomic status can play a role in study participation. Research has indicated that individuals of lower socioeconomic status are less likely to participate than those of middle and higher socioeconomic status.[15]

As a result, sample characteristics are an important consideration in the selection of a data collection method.

Accuracy   Accuracy refers to the extent to which the data collected in the research study is free from errors. Data accuracy can be affected by faulty interviewers, poor question wording, or confusing questionnaire design. Each of these causes of poor data accuracy are discussed later in the text. In addition to these causes, data accuracy, particularly the accuracy of responses to sensitive questions, can be affected by the method of data collection.

Research has shown that respondents tend to be more honest and candid in telephone and mail versus personal interviews. *First, telephone interviews tend to elicit fewer "socially acceptable" responses.* Krysan, for example, conducted personal and mail surveys among comparable groups of African-American and white respondents. She found that mail survey respondents expressed more negative attitudes toward racial integration and affirmative actions than did those interviewed in a personal setting.[16] Along these same lines, Hochstim and Colombotos each discovered lower levels of "socially acceptable" responses in telephone versus personal interviews. Hochstim found that women were more likely to be candid about drinking habits.[17] Colombotos found that physicians were less likely to over report publications and the number of professional journals read.[18] *Second, respondents appear to be more likely to reveal personal information over the telephone versus a face-to-face interview.* O'Dell found significant underreporting of behaviors in personal areas when responses were collected in person versus through the mail.[19]

While telephone and mail surveys appear to be the better means for collecting sensitive information and for avoiding socially desirable responses, personal interviews appear to be a better means for collecting complete and considered responses.[20] The personal nature of the interview situation, coupled with the physical presence of

---

[13] Maria Krysan et al., "Response Rates and Response Content in Mail Versus Face to Face Surveys," *Public Opinion Quarterly* 58 (1994): 381–99.

[14] For a review of these studies see Leslie Kanuk and Conrad Berenson, "Mail Surveys and Response Rates: A Literature Review," *Journal of Marketing Research* 12 (November 1975): 440–53.

[15] Lee N. Robins, "The Reluctant Respondent," *Public Opinion Quarterly* 27 (Summer 1961): 276–86.

[16] Maria Krysan et al., "Response Rates and Response Content."

[17] J. R. Hochstim, "A Critical Comparison of Three Strategies of Collecting Data From Households," *Journal of the American Statistical Association* 62 (September 1987): 976–89.

[18] J. Colombotos, "Personal Versus Telephone Interviews' Effect On Responses," *Public Health Report* 34 (September 1969): 773–82.

[19] William D. O'Dell, "Personal Interviews or Mail Panels," *Journal of Marketing* 26 (1962): 16–21.

[20] Jeanne Brett Herman, "Mixed Mode Data Collection: Telephone and Personal Interviewing," *Journal of Applied Psychology* 62 (1977): 399–404; E. Telser, "Data Exorcises Bias," 6–7.

an interviewer, appears to better motivate consumers to consider each question and avoid quick and simple responses.

Complexity of the Topic and Questionnaire   Some research *topics* are inherently more complex than others. Research exploring consumers' attitudes toward government plans to revise health care or welfare address more complex issues than research designed to obtain reactions to a television advertisement. Additionally, regardless of the complexity of the topic, some *questionnaires* are more complex than others. Questionnaire complexity tends to increase as the number of skip patterns and verbally complex questions increases. A skip pattern instructs the respondent or interviewer to jump from one point to another on the questionnaire depending on an individual's response. Verbally complex questions are questions that require a respondent to expend a great deal of cognitive energy to process and remember elements or demands of the question, for example,

- multiple choice questions that have many possible choices for their answer,
- ranking questions that ask the respondent to remember a large set of objects and then place them in ranked order,
- constant sum questions that ask respondents to allocate points to a set of objects, and
- questions that have long lead-ins or provide information that must be remembered prior to answering.

Personal interviews are most appropriate when *both* the topic and questionnaire are complex. The personal nature of the interview provides the best setting for the discussion of complex issues, particularly because of the ease of presenting and probing responses to open-ended questions. Additionally, complex questions can be shown to the respondent reducing the demands on verbal memory.

Telephone interviews work well when the issue is complex and questionnaire complexity is entirely due to skip patterns. As with personal interviews, the interactive nature of the interview provides a good setting for the discussion of complex issues and for the use of open-ended questions. The use of computers to assist in the conduct of the interview (see the discussion of CATI presented earlier in this chapter) automates and minimizes errors in skip patterns and checks the appropriateness of responses. Telephone interviews are not appropriate when questionnaire complexity is due to verbal or question complexity. A respondent's inability to see a complex question may reduce his understanding of the question, thereby reducing the quality of the information provided.

Electronic interactive interviews are appropriate for relatively simple topics with or without questionnaire complexity. The impersonal nature of the interview makes it difficult to use open-ended questions to probe attitudes in complex areas (especially since answers to these questions must be typed into the computer). However, a respondent's ability to see the questions and be guided by the computer permit relatively high levels of questionnaire complexity. Similar to computer assisted telephone interviewing, the computer program can make certain that responses to more complex questions are appropriate given the demands of the question.

Mail interviews are appropriate for relatively simple topics and relatively simple questionnaires because of the lack of an external check on responses, respondent's in-

ability to clarify questions, and the inconvenience of having to write down responses to open-ended questions.

Interview Length *Interview length* refers to the amount of time required for a typical respondent to complete the survey. Interview length tends to increase as the absolute number of questions, question complexity, and the number of open-ended questions rises.

Personal contact is essential for longer surveys. The personal, face-to-face nature of the interview permits an interviewer to keep the respondent interested, attentive, involved, and a continuing participant in the research. Thus, longer interviews, especially those with many open-ended questions, generally use personal interviews as the data collection method. Mail, telephone, and interactive data collection techniques are generally appropriate only for shorter interviews.

- Lengthy mail interviews are visually overwhelming and require a considerable commitment of time and energy on the part of the respondent. Most respondents are unwilling to give such a commitment.
- Telephone interviews compete with other home or business activities, making it difficult to maintain respondent participation for more than five or ten minutes.
- Lengthy interactive interviews share many of the same problems as mail interviews, that is, they require a commitment of time and energy that most respondents are unwilling to give.

Response Rate *Response rate* refers to the percentage of the valid sample who participate in the research by completing an interview or survey. Response rates vary across data collection techniques. Yu and Cooper analyzed 93 published surveys and found that the response rate for personal interviews average 82 percent, telephone interviews average 72 percent and mail surveys average 47 percent.[21] Other researchers have found similar patterns: personal interviews tend to have the highest response rate, followed by telephone interviews and mail surveys.

Response rate is a crucial element of a research study. A low response rate can severely decrease the validity and generalizability of collected data, thereby reducing the ability of the data to positively and accurately contribute to the decision-making process. Response rate, and its implications for nonresponse error, are so critical that they are discussed in detail in the following section.

RESPONSE RATE, NONRESPONSE RATE, AND NONRESPONSE ERROR

Response and nonresponse rates are important ways to evaluate the integrity of survey data. A *response rate* is calculated by dividing the number of respondents completing the survey by the number of respondents in the valid sample. A *nonresponse rate* is the

---

[21] J. Yu and H. Cooper, "A Quantitative Review of Research Design Effects on Response Rates," *Journal of Marketing Research* 20 (February 1983): 36–44.

complement of response rate and is calculated by dividing the number of individuals in the valid sample not completing the survey (for whatever reason, for example, refusals or language problems) by the total number of respondents in the valid sample.

Figure 6.5 illustrates the calculation of response and nonresponse rates for a hypothetical telephone survey. One thousand two hundred (1,200) homes were contacted through random digit dialing. One hundred fifty of these contacts fell outside of the desired sample due to the telephone number being a disconnected number, a fax machine, or business. These numbers are subtracted from the total sample, leaving a working sample of 1,050 contacted homes. Of these remaining homes, 250 failed to meet at least one sample characteristic. These homes are also eliminated from the working sample, leaving a *valid* sample of 800 homes. Of these remaining 800 homes, 100 refused to participate in the interview and 150 were not at home. Interviews were therefore conducted with individuals in the remaining 550 homes. The response rate was 68.8 percent and the nonresponse rate was 31.2 percent.

Response and nonresponse rates are important indicators of data integrity. A high response rate, and thus a low nonresponse rate, generally indicates that there are no meaningful differences between those who responded to the survey and those who did not. A low response rate, and thus a high nonresponse rate, generally indicates a significant problem with the source of the data. It indicates that there is probably bias in the data, reflecting the fact that the characteristics of those who participated in the research are different from those who did not participate.

The tables shown in Table 6.1 (page 130) illustrate the danger of a nonresponse error. The data in the upper table presents the hypothetical results of an opinion survey taken before the start of an antismoking advertising campaign. The response rates for men and women are high and equivalent, leading us to accept the findings, especially

Begin with original sample	1,200
Remove those not valid	(150)
Subtotal to obtain working sample	**1,050**
Remove those failing to meet sample definition	(250)
Subtotal to obtain valid sample	**800**
Subtract refusals	(100)
Subtract not-at-homes	(150)
Subtract other noninterviewed contacts	(0)
Subtotal to obtain number of responders	**550**

To obtain *response rate* divide number of responders by total valid sample:
$$550 \div 800 = 68.8\%$$

To obtain *nonresponse rate* divide number of nonresponders in valid sample by total valid sample:
$$250 \div 800 = 31.2\%$$

FIGURE 6.5
Calculation of response and nonresponse rates.

TABLE 6.1 Precampaign Measures			
Survey Question	**Men** (base = 180) (resonse rate = 90 percent)	**Women** (base = 180) (response rate = 90 percent)	**Average** (base = 360) (response rate = 90 percent
The "antismoking" advertising is believable	35%	53%	44%
Smoking is a dumb thing to do	34%	52%	43%
I should stop smoking	23%	43%	33%

Postcampaign Measures			
Survey Question	**Men** (base = 50) (resonse rate = 25 percent)	**Women** (base = 150) (response rate = 75 percent)	**Average** (base = 200) (response rate = 50 percent
The "antismoking" advertising is believable	35%	53%	48.5%
Smoking is a dumb thing to do	34%	52%	47.5%
I should stop smoking	23%	43%	38.0%

Note: Data represents percent "strongly" or "slightly" agreeing.

the overall averages, as representative of the population from which the sample was drawn. The data shown in the lower table represents opinions obtained after the campaign had aired for six months. Notice how men's and women's opinions are unchanged from the first measure. However, because of the nonresponse error (i.e., a low proportion of responses from men) it appears that the campaign has exerted a positive impact on attitudes. The overall averages indicate that a greater percentage of the sample believes that the campaign is believable, that smoking is dumb and that personal smoking should stop. The conclusion that the campaign has been effective, however, is incorrect and is directly due to the effects of the nonresponse error.

Causes of Nonresponse Errors

The two main sources of nonresponse errors are refusals and not-at-homes. A refusal occurs when a participant declines to participate in the research study or fails to complete a survey once it has begun. The number of refusals varies from study to study and is influenced by a number of factors, for example, the personality of the interviewer, the type of survey being conducted, a respondent's level of interest in the subject matter of the survey, the time of day the respondent is contacted, and the way in which the survey is introduced. Not-at-home nonresponse bias occurs when a respondent is unavailable at the time of potential contact. While, refusals have always been a primary cause of nonresponse bias, societal and lifestyle changes have increased the incidence of not-at-home bias.

Reducing Nonresponse Errors

An understanding of the sources of nonresponse errors provides a foundation for planning ways to reduce this type of problem in a particular survey. The primary approaches to reducing nonresponse bias due to refusals and not-at-homes are advance notification, incentives, callbacks, and recontacts. These approaches are implemented somewhat differently in personal, telephone, and mail surveys.[22]

Reducing Nonresponse in Personal Interviews and Telephone Surveys
Refusals are a problem in both personal interviews and telephone surveys. Most refusals occur immediately after initial contact. Thus, it is important at this beginning point of the interview that steps must be taken to try and ensure the cooperation of the potential respondent. Techniques that have successfully increased cooperation (and thus reduced error due to nonresponse) in personal interviews and telephone surveys are to

- explicitly mention the interview topic and describe why the topic is important and relevant to the respondent.
- effectively and accurately describe the purpose and goal of the research, noting the importance of the individual's responses to achieving the goal.
- make certain that respondents do not feel threatened by participation in the research or by how their responses will be used.
- use incentives at levels appropriate to the demands of the survey. A $10 incentive increased the response rate in a research project that asked respondents to watch a particular television program[23] while $2 or a small gift may be sufficient to effectively increased the response rate in a relatively short mall intercept study.
- use advance notification. Contact respondents in advance of the interview in order to gain cooperation and schedule the interview at a time convenient to the respondent.

In addition to these respondent-centered techniques, careful training and monitoring of interviewers can reduce refusal rates.[24] Here, it is important to make certain that interviewers are

- successfully trained to establish quick rapport with respondents. The tone of the interviewers voice has been shown to affect respondent cooperation and participation.
- carefully monitored with regard to their individual refusal rates. Interviewers who have exceptionally high refusal rates should be immediately retrained or replaced.

---

[22] From a methodological perspective, it is best to try and maximize response level and minimize the nonresponse error. The techniques described in this section present ways to accomplish this. When response rates remain low in spite of a researcher's efforts, statistical techniques can be used to compensate and adjust the data. These techniques, however, rely on many assumptions and may or may not *in actuality* increase the validity and respresentativeness of the data. For a discussion of these techniques see G. Kalton, *Compensating for Missing Survey Data* (Ann Arbor, MI: University of Michigan Institute for Social Research, 1983). For a current review of nonresponse errors and procedures for reducing nonresponse errors see Nejdet Delener, "An Integrative review of Nonresponse Errors in Survey Research: Major Influences and Strategies," *Research in Marketing* 12 (1995): 49–80.

[23] E. G. Goetz, T. R. Taylor, and F. L. Cook, "Promised Incentives in Media Research," *Journal of Marketing Research* 21 (May 1984): 148–54.

[24] A fascinating discussion of training interviewers to be sensitive to respondent's needs and cognitive styles (thereby reducing respondent anxiety and increasing study participation) is presented by Robert M. Groves, Robert B. Cialdini, and Mick P. Couper, "Understanding the Decision to Participate in a Survey," *Public Opinion Quarterly* 56 (1992): 475–95.

Nonresponse error due to respondent unavailability can be significantly reduced when callbacks, multiple attempts to reach a specific respondent, are used. Researchers have found that a second round of callbacks can double the response rate.[25] The following guidelines have demonstrated effectiveness in increasing the success rate of callbacks:

- Attempt recontact between three and six times.
- Vary the time of day calls are made. Use weekday evenings and weekend days to contact individuals who work full-time outside the home.

A recent Times Mirror Survey described their attempt to reduce nonresponse bias as follows:

> "At least three attempts were made to complete an interview at every sampled telephone number. The calls were staggered over times of day and days of the week to maximize the chances of making a contact with a potential respondent. All interview breakoffs and refusals were recontacted at least once in order to attempt to convert them to completed interviews."[26]

Reducing Nonresponse in Mail Surveys   The causes of nonresponse in mail surveys are different than that of personal interviews and telephone surveys. Researchers using mail surveys, assuming their list of names and addresses is accurate, have little problem in reaching respondents. The major problem in mail surveys relates to refusals, that is, many recipients of mail surveys simply do not take the time to complete and return the survey. As a consequence, great effort should be make to gain compliance and cooperation.

Advance notification is an effective means of inducing respondent cooperation and study participation. An advance notice briefly informs a respondent of the nature and importance of the study, the fact that they have been selected to participate, and the date around which they can expect to receive the survey questionnaire.

The mailing itself can be constructed to increase the potential for study participation. Techniques that have been shown to increase response rate are to

- Use a cover letter that clearly states the interview topic, describes why the topic is important and relevant to the respondent, effectively and accurately describes the purpose and goal of the research, and explains the importance of the individual's responses.
- Include a postage-paid return envelope.
- Prepare and print the questionnaire to maximize visual simplicity and professionalism.[27]
- Enclose monetary incentives with the questionnaire. Prepaid monetary incentives are the most powerful means of increasing response rates in both business and consumer mail surveys. Although larger incentives (those of $5.00 or more) tend to have a stronger effect than smaller ones ($1.00 or less) the actual difference is actually

---

[25] William C. Dunkleberg and George S. Day, "Nonresponse Bias and Callbacks in Sample Surveys," *Journal of Marketing Research* 10 (May 1975): 440–54.

[26] Times Mirror Center for The People & The Press, *Voter Anxiety Dividing GOP; Energized Democrats Backing Clinton* (1995): 68.

[27] A. Linzsky, "Stimulating Response to Mailed Questionnaires: A Review," *Public Opinion Quarterly* 39 (1975): 82–101.

quite small. Many researchers have found that $1.00 is sufficient to influence response rates.[28]

Finally, after the surveys have been mailed, recontact is an effective means of increasing response rate. A respondent is sent a postcard or letter requesting that he or she complete and return the questionnaire that had been sent earlier. However, given the fact that many respondents may no longer possess the originally mailed questionnaire, many researchers include a second questionnaire in the recontact mailing. Research has demonstrated that a significant increase in response rate is achieved with a single follow-up mailing.[29]

Summary

Primary research is conducted when secondary research is either nonexistent, unreliable, or too costly. Qualitative primary research, typically personal interviews or focus groups, is most appropriate when there is a need to obtain in-depth information on consumers' attitudes and behaviors and to "get close to the data," to see and hear respondents express their thoughts in their own words. Quantitative research is used when there is a need to understand and describe populations in terms of numerical descriptors and to confidently generalize and project the results of the research to the population from which the sample was drawn.

There are three types of quantitative research: observation, physiological measures, and surveys. *Observation research* is the recording of objects, events, situations, or people's behaviors. Observations can take place in either a natural or contrived situation where the presence of the observer may or may not be known. *Physiological research* entails the direct measurement of an individual's physical responses to stimuli such as an advertisement. Observation is most appropriate in circumstances where the data cannot be reliably obtained through verbal reports and when the emphasis is on *what* is happening rather than *why*. *Physiological research* measures both voluntary (such as eye movements) and involuntary responses (such as brain waves and galvanic skin response). Only eye movement research is widely accepted. *Survey research,* the most common form of quantitative research, is the systematic collection of information from respondents through the use of questionnaires. Surveys are most commonly administered over the telephone, through the mail, or in person to person interviews. Electronic interactive surveys may also take place.

No survey research technique is inherently better than another. Each technique has its own set of strengths and weaknesses and each is more or less appropriate for a

---

[28] Experimental studies have found that incentives enclosed with the questionnaire are more effective than the promise of a reward when the questionnaire is completed and returned (see Mark L. Brek et al. "The Effect of Prepaid and Promised Incentives: Results of a Controlled Experiment," *Journal of Official Statistics* 3 (1987): 449–57; Michael S. Goodstadt et al., "Mail Survey Response Rates: Their Manipulation and Impact," *Journal of Marketing Research* 14 (1977): 391–95). Moreover, monetary rewards appear to be more effective than nonmonetary rewards (see Robert A. Hansen, "A Self-Perception Interpretation of the Effect of Monetary and Nonmonetary Incentives on Mail Survey Response Behavior," *Journal of Marketing Research* 17 (1980): 77–83). For a comprehensive review of the effect of incentives on mail survey response rates see Allan H. Church, "Estimating the Effects of Incentives on Mail Survey Response Rates: A Meta-Analysis," *Public Opinion Quarterly* 57 (1993): 62–79.

[29] J. Yu and H. Cooper, "Research Design Effects"; Kanuk and Berenson, "Mail Surveys and Response Rates."

specific research study. The strengths and weaknesses of each approach for a particular research study are evaluated in terms of eight criteria: cost, timing, control, sample characteristics, accuracy, complexity of the topic and questionnaire, interview length, and response rate.

Response rate is an important way to evaluate the integrity of survey data. A high response rate, and thus a low nonresponse rate, generally indicates that there are no meaningful differences between those who responded to the survey and those who did not. As a consequence, in the absence of other methodological problems, a researcher can confidently apply the data and findings to the research problem. A low response rate, and thus a high nonresponse rate, generally indicates a significant problem with the source of the data and severely limits the extent to which a researcher can generalize study findings to the sample population. Response rates can be increased by taking action targeted toward reducing refusals and not-at-homes.

Review Questions

1. When should primary research be conducted?
2. What are the two main approaches to primary research?
3. When should qualitative research be used?
4. What are similarities and differences between personal interviews and focus groups?
5. What are the three main forms of quantitative research? Briefly describe the characteristics of each.
6. When should observation be conducted?
7. What are the three characteristics of observation? Briefly describe the two dimensions of each characteristic.
8. What are the forms of physiological measurement? What is the current state of appropriateness of each form for advertising research?
9. What are the principal ways of conducting surveys?
10. What are intercept interviews?
11. What are the advantages and disadvantages of personal interviews?
12. How are telephone interviews conducted?
13. What are the advantages and disadvantages of telephone interviews?
14. How are mail surveys conducted?
15. What are the advantages and disadvantages of mail surveys?
16. How are electronic interactive surveys conducted?
17. What are the advantages and disadvantages of electronic interactive surveys?
18. What eight criteria should be considered when evaluating methods of survey data collection? Briefly describe the nature of each criteria.
19. What is response rate, nonresponse rate, and nonresponse error? How is response rate and nonresponse rate calculated?
20. How does nonresponse rate affect data integrity?
21. What are the main causes of nonresponse errors?
22. How can nonresponse rates be reduced in personal interview and telephone surveys?
23. How can nonresponse rates be reduced in mail surveys?

Application Exercises[30]

1. Consider each of the primary research situations shown below. For each situation, indicate whether you would recommend the use of qualitative or quantitative research. Provide an explanation for the selection of your research approach.

    a. The agency has just been invited to complete a "pre-pitch" questionnaire for a banking client. One question on the questionnaire asks for an agency point of view on the bank's current advertising campaign.

    b. The agency is about to begin the strategic planning process for one of its clients, a manufacturer of no fat/no cholesterol frozen entrees. Meetings will begin to be held in about one month. Three years ago the agency conducted a large quantitative study of consumers' attitudes, product trial, and usage and category purchase behaviors. The agency now wants to determine if consumers' attitudes, product trial, and usage and category purchase behaviors have changed since the initial study was conducted.

    c. The creative team is about to begin creative development for a new advertising campaign. Prior to beginning work on the campaign, they feel the need to "touch base" with their target audience. Specifically, they want to see and hear the target audience discuss their experiences with their clients' and competitive brands of cake mixes.

    d. The agency has developed two new advertising campaigns. Research has been recommended to help the agency select the strongest campaign (where "strongest" will be evaluated in terms of "liking" and "purchase intent").

    e. The agency's client, a gasoline manufacturer, has decided that their new advertising campaign should not be directed toward "all gasoline purchasers" (as it has in the past) but rather to a smaller and much better defined segment of purchasers. Research is needed to identify the size and characteristics of different segments of gasoline purchasers.

2. Consider each of the following primary *quantitative* research situations. For each situation, indicate whether you would recommend the use of observation, physiological measurement, or surveys to collect the appropriate data. Provide an explanation for the selection of your research approach and a brief description of the characteristics of the research.

    a. Reddi-Vegee is a manufacturer of vegetarian (soy and vegetable based) cold cuts. They wish to determine vegetarians' reactions to their line of products (pepperoni, salami, chicken, and turkey). They are specifically interested in each product's appeal and in the target audience's purchase intent.

    b. McDonald's has introduced a new menu display in several test stores. This menu shows how many of each item is currently available and how long the wait is for obtaining various items. McDonald's is interested in their customers reactions to this new menu display.

    c. John Kyle is running for the California Senate. Prior to the development of his advertising campaign he wishes to understand what the most important issues to the individuals in his district are.

---

[30] All situations are hypothetical. Specific manufacturer and brand names are either fictitious or used for illustrative purposes only.

   d. Jack in the Box has introduced the "Big Jack," a ½ pound hamburger. They wish to determine consumers' reactions to this product, especially as they first begin to eat the product.

   e. Kellogg's has developed three packages for a new cereal. They wish to determine consumers' reactions to the package particularly likes/dislikes and readability. Kellogg's also wishes to determine the extent to which each package is able to attract a consumer's attention.

3. It has been decided that each of the following situations are best met through survey research. Consider each situation and then decide if you would recommend that the research be conducted through personal interviews, telephone interviews, mail surveys, or interactive computer (either through a freestanding computer or through the mailing of a computer disk). Your recommendation should reflect your decision as to the best means of data collection given each approach's relative strengths and weaknesses. Fully explain and justify your decision.

   a. Yolin Labs is a manufacturer of prescription drugs. Their latest product, which just received FDA approval, is a diet pill that curbs appetites for at least eight hours. The pill is intended for individuals who are seriously overweight (defined as at least 75 pounds over the average weight for their age and height.) Prior to the development of the advertising campaign, the agency and client wish to determine their target audience's current dieting practices and their reaction to this new medication.

   b. The editors of Woman's Day Magazine have just completed a redesign of the magazine. The newly redesigned magazine will go on sale in about one week. The editors wish to determine their readers' reactions to the redesign three months after the introduction.

   c. Ford is introducing three new minivans at the Detroit auto show. Ford wishes to obtain reactions to these new models.

   d. Apple Computer is planning to specifically target primary and secondary school teachers in one part of their new advertising campaign. Prior to the development of the campaign Apple needs to understand computer ownership among these individuals, computer brand perceptions, and the dimensions along which brands of computers are evaluated.

   e. Budget Rent A Car has decided to conduct research among travel agents. Budget wishes to find out how often, and in what circumstances, travel agents recommend Budget to their clients.

4. You are conducting a national survey among doctors and have expressed concern about the response rate. (The survey asks about the influence of advertising on doctor's prescribing behaviors.) First, select and defend a methodology to collect the data. Second, present a discussion of the nonresponse error and its likelihood to occur in the methodology you select. Third, explain why it is necessary to keep nonresponse errors to a minimum. Fourth, present specific recommendations for reducing nonresponse errors within the methodology you selected.

CHAPTER

7

EXPERIMENTATION

The research techniques described in the prior two chapters are primarily descriptive. Descriptive research lets advertisers take a "snapshot" of the consumer or marketplace to understand consumers' attitudes and behaviors better and also marketplace or product-related conditions. There are times, however, when advertising-decision makers require more than a description. These situations require an understanding of how changes in advertising, products or marketplace conditions affect consumers' attitudes, beliefs, and behaviors or marketplace conditions. This understanding is obtained using experimental research in which a researcher changes or alters something in the consumers' or product's environment to see what happens. This chapter discusses the role of experiments in advertising research.

After reading this chapter, you will be able to

■ Identify characteristics of experiments.

■ Explain the factors that influence an experiment's ability to provide a sound basis for decision making.

■ Describe the options a researcher has in designing experiments.

■ Describe how advertisers use both laboratory and field experiments to make product, advertising, and media decisions.

Advertisers and marketers have two ways of understanding the consumer, the product, and the marketplace. Descriptive studies provide a look at consumers' attitudes, beliefs, lifestyles and behaviors at a particular point in time. A descriptive study, for example, might survey individuals in the advertiser's target audience to determine the extent to which they are aware of the advertising and can recall key ideas communicated by the advertising. An experimental study moves beyond description. *The goal of an experiment is to determine causality—the effect of changes in one area on one or more other areas.* An experiment might vary the amount of advertising placed in particular markets to determine how advertising weight affects target audience advertising awareness and message recall. Some individuals would be exposed to a great deal of advertising while other individuals would be exposed to very little advertising. The ex-

periment would try to answer the question: "To what extent does the amount of advertising exposure affect advertising awareness and message recall?"

This chapter discusses experimentation. We begin by discussing the characteristics and components of experiments paying particular attention to the requirements that must be satisfied for one to accept the causality inferred from an experiment. Next, we present the concept of internal validity. The internal validity of an experiment determines the extent to which we have confidence that observed results are due to the experimental manipulations. The discussion of internal validity is followed by a presentation of experimental design options and a discussion of how different experimental designs can increase internal validity, thus improving the value of the information provided by the experiment. Next, we examine the settings for experiments, laboratories and the field, noting the strengths and weaknesses of each approach. Experimental setting affects an experiment's external validity, the extent to which the experimental results are generalizable to the "real world." We conclude the chapter by discussing the characteristics of external validity within the context of three common settings of experimentation in advertising: field test markets, electronic test markets, and simulated test markets.

THE CHARACTERISTICS OF EXPERIMENTS

Experiments are appropriate whenever one needs to understand causation, the effect of changes in one variable on other variables. Every experiment consists of four basic steps, regardless of who is conducting the experiment or the subject matter that the experiment addresses. When you conduct an experiment you

- identify what you need to learn,
- take the relevant actions (conduct the experiment by manipulating one or more variables),
- observe the effects and consequences of those actions on other variables, and then
- determine the extent to which the observed effects can be attributed to actions taken.

Each of these parts of an experiment are illustrated in the following example of a daily-life experiment:

Peter wants to develop a pizza crust with better texture than the crusts he has made in the past. So, he conducts an experiment to see how the amount of water added to the batter affects crust texture. Peter mixes three different batches of crust, making certain that he uses the same ingredients in the same quantity in each crust except for the amount of water. Crust A is made with one cup of water, Crust B contains 1½ cups of water while Crust C contains two cups of water. All ingredients are added and mixed in the same order. Peter's oven is large enough to hold one crust at a time. He bakes each crust for the same amount of time at the same temperature. He mixes each crust batter immediately before baking and lets the oven cool down between each baking. Peter then observes and evaluates each crust when it comes out of the oven. He decides that Crust C has a better texture: it is firmer, crisper (without burning), and has a better color. Peter decides that the recipe for Crust C is the better of the three recipes.

Peter's pizza crust experiment illustrates the four steps underlying the conduct of an experiment. Peter decided that he wanted to understand the effect of water con-

tent on crust texture, he took the relevant action by varying the amount of water in the recipes, he observed the effect of water variation on crust texture and he decided (because of the care he took in the design and conduct of the experiment) that he could have confidence in the conclusion that the amount of water in Crust C results in the best crust.

Beyond the characteristics of an experiment, Peter's pizza experiment also illustrates the components of an experiment and the requirements needed for one to accept the causality inferred by an experiment.

Components of an Experiment

Every experiment has at least one dependent variable, one independent variable, and manipulation. The *dependent variable(s)* is what the researcher is interested in explaining. The dependent variables in Peter's crust experiment were observational ratings of crust firmness, crispness, and color. The *independent variable(s)* is used to explain changes in the dependent variable. The amount of water in Peter's crust experiment was the independent variable. The *dependent variable(s)* in an experiment is the criterion or measure used to evaluate the influence of the independent variable. Finally, independent variables are *manipulated* in some systematic way. Variations in the amount of water in each crust reflected manipulation of the independent variable.

Requirements for Causality

Experiments permit one to attribute causality, that is, to presume that the cause of changes in the dependent variable(s) are due to manipulations of the independent variables(s). However, before this causal relationship can be accepted three criteria must be satisfied.

1. *Events must take place in the proper order*—For one event to cause another it must precede it. Peter's experiment satisfies this criterion because his manipulation of water content preceded crust evaluation.[1]

2. *Events must take place at the same time*—This attribute of causation, labeled concomitant variation, requires that causes and effects must occur or vary together. Peter's experiment satisfies this criterion because crust quality and water manipulation varied together.

3. *Alternative explanations must be reduced*—While it is impossible to eliminate all alternative explanations for experimental results, you must structure your experiment so that you eliminate as many alternative causal factors as possible. When all reasonable alternative explanations for the results are eliminated then you can have confidence that the manipulations of the independent variable caused the observed changes in the dependent variable. Consider what happens when Sally conducts her own pizza experiment in this way:

---

[1] While this criterion appears to reflect common sense intuition, it is nevertheless important because cause and effect can, at times, become quite confused. Consider an experiment in which one varies the amount of advertising exposure and then measures consumers' awareness of the advertising and product purchase. Assume that both measures rise. One could conclude that increases in advertising awareness (and thus more exposure and attention to the advertising) caused more people to try the product. However, it is also possible that as people increasingly purchased the product they became more aware of the product's advertising. Which event, advertising awareness or product purchase preceded the other?

Sally begins her experiment in exactly the same way as Peter. She carefully prepares each recipe manipulating only the water content. However, because she is pressed for time and has a shortage of pizza pans, she bakes Crust A in her oven and pan, she bakes Crust B in a neighbor's oven in a different brand of pizza pan, and she bakes Crust C in a second neighbor's oven using a third brand of pan.

This experiment fails to eliminate two reasonable alternative explanations of the results. The differences in crust quality could be due to differences in the ovens or to differences in the pans.

While all three criteria for the acceptance of causation are essential, the third criterion is perhaps the most crucial because it affects an experiment's internal validity. *Internal validity* refers to the extent that one can eliminate alternative explanations for the observed experimental results. The greater a researcher's ability to show that the manipulation of the independent variable caused the observed changes in the dependent variable the higher the level of experimental internal validity. Peter's pizza experiment had high internal validity because of the care he took in the preparation and baking of each crust. Consistency in these areas helped to eliminate alternative explanations. Sally's pizza experiment lacked internal validity because there were several alternative explanations of the results. Crust differences in Sally's experiment could be attributed to differences in ovens or pans.

The next section discusses the factors that can affect the internal validity of an experiment.

PROBLEMS AFFECTING INTERNAL VALIDITY

Internal validity is reduced whenever alternative explanations of the results are present. Researchers have identified seven different types of threats to an experiment's internal validity:

- premeasurement
- interaction
- history
- maturation
- instrumentation
- selection
- mortality

The presence of these threats in an experiment *reduces* the likelihood that decisions based on the findings are the correct decisions because they reduce one's confidence in the cause and effect relationship of the experimental manipulation and outcome.

The remainder of this section discusses each of these threats to the internal validity of an experiment. The next section discusses how these threats may be eliminated by using experimental design.

Premeasurement and Interaction Premeasurement and interactional threats to internal validity are closely related. Either or both may occur whenever individuals are interviewed before the experimental manipulation and exposure to the independent

variable. *Premeasurement* threats occur whenever the interview administered at the start of the experiment has a direct effect on the respondent's actions or behaviors as reflected in the interview administered after the experimental manipulation. *Interactional* threats occur whenever the interview administered before the start of the experiment affects a respondent's sensitivity or responsiveness to the independent variable, thus affecting how he or she responds to measures of the dependent variable.

The following hypothetical situations illustrate premeasurement and interactional threats to internal validity:

PREMEASUREMENT:
Tom resides in a test market selected by Wisk, a manufacturer of laundry detergent. Wisk is about to conduct a test of a new advertising campaign in the test market. Tom is selected to participate in the research study that will track changes in product perceptions and purchase behaviors. Before the start of the study Tom completes a questionnaire that asks him to rate five brands of laundry detergent and to describe his purchase behaviors of the past four months. After he completes the questionnaire, he says to himself: "I've recently tried all the brands the questionnaire asked me about except Wisk. I haven't bought Wisk in a long time. I wonder why? Next time I think I'll get some." Tom's next purchase of laundry detergent is Wisk. Four weeks later Tom fills out another questionnaire that shows he has purchased Wisk.

Wisk attributes this positive shift in Tom's behavior to the effects of the advertising. However, Tom's purchase had nothing to do with the advertising test. **In fact, he did not even see any Wisk advertising.** Tom's purchase was directly affected by the questionnaire he filled out before the start of the test.

INTERACTION:
Tom's neighbor, Mary, is selected to participate in another research study. This study is designed to probe the influence of heath care advocacy advertising on consumer attitudes. Before the start of the study and the advertising campaigns, Mary completes a questionnaire that explores her attitudes toward health care reform and health care-related advocacy advertising. At the end of three months, during which time the advertising appears, Mary completes another survey that again explores her attitudes toward health care reform and health care-related advocacy advertising. Mary shows a large shift in attitude between the first and second questionnaires.

The study sponsor attributes the changes in Mary's attitudes to the impact of the advertising and generalizes these changes to the broader population. But, Mary is not representative of the broader population. After Mary completed the first questionnaire, she said to herself: "That's an interesting topic. I haven't seen any advertising about health care reform, yet. I'd better watch out for it." The first questionnaire sensitized Mary. She was much more likely than the average consumer to watch for this advertising. Because her change in attitude may be larger than the typical consumer who was not sensitized and who paid less attention to the advertising than did Mary.

In the cases of Tom and Mary, decision makers have attributed changes in the dependent variable (purchase behavior and attitudes) to the advertising exposure (the independent variable). But this linkage may not be true (and in these cases are *not* true) given the presence of the two uncontrolled threats to internal validity. The presence of these threats to internal validity obscure the interpretation of the findings and reduce our confidence in attributing changes in the dependent measures to the independent variable.

Finally, while premeasurement and interactional threats to internal validity are related, it is important to understand their differences. The threat of premeasurement to

validity occurs *without* exposure to the independent variable. All observed attitudinal or behavioral changes are the result of exposure to the initial measurement instrument. Interactional threats to validity do not require any direct effects from the initial measurement. Interaction occurs whenever the independent variable is more likely to be noticed and reacted to then it would be without the initial measurement. Thus, interactional threats occur when the premeasurement *and* the independent variable have a unique, combined effect on the dependent variable. This distinction is important for the design of experiments. As you will see in the next section, some experimental designs control the premeasurement threats without controlling the interaction threats.

History *History*, within the context of experimentation, refers to any events or influences beyond those intentionally manipulated by the researcher that occur during the experiment *and* that have the potential to affect the experimental outcome as measured by the dependent variable(s). Historical threats to an experiment's internal validity come from several sources. Some historical threats are the result of circumstances beyond any person's control. For example, an experiment designed to measure the effect of various promotions on soft drink consumption might be distorted by several weeks of unexpected unseasonably hot or cold weather. Some historical threats are the result of deliberate actions taken by others. Wondra hand lotion, for example, was test marketed in Milwaukee. During the test, large and atypical discounts were offered by Wondra's competitor, Vaseline Intensive Care lotion.[2] The ability of a company to affect the results of the competitor's experiments (commonly referred to as "competitive jamming") is one reason why simulated (or laboratory) test markets are increasing in popularity. (Simulated and laboratory test markets are discussed later in this chapter.)

Maturation Respondents' attitudes, behaviors, and physiology change during an experiment. They can become tired, hungry, thirsty, bored, and/or disinterested as the experiment progresses. *Maturational* threats to internal validity refer to these types of changes, all of which have the potential to affect and distort the levels of the dependent variable. Respondents at the end of an experiment may be less interested in the experiment and the experimental topic than when they began. This may cause them to provide superficial answers on the questionnaire administered at the end of the experiment. An analysis of these answers might incorrectly interpret the depth of their attitudes and interest in the test product, when in fact they are *more* interested in the product but they simply answered the questionnaire quickly so that their participation in the experiment would end.

Instrumentation *Instrumentation* refers to changes made to the measurement instrument (for example, the questionnaire) or data recording techniques during the experiment. Such changes affect the internal validity of the experiment because one does not know whether to attribute differences in attitudes or behaviors observed before and after the experimental manipulation to the manipulation itself, or to changes in the measurement instrument, recording techniques, data collection methods, or inconsis-

---

[2] N. Howard, "Fighting It Out In The Test Market," *Dun's Review* (June, 1979): 69.

tent interviewing. An example of each of these sources of instrumentation threats is presented in Figure 7.1.

Selection and Mortality   *Selection and mortality* threats to internal validity are related to the composition and characteristics of the groups comprising the experimental study.

Most experimental designs require at least two groups of individuals, a test group and a control group. The control group is not exposed to the experimental manipulation and serves as a basis of comparison for the test group, which is exposed to the experimental manipulation. *Selection* threats to internal validity occur whenever the characteristics of these two groups are not equivalent before the start of the experiment.

Changes in the Measurement Instrument

Harris Toys is interested in determining the effects of two advertising campaigns on product perceptions and purchase behaviors. They select four comparable markets. The new campaign will be shown in two markets, the remaining markets will not receive any advertising. Prior to the start of the campaign study participants are questioned about their current product perceptions. One of the key scale questions, which probes the value of Harris' toys, is found to be confusing and difficult for respondents to answer. This question is changed and the new, revised version appears on the questionnaire used to measure attitudes and behaviors at the conclusion of the experiment. The change in the question makes it impossible to accurately compare attitudes on the pretest with attitudes expressed on the posttest.

Changes or Noncomparability in Recording Techniques

Harris Toys has also developed two new versions of a preexisting toy. First they take the old version, give it to children, and note their reactions by recording their play behavior on an observation protocol. Three days later, they give each of the new versions to the same children and again record their reactions. However, different individuals record the children's reactions. Because the recording requires judgment, a subjective analysis of the behaviors being displayed, there is no assurance that the judgment used to obtain ratings of the old toy is comparable to the judgment used to rate reactions to the revised toy.

Changes in Data Collection Methods

In January 1995 Talpin Bank conducts a study of consumers' attitudes toward Chicago banking and financial institutions. The study uses face-to-face personal interviews conducted among a representative sample of the target audience. While the study collected a great deal of valuable information, the use of face-to-face interviews was very costly and time consuming. One year later, in January 1996, the bank uses the same questionnaire but conducts the study by mail among a second representative sample. The differences in data collection methods prevents the bank from confidently comparing attitudes in 1995 and 1996.

Inconsistent Interviewing

The Remmie Corporation has hired a field service to conduct 300 mall intercept interviews. The interviews need to be completed within two weeks. After one week, 100 interviews had been completed. A discussion with the interviewers reveals that a great deal of time is devoted to clarifying questions and to probing answers. In the interest of meeting the time deadline, interviewers are told to minimize these activities. The change in interviewing can have a dramatic effect on information content and quality and thus affects the internal validity of the research.

FIGURE 7.1
Examples of instrumentation threats to internal validity.

Selection threats occur whenever the test and control groups differ in relevant demographics, attitudes, behaviors, their initial level with regard to the dependent variable or in their likelihood to respond to the independent variable. Selection threats to internal validity can be reduced by using random selection and assignment of individuals to the test and control groups.[3]

Mortality threats to internal validity occur whenever the characteristics of the test and control groups differ in terms of relevant demographics, attitudes, behaviors, their initial level with regard to the dependent variable, or in their likelihood to respond to the independent variable at the conclusion of the experiment. Mortality threats typically arise when different types of individuals from each group drop out of the study. For example, assume that a test and control group are well matched before the start of the study and that each group consists of a representative sample of the U. S. adult population. During of the study 10 percent of the individuals in both groups drop out of the study. However, in the control group the dropouts are individuals aged 18 to 24 (thus increasing the mean age of this group) while in the test group the dropouts are individuals aged 45 and older (thus decreasing the mean age of this group). Consequently, differences in attitudes or behaviors at the conclusion of the experiment cannot unambiguously be attributed to the influence of the independent variable. The difference in mean age between the two groups may have affected responses to the dependent measures.

EXPERIMENTAL DESIGN

The seven threats to internal validity discussed in the prior section can, to a greater or lesser extent, be controlled with experimental design. Some experimental designs attempt to control all threats to internal validity while other designs attempt (or are able to) control only a few, as shown in Table 7.1.

Usually, information accuracy and cost increase as more controls are built into the experimental design. Given this relationship between cost and control, it is not necessarily the case that a researcher always wants to select the design that controls all seven threats to internal validity. Good research design requires a balance between the accuracy of the information collected and the cost required to collect that information. A researcher must identify the experimental design that, given the magnitude of the decision and informational needs, provides the best balance between accuracy and cost.

This section discusses each of the experimental designs listed in Table 7.1, noting the strengths and weaknesses of each design. Each experimental design will be discussed in the context of the hypothetical situation shown in Figure 7.2 (page 146).

Quasi-Experimental Designs

The effectiveness of the direct mail campaign conducted by the American Savings Association (see Figure 7.2) could be evaluated by one of the two quasi-experimental de-

---

[3] A random sample is the result of probability sampling in which each element in the target population has a known and equal chance of being selected to participate in the research. Random or probability samples are discussed in greater depth in Chapter 8.

TABLE 7.1 Experimental Research Designs: Relative Ability to Control Threats to Internal Validity

Experimental Design	Premeasurement	Interaction	History	Maturation	Instrumentation	Selection	Mortality
Quasi-Experimental							
One group posttest-only	✓	✓			✓		
One group pretest-posttest						✓	
True Experimental							
Simulated pretest-posttest	✓	✓					✓
Posttest only with control	✓	✓	✓	✓	✓		
Pretest-posttest with control	✓		✓	✓	✓	✓	
Solomon four-group design	✓	✓	✓	✓	✓	✓	✓

signs listed in Table 7.1. These designs are called quasi-experimental because they are not true experiments. Quasi-experimental designs are difficult to interpret because they offer little or no control over threats to internal validity, and are only slight improvements over descriptive studies as a basis for decision making, as opposed to true experimental designs. Thus, while these designs are commonly and appropriately used for specific types of advertising and marketing research (such as advertising pretesting, concept testing, etc.) they are generally inappropriate for use in experimental research. Marketers and advertisers who use these designs in an experimental context do so at their own risk.

One Group Posttest-Only   The *one group posttest-only* design takes a single group of individuals, exposes them to the treatment or experimental manipulation (the independent variable) and then measures the dependent variable(s) as part of the posttest. Symbolically, this design is represented as

Group 1:   Treatment ⋯⋯⋯⋯➤ Posttest

The use of this design in the American Savings Association direct mail campaign would result in the following experiment and observations: The American Savings Association mails its direct mail pieces to a group of selected individuals. Two weeks after the last mailing, each individual is contacted by phone and is asked to provide his or her perceptions of the stability, friendliness, and community involvement of their community's Savings & Loans. The American Savings Association looks at the opinions expressed on the questionnaire and then decides whether the mailing was successful.

As this scenario illustrates, there are three important flaws with this design. First, the Association is forced to rely entirely on judgment to interpret the results. For example, assume that "friendliness" is measured using a five-point scale in which a '1' is extremely friendly and a '5' is extremely unfriendly. Is an average friendliness rating of 3.0 good or bad? The Association has no way of knowing because it did not know

The American Savings Association, an association of Savings & Loan institutions, has developed a direct mail campaign designed to foster positive perceptions of the stability, friendliness, and community involvement of local Savings & Loans. Consumers' ratings of Savings & Loans in each of these areas are the dependent variables. The campaign consists of four direct mail pieces. Each direct mail piece addresses stability, friendliness, and community involvement.

The outside of the envelopes are shown below. The direct mail campaign is structured so that one envelope per week is mailed to each respondent. Thus, at the end of a four-week period each respondent will have received all four envelopes. (Exposure to the direct mail campaign is the independent variable.)

At the end of the mailing, the association will assess the effectiveness of the mail campaign by evaluating consumers' attitudes toward Savings & Loan stability, friendliness, and community involvement.

Following are the four envelopes used in the direct mail campaign.

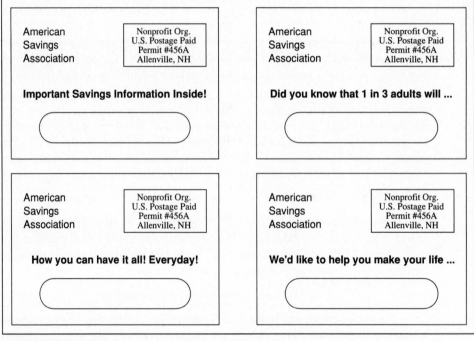

FIGURE 7.2
Core situation for discussion of experimental design.

how "friendly" Savings & Loans were perceived to be *prior* to the start of the campaign. Second, there is no control group, so the Association cannot determine the extent to which any attitude change is specifically attributable due to receipt of the mailing versus other influences on the consumer. This represents a history threat to internal validity. Third, the design fails to control for several additional threats to internal validity, specifically maturation, selection, and mortality.

One Group Pretest-Posttest   The one group pretest-posttest also called the "before and after without control design," is similar to the one group posttest-only design just

discussed except that a premeasure is taken before experimental manipulation of the independent variable. Symbolically, this design is represented as

Group 1:   Pretest ················➤ Treatment ················➤ Posttest

This design is frequently utilized for tests of product pricing, packaging, and advertising response, as follows:

Measure product brand share ······➤ Alter pricing ································➤ Measure product brand share

Measure customer satisfaction ·····➤ Alter product formulation ···············➤ Measure customer satisfaction

Measure product perception ········➤ Run new advertising campaign ····➤ Measure product perceptions

In each case, the impact of the experimental treatment is made by comparing levels of the dependent measure in the posttreatment measure to levels observed in the pretreatment measure.

The use of this design for the research described Figure 7.2 would be: The American Savings Association selects a group of individuals for study participation. Each individual is contacted by telephone and interviewed regarding their perceptions of Savings & Loan stability, friendliness, and community involvement before the first mailing. The Association begins its mailing one week after the conclusion of pretest interviews. Two weeks after the last mailing, each individual is contacted by telephone and is asked to provide his or her perceptions of the stability, friendliness, and community involvement of their community's Savings & Loans. The American Savings Association looks at the levels of opinion expressed on the postmailing interview in relation to premailing levels and then decides whether any changes between the pretest and posttest levels are indicative of a successful campaign.

As with the prior design, the weakness of this approach to experimentation becomes evident when we try to interpret the findings. We cannot confidently attribute any observed changes in pretreatment to posttreatment levels to the mailing because (1) we cannot isolate the effects of the mailing from other influences and (2) the design fails to control for all other threats to internal validity with the exception of selection.

True Experimental Designs

True experimental designs differ from quasi-experimental designs in two important ways. True experimental designs have a control group and use random assignment of units (i.e., individuals, retail outlets, etc.) to the control and test groups. (Random assignment occurs when each member of the population has a known and equal chance of being selected for inclusion in the research.) The use of random assignment is particularly important because randomization helps to control many threats to internal validity. Thus, in spite of the fact that true experimental designs are more costly and time consuming versus quasi-experimental designs, they tend to collect information that provides a sounder basis for decision making. The four most common types of true experimental designs are[4]

---

[4] For an extremely clear and detailed discussion of quasi- and true experimental designs see Donald Campbell and Julian Stanley, *Experimental and Quasi-Experimental Designs For Research* (Chicago, IL: Rand-McNally Company, 1963).

- simulated pretest–posttest
- posttest-only with control
- pretest–posttest with control
- Solomon four-group design

As illustrated in Table 7.1 while each of these designs controls for different threats to internal validity, all are more sound than quasi-experimental designs.

Experimental designs' greater control of threats to internal validity generally entail greater expenditures of time and money, primarily because of the need for more measurements and groups of respondents. The researcher, therefore, must select the design that provides the best balance given the current set of informational needs.

Two Groups—Two Measure Designs

The two most common forms of experimental advertising research are designs that require two groups of respondents and two measurements. These designs, the *simulated pretest—posttest* and *posttest only with control*, are popular because of their ability to control most threats to internal validity while minimizing the number of required groups of respondents and measurements. Both designs are able to minimize the number of groups and measurements because they assume that the random assignment of individuals to the two groups results in equivalency across groups.

Simulated Pretest—Posttest The *simulated pretest—posttest* experimental design was developed to control for premeasurement and interactional threats to internal validity particularly in experiments dealing with consumer attitudes and knowledge.[5] The experimental design controls these threats to validity by using one group of randomly assigned respondents for the pretest measurement and a second group of randomly assigned respondents for the treatment and posttest measurements, as follows:

Group 1 (Random)   Pretest

Group 2 (Random)   Treatment ·············► Posttest

Because different individuals are administered the pretest and the posttest, premeasurement or interactional threats to validity cannot arise. However, other threats, such as history, maturation, instrumentation, and selection can still occur.

Data analysis in this design compares levels of posttest measures to pretest measures. In the absence of other explanations, differences in these measures are attributed to the experimental treatment because the design assumes that the control and test groups (Group 1 and Group 2, respectively) are equivalent.

The American Savings Association would use this design as follows: Two nationally representative samples of adults would be constructed by random assignment from the larger population. The first group would be administered a questionnaire that measures their attitudes toward Savings & Loans. The second group of respondents would receive the direct mail campaign. After the last mailing in the campaign, the second group would be administered the same questionnaire as the first group. If the

---

[5] Donald S. Tull and Del I. Hawkins, *Marketing Research; Measurement and Method (Fifth Edition)* (New York: Macmillan Publishing Company, 1990): 195.

groups are large enough, and the random assignment and selection of respondents were performed properly, then any differences in the two groups' attitudes can be attributed to the effects of the direct mail campaign in addition to any effects products by either history, maturation, instrumentation, or selection.

Posttest-Only With Control   The *posttest-only with control* experimental design also utilizes two groups of respondents and two measures. Its cost for an equivalent sample size is roughly equivalent to the simulated pretest—posttest.

The posttest-only with control design differs from the simulated pretest–posttest in the way that it measures the treatment effects. The simulated pretest–posttest design estimates treatment effects by comparing levels of pretest and posttest measures. The posttest-only with control design estimates treatment effects by comparing postmeasures, one postmeasure obtained from the treatment group and one obtained from the control group, as follows:

Group 1 (Random)	Posttest
Group 2 (Random)	Treatment ··············► Posttest

In the absence of other explanations, differences in the two groups' posttest measures are attributed to the experimental treatment because there is an assumed pretreatment group equivalency.

The posttest-only with control design is a more powerful design than the simulated pretest—posttest design because it controls for a greater number of threats to internal validity. Because both postmeasures are taken at the same time, this design is able to control for history, maturation, and instrumentation, as well as premeasurement, and interaction.

The American Savings Association would use this design as follows: Two nationally representative samples of adults would be constructed by random assignment from the larger population. Individuals in the second group would receive four direct mail mailings. After the last mailing, both groups of individuals would be administered the same questionnaire. Since it is assumed that random assignment of individuals to the two groups resulted in equivalency in terms of pretreatment attitudes, any differences in the two groups' posttest measures can be attributed to the effects of the treatment, the direct mail campaign.

Two Groups–Four Measures: The Pretest–Posttest with Control

The prior design assumed, but never verified, that random assignment resulted in equivalent pretreatment attitudes in the two experimental groups. The *pretest–posttest with control* design makes certain that there is equivalency between the treatment and nontreatment (control) group before the start of the research. This certainty is obtained by testing both groups before the start of the research, as follows:

Group 1 (Random)	Pretest ··············►	Treatment ··············►	Posttest
Group 2 (Random)	Pretest ·································	····················►	Posttest

This design is appropriate whenever a researcher needs explicit evidence of group equivalency before the start of the treatment or whenever there is some doubt as to the extent of group equivalence.

The pretest–posttest with control design is quite powerful. The use of a control group coupled with two pretest measures allows for the control of all potential sources of experimental error except mortality and interaction. Moreover, the design is able to compensate for differences in group pretest levels should these be discovered after the start of the research. This compensation for initial inequalities is achieved by making the statistic of interest the difference in the differences of each group's posttest and pretest, estimated using the following calculation:

(Group 1 Posttest minus Group 1 Pretest) minus (Group 2 Posttest minus Group 2 Pretest)

This power of the pretest-posttest with control design is not without cost, however. The use of two groups and four measures makes this design more costly than comparable two group–two measure designs.

The American Savings Association would use this design as follows: Two nationally representative samples of adults would be constructed by random assignment from the larger population. Individuals in both groups would be administered a questionnaire before the start of the survey. The first group of individuals would then receive four direct mail mailings. Both groups of individuals would be administered the same questionnaire after the last mailing.

The pretest–posttest with control design is an alternative to the posttest-only with control design. Both experimental designs control for premeasurement, history, maturation, and instrumentation threats to internal validity. However, the posttest-only with control eliminates interactional threats while the pretest–posttest with control eliminates selection threats. Neither design eliminates challenges to internal validity due to mortality. Consequently, design selection reflects a researcher's informational needs, anticipated threats to validity and budget.

Four Groups–Six Measures: The Solomon Four-Group Design

The *Solomon four-group design* is the most powerful and the most resource intensive, experimental design. The design is powerful because it controls for all seven threats to an experiment's internal validity. It accomplishes this by combining a pretest—posttest with control design with a posttest—only with control design:

Group 1 (Random)	Pretest ···········►	Treatment ···········►	Posttest
Group 2 (Random)	Pretest ································►		Posttest
Group 3 (Random)		Treatment ···········►	Posttest
Group 4 (Random)			Posttest

The number of measurements taken as part of this design allows for a variety of comparisons during data analysis, for example:

- Group 1 Pretest v. Group 1 Posttest
- Group 1 Posttest v. Group 2 Posttest
- Group 1 Posttest v. Group 3 Posttest
- Group 2 Posttest v. Group 4 Posttest

The American Savings Association would use this design as follows: Four groups, each consisting of a nationally representative sample of adults would be formed by random selection from a larger population. Individuals in groups one and

two would be administered a questionnaire before the start of the survey. Individuals in groups one and three would receive four direct mail mailings. All groups of individuals would be administered the same questionnaire after the last mailing.

It should be noted that in spite of its experimental power, the Solomon four-group design is rarely applied advertising and marketing research, primarily due to its complexity, cost, and timing.

More Complex Experimental Designs

The prior examples presented the most basic forms of experimentation. There was only one independent variable and this variable had only one level (present or absent). Advertising research often requires more complex experimental designs in which different levels of an independent variable are manipulated, or two or more independent variables are manipulated at the same time.

More Than One Level of a Variable

A true experimental design can be expanded for circumstances in which different levels of one independent variable need to be studied. Imagine that the American Savings Association wanted to test the extent to which the *number of different mailings* affected a person's attitudes toward Savings and Loans. In this situation, the independent variable would have four levels, each level representing the number of mailings a respondent receives. An experimental design addresses this situation by expanding to include a treatment group for each level of the independent variable. The *pretest—posttest with control* design, for example, would take the following form consisting of four treatment groups and one control group:

Group 1 (Random)   Pretest ·············►Treatment 1·············► Posttest

Group 2 (Random)   Pretest ·············►Treatment 2·············► Posttest

Group 3 (Random)   Pretest ·············►Treatment 3·············► Posttest

Group 4 (Random)   Pretest ·············►Treatment 4·············► Posttest

Group 5 (Random)   Pretest ··► Posttest

As in the prior cases, each group consists of a nationally representative sample of adults formed by random selection from a larger population. Individuals in all five groups would be administered a questionnaire before the start of the survey. All mailings take place over the course of a week. Individuals in Group 1 receive one mailing, individuals in Group 2 receive two mailings, etc. Individuals in Group 5, the control group, receive no mailings. One week after the last mailing, all five groups of individuals would be administered the same questionnaire, and posttest levels across all five groups would be compared.

Factorial Designs: More Than One Manipulation

There are times when an advertising researcher needs to manipulate and observe the effects of two or more independent variables at the same time. Imagine, for example, a creative team in the following situation:

We have debated for days our executional options for the new advertising campaign. Two problems remain. First, we cannot decide if we should use a celebrity or an ordinary person as the spokesperson in the commercial. Second, we cannot decide if the tone and manner should be humorous or serious. We need research to answer three questions for us. In terms of the persuasiveness of the commercial:

1. What is the effect of varying the spokesperson in the commercial?
2. What is the effect of varying the tone in the commercial?
3. What is the effect of varying the spokesperson and tone at the same time? That is, is there an interaction between spokesperson and tone?

A factorial design could be used to answer these questions. A *factorial design* is an experimental procedure that simultaneously measures the effect of two or more independent variables, each with different levels, on one or more dependent variables.

Factorial designs consist of main effects and interactions. A main effect is the separate influence of each independent variable on the dependent variable(s). In this example, the main effects are the spokesperson (two levels: celebrity and ordinary person) and tone (two levels: humorous and serious). The effect of *combinations* of main effects on the dependent variables(s) is the interaction. Interaction occurs when the simultaneous effect of two or more independent variables is different from the sum of their independent effects. In this example, an interaction would occur if responses to a particular spokesperson-tone combination was different from independent responses to spokesperson alone or tone alone.

The factorial design that would be used to address the issues of spokesperson and commercial tone is graphically represented on the top of Figure 7.3. The columns represent the levels of one main effect while the rows represent the levels of the second main effect. The total sample consists of 240 respondents who are randomly assigned to one of the experimental conditions, represented by one of the cells in Figure 7.3. Each respondent will see one ad. Respondents assigned to the upper left cell will see a humorous ad with a celebrity spokesperson while respondents assigned to the lower right cell will see a serious ad with an ordinary spokesperson.

After all the ads are seen, the responses of the individuals in each cell are averaged. The chart shown on the bottom of Figure 7.3 shows the average persuasiveness score for each level of each main effect (shown on the outside of the cells) and each individual cell in the factorial design. The average score for each level of the main effect "spokesperson" is calculated by averaging the commercial tone scores. Conversely, the average score for each level of the main effect "commercial tone" is calculated by averaging the spokesperson scores. Statistical analyses of the data indicate that neither main effect is significant.

- The average score for humor (2.4) is not significantly different than that of the average score for serious (2.1).
- The average score for celebrity spokesperson (2.2) is not significantly different than that of the average score for ordinary spokesperson (2.3).

But, a visual examination of the persuasiveness scores for each cell indicates that differences do exist. (Compare, for example, the persuasiveness score in the humor-ordinary spokesperson cell to that of the serious-ordinary spokesperson cell.) Statistical analyses indicate that there is a significant interaction effect. The average persuasiveness score for the humor-ordinary spokesperson cell is significantly higher than the score obtained in each of the three remaining combinations. Thus, while neither the

Factorial Design: Factors and Number of Respondents Per Cell

Commercial Tone

Spokesperson:	Humor	Serious
Celebrity	60	60
Ordinary	60	60

Factorial Design: Average Persuasiveness Scores Per Factor

Commercial Tone

Spokesperson:	Humor	Serious	
Celebrity	2.1	2.3	**2.2**
Ordinary	2.7	1.9	**2.3**
	2.4	**2.1**	

FIGURE 7.3
Characteristics and data from a factorial design.

type of spokesperson nor commercial tone *independently* affected commercial persuasiveness, these two factors *together* exerted a significant influence.

As can be seen, the power and usefulness of factorial designs lies in their ability to identify the influence of separate independent variables as well as the influence of their interaction.

INTERNAL VALIDITY: A BROADER VIEW

The prior section shows how experimental design affects internal validity by allowing or eliminating alternative explanations of the experimental results. Internal validity improves as more threats to internal validity are eliminated. Beyond these specific aspects of internal validity, Krathwohl[6] argues that an experiment's internal validity is also af-

---

[6] The points presented in this section are from David R. Krathwohl, *Social and Behavioral Science Research: A New Framework for Conceptualizing, Implementing and Evaluating Research Studies* (San Francisco, CA: Jossey-Bass Publishers, 1985): 92–97.

fected by the nature of the experiment's predictions and results. This broader view of internal validity suggests that an experiment's internal validity improves under the following circumstances:

1. *Internal validity increases with stronger predictions*—Strong predictions state the direction and size of changes that will occur in response to the experimental manipulations. "Indicating simply when the effect will occur is the weakest prediction. A stronger prediction adds the direction of effect, a still stronger one the size and nature of the change." A researcher, for example, might wish to explore the relationship between advertising exposure and brand attitudes. A statement that "exposure will affect attitudes" is the weakest prediction because it does not specifically identify the nature of the relationship between exposure and attitudes. A stronger prediction would add directionality (i.e., "increased advertising exposure will positively improve brand attitudes") while an even stronger prediction would address the nature of the change (i.e., "increased advertising exposure will improve brand attitudes in the areas of product performance and quality").

2. *Internal validity is greater when a change in the cause is followed by large changes in effect*—The results of experiments are typically evaluated by the use of inferential statistics that determine if there are statistically meaningful differences among experimental conditions. However, not all statistical significant differences are meaningful and not all meaningful differences are statistically significant. As a consequence, studies that exhibit large changes in the dependent variable(s) tend to produce results that are both meaningful and statistically significant, thereby improving the experiment's internal validity.

3. *Internal validity is greater when the effect reverses a prevailing tendency or condition than when the change simply produces more of the same*—An experiment that improves brand attitudes among those negative toward the product tends to have more internal validity than an experiment that improves brand attitudes among those who are already positive.

We agree with Krathwohl and recommend that these factors be considered during the planning stages of any experiment.[7]

EXPERIMENTAL SETTING

All experiments strive for the highest level of internal validity given time and budget constraints. However, beyond considerations of experimental design and internal validity, a researcher must also determine the best setting for the planned experiment.

---

[7] Krathwohl, *Social and Behavioral Science Research*, presents five additional criteria for the evaluation of internal validity. Internal validity is believed to increase: "With controlled application of the cause, treatment or instigating condition"; "The more a complexly patterned cause is predictably mirrored by the effect"; "If an instigating condition or cause can be controlled at will, producing a pattern of cause on demand"; "The greater the range of instigating conditions over which the predictions can be shown to hold"; "The more time elapses between the instigating condition and the effect, assuming one can accurately predict the time of appearance of the effect." The reader is encouraged to use this source for an extended discussion of these issues.

Experiments can be conducted in either a laboratory or field setting. Consider, for example, two approaches to evaluating reactions to a new package design:

- Individuals are seated in front of a computer screen and told that they are about to take a "virtual" shopping trip. They use a joystick to "move" down the grocery store aisle. They can stop where they like and zoom in on any product of interest.
- A new product package is placed on actual grocery store shelves. Shoppers who pass by the product are interviewed to see if they noticed the product and, if so, to learn their reactions to the new package.

The first approach is a *laboratory* experiment while the second is a *field* experiment.

Laboratory Experiments

Laboratory experiments have the potential to play an important role in marketing and advertising decision making. Laboratory experiments are most commonly used by advertisers and marketers when there is a need to evaluate package designs, pricing levels, alternative product formulations, and advertising creative, for example:

- Laboratory package tests often use eye tracking, tachistoscopic, or photographic displays to assess the ability of proposed package designs to attract attention and break through shelf clutter as well as communicate the brand name and other desired product information.
- Laboratory advertising tests may involve physiological measures such as eye tracking, tachistoscopes, or galvanic skin response. Other forms of advertising laboratory tests include some version of theater tests in which prerecruited respondents come to a central facility (such as an office complex, hotel, or convention center) to view advertising in the context of actual television programs. (The use of laboratory experiments to evaluate advertising creative is discussed in Chapter 23.)
- Laboratory product tests generally involve some form of blind usage. Here, consumers are given unlabeled products and are asked to rate performance, appeal, etc. While blind taste tests are quite informative, they do have the potential to be misleading if the brand name provides significant and influential cues to the consumer, as was the case of Coca-Cola and new Coke.

Field Experiments

Advertisers often use marketplace or field experiments to help answer questions related to new product introductions, product packaging, advertising content, media mix, and advertising spending, for example:[8]

- Brown-Forman Beverages Worldwide conducted a test a of new line of prepared cocktails called Tropical Freezes in Birmingham, St. Louis, Phoenix, and Houston.[9]

---

[8] In addition to the examples noted see also Alexa Bell, "Will KFC's Latest Test Spawn a Big Chance?" *Restaurant Business* (June 10, 1993): 23–24; Don Nichols, "Taco Bell Expands All Night Test in Seattle," *Restaurant Business* (May 1, 1993): 30; Michael J. McCarthy, "PepsiCo is Set to Test Two Lines of Fruit Flavored Drinks This Week," *Wall Street Journal* (April 22, 1993): B6.

[9] Eric Hollreiser, "New Products: Brown-Forman Tests New Markets for Wine Based Drinks," *Brandweek* (October 24, 1994): 4.

- Sega of America tested a joint venture with Blockbuster Entertainment and IBM to offer video game rentals on demand. The test was conducted in one Southwest market and lasted about four months.[10]

- Coors Brewing tested a new "value-added" brand of lager and light beers in Kansas and Oklahoma. The test was designed to determine if the introduction of these products could increase Coors' share of the lower-priced beer segment.[11]

- Perrier initiated a test market of its new Celestial Seasons brand of ready-to-drink iced teas in Dallas, Denver, Houston, Miami, San Francisco, and Tampa. The product test was supported by television, radio, and outdoor advertising.[12]

- Evian tested vending machine availability of its bottled water at beaches, health clubs, and college campuses in New York, Dallas, Boston, Los Angeles, and Phoenix. The machines contained either 11.2 oz. or 16.9 oz. PET bottles. Product pricing was set to be comparable to local convenience stores.[13]

Field experiments such as these are often expensive and long-term. These disadvantages are outweighed by the experiment's "real world" context. Advertisers can be confident that the results of a well planned and conducted marketplace experiment provide sound guidance for making decisions related to the broader marketplace.

Laboratory and Field Experiments: The Issue of External Validity

External validity refers to the representativeness or generalizability of experimental findings.[14] A high degree of external validity gives us confidence that the conclusions

> claimed for the relationship across subjects, situations, independent variables or ways of administering treatments, measuring instruments, times, study designs and procedures is supported by the evidence and is the only appropriate interpretation of that evidence with regard to generality.[15]

Researchers have a great deal of control in laboratory experiments because they are able to design the physical conditions under which the experiment will take place and can manipulate "one or more independent variables under rigorously specified, operationalized, and controlled conditions."[16] However, the artificiality of the experimental setting often results in an environment that is distinct from a real-life situation. Respondents may react differently to an independent variable in the laboratory versus how they would react to that variable under more natural conditions. As a consequence, well-designed laboratory experiments tend to have high degrees of internal validity and relatively low degrees of external validity. Field experiments are just the opposite. Field experiments tend to have relatively lower degrees of internal validity (because not all factors can be isolated or controlled) but higher degrees of external validity.

---

[10] Jeffrey D. Zbar, "Hey Kids! It's Sega On Demand," *Advertising Age* (June 6, 1994): 21.

[11] Wall Street Journal Staff, "Coors to Test Market Lower Priced Beer in Kansas, Oklahoma," *Wall Street Journal* (August 11, 1994): A4.

[12] Terry Lefton, "Test Markets: Perrier, Celestial Sample Teas," *Brandweek* (July 13, 1993): 10.

[13] Larry Jabonsky, "Evian Tests Vending Waters," *Beverage World* (March 1993): 76.

[14] Robert J. Kibler, "Basic Communication Research Considerations," In Philip Emmert and William D. Brooks eds., *Methods of Research Communication* (Boston, MA: Houghton Mifflin Company, 1970): 9–50.

[15] Krathwohl, *Social and Behavioral Science Research*, 113.

[16] F. N. Kerlinger, *Foundations of Behavioral Research* (New York: Holt, Rinehart, and Winston, Inc., 1973): 398.

Controlling Threats to External Validity

Researchers have identified two principle threats to an experiment's external validity. Designing an experiment to control for these threats can increase the experiment's external validity.

Surrogate situation threats occur when the sample or experimental manipulation are not representative of the population or conditions to which the results are to be generalized. Surrogate situation threats occur, for example, when the effects of advertising are determined by forced-exposure in a laboratory setting. The viewing situation in the experiment is clearly different than that of one's home. Fortunately, these types of surrogate situation threats to external validity can be eliminated or reduced by using appropriate study sampling (see the next chapter) and control of treatment characteristics. Other surrogate situation threats, such as those related to the artificiality of the experimental situation, typically arise in laboratory experiments. This type of threat to external validity is inherent to the laboratory environment and is extremely difficult to eliminate.

Reactive threats occur when the artificiality of the experimental situation or the behaviors of the experimenter change a respondent's behaviors so that the respondent reacts to the experimental situation itself rather than to the independent variable. This type of threat is primarily associated with laboratory experiments. Reactive threats may occur when respondents try to guess the nature of the experiment and act accordingly (either positively or negatively) or when they try to act the way in which they think the experimenter wants. There are two types of reactive threats, each can be reduced with control of the experiment's structure.

- Reactive threats due to the experimental situation can be reduced by eliminating cues that signal either the intent of the study or the types of behaviors that are "expected" of the respondent.
- Reactive threats due to the experimenter can be reduced by controlling experimenter behaviors. These threats can be reduced with rigorous experimenter training, the creation of experimental protocols (e.g., scripts that state what is to be said to each group of respondents), and increasing experimenter sensitivity to nonverbal signals and cues.

APPLICATIONS OF EXPERIMENTATION: TEST MARKETS

Advertising experiments explore a broad range of issues. A test market experiment duplicates planned or potential national actions and then evaluates the results of these actions in terms of business (e.g., sales, distribution) and consumer (i.e., attitudes, brand perceptions) impact. Test marketing represents a "cautious and usually prudent step"[17] when evaluating a new product introduction, strategic alternatives and advertising campaigns prior to a national rollout because it provides the opportunity to evaluate different courses of actions without the financial commitment to a national program.

This section describes three types of test market experiments: field test markets, simulated test markets, and electronic test markets. These options provide a basis for

---

[17] René Y. Darmon, Michèl Laroche, and K. Lee McGowan, *Marketing Research In Canada,* (Scarborough, Ontario, Canada: Gage Educational Publishing Company, 1989): 371.

understanding how experiments are planned and conducted and the trade-offs advertisers make between experimental internal and external validity.

Field Test Markets

A field experiment is conducted in the marketplace, where some factors are under the advertiser's control while other factors are not. As a result, a well-designed field test market experiment tends to have a relatively high level of external validity and a moderate degree of internal validity.

The success of a field test market experiment rests, in great part, on the geographic areas selected. Typically, purposive sampling of geographic areas is performed with the goal of selecting representative, comparable cities or other defined geographic areas. Suggested criteria for the evaluation and selection of geographic areas for a field test market experiment include the following:[18]

- Markets should not have been used for prior test market research.
- Markets should be average in terms of the overall category. Category sales or participation should neither be over nor under developed.
- Brand shares for both the test brand and competitors should be representative of the overall product category.
- Markets should be relatively isolated in terms of media spill-in. Few media signals from other markets should be available.
- Media usage should be similar to national patterns.
- Markets should be of average size. Markets should not be extremely small or extremely large.
- Demographic profiles should be comparable to each other and to national patterns.

Once a set of potential markets is selected, the next step in the experiment assigns markets to experimental conditions. Here, it is recommended that each experimental condition contain at least two markets. Additionally, if national projections are desired, the experimental and control groups should each contain four markets, one from each geographic region of the country.

Finally, cost and timing are considered. A typical test market can run anywhere from one month to a year or more. The actual time a specific test runs is often affected by the following "rules of thumb":

- A test should run long enough so that a sufficient number of repeat purchase cycles can be observed and measured. In general, the shorter the purchase cycle the shorter the duration of the test.
- Test length should not jeopardize the product's or marketing program's national success. The quicker one anticipates competitive response the shorter the test should be.
- The value of information obtained from the test must be reasonable in light of the funds necessary to obtain that information. Longer tests cost more. As a result, additional insights obtained from additional test months must be reasonable in light of the expenditures necessary to obtain those insights.

---

[18] F. Ladik, L. Kent, and P. C. Nahl, "Test Marketing of New Consumer Products," *Journal of Marketing* (April 1960): 40.

These general guidelines for field test marketing are illustrated in the following example.

Exploring Alternative Advertising Campaigns for a New Product   Imagine that you are a manufacturer and advertiser of fresh pasta. You have just developed a new line of flavored, all natural fresh pasta and wish to introduce the line nationally with significant advertising support. Your agency has developed two advertising campaigns and has recommended that a test market experiment be used to determine reactions to the product in the marketplace and to identify the advertising campaign that should be selected. You agree to conduct such an experiment.

The design and execution of the test consists of the following steps:

- experimental preplanning
- collect pretest data (if called for by the experimental design)
- conduct the test
- collect posttest data
- analyze the data and determine the effects
- apply results to future planning

Experimental Preplanning   Planning for this test market experiment begins with discussion and decisions in four areas: identification of the experimental variables, experimental design, locations, and assignment of locations to experimental treatments.

There will be one independent and two dependent variables. The independent variable is the advertising campaign shown in the market. There will be two dependent variables: sales and attitudes toward the product. Sales will be measured by manufacturer shipments to each market. Consumer attitudes toward the product will be measured using a questionnaire.

One appropriate experimental design is the posttest-only with control. No pretest measures are necessary because in all markets sales begin at zero. Moreover, there is an absence of consumer attitudes toward the advertising and brand because neither has been introduced into the test markets. As shown in Table 7.1, the posttest-only with control design also eliminates many important threats to the experiment's internal validity. Schematically, the design would be

Market Group 1:	No advertising	··► Posttest
Market Group 2:	Advertising Campaign A	·······························► Posttest
Market Group 3:	Advertising Campaign B	·····························► Posttest

(Note how Market Group 1 serves as the control group.)

Locations where the test will be conducted are selected in accordance with the guidelines presented earlier. In this example, given the need to generalize to the entire country, twelve markets will be selected, three from each of four geographic regions (North, South, East, and Western United States). Within a geographic region markets will be matched using criteria related to population demographic characteristics, population media habits, television spill-in, and category development. Once this is done, one market from each trio of markets is randomly assigned to one of the three experi-

mental conditions. Thus, each experimental condition consists of four cities, one from each region of the country.

Conduct the Test   Comparable media plans are developed and enacted in the experimental treatment conditions. The product is shipped in response to grocer orders. Levels of promotional and other support are held constant across the test cities.

Collect Posttest Data   At the planned end of the experiment (for example, at the end of six months) a randomly selected, representative sample of respondents in each market is interviewed. Shipments to each market are also tallied in order to determine total market sales.

Analyze the Results and Determine the Effects   The principal analysis in this experimental design compares posttest levels across the three experimental conditions. Given assurances that the sampling was done properly and that there were no selection or maturation threats to internal validity, any observed differences on the dependent variables can be attributed to the independent variable—type of advertising campaign appearing in the marketplace.

Apply Results to Future Planning   The final step in any test market experiment is application of the results to future planning. In this example, consumer attitude and sales data would be used to determine the differential impact of each advertising campaign (especially versus the no advertising condition) and, if appropriate, to select the campaign that will air nationally.

Simulated or Laboratory Test Markets

A simulated test market is test marketing conducted in a laboratory. As such, this approach reflects the strengths and weaknesses of laboratory experiments discussed earlier: a relatively high degree of internal validity and a relatively low degree of external validity.

Five marketing research companies perform the vast majority of simulated market tests. These companies and their product's names are: Burke Marketing Research (BASES), M/A/R/C (Macro Assessor), Yankelovich, Clancy Shulman (Litmus), Market Simulations (STM System) and Elrick & Lavidge (Comp/Comp Plus). Although there are some methodological variations among these companies, overall, most take similar steps to use the laboratory setting to simulate an actual field test market, as follows:

1. Target audience consumers are identified and recruited. These individuals may either be prerecruited and invited to a company's test facility or may be recruited via mall intercept or other convenience sampling technique.
2. Respondents are exposed to advertising. This advertising may be only for the test product or a combination of the test product's and competitor's advertising. The level of exposure generally reflects anticipated marketplace levels as represented in the products' media plans.
3. Respondents are allowed to shop and select the products they wish to take home. The shopping experience may be a "virtual" trip using film and slides of an actual store or a trip in a real store.

4. Respondents are interviewed about their selection. Reasons for product selection and nonselection are probed.

5. Each respondent is given the product to take home. Respondents are interviewed again after using the product at home. This interview focuses on usage occasions, product satisfaction, purchase intent, anticipated purchase quantity, and purchase frequency.

6. The research company uses the data from the shopping trip and both personal interviews as input into a mathematical model. The models analyze this data and then predict product trial, repeat purchases, sales volume, and brand share.

Simulated test markets provide advertisers with several advantages over field test markets. Advertisers have a higher degree of control over extraneous variables, results can be obtained more quickly and costs are lower. However, it is important to use these systems cautiously, acknowledging their limitations prior to the start of the research. As mentioned earlier, one limitation is that of all laboratory experiments, the artificiality of the situation and forced exposure to advertising may result in behaviors that are not representative of those that will be exhibited in the real world. A second limitation relates to the model used to predict trial, usage, volume, and share. The predictions from a model are only as good as the model itself. Since each company uses a different model, an advertiser using these systems must carefully evaluate the validity of each model's underlying assumptions.

Electronic Test Markets

Electronic test markets are a recent attempt to improve marketplace experimentation. The goal of an electronic test market is to increase control over the experimental situation without sacrificing generalizability or external validity.

An electronic test market is a market in which a marketing research company has established the ability to control the advertising that is transmitted to each individual's home in the market *and* to track the purchases make by individuals in each household.[19] Thus, research conducted in an electronic test market is able to relate the type and quantity of advertising exposure to purchase behavior.

The electronic test markets established by BehaviorScan® are representative of this approach to experimentation.

Market Selection   Electronic test markets are generally markets that are large enough to generalize to the larger population but still small enough to control advertising exposure, track individual purchase patterns, and monitor and control marketplace variables such as product pricing, distribution, and promotions. Current BehaviorScan® markets are Pittsfield, MA; Marion, IN; Eau Claire, WI; Midland, TX; Grand Junction, CO; and Cedar Rapids, IA.

Consumer Selection and Purchase Tracking   Individuals in cable TV households are recruited for the BehaviorScan® panel. Once recruited, information related to demographic characteristics, brand usage, and shopping behaviors is collected. Each re-

---

[19] Manipulation of the television signal and purchase tracking takes place only in those households that have agreed to become members of the participating panel. Research firms that offer electronic test market opportunities are Information Resources Inc. (IRI-Behaviorscan®, A. C. Nielsen (ERIM), and SAMI/Burke (Ad Tel/View Scan).

cruited individual is then placed on the BehaviorScan® panel and given a plastic identification card. Panel members show this ID card when they shop at each of the scanner-equipped stores in the market. This allows BehaviorScan® to electronically associate individual brand purchases with individual panel members.

Experimental Design and Treatment Research conducted in electronic test markets generally use a pretest-posttest with control design, as follows: Two or more groups (depending on the levels of each independent variable and the total number of independent variables) are drawn from the total BehaviorScan® panel. Members of each group are selected in a way that assures that the overall composition of the test and control groups are balanced and/or equivalent in terms of demographics, current and past brand usage behaviors, product category involvement, grocery stores utilized, and television viewing habits. This matching procedure, in the context of the pretest-posttest with control design, reduces many threats to internal validity and makes it easier to attribute observed differences among the groups to experimental treatment effects rather than to preexisting differences among the groups. Finally, because panel participants show their ID card each time they shop, pretest information on all participants resides in the BehaviorScan® database.

The experimental treatment is accomplished by manipulating the cable TV signal transmitted to each participant's household. BehaviorScan® uses split cable technology that allows commercials to be substituted at the individual household level. This allows the test group to be exposed to a test commercial or greater advertising weight while the control group is *at the same time* exposed to control ads.

Research studies conducted in electronic test markets typically last between six and twelve months.

An Example Electronic Test An electronic test market assessment of the effectiveness of two potential advertising campaigns could be conducted as follows:

- Three groups of individuals within the marketplace are formed. The groups are drawn from all individuals in the panel and are assigned to groups in a way that ensures group equivalence in terms of demographics, brand and category usage, and television viewing habits.
- By manipulating the cable signal into each individual's household, individuals in Group 1 receive no brand advertising, individuals in Group 2 receive advertising campaign "A" and individuals in Group 3 receive the advertising campaign "B."
- When the individuals in each group go shopping, they show their special ID card.
- At the end of a predetermined period the purchase behaviors of the three groups are compared and the effectiveness of the advertising (in general) and each campaign (in particular) is evaluated.

Summary

Advertisers conduct experiments to determine how different actions (the independent variables) affect consumer attitudes, beliefs, or behaviors (the dependent variables). They use experimentation to help them answer questions related to new product introduction, product packaging, advertising content, media mix, and advertising spending.

The extent to which an advertiser can confidently conclude that actions affect outcomes is dependent on how well the experiment is planned and conducted. Experimental designs that reflect better planning and control, and thus increase confidence in the results, are simulated pretest-posttest, posttest-only with control, pretest-posttest with control and Solomon four-group. These designs, versus quasi-experimental designs, increase confidence because they eliminate many of the seven threats to internal validity (i.e., premeasurement, and interaction, history, maturation, instrumentation, selection, and mortality).

Experiments can be classified according to the degree of realism in the experimental setting or environment. Laboratory experiments are characterized by low degrees of realism. Their advantages are relatively high levels of control but relatively low levels of generalizability. They are most commonly used in evaluating package designs, pricing levels, product preferences (such as taste tests), and advertising testing. Field experiments are characterized by high degrees of realism. These experiments have high levels of generalizability but may suffer from one or more threats to their internal validity. Marketers and advertisers often use marketplace or field experiments to help then answer questions related to new product introduction, product packaging, advertising content, media mix, and advertising spending.

Test markets and electronic test markets are specific types of field experiments. Test market experiments involve duplicating planned or potential national actions in a limited set of geographic areas, typically cities, and then evaluating the results of these actions in terms of business (e.g., sales, distribution) and consumer (i.e., attitudes, brand perceptions) results. An electronic test market conducts the experiment in a limited number of markets in which the television signal to individual homes can be controlled and the purchase behaviors of individuals in those homes can be monitored.

Review Questions

1. What are the four basic steps in an experiment?
2. What is meant by the term *causality*? What are the requirements for one to assume causality?
3. What is an *independent* variable?
4. What is a *dependent* variable?
5. Why is it important that an experiment control threats to internal validity?
6. What is a *premeasurement* threat to internal validity? Provide an original example.
7. What is an *interactional* threat to internal validity? Provide an original example.
8. How are premeasurement and interactional threats to internal validity similar? How are they different?
9. What is an *historical* threat to internal validity? Provide an original example.
10. What is a *maturation* threat to internal validity? Provide an original example.
11. What is an *instrumentation* threat to internal validity? Provide an original example.
12. What is a *selection* threat to internal validity? Provide an original example.
13. What are *selection* and *mortality* threats to internal validity? Provide an original example of each.

14. How does a true experimental design differ from a quasi-experimental design?

15. Name and describe the characteristics of two quasi-experimental designs? What are the strengths and weaknesses of each design?

16. Name and describe the characteristics of four true experimental designs? What are the strengths and weaknesses of each design?

17. What are the characteristics of a factorial design and in what circumstances is this design most appropriate?

18. What is the difference between main effects and interactions effect in a factorial design?

19. What are the relative advantages and disadvantages of laboratory versus field experiments? How do these advantages and disadvantages relate to the concepts of internal and external validity.

20. What are two common threats to an experiment's external validity? How does one control each threat?

21. What are the relative advantages and disadvantages of field, simulated, and electronic test markets?

Application Exercises[20]

1. Spritzz is a wine cooler that has been distributed in three states: Delaware, New Hampshire, and Maine. It has been successful in these states, in spite of the fact that it has never been advertised. Its average share of the wine cooler market in these states is about 15 percent.

   A new management team at Spritzz has identified two goals for the upcoming year. First, they want to increase Spritzz's market share in Delaware, New Hampshire, and Maine. Management believes that one way to increase market share is to begin advertising in these states. Second, management wants to expand Spritzz's area of distribution. They believe that they can successfully market the brand in denser, more urban states such as New York and New Jersey. Management believes that consumers in these areas would respond well to Spritzz's natural taste.

   As the Research Director at Spritzz you realize that you have no way of knowing whether management's assumptions are correct. You convince management to explore the truth of these assumptions using experimentation.

   Prepare a memo to Spritzz management that proposes two experimental designs. The first design should help answer the question: "To what extent will increased advertising in existing markets affect market share?" The second design should address the questions: "How successfully can Spritzz be marketed in urban areas?" Be certain to clearly explain and justify your recommendations. Remember, individuals in management are not researchers, so be certain to provide sufficient detail (explained in clear language) to help them understand both the methodology you recommend and what they will learn from the experiment.

2. You are an advertising researcher who wishes to explore the effect of television commercial exposure on children's play behavior. You think that there is a relationship between exposure to children's toy commercials and possessiveness during play. Specifically, you hypothesize that the more toy commercials a child sees the more possessive he or she will become.

---

[20] All exercises are hypothetical. Data are fictitious and are presented for illustrative purposes only.

You have access to a day care center with 200 children. In addition to a large, common area play room, the center has eight individual rooms. Each individual room has a video tape player, a television set, many toys and games, and a one-way mirror, through which you can unobtrusively watch the children in the room.

Present and defend a research design, including key measures, that you would use to experimentally determine if there is a relationship between exposure to children's toy commercials and possessiveness during play.

3. Pizza Pie, a local pizza chain, wants to determine consumers' reactions to three different coupon offers. Pizza Pie creates two groups of individuals from a list of past customers. Each group of 400 receives one of the coupons. A third coupon is placed in the Sunday paper. A count of redeemed coupons is conducted for two weeks after mailing or publication. Evaluate this methodology. Is it a proper experiment? Can the results confidently be used for future planning? What experimental problems exist? What threats to internal validity are uncontrolled? Evaluate Pizza Pie's approach and then propose an improved experimental design to answer their informational need.

4. The Norris Agency has prepared two new advertising campaigns for their client, the Old World Rice Company. Old World likes the current campaign, but has said, "We'll run either of the new campaigns if you can prove to us that it is better than the current one. But, you pay for the test." The agency has allocated enough money to conduct and analyze a *total* of 1,500 interviews. With this budget constraint in mind, propose and defend an experimental design to determine the campaign that is the strongest in terms of changing consumer attitudes toward the brand and in motivating consumers to purchase the product.

5. Several marketer's use of test marketing was discussed earlier in this chapter. Select one of these examples, or one of your own choosing, and read the entire description of the test market. Then, evaluate the strengths and weaknesses of the approach used? What specific recommendations do you have for increasing confidence in (and generalizability of) the results of the test?

6. Select an advertising-related experiment from one of the following academic journals: *Journal of Advertising*, *Journal of Advertising Research*, *Journal of Marketing*, *Journal of Marketing Research*, *Journal of Consumer Behavior*, and *Journal of Consumer Marketing*. Evaluate the strengths and weaknesses of the design used in the study. What threats to internal validity were controlled for? Which threats were not? Was the design appropriate for the type of information needed and research question explored? Why or why not? Explain and justify your point of view. How does the laboratory field setting of the experiment affect the interpretation and generalizability of the results? If the research was conducted in the field, present a plan for exploring the research question in a laboratory setting. If the research was conducted in the laboratory, present a plan for exploring the research question in a field setting.

7. Electronic test markets generally use a pretest-posttest with control design. Why do you think this design is the most commonly used? What are the relative advantages and disadvantages of this design in an electronic test market setting versus other true experimental designs?

CHAPTER

8 | SAMPLING

Sample—A portion, piece, or segment regarded as representative of the whole; a small part of anything designed to show the style, quality, and nature of the whole.[1]

Advertising research uses sampling, which is the observation or interviewing of a subset of a population to draw conclusions about the larger population. The quality of conclusions drawn from a sample is in great part dependent on the thoughtfulness and appropriateness of the decisions that underlay the sampling process.

After reading this chapter, you will be able to

■ Make well-considered and appropriate sampling decisions.

■ Describe the role of sample definition and sample frames in the sampling process.

■ Explain the difference between probability and nonprobability sampling.

■ Identify the strengths and weaknesses of different forms of probability and nonprobability sampling.

■ Determine sample size.

Sampling is a common process. When you *sample*, you select and examine elements of a population in order to draw conclusions about the larger population of which these elements are members. For example:

• You are unsure whether to take a particular class at school. You talk to seven of the thirty people who took the class last semester. Six of the people provide similar comments: the class was very interesting, the content seems appropriate to your career goals, and the professor was accessible and well prepared. You decide to take the course and find that these observations are indeed true.

---

[1] The author's composite definition based on several standard dictionary definitions of sampling.

- You go to the local Blockbuster Music store. You listen to ten of twelve tracks on a new CD. You like what you hear and decide to buy the CD. When you finally listen to the entire CD you are quite pleased.

- You are shopping in a local supermarket that is promoting grapes this week. They offer you three grapes to taste. The grapes are sweet and delicious. You buy another bunch from the same carton. When you try the grapes at home you find them to be tart and unpleasant to eat.

These situations illustrate three important characteristics of a sample and the sampling process. First, a sample can consist of animate or inanimate objects. A sample does not necessarily have to consist of individuals. Second, a sample can be evaluated in terms of its *efficiency*. A good sample is one in which the cost and time required to select the members of the sample are minimized. Third, a sample can be evaluated in terms of the *generalizations* that it provides. A good sample is one that provides *reliable* generalizations about the population from which it is selected. The first example satisfies each of these criteria. The sample is efficient and provides reliable generalizations about the class. The second example illustrates good generalization but low efficiency; nearly the entire population (in this case, songs on the CD) was included in the sample. The third example illustrates good efficiency but poor reliability of generalization.

Successful sampling requires a balance of efficiency and reliability of the generalization. A sample's ability to balance these needs, that is, to efficiently gather information and to provide accurate generalizations about the sampled population, increases when key issues in the sampling process are addressed in a sequential and systematic manner. The sequence of issues commonly addressed in the sampling process are shown in Figure 8.1 (page 168). The remainder of this chapter follows the flow of this figure and discusses each issue as follows: First, we discuss how to determine the nature of the surveyed population, that is whether a sample or a census should be used. Next, we discuss a target population definition, a task required for both probability and nonprobability sampling. This discussion is followed by an exploration of probability sampling, specifically the selection of the sample frame, the different types of probability samples, and how to determine appropriate sample size. Finally, we discuss the different types of nonprobability samples and how to determine sample size for nonprobability samples.

SAMPLE OR CENSUS

The first step in the sampling process decides whether a sample will be used. A decision to take a sample results in a *subset* of the population of interest participating in the research. A decision to take a census results in every member of the population of interest participating in the research.

A sample, rather than a census, is used in the vast majority of research situations. When dealing with large populations, such as adults aged 18 and older or purchasers of a particular product, the time and cost involved in surveying all members of the target population exceeds the value of any information or insights obtained from the research. Additionally, even if funds and time were available, a census of the popula-

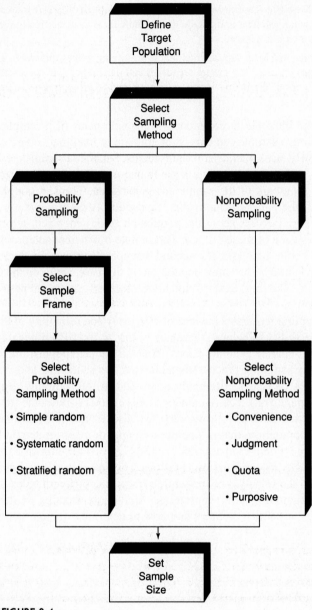

FIGURE 8.1
The sampling process.

tion may still be impossible. Members of the population may be out of the country, institutionalized or otherwise inaccessible. Beyond target population size and accessibility there are times when a census destroys the population so that additional research is impossible. Several experimental designs discussed in the prior chapter, for example, would not be possible if all members of the population were surveyed before the treatment. Finally, as you will see later in this chapter, there is rarely a need

to take a census. A well-selected sample can provide information comparable to that of a full census.

There are some situations, however, when a census is preferable. A census is preferable to a sample when

- the population of interest is small and identifiable,
- sampling might eliminate important cases from the study, and
- credibility requires the consideration of all members of the target population.

For example, a chain of restaurants might have thirty-five franchisees. A survey of the franchisees' reactions to the chain's new advertising campaign would likely be a census. The sample of franchisees is small, all franchisees' opinions would be heard and the study would be more credible than a sample because all the the franchisees participated (i.e., no one can say "Well, the results are wrong. Just look at who was interviewed. They didn't ask me!").

DEFINE TARGET POPULATION

Once it is determined that a sample is appropriate, the first step in the actual sampling process requires that you define the *target population,* the group of individuals or things in which you are interested. This is a critical step for all forms of advertising research and is therefore required for all types of samples. The adequacy of a target population definition is evaluated in terms of how well the definition (1) unambiguously describes the group of interest and (2) serves to differentiate those things or individuals who are of interest from those who are not. The following two examples illustrate the care needed to satisfy these criteria.

An Inanimate Population

Imagine a brainstorming session in which account executives and creatives are trying to identify new benefits and competitive positionings for their client, a manufacturer of ibuprofen-based pain relievers. One of the creatives says: "Price is always an important benefit. Especially when we can relate it to value. So, can we make the claim that our product is the lowest priced name brand pain reliever?" It is agreed that research will be conducted to determine the viability of this claim. The agency researcher says that she will "obtain a random sample of the retail prices of the leading brands of pain relievers in stores across the United States."

Ambiguity and incompleteness make this target population definition inadequate. Consider each of the key components of the definition:

- *Retail price*—Does this refer to the regular selling price or a sale price? Is the retail price the manufacturer's recommended price, perhaps as marked on the package, or the actual price at which the outlet normally sells the product?
- *Leading brands*—On what basis will leading brands be identified and selected? Is "leading brand" defined on the basis of sales, distribution, advertising expenditures, or consumer awareness?
- *Stores*—What types of stores will be sampled? Any store that sells pain relievers? Drug stores only? Drug stores and grocery stores only?

- *Pain relievers*—Any product designed to relieve any type of pain? Ibuprofen-based products only? Any product containing aspirin, acetaminophen or ibuprofin? What about combination products, for example, acetaminophen plus anithistimine?
- *Across the United States*—Where across the United States? In every city? In major metropolitan areas? In cities over or under a certain size?

Every combination of answers to the prior questions leads to a different definition of the target population. The "right" target population definition is the one that all involved in the research agree unambiguously defines the target population and best responds to the informational need motivating the research. In this example, the research team might decide to refine the prior target population definition as follows:

The research will determine the average price of leading brands of pain relievers where

- *Price* refers to the usual selling price as indicated on the item's shelf description,
- *Pain relievers* refer to any aspirin, acetaminophen- or ibuprofen-based product specifically sold to relieve headache or muscle pain and the product cannot contain any additional ingredients beyond aspirin, acetaminophen or ibuprofen,
- *Leading brands* are defined as the five top selling brands of pain relievers (as defined previously) based on 1996 unit sales.

Prices will be sampled in grocery and drug stores in twelve cities where

- *Grocery store* refers to any store whose merchandise primarily consists of food items. This includes traditional grocery stores and includes some warehouse stores. Drug store refers to any store not included in the prior definition that dispenses prescription medicine.
- *Twelve cities* refer to four cities among the top ten cities as measured in the 1990 population census, four cities among those ranked eleven to twenty, and four cities among those ranked twenty-one to thirty.

Finally, prices of the following sized packages will be sampled: 100 and 250 regular tablet and thirty tablet gelcap. These are the leading sizes based on unit sales.

As can be seen, this target population definition explicitly and unambiguously (with explanation and justification from external sources) defines the target population.

A Human Population

Populations of individuals are typically defined in some combination of demographic, geographic, product, and category relevant behaviors.

- The *demographic* component of the target population definition specifies relevant age, gender, income, or other related characteristics of the population of interest.
- The *geographic* component specifies the geographic area(s) in which the target population resides. The geographic area can, for example, reflect where a particular product has distribution, where the advertising campaign has aired, or the particular cities or states where the target audience resides.
- The *behavioral* component specifies relevant category- or product-related behaviors. Here, for example, the population of interest can be defined in terms of purchase patterns (i.e., "brand loyalists," defined as individuals whose three of the past four purchases were of the same brand), category participation (i.e., have taken three or more cruises in the past ten years), or purchase frequency (i.e., have purchased four six-packs of imported beer within the past two weeks).

Consider the following hypothetical circumstance. Imagine that within the past six months Marvel Comics has added five additional pages of advertising to its series of X-Men comics. These pages have been added on a test basis and were only included in comics sent to retail outlets and subscribing homes that are in the city of Chicago. Marvel now wants to assess perceptions of the advertising in these comics, specifically, whether readers believe there is *currently* too much, not enough, or just the right amount of advertising in these comics. The opinions of individuals who read the test issues will be compared to those who receive the regular issue. Two population definitions are required, one for the test and one for the nontest conditions. Six researchers each present a different definition of the target population for the test condition.

Sample definition A: Purchasers of Marvel X-Men comic books.

Sample definition B: Subscribers to Marvel X-Men comics.

Sample definition C: Readers of Marvel X-Men comic books.

Sample definition D: Individuals who have read any Marvel X-Men comic book within the past 30 days.

Sample definition E: Individuals between the ages of 7 and 17 who have read at least three new issues of Marvel X-Men comics within the past four months.

Sample definition F: Individuals over the age of 7 who have read at least three new issues of Marvel X-Men comics within the past four months.

All six definitions are inadequate because they fail to describe the geographic boundaries of the test area (for example, the city of Chicago). Additionally, each fails to (1) clearly identify and define the individuals who would provide the most relevant information on the test issues of X-Men comic advertising and (2) separate individuals of interest from those not of interest.

- Definitions A and B are too broad. A "purchaser" of a comic book is not necessarily the reader of the comic. Similarly, a subscriber is not necessarily the reader (for example, if the parent subscribes to the comic on behalf of the child.) Since, it is the *reader's* opinions that are of interest these definitions are unacceptable.

- Definitions C and D are vague and ambiguous. In these definitions, a "reader" is anyone who has *ever* read an X-Men comic. This includes those who have read the most recent issue and those who read an issue four years ago but not since. Similarly, "any X-Men comics within the past 30 days" does not necessarily mean that the comic read is one of the more recent issues. "Any X-Men comic" can refer to a recent issue or an issue that is ten or more years old. These definitions are inadequate because Marvel is interested in responses to advertising in recent issues.

- Definition E solves many problems of the prior definitions. This definition defines a reader in terms of recent reading ("new issues") and the three of four issue criterion helps to assure that the reader has adequate experience with the test issues so that reasonable opinions can be formed. However, the age boundaries make this definition unacceptable. This sample definition would bias the survey because younger and older individuals meeting the readership criterion are excluded from the study.

- Definition F is the best option among the presented definitions. The lower age boundary is reasonable from an interviewing perspective. It is very difficult to interview individuals below this age. However, while this definition adequately defines the sample population in terms of recent readership it does not provide any guidance in terms of demographic or geographic information. The term, "individuals," for example is still quite vague.

A more complete target population definition might be:

> Men and women over the age of seven who have read at least three new issues of Marvel X-Men comics within the past four months. These individuals will either (a) obtain their comics by subscription and reside within the Chicago city limits or (b) purchase the minimum of three new issues of X-Men comics from retail outlets found within the Chicago city limits.

SELECT SAMPLING METHOD

Once the population is defined, you then determine which of two types of sampling methods will be used to identify items or individuals for study inclusion. A *probability sample* is a sample in which each individual, household, or item (generally called a sample element) comprising the universe from which the sample is drawn has a known chance or probability of being selected for inclusion in the research. The selection of sample elements is done purely by chance, for example, with a table of random numbers or through random digit dialing. When a probability sample is used, the selection of elements from the sample universe continues until the required number of elements has been selected and observed or interviewed. A *nonprobability sample* is a sample of elements that is not selected strictly by chance from the universe of all individuals, but are rather selected in some less random, more purposeful way. Here, the selection of elements for study inclusion may be made on the basis of convenience or judgment.

The choice of a sampling method is influenced by several factors: the type of generalization required, the researcher's need to minimize sampling error, study timing, and cost. The relative advantages and disadvantages of probability or nonprobability samples mirror each other in these areas.

- Probability samples let a researcher estimate sampling error, calculate reliability, statistically determine the sample size required for a specified degree of confidence, and confidently generalize the findings to the sample universe. Research using probability samples, however, tend to be expensive and take considerable time to plan and conduct.
- Nonprobability samples are quick and inexpensive to obtain. Research conducted among nonprobability samples is easy to design and carry out. However, a researcher using a nonprobabilty sample cannot calculate sampling error or reliability and has very limited confidence in generalizing the findings to the sample universe.

PROBABILITY SAMPLING

Probability sampling is the process of selecting elements or groups of elements (such as households or individuals) from the population described in the target population definition in a way that gives each element in the population a known, calculable non-zero probability of inclusion in the sample.[2]

The first step in obtaining a probability sample is selection of the sample frame. (Sample frames are not necessary for nonprobability samples.)

---

[2] Martin R. Frankel and Lester R. Frankel, "Probability Sampling," In Robert Ferber ed., *Handbook of Marketing Research* (New York, NY: McGraw-Hill Book Company, 1974), Section 2, p 231.

Sample Frame

A *sample frame* specifies the method you will use to identify the households, individuals, or other elements specified in the target population definition. You can take one of two approaches to specifying the sample frame. You can either construct or obtain a list to represent the target population or, when lists are incomplete or unavailable, you can specify a procedure such as random digit dialing for identifying and contacting target individuals.

The adequacy of a sample frame is evaluated in terms of how well the frame represents the target population.

A perfect sampling frame is identical to the target population, that is, the sample frame contains every population element once and only once *and* only population elements are contained in the sampling frame. Additionally, a perfect sample frame contains complete and accurate information on each element in the target population. As might be expected, perfect sample frames are quite rare in actual practice.[3] Typically, sample frames will either overregister or underregister the target population.[4] A sample frame that consists of all the elements in the target population plus additional elements suffers from *overregistration*. An overregistered sample frame is too broad. A sample frame that contains fewer elements than the target population suffers from *underregistration*. An underregistered sample frame is too narrow and excludes elements from the target population. Examples of sample frames having under- and overregistration as well as perfect registration are provided in Figure 8.2 (page 174).

Neither over- nor underregistration is necessarily fatal to the integrity of an advertising research study, but knowledge of their existence permits you to adjust your planning to improve the sampling process. If overregistration is believed to be the case, and the elements that fall outside the target population can be identified, then it might be possible to eliminate the effects of overregistration by modifying your sampling plan or by using a screener to eliminate individuals not in the target population. If underregistration is believed to be the case, then it might be possible to modify the sample frame by updating or some other procedure that adds omitted units.

Forms of Probability Sampling

Once you know the characteristics of the population of interest (the target population) and how the population will be identified (the sample frame), you next need to determine the specific probability sampling procedure by which individuals are selected for study inclusion. The three most common forms of probability sampling used in advertising research are: simple random, systematic random, and stratified random.[5]

---

[3] Rober A. Peterson, *Marketing Research* (Plano, TX: Business Publications, Inc., 1982), 344.

[4] Richard M. Jaeger, *Sampling in Education and the Social Sciences* (New York, NY: Longman, 1984), 28.

[5] A fourth sampling method is cluster sampling, which is primarily used for research with data collection needs that require personal, at-home interviews. Cluster sampling is appropriate to this form of data collection because it shifts data collection to groups of sampling units rather than individual sampling units. Cluster sampling works as follows: First, the universe described in the sample universe definition is divided into groups, or clusters where every element of the universe is contained in one and only one cluster. Second, clusters are examined for internal representativness. Each cluster should be a "miniuniverse," that is, the characteristics of the cluster should mirror the characteristics of the total universe. Third, clusters are examined for external comparability. Clusters should be equivalent to each other with regard to important characteristics. Fourth, one or more of the clusters is selected to represent the total universe. Fifth, simple, systematic, or stratified sampling is used to select elements within the cluster. For further discussion of cluster sampling see Thomas T. Semon, "Basic Concepts," In Robert Ferber ed., *Handbook of Marketing Research* (New York, NY: McGraw-Hill Book Company, 1974), Section 2, 217–29.

Perfect Registration

A manufacturer of paper goods wishes to conduct a survey of attitudes and purchasing behaviors among his current clients. The target population is defined as companies that have purchased at least $100 worth of goods within the past three months. The names of all clients meeting these criteria are selected from the manufacturer's data base and are placed on a separate list (the sample frame) from which study participants will be selected.

Overregistration: Sample Frame Larger Than Target Population

You have just completed a six-month advertising test in metropolitan Atlanta and wish to determine levels of advertising and product awareness as well as brand perceptions. You decide to use random digit dialing among prefixes that are identified as "Atlanta." There are two overregistration problems. First, because of the way telephone companies assign telephone prefixes, not all telephones with an Atlanta prefix actually are in metropolitan Atlanta. Second, the research should be conducted among individuals who have lived in metropolitan Atlanta for at least six months, the time of the advertising test. Random digit dialing will not discriminate between those who have and have not resided for the required amount of time in Atlanta. A screener can be used to adjust the sample frame to better correspond with the target population.

Underregistration: Sample Frame Smaller Than Target Population

You want to assess teachers' reactions to corporate-sponsored educational materials. You select a list of members of the American Federation of Teachers as the sample frame. This frame suffers from underregistration because not all teachers are members of the Federation.

You want to conduct a telephone survey of individuals residing in New York. One potential sample frame might be the telephone book. However, this sample frame is incomplete and suffers from underregistration because a telephone book does not contain individuals with unlisted telephone numbers.

FIGURE 8.2
Relationship of target population and sample frame.

Simple Random Samples   *Simple random samples* are frequently used in advertising research. Here, each member of the population (as represented in the sample frame) has a known and equal chance of being selected for inclusion in the research.[6] You can think of random sampling as a drawing where the name of each member of the population is placed on a ticket and then placed into a drum. Individual names are selected from the drum. Every name in the drum has an equal chance of being selected. In practice, random number tables are used instead of drums and lotteries to select study participants from the sample frame (see Table B.1 in Appendix B).

Simple random sampling works as follows: Imagine that the S. E. Johnson Company wants to measure levels of Raid purchase after a six-month advertising test. The S. E. Johnson Company will ask the primary shopper in each sampled household: "How many cans of Raid have been purchased for your household in the past thirty days?" The target population consists of households with or without children in both urban and suburban areas. In this example the sample frame and target population are identical and consist of the twenty households shown in Table 8.1. As you can see from the bottom of the table, if we were to interview every household we would find that the average number of cans purchased is 2.0.

---

[6] The chance or probability of being selected is calculated as $^1\!/_N$ where N represents the total number of elements in the sample frame.

TABLE 8.1	Hypothetical Sample Universe for Study of Raid Purchase Behaviors		

Household Number	Geography	Presence of Children	Cans of Raid Purchased
1	urban	no	2
2	urban	no	0
3	urban	no	3
4	urban	no	2
5	urban	no	2
6	urban	yes	2
7	urban	yes	2
8	urban	yes	2
9	urban	yes	3
10	urban	yes	2
11	suburban	no	2
12	suburban	no	1
13	suburban	no	1
14	suburban	no	3
15	suburban	no	2
16	suburban	yes	2
17	suburban	yes	2
18	suburban	yes	2
19	suburban	yes	2
20	suburban	yes	3
Overall Average:			**2.0**

Nevertheless a simple random sample can provide comparable estimates without having to survey the entire population. A table of random numbers can be used to select simple random samples of five households. As shown in the following table, different random samples taken from the universe shown in Table 8.1 provide purchase levels comparable to the population as a whole.

Household Numbers	Average Cans of Raid Purchased
1, 4, 7, 11, 16	2.0
3, 7, 12, 17, 19	2.0
5, 12, 14, 15, 20	2.2

Thus, by randomly selecting households from the sample universe we can accurately estimate the purchase behaviors of the entire target population. In this circumstance, a simple random sample satisfies the two characteristics of good sampling described earlier in this chapter: it is efficient and it provides reliable generalizations about the population from which the sample is taken.

Systematic Random Samples   A variation of a simple random sample is a *systematic random sample*. Systematic random samples typically provide data identical to

simple random samples with the added advantage of simplicity—no table of random numbers is needed.

Like a simple random sample, a systematic sample begins with a sample frame, typically a list that represents the sample universe. The following steps are taken once the list is obtained:

- Count the number of elements on the list,
- Determine the desired sample size,
- Compute a skip interval,
- Select a random place on the list,
- Select and interview each element at the appropriate skip interval.

For example, imagine that we had a list of 10,000 doctors and required a final sample size of 500. The skip interval would be twenty (calculated as 10,000 ÷ 500). We would begin at a random place on the list, perhaps at doctor number 16 and then select every twentieth doctor from this point on (for example, doctor 36, 56, etc.).

Refer again to the universe shown in Table 8.1. As shown in the following table a systematic sample provides accurate estimates of the overall population average. (The first number in each systematic random sample of households is the starting point. The skip interval is four.)

Household Numbers	Average Cans of Raid Purchased
1, 5, 9, 13, 17	2.0
2, 6, 10, 14, 18	1.8
11, 15, 19, 3, 7	2.2

Stratified Random Samples   In the prior example, simple and systematic random sampling techniques worked well. They were efficient and provided reliable generalizations about the total population. However, these forms of sampling worked well *only* because the universe was homogeneous with respect to what was being measured. That is, there was little variation in purchase patterns among households. The *overall* average of 2.0 cans of Raid purchased did not significantly vary in response to the two subgroup characteristics of geographic location and presence of children, as shown in the following table.

Subgroup	Average Cans of Raid Purchased
Urban	2.0
Suburban	2.0
No children present	1.8
Children present	2.2
Urban, no children present	1.8
Urban, children present	2.2
Suburban, no children present	1.8
Suburban, children present	2.2

TABLE 8.2 Hypothetical Sample Universe for Study of Furniture Wax and Polish Purchase Behaviors

Household Number	Geography	Presence of Children	Cans of Wax or Polish Purchased
1	urban	no	0
2	urban	no	1
3	urban	no	2
4	urban	no	1
5	urban	no	1
6	urban	yes	2
7	urban	yes	3
8	urban	yes	2
9	urban	yes	2
10	urban	yes	1
11	suburban	no	2
12	suburban	no	4
13	suburban	no	4
14	suburban	no	5
15	suburban	no	5
16	suburban	yes	6
17	suburban	yes	5
18	suburban	yes	4
19	suburban	yes	5
20	suburban	yes	7
Overall Average:			**3.1**

However, simple and systematic random samples provide fewer reliable generalizations about the total population when population homogeneity decreases and differences among population subgroups increase.

Consider the data shown in Table 8.2. The target population and sample frame consists of the same twenty households used in the Raid example. Imagine that now the S. E. Johnson Company wants to assess household purchase levels of furniture waxes and polishes over the past three months. As shown in the following table, simple random samples from this universe vary greatly and provide inconsistent and inaccurate generalizations of the purchase behavior of the total population. (A similar pattern would be expected had the households been selected using a systematic random sample.)

Household Numbers	Average Cans of Wax or Polish Purchased
1, 5, 7, 13, 17	2.6
10, 11, 17, 19, 20	4.0
3, 12, 14, 16, 19	4.4

Simple random sampling works poorly in this case because there is wide variability in the population, *and* this variability is due to identifiable demographic or ge-

ographic characteristics, in this case, geographic location and presence of children. Purchase frequency is not at all consistent among these factors.

Subgroup	Average Cans of Wax or Polish Purchased
Urban	1.5
Suburban	4.7
No children present	2.5
Children present	3.7
Urban, no children present	1.0
Urban, children present	2.0
Suburban, no children present	4.0
Suburban, children present	5.4

Stratified random sampling must be used when you suspect that there is large variation in the variable being studied and that this variation is due to or correlates with observable characteristics in the universe being sampled. Given that you might suspect that households without children would use the product less than households with children (fewer fingerprints) and that urban households would use the product less than suburban households (smaller homes and apartments with less furniture) you might decide to stratify the sample, that is, divide the households in the target universe into four classes (or strata) and then randomly sample from each strata individually.[7] Each stratum is treated and sampled as if it were an independent universe.

Stratified sampling is thus a three-step process:

- First, the classification criteria that define the strata are identified. These classification criteria should define independent strata that do not overlap. The classification criteria for the population shown in Table 8.2 are residence type and presence of children. Taken together these criteria result in four independent strata: Stratum 1—urban without children, Stratum 2—urban with children, Stratum 3—suburban without children, and Stratum 4—suburban with children.
- Second, each element in the sample frame is assigned to one and only one stratum. The households shown in Table 8.2 would be assigned as follows: Stratum 1—households 1–5, Stratum 2—households 6–10, Stratum 3—households 11–15 and Stratum 4—households 16–20.
- Third, independent random samples (using either simple or systematic sampling methods) are selected from each stratum.

The third step, sampling from each stratum, presents two options regarding the number of elements selected *from each stratum*. Either proportionate or disproportionate sampling may be used.

Proportionate stratified sampling selects individuals in proportion to their stratum's size within the total target population. For example, each of the four strata in the

---

[7] The notion underlying stratified sampling is that variation within a strata will be less than the variation among strata. In other words, levels of the measured variable should be relatively homogeneous within any specific strata. If this is not the case, then the statification used to divide the population is inappropriate. Note how in our example the deviation within each individual stratum is less than the deviation of the population as a whole.

universe shown in Table 8.2 represents 25 percent of the total population. As a result, proportionate stratified sampling would select 25 percent of the total study sample from each stratum. Proportionate stratified sampling works well when the total number of strata is small and the sizes of the strata are relatively equivalent.

Problems arise with proportionate stratified sampling when the absolute number of strata is large and when strata sizes are not comparable. When some strata are small, proportionate sampling may not result in sufficient numbers of observations or interviews in these smaller strata to permit reliable data analysis. In these cases, disproportionate stratified sampling is used.

Disproportionate stratified sampling selects a predetermined number of elements from each stratum despite the relative size of those strata. Selection is based on analytical considerations, that is, the sample size required for reliable data analysis, as opposed to population considerations, that is, the size of the stratum within the total universe. When disproportionate stratified sampling is used, the data obtained from an individual stratum must be weighted to compensate for stratum size differentials in the actual sample universe before total sample findings are reported. An example of disproportionate stratified sampling and the weighting of strata data to determine overall population characteristics is shown in Figure 8.3.

Kylito's Pizza wishes to determine consumers' perceptions of product quality. The sample universe has been divided into the following three strata:

- Individuals who have tried and repurchased the product at least once (estimated to be 65 percent of the population);

- Individuals who have tried the product but have not repurchased (estimated to be 30 percent of the population);

- Individuals who have never tried the product (estimated to be 5 percent of the population).

For analytical purposes 100 individuals in each strata will be interviewed and asked: "On a scale of 1 to 10, where ten is the most positive, how would you rate the quality of Kylito's Pizza?"

The mean score for each stratum is

Stratum	Number Sampled	Percent of Universe	Average Quality Rating
Repurchasers	100	65%	7.7
Rejectors	100	30	2.3
Non-triers	100	5	4.7
Overall Population Average:			**5.93**

The average overall population average of 5.93 is calculated as: $(7.7 \times 0.65) + (2.3 \times 0.30) + (4.7 \times 0.05)$.

FIGURE 8.3
Disproportionate sample selection.

Sample Selection Bias in Probability Samples

The goal of probability sampling is the selection of a group of individuals or objects that represent the population from which they were selected. Researchers need to be careful, however, that individuals or objects identified for participation in the research are selected in a way that does not introduce bias. The elimination of bias is important, because only without bias can a researcher confidently generalize the research results to the sampled population.

Sample bias occurs when members of the population of interest are selected in violation of the basic principle of random sampling, that is, where each observation has a known and equal chance of being selected for inclusion in the sample. The use of telephone books as the source of numbers for a telephone survey is, for example, likely to lead to sample bias. Even if random sampling is used to select the names and numbers from the telephone book, the sample is still biased because those who do not have listed numbers are systematically excluded from the research. These individuals can never be selected. (This is the reason for random digit dialing.) Additional examples of sample selection bias are[8]

> Imagine that you wish to select a random sample of students from your university. You make a conscientious effort to interview every tenth student who enters the cafeteria. You chose the cafeteria because most students go there at least once during the day. However, because different types of students visit the cafeteria with different frequencies, and not all visit at least once, the sample would be biased. It would over represent the type of student who uses the cafeteria.
>
> Now imagine that the *entire* student body is gathered in the stadium to watch the championship football game. You decide to interview a random sample of the students. However, you avoid interviewing those dressed in "hippie clothes" because you feel they might not take the research seriously and you avoid interviewing those in the fraternity and sorority seats because you feel their opinions are not indicative of the "average" student. The systematic exclusion of these individuals violates the principle of random selection and introduces a great deal of bias into the research.

In sum, sample selection bias prevents the conduct of sound research and can lead to inappropriate conclusions about a sampled population. The sampling planning process should therefore include an explicit discussion of how sample bias might be introduced into the study and how strict adherence to random sampling techniques can eliminate identified potential sources of bias.

Sample Size in Probability Samples

Confidence in the generalizations drawn from a probability sample is directly affected by sample size. Generally, larger samples permit greater confidence in population estimates and generalizations. But, increases in confidence do not increase in a linear, one-to-one relationship with increases in sample size. Quite large increases in sample size are required for small increases in confidence. The goal in determining sample size, therefore, is the determination of the minimal sample size that will provide the desired degree of confidence in the population estimates.

The concept of confidence in sample estimates and generalizations is expressed in terms of the confidence interval and the confidence level. A *confidence interval* is an es-

---

[8] These examples are adapted from Earl Babbie, *The Practice of Social Research, Fourth Edition* (Belmont, CA: Wadsworth Publishing Company, 1986), 140–41.

timate, plus or minus, of the value of the population estimate; it states the range in which we believe the true population estimate lies. For example, it is common to read or hear that: "Eighty percent of all adults surveyed agree that there need to be major changes to the income tax code. The confidence interval is ± 2 percent." This means that the true percentage of voters agreeing with the statement probably lies between 78 percent and 82 percent. The *confidence level* is the mathematical expression of our confidence that the population estimate lies within the confidence interval. For example, a confidence level of 95 percent means that there is a 95 percent probability that the population estimate from the research lies within the identified confidence interval.

Sample size is determined in light of confidence intervals and confidence levels. Greater precision in either or both levels requires larger sample sizes. Thus, the most important step in sample size determination occurs when you explicitly state your desired confidence interval and confidence level. Once this is done, there are several ways for determining the appropriate sample size.

Sample Size When the Estimate Is a Proportion When the results of a survey question are presented as proportions, then a table such as that shown in Table 8.3 may be used to determine the appropriate sample size. (All of the information presented in this table is based on a 95 percent confidence level.) To use this table you need to have some estimate of the sample's level of response. For example, assume that there are three agree/disagree key questions on a study and that you expect 10 percent of the sample to agree with one question, 20 percent to agree with the second and 85 percent to agree with the third. Additionally, assume that you want to have a small confidence interval, no more than ± 3% for any of the three independent questions. The table

TABLE 8.3 Confidence Intervals for Various Sample Sizes and Expected Level of Response (Confidence Level = 95 Percent)

Sample Size	5% or 95%	10% or 90%	15% or 85%	20% or 80%	25% or 75%	30% or 70%	35% or 65%	40% or 60%	45% or 55%	50%
100	4.4	6.0	7.1	8.0	8.7	9.2	9.5	9.8	9.9	10.0
200	3.1	4.7	5.0	5.7	6.1	6.5	6.7	6.9	7.0	7.2
300	2.5	3.5	4.2	4.6	5.0	5.3	5.5	5.7	5.7	5.8
400	2.2	3.0	3.6	4.0	4.3	4.6	4.8	4.9	5.0	5.0
500	1.9	3.0	3.2	3.6	3.9	4.1	4.3	4.4	4.5	4.5
600	1.8	2.5	2.9	3.3	3.5	3.7	3.9	4.0	4.0	4.1
700	1.6	2.3	2.7	3.0	3.3	3.5	3.6	3.7	3.8	3.8
800	1.5	2.2	2.5	2.8	3.1	3.2	3.4	3.5	3.5	3.5
900	1.4	2.0	2.4	2.7	2.9	3.1	3.2	3.3	3.3	3.3
1,000	1.4	1.9	2.3	2.5	2.7	2.9	3.0	3.1	3.1	3.2
1,500	1.1	1.5	1.8	2.0	2.2	2.4	2.5	2.5	2.6	2.6
2,000	1.0	1.3	1.6	1.8	1.9	2.0	2.1	2.2	2.2	2.2
3,000	.8	1.1	1.3	1.5	1.6	1.7	1.7	1.8	1.8	1.8
5,000	.6	.8	1.0	1.1	1.2	1.3	1.3	1.4	1.4	1.4

shown in Table 8.3 indicates that a confidence interval of no more than ± 3% for an expected response level of

- 10 percent requires a sample of 400,
- 20 percent requires a sample of 700, and
- 85 percent requires a sample of about 600.

Given these parameters, a sample of about 700 is needed (the largest of the three required sample sizes).

There are times when you will want to set a different confidence level and a table such as that shown in Table 8.3 is not available. In these cases, sample size can be determined through the formula:

$$sample\ size = \left(\frac{z}{e}\right)^2 \bullet (p) \bullet (1 - p)$$

where z represents the z score for a specific confidence level and e represents the desired confidence interval. Z scores for specific confidence levels are as follows:

Confidence Level	Z Score
99%	2.57
95%	1.96
90%	1.64

(A detailed discussion of the derivation of Z scores and confidence levels is presented in Chapter 16.) For example, imagine that you ask a group of respondents "Are you aware of advertising for Lanier office equipment?" and you anticipate the proportion saying "yes" to be 35 percent. Additionally, you want to be 99 percent confident that the actual proportion estimated by the research is within ± 2%. The required sample size for these desired levels of confidence would be

$$sample\ size = \left(\frac{z}{e}\right)^2 \bullet (p) \bullet (1 - p)$$

$$= \left(\frac{2.57}{.02}\right)^2 \bullet (.35) \bullet (1 - .35)$$

$$= (128.5)^2 \bullet (.35) \bullet (.65)$$

The sample size is large because the confidence level and confidence interval demand a high level of precision. Sample size drops dramatically, however, when the confidence interval is raised to ± 4% and the confidence level is lowered to 95%:

$$sample\ size = \left(\frac{z}{e}\right)^2 \bullet (p) \bullet (1 - p)$$

$$= \left(\frac{1.96}{.04}\right)^2 \bullet (.35) \bullet (1 - .35)$$

$$= (49)^2 \bullet (.35) \bullet (.65)$$

$$= 546$$

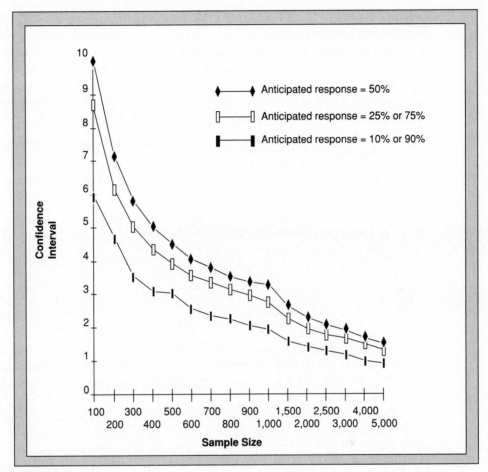

FIGURE 8.4
Relationship of sample size and confidence level at three levels of anticipated response and 95 percent confidence level.

Table 8.3 also illustrates this relationship between confidence intervals and sample size. As can be seen, when we hold the confidence level constant, it takes a fourfold increase in sample size to reduce the confidence interval by half. For example, at the 20 percent level of expected response a sample of 100 provides a confidence interval of ± 8%, a sample of 400 provides a confidence interval of ± 4% and a sample of about 1600 provides a confidence interval of about ± 2%. The relationship between accuracy (as reflected in smaller confidence intervals) and sample size is illustrated in Figure 8.4. As can be seen, large increases in accuracy are achieved by small increases in sample size up to sample sizes of about 1,000. However, increases in accuracy slow significantly at sample sizes of more than 1,000. This is why most consumer, marketing, and advertising research studies rarely exceed a sample of 1,000 individuals.[9]

[9] The relationship between sample size and confidence interval is independent of the size of the target population. A sample of 1,000 will provide the same confidence interval regardless of whether the target population consists of 10,000, 1,000,000, or 10,000,000 individuals.

Sample Size When the Estimate Is a Mean Sample sizes for estimates that are means or averages can be computed. In these cases an estimate of the range of response is required in addition to the specification of a confidence level and confidence interval. (The range of response is expressed as a "standard deviation." See Chapter 15 for a detailed discussion of the computation and interpretation of this measure.) Because the population standard deviation is rarely known, it is typically estimated in one of three ways:

1. Estimate the standard deviation from a prior, similar study conducted among the same population,

2. Conduct a small pilot study, use the standard deviation from the pilot study as the estimate of the population standard deviation,

3. Divide the range of response by four, that is, add the values of the two most extreme response options and then divide the sum by four.

Once the standard deviation is estimated and the confidence interval and confidence level are determined, sample size can be estimated through the formula:

$$sample\ size = \frac{z^2 \cdot s^2}{e^2}$$

where, as in the previous formula, z represents the z score for a specific confidence level (taken from the table shown earlier) and e represents the desired confidence interval. The new term in this equation, s, represents the estimate of the population standard deviation.

Consider an example similar to the one just discussed. Imagine that you ask a group of respondents "On a scale of one to five, please rate the believability of Lanier office product advertising?" You want to be 95 percent confident that the average rating estimated by the research is within plus or minus .2 points of the true population average. You estimate the sample standard deviation to be 1.5, derived by adding the extremes of the rating scale and dividing by 4 (i.e., $5 + 1 \div 4 = 1.5$). The required sample size for these desired levels of confidence would be 216, calculated as:

$$sample\ size = \frac{z^2 \cdot s^2}{e^2}$$
$$= \frac{1.96^2 \cdot 1.5^2}{.2^2}$$
$$= \frac{3.84 \cdot 2.25}{.04}$$
$$= 216$$

As with the prior formula, changes to the confidence level and confidence interval result in changes to required sample size. For example, the required sample size increases significantly if we raise the confidence level to 99 percent and lower the confidence interval to .1:

$$sample\ size = \frac{z^2 \cdot s^2}{e^2}$$
$$= \frac{2.56^2 \cdot 1.5^2}{.1^2}$$
$$= \frac{6.55 \cdot 2.25}{.01}$$
$$= 1474$$

In sum, the relationship between sample size and accuracy in the survey results is an important consideration when attempting to balance sample size and confidence. When evaluating alternative sample sizes you need to ask: "Is the increased cost of precision justified by the increased costs of data collection? For example, is a reduction in the confidence level from ± 3% to ± 1.5% justified given a quadrupled increase in the cost of interviewing?"

The Central Limit Theorem

Confidence intervals are one consideration in the selection of sample size. As you have seen, confidence intervals decrease as the overall sample size increases. An additional consideration in the selection of sample size relates to the types of statistical tests that can be used to analyze the data. Some statistical tests are only appropriate for samples of thirty or more while other tests are only appropriate for smaller samples of less than thirty (see Chapter 16). The differentiation between large and small samples is a reflection of the Central Limit Theorem that states that when the sample is large, at least thirty, the distribution of the sample means (or averages) closely approaches a normal distribution without regard to the distribution of the population from which the sample is drawn. Thus, because sample size affects statistical tests and the interpretation of results, the implications of the Central Limit Theorem for sample selection should be considered during development of the sampling plan and determination of sample size.[10]

NONPROBABILITY SAMPLING

The previous section discussed three types of probability samples: simple random, systematic random, and stratified random. Each of these forms of sampling obtains probability samples because all elements in the defined universe have a known and equal chance of being selected.

However, in spite of its advantages, not all advertising research uses probability sampling. Some informational needs do not require the precision and generalizability of probability samples while other needs cannot justify the time and expense of probability sampling. In these cases, other forms of selection are used. These forms of selection, la-

---

[10] For a more detailed discussion of the Central Limit Theorem see James T. Walker, *Using Statistics for Psychological Research* (New York, NY: Holt Rinehart and Winston, 1985), 169–72.

beled nonprobability sampling, select elements in some nonrandom way. The major forms of nonprobability sampling are convenience, judgment, quota, and purposive.

Forms of Nonprobability Sampling

Convenience Sampling *Convenience sampling* is just what the name implies: study participants are selected because they are convenient and accessible. Interviewing friends, associates or individuals walking down the street are forms of this type of sampling as are selecting the last thirty transactions because the records are handy. Convenience sampling, as might be expected, is uncomplicated, quick, and low in cost.

Convenience sampling also has great potential to provide extremely unreliable information and, therefore, should only be used when there is absolutely no need to generalize the attitudes and behaviors of the convenience sample to the broader population. This is because there is never any assurance that the characteristics of the convenience sample are in any way representative of the larger universe. As a result, it is only appropriate to use convenience sampling for exploratory research or for quick, nongeneralizable information relevant to a specific research need, such as questionnaire pretesting.

Judgment Sampling In *judgment sampling* individuals are selected from the target population based on an expert's judgment of the characteristics of a representative sample. The expert may be the researcher, others at the agency, the client, or a specialist with particular expertise. A storekeeper, for example, may decide to sample what he considers the "typical" customers of his business.

One's confidence in the results of the research conducted with judgment samples is directly proportionate to the expertise used to identify and select the sample. The greater the expertise the more likely the results can be trusted. For example, the selection of cities for test marketing a new product is almost always made on judgment. Individuals who are knowledgeable about the product and of cities in the United States are more likely to choose appropriate cities versus random selection. On the other hand, an expert may believe that the most appropriate targets for a college savings program are parents with children aged 10 to 17. If this judgment is wrong, then research conducted among these targets is likely to provide misleading direction. Judgment samples are recommended only when there is absolute confidence in the expert's opinion or, similar to convenience sampling, when only preliminary, exploratory information is required.

Quota Sampling *Quota sampling* is a more sophisticated form of nonprobability sampling. Quota sampling attempts to ensure that demographic characteristics of interest are represented in the sample in the same proportion as they are in the target population. Quota samples are executed through the following five steps:

1. Determine the defining characteristics of the key subgroups,
2. Determine the percent of the total population represented by each defining characteristic,
3. Determine the percent of the total population represented by each quota cell,
4. Translate the percent into a sample size,
5. Sample the population.

Table 8.4 illustrates the outcome of following the prior steps. First, the universe was divided based on gender and education. Second, the percent of the total population represented by each characteristic is determined and placed in the margins of the table. Third, because the two characteristics are assumed to be independent, the percent of the total sample represented by each cell is calculated by multiplying the appropriate marginal values. For example, the percent of men with less than a high school education is the product of 0.21 (the percent of the total population that has less than a high school education) and 0.48 (the percent of the total population that are men). Third, the total sample of 400 individuals is allocated on a percentage basis. (In this example, a total sample of 400 permits sufficient size in each quota cell for subgroup analysis. Were this not the case, total sample size would have to be increased.) Finally the sample is selected so that each cell's quota is filled.

Purposive Sampling   Purposive sampling is explicitly chosen to be nonrepresentative to achieve a specific analytical objective, typically to make certain that there are sufficient numbers of elements (for example, households or individuals) in key subgroups to permit reliable analysis of subgroup data. Here, similar to quota samples, a researcher divides the universe into a number of segments in which a predefined, but arbitrary, number of interviews will be conducted. This form of sampling entails the following three steps:

- Determine defining characteristics of the key subgroups,
- Determine the number of individuals required in each group, from the perspective of data analysis,
- Sample the population.

TABLE 8.4   Sample Size Determination in Quota Sampling
Percent of the Target Population Falling Into Each Quota Cell

	Education				
Gender	*Less Than High School*	*High School*	*Some College*	*College and Above*	*Total %*
Men	10	17	11	10	**48**
Women	11	18	12	11	**52**
Total %	**21**	**35**	**23**	**21**	**100**

Sample Size for Each Cell, Given a Total Sample Size of 400

	Education				
Gender	*Less Than High School*	*High School*	*Some College*	*College and Above*	*Total %*
Men	40	68	44	40	**192**
Women	44	72	48	44	**208**
Total	**84**	**140**	**92**	**84**	**400**

On the surface, purposive sampling resembles quota sampling. But, these surface appearances mask an important difference. Data obtained from quota sampling can be directly generalized to the population universe. No intervening data manipulation is required. Purposive sampling, similar to disproportionate stratified sampling, must be weighted before drawing conclusions about the population universe.

Sample Size in Nonprobability Samples

As the prior discussion has implied, sample sizes in nonprobability research are determined based on different forms of judgment. The nature of nonprobability samples precludes the use of statistical techniques to determine confidence intervals and associated sample size. Some forms of judgment, however, are better than others.[11]

Unaided Judgment   Unaided judgment is the most arbitrary approach to nonprobability sample size determination. Here, the client or researcher simply says: "A sample of fifty (or 100 or 1,000) will do. This is a good number. One that I feel comfortable with." While the researcher or client may "feel comfortable" with sample sizes selected in this way, there is no assurance that the sample is sufficient to satisfy informational needs. Consequently, this approach should be avoided.

What Is the Budget?   A second approach reflects budget considerations. The amount of funds available for sampling is divided by the cost per sample unit (for example, the cost to interview one individual) and the result is used to set the sample size. At ten dollars per interview, for example, a budget of $1,000 dictates a sample size of 100.

This approach should also be avoided. Buying the largest sample size that the you can afford has a high potential to produce samples that are either too large or too small given the research's informational needs.

Frame of Reference   A more reasonable approach to nonprobability sample size determination is to follow the practices of others. Here, you would first determine the sample sizes others have used for similar types of research and would then select samples of comparable size. The strength of this approach lies in the fact that there is often merit in historical precedence. A weakness, however, is that you may not know the validity of the rationale underlying initial decisions of sample size.

Analytical Requirements   The best method for determining nonprobability sample size is in response to analytical needs. It is recommended that the total number of individuals or observations in major study subgroups total at least 100 while there be a minimum of twenty to fifty individuals in minor analytical groups. These requirements are met, for example, in the quota sample shown in Table 8.4.

---

[11] This discussion is adapted from Donald S. Tull and Del I. Hawkins, *Marketing Research: Measurement and Method, Fifth Edition* (New York, NY: MacMillian Publishing Company, 1990), 492–93.

Summary

The sampling process involves the selection and examination of the elements of a population for drawing conclusions about the larger population of which these elements are members. A good sample is efficient and provides reliable generalizations about the larger population.

All sampling begins with a definition of the target population, the group of elements about which you wish to make inferences and draw generalizations. A well-defined target population unambiguously describes the group of interest and clearly differentiates those things or individuals who are of interest from those who are not.

A determination of the sampling method occurs next. Given the informational needs motivating the research, and the time and financial considerations, either a probability or nonprobability sampling technique will be selected. A probability sample is when each individual, household, or item comprising the universe from which the sample is drawn has a known chance, or probability, of being selected for inclusion in the research. The selection of sample elements is done purely by chance. A nonprobability sample is when the elements are not selected strictly by chance from the universe of all individuals, but are rather selected in some less random, often more purposeful way.

Probability Sampling

Probability sampling techniques require an additional three planning steps. First, a sample frame must be determined. A sample frame specifies the method you will use to identify the households, individuals, or other elements specified in the target population definition. You can take one of two approaches to specifying the sample frame. You can either construct or obtain a list to represent the target population or, when a list is incomplete or unavailable, you can specify a procedure such as random digit dialing for identifying and contacting target individuals. Once a sample frame is selected, it is compared to the target population. A perfect sample frame is identical to the target population, that is, the sample frame contains every population element once and only once *and* only population elements are contained in the sampling frame. Typically, however, sample frames are either too broad (overregistration) or too narrow (underregistration). In these latter instances, modifications in the sampling plan can be made to take into account the sample frame's characteristics.

Second, a specific probability sampling technique is selected. The most common forms of probability sampling are simple random samples, systematic random samples, and stratified random samples. Simple and systematic random sampling work well when the target population displays little variability among demographic, geographic, or behavioral subgroups. When wide variability is thought to exist, stratified random sampling (using either proportionate or disporportionate sample selection) is recommended.

Third, statistical techniques are used to determine the most appropriate balance between required sample size and confidence intervals, that is the range of measurement error.

Nonprobability Sampling

Two additional steps are required for nonprobability sampling. First, a specific non-probability sampling technique is selected. The most common forms of nonprobability sampling are convenience sampling, judgment sampling, quota sampling, and purposive sampling. Convenience sampling should be used with great caution and it is only appropriate to use a convenience sample for exploratory research or for quick, non-generalizable information relevant to a specific research need, such as questionnaire pretesting. Judgment sampling should also be used with caution, and only when there is great confidence in the judgment of the expert making the sample recommendation. Quota and purposive samples are the recommended forms of nonprobability sampling.

Second, sample size is determined based on analytical requirements and reflects the minimum number of observations required for each major and minor analytical subgroup.

Review Questions

1. What is the purpose of a *sample?*
2. What are the three important characteristics of a *sample?*
3. How does a sample differ from a *census?* In what types of situations is a census more appropriate than a sample?
4. What are the two characteristics of a well-written target population definition?
5. On what basis are populations of individuals typically defined? Provide appropriate examples.
6. What is a *probability* sample?
7. What is a *nonprobability* sample?
8. What are the relative advantages and disadvantages of probability and nonprobability sampling?
9. What types of sampling require a sample frame?
10. What is a *sample frame?*
11. What are two common forms of sample frames?
12. On what basis do you evaluate the adequacy of a sample frame?
13. What are *over-* and *underregistration?* How can each be addressed if identified early in the sample design process?
14. What are the three primary forms of probability sampling used in advertising research?
15. What are the characteristics of a *simple random sample?*
16. How are observations or individuals selected when one uses simple random sampling?
17. What is a *systematic random sample?* How is this type of sample similar and dissimilar to a simple random sample?
18. How are observations or individuals selected when one uses systematic random sampling?

19. Under what conditions does a simple or systematic random sample provide accurate estimates of the target population? When are estimates from these sampling methods more questionable and probably less reliable?

20. What is a *stratified random sample?* When is this type of sampling method most appropriate?

21. How are observations or individuals selected when one uses stratified random sampling?

22. What is the difference between *proportionate* and *disproportionate* stratified random sampling? Under what types of conditions is each most appropriate?

23. What are *confidence intervals* and *confidence levels?*

24. What is the relationship between confidence intervals, confidence levels, and sample size?

25. What are the steps underlying determination of the size of a probability sample when the response is a proportion? What are the steps underlying determination of the size of a probability sample when the response is a mean or average?

26. What are the major forms of nonprobability sampling?

27. Explain *convenience* and *judgment* samples? How are the similar and dissimilar? Under what types of circumstances should each be used?

28. What is a *quota sample?*

29. How is a quota sample selected?

30. What is a *purposive sample?*

31. How is a purposive sample selected?

32. How are quota and purposive samples similar and dissimilar?

33. What is the recommended way to identify appropriate sample size when using nonprobability sampling?

Application Exercises[12]

1. The local chapter of the Arthritis Foundation is preparing for their annual fund-raiser. It is recommended that to better target this year's efforts, research on donor characteristics from last year's fund-raiser be examined. Specifically, the research must describe the demographics of last year's donors. Time is of the essence.

   Two lists are available. First, a list of the names and addresses of all 11,000 individuals who donated from the prior year is stored in the chapter's archives. The file summary of this list shows that the percent of all last year's donors who donated at various levels is:

Supporter (under $25)	39%
Bronze Club ($25–$99)	11
Silver Club ($100–$500)	45
Gold Club ($1,000 or more)	5

   It would take about ten days to retrieve this list. A second list is also available. This list, stored in the chairman's files, lists the first 150 and last 300 donors from the past year.

---

[12] All application exercises are hypothetical.

You have been asked to recommend a sampling plan. Present your recommendations for sampling this population and provide a discussion of the strengths and weaknesses (if any) of your recommendation. Be certain that your discussion addresses target population definition, sampling method, sample frame (if appropriate), specific sampling approach, and sample size.

2. Tom's Buns N' Burger is a national chain of hamburger restaurants. Tom's wants to conduct research to determine consumers' reactions to their newly revised menu. During the week of March 4 they give each customer a coupon for a free hamburger and drink. However the coupon is not valid until the customer calls an 800-number, answers some survey questions, and obtains a validation code. Tom's will use the information they gather to plan future revisions to their menu.

Comment on Tom's sample plan. Do you agree that the plan is appropriate? Why or why not? If you do not feel that it is appropriate, propose, describe, and justify an alternative sampling plan. Be certain to address all applicable elements as shown in Figure 8.1.

3. The Weekly World Reporter conducts weekly surveys to determine the best-selling video games. A description of their methodology follows:

Interviews are conducted with a national sample of 100 discount stores, 250 toy stores, fifty warehouse stores and five video mail order companies.

Interviews with retail outlets are conducted in each of the fifty states on a proportionate basis (that is, two discount stores, five toy stores, and one warehouse store are surveyed in each state.) Stores are all in the second largest city in each state. Specific stores selected are identified by using the city's newspaper. Stores that advertise (that are most likely the larger stores) are selected to be interviewed.

Mail order companies are selected from among all mail order advertisers in the current month's Nintendo magazine.

Interviews are conducted by telephone. The individual who answers the phone is asked "What are your five highest selling games in the past week?" The highest selling game is awarded five points, the next best selling four points, etc. Points are then summed among all outlets."

Comment on this sampling plan. Do you agree that the plan is appropriate? Why or why not? If you do not feel that it is appropriate, propose, describe, and justify an alternative sampling plan. Be certain to address all applicable elements as shown in Figure 8.1.

4. Imagine that you are a research consultant. A client comes to you and says that his company has just developed a new financial planning program to help parents plan and save for their child's college education. The plan is structured to help parents start with a minimum of investment and build up the balance without undue pressure on the family's monthly budget. No research has ever been done for this client for this product. All you and the client's researcher have to go on are assumptions that you think are correct.

The client recommends that research be conducted to determine the reactions to various ways in which the program can be marketed and advertised. The client sends you a recommendation for who should be included in the study. The recommendation reads as follows:

I recommend that we conduct a telephone study among parents. Further, because the study is an attempt to assess these parents' interest in programs to help them get an early start in planning for their children's college education I recommend

that the interviews, for the sake of efficiency, be conducted among those I feel would most likely to be interested in, and have the resources for, participation in such a college planning program, namely those households with small children with total household incomes more than $45,000 per year. We can purchase a comprehensive list of households meeting these criteria from a list supplier and then randomly sample from the list.

Respond to the target universe and sample frame recommendations. Would you accept them as presented or would you suggest any revisions or modifications? Describe and justify any recommended modifications or revisions.

5. Assume that Family Magazine is one of the country's leading women's magazines and has a national circulation of more than 7,000,000 per copy. Its readers are primarily women. The editors of the magazine decide that they want to do a study of the views and attitudes of the American woman. Specifically, they want the research to be a definitive study and report national trends. They will call this study "The American Woman: What She Thinks and Feels." To collect data for the study the editors hire an independent research company to write the questionnaire. The editors then take the questionnaire and insert it in one issue of the magazine. The questionnaire is a self-mailer. Readers can indicate their opinions (anonymously) and then return the questionnaire postpaid. Response is exceptional. Nearly two hundred thousand readers return a questionnaire. The research company analyzes the data and editors print the results.

   Assess the acceptability or unacceptability of this method of data collection given the aims and goals of the magazine's editors.

6. Your client, Tastee-Good Ice Cream is ready to bring their new ice cream to market. This ice cream will provide all the flavor and richness of other premium ice creams (such as Hagen-Daas) without fat, calories, or artificial ingredients or sweeteners.

   The agency has been asked to think of some ways to advertise this product. The creative staff has, after an extensive review of consumer research created three different creative approaches. Each approach has been turned into a sample commercial. Note, however, that while the creative approaches (i.e., commercials) are different the intent of all three commercials is the same. The commercials are designed to make women (actually women with specific characteristics) try the ice cream.

   You need to know which creative approach, as represented in the three commercials, is the one that should be selected for production. Each commercial needs to be tested among the target audience in finished form. The target audience has been defined in terms of demographic, psychographic, and brand specific characteristics as follows:

   All of the women we want to talk to *must*

   • be between the ages of 25–34,
   • live in a household with an annual income of between $40,000–$50,000,
   • be concerned about their weight,
   • view ice cream as an indulgence or a treat,
   • not be price-conscious when it comes to the price that they pay for packaged ice cream.

   Moreover, these women may or may not currently be regular eaters of ice cream. In addition to satisfying all of the previously mentioned characteristics they must also satisfy *one* of the following:

- If they eat packaged ice cream regularly then they must usually eat premium ice cream. (Note, the word "premium" is a trade word, consumers may not use that word to describe the higher end ice creams.)
- If they do eat packaged ice cream regularly then it does not matter what type of packaged ice cream they eat. However, the main reason they are not regular eaters of ice cream must be that they are concerned about the perceived negative effects of ice cream on their weight or health.

It is very important that we understand the views of these women in a way that provides a high degree of confidence in the insights and generalizations drawn from the interviews.

To respond to the agency's needs please do the following. First, comment on the adequacy of the target population definition. Feel free to modify the target definition to eliminate problems associated with lack of clarity. Second, recommend a sampling approach and, if needed, the sample frame. Third, recommend and justify a specific sampling technique. Finally, present your recommendations in terms of sample size.

7. Define the target population and sample frame for each of the following situations:
   a. You wish to evaluate the effectiveness of the Partnership for a Drug Free America antidrug advertising campaign.
   b. You have just introduced a new luxury sports car. You wish to determine perceptions of the car after exposure to the car's television advertising. The advertising is presented nationally.

8. You are exploring automobile tire purchasers' buying habits. You are specifically interested in exploring habits as a function of type of tire purchased and a census region (that are assumed to be independent of each other). The percent of the population residing in each census region is

Northeast	21%
North Central	24
South	34
West	21

The percent of tire purchasers that have purchased each type of tire in the past twelve months is

Radial	79%
Bias Belted	11
Bias Ply	10

You decide to quota sample the population. What percent of the total sample will fall into each quota cell? Given the percent represented in each call, what is your recommendation for the minimum total sample size?

CHAPTER

9

QUALITATIVE RESEARCH

Qualitative research techniques, characterized by small sample sizes and probing open-ended questions, provide in-depth insights into consumers' attitudes, beliefs, motivations, and lifestyles. Qualitative research helps researchers to get "beneath the surface" by providing feelings, textures, a sense of intensity, and a degree of nuance beyond the numeric descriptions provided by quantitative research. This chapter discusses the characteristics of qualitative research.

After reading this chapter, you will be able to

■ Describe the appropriate uses of qualitative research.

■ Identify the characteristics, advantages, and disadvantages of the most common qualitative research techniques: in-depth interviews, focus groups, and minigroups.

■ Describe the techniques used to conduct qualitative interviews.

Qualitative advertising research entails the intensive observation or interviewing of a small number of individuals to acquire detailed, in-depth insights into their attitudes, beliefs, motivations, and lifestyles. The goal of qualitative research is to help develop a better understanding of *why* individuals act as they do rather than developing numeric descriptions of *what* people do.[1] Thus, qualitative research focuses on the nature or structure of attitudes and motivations rather than their frequency or distribution.[2]

The characteristics and goals of qualitative research make it especially well-suited for satisfying several types of advertising informational needs. Qualitative research is appropriate whenever there is a need to

- understand the underlying relationship between consumers' feelings, attitudes, beliefs, and their behaviors, *especially* when information on this relationship cannot be obtained through direct, structured, primarily closed questioning;

---

[1] See, for example, Joe Whalen, "Qualitative Research Adds the 'Why?' to Measurement," *Marketing News* (May 9, 1994): 8–9.

[2] Alfred E. Goldman and Susan Schwartz McDonald, *The Group Depth Interview: Principles and Practice* (Englewood Cliffs, NJ: Prentice-Hall, 1987), 7.

- complement quantitative research, either in the preliminary or postresearch stages. Qualitative research can help to
  - better define and understand a marketing or advertising problem before the quantitative research is conducted;
  - develop hypotheses before the planning and initiation of quantitative research;
  - evaluate the appropriateness of a proposed quantitative research design or sampling plan, for example, when determining the inclusion or exclusion of consumers with certain demographic or behavioral characteristics;
  - pilot test questionnaires or similar forms of survey research instruments;
  - amplify, explain, or further explore points emerging from a quantitative study without having to repeat the quantitative study.
- obtain preliminary or background information when little is currently known;
- listen to consumers express their ideas in their own words and/or have first-hand observation of consumers' responses.

Qualitative research is an appropriate response to a wide range of advertising informational needs. It works well in these situations for several reasons. First, and most important, qualitative research is appropriate for these types of situations because of the type of information it collects and the types of insights it provides. Goldman and McDonald point out that

> Although qualitative research does not tell you how widely distributed an attitude or motivation might be, it does tell you—and in ways surveys cannot—from where those attitudes arise, how they are structured, and what broader significance they may have for consumer behavior. The rich qualitative insights that spring from close inspection of individuals can never be duplicated by large-scale surveys, which view the market from a more distant vantage point.[3]

Second, qualitative research provides an opportunity to "get close to the data," to see and hear consumers express their thoughts in their own words. The insights that occur from seeing and hearing the consumer are often a missing component of the numeric summaries reported in quantitative research.

Third, qualitative research allows one to draw insights and explanations from respondents themselves, rather than having to predetermine areas of response or importance. Filstead notes that qualitative methods allow the researcher to develop the "analytical, conceptual and categorical components of explanation from the data itself—rather than from the preconceived, rigidly structured and highly quantified techniques that pigeonhole the empirical social world into the operational definitions that the researcher has constructed."[4]

Fourth, qualitative research is often quicker and less costly than quantitative research, especially for satisfying informational needs that do not require numeric, statistically projectable data.

Finally, qualitative research is more flexible than quantitative research. Qualitative research permits you to change course, such as modifying the interview guide or probing new areas, depending on the nature of consumer response.

---

[3] Ibid., 8.

[4] W. J. Filstead, ed., *Qualitative Methodology* (Chicago, IL: Markham, 1970), 6.

Qualitative research also has three specific limitations that make it an unacceptable procedure for satisfying some forms of advertising-related informational needs. First, and perhaps most important, generalizations obtained from qualitative research are severely limited. In fact, one can confidently generalize the results of a quantitative study only to those individuals who participated in that study. There is no assurance that the small number of individuals who participated in the research are in any way representative of the larger population from which they were drawn. Given this limitation, the results of qualitative research should be treated as directional rather than definitive. Second, the small sample sizes used in qualitative research prevent the numeric description of findings. Thus, qualitative research should be avoided when numeric descriptions of population characteristics are required. Third, the interpretation of qualitative research data is more subjective than the interpretation of quantitative data because the basis of qualitative analysis is individuals' comments and verbal responses as opposed to numeric ratings or rankings. As a result, qualitative research should not be used when a nonsubjective and detached description of findings is required.

TYPES OF QUALITATIVE RESEARCH

Qualitative advertising research typically utilizes either personal or small group interviews.[5]

Personal Interviews

Personal interviews (also known as one-on-one, depth or in-depth interviews) typically take between thirty and sixty minutes and consist of a private, face-to-face conversation between a trained qualitative interviewer and a respondent. Given the time and expense associated with this form of qualitative research (the two most significant drawbacks to personal interviews), most studies utilizing personal interviews have samples of between five and fifteen individuals.

A personal interview is a free-flowing, yet structured, conversation between the interviewer and the respondent. While the interviewer and the respondent know the specific topics to be addressed during the interview, the interviewer is free to pursue each topic in different ways with different respondents. Moreover, during the interview, the interviewer is free to create questions and to probe responses that seem interesting and relevant to the goals and informational needs motivating the research. Thus, within a specific research study, the informational goals of each personal inter-

---

[5] While personal interviews, minigroups, and focus groups are the primary forms of qualitative advertising research, a wide range of other forms of qualitative research exist. These include ethnomethodology, symbolic interactionism, cultural studies, historiography, and oral traditions. For discussions of these approaches to qualitative research see Thomas R. Lindloff, *Qualitative Communication Research Methods* (Thousand Oaks, CA: SAGE Publications, 1995) and Bruce L. Berg, *Qualitative Research Methods for the Social Sciences* (Boston, MA: Allyn and Bacon, 1995).

view remain constant although the actual structure of the interviews typically varies among respondents.

Personal interviews are appropriate for situations in which *extensive*, *detailed* probing of attitudes, behaviors, motivations, or needs is required. This is because personal interviews provide "more detail, point out personal preferences and idiosyncrasies and describe subtleties, nuances, and shades of difference that are masked in a group setting."[6] Beyond this informational advantage of personal versus group interviews, personal interviews are also more appropriate than group interviews in the following circumstances:

- The subject matter of the interview is likely to be seen as highly confidential (e.g., family or personal finances, business practices), emotionally charged (e.g., sexual behaviors) or embarrassing (e.g., personal hygiene products);
- Antitrust restrictions prohibit group discussion (it is illegal, for example, to convene a group of CEOs from the same industry to discuss business practices and approaches to product pricing);
- Group pressure or the presence of others is likely to alter or discourage response honesty;
- There is a need to acquire a detailed or step-by-step understanding of complicated behaviors or decision-making patterns (e.g., the process underlying the evaluation and selection of a new automobile);
- Longer amounts of time and increased interviewer-interviewee rapport are required to understand target attitudes and behaviors.

Focus Groups and Minigroups

Focus groups and minigroups are the focused discussion of a *group* of individuals led by a trained moderator. The moderator's role is to facilitate the discussion among members of the group in subjects relevant to the areas of study and informational needs. The flexibility of focus groups makes it a common approach for meeting many marketer and advertiser informational needs, particularly in the areas of new product idea generation, product positioning and product perceptions, creative, product and package screening, and explorations of consumers' attitudes, beliefs, needs, and motivations.

Focus groups and minigroups are similar in orientation and structure. Each lasts about one and one-half to two hours and uses a moderator who relying on a discussion guide moves the discussion through desired topic areas. The primary difference between focus groups and minigroups is in the number of participants. Focus groups generally consist of between eight and twelve individuals. Minigroups are smaller, generally consisting of between three and six individuals.

Advantages of Focus Groups   The group nature of a focus group discussion gives advertising researchers five specific advantages over personal interviews.

First, the interactive nature of the discussion helps focus group participants expand on and refine their own opinions. It is common for all individual's comments in a focus group to

---

[6] M. S. Payne, "Individual In-Depth Interviews Can Provide More Details Than Groups," *Marketing Today* (Chicago, IL: Elrick and Lavidge, 1982).

- stimulate thoughts in other respondents,
- cause other respondents to view things differently,
- stimulate greater depth of discussion,
- remind individuals of things they may have forgotten, or
- help other respondents better verbalize their thoughts and opinions.

These positive outcomes of focus group discussion are illustrated in Goldman's exploration of womens' grocery store perceptions:

> Some of the women in each of four group sessions were adamant in their intention not to shop in one of the markets, although they did not appear able to express their reasons in a clear and consistent manner. Some mentioned a vague feeling that the market in question was somehow messy or even dirty. Yet, upon further exploration, these same women agreed that the shelves were neatly stacked, the personnel clean, the floors swept, the counters well dusted. They could not point out anything to support their charges of uncleanliness. Further, they readily agreed that the store they did shop in was more messy than the one in which they refused to shop. A casual reference by one of the women to a peculiar odor evoked immediate recognition from the others. This occurred spontaneously in several of the groups and led to the consensus that it was a "bloody" or "meaty" odor. This process of "consensual validation" suggested that this vague impression of untidiness stemmed not from anything that could be seen, but rather from this faint yet persuasive and offensive odor.[7]

Second, focus groups are more stimulating and exciting for participants versus depth interviews. The heightened interest that results from participating in a group discussion increases the likelihood that participants will pay attention, participate in the discussion, and provide more than superficial responses.

Third, focus groups are more spontaneous than personal interviews. A well-moderated group encourages respondents to express their opinions and fosters active, positive interchanges between respondents. This spontaneity reduces defense mechanisms and self-editing and encourages respondents to share actual opinions. Further, because there are always other participants in the group, the spontaneity of the group reduces the chances of participants "making-up" answers because they feel pressure to do so.

Fourth, focus groups are quicker to conduct and analyze versus personal interviews. Broom and Dozier point out that

> Because small, purposive samples are generally used, research firms can use existing sample frames to quickly draw participants of desired characteristics. A screening questionnaire is used to ensure that focus group participants qualify for the purposes of the study. A competent supplier can put together a focus group in seven to ten days. A final report of findings can be generated within a day or two of the groups.[8]

Fifth, the per respondent cost of focus group studies is generally less than the per respondent cost of personal interviews. A typical focus group costs between $1,700 and $2,500 including the moderator's fee, the fee to the focus group facility, and compensation for respondents.

---

[7] A. E. Goldman, "The Group Depth Interview," *Journal of Marketing* (July 1962): 61.

[8] Glen M. Broom and David M. Dozier, *Using Research in Public Relations* (Englewood Cliffs, NJ: Prentice-Hall, 1990), 147–48.

Disadvantages of Focus Groups   In addition to the problems of generalizability shared by all qualitative research, focus groups have four significant disadvantages versus personal interviews. First, there is always the possibility that one respondent will dominate the discussion or impose a particular point of view setting a tone and direction counter to that of the group's or moderator's preference. For example, it will be difficult for participants to admit serving their children sugared cereal if one respondent begins the discussion by saying "Only mothers who don't care about their children's health serve their children cereal loaded with sugar."

Second, beyond the bias introduced by dominant respondents, there is the potential for moderator-introduced bias. A moderator can introduce significant bias into the group and the direction of the group's discussion by shifting or introducing topics too rapidly, implicitly or explicitly encouraging certain points of view, or by failing to introduce or probe topics or responses.

Third, there is the possibility that group pressures can distort the expression of individual opinions. Some respondents may be reluctant to express extreme opinions that they feel deviate from accepted or expressed group norms while others may not verbalize opinions that they feel run counter to group consensus.[9]

Fourth, the data obtained from focus group discussions represents *group,* not individual, data. Focus group data reflects the "collective notions shared and negotiated by the group"[10] and, therefore, focus groups do not provide the depth of individual detail commonly obtained from personal interviews.

Obtaining Qualitative Insights

Whether conducted through personal or group interviews, the goal of qualitative research is to uncover respondents' underlying thoughts, attitudes, beliefs, and motivations and to determine how these personal attributes and characteristics influence behaviors and perceptions. The probability of obtaining these insights is increased when the interviewer

- is adequately prepared for the interview or focus group,
- uses appropriate questioning and projective techniques, and
- conducts the interview or focus group in the proper environment.

The remainder of this chapter address each of these issues.

PREPARING FOR THE QUALITATIVE INTERVIEW OR FOCUS GROUP

Qualitative research begins similarly to quantitative research. Discussions related to problem identification and informational needs precede the design and execution of the research (see Chapter 2). Once these issues are addressed, preparation for the personal interviews or focus groups begins.

The first step in the preparation process determines, for each informational need, the types of questions or techniques most likely to elicit insightful, relevant informa-

---

[9] See D. L. Morgan, *Focus Groups as Qualitative Research* (Newbury Park: CA: SAGE, 1989).
[10] Berg, *Qualitative Research Methods,* 78.

tion. Some informational needs, for example, might be addressed best through direct, open-ended questioning and subsequent discussion while other informational needs might be addressed best through projective techniques.

The successful specification of an approach to each informational need is followed by the creation of an interview guide (for personal interviews) or a discussion group guide (for focus groups and minigroups). Both guides serve the same two purposes: to provide a framework and path for conducting the interview, and to provide a reminder to the interviewer or moderator as to how the interview is to be conducted. Interview and discussion guides generally begin as an outline, listing the broad topics and categories that are to be addressed. The outline permits the interviewer or moderator to visualize the flow of the discussion and to structure the discussion in a logical flow from topic to topic. Next, specific questions and techniques are added to the outline to illustrate the manner in which information and reactions will be elicited. Finally, probes are added as reminders. The explicit addition of probes to the guide makes certain that all important areas will be addressed. An excerpt from a focus group discussion guide is shown in Figure 9.1 (page 202).

Concluding preparatory steps relate to interview or discussion guide evaluation and revision. The guide is circulated to key individuals in the project for examination and comment. Revisions are enacted in response to comments. Next, the guide is pretested using one or two individuals to evaluate the clarity, appropriateness, and logical flow of the questions and issues. The results of the pretesting are considered and a final copy of the guide is created.

ELICITING QUALITATIVE INSIGHTS: VERBAL QUESTIONING TECHNIQUES

Qualitative interviews, whether in focus groups or one-on-one interviews, try to elicit respondents' experiences, attitudes, and feelings in words that are natural to the respondents. Several types of verbal questions work well to elicit these types of responses. These question types include the following:

- direct and factual
- structural
- grand tour
- idealization
- contrast
- hypothetical-interaction
- third-person[11]

Direct and Factual Questions

Direct and factual questions are explicit requests for specific pieces of information or feelings and are most useful in providing background information or the foundation for

---

[11] The typology of question types is primarily based on Lindloff, *Qualitative Communication Research Methods*, 187–93.

TOPIC: Children's cereals: reactions to current positionings, promotions, and advertising. Effect of these perceptions and other factors on product evaluation and purchase.

Group 1: Mothers of children under age 5, regular purchasers of sugared children's cereal.

I. Introduction

Moderator name and who I am, what I do
Explain focus groups—why we are here, what we will be doing
Explain moderator's role
Participant's rules:
   speak one at a time
   first names only
   speak to each other
   be truthful, no right or wrong answers
   all opinions count
   don't try to please me
Explain the setting:
   one-way mirror
   tape recorder
   observers behind one-way mirror
Explain usage:
   for internal use only
   not for commercials
   no one will be quoted by name
   strictly confidential
Introduce topic: children's foods, with specific emphasis on children's cereals

II. Personal Introductions

Participants invited to introduce themselves
Provide name, age, number, and ages of children
Name children's cereals purchased on most recent shopping trips, typical or not typical

III. Perceived Structure of Children's Cereal Market

What are the different types of children's cereals on the market?
On what basis are differentiations made?
What are the most important attributes of different types or segments?
   Probe if no "sugared" segment is mentioned
   Probe if no "slightly sugared" segment is mentioned
Is there a difference between sugared and lightly sugared cereals? What?
   Probe: Is difference meaningful?
What brand names come to mind within each segment?
   Make certain to elicit specific brand names
   Probe if "Honey Nut Cheerios" not mentioned?
   Probe if "Trix" not mentioned
   Probe if "Captain Crunch" not mentioned

IV. Reactions to Children's Cereal Advertising—Mother's Point of View

Awareness of children's cereal advertising
Overall reactions to advertising:
   Probe for specific likes and dislikes
   Probe for truthfulness, appropriateness
Reactions to specific brand advertising:
   Brands seen advertised recently; in the past
   Take brands one by one, probe for specific likes, dislikes, truthfulness, appropriateness
Influence of advertising on purchase decision:
   Positive influences?
   Negative influences?
Idealization: Describe characteristics of ideal children's cereal advertising?
   Take individual mentioned brands and compare to ideal.
Hypothetical-interaction: If [insert brand name]'s director of advertising were here in this room what would you say or ask? What responses would you expect to receive? If you could recommend and have accepted one wish (regarding children's cereal advertising) what would it be?

FIGURE 9.1 Excerpt from a focus group discussion guide.

more extensive discussion. In spite of their direct and factual nature, however, these questions are still asked in an open-ended manner, for example:

> What are the names of all the brands of beer you have consumed within the past week?
>
> What are the most important reasons why you purchase your current brand of shampoo?
>
> Why did you stop using your old brand of dish washing detergent?
>
> How did you feel when you discovered the chips had no fat but 180 mg of sodium per serving?

Structural Questions

Structural questions take a step beyond direct and factual questions and help an interviewer understand how a respondent has organized his or her feelings and knowledge within a particular area.[12] Here a respondent might be asked to explain "What are all the different ways that you discuss the taste of different beers with your friends?" or "What are all the different ways to describe how you evaluate various brands of coffee?"

Direct, factual, and structural questions are straightforward ways to elicit information. The interviewer or moderator clearly and narrowly defines the area of discussion and the types of information sought. Other types of questions are more open-ended allowing for a range of responses.

Grand Tour Questions

Grand tour questions ask a respondent to reconstruct a routine, procedure, activity, or event that took place at a particular time in his or her life. The respondent is the tour guide, describing for the "uninformed" interviewer the steps taken and the thoughts or feelings associated with each step. The respondent begins at the specified point in the question and continues until the experience or event is fully described, for example:

> You mentioned that you purchased a new VCR within the past month. Tell me about the events that led up to the purchase of the VCR. Tell me what you did and what your thoughts were from the time you decided you needed a new VCR to the time of the actual purchase.
>
> Tell me about the first time you tried a no fat ice cream. Start at the time you decided to purchase this type of ice cream and continue through your first tasting. Try to describe what you were doing and thinking at each point in the process.

Grand tour questions are excellent ways to move beyond direct and factual questions because they are nonthreatening, have no single correct answer, show that the interviewer is interested in the respondent's experiences and, finally, they allow the respondent to demonstrate his or her expertise and experiences.

---

[12] J. P. Spradley, *Participant Observation* (New York, NY: Holt, Rinehart & Winston, 1980), 60.

Idealization Questions

Idealization questions ask a respondent to speculate about "the ideal," for example, the ideal product or ideal type of product category advertising. Once the ideal is described, then specific, existing instances are discussed in the context of the ideal. For example, a respondent might be asked to "describe the ideal dish washing detergent" after which the characteristics of specific dish washing products are compared to the ideal. In this example, the gap between existing and ideal product characteristics provides direction for identifying potential product gaps and new product opportunities. Alternatively, the interviewer can propose or describe the characteristics of the "ideal" and ask the respondent to evaluate and respond to the description. The interviewer might say "Here are some characteristics of what might be considered an ideal dish washing detergent. It is extremely mild on the hands and is biodegradable. It works on all types of baked-on stains. How does this description match with your ideal dish washing product?"

Contrast Questions

Closely related to idealization questions are contrast questions. *Contrast questions* help uncover differences in attitudes and perceptions by setting and comparing one item or object to another. One form of contrast questioning, laddering, asks respondents to distinguish among brands and concepts by asking questions of the form "In what ways is a Honda different from a Toyota?" Each attribute mentioned in response to this question is noted and then probed to determine the extent to which that attribute is important and meaningful. Each of these new reasons is then probed. The process continues until meaningful response has ended. The continuous and systematic probing of responses can lead to the discovery of a "network of meanings" associated with a set of brands or products.[13] A second form of contrast questioning asks respondents to describe the opposites of an item, brand, or product. Respondents might be asked, for example, to describe the opposite of a Volkswagen. Responses would then be interpreted to discover the perceptions of Volkswagens.

Hypothetical-Interaction Questions

Hypothetical-interaction questions present a plausible situation and ask the respondent to verbalize how he or she would respond in that situation. The situation can describe a respondent's interaction with other individuals, with a specific product or with a product category, for example:

> Imagine that the director and creator of Calvin Klein's jeans advertising were sitting across the table from you. Describe how you would feel and what you would be thinking. What types of questions might you ask these people? What would you anticipate their answers to your questions might be?

Grand tour, idealization, and hypothetical-interaction questions draw on a respondent's imagination and experiences. An interviewer using these types of questions works cooperatively with the respondent(s) to elicit underlying beliefs and at-

---

[13] T. Reynolds and J. Gutman, "Advertising is Image Management," *Journal of Advertising Research* (February 1984): 1–13.

titudes and the reasons for beliefs, attitudes, and behaviors. When used in a focus group setting, the moderator can use one person's grand tour or responses to an idealization question as the stimulus for further discussion. Grand tour, idealization, and hypothetical-interaction questions are often advantageously followed by third-person questions.

Third-Person Questions

Third-person questions follow up self-disclosures with nonthreatening challenges couched in the form of detached questions. A *third-person question* asks for elaboration within the context of an anonymous, nonpresent person, for example,

> You said that you think economy is the most important factor in the selection of a shampoo. You said that the shampoo should be reasonably priced and that a little bit should go a long way. Others whom I have talked to have said the same thing. But, in my last group several people said that price and economy were really far less important than leaving hair shiny and manageable. What do you think about this point of view?

ELICITING QUALITATIVE INSIGHTS: PROJECTIVE TECHNIQUES

The types of verbal questions discussed in the prior section are a direct means of exploring individuals' attitudes and beliefs. There are times when verbal, direct questions fail to get beneath the surface or when respondents cannot verbalize their thoughts and feelings. In these cases, projective techniques are often a successful alternative to direct questioning.

Projective techniques have their roots in clinical psychology and are based on the *projective hypothesis,* which proposes that when people attempt to understand an ambiguous or vague stimulus, their interpretation and response to that stimulus reflects a projection of their needs, feelings, attitudes, and experiences. For example, when a young child hears a sound in another room late at night that he interprets as a "monster walking," he is projecting his fears onto the sound. The sound itself is an ambiguous, vague, but neutral stimulus. It is, in and of itself, neither good nor bad, fearsome nor friendly. What the child hears and verbalizes is a reflection of his underlying fears and attitudes. Projective techniques used in advertising and marketing research rely on the same projective principle.

The projective techniques used in advertising research can be divided into three groups:

- Techniques that use verbal stimuli and responses (word association, sentence completion, and story completion),
- Techniques that require the use of imagination or scenarios (personification, anthropomorphism, role playing, and shopping lists), and
- Techniques that use pictures as stimuli (picture projection, picture sorts, and picture collage).

Each of these techniques, which can be used in both group and personal interview settings, are discussed in the following sections.

Word Association

Word association asks an individual to quickly respond to the presentation of words or phrases with the first thing or things that come to mind. This technique is commonly used to assess reactions to potential brand names, advertising campaign themes, and advertising slogans. Word association works as follows: A respondent is first read (one at a time) neutral terms to help establish the demands of the technique. Then, words or phrases of interest to the advertiser are presented (again, one at a time), each of which is separated by several neutral terms (to reduce any bias due to anticipation or defense mechanisms). For example, an airline might ask interviewees to respond to four potential tag lines: "best in the sky," "on time, every time," "your friend in the sky," and "the airline of pampered passengers." Responses to each tag line would be examined in terms of valence (positive, negative, or neutral response) and typicality of response (more common versus less common response).

Sentence and Story Completions

Sentence and story completions, considered by many researchers to be the most useful and reliable of all projective techniques, require a respondent to draw on his or her own attitudes and beliefs to complete an incomplete sentence or story.

Sentence completion requires a respondent to complete a sentence with the first phrase that comes to mind or anything else that makes sense. For example, an individual might be asked to complete the sentence "The type of people who really like to eat reduced calorie ice cream are . . ." At first glance it might appear that sentence completion is merely another way of asking an open-ended question (for example, "What kind of people like to eat reduced calorie ice creams?"). However, while open-ended and sentence completion formats are similar, each elicits different types of information. In direct questioning through open-ended questions, respondents typically give their answers after logical consideration and evaluation. However, because of the emphasis on speed of response in sentence completion tasks, internal defenses and self-editing tends to be greatly reduced. Kassarjian illustrates the differences in response to direct and sentence completion questions in the context of a study of smokers' attitudes:

> The majority [of smokers] gave responses [to direct questions] such as "Pleasure is more important than health," "Moderation is OK" and "I like to smoke." One gets the impression that smokers are not dissatisfied with their lot. However, in a portion of the study involving sentence-completion tests, smokers responded to the question, "People who never smoke are _____" with comments such as "better off," "happier" [and] "wiser, more informed." To the question, "teenagers who smoke are _____" smokers responded with "foolish," "crazy," "uninformed," "stupid," "showing off," "immature" [and] "wrong."[14]

The sentence completion task showed that smokers were not as satisfied with their decision to smoke as their answers to direct questions might have indicated.

Story completion is an expanded version of sentence completion. Story completion begins with the interviewer reading part of a story to the respondent. At some point

---

[14] H. H. Kassarjian, "Projective Methods," In R. Ferber, ed., *Handbook of Marketing Research* (New York, NY: McGraw-Hill Book Company, 1974), Section 3, 85–100.

the narrative ends and the respondent is then asked to provide the end of the story. As with other projective techniques, it is hoped that the respondent will incorporate his or her own attitudes, beliefs, and experiences in the story ending. Imagine, for example, that First Savings Bank has aired an advertising campaign designed to increase favorable perceptions of the friendliness and responsiveness of their loan officers versus their major competitor, the First National Trust. A researcher could use direct questioning to examine differences in perceptions or he or she could use story completion, as follows:

> Think about a man and woman who have been married for five years. They own their own home and have acquired enough equity in their home to obtain a home equity loan. They wish to use the loan to finance a vacation.
>
> The husband, Tom, and wife, Mary, are discussing their own options after dinner one evening. They are trying to determine which banks to approach for the loan. They pick up the day's newspaper and see ads for First Savings Bank and First National Trust. They begin to discuss these banks.
>
> Tom says to Mary, "What about First Savings Bank?" Mary says _____.
> _____.
>
> (PROBE FOR DETAIL. ASK FOR DIALOGUE FROM BOTH TOM AND MARY. AFTER THIS SEGMENT IS COMPLETED, CONTINUE.)
>
> After they discuss the First Savings Bank, Mary says, "What about First National Trust?" Tom says _____ .
>
> (PROBE FOR DETAIL. ASK FOR DIALOGUE FROM BOTH TOM AND MARY. AFTER THIS SEGMENT IS COMPLETED, END.)

Personification and Anthropomorphism

Personification and anthropomorphism are techniques that "seek to establish the image and character of a company or brand by relating it to some well-known person, theatrical character or even an animal. [These approaches] help participants communicate subtle characteristics of company or brand image that would otherwise require unusual verbal facility or insight."[15]

Personification can take one of two forms. First, respondents can be asked a series of questions of the form:

> Think about a Jeep automobile. If a Jeep were to turn into a celebrity or other famous person, who would it be? Write down your first thought on the pad in front of you. Now, think about Chevrolet automobiles. If a Chevrolet were to turn into a celebrity or other famous person, who would it be? Write down your first thought on the pad in front of you.[16]

Clearly, the brands would have different images (to be probed by the interviewer) if the response to Jeep was "Arnold Schwarzenegger" and the response to Chevrolet was "Archie Bunker." Second, respondents can be presented with a brand name and then asked to describe the brand as if were a human being, that is, to describe what types of human characteristics the brand might have. Respondents might be asked to describe

---

[15] Goldman and McDonald, *The Group Depth Interview,* 127.

[16] Respondents are asked to write down their answers for several reasons. First, it makes certain that they do not change their mind at this time of discussion. Second, it makes certain that they are not influenced by other people's responses. Third, it provides a basis for respondents to contrast and compare their own responses prior to discussion.

the brand's gender, age, hobbies, favorite vacations, foods, etc. Differences in characteristics among brands reflects underlying differences in brand perceptions.

Respondents can also be asked to select an animal to represent a particular brand or company. As with personification techniques, the interviewer probes each mention to discover the underlying symbolism or meaning. Goldman and MacDonald provide an example of how this technique helped to discern differences in corporate perceptions:

> One company was associated with a teddy bear, an image that suggested the ingratiating friendliness of the company's sales representatives but reflected little respect. Other companies were seen as a mole (". . . because the salesman always goes around me to the boss."), a bat ("They do all their business by mail; like bats they hide in dark caves."), a snake (. . . can't trust them.") and a unicorn ("People know about them, but you can never see them.").[17]

Role-Playing

One of the easiest projective techniques is role playing. Here, rather than directly asking a person what he or she thinks, the question is couched in terms of "What would your neighbor think?" or "How do you think the average person would react?" This technique works well when the area under exploration is sensitive or responses may run counter to social or other norms. For example, a focus group might be composed of mothers, all of whom consistently serve their children sugared cereals for breakfast. They participate in this behavior even though they know there are better options and, therefore, they may be reluctant to admit the extent to which they participate in this behavior. In this instance it might be better to ask "Why do you think many mothers serve their children sugared cereal?" rather than asking "Why do you consistently serve your children sugared cereal?" Similarly, while an interviewer could ask respondents to describe how they feel they are treated by the counter personnel of various department stores, it might be more insightful to ask each respondent to play the role and exhibit the behaviors of various stores' clerks.

Shopping Lists

Shopping lists ask respondents to speculate about the characteristics of different types of individuals based on the types of products they purchase. Here, it is assumed that respondents' feelings toward the products on the list will be reflected in their descriptions of the shopping list's owner or originator. Haire reports a classic example of the use of this technique:

> The introduction of instant coffee was initially met with much skepticism and resistance. The most common reason why was "It just doesn't taste good." Haire believed that there were deeper, more logical reasons for the nonacceptance of instant coffee. He constructed two identical shopping lists except that one list contained "Nescafé instant coffee" while the other list contained "Maxwell House drip grind coffee." Respondents were shown one of the lists and were asked to write a brief description of the personality and character of the woman who would be likely to purchase the items on the list.
>
> The differences in the descriptions was remarkable. The owner of the list with Maxwell House was generally described as average. The owner of the Nescafé list, how-

---

[17] Goldman and McDonald, *The Group Depth Interview,* 129.

FIGURE 9.2
Stimuli for picture projection.
Courtesy of Danna L. Givot.

ever, was characterized as being lazy, a spendthrift and a poor cook. These latter responses were much more revealing about attitudes toward instant coffee than the logical, rational response, "It doesn't taste good."[18]

Picture Projection

Picture projection techniques use visual rather than verbal stimuli as the basis for respondent constructed stories or descriptions. A respondent is shown a picture and is then asked to provide the dialogue, thoughts, or feelings of other individuals in the drawing. The drawing shown in Figure 9.2 is an example of this type of projection technique and illustrates another way to assess perceptions of First Savings Bank loan officers. Respondents might be shown pictures (in sequence) with the following introductions:

Picture A: This couple is thinking about applying for a loan. What financial institutions do you think they are considering? Why are they considering these institutions? Are there any institutions that they have explicitly eliminated from consideration? Why have they been eliminated?

Picture B: This second couple is about the enter First Savings Bank to apply for a loan. What thoughts do you think are going through their minds? What sorts of feelings do you think they are experiencing?

Picture C: (Show picture in Figure 9.2) This third couple is applying for a loan at First

---

[18] M. Haire, "Projective Techniques in Marketing Research," *Journal of Marketing* (April 1950): 649–56.

Savings Bank. How are they being treated? What thoughts are going through their minds? What feelings are they experiencing? Are they happy or unhappy with the process and how they are being treated? Why do you think they feel this way?

Picture projection can also be used with more complex drawings or even photographs. In these cases, similar to simpler line drawings, the pictures should be relatively vague to increase the chances of the respondent using his or imagination to describe what is occurring.

Picture Sorts

Picture sorts are used to identify the different ways consumers view other individuals, brands, products, places, and activities. The approach and goals of a picture sort are illustrated in the directions given to the respondent. For example, the directions and approach for a study on pain relievers would be the following:[19]

> I am conducting research to determine what people think and feel about different pain relievers. Here are pictures of pain reliever brands. Please look through the pictures and familiarize yourself with them.
>
> SHUFFLE PICTURES AND HAND TO RESPONDENT. WHEN RESPONDENT IS DONE EXAMINING PICTURES, CONTINUE.
>
> Please look at the pictures and sort them into groups in such a way that all the pictures in any group are similar to each other in some important way and different from those in the other groups. You can sort the pictures into as many groups as you like and you can put as many or as few pictures in a group as you like. Remember, there is no right or correct answer. I am interested in what **you** think. You can begin whenever you are ready. Remember, you can change your mind and move pictures from pile to pile. Just let me know when you are done.
>
> WHEN RESPONDENT IS DONE, RECORD PICTURE GROUPINGS ON TALLY SHEET.
>
> You divided the pictures into [NUMBER OF GROUPS] groups. Can you tell me the basis that you used to sort the pictures, that is, what criterion you used to sort or divide the pictures.
>
> RECORD RESPONSE. PROBE AS NECESSARY.
>
> POINT TO PICTURE GROUP 1. Can you tell me what the pictures in this group have in common? RECORD RESPONSE. BE CERTAIN TO PROBE RELATIONSHIP OF RESPONSE TO OVERALL SORTING CRITERION. CONTINUE WITH SAME QUESTION FOR REMAINING PILES OF PICTURES.
>
> COLLECT CARDS AND SHUFFLE. HAND CARDS BACK TO RESPONDENT. Can you please sort the pictures again using whatever *different* criterion you might wish to use?
>
> FOLLOW PRIOR RECORDING AND QUESTIONING PROCEDURES FOR EACH ADDITIONAL SORT. CONTINUE UNTIL RESPONDENT SAYS THAT NO FURTHER SORTS ARE POSSIBLE.

---

[19] The instructions are an extended version of the instructions provided by David Canter, Jennifer Brown, and Linda Groat, "A Multiple Sorting Procedure for Studying Conceptual Systems," In Michael Brenner, Jennifer Brown, and David Canter eds., *The Research Interview: Uses and Approaches* (New York, NY: Academic Press, 1985), 79–114.

The sorting procedure, coupled with the respondents verbal explanation provides three different types of insights. First, responses to the question, "On what basis did you sort the objects?" provides an explicit identification of the attributes by which objects in the category are evaluated. This information fosters an understanding of how the consumer organizes the category and has implications for brand positioning. Second, responses to the question, "How are the objects in this pile alike and different from objects in other piles?" provides insights into the arrangement of objects within a particular category and, as a result, helps the advertiser understand the brand's competitive set from the perspective of the target consumer. Third, the relative importance of criteria or characteristics can be inferred from the order in which they selected as the basis of a sort. Criteria used in earlier sorts are likely to be more salient to the individual and, therefore, may be more important for evaluating objects in the category. This information helps the advertiser understand the relative importance of category benefits and the brand's competitors in terms of these benefits.

Collage

A collage is a visual image formed from the selection and arrangement of many smaller images. Individuals in personal interviews and focus groups can use small pictures to create a collage that expresses their underlying feelings and attitudes toward themselves, a particular brand, or an entire product category. Once constructed, the interviewer or moderator looks for themes and may ask the individual who created the collage to explain the reasons for his or her picture choice and arrangement.

The advertising agency D'Arcy Masius Benton & Bowles (DMB&B), for example, used the collage technique to assist in the planning of Cadillac advertising. Participants in focus groups (that explored attitudes toward the Cadillac Seville STS) made collages that they felt described themselves and their lifestyle. The resulting collages were physically very neat, emphasized health, exercise, and a desire for quality and expressed "discriminating choices" in both lifestyle and product selection. The DMB&B creative team used the collages as a basis for Cadillac Seville STS creative. DMB&B produced a 30-second commercial that featured Olympic gold medalist Edwin Moses and other high achievers. The spot ended with a theme line designed to reflect the attitudes expressed in the collages: "The great performers are always creating a higher standard."[20]

ELICITING QUALITATIVE INSIGHTS: ACTIVE LISTENING AND PROBES

Direct verbal questions or projective techniques are the initial stimulus in a personal interview or discussion group. Probes and follow-up questions provide the opportunity for a deeper exploration of responses, for the clarification of issues, and for "pushing" respondent's to provide deeper, more meaningful responses.

A prerequisite to the meaningful probing of responses is active (as opposed to simple) listening on the part of the interviewer or moderator. Simple listening shows the respondent that what he or she is saying is important. Verbal responses, such as

---

[20] Leah Rickard, "Focus Groups Go To Collage," *Advertising Age* (November 14, 1994): 39.

"Yes, tell me more," "that's interesting, what else," and "I see" as well as nonverbal responses such as attentive body language, nods, smiles, and the maintenance of eye contact show a respondent that the interviewer is interested in what is being said and places value on the content being communicated. Active listening goes beyond simple listening. Active listening means hearing and responding to the *significance* of the respondent's remarks. Here, the interviewer attends to the "emotive aspects of what is said, the figures of speech, the inconsistencies, the buried connections, the obscure references, the startling insights, and the repetitions [in order to determine] what the person might have meant and what that person's remark might mean outside its immediate context."[21]

Active listening is important for several reasons. First, active listening shows that the interviewer is interested in and is paying close attention to what is being said. This communicates to respondents that what they are saying is important. One way to indicate active listening is to use the respondent's own words in probes and follow-up questions, for example:

> Tell me more about why you feel all gasolines are the same except for Amoco.

> You mentioned that advertisers don't usually tell the whole truth about their products. Can you give me an example of when you saw this happen?

Drawing attention (in a nonthreatening and nonjudgmental way) to conflicting statements is another way to demonstrate this aspect of active listening, for example:

> Mary, at one point earlier in the group you said that you would never consider purchasing a luxury car. Just recently, however, you said that you might consider purchasing a Lexus or an Infiniti. Could you please help me understand your point of view? Can you please try and explain for me your attitudes toward purchasing luxury cars in general and purchasing an Infiniti or Lexus in particular.

Second, active listening tends to reinforce respondents' perceptions that they and the interviewer are working on a common problem and that the interviewer is interested in truly understanding their unique points of view. Finally, the probes and follow-up questions that result from active listening increase the quality and depth of information communicated by the respondent.

Probes and follow-up questions accomplish these goals and provide the means for deeper information only if used appropriately. As a consequence, qualitative researchers recommend the following guidelines for the use of probes and follow-up questions:[22]

- Follow up on what the respondent says using the respondent's own words;
- Ask follow-up questions to resolve ambiguity and to increase clarity;
- Do not ask probes or follow-up questions for their own sake. Each must have a role in advancing the interview or discussion;
- Try not to interrupt or cause the respondent to lose his or her train of thought. Probe and follow up at logical stopping or transition points;

---

[21] Lindloff, *Qualitative Communication Research*, 183.

[22] I. E. Seidman, *Interviewing As Qualitative Research* (New York, NY: Teacher's College Press, 1991), 56–71; Goldman and McDonald, *The Group Depth Interview*, 111–22.

- Use probes to add depth by asking for concrete details;
- Use probes that are simple, direct, and easy for the respondent to understand;
- Use probes and follow-up questions to stimulate affective as well as cognitive responses.

THE ENVIRONMENT FOR QUALITATIVE RESEARCH

Verbal questions, projective techniques, and probes attempt to draw information and insights from respondents. However, the success of these techniques depends on the environment in which they are asked. The potential for a successful qualitative research interview or focus group increases when the interviewer or moderator creates the proper environment.

Successful qualitative research is conducted in an environment in which respondents feel safe, comfortable, and free to express their opinions. This type of environment is most likely to occur when the interviewer or moderator

- personally does not act (and prevents others from acting) in a judgmental manner,
- establishes rapport, between him or herself and the respondents and, in a group discussion, among the respondents themselves.

Nonjudgmental Manner

The interviewer or moderator must interact with respondents in a nonjudgmental manner, that is, he or she must ask questions, probe responses, and react to provided information without explicit or implicit indications of what is the "right," "better," or expected response. The best interviewers or moderators take a neutral stance. They do not let their own opinions be known and they do not evaluate the responses of others. This does not mean, however, that the moderator must be distant or poker-faced. On the contrary, a relaxed, interested, and pleasant *but neutral* manner is very effective in encouraging respondents to feel comfortable expressing intimate or socially unacceptable sentiments as well as opinions that simply may run counter to prevailing group consensus.

The avoidance of *explicit* judgments (and the subsequent bias they cause) is relatively simple. The interviewer or moderator avoids leading or evaluative questions and probes, for example:

John, do you *really* mean to say that you actually believe what that advertiser said in his commercial?

How many others in the group participate in these sorts of unusual behaviors?

The avoidance of implicit judgments is also important, but is often more difficult to control. Here, for example, body language and note taking can introduce judgmental bias. Changes in the interviewer's body language, the tilting of an eyebrow, or the loss of eye contact can all signal evaluative judgments. Further, if notes are taken sporadically, respondents may infer that comments that are written down are more important or more correct than comments not written down.

Rapport

The establishment of rapport between interviewer and respondent(s) is an important component of the interview or group setting. Lindlof[23] characterizes rapport as the "ability of both parties to empathize with each other's perspective . . ." occurring when the "interviewer and interviewee are in basic accord on communication style and the subject matter that can and cannot be talked about." He goes on to point out that rapport is important because "it clears away the burden of having to translate what one wants to say into a formal or foreign style. It clears away the fear of being misunderstood. It means that, for this occasion, conditions are right for disclosing thoughts and feelings more readily."

Interview conditions and interviewer's actions affect the establishment of rapport. In terms of interview conditions, rapport is more likely to be established when the interview is conducted in comfortable surroundings and when initial contact between interviewer and respondent is positive (for example, greetings are exchanged, hands are shaken, etc.). In terms of interviewer actions, rapport is more likely to be established when the interviewer

- pays attention to and follows up on what the respondent says,
- asks questions to clarify and expand on the respondent statements,
- probes for further information on respondent's cognitive *and* affective statements,
- follows up to learn more but does not interrupt to do so,
- displays appropriate emotions (for example, laughs at respondent's jokes),
- tolerates silence and does not force responses,
- is attentive and appropriately responds to respondent's body language.

The creation of rapport between interviewer and respondent does not imply that interviewer neutrality needs to be abandoned. Patton explains the difference between these characteristics:

> Rapport is a stance vis-à-vis the *person* being interviewed. Neutrality is a stance vis-à-vis the *content* of what that person says. Rapport means that I respect people being interviewed, so that what they say is important because of who is saying it . . . Yet, I will not judge them for the content of what they say to me. [emphasis added][24]

Focus groups and minigroups also require rapport among the group members. Respondents are more likely to express their true opinions if they believe they have things in common with other members of the group and that other members of the group will not judge the "correctness" of their attitudes and beliefs.

Summary

Qualitative advertising research entails the intensive observation and interviewing of a small number of individuals in order to acquire detailed, in-depth insights into their attitudes, beliefs, motivations, and lifestyles. The goal of qualitative research is to help

---

[23] Lindloff, *Qualitative Communication Research*, 180.

[24] Michael. Q. Patton, *Qualitative Evaluation and Research Methods*, 2nd ed. (Newbury Park: CA: SAGE, 1990), 317.

develop a better understanding of *why* individuals act as they do, rather than developing numeric descriptions of *what* people do.

Qualitative research has several strengths and weaknesses versus quantitative research. Strengths include the depth of information provided, the opportunity to "get close to the data" by observing respondents themselves, and its cost and time efficiency. Weaknesses relate to problems of generalizability and projectability, the absence of numeric summaries and greater potential for bias in findings interpretation.

Qualitative advertising research generally uses personal interviews or groups. Personal interviews, where individuals are interviewed one at a time, provide the greatest depth of detail and are most appropriate when

- the subject matter of the interview is confidential,
- group pressure is likely to distort responses,
- there are legal or confidentiality constraints on group discussion,
- a longer amount of time is required to establish rapport or an understanding of target attitudes and behaviors.

Focus groups, however, are appropriate when the spontaneity and interaction of the group discussion is desired.

The interviewer or focus group moderator is the key to obtaining valuable insights from the qualitative research study. The interviewer or moderator is more likely to conduct research that leads to valuable insights when he or she is well prepared, conducts the interviews appropriately, and uses appropriate questioning and projective techniques. Preparation for the interview entails obtaining an accurate and complete picture of the research study's background and informational needs, determining the most advantageous ways to obtain desired information and preparing a well-tested and constructed discussion guide. Appropriate conduct of the interview or focus group entails using a nonjudgmental manner, establishing rapport, and being an active listener. Appropriate questioning techniques entail understanding and using the types of questions (direct and factual, structural, grand tour, idealization, contrast, hypothetical-interaction, and third-person) and projective techniques (word association, sentence and story completions, personification, anthropomorphism, role-playing, shopping lists, picture projection, picture sorts, and collage) are most likely to uncover desired insights and information.

Review Questions

1. What are the basic characteristics of qualitative research?
2. What is the primary difference between qualitative and quantitative research?
3. In what types of circumstances is qualitative research most appropriate? Why is it appropriate in these circumstances?
4. What are the two most common types of qualitative advertising research?
5. What are the basic characteristics of personal interviews?
6. In what types of circumstances are personal interviews most appropriate?
7. What are the basic characteristics of minigroups and focus groups?

8. In what types of circumstances are focus groups most appropriate?

9. What are the relative strengths and weaknesses of focus groups versus personal interviews?

10. What are the steps an interviewer or moderator should take when preparing for qualitative research?

11. What are the seven different types of verbal questions used in qualitative interviewing? What types of insights are provided by each type of question?

12. What are projective techniques? What is their role in qualitative advertising research?

13. What are the most common types of projective techniques used in qualitative advertising research? Provide an example of each.

14. What is *active listening* and why is it important?

15. How can an interviewer or moderator demonstrate active listening?

16. What does "establishing the proper environment" for an interview or group mean?

17. Why is it important for the interviewer or moderator to act in a nonjudgmental manner?

18. What is *rapport* in the context of interviewing and why is it important?

Application Exercises[25]

1. You are the supervisor of a qualitative research study. One of your assistants has just conducted a qualitative interview. The objective of the interview was to determine people's reactions to the political advertising shown in a prior presidential campaign.

   You must provide a critique of the interview to your assistant, pointing out areas where your assistant performed well and areas in which there were problems. In other words, you want to help your assistant improve her qualitative interviewing skills. Read the following interview and then prepare a written analysis of the interview. NOTE: Your job is to assess how well your assistant *conducted* the interview. You are not interested in the content of the interview per se. Also, the transcript begins after rapport, etc. was established. Take each interviewer comment, question, or reply (in turn) and discuss whether the interviewer's comment, question, or reply was or was not appropriate. Justify your answer. If it was appropriate, why? If it was not appropriate, what advice would you give the interviewer to improve her performance. (In the interview transcript an "I" stands for the interviewer and a "R" stands for the respondent. The transcript begins in midinterview. The number after the I represents the number of the interviewer interaction and can be used as a reference in your answer. The respondent has been appropriately screened.)

   I (1): Let's turn our attention to the almost overwhelming number of political ads shown over the past three months. Specifically, I'd like to get your reactions to the advertisements for the presidential candidates. All right?

   R: Fine.

   I (2): Over the past three months, would you say that you saw more advertising for Clinton, Perot, or Dole?

---

[25] All application exercises are hypothetical.

R: Clinton.

I (3): All right, let's focus on the advertising for Clinton. In thinking back about his particular advertising, what thoughts or feelings come to mind?

R: I think that his advertising was the most straightforward.

I (4): What do you mean by straightforward?

R: I think that it addressed the issues that needed to be addressed. His ads really didn't go into a lot of character attacks or go off on any tangential issues like the other advertisements did.

I (5): Any other thoughts or feelings?

R: You know, I really don't like all that shrill stuff—the yelling and the name calling. There's one ad that really got me mad. I remember saying to myself "What kind of person would put an ad like that on the air?"

I (6): Let's get back to Clinton's ads. Many people liked the ad that he aired the day before the election. The thirty-minute infomercial. Did you happen to see this particular ad?

R: Yup.

I (7): How would you compare this ad to the thirty-minute infomercials of Ross Perot?

R: I liked them both. They really touched me.

I (8): In what way?

R: Different ways.

I (9): Can you be more specific?

R: Well, Clinton's ad touched me emotionally. Perot's ad, on the other hand, was very different and had a completely different effect on me. Almost the opposite effect. Perot's ad was very intellectual and thought-provoking.

I (10): That's interesting. But in terms of who you finally wound up supporting, you know, the candidate that you wound up voting for, just how much did the ads that you saw influence your final decision?

R: They didn't influence me at all. Not one iota. Not even one little bit. I just don't pay any attention to the ads. They don't have any impact at all.

2. Select an interview topic and prepare a discussion guide. (Plan on conducting the interview for approximately twenty minutes.) Tape record the interview. After the interview is complete listen to the tape and prepare an assessment of how well you

   • were prepared for the interview and how this preparation affected the interview,

   • established rapport,

   • appropriately and successfully probed responses, and

   • appropriately and successfully used questioning and projective techniques.

   Additionally, discuss what you believe to be the strengths and weaknesses of your performance as an interviewer. Provide examples. Discuss how you would use this experience to improve your skills in future qualitative interviews.

3. Select four individuals with whom you can conduct personal interviews. Two individuals should be regular consumers of diet soft drinks while the remaining two individuals should be occasional or nondrinkers of diet soft drinks. Your goal in each interview is to explore: (1) differences in perceptions of different brands of diet soft drinks, with particular attention to Diet Coke and Diet Pepsi; and (2) how perceptions relate to

levels of diet soft drink consumption. Your interviews should use each of the question techniques discussed in this chapter. You may customize the questions and techniques to meet the specific diet soft drink usage characteristics of each interviewee.

When you have completed all four interviews, prepare a summary of what you have learned about the types of insights provided by each different type of questioning technique.

4. Select four individuals with whom you can conduct personal interviews. Two individuals should be owners of sport/utility vehicles while the remaining two individuals should be owners of sedans. Your goal in each interview is to explore each individuals self-image, the image of their vehicle, and the relationship between the individual and his or her vehicle. Your interviews should use at least one of each type of projective technique (verbal stimuli and response, use of imagination or scenarios, and pictorial) discussed on pages 205–213.

When you have completed all four interviews, prepare a summary of what you have learned about the types of insights provided by each different type of projective technique.

10 FOCUS GROUPS

As discussed in Chapter 9, focus groups are probably the most common form of qualitative advertising research. As a form of qualitative research, focus groups are appropriate when informational needs require deep insights into individuals' thoughts and attitudes and direction for understanding how these thoughts and attitudes influence behavior. Focus groups are an inappropriate research technique when informational needs require numeric descriptions, they are used as a substitute for more complex quantitative research, or they are used simply because there is a feeling that we should do "something" (i.e., any) research before we have to make a decision.

After reading this chapter, you will be able to

■ Plan and conduct focus groups once it has been decided that they are an appropriate research technique for satisfying current informational needs.

Focus groups begin with the same planning and decisions as other types of research. The situation motivating the research is examined, a problem statement is formulated, informational needs are specified, and the selection of focus groups as a means of satisfying informational needs is made.[1] Once these decisions are made, focus group planning begins. The steps involved in the planning and conduct of focus group research are shown in Figure 10.1 (page 220).

Select a Moderator

Focus group planning begins with two simultaneous sets of activities. Figure 10.1 shows that one line of activity in the planning process relates to the group moderator and moderator-related activities. The success of any focus group research is directly dependent on the skill and performance of the selected moderator. For this reason, this line of activity begins with the evaluation of potential moderators and the selection of the one moderator who will conduct the groups.

---

[1] See, for example, Robert Ferguson, "Focus Groups May Provide Unfocused Marketing Direction," *Advertising Age* (June 12, 1995): 26.

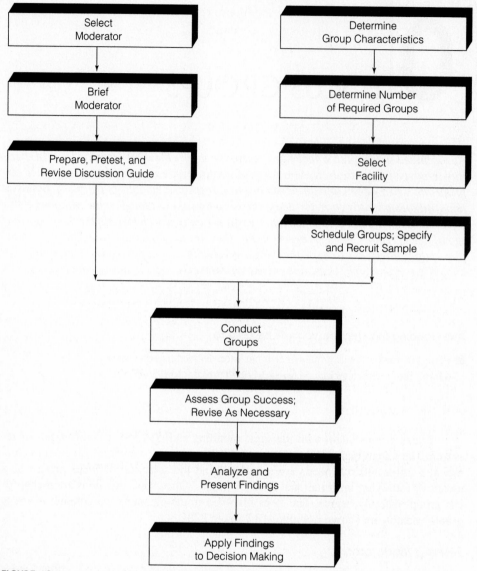

FIGURE 10.1
Steps in planning and conducting a focus group.

Several different aspects of moderator characteristics should be considered during the selection process. First, there are personality characteristics. Moderators who demonstrate excellence in focus group facilitation generally are

- genuinely interested in hearing other people's thoughts and feelings,
- able to verbalize and clearly express their own feelings,
- animated and spontaneous conversationalists,
- active listeners,

- able to understand how others feel and are able to see life from others' perspectives,
- cognizant of, and able to control, their own biases,
- inquisitive about "what makes people tick,"
- flexible and able to respond quickly to changing situations,
- innovative and able to see new ways to explore issues and facilitate the group discussion.[2]

Second, it is important that group members be comfortable with the demographic characteristics of the moderator. Thus, for example, it may be a poor decision to have a male moderator conduct groups with women who will be asked to discuss their use of personal health and beauty aids. Third, it is important that the moderator have good advertising and business sense. The moderator must be able to understand, from an advertising or business perspective, why the groups are being conducted, the types of information required, and how this information will be used for advertising decision making.

Beyond personality and demographic characteristics, the moderator's fee is also a consideration in moderator evaluation and selection. Moderator's fees vary greatly from moderator to moderator. Typical fees for moderating (not including the preparation and presentation of findings) range from about $500 to over $1,000 per group. The moderator's fee is not always an indicator of moderator quality. Many excellent moderators charge on the low end of the continuum while many poor moderators charge on the high end. As a result, we recommend you obtain and use referrals from prior moderating projects rather than relying on fee as a gauge of moderator quality.

Brief the Moderator

Once selected, the moderator is briefed on the research problem, research goals, informational needs, timing, and other study parameters and products, materials, or other tangible items (such as products to be taste tested) to be used during the focus group research. This briefing typically takes several hours and helps the moderator understand what needs to be learned from the groups so that he or she is in the best position to keep the discussion focused on important areas and to circumvent or minimize irrelevant discussion. Remember that

> the objective of the moderator briefing should not be to try and make the moderator an expert in the area being researched, which could inhibit discussion by the respondents. Rather, the moderator should be sufficiently familiar with the material so that he or she can probe the important areas and become familiar with the language of the consumer with regard to the area being surveyed.[3]

Finally, moderator briefings are most productive when the moderator receives the documentation on the research study's background and informational needs for review before the briefing.

---

[2] Adapted from J. Langer, "Clients: Check Qualitative Researcher's Personal Traits to Get More," *Marketing News* (September 8, 1978): 10–11.

[3] Thomas L. Greenbaum, *The Practical Handbook and Guide to Focus Group Research* (Lexington, MA: D. C. Heath and Company, 1983), 29–30.

Prepare, Pretest, and Revise Discussion Guide

The discussion guide is typically drafted by the focus group moderator. (The steps underlying the creation and revision of the discussion guide are presented in Chapter 9.) Once the guide is drafted, it is recommended that involved individuals from the agency meet with the moderator to discuss and, if necessary, revise the discussion guide.

Determine the Group Characteristics

As illustrated in Figure 10.1, decisions related to group characteristics and the logistics of the research proceed at the same time the moderator is being briefed and the discussion guide is being developed and revised. The first decision reached in this area of planning relates to group composition.

There is a wide range of opinions with regard to the need for homogeneity within a focus group. Some recommend near complete homogeneity, that is, group members share a wide range of attitudinal, demographic, and behavioral characteristics. Keown, for example, states that "Homogeneous groups... are generally more comfortable and open with each other, whereas mixed sex, ethnic, or socioeconomic groups make it more difficult to achieve a high degree of group interaction."[4] Others, however, recommend that group homogeneity need only extend to those areas that have the potential to affect a group member's interpersonal comfort or self-disclosure.

> The goal is homogeneity in background, not homogeneity in attitudes.[5]

> A number of individuals may be very different in national origin, religious beliefs, political persuasion and the like; but if they share a common identity relevant to the discussion. . . a group can form.[6]

Our experience as well as recent empirical findings[7] leads us to agree with this latter view. However, because there are no hard and fast rules for determining group composition in any particular research situation, common sense and professional judgment must be relied on to isolate those characteristics most likely to affect discussion and group cohesion, for example:

- *Attitudes may be the defining characteristic in some circumstances.* Focus group exploration of Tom Smith's political advertising might entail seeking the reactions of those who are favorable toward candidate Smith and those who are neutral or unfavorable. (Smith is seeking the senatorship from Illinois.) It would likely be best to separate these two groups of individuals. Other respondents' characteristics such as age, sex, and income appear to be related less to Smith support, and thus are not a consideration in group composition. Thus, Smith will have two types of groups: one focus group of "supporters" and one group of "nonsupporters." Similarly, groups probing perceptions of different types of wine might require separating those who consider themselves wine "connoisseurs" from those who consider themselves casual wine drinkers.

---

[4] Charles Keown, "Focus Group Research: Tool for the Retailer," In Thomas J. Hayes and Carol B. Tathum eds., *Focus Group Interviews: A Reader* (Chicago, Il: American Marketing Association, 1983), 64–70.

[5] David L. Morgan, *Focus Groups as Qualitative Research* (Beverly Hills, CA: SAGE, 1988), 46.

[6] Alfred E. Goldman, "The Group Depth Interview," *Journal of Marketing* (July 1962): 61–68.

[7] Kim P. Corfman, "The Importance of Member Homogeneity to Focus Group Quality," *Advances in Consumer Research* 22 (1995): 354–9.

- *Demographics and product usage may be the defining characteristics in other circumstances.* Focus group exploration of hair coloring might entail seeking the reactions of men and women who do and do not color their hair. Because of gender differences in hair coloring, men and women would likely feel more comfortable in a same gender group. Moreover, the personal nature of hair coloring might make participants more comfortable if they were in a group with others of the same behavior. Thus, four types of groups are required in this product category: (1) women who color their hair, (2) women who do not color their hair, (3) men who color their hair, and (4) men who do not color their hair. Other demographic criteria (such as age and income) do not appear to be relevant to this set of group's composition.

Determine the Number of Required Groups

The specification of group characteristics has implications for the total number of groups required. In the case of Smith's political advertising, two distinct groups are needed. Once the number of distinct groups is determined, it must then be decided how many groups will be conducted in how many locations.

It is generally unwise to conduct only one set of groups per location. Given small sample sizes and nonrandom sampling procedures, it is dangerous to rely on the perceptions, attitudes, and behaviors of one group of individuals. Thus, it is generally recommended to conduct two groups per location.

The number of locations selected for the groups reflects the extent to which it is believed that geographic differences affect salient attitudes and behaviors. Where geographic differences are felt to exist, sets of groups should be held in geographically diverse locations. Candidate Smith may decide that upstate voters are different than downstate voters, and so may want to conduct one set of groups in each part of the state. This would result in a total of eight groups: two upstate groups with "supporters," two downstate groups with "supporters," two upstate groups with "nonsupporters," and two downstate groups with "nonsupporters."

In general, geographic diversity provides greater insights and reduces the likelihood of respondents from a single geographic area skewing the results. However, geographic diversity becomes less important in the following circumstances:

- The groups are designed to provide preliminary creative guidance;
- The groups are designed to confirm or extend actions based on more extensive prior research, for example, the revision of product positioning or a change in product labeling;
- The research is designed to support questionnaire development;
- Sales data suggest that there are no regional variations in product purchase behaviors;
- Prior quantitative data suggest that there are no regional variations in relevant perceptions or attitudes.[8]

Select the Facility

The focus group facility is the place where the groups will physically be held. While some advertising agencies have their own in-house facilities, most focus groups are

---

[8] Alfred E. Goldman and Susan Schwartz McDonald, *The Group Depth Interview: Principles and Practice* (Englewood Cliffs, NJ: Prentice-Hall, 1987), 33.

DIRECTIONS TO RECRUITER: You are recruiting respondents for four focus groups. Group meeting times are

Tuesday, June 23	Group A	6 p.m.
	Group B	8 p.m.
Wednesday, June 24	Group C	6 p.m.
	Group D	8 p.m.

Respondents will be women between the ages of 25 and 44 who work full-time outside the home and who have a personal annual income of at least $30,000. In addition to these general characteristics, women in Groups A and B must have at least one current brokerage account in their own name (or joint tendency) *and* must have executed at least one trade within the past 30 days. Women in Groups C and D cannot have had any active brokerage account within the past five years *and* must express an interest in investing stocks.

SCREENER:
IF WOMAN ANSWERS THEN BEGIN. IF MAN ANSWERS, IDENTIFY YOURSELF AND ASK IF THERE IS A WOMAN IN THE HOUSE BETWEEN THE AGES OF 25 AND 44, AND, IF SO, CAN YOU TALK TO HER. WHEN WOMAN ANSWERS BEGIN.

Hello, my name is_____ from _____, a marketing research company. Can I ask you just a few questions as part of a marketing research study? I assure you that all your answers are confidential and that I am not trying to sell you anything.

1. First, can you please tell me into which of the following categories your age falls?

24 and under	[ ]	⟶ THANK AND DISCONTINUE
25 to 34	[ ]	⟶ CONTINUE WITH Q. 2
35 to 44	[ ]	⟶ CONTINUE WITH Q. 2
45 and older	[ ]	⟶ THANK AND DISCONTINUE

2. Are you currently...

employed full-time outside the home	[ ]	⟶ CONTINUE WITH Q. 3
employed part-time outside the home	[ ]	⟶ THANK AND DISCONTINUE
not employed outside the home	[ ]	⟶ THANK AND DISCONTINUE

3. Do you or any member of your household have a job that entails...

advertising	[ ]	⟶ THANK AND DISCONTINUE
marketing	[ ]	⟶ THANK AND DISCONTINUE
the sale of stocks or other securities	[ ]	⟶ THANK AND DISCONTINUE

4. Into which of the following categories does your personal annual income fall?

under $30,000	[ ]	⟶ THANK AND DISCONTINUE
$30,000 to $49,999	[ ]	⟶ CONTINUE WITH Q. 5
over $50,000	[ ]	⟶ CONTINUE WITH Q. 5

5. Do you currently have a brokerage account that is registered in your name alone or in joint tenancy with another?

yes	[ ]	⟶ CONTINUE WITH Q. 6
no	[ ]	⟶ CONTINUE WITH Q. 8

6. Have you made a trade in this account within the past 30 days?

yes	[ ]	⟶ CONTINUE WITH Q. 7
no	[ ]	⟶ THANK AND DISCONTINUE

(continued)

7. Have you participated in a focus group or other form of market research within the past 30 days?

       yes   [   ] ——▶ THANK AND DISCONTINUE

       no   [   ] ——▶ CHECK QUOTAS, INVITE TO GROUP A OR
                                      GROUP B. END SCREENER

8. Have you had a brokerage account that is registered in your name alone or in joint tenancy with another individual within the past five years?

       yes   [   ] ——▶ THANK AND DISCONTINUE

       no   [   ] ——▶ CONTINUE WITH Q. 9

9. How interested or uninterested are you in purchasing stocks or other securities for your own personal investment? Are you...

    Extremely interested   [   ] ——▶ CONTINUE WITH Q.10

    Somewhat interested   [   ] ——▶ CONTINUE WITH Q.10

    Somewhat uninterested   [   ] ——▶ THANK AND DISCONTINUE

    Extremely uninterested   [   ] ——▶ THANK AND DISCONTINUE

10. Have you participated in a focus group or other form of market research within the past 30 days?

       yes   [   ] ——▶ THANK AND DISCONTINUE

       no   [   ] ——▶ CHECK QUOTAS, INVITE TO GROUP C OR
                                      GROUP D. END SCREENER

FIGURE 10.2
Sample focus group screener.

held at facilities specially designed for the conduct and viewing of focus groups. Regardless of where the facility is located, it should have at minimum: a reception area in which to greet and organize respondents prior to the group, a conference room with a one-way mirror in which the group will be held, video and/or audio recording capabilities, and a viewing room.

    Beyond the physical layout of the facility, a facility should be selected with the characteristics of the group participants in mind. The facility should be located in a place that is conveniently located for the group participants.

Schedule Groups, Specify Sample, and Recruit Participants

Focus groups among those not employed outside the home may be conducted in either the day or the evening. Groups conducted among those employed outside the home typically take place in the evening (common group times are 6 P.M. and 8 P.M.).

    Most focus group facilities have the capability to recruit respondents. Here, the researcher specifies the characteristics of individuals required for each group and the facility locates and recruits the respondents. A sample screener is shown in Figure 10.2. Note how the screener not only identifies desired participants and assigns each different type of participant to a different group, but also eliminates "undesirable" respondents who are

- professional focus group participants (Questions 7 and 10),
- involved in the advertising or marketing professions (Question 3), and

- employed in the industry or professionally involved with the brand or product category being studied (Question 3).

An important part of respondent recruitment is the incentive. An *incentive* is a fee paid to respondents for participating in a focus group. The amount of an incentive generally reflects the difficulty in respondent recruiting. Easy to recruit respondents may be paid $30–$40 while harder to recruit respondents, such as those in specialized businesses, may be paid upwards of $150.

Conduct the Groups

Figure 10.1 shows that the successful conclusion of both planning paths is the conduct of the first set of groups. While the specific discussion in every group is different, there are nevertheless commonalties among the groups. Focus groups tend to follow the same progression, as outlined next.

Prefatory remarks welcome the respondents, introduce the moderator, and explain the focus group setting and the rules that will govern the next two hours of discussion. Most prefatory statements contain the following elements:

- Introduction of the moderator by name;
- Refreshments (soft drinks, coffee, sandwiches for dinner groups);
- Explanation of the moderator's role ("to keep the discussion moving," "to help bring out thoughts and opinions," etc.);
- Specification of the topic under discussion ("tonight we will be discussing. . .");
- Rules for participants: do not speak at the same time, address each other and not the moderator, be candid and truthful, do not try for the right answer—there aren't any! and do not talk at the same time;
- Characteristics of observation: one-way mirror, tape recording and/or audio recording, observers behind the one-way mirror;
- Rules for reporting: participants will not be quoted by name, all information is confidential and is only for internal agency for client usage.

Introductions and personal information follow prefatory remarks. Here, each member of the group is invited to state his or her name and to tell something about him or herself that is related to the focus of the discussion. If appropriate, each respondent may also be invited to share basic demographic information, such as marital status, number of children, occupation, etc. There are three reasons for beginning the group in this way. First, it provides an opportunity for each respondent to talk, implicitly communicating that each person and his or her opinion is important. Second, it helps to establish group rapport by demonstrating similarities in important characteristics among the respondents. Third, shared information related to the topic of the groups begins to focus respondents on the area of group discussion and inquiry.

Setting the context for discussion follows next. It is important for both the moderator and observers to understand the context of each individual's comments. Thus, groups often begin with a short series of questions that probe attitudes and behaviors specific to the topic of the group. Imagine a group designed to assess mothers' reac-

tions to new children's cereals and positionings. At this stage in the group, to better understand the discussion that follows, the moderator might ask respondents to summarize their children's cereal related behaviors, for example, the brands they typically buy, how often they purchase each brand, etc.

The majority of group time is then devoted to the *main discussion*. The moderator uses the open-ended questioning, probing and projective techniques discussed earlier to stimulate and lead the discussion.

A moderator, at the end of the main discussion, often develops and presents a *summary* to confirm his or her understanding of the group's primary comments and perspective. For example, at this point (near the end of the group) a moderator might say:

> We have covered a lot of ground tonight and I want to thank you for sharing your thoughts and opinions with me. We are close to finished, but before we disband I would like to take just a few moments to make certain that I correctly understand what you have said. OK. First, it seemed that almost all of you felt that children's cereal advertisers place too much emphasis on the premiums contained in the box. The group, fairly consensually, I think, believed that this was an unfair way to sell the cereal. Is this right?

This type of recap serves three purposes. First, and perhaps most important, it makes certain that what the moderator thinks he or she heard is, in fact, correct. Second, group participants have one final opportunity to make their opinions known. Third, a clear and concise summary is provided for individuals in the viewing room.

Moderators often excuse themselves from the discussion room just before the end of the group discussion to take viewing room questions. At this time, the moderator might say:

> You will recall that there were individuals in the viewing room watching the group. Before I let you go, let me just check to see if they have any questions that they would like me to ask you.

The moderator would then do a *viewing room check* to see if those in the viewing room have any important, unresolved issues that need to be addressed. A viewer might say, "The lady in the red dress said that she would never ever buy our product again. But, others prevented her from saying why. Can you see what the main reasons are?" The moderator takes questions from the viewing room and, if appropriate, communicates them to the group.

The group then ends with a thank you and the payment of incentives.

Assess Group Success and, If Necessary, Revise the Discussion Guide

Focus groups should be viewed as a dynamic rather than a static process and, consequently, the discussion guide should be viewed as a fluid document subject to revision and modification as necessary. At the end of the first set of groups it is often advantageous to evaluate what transpired and to plan for the next set of groups. At this point, it is important to prepare for the upcoming set of groups by noting

- information areas that should be probed in the same way in upcoming groups,
- information areas that should be explored differently in upcoming groups because the questioning or projective techniques were unsuccessful,

- new question areas that should be explored in upcoming groups,
- question areas that should be eliminated in upcoming groups.

Each of these modifications is reflected in a revised discussion guide.

Analyze and Present Findings; Apply Findings to Decision Making

Focus group research concludes similarly to other advertising research. The data, in this case the group discussions, are analyzed, the major findings are presented and the findings are used to assist in the decision-making process. Each of these tasks is discussed in Chapter 11.

VIEWING FOCUS GROUPS

As noted earlier in this chapter, one of the great advantages of focus groups is the ability for individuals at the agency and client to see and hear the target consumer. Mere viewing, however, is not enough to provide insights into the meaning of the discussion. Focus group viewers must view the groups in a way that fosters an understanding of what is being said and that focuses on important aspects of the group's discussion. Viewer adherence to the following eight recommendations helps increase the likelihood of a positive, rewarding, and insightful viewing experience.

1. *Come prepared.* Informed, prepared viewers are in the best position to participate in meaningful, productive group viewing and post group discussions. At minimum, viewer preparation requires
   - familiarity with the research project's background, goals and informational needs, and
   - that all required materials are handy and accessible (for example, paper and pencil to take notes, a copy of the moderator's guide, etc.).

2. *Start watching from the beginning.* The first brief sections of the focus group (introduction, personal information, setting the context) provide a great deal of meaningful background information and make explicit the context within which more detailed discussion will take place. It is important to pay attention to what is said in these early group discussions.

3. *Focus on the big picture.* Focus group viewers often lose the forest by focusing on the trees. They may pay attention to the few unusual things that are said or they may become fixated on the comments from one or two individuals. Both viewing behaviors are dangerous. While detail is always important, it is most important to watch with an eye toward broad areas of group agreement and disagreement.

4. *Listen to everyone.* Focus group viewers have a tendency to listen to and give more credence to individuals in the group who agree with their position and to discount the comments of those with whom they disagree. It is important that the opinions of all members of the group be given equal attention and consideration.

5. *Listen to all comments.* A related viewer behavior is selective listening. Here, regardless of which participant expresses the thought, viewers tend to hear comments that agree with their position and to eliminate from consideration comments that run counter to their opinion. It is not unusual, for example, for a supporter of a particular point of view to quote all of the comments that agree with his or her point of view, even

if there were an equal (or greater) number of counter comments. Selective listening has the potential to greatly distort the conclusions drawn from a group discussion and should be avoided.

6. *Do not jump to premature conclusions.* Viewers should concentrate on listening to and interpreting the group discussion. Greenbaum notes that:

> the focus during the groups should be on intensive listening to the discussion, so that the observers can write down their interpretations of the discussion on the topics being discussed. After the groups, there is adequate time to review the notes and gather one's thoughts about the discussion in order to develop conclusions. This is an important point; many focus group observers jump to conclusions during the group discussion and therefore lose their objectivity. They then listen to the balance of the discussion (after their conclusion has been generated) with a biased mind, tending to hear only discussion points that support what they have already concluded.[9]

7. *Do not let character judgments affect how the group members' comments are perceived.* Some viewers have a tendency to equate the value of the respondents' comments with the respondents' personal characteristics. In these cases, viewers believe that the comments of the more attractive, articulate, or entertaining respondents are more valid and insightful. This is a dangerous perspective and should be avoided.

8. *Do not be biased by dominant personalities.* As discussed earlier, one risk of focus group research is the dominant personality, the person who speaks first (and often) and, in doing so, influences the direction and tone of the group's discussion. Viewers must be careful not to let this "louder voice" affect their interpretation of the overall group's perspective.

TECHNOLOGY AND FOCUS GROUP RESEARCH

The vast majority of focus group research is conducted in the way described in this chapter. Individuals in the target audience are prerecruited, a focus group is held in a focus group facility, the group is conducted by a moderator, and observed by individuals from the client and agency. However, new electronic technologies have widened the range of focus group options for marketers and advertisers with special needs.[10]

- Videoconferenced focus groups are being used as a way to reduce agency and client travel costs. Here, the focus group is televised to geographically dispersed viewing locations rather than having individuals from different locations travel to the focus group facility.

- Telephone focus groups are being used when the target audience is geographically dispersed (such as farmers) or when privacy needs discourage face-to-face contact (such as corporate purchasing agents). Here, respondents are prerecruited and told to call an 800-number at a certain time to participate in the group. Telephone focus groups are conducted by specially trained focus group moderators.

- BKG America, a New York research company, conducts focus groups with America Online's subscribers. Participants (who are paid $15 to $90 per session), log onto Amer-

---

[9] Greenbaum, *The Practical Handbook,* 141.

[10] The material in this section is based on Leslie M. Harris, "Technology, Techniques Drive Focus Group Trends," *Marketing News* (February 27, 1995): 8 and Cyndee Miller, "Focus Groups Go Where None Has Been Before," *Marketing News* (July 4, 1994): 2,14.

ica Online and then proceed to one of the "rooms" reserved for BKG Research. Respondents are then screened for target audience characteristics, and once a group has been formed, a "cyberspace" focus group takes place.

Summary

Focus groups are the most common form of qualitative advertising research. Focus group planning begins with two parallel activity paths. The first path relates to the moderator and consists of moderator selection and briefing and the creation of the focus group discussion guide. The second path relates to the logistics of the groups. Here, decisions are reached with regard to group characteristics, the number and location of the groups, facility selection, and participant recruitment. The successful completion of these two paths leads to the conduct of the groups themselves. A typical focus group passes through seven stages:

1. prefatory remarks
2. introductions and personal information
3. setting the context for discussion
4. main discussion
5. summary
6. viewing room check
7. conclusion

The process concludes with an assessment of the success of the first set of groups, modifications and revisions (if necessary), analysis, presentation, and application to decision making.

The quality of information derived from focus groups, in particular, is affected by observers' viewing behaviors. Observers should make certain that they

- come prepared,
- start watching from the beginning,
- focus on the big picture,
- listen to everyone,
- listen to all comments,
- do not jump to premature conclusions,
- do not let character judgments affect how the group members' comments are perceived,
- are not biased by dominant personalities.

Finally, new technologies such as videoconferencing, telephone focus groups, and "cyberspace" groups are expanding the options of advertisers whose special needs may prevent them from conducting traditional focus groups.

Review Questions

1. What are important considerations in the selection of a focus group moderator?
2. What is the purpose of the *moderator briefing*? What topics are typically covered in the briefing?

3. What is a *discussion guide*? Describe the process by which it is developed?

4. What are important considerations in determining focus group composition? Why are different considerations appropriate for different types of groups?

5. How is the total number of required focus groups determined?

6. What are the key characteristics of a focus group facility?

7. What types of respondent characteristics prevent participation in a focus group?

8. What are the main stages in a focus group? What events occur at each stage?

9. What are the guidelines for focus group viewing? Why is each guideline important?

10. What technological trends are affecting how focus groups are conducted?

Application Exercises[11]

1. You are the researcher working on the National Dairy Board Account. The National Dairy Board is the group that sponsors advertising designed to promote the drinking of milk. Their advertising stresses the benefits of milk and ends with the tag line "Milk. It does a body good." The Dairy Board has created this advertising in an attempt to appeal to men and women aged 25–44. You, as the researcher, have decided to hold focus groups to determine target consumers' perceptions of milk versus other drinks, reasons for drinking or not drinking milk, and reactions to the current advertising. The groups will be held next week. Your client, however, has never been to a focus group. Write the client a letter to explain what has happened so far and what is about to happen. In your letter be certain to address

   • What you have done so far to prepare for the groups? For example, how will you assure the client that the appropriate people will be attending and that the groups will be conducted in a beneficial and professional manner?

   • What the client can expect as he watches the groups? Discuss in detail, specific to these groups, the stages or progression the groups might proceed through, paying particular attention to the specific types and focus of discussion that will occur at various points throughout the groups. Be specific. Explain what will happen when the groups first begin, what you expect to happen next, etc.

   • What is the best way to listen to, learn from, and draw conclusions from the group's discussion? Again, be concrete; avoid pure generalizations.

2. You are the researcher working on the account team responsible for the advertising for K-Mart. K-Mart has decided to reposition itself. K-Mart's traditional appeal and customer base has been "middle-American" women aged 25–49, full-time homemakers, "working-class" households with total annual incomes between $15,000 and $35,000. K-Mart now wishes to appeal to a more contemporary, upscale clientele. Its new target includes both men and women aged 25–49, employed in white collar jobs with annual household incomes of more than $40,000. K-Mart believes that it can appeal to this new target while at the same time keeping its traditional customer base.

   Your client, K-Mart, has authorized up to eight focus groups. How many groups do you recommend be conducted? Why? What are the *specific* characteristics of the people who would be attending each group? Why? Avoid generalities in your discussion. Be specific and provide a sound rationale for your decisions as to the number of groups you recommend and the characteristics of those attending.

---

[11] All application exercises are hypothetical. Actual organizations are used for illustrative purposes only.

3. Examine the recommended characteristics of the set of focus groups from the prior question. Write a screener that could be used to recruit group participants.

4. Consider each of the following situations. Then, for each situation, decide whether you would recommend face-to-face, telephone, or "cyberspace" focus groups. Explain and justify your recommendation.

   a. John Deere wishes to obtain farmers' reactions to its latest advertising campaign for farm tractors and to explore reactions to potential creative themes for a new campaign.

   b. Kraft General Foods wants to explore reactions to their trade advertising campaigns in focus groups with grocery store purchasing managers.

   c. Revlon wants to explore reactions to several new make-up formulations. The target consists of women aged 25–44 who have purchased blush or eye shadow in the past sixty days. Group participants will (for each new product: be exposed to a description of the product, try the product, evaluate the product, and discuss the relationship between the new product description and actual product performance.

   d. Toys "Я" Us wishes to probe what is "hot" in the video game market. Specifically, Toys "Я" Us seeks to better understand perceptions of video games (both in general and in terms of specific titles) among boys aged 12–16.

CHAPTER
11
ANALYSIS OF QUALITATIVE DATA

A qualitative research study collects words. Tens of thousands of words that describe respondents' attitudes toward a particular object, express respondents' thoughts and opinions, and communicate respondents' feelings and emotions. Qualitative analysis attempts to make sense out of this verbal data by going beyond the literal words themselves to discover underlying themes and also commonalties and differences among respondents. This chapter introduces you to the procedures underlying the analysis of qualitative data.

After reading this chapter, you will be able to

■ Define the characteristics of qualitative data analysis.

■ Identify the techniques by which insights are obtained and conclusions are drawn from qualitative data.

The goals of qualitative analysis, as with any form of data analysis, are to produce findings that relate to the problem motivating the research and to provide insights that contribute to the decision-making process. These goals can be achieved only when the vast amount of verbal data collected during a qualitative research study is reduced to a set of well-defined and clearly explained patterns and themes. Unfortunately, there are few agreed on, externally objective techniques for accomplishing this. There are, for example, no formulas for determining statistical significance. There are no straightforward tests for reliability and validity. There is no way to replicate perfectly the process by which an individual analyst infers themes from the data. In short, there are no absolute rules except "to do the very best with your full intellect to fairly represent the data and communicate what the data reveal given the purpose of the study."[1] Thus, the extent to which a qualitative research study produces relevant, accurate findings is in great part dependent on the skills of the researcher who conducts the analysis.

---

[1] Michael Q. Patton, *Qualitative Evaluation and Research Methods* (Newbury Park, CA: SAGE Publications, 1990), 372. The discussion in the introduction of this chapter is also adapted from this source.

This is not meant to imply that qualitative data analysis is haphazard or subject to the whims of each individual analyst. Nothing, in fact, is farther from the truth. While there are no hard and fast rules governing the analysis of qualitative data, guidelines do exist. It is the *application* of these guidelines that affect the outcome of a qualitative analysis. The greater the extent to which an analyst systematically applies these guidelines the greater the likelihood that the analysis will accurately reflect trends and patterns in consumer response. Patton, in this regard, points out the relationship between analytical procedures, analyst skills and outcomes of the analysis:

> guidelines and procedural suggestions are not rules. Applying guidelines requires judgment and creativity. Because each qualitative study is unique, the analytical approach used will be unique. Because qualitative inquiry depends, at every stage, on the skills, training, insights and capabilities of the researcher, qualitative analysis ultimately depends on the analytical intellect and style of the analyst. The human factor is the great strength and the fundamental weakness of qualitative inquiry and analysis.[2]

The remainder of this chapter presents strategies that can be used to guide the analysis, interpretation and presentation of qualitative data. These strategies have been incorporated into a structured approach to qualitative data examination, analysis, and presentation that, as shown in Figure 11.1, divide the analysis and presentation of qualitative data into four main stages:

- activities conducted before data examination
- data examination
- theme identification, evaluation, and revision
- reporting

The next section addresses the activities conducted before data examination, the first stage of the analytical process.

ACTIVITIES CONDUCTED BEFORE DATA EXAMINATION

Figure 11.1 shows three important activities taking place during this stage. These activities pertain to (1) review of the research problem and informational needs, (2) confirmation and final listing of areas in which the analysis will focus, and (3) evaluation of the study sample.

Review Problem Definition and Informational Needs

A useful qualitative analysis responds to the problem(s) motivating the conduct of the research and the type(s) of information required for relevant marketing or advertising related decision(s). Thus, the first step in this stage of analysis conducts a formal review of the problem definition and informational needs. Notes and documents from agency and client meetings as well as the research proposal itself are reviewed. The outcome of the review is a list of specific areas that the analysis will address and the types of information that the analysis will provide. An excerpt from a list of areas to be

---

[2] Ibid., 372.

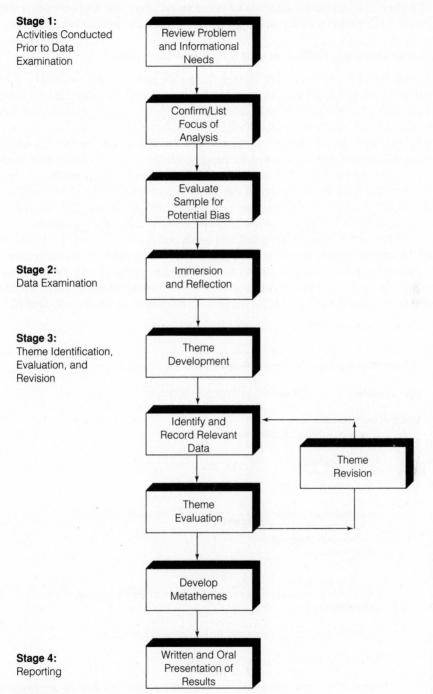

Stage 1:
Activities Conducted Prior to Data Examination

Review Problem and Informational Needs

Confirm/List Focus of Analysis

Evaluate Sample for Potential Bias

Stage 2:
Data Examination

Immersion and Reflection

Stage 3:
Theme Identification, Evaluation, and Revision

Theme Development

Identify and Record Relevant Data

Theme Revision

Theme Evaluation

Develop Metathemes

Stage 4:
Reporting

Written and Oral Presentation of Results

FIGURE 11.1
The process of qualitative data analysis and presentation.

addressed in a qualitative analysis of reactions to three product concepts is shown in Figure 11.2. Notice how the descriptions are specific and explicitly stated.

Confirm Problem Definition and Informational Needs

Informational needs sometimes change during a qualitative research study. Some initial informational needs may become less important and new informational needs may arise during the research. Additionally, it is possible that some important informational needs may not have been explicitly specified in initial discussions and research planning meetings. As a result, it is recommended that the analyst, before the start of data analysis, confirm that the focus of the proposed analysis (as described in the prior step) will satisfy the *current* set of informational needs. Confirmation can be accomplished in a meeting with the end users of the research and other involved individuals where the proposed focus of the analysis is presented and discussed. The outcome of this meeting is either acceptance or revision of the list of areas of the analysis.

The confirmation of informational needs and revision (if any) of the list of areas of the analysis serves two important purposes. First, it provides an outline and focus for subsequent data analyses. As such, it lets the analyst focus on a well-defined set of topics. Given the vast amount of data collected by most qualitative research studies, the ability to focus the analysis is an important component of success. Kruger points out that:

General Problem Area: Reactions to new product line extension concepts

Specific Area: Reactions to "Dual Disk Walkman"

Informational Needs:
Overall reaction, with reasons for
- Likes
- Dislikes
- Appeal
- Weaknesses

Reactions to specific concept element—dual disk—with reasons for
- Appeal
- Lack of appeal
- Likes
- Dislikes

Perceptions of product uniqueness, with reason for perceived uniqueness or lack of uniqueness

Interest in purchase, with reasons for interest of lack or interest

Influence of pricing on interest in purchase

For all of the above, differences related to demographic, attitudinal, or brand-related characteristics

---

FIGURE 11.2
Degree of specificity required for informational need listing.

The challenge to the researcher is to place primary attention on questions that are at the foundation of the study. Focused analysis conserves resources, but more importantly it enables the analyst to concentrate attention on areas of critical concern.[3]

Second, an agreement of informational needs and analytical focus before data analysis verifies for the research end users the types of information that will be addressed in the presentation of the study's findings and conclusions. This agreement greatly reduces the probability of a dissatisfied end user stating during a presentation: "This report is not complete. You should have looked at . . . ? I need to know about . . . ! Why is that information not here!"

Evaluate the Sample and Note Any Limitations

Next, the sample of respondents participating in the research is evaluated in terms of its "goodness" for providing reliable information relevant to the problem. The analyst assesses the extent to which the sample can provide accurate and appropriate information.

As discussed in earlier chapters, qualitative research rarely uses probability sampling, and therefore, it is typically acknowledged "up-front" that representativeness and generalizations to the broader population are limited. However, even when acknowledging these limitations, respondent characteristics must be still examined to confirm that the sample (1) possesses the desired set of demographic, brand-related and/or attitudinal characteristics, and (2) that there is an absence of bias or confounding effects. The following scenario illustrates the importance of this step.

> Imagine that Sony conducts a set of focus groups to probe college students' reactions to, perceptions of and experiences with various brands of portable CD players. Sony wishes to know the perceptions of those who currently own a Sony and those who own a competing brand. There are no problems with the respondents recruited for the Sony-owners group. Respondents represent a good cross-section of the male and female college population and they possess specified brand and demographic characteristics. Moreover, these respondents did not know each other prior to attending the group. Recruitment for the group that owns other brands' products is a problem, however. All of the participants in this group own the same competing brand (thus limiting the range of experiences with competing brands) and all have been recruited from one fraternity and one sorority on campus (thus even further limiting the representativeness of the groups.) These limitations must be kept in mind during the analysis and must be acknowledged during the presentation of the findings.

DATA EXAMINATION

The next stage in qualitative data analysis entails a review and examination of the raw data. Here, audio or video tapes or transcripts of the personal interviews or focus groups are examined in addition to any notes that might have been taken.[4] At this stage

---

[3] Richard A. Krueger, *Focus Groups, Second Edition* (Thousand Oaks, CA: SAGE Publications, 1994), 130.

[4] The basis of the review can either be audio tapes or transcripts. While both work well, we nevertheless recommend that tapes be utilized whenever possible. Tapes permit a greater understanding of the tone, conviction, and expression associated with individual consumers' responses. Imagine, for example, two respondents who answer a question "This one was good." The transcript merely reports their words. However, a tape recording provides a better understanding of the underlying meaning, for example, compare "This ONE was good." (meaning "This one in particular was good, the others were not.") to "This one WAS good." (meaning "This one was at one time good, but it no longer is.").

the analyst immerses him or herself in the data in an attempt to experience the texture, tone, mood, range, and content of respondents' verbal (and if available nonverbal) communications. This immersion is not a results-oriented process, however. The goal is not to determine what the data *means,* but rather, the goal is to become more familiar with what the data *says.* Moustakas notes that this type of immersed data review lets an analyst "savor, appreciate, smell, touch, taste, feel [the information] without concrete goal or purpose."[5]

The goal of data review, therefore, is an understanding of what respondents communicated during interviews or focus groups. This understanding is facilitated when the following guidelines are kept in mind during the review process.[6]

Review the data with an open mind. Your goal is to review and refamiliarize yourself with what the respondents did and said. Review their comments without bias. Open yourself up to letting the patterns of response reveal trends, commonalties, and differences. Do not selectively look for patterns of response that either confirm or disconfirm preconceived notions.

Try to understand the reasons underlying attitudes and behaviors. Statements of opinion or descriptions of a particular set of behaviors provide one level of information. An informed understanding of attitudes and behaviors, however, requires that the analysis be conducted on a second, deeper level. Here, it is necessary to get "beneath the surface" and understand *why* opinions are held or behaviors are exhibited. Thus, the initial review of the data should pay particular attention to the reasons individuals give for their attitudes and behaviors. Many respondents, for example, might state that they are offended by current approaches to perfume advertising. The widespread dislike of the advertising provides insights on one level. However, the implications of these stated attitudes for marketing and advertising would vary under the following conditions of *underlying* attitudes:

- Most respondents object because the advertising is felt to degrade women, portraying them as sexual objects;
- Most respondents objected because the advertising is felt to exclude them, being targeted to a much younger audience;
- Most respondents object because they believe the advertising leads to increased promiscuity.

Respondents are often able to explain the reasons underlying their attitudes and behaviors. There are times, however, when respondents cannot verbally explain why they feel or act as they do. In these cases, underlying reasons can often be inferred from the words and analogies respondents use to describe the reasons for their opinions. Goldman and McDonald provide the following example:

> A [focus group] participant who is unable to explain why he dislikes a creamy spread but offhandedly compares it to a toothpaste in a tube, is communicating something important about [the spread's] perceived inedibility and perhaps artificiality.[7]

---

[5] Clark Moustakas, *Rhythms, Rituals and Relationships* (Detroit, MI: Center for Humanistic Studies, 1981), 56.

[6] Several of the guidelines presented in this section are adapted from Alfred E. Goldman and Susan S. McDonald, *The Group Depth Interview: Principles and Practice* (Englewood Cliffs, NJ: Prentice-Hall, 1987), 163–9; Krueger, *Focus Groups,* 149–51.

[7] Goldman and McDonald, *Group Depth Interview,* 165.

Thus, an initial review of the data must be sensitive to both the direct and indirect methods that respondents use to express the reasons why they hold a particular belief or participate in certain behaviors.

Try to understand the intensity of respondents' feelings and points of view. Qualitative data analysis often seeks to uncover areas in which consensus of opinion does or does not exist among the sample of respondents. However, it is important to note the *extent* of consensus and the *strength* or *conviction* with which expressed views are held. It is possible, for example, to use individual interviews to determine the initial appeal of two proposed advertising slogans. The pattern of responses to these slogans may indicate an overall consensus. Most respondents may have liked both slogans while a small portion of those interviewed may not have liked either slogan. This finding might suggest that either slogan can be selected. However, the *intensity* of respondents' reactions provide additional insights and can greatly influence the decision-making process. An examination of the intensity of responses might indicate the following:

> Slogan 1: Most respondents liked (although in a quite lukewarm fashion) this slogan. A few respondents disliked this slogan very much. These respondents were quite outspoken in their distaste for the slogan.

> Slogan 2: Most respondents liked this slogan very much. Respondents spent a long time describing the positive feelings evoked by the slogan. A few respondents disliked the slogan, but this dislike was not very strongly felt.

Thus, while the relative number of individuals liking and disliking each slogan were comparable, the intensity of opinions strongly suggests differences in the underlying reactions to each slogan. While the slogans appear equal on the surface (both appear to be liked by about the same proportion of respondents) the intensity of opinion clearly favors selection of Slogan 2 over Slogan 1.

Inferences of belief intensity can be drawn from the way in which a belief is expressed. Clear, unambiguous, forceful language is often an indicator of strong, intense feelings. A respondent who forcefully states "I hate that ad!" leaves little doubt that the opinion is genuine and intense. Repetition, where a respondent provides the same answer to several different (or differently worded) probes and questions, can also be a sign of belief intensity. Finally, respondents may signal a strongly held belief through irony, metaphor, or derisive humor. A respondent who looks at a new product concept and states (with a great deal of irony): "Oh, yeah sure, I'd buy this product. I've been waiting all my life for this product. Where, oh where, has it been?" is signaling a strongly held opinion.

Try to understand the respondent not the individual responses. Most respondents try to provide truthful responses to the questions they are asked. Sometimes opinions change during the interview or focus group, or initial statements do not present a complete view of an individual's beliefs. Thus, it is important to look at trends in the entire corpus of data rather than reviewing comments and statements on a response by response basis. The importance of this approach to data review becomes most apparent when self-contradictory statements are examined.

A self-contradiction occurs when statements made by a respondent at one point in the group or personal interview contradict statements made at other times. For example, a conversation early in a focus group could take this form:

> Respondent 1: I never buy or use shampoos from the grocery store. They're really low in quality and they damage your hair.
>
> Respondent 2: That's right. You really need to buy a salon shampoo. I know that's all I use. It's worth the price.
>
> Respondent 1: There's just no comparison with how your hair looks.The shine and appeal is just so much greater after you shampoo with a salon shampoo. No grocery store brand can compare. So, I just don't buy them.

Later in the group, this conversation could take place:

> Respondent 2: So what do you do?
>
> Respondent 1: I buy it. There are times when I'm in the grocery store and I see a well-known brand. And it's on sale for a really good price. So I'll buy it. I really don't notice any short-term harm. And when I'm done with the bottle, I go back to my salon brand.

Respondent 1 provided self-contradictory statements. This respondent's initial comments were not attempts to mislead the moderator, but rather, they were an honest expression of her point of view. The respondent's initial comments were overstated and did not provide insights into her overall pattern of behavior. Only by examining the totality of this respondent's statements, especially her later statements in the context of earlier statements, can true insights into her attitudes and behaviors be understood.

Review with a critical eye and ear. Most respondents try to tell the truth. They try to honestly express their attitudes and opinions and they try to accurately report their behaviors. However, some respondents, in some instances, will either intentionally or unintentionally not tell the truth. The challenge in qualitative analysis is to determine when to take respondents' comments at face value and when to discount or distrust their comments. It is important, for example, to distinguish between respondents who truly dislike a proposed television execution and those who may really like it but express negative reactions because all other group respondents express dislike.

Distinguishing between truth and falsity in respondents' comments is one of the great challenges of qualitative analysis. As seen, self-contradictory statements provide some direction for distinguishing between truth and falsity. Here, one looks at the totality of response and infers the nature of true opinions. Other clues to false statements relate to social norms and social acquiescence. This occurs when respondents provide answers that they think the interviewer, moderator, or other group members want to hear. Responses that signal this type of false statement include the following:

- Simple responses (such as "Yes, that's true." and "No, I don't think so.") offered in response to probes but seldom volunteered.
- Responses that suggest either hostility or personal allegiance (such as "I've already said that twice!" and "You've convinced me.").
- Evasive responses that fail to explain a point of view (such as "It's like I said." and "You know what I mean.").[8]

Keep an eye and ear open for what is not said. Respondents can fail to mention a topic or provide a piece of information for one of four reasons. First, respondents may

---

[8] Ibid., 168.

feel that the topic is not at all important and therefore, they may feel that there is little need to discuss and explore the topic. Second, respondents may assume that the topic is *so* important that it is unnecessary to mention, discuss, or explore it. (Respondents, for example, may not mention "avoidance of crashes" when asked to list the things they consider important in an airline. They assume the importance of this characteristic is already known.) Third, the topic may be so personal or sensitive that the respondent does not feel like "opening up" in that particular area. The analyst, during the review process, must try to determine which of these causes is the reason why a particular topic has not been mentioned.

The fourth reason is relatively easy to identify. Respondents will talk around the issue, talk in the third person or otherwise avoid directly confronting the issue. Respondents may also explicitly state that they do not wish to pursue the topic. Distinguishing the first from the second situation is more difficult. Here, the analyst must look for cues in the discussion that point either toward or away from topic importance. When these cues are not present or are ambiguous, the analyst must be careful not to let his or her own biases influence inferences drawn from the interviews.

Reflection

Reflection is the final activity in this stage of data analysis. This is a time of "quiet contemplation . . . where the researcher deliberately withdraws" from the formal analytical process.[9] During this period (that typically lasts from one to several days) impressions and meanings from the prior review of the data "incubate" without structure or guidance as a prelude to the formal analysis, which takes place in the next set of activities.

THEME IDENTIFICATION, EVALUATION, AND REVISION

A theory is a verbal or mathematical statement that organizes and explains a variety of associated facts.[10] (Darwin's Theory of Evolution, for example, summarizes and explains a wide range of facts and observations in the area of species development and survival.) Qualitative analysis typically centers around themes, which in this context serve a function very similar to theories. In the context of the qualitative data analysis, an identified theme

- provides a summary statement of facts that are believed to be true about the respondents and their world, thereby facilitating understanding and comprehension;
- reflects an interpretation of the facts' meaning, thereby facilitating use of the research findings in the decision-making process.

Themes thus help the end users of the research to "see the forest" and understand the trends and patterns suggested by the data.

The third major step in qualitative data analysis relates to theme development, evaluation and revision. As shown in Figure 11.1, the specific steps underlying ac-

---

[9] Patton, *Qualitative Evaluation,* 409.

[10] Paul C. Cozby, *Methods in Behavioral Research, Third Edition* (Palo Alto, CA: Mayfield Publishing Company, 1985), 18–19.

tivities at this stage are: theme development, data identification and recording, theme evaluation, theme revision (if necessary), and development of metathemes. It is important to note that the activities conducted during this state of analysis generally do not follow a linear path. As illustrated in Figure 11.1, the development and evaluation of themes is a circular process entailing continuous data examination and theme revision.[11]

Theme Development

Theme development begins with the list of areas to be addressed. (You will recall that this list was developed earlier in the process of data analysis, see Figure 11.1 and the example shown in Figure 11.2). Specifically, based on a review of the raw data conducted in the prior steps, a theme describing the findings is proposed for each listed area. The theme represents the analyst's intuitive and informed judgment as to the content and pattern of findings in each topic area and, where appropriate, a specification of the underlying causes. The following illustrates a theme developed to respond to the informational needs shown in Figure 11.2. Note how the theme is clear, concise, unambiguous, and oriented to underlying causes.

> Theme: Overall, respondents reacted positively to the "Dual Disk Walkman" product concept. The product was seen as unique and many expressed an interest in purchase when the product was priced under $90. Primary reasons for enthusiasm related to convenience and value. Neither gender nor income status appear related to response.

Recording Relevant Data

The themes proposed by the analyst provide a concrete, tangible point of view that can be used to organize the findings and can be confirmed or disconfirmed based on the trends in the raw data. The next step in the analytical process collects and examines the raw information relevant to each theme to determine the theme's correctness. A record sheet of the type shown in Figure 11.3 facilitates this process. The top of the form presents the theme—the analyst's view of a major pattern of response or finding. The theme shown on the top of the form in this example is the theme presented earlier in this section. The form following the theme is divided in half. Evidence from the raw data that supports the theme is transcribed on the left side of the page while evidence that disconfirms or contradicts the theme is transcribed on the right side of the page.

When recording responses, it important to record respondents' verbatim comments as well as any relevant demographic, attitudinal, or brand information. Verbatim, as opposed to paraphrased comments, are recorded for two reasons. First, the comments will be used later to provide the detail and substantiation for conclusions drawn

---

[11] The sequence of analysis proposed in this chapter is one where, after data review and reflection, themes are proposed, the data relevant to the evaluation of the theme is collected, and based on the data the theme is accepted, rejected, or modified. It can be argued that this is the reverse of the "proper" process where data is organized first without any conclusions or themes in mind and *then* the theme is allowed to "flow" out of the data. This reverse procedure will certainly, at the conclusion of the analysis, produce a set of findings. However, we recommend the theme → data → evaluation → revision procedure for several reasons. First, after data review and reflection an analyst will certainly have themes in mind. It makes little sense (to us) to ignore these insights at the beginning of formal data analysis. Second, the uses of themes at the beginning of data analysis provides a tangible focus for the collection and evaluation of the data. Finally, the recommended process entails more extensive data analysis as one makes multiple passes through the data to confirm or disconfirm proposed themes.

> **Theme:** Overall, respondents reacted positively to the "Dual Disk Walkman" product concept. The product was seen as unique and many expressed an interest in purchase when the product was priced under $90. Primary reasons for enthusiasm related to convenience and value. Neither gender nor income status appeared to be related to response.
>
> ***Evidence in support of theme***   ***Evidence in opposition of theme***

FIGURE 11.3
Sample format for recording verbatim responses to a specific theme.

in the written or oral presentation. Second, the verbatim comments shown on the record sheets provide a way for the analyst to justify and explain conclusions drawn from the data. (This aspect of the analysis is discussed in the next section.) Both uses of respondents' comments require the use of original, unaltered comments.

Theme Evaluation

Once all the comments relevant to a theme have been recorded, the analyst reexamines the theme in light of the recorded data to determine the extent to which the theme should or should not be accepted given the pattern of the underlying data. An acceptable theme is one that accurately reflects the content of the recorded data. An unacceptable theme is one that does not accurately reflect the content of the recorded data and therefore must be rejected or revised. The process of theme evaluation proceeds as follows:

> The data is examined by the analyst. The theme is strengthened each time a piece of data is found that supports the theme. But, if some aspect of the data disconfirms the theme or relates to it ambiguously then the analyst redefines or restates the theme to accommodate the contrary data. The analyst keeps considering each piece of data and, as necessary, revising the theme until all the relevant data has been examined.[12]

This procedure of theme revision tends to produce themes that are highly accurate descriptors of the underlying data. Moreover, the process itself is an effective means of increasing and demonstrating the validity of conclusions reached, especially in light of the perceived subjective nature of qualitative data analysis.

As might be expected, few themes at this point are completely accepted in their original form or completely rejected. More typically, themes are modified or revised to improve clarity and increase accuracy. Based on an examination of the relevant data, for example, the theme presented earlier in this section might be revised to read:

> Revised Theme: Respondents' reactions to the "Dual Disk Walkman" were generally positive. Women and men expressed positive reactions to the concept before the mention of price, although more women than men were favorable. The primary product appeal to both men and women was convenience. Women also displayed a positive response to two specific product features: the sound quality and the technological advancement of the

---

[12] This process is an adaptation of a qualitative analytical procedure known as negative case analysis. See Thomas R. Lindloff, *Qualitative Communication Research Methods* (Thousand Oaks, CA: SAGE Publications, 1995), Y. S. Lincoln and E. G. Guba, *Naturalistic Inquiry* (Thousand Oaks, CA: SAGE Publications, 1985).

product. Respondents' favorable comments generally disappeared when the product was priced at $115. At this price level it was generally felt that the value (primarily provided by the convenience) was just "not there." Respondents felt that the appropriate price for the product was $90, a point at which there was a great deal of value. Beyond a lack of value related to price, primary reasons for negative response related to lack of a real need and perceptions that it is "just a gimmick."

Metathemes

Up to this point, individual themes describing trends and patterns in the data have been developed and evaluated. Moreover, individual themes have been modified to ensure that they are an accurate reflection of the data. One additional step is necessary to make the results of qualitative study maximally useful to those who use the information for decision making. The *interrelationships* of the individual themes must be made explicit to facilitate understanding of the *overall* trends and patterns in the data. Thus, for example, the individual themes describing reactions to each of Sony's three new product concepts can be related to form a metatheme. This metatheme would summarize similarities and differences among each of the individual themes, as follows:

> Metatheme: Overall, reactions to all three concepts were positive. Men and women, however, displayed different patterns of response.
>
> Women tended to respond to each concept more favorably than men. They tended to react to the specific characteristics of each proposed concept and identified specific product attributes that led to product appeal. Additionally, women felt that all three concepts presented products that were "cutting edge" and that "would make their life better or more enjoyable."
>
> Men, on the other hand, were impressed by each product's convenience. Additionally, men were more price sensitive than women, often noting that the product was "just a gimmick" that in terms of the cost was just "not worth it."

Serendipitous Discoveries

The prior steps reflect a sequence of theme development, evaluation, modification, revision, and ultimate selection. The themes evaluated in this process are those that have been explicitly formulated in response to preidentified areas of inquiry or informational need. However, one of the great advantages of qualitative analysis is the opportunity to gain insights in unanticipated areas. During each of the activities conducted in this stage of analysis, an analyst must be sensitive and open to unforseen or unanticipated insights. These insights should be recorded on forms similar to that shown in Figure 11.3 and evaluated similarly to other preidentified themes.

REPORTING THE RESULTS

A report of qualitative findings contains many of the characteristics of research reports presented in Chapter 4.

- The written and oral presentation of the findings and implications should satisfy the characteristics of good writing (e.g., clear, concise, complete, correct grammar, coherent).
- The written report should contain all required elements (e.g., title page, table of contents, executive summary, background, methodology, findings, limitations, recommendations, next steps).

- The oral report should reflect the characteristics of good oral reports (e.g., adequate use of audiovisual materials, verbal "road maps," etc.).

Beyond these characteristics of all research reports, an analyst must keep several additional guidelines in mind when developing the content and structure of qualitative reports. The additional considerations are discussed in the remainder of this section.

Use Metathemes as the Organizing Framework

Metathemes provide end users with the "big picture." As such, they provide an excellent framework for the organization and presentation of findings. Begin each major section of the report with a metatheme. Explore the characteristics of the metatheme and its implications. Next, move to the more detailed level of individual themes. Present each theme underlying the metatheme and the evidence that supports acceptance of that theme. Your goal is to communicate major findings and conclusions, using detail to convince the audience that the communicated findings are justified by the data.

Focus On Meaning and Relationships Rather Than Literal Description

As discussed earlier, end users of research are more interested in what the data means than what it literally says or how it was collected. Thus the presentation of themes and findings should focus on the meanings rather than descriptions. The following illustrates a misplaced emphasis and a lack of meaningful analysis in the reporting of qualitative findings.

> The moderator stopped the discussion of product usage and then told the group that they would now see three concepts for brand line extensions. Each concept described a line extension for the Sony Walkman. Concepts were presented and discussed one at a time.
>
> With regard to the first concept, the "Dual Disk Walkman": One respondent, Mary, a 23-year-old, said that the concept was a "really neat idea." She liked the idea of being able to store and play two disks at once. John, a 32-year-old, disagreed. He felt that it was just "a gimmick" that was "a new way for Sony to make money." Others in the group tended to agree with Mary. Ron, for example....

Use Quotes Appropriately

A report of qualitative research findings must strike a balance between too much and too little support (in the form of verbatim quotes) for identified themes, trends, and patterns. A sufficient amount of direct quotations should be used so that the end user can visualize the context of the comments, understand the thoughts and feelings of the individuals represented in the report, and believe that the presented findings are justified. On the other hand, the use of verbatim quotes should stop short of becoming trivial, mundane, and repetitive. The audience does not have to know absolutely everything that was done or said. Thus, only use quotes when they advance your argument or provide important insights. Moreover, select the quotes wisely. The best quotes are those that allow the audience to hear and understand respondents' voices, feelings, and points of view.[13]

---

[13] For a more detailed discussion of the selection of quotes and exemplars see Lindloff, *Qualitative Communication*, 229–30.

Do Not Use Numeric Descriptions

Qualitative research is almost always conducted with small, nonrandom samples of individuals. As a result, it is inappropriate to use numbers in the reporting of qualitative findings. Numbers both imply a sufficiently large base of respondents and reasonable projection to a larger population. The results of qualitative research should be expressed using nonspecific quantifiers such as "several," "most," "many," "almost all" and "very few." These nonspecific quantifiers communicate the relative size of groups of individuals without falsely communicating higher levels of accuracy than actually exist.

Do Not Use Names

The names of respondents should not be reported. First, and most importantly, respondents were assured confidentiality of response, and as a consequence, associating their names with specific comments violates this assurance. Second, from a more pragmatic perspective, end users of the research are not interested in which stranger said something, they are only interested in what that person had to say. Constant reference to an individual by name soon becomes an annoying distraction.

Be Certain to Provide Alternative Explanations Rather Than Arbitrarily Selecting One

No matter how hard an interviewer or moderator tries to make underlying causes and beliefs explicit, there are times when no single cause can be identified to explain a particular point of view or behavior. There may be no explicit identified cause or several causes may be equally plausible. In these instances, the integrity of the research dictates that the analyst present an examination of the plausibility of each reasonable alternative rather than selecting one for the sake of efficiency or closure.

Be Complete and Enlighten

Your goal in data analysis and presentation is enlightenment, to provide important insights to end users of the research. You enlighten your audience by first conducting a complete and thorough analysis of the data and then presenting findings that

- make the obvious obvious, that is, use the data to confirm a previously held belief about an area explored in the research,
- make the obvious dubious, that is, use the data to disconfirm a previously held belief about an area explored in the research,
- make the hidden obvious, that is, illuminate areas that the audience previously did not know but needs to know.[14]

USING A "COGNITIVE MAP" TO COMMUNICATE THE FINDINGS OF QUALITATIVE RESEARCH

The findings and implications of qualitative research are typically presented in either written or oral form where the communication is text-based, that is, where words are

---

[14] P. Schlechty and G. Noblit, "Some Uses of Sociological Theory in Educational Evaluation," In Ron Corwin ed., *Policy Research* (Greenwich, CT: JAI, 1982).

the medium of communication. There are times when the communication of qualitative data is facilitated by the use of a "cognitive map," a pictorial representation of the findings. Cognitive maps are effective tools for the presentation of qualitative findings because they provide a visual, all-encompassing representation of the study's results on a single sheet of paper, thereby helping the audience to understand the trends and interrelationships of the findings. This section explains how to create and present a cognitive map.[15]

Constructing a Cognitive Map

A cognitive map is a visual representation of the interrelationships between specific facts, themes, and metathemes (see Figure 11.4, page 248). The information in a cognitive map is arranged to help members of the research audience clearly understand the key findings in each area of exploration and the interrelationships of these findings. Moreover, the pictorial format helps the audience understand how individual beliefs and attitudes lead to themes and metathemes.

Construction of a cognitive map begins after the process of data analysis described earlier in this chapter. Once themes and metathemes have been identified, the map is developed as follows:

1. Draw a small circle in the center of a large sheet of paper or poster board. Write the name of the area, category, product, or brand under exploration.

2. Identify three to five broad areas in which findings will be presented. Each identified area should reflect an area of informational need explored in the research.

3. Divide the paper into equal sections. There should be one section for each area of focus.

4. Identify the area of focus with a descriptive label.

5. Address areas of focus sequentially, completing one area before beginning work on another area. *Within each area* develop the cognitive map by

   • recording the most important individual facts or details closest to the outside of the page. Facts and details that lead to or support a theme should be placed adjacent to each other;

   • moving inward (toward the center of the page) and recording themes above or near their constituent facts or details. Use lines to connect themes to their supporting details and facts;

   • moving inward further and, close to the small inner circle, record and circle metathemes above their constituent themes. Use lines to connect metathemes to their constituent themes.

   The requirement that all pertinent data fit into a specified small space is intentional. The space limitation forces a researcher to identify and present only the *most important* findings.

6. Finish the cognitive map. Use shading, color, and/or alterations in type size to visually distinguish metathemes, themes, and facts/details (see Figure 11.4).

---

[15] This section is adapted from an earlier presentation of cognitive mapping. See Joel J. Davis, "Cognitive Mapping: A Qualitative Multidimensional Approach For Formulating Advertising and Creative Strategies," in Joey Regan ed., *Applications of Research to the Media Industries* (Ames, IA: Kendall Hunt, 1992), 73–94.

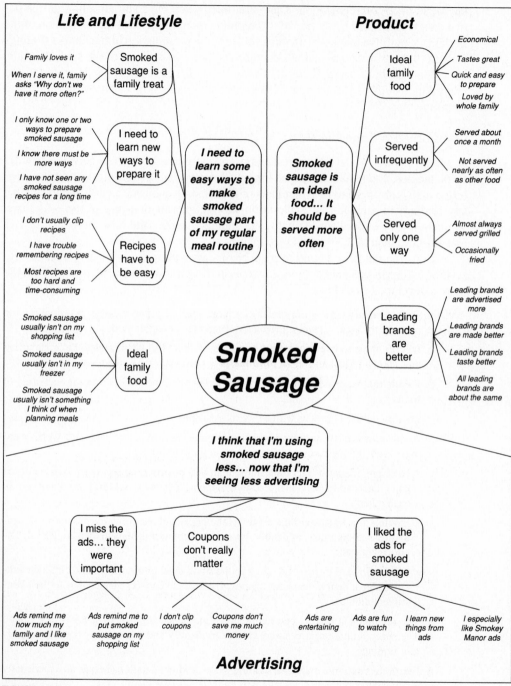

FIGURE 11.4
A cognitive map.

Presenting and Interpreting a Cognitive Map

As with all reports of research findings (see Chapter 4), the presentation begins with general information on the respondents, research methodology, sampling, etc. Next, a brief overview of the characteristics of a cognitive map is provided. Following this introduction, the researcher identifies the focus of the research (by pointing to the small center circle in the center of the map) and the specific areas that will be addressed (by pointing to the labels of each map section).

Next, each area of analysis is explored in detail. Cognitive maps are presented as a narrative, typically from the respondent's point of view. As a result, within each area, the metatheme is read, followed by its first constituent theme, and that theme's constituent facts and details. As each metatheme, theme, or fact is read, the presenter points to the appropriate space on the cognitive map. Extended comments from specific questions or projective techniques can be used to clarify and elaborate on points made by themes and metathemes.

The presentation of a cognitive map requires more than just reciting the findings and sequentially reading themes and details. The findings (in general) and themes (in particular) must be placed in context. Consequently, when presenting a cognitive map one must be careful to

- refer back to the marketing and/or advertising questions that initially prompted the research. As with all research, findings and insights on a cognitive map must be seen as a means of responding to the informational needs that motivated the research;
- point out patterns that exist within and among the areas of focus. Insights that complement each other but appear in different domains should be made explicit;
- make certain that the implications of the findings for decision making are made explicit.

With this in mind, the cognitive map shown in Figure 11.4 could be presented as follows:

Today we are here to discuss the results of qualitative research conducted to help us better understand our target consumer and smoked sausage. To refresh your memory, this presentation reflects the results of thirty personal, in-depth interviews conducted among our target audience of married women aged 35 to 54 who are the principal family shopper and meal preparer. Our target self-classifies herself as a "regular" user of smoked sausage. She is moderately well educated and lives with her husband and several children in a blue collar household. Household income is between $30,000 and $40,000 annually.

To improve our understanding of the target we are using a technique known as cognitive mapping. This technique attempts to replicate on paper our target's mind-set—how she feels and thinks—about smoked sausage. We'll look at the thoughts, opinions, and perceptions of our target in three main areas: (1) the product itself, (2) how the product fits into her life and lifestyle, and (3) what she thinks about and how she reacts to our own and our competitors' advertising.

Let's begin by exploring how our target thinks about the smoked sausage category and specific products within the category. This is the PRODUCT area. In thinking about smoked sausage our target believes that "smoked sausage is a terrific food and *should* be served more often." She feels that it should be served more often because it is "an ideal family food." It does everything an ideal food should do: it is "economical" and "tastes great"; it is "quick and easy to prepare"; and, importantly, it is "loved by everyone in the family." In spite of all of these positive product attributes it is "served infrequently,"

"about one or twice a month," "not nearly as often as other foods." When it is served it is almost always "grilled" or occasionally "fried." Keep in mind that all these women, at the onset of the research, said that they considered themselves "regular" users of smoked sausage. Evidently, regular usage is not very often.

Our target likes the product, but she isn't serving it very often. The problem doesn't seem to lie within the product itself. This is good; we do not have to sell her on the product. All of our competitors' advertising, which seeks to convince current users that the product is healthy and nutritious, seems to be off the mark. A headline, used by one of our competitors, which states "You know the taste, now you know how well it is made," appears to be inappropriate and irrelevant to this target.

So why isn't smoked sausage being served more often? Understanding why will help us understand why sales in the category remain flat and what must be done to grow the market.

Increasing sales after a long period of flat or stagnant sales in difficult. Is our client, Smokey Manor Smoked Sausage, positioned in a way that it can be the stimulus for stimulating category sales and be the brand that benefits from increased category sales? Our interviews lead us to believe that the answers are "yes." Our target prefers to buy and serve leading brands. She believes that leading brands are "made better" and "taste better" than nonleading brands. She equates advertised brands with leading brands. In essence, the more a brand advertises, the more leading that brand is perceived to be. However, at the moment, she feels that among the set of leading brands, all are about the same. Our task, therefore, is to distinguish Smokey Manor from the other leading brands. I'll address how this might be done after we have seen the remainder of the cognitive map.

The answer to why smoked sausage isn't served more often can be found in our second area of focus: the target's LIFE AND LIFESTYLE. After all, if smoked sausage is perceived to be such an ideal food, why isn't it served more often?

Our target answers for us. She believes that "I need to learn some easy ways to make smoked sausage part of my regular meal routine." Right now, smoked sausage is a "family treat" that the family loves and always asks "Why don't we have it more often?"

It isn't served more often because it not part of our target's regular meal routine. The product is ideal, but our target hasn't yet incorporated it into her pattern of regular meal planning and preparation.

What can be done to make smoked sausage part of our target's regular routine? Several things. First, we can show her new and different ways to prepare smoked sausage. She freely admits that, "I really need to learn new ways to prepare it." At this point she only "knows one or two ways" but acknowledges that "there have to be more ways." She's stuck, in part, because she "hasn't seen any smoked sausage recipes for a long time."

However, if and when we do show her new ways to prepare the product, we have to make this learning easy. The recipes have to be "easy to remember." Our target "doesn't usually clip recipes" and she has "trouble remembering new recipes that she has seen." Moreover, she thinks that most recipes are "just too hard and time consuming."

Finally, we have to make smoked sausage more top-of-mind. It isn't a "staple." It is now a product that is "not on her shopping list," she "doesn't keep it in her freezer" and she really "doesn't think about (it) when planning meals."

These two related needs, to make the product more top-of-mind and to incorporate the product into regular meal planning, were expressed by many women in response to the two projective stimuli, especially the sketch of the woman standing in front of the smoked sausage section of the grocery store. These women *want* to prepare and serve the product more often, they just forget.

The task of increasing top-of-mind awareness of smoked sausage and reposition-

ing the product as part of our target's regular meal planning routine will in large part be assigned to the advertising.

Our target realizes that there is now less advertising for smoked sausage, and that this *has had* an effect on her product usage. Again, we see a reduced frequency of usage related to a lack of top-of-mind awareness. Our target's most general belief about advertising is "I think that I'm using smoked sausage less, now that I see less advertising." Why is this so? Why does our target believe that less advertising has reduced her product usage? Our target says "I miss the ads—they were important" because "they reminded me of how much I liked smoked sausage," and they "reminded me to put smoked sausage on my shopping list."

It is the advertising that was important, not as some at the agency believed, the coupons. "Coupons," says our target "don't really matter," "I don't clip them" because "they don't save me very much money."

Beyond this impact on product usage, it is also important to note that our target likes watching smoked sausage ads. She says "I like the ads for smoked sausage," They were "entertaining," "fun to watch," and "I learned new things." It is nice to hear that they "especially liked Smokey Manor ads."

So, what does this research mean for the decision we need to reach. I would suggest that, based on the research, we consider the following.

First, in terms of advertising content, I believe the research suggests that our advertising should reinforce the positive perceptions of smoked sausage currently held by this target. However, this reinforcement should be communicated within the context of advertising that presents memorable, easy-to-prepare smoked sausage recipes and dishes. These recipes would provide the means for moving smoked sausage into the regular meal planning routine. Let's consider breaking away from our competitors' messages of ingredients and health/nutrition.

Second, I believe that the research indicates a need to reexamine our media schedule. The majority of smoked sausage advertisers, Smokey Manor included, schedule their advertising in flights, a few weeks on the air and a few weeks off. This helped to make limited media dollars go farther. The cognitive map, however, indicated that a major barrier to increased product usage and its eventual incorporation into the regular meal routine was its lack of top-of-mind awareness. As a result, I would suggest that we consider a continuous, rather than flighting schedule. The additional funds might come from promotional efforts, such as couponing, which appear to have little appeal to the target.

Third, there is the issue of advertising exposure. The target believes that leading brands are better and that brand leadership is reflected in advertising exposure. Simply put, leading brands do more advertising. Thus, to sell Smokey Manor and not the smoked sausage category, we need to position ourselves as the leading brand (that our target believes is better). Thus, we should consider a media plan that increases frequency of advertising exposure.

Summary

The analysis and presentation of qualitative research proceeds best when the analyst adopts a systematic approach. One approach, shown in Figure 11.1, divides the process into four main stages.

Three events occur in the first stage, *activities conducted prior to data examination*. These activities pertain to the following:

1. Formal review of the research problem and informational needs. The result of this activity is a preliminary list of areas in which the analysis will focus.

2. Confirmation and final listing of areas in which the analysis will focus. This activity gathers and responds to feedback from the research study's end users.

3. Evaluation of the study sample to determine any bias or other limitations that may affect conclusions drawn from the data.

The second stage, *data examination,* entails a review and examination of the raw data. Here, the analyst immerses him or herself in the data in attempt to become familiar with and better understand what the data *says* (rather than what the data means). This understanding is facilitated when the following guidelines are kept in mind during the review process:

- Review the data with an open mind,
- Try to understand the reasons underlying attitudes and behaviors,
- Try to understand the intensity of respondents' feelings and points of view,
- Try to understand the respondent not the individual responses,
- Review with a critical eye and ear,
- Keep an eye and ear open for what isn't said.

The final activity during this stage is reflection—quiet contemplation of the data.

The third stage, *theme identification, evaluation, and revision,* attempts to determine what the data *means.* The first activity in this stage is theme development, where a theme (1) provides a summary statement of facts that are believed to be true about the respondents and their world and (2) reflects an interpretation of the facts' meaning. Theme development is followed by the identification and recording of relevant data, theme evaluation and, if necessary, theme revision. The final activity uses identified themes to develop metathemes—themes that describe the interrelationships of individual themes.

The final stage, *reporting the results,* creates a written and/or oral presentation of the findings and implications. While the presentation of qualitative research findings share many of the characteristics of all reports (see Chapter 4), there are several considerations unique to the presentation of qualitative data.

- Use metathemes as the organizing framework. Move from metathemes to levels of increasing detail and support.
- Focus on meaning and relationships rather than literal description.
- Use quotes appropriately.
- Do not use numeric descriptions.
- Do not use names.
- Be certain to provide alternative explanations rather than arbitrarily selecting one.
- Be complete and enlighten.

Review Questions

1. What are the two goals of qualitative research?
2. What factors make qualitative research particularly difficult, especially when compared with the analysis of quantitative data?

3. What are the four broad stages of qualitative analysis?

4. What three key activities take place before the start of formal data analysis? Briefly describe the outcomes of each activity.

5. Why should an analyst always confirm problem definition and informational needs with the end users of the research?

6. Why it is important to evaluate sample characteristics prior to the start of data examination and analysis?

7. What guidelines can an analyst use to facilitate the process of data review? Briefly describe why each guideline is important.

8. What is a theme? What are the roles of a theme in the analysis of qualitative data?

9. What is the process by which a theme is identified and refined?

10. What is a metatheme? What is the role of a metatheme in the analysis of qualitative data?

11. What considerations should an analyst keep in mind during the oral or written presentation of qualitative research? Briefly describe how each consideration leads to a better presentation of the results?

Application Exercises[16]

1. The Sony Playstation advertising account has just been placed into review. Sony sends twenty agencies a questionnaire. Sony will examine responses to their questions and then select the four agencies that will participate in the "pitch." Your agency receives one of the questionnaires.

   Several of the questions on the questionnaire ask for your agency's analysis of Sony's and competitive brands' advertising. It is decided that to respond to these questions two types of research are required. First, several creatives and account executives will collect, examine, and review the advertising. This review will lead to the preparation of a point of view of the advertising's strengths and weaknesses from a professional advertiser's perspective. Second, the advertising will be shown to individuals in the advertising's target audience. Three focus groups will be held with these individuals, at that time they will be shown the advertising and their reactions will be explored. The reactions of the focus group participants will also be used to respond to Sony's questionnaire.

   Timing is tight. The groups will be held in two days. Three days later the questionnaire must be submitted to Sony. Your supervisor says (not altogether jokingly) that you will have to begin writing the report of the findings from the focus groups while you are in the process of watching the groups. Describe each of the steps or actions that you will take from this point (two days prior to the groups) forward to ensure that the task of providing reliable, appropriate information is accomplished successfully.

2. A series of personal interviews have been held with individuals who are frequent car renters. Selected portions of the interviews are shown next. Review the set of interviews. Then analyze the data to discover underlying themes. Prepare a memo that presents each identified theme and your support for the validity of that theme.

---

[16] All situations are hypothetical. Actual company names are used for illustrative purposes only.

Sally   Age 23   You know, after renting quite a number of cars I've realized a couple of things. You get what you pay for. And what I pay for, and what I expect to get, are attendants who are polite, bills that are right, and cars ready for me when I get to the rental counter. I've found I can get this from Avis or Hertz. Budget is just what it says it is.

Jim   Age 53   I hate traveling out of town, but lately I'm doing it more and more. So, I guess when I travel I try to make it as easy on myself as possible. I stay at the nicer hotels and I try to keep things going smoothly. The last thing I need after getting off an airplane is rental car problems. I've had cars that were dirty, that needed gas, that smelled like cigarettes, that broke down. Usually from the cheapie, budget companies. Now I try to avoid these companies. I want, need, things to go smoothly. No hassles. Not with the car. Not with getting the car. A smile from behind the counter is so nice. Someone who knows what they are doing is even nicer. I get this with Hertz, usually Avis. Not very many of the other companies.

Adam   Age 28   I like the smell of a clean car. Of a car that has the floors swept and the windows cleaned. I also hate standing in line. The men and women behind the counter need to be fast and efficient. I truly hate standing in line while some tourist takes three hours to fill out the rental papers. It's nice when there's a window or a club just for renters like me. Avis and Hertz have one. I don't think that Budget does.

Matthew   Age 31   What's important to me. No hassle. No problems. A car that is prepared and ready for me. Attendants and counter people that know what they are doing. And that are helpful. And courteous. And have a smile. I rent from the big companies—except for Budget.

Kathy   Age 54   After all these years it's still important that I make a good impression with my boss at work. One way I do this is by showing that I'm responsible in the way that I spend the company's money. Where do I rent? Budget.

Melanie   Age 32   You know, I think that I've rented at least 75 cars. And things have clearly gotten worse. All the things that I used to look for and take for granted just a few years ago: nice people, smiling people, people who know what they are doing, just don't seem to exist anymore. Or at least there's not very many of them. I think that Hertz has hired the last of them.

Todd   Age 53   I'll never forget the first time I rented a car. Now I'm an old pro, I guess. I've learned that there certainly are differences in what a rental company delivers. Their people, for example. Hertz and Avis must spend a lot of time training their people. They know what they're doing. And they do it well. I've come to expect and want this kind of treatment. Boo on Budget. Also, I like driving new cars. So it's important that the car I rent is ready for me. Not only there in the lot, but clean and gassed.

Diana   Age 49   A car is a car. It gets you from here to there. It's just trans- portation. I don't need or expect anything special. I just don't want the price to take me "for a ride." All the companies are about the same, but I usually wind up renting from Budget.

3. Each of the following excerpts appeared in a preliminary draft report of focus group findings. Read each excerpt and then decide if it is acceptable as written. If it is not acceptable, explain why and then rewrite the excerpt, correcting identified problems.

   1. Qualitative research, a methodological approach to the collection of in-depth information on consumers' attitudes, beliefs, and perceptions (noting the relationship of these attitudes, beliefs, and perceptions to subsequent behaviors) was the method used to collect the data. Twenty interviews were conducted. These conducted interviews took place among a sample of nine men and eleven women, these men and women all being consumers of the target product. The target product was sport utility automobiles.

   2. At this point in the groups the moderator asked the respondents who were participating in the group to imagine what the product would be if the product were an animal. (The product was a Jeep 4 × 4.) Each person in the group wrote down his or her answer and then provided his or her answer when asked by the moderator. There were ten people in the group. Here are their responses:

Mary: elephant

Sue: rhinoceros

Ellen: elephant

Theresa: hippopotamus

Martha: ox

John: jaguar

Max: cougar

Joe: lion

David: lion

Glen: tiger

As you can see, five respondents (100% of the women) picked large, lumbering animals while five respondents (100% of the men) picked fast, sleek, aggressive animals. There were two pairs of agreement, one among the men and one among the women.

The moderator then asked each person why they picked this animal. Here are the answers:

Mary: because the car can go anywhere, and so can an elephant

Sue: a rhino is heavy and chunky, and so is a Jeep

Ellen: an elephant is big and boxy and can go along where ever he wants to go

Theresa: hippos are big, boxy and ugly

Martha: slow, lumbering, and good for doing a lot of heavy work

John: fast, manly, uncontrollable

Max: sleek, in charge, fast

Joe: the king of the beasts, and a Jeep is king of cars

David: uncontrollable, just like you feel when driving a Jeep

Glen: rough and tough

It is obvious what these people see in a Jeep 4 × 4.

3. The group's reactions to the three new product recipes were mixed. The group's reactions, noting specific patterns of response by gender, are presented as follows:

Recipe One

	M*	M	M	M	M	F†	F	F	F	F	F	Total
Positive	x	x	x	x	x	x	x					7
Neutral								x	x			2
Negative										x	x	2

Recipe Two

	M	M	M	M	M	F	F	F	F	F	F	Total
Positive	x		x		x	x						4
Neutral		x					x	x				3
Negative				x					x	x	x	4

Recipe Three

	M	M	M	M	M	F	F	F	F	F	F	Total
Positive							x		x	x	x	4
Neutral			x	x	x							3
Negative	x	x	x					x				4

*M = Male; †F = Female.

4. Select ten individuals who consume at least five cans of soft drinks per week. Five individuals should consume diet soft drinks most often and five individuals should consume regular (i.e., not diet) soft drinks most often. Conduct personal interviews with these individuals using the following guide. Prepare a written report of the findings.

I. Introduction
  - Study of soft drink consumption and perceptions
  - Being used for class project
  - Confidential

II. Purchase Behaviors
  - What flavors are purchased? Why?
  - What flavors are avoided? Why?
  - What brands are purchased? Why?
  - What brands are avoided? Why?
  - Where primarily purchased? Why? Other places purchased?
  - Form (cans, bottles, etc.) in which purchased? Most often form? Why?
  - Influence of price? Brand switching (if any) based on sales, etc.?

III. Consumption Behaviors
  - Places typically consumed
  - Situations drinks consumed in (alone, with friends, etc.)
  - Most common consumption situations

- Number of units (cans, bottles) typically consumed at one time
- Different drinks for different situations? Why?

IV. Trend in Consumption Behaviors

- Changes in flavor preference over past year? Why?
- Changes in brand preference over past year? Why?
- Extent of brand loyalty over past year?
- Extent of flavor loyalty over past year?

V. Importance of Specific Product Attributes

- taste (overall)
- sweetness/tartness
- calories
- other

5. Using your interviews from the prior exercise, prepare a cognitive map to communicate key insights and findings.

CHAPTER

12

MEASUREMENT IN ADVERTISING RESEARCH

Quantitative advertising research is concerned with the collection, analysis, and interpretation of numerical data. The ability of numerical data to provide useful, reliable insights into an advertising problem is in great part dependent on the rigor underlying the measurement process. Not all measurements are appropriate for all situations. Not all measurements provide useful and reliable information. The quality of the measures you make directly determine the depth and quality of the insights you obtain. This chapter introduces you to the concept of measurement.

After reading this chapter, you will be able to

■ Describe the measurement process.

■ Explain the four different levels of measurement.

■ Determine a measure's reliability and validity.

Measurement can be defined as the way that abstract, typically unobservable concepts are linked to observable events.[1] It is the way researchers use an observable event, such as a check mark on a questionnaire, to draw inferences about concepts that may not be directly observable, for example, attitudes toward a particular brand or advertiser. The process by which a researcher moves from an unobserved concept to an

---

[1] This definition of measurement is taken from Edward G. Carmines and Richard A. Zeller, *Measurement in the Social Sciences: The Link Between Theory and Data* (New York, NY: Cambridge University Press, 1980); M. W. Riley, *Sociological Research: A Case Approach* (New York, NY: Harcourt Brace Jovanovich, 1963). It should be noted that this definition is different than the traditional definition of measurement presented in many texts, where measurement is defined as "the assignment of numbers to objects and events according to rules." Carmines and Zeller present a persuasive argument why this latter definition is inappropriate for social science research. See Edward G. Carmines and Richard A. Zeller, *Reliability and Validity Assessment* (Beverly Hills, CA: SAGE Publications, 1979). The discussion in this introductory section is based on that presented by Carmines and Zeller, *Reliability and Validity Assessment.*

observable event is an important one. A systematic approach of moving *from* a concept *to* an event increases the likelihood that the inferences drawn from the observed event about the underlying concept are appropriate, reliable, and valid. The remainder of this chapter describes a systematic approach to the measurement process.

THE MEASUREMENT PROCESS

The steps comprising the measurement process are shown in Figure 12.1 (page 260). These steps, which are followed for each area explored and measured in a research study, can be grouped into the following three major tasks:

- Identify and define the concept of interest
- Specify an observable event
- Evaluate and revise the observable event

Stage One: Identify and Define Concept of Interest

The first stage of the measurement process is refinement. As shown in Figure 12.1, this stage begins with a general notion of the area to be explored and ends with a detailed, explicit operational definition of what is to be measured.

Identify Concept of Interest Survey questions or observations represent an attempt to measure a characteristic, behavior, or attitude of interest. To ensure that the questions or observations provide the required information and desired insights, the measurement process begins by identifying the concept (sometimes called a construct) of interest for study and exploration.

A *concept* is an invented name for a property of an object, person, state, or event. Some concepts, such as age, gender, and income, present few measurement problems because they have well-defined meanings and can be easily observed, reported, and quantified. Other concepts explored in advertising research, such as advertising awareness, brand loyalty, communication recall, and reactions to an advertisement, cannot be explicitly observed and, as a result, are less concrete and present greater measurement challenges. In these types of cases it is important to clearly define the concept and specific observable events that might be used to define the concept. This refinement of the concept of interest is accomplished through the creation of a conceptual, and then an operational, definition of the concept.

Develop Conceptual Definition A *conceptual definition* expresses the central or core idea of the concept. It clearly states the major characteristics of the concept and distinguishes the target concept from similar, but different, concepts. Attitude toward an advertisement, for example, has been conceptually defined as "a predisposition to respond in a favorable or unfavorable manner to a particular advertising stimulus during a particular exposure situation."[2] This definition clarifies what an author means

---

[2] Scott B. Mackenzie, Richard J. Lutz, and George E. Belch, "The Role of Attitude Toward the Ad as a Mediator of Advertising Effect: A Test of Competing Explanations," *Journal of Marketing Research* 23 (May 1986): 130–43.

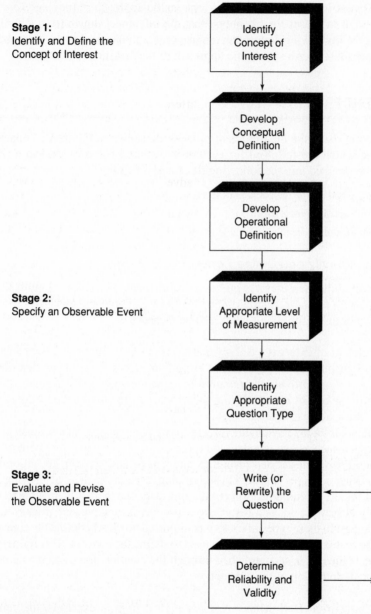

Stage 1:
Identify and Define the
Concept of Interest

Identify
Concept of
Interest

Develop
Conceptual
Definition

Develop
Operational
Definition

Stage 2:
Specify an Observable Event

Identify
Appropriate Level
of Measurement

Identify
Appropriate
Question Type

Stage 3:
Evaluate and Revise
the Observable Event

Write (or
Rewrite) the
Question

Determine
Reliability and
Validity

FIGURE 12.1
The measurement process.

when he or she says that the research probes attitudes toward an advertisement. The conceptual definition also clearly distinguishes the research focus from similar but different research such as overall attitudes toward advertising.

Develop Operational Definition   Once a concept has been identified and conceptually defined, it is then operationally defined. An *operational definition* translates the

concept into one or more observable events by explicitly describing the most important observable, defining characteristics of the concept. An operational definition serves as a bridge between the abstract, theoretical concept and real-world data collection.

However, while there is often little debate among researchers over the substance of a conceptual definition of the concept, there can be great diversity of opinion as to the operational definition of the concept. Differences in perspective among researchers lead to differences in operational definitions. Figure 12.2 (page 262) shows how an accepted conceptual definition can lead to several different operational definitions. The figure demonstrates how several researchers, all starting with the same conceptual definition of attitude toward the advertisement as "a predisposition to respond in a favorable or unfavorable manner to a particular advertising stimulus during a particular exposure situation," diverge as they operationalize the concept.

While the operational definitions shown in Figure 12.2 are different from one another, together they illustrate the process of moving from the concept of interest to an operational definition. The following tasks underlie the process:[3]

1. Specify the area of interest. In this example, the area or concept of interest is attitude toward the advertisement.

2. Think about the concept of interest. Ask yourself: "What do I mean by (concept of interest)? What do others mean when they say (concept of interest)?" In this example, the answers to these questions led to the conceptual definition: "a predisposition to respond in a favorable or unfavorable manner to a particular advertising stimulus during a particular exposure situation." The most important portion of this conceptual definition is the specification of response as "favorable" or "unfavorable."

3. Think about the key components of the operational definition. Ask yourself: "How will I observe (conceptual definition)? How have others observed (conceptual definition)?" In this example, the answers to these questions require one to specify how favorable or unfavorable predispositions can be operationalized and made more concrete.

4. Evaluate and select one or more of the alternatives identified in the prior step. The selected alternative or alternatives become your operational definition. In this example, the first operational definition shown in Figure 12.2 specifies that favorable and unfavorable predispositions toward an advertisement can be observed by asking a respondent about five dimensions of the ad: good/bad, interesting/boring, creative/uncreative, liked/disliked, and informative/uninformative.

Stage Two: Specify an Observable Event

The second stage of the measurement process creates the observable events. Here, a researcher determines the nature of the information needed and the most appropriate means for collecting this information. Finally, the actual research question or data collection instrument (the observable event) is created.

Identify the Appropriate Level of Measurement The nature of the information obtained from any particular observable event, such as a survey question, is dependent on the event's level of measurement. There are four *levels of measurement*: nominal, or-

---

[3] This process reflects the work of G. A. Churchill, Jr., "A Paradigm for Developing Better Measures of Marketing Constructs," *Journal of Marketing Research* (February 1979): 64–73.

Concept of Interest: Attitude toward the advertisement.

Conceptual Definition: A predisposition to respond in a favorable or unfavorable manner to a particular advertising stimulus during a particular exposure situation.

Operational Definitions: Favorable or unfavorable attitudes will be evidenced in terms of the dimensions of

• Five dimensions: good/bad, interesting/boring, creative/uncreative, liked/disliked, and informative/uninformative,[a]

• Four dimensions: good/bad, like/dislike, not irritating/irritating, and interesting/uninteresting,[b]

• Two dimensions: favorable/unfavorable and good/bad,[c]

• Thirteen dimensions: pleasant/unpleasant, refined/vulgar, likable/unlikable, interesting/boring, tasteful/tasteless, entertaining/unentertaining, artful/artless, familiar/novel, good/bad, uninsulting/insulting, believable/unbelievable, convincing/unconvincing, and informative/uninformative.[d]

FIGURE 12.2
Operational definitions of "attitude toward the advertisement."
[a] Gabriel Biehal, Debra Stephens, and Eleonara Curlo, "Attitude Toward the Ad and Brand Choice, *Journal of Advertising* 21 (1992): 19–36.
[b] Meryl P. Gardner, "Does Attitude Toward the Ad Affect Brand Attitude Under a Brand Evaluation Set?" *Journal of Marketing Research* 22 (May 1995): 192–8.
[c] Mita Sujan, James R. Bettman, and Hans Baumgartner, "Influencing Customer Judgment Using Autobiographical Memories: A Self-Referencing Perspective, *Journal of Marketing Research* 30 (November 1993): 422–36.
[d] Sunendra N. Singh and Catherine H. Cole, "The Effect of Length, Content and Repetition on Television Commercial Effectiveness," *Journal of Marketing Research* 30 (February 1993): 91–104.

dinal, interval, and ratio. Table 12.1 shows the uses and characteristics of each level of measurement and lists the types of survey questions commonly asked at each level. Note how each succeeding level of measurement provides different types of information and includes all the information provided by all lower levels. (Different levels of measurement also require different types of analyses. The analytical procedures appropriate for each level of measurement are discussed in Chapters 15 and 16.)

Nominal Level of Measurement   Measurement on the nominal level is very common in advertising and marketing research. *Nominal measurement* occurs whenever the goal is only classification of the measured characteristic or attribute. A nominal level measure classifies by assigning each level of a characteristic or attribute to a distinct category, for example:

RECORD GENDER OF RESPONDENT

    Male _____ (1)   Female _____ (2)

This nominal level measure divides individuals into one of two categories based on the characteristic of gender: male or female.

TABLE 12.1 Levels of Measurement

Level of Measurement	Classifying	Putting in Order	Determining Differences	Determining Ratios	Common Examples	Measure(s)
	Permissible Uses					
Nominal	x				Gender, age, income, product purchaser/ nonpurchaser, commercial aware/not aware	Dichotomous, multiple choice, checklist
Ordinal	x	x			Preferences or any set of ranks along any specific dimension	Ranking
Interval	x	x	x		Measurement of attitudes, beliefs, and perceptions	Rating, semantic differential, Stapel, Likert
Ratio	x	x	x	x	Measurement of attitudes, beliefs, and perceptions	Constant sum

The nominal level of measurement has three defining characteristics, each of which is illustrated in the prior example. First, categories in nominal measurement are mutually exclusive and collectively exhaustive. This means that every level of the characteristic or attribute fits into one and only one category *and* that every characteristic or attribute fits somewhere. In this example, the categories are mutually exclusive (no one can be both male and female) and exhaustive (everyone must be either male or female, there are no other options). Second, for purposes of data analysis, numbers are assigned to each category of response. However, on this level of measurement, the numbers are labels for the categories that they represent. Thus, in terms of gender in the prior example, a '1' represents the category of individuals classified as male while a '2' represents the category of individuals classified as female. Third, nominal measurement assumes internal category equivalence. All objects assigned the same category and represented by the same number are assumed to be the same. For example, in terms of gender, all individuals classified as '1' are assumed, in terms of male gender, to be equivalent to all other individuals classified similarly.

Ordinal Level of Measurement Measurement on the *ordinal level* arranges characteristics or attributes according to their magnitude in an *ordered* relationship along

some explicit dimension, typically from greater to smaller or from more to less, for example:

> Think about the taste of the five soft drinks that you just tasted. The name of each soft drink is shown below. Please rank the soft drinks to indicate your **taste** preference. Place a '1' next to the soft drink whose taste you most preferred, a '2' next to the second best preferred all the way through '5', which represents the drink whose taste you least preferred. Please use each number from 1 to 5 only once (there can be no ties).
>
> Coke   _____
> Dr. Pepper   _____
> Pepsi   _____
> Seven-Up   _____
> Sunkist   _____

This question asks respondents to rank (that is, place in order) five soft drinks according to taste preference (the dimension) from most to least preferred (more to less).

An individual might provide the following responses to soft drink ranking question:

> Coke   1
> Dr. Pepper   4
> Pepsi   3
> Seven-Up   2
> Sunkist   5

As opposed to numbers on the nominal level, numbers provided by the respondent on the ordinal level have some mathematical meaning. On this level of measurement a number represents an object's position along the dimension of interest relative to all other objects. An analysis of this question would include the assumption, therefore, that this individual most prefers the taste of Coke and least prefers the taste of Sunkist.

Ordinal measures thus provide insights into the relative standing of ordered characteristics. That is the extent of ordinal measure's interpretive value. *Ordinal measures cannot provide any insights into the relative distance between ranked objects.* It is tempting in this example to believe that the difference in taste preference between Coke and Seven-Up (ranked '1' and '2', respectively) is the same as the difference in taste preference between Seven-Up and Pepsi (ranked '2' and '3', respectively). After all, in the "real-world" the distance between number 1 and number 2 is the same as the distance between 2 and 3. But, this interpretation would be wrong. On the ordinal level of measurement numbers are symbols that represent a place in an ordered array. As such, they are not subject to mathematical computations such as addition and subtraction.

Interval Level of Measurement   *Interval measurement* contains all of the features of ordinal measurement with the additional characteristic that the distance or magnitude between any two adjacent points on the scale (or the numbers that represent the points on the scale) is equivalent. Consequently, interval measures permit you to determine the relative ranking of objects and the distance between the objects.

The most obvious example of an interval scale is a thermometer. The difference in temperature between 34°C and 35°C is exactly the same as the difference between

64°C and 65°C. Similarly, time is measured on an interval scale. The same amount of time passed between the years 1901 and 1903 as passed between the years 1979 and 1981. Interval measures thus reflect the formal property of equal differences; that is, numbers are assigned to the positions of objects on an interval scale so that they carry a mathematical meaning and can be manipulated with arithmetic operations such as addition and subtraction.

Some interval scales, such as temperature and calendar years, are intuitively reasonable. Common sense dictates that no assumptions need be made as to the equivalence between points on the scale. Other scales, if constructed properly, have the *assumption* of equivalence between points even if this equivalence cannot be externally verified, for example:

> Think about the commercial that you just saw. Compared to other shampoo commercials how would you rate the believability of this specific commercial?

> Very believable   _____ (1)
> Slightly believable   _____ (2)
> Slightly unbelievable   _____ (3)
> Very unbelievable   _____ (4)

This type of scale assumes that response options represent a continuum on which the distance between points is equivalent. (For purposes of data analysis, each point is assigned a number in sequence.) The scale shown assumes that the distance between "very believable" and "slightly believable" is the same as the distance between "slightly believable" and "slightly unbelievable." Therefore, the distance between a '1' that represents very believable and a '2' that represents slightly believable is the same as the distance between a rating of '2' and a rating of '3'.

Interval level measurement is very powerful. It permits you to draw all of the inferences allowed by ordinal and nominal scales while providing additional information on the distance between objects. There is, however, a limitation to the interpretive power of interval measures. Because an interval measure does not have a true, nonarbitrary zero point it cannot be used to make *comparative* judgments. We know, for example, that the world is five hundred years older in the year 1,000 versus the year 500. But, we cannot say that the world was twice as old in the year 1,000 as in the year 500. The inability of interval measurements to make comparative judgments also holds true in research. One cannot conclude from an interval scale that one response option indicates twice as much of the measured quantity (such as liking) as another response option even if the numbers assigned to those options are '4' and '2', respectively.

Ratio Level of Measurement   As shown in Table 12.1, *ratio measures* have all the power of nominal, ordinal, and interval measures with the added, unique power that permits researchers to make comparisons among quantities. This is because ratio measures have equal distances between points on the scale (as in interval measurement) *and* have a meaningful zero point on the scale.

A common form of ratio measure is the constant sum scale. Here, a respondent is given a number of points and is told to distribute those points among a set of objects according to a specific criterion, for example:

Think about the reasons why you purchase a particular children's cereal. Many potential reasons are listed below. We are interested in knowing the relative importance of these reasons in your purchase decision. Assume that you have 100 points. Divide the points among the reasons below to indicate each reason's relative importance. The more points you give something, the more important it is. You can give as many or as few points as you wish to each reason. Please make certain that your total equals 100 points.

All natural   _____
Children like it   _____
Contains fruit   _____
Low Price   _____
Low/no fat   _____
TOTAL   __100__

As this question illustrates, numbers on the ratio level of measurement indicate the actual amount of the property being measured. A measure of zero on a ratio measure truly indicates the total absence of the characteristic or attribute being measured. Common characteristics or attributes measured on the ratio level include advertising awareness, number of commercials seen in the past 24 hours, and number of brand purchasers.

Summary: Selecting a Level of Measurement   We have seen that each of the four levels of measurement provides different types of information. On what basis, then, do you determine the appropriate level of measurement?

Level of measurement can be determined by the characteristic(s) or attribute(s) being measured and the desired depth of detail. However, because higher levels of measurement contain all the descriptive power of lower measures *a general rule of thumb is try to collect information at the highest appropriate level of measurement*. For example, both nominal and ratio level measures can be used to determine an individual's age:

Nominal: Into which of the following groups does your age fall?

Under 18	_____	(1)
18–29	_____	(2)
30–39	_____	(3)
40–49	_____	(4)
50–59	_____	(5)
60–69	_____	(6)
70 and older	_____	(7)

Ratio: What is your age? _____

Notice that the age groupings in the nominal level question represent the extent of understanding. One cannot determine, for example, the distribution of individuals within the 18- to 29-year-old age groups. However, the ratio level measure provides more detail and collects data that can always be grouped so that it is equivalent to the nominal data. Additionally, ratio level measures (versus nominal level measures) can be examined with more powerful statistical techniques (see Chapter 16). Thus, the ratio level might be the better choice for collecting age information, illustrating the power of using the highest appropriate level of measurement.

Identify Appropriate Question Type   Once concepts have been operationally defined and the appropriate level of measurement selected, specific questions or observational instruments are written to collect and record the desired information. However, before a specific question or observational instrument can be written to reflect the

concept's operational definition, you must first determine whether an open-ended versus a closed-ended question is the better means for obtaining the desired information.

Open-ended questions collect information by allowing an individual or observer to reply in his or her own words without use of a fixed, predetermined set of answers. Typical open-ended questions are

Tell me in your own words what the commercial said or showed about the advertised product?

What do you think are the principle benefits of a hair care product that combines shampoo and conditioner?

Why have you stopped using generic children's aspirin?

Open-ended questions have several advantages over closed-ended questions. First, and most obviously, open-ended questions permit an individual to answer a question in his or her own words. An individual can state exactly what is on his or her mind without influence, as might occur when that individual must select an answer from a predetermined list of response options. Thus, open-ended questions are well-suited for exploring circumstances in which you are unable (or unwilling) to list all potential responses. Second, open-ended questions can provide a context for interpreting an individual's answers to closed-ended questions, as follows:

1. Please use the following scale below to indicate the extent to which you liked or disliked the commercial you just saw.

Strongly liked	_____ (1)	CONTINUE WITH Q. 2
Slightly liked	_____ (2)	CONTINUE WITH Q. 2
Slightly disliked	_____ (3)	CONTINUE WITH Q. 4
Strongly disliked	_____ (4)	CONTINUE WITH Q. 4

2. What, in particular, did you like about the commercial?

3. What, if anything, did you dislike about the commercial?

SKIP TO Q. 6

4. What, in particular, did you dislike about the commercial?

5. What, if anything, did you like about the commercial?

6. INTERVIEW CONTINUES

Third, open-ended questions are a good way to introduce a topic area. Once a subject is introduced, the questionnaire can then systematically reduce the breadth and increase the specificity of subsequent questions. Finally, because you need not know all possible answers in advance, open-ended questions tend to be easier to write versus many types of closed-ended questions.

Although the advantages of open-ended questions are significant, this type of question also has several disadvantages. First, responses can be incomplete, irrelevant and/or incomprehensible. Second, open-ended questions take more time to administer and place a greater demand on the verbal skills of the respondent. Third, and most important, the analysis of responses to open-ended questions is more time consuming and difficult versus the analysis of closed-ended questions.

Closed-ended questions present a set of fixed alternative answers. Consequently, closed-ended questions versus open-ended questions tend to

- produce less variability in the range of response,
- be easier for a respondent to answer,
- be quicker to administer,
- be easier to examine and analyze.

The relative advantages of open-ended and closed-ended questions provide some direction for determining which is most appropriate for a particular research situation.

Additional considerations relevant to the evaluation and selection of question type relate to researcher knowledge and respondent priming. Closed-ended questions should only be used when you are convinced that you have presented the full range of options. When presented with a list of items, respondents will generally use the list provided to answer the question; if the list is incomplete the potential of the research to mislead judgment dramatically increases. Beyond list completeness, closed-ended questions have the potential to "prime" or "cue" the respondent. Open-ended questions are appropriate when the measurement goal is the attainment of unaided recall, opinions, or attitudes. Closed-ended questions are appropriate when the measurement goal is the attainment of aided recall, opinions, or attitudes. The difference between unaided and aided measurements, in this case advertising awareness, is illustrated in the following two questions:

Unaided advertising awareness:	Think about all the advertising that you have seen or heard in the past week. Please name any batteries that have advertised themselves as "environmentally-sensitive" or "better for the environment."
Aided advertising awareness:	Think about all the advertising that you have seen or heard in the past week. Which, if any, of the batteries listed have advertised themselves as "environmentally-sensitive" or "better for the environment?" Please check as many or as few as are appropriate.

Energizer _____ (1)
Eveready _____ (2)
Ray-O-Vac _____ (3)
Other (specify) _____ (4)

Stage Three: Evaluate and Revise the Observable Event

Develop the Measurement Instrument   Open-ended and closed-ended question formats provide different means of collecting needed information. Once you have chosen the format most appropriate to a specific informational need, the question itself must be written. The next chapter presents detailed guidance for developing open-ended and closed-ended questions.

Evaluate and Revise Instruments   A specific survey question or observational instrument yields useful, accurate information only if it is reliable and valid. Thus, before initiating any research study, pilot research should be conducted to assess the reliability and validity of any untested measures. Reliability concerns the extent to which

a survey question or other measurement procedure yields the same results over repeated trials. Validity concerns the extent to which the survey question or measurement procedure actually measures what it is intended to measure.

The determination of a measure's reliability and validity is a critical step in the measurement process. Figure 12.2 shows that only reliable and valid measures should be used in the actual conduct of research. Measures that are either unreliable, invalid, or both are rewritten and are then subjected to further assessment of reliability and validity before they are used in a research study.

Reliability   *Reliability* is the degree to which a measure is *stable*, that is, free from random error and yields consistent results over multiple administrations. The test-retest and alternative forms of methods can be used to determine the reliability of *individual* survey questions.

Test-retest reliability is a common way of assessing an item's reliability. An estimate of *test-retest* reliability is obtained by repeating the administration of the test item under equivalent conditions to the same group of people. The results of the two administrations are then compared. The greater the similarity in response between the two administrations the greater the item's reliability. Imagine, for example, that a group of individuals is asked to (1) rank five brands of frozen dinners according to value (an ordinal measure) and (2) rate the taste of five brands of frozen dinners (an interval measure) as part of a survey administered on February 1 and February 14. The ordinal measure would have test-retest reliability if the relative order obtained in both administrations was consistent while the interval measure would have test-retest reliability if the relative order and the relative distance between brands was consistent.

The *alternative form* method of reliability estimation is similar to the test-retest method in so far as the same individuals participate in multiple administrations. However, this method differs from test-retest in one important regard: the same test is not given on the second testing. Rather, an alternative form of the first test is administered. Because it is assumed that the two forms of the test are designed to measure the same thing, reliability is estimated by comparing the responses to the two forms. The greater the correspondence in response between the two forms the greater the reliability.[4]

There are cases in which a single measure cannot by itself carry out the operational definition of a concept or when sensitivity in measurement is desired beyond that which can be provided by a single question. As seen earlier in this chapter, measurement of attitude toward an advertisement may require asking several similar but not identical questions. A set of questions is considered reliable if there is *internal consistency* in response. Consider the following questions used to measure consumers' attitudes toward a celebrity product endorser's attractiveness:[5]

---

[4] Test-retest and alternative form reliability are typically assessed through the use of correlation, denoted as r_{xy}. Chapter 16 provides a detailed discussion of the correlation coefficient, but for the present discussion you need only to understand that r_{xy} is a number that falls in the range of -1.0 to $+1.0$ and reflects the strength of relationship between two variables or measures. In evaluating the reliability of a measure we look for a high positive correlation, that is a r_{xy} which approaches $+1.0$.

[5] Roobina Ohanian, "Construction and Validation of a Scale to Measure Celebrity Endorser's Perceived Expertise, Trustworthiness and Attractiveness," *Journal of Advertising* 19 (1990): 39–52.

Below are five scales. Use each scale to indicate how you feel about the celebrity which you just saw in the advertisement. Place a check in the space in each scale that best represents your feeling.

The celebrity was . . .

attractive								unattractive
	(1)	(2)	(3)	(4)	(5)	(6)	(7)	
not classy								classy
	(1)	(2)	(3)	(4)	(5)	(6)	(7)	
beautiful								ugly
	(1)	(2)	(3)	(4)	(5)	(6)	(7)	
elegant								plain
	(1)	(2)	(3)	(4)	(5)	(6)	(7)	
not sexy								sexy
	(1)	(2)	(3)	(4)	(5)	(6)	(7)	

These scales would be internally consistent, and thus reliable, if individuals with positive attitudes tend to answer all questions positively while those with negative attitudes tend to answer all questions negatively.[6]

Validity A reliable measure consistently measures something. But, this something may or may not be what you want to measure. In other words, it is entirely possible that a survey item is reliable but not at all valid. Only valid measures actually measure what we want or, put in more formal terms, validity occurs when there is a high degree of correspondence between a concept's operational definition and the specific observable event used to record the concept.

Validity is commonly determined in one of three ways: content, criterion, or construct.

Content validity is the simplest form of validity assessment. A measure is considered to have content validity when the subjective judgment of professionals agrees that the measure accurately translates the operational definition into an observed event, in other words, when there is a consensus that a question does in fact measure what it is supposed to measure. Clear, unambiguous questions such as "Do you recall seeing any advertising for the Ford Taurus?" are generally felt to have content validity (in this case for the measurement of advertising recall). A question that attempts to measure brand loyalty by asking "Which brand is the best value for the money?" would lack content validity because the characteristic probed in the question (brand value) is different from the characteristic specified in the conceptual and operational definition (brand loyalty).

Criterion validity can take one of two forms: concurrent and predictive.

- *Concurrent validity* is estimated by comparing the results obtained from a new measurement with the results of an accepted measurement taken at the same point in time. For example, assume that researchers have developed a ninety-six item test that predicts how specific individuals will react to different types of advertising. The predictive abil-

---

[6] The statistical technique most commonly used for determining the reliabiliy of multiple items is the coefficient alpha. For a discussion of this measure's characteristics, computation, and measurement see L. J. Cronbach, "Co-efficieint Alpha and the Internal Structure of Tests," *Psychometrika* 16 (1951): 297–334; Carmines and Zeller, *Reliability and Validity Assessment*. Coefficient alpha is discussed in Chapter 15.

ity of this test is high, but the test takes a long time to administer. Consequently, you develop a new, shorter test consisting of only fifteen items. The new test will have concurrent validity if its scores highly correlate with that of the existing test.

- *Predictive validity* is estimated by determining the extent to which performance on one variable (measured today) accurately predicts performance on another variable (to be measured in the future). For example, you might be interested in understanding the effects of product quality perceptions on purchase behaviors. Consequently, you might develop a set of survey questions that measure product quality perceptions and a procedure for tracking brands purchased. Predictive validity will reflect the extent to which the first set of measures accurately predicts the brands purchased.

Construct validity is the most complex and most important form of validity. This form of validity is theory-based and is "concerned with the extent to which a particular measure relates to other measures consistent with theoretically-derived hypotheses concerning the concepts (or constructs) being measured."[7] To prove construct validity, the test measure(s) must

- correlate positively with other measures of the same concept,
- show little or no correlation with theoretically unrelated concepts,
- correlate in a theoretically consistent way with measures of different but related concepts.[8]

Assume that an advertiser wishes to develop a scale that measures an individual's inclination to respond to infomercials and purchase the advertised product. The advertiser theorizes that the inclination to purchase is caused by three personality variables: low-self esteem, high materialism, and a high need for immediate gratification. Further, the advertiser believes that the inclination to respond is unrelated to disposable household income or the need for status. Evidence of construct validity would exist if the scale designed to measure inclination to purchase has

- a high correlation with other measures of purchase intent,
- a low correlation with theorized unrelated measures, such as household income and need for status,
- a low correlation with measures of self-esteem and high correlations with measures of materialism, and the need for immediate gratification.[9]

Summary

The measurement process links concepts such as beliefs and attitudes to observable events such as responses to questionnaire items. The measurement process, consists of seven steps representing three major stages (see Figure 12.1).

The first stage, *identify and define the concept of interest*, is one of refinement. This stage begins with a general notion of the area to be explored (the concept of interest) and ends with an explicit operational definition of what is to be measured. The

---

[7] Carmines and Zeller, *Reliability and Validity Assessment*, 23.

[8] Donald S. Tull and Del I. Hawkins, *Marketing Research: Measurement and Method* (New York, NY: Macmillan Publishing Company, 1990), 276.

[9] Ibid., 276–7.

second stage, *specification of the observable event,* actually creates the measurement instrument. During this stage a researcher determines the nature of the information needed and the most appropriate means for collecting this information. Here, decisions relate to the appropriate level of measurement (nominal, ordinal, interval, and ratio) and the appropriate question type (open-ended versus closed-ended).

- Nominal level measures assign responses to mutually exclusive and exhaustive categories.
- Ordinal level measures arrange characteristics or responses according to their magnitude in an ordered relationship along an explicit dimension.
- Interval level measures contain all of the features of ordinal measurement with the additional characteristic that the distance between any two points are equivalent.
- Ratio level measures have all the characteristics of all the prior levels with the added quality of having a true, nonarbitrary zero point.

The third stage, *development and revision*, evaluates the measurement instrument. Acceptable measurement instruments are those that are both reliable and valid. Measurement instruments that are not reliable or valid are revised or eliminated before they are used in the research study.

Review Questions

1. What does the term *measurement* mean?
2. What are the three main stages of the measurement process? What key events occur at each stage?
3. What is a *conceptual definition*?
4. What is an *operational definition*?
5. Why is an operational definition important?
6. Describe the process by which one moves from a concept of interest to an operational definition.
7. What is *nominal* measurement?
8. What are the characteristics of nominal measurement? Provide an example of a survey question written at the nominal level of measurement.
9. What is *ordinal* measurement? Provide an example of a survey question written at the ordinal level of measurement.
10. What is *interval* measurement? Provide an example of a survey question written at the interval level of measurement.
11. What is *ratio* measurement? Provide an example of a survey question written at the ratio level of measurement.
12. What are the relative advantages of *open-ended* versus *closed-ended* questions?
13. What is the definition of *reliability*?
14. What are the two ways by which reliability is estimated? Provide a brief description of each.
15. What is the definition of *validity*?
16. What are the three ways by which validity is estimated? Provide a brief description of each.

Application Exercises[10]

1. Three researchers proposed methods for measuring brand loyalty. They began with the same conceptual definition: brand loyalty is a consumer's preferential behavioral response to one or more products in a product category expressed over a period of time. They wrote the following three questions:

   Terry: Think about all of the laundry detergents that you have purchased during the past year. What percent of your purchases were of each of the following brands shown? Fill in a percentage beside each brand to indicate that brand's percentage of total purchases.

All	_____
Cheer	_____
Tide	_____
Wisk	_____
Generic	_____

   Richard: Think about your purchase of laundry detergent. Would you say that you . . .

Consistently purchase the same brand	_____	(1)
Do not consistently purchase the same brand	_____	(2)

   Staci: I am interested in learning how brand loyal you are to your laundry detergent. Would you say that you are

Extremely loyal	_____	(1)
Usually loyal	_____	(2)
Usually loyal except when I have a coupon	_____	(x)
Slightly loyal	_____	(3)
A little loyal	_____	(4)
Not at all loyal	_____	(5)

   Take this definition and (1) prepare an operational definition that reflects the approach taken by each researcher, (2) evaluate how numbers are used (properly or improperly), and (3) revise each question to reflect the operational definition. Discuss how your revised questions satisfy your assumptions as to the nature of the operational definition.

2. Advertising-related research is published in journals such as the *Journal of Advertising*, the *Journal of Advertising Research*, the *Journal of Consumer Research*, the *Journal of Marketing*, the *Journal of Marketing Research*, and *Journalism Quarterly*. Concepts frequently explored in articles published in these journals include: attitudes toward the advertising, attitudes toward the brand, purchase intent, and attitudes toward the advertiser. Select one of these concepts, or another relevant to advertising research, and provide at least three different examples from the academic literature illustrating how the concept has been operationally defined. Present a point of view on the relative strengths and weaknesses of each approach.

3. Select one of the approaches identified in the prior question. How did the researcher address issues related to reliability and validity? Present a point of view on the adequacy of the procedures the researcher used.

4. Examine each of the following questions. Then, for each question: (1) identify the question's level of measurement and (2) present a point of view as to whether the ques-

---

[10] All application exercises are hypothetical.

tion adheres to the principle of "collecting information at the highest appropriate level of measurement." If you feel that the question does not collect information at the appropriate level, present an alternative. Be certain to explain your recommendation.

a. Think about the following three products: Spiffo, Boffo, and Waxo. Which of these three products do you think cleans dirty floors the best? CHECK ONE.

Spiffo   _____
Boffo   _____
Waxo   _____

b. Into which of the following categories does your annual household income fall? CHECK ONE.

Under $25,000   _____
$25,000–$49,999   _____
$50,000–$74,999   _____
$75,000–$99,999   _____
$100,000 or above   _____

c. How many children under the age of 18 are currently living full-time in your household?

Fill in number of children   _____

d. Please tell me whether you liked or disliked the advertising?

Liked   _____
Disliked   _____

e. Please use a scale of '1' to '10', where '10' is the most favorable response, to rate the value of . . .

Toyota automobiles   _____
Ford automobiles   _____
Chevrolet trucks   _____

f. Think about what is important to you in a toothpaste. Now, please use of a scale of '1' to '10', where '10' represents extremely important, to rate the importance of each of the following in your toothpaste purchase decision. How would you rate the importance of . . .

Taste   _____
Cavity-fighting   _____
Fights gum disease   _____
Good for both kids and adults   _____
A brand name   _____

5. Imagine that you are hired as the consultant to your regional mass transit authority. The transit authority has allocated funds to develop and air an advertising campaign intended to increase mass transit ridership. In preparation for the campaign they ask you to conduct some research that will help them better understand (1) attitudes toward riding mass transit and (2) attitudes toward car pooling.

Write a letter to the transit authority that explains how you will move from each general area of interest, to operational definition, to valid and reliable survey questions. Be specific in explaining the decisions and procedures that you will use at each stage of the measurement process.

CHAPTER

13

QUESTION DEVELOPMENT

The types and quality of questions you ask in an interview will determine the depth and quality of the insights you obtain. In this chapter you will learn about procedures and guidelines for writing questions that provide the information and insights required for sound advertising decision making.

After reading this chapter, you will be able to

■ Describe the options for closed- and open-ended question form and content.

■ Explain why and how some types of questions work better in certain situations than others.

■ Recognize well-written and poorly written questions.

Quantitative advertising research uses two types of questions, closed-ended and open-ended. A closed-ended question gives the respondent a predefined set of response options from which he or she can choose. An open-ended question permits the respondent to answer in his or her own words. Both types of questions provide valuable insights into a respondent's thoughts, beliefs, and attitudes. This chapter begins with a discussion of the types and characteristics of closed-ended questions, followed by a discussion of open-ended questions. The chapter concludes with the presentation of special considerations for open- and closed-ended question development.

DEVELOPING CLOSED-ENDED SURVEY QUESTIONS

The prior chapter discussed the four levels of measurement: nominal, ordinal, interval, and ratio. In this section we discuss the common forms of closed-ended questions advertising researchers use at each level of measurement.

275

Nominal Level Questions

Questions at the nominal level of measurement seek to categorize responses through assignment to mutually exclusive categories. Three common types of nominal level questions are dichotomous questions, multiple-choice questions, and checklists.

Dichotomous Questions A *dichotomous question* is the simplest type of measurement on the nominal level. It is used to classify individuals, objects, attitudes, or other responses into one of two exhaustive, mutually exclusive groups. The most common form of classification in dichotomous questions uses "yes" and "no" responses, for example:

Did you see any advertising for Bubble Yum before purchasing the product?
Yes _____ (1)   No _____ (2)

Are there currently any children under the age of 18 living full-time in your household?
Yes _____ (1)   No _____ (2)

Dichotomous questions, however, are not limited to yes and no response options. For example:

Do you prefer diet soft drinks flavored with NutraSweet or Aspartame?
Nutrasweet   _____ (1)
Aspartame   _____ (2)

Dichotomous questions have several advantages over more complex questions: (1) they are easy for a respondent to answer. (Respondents generally find it faster and easier to select from two choices than to select from ten options); (2) they are very simple to edit, code, tabulate, and analyze; and (3) they work well to direct skip patterns within the questionnaire. For example:

1. Are you currently married or single?
   Married   _____ (1)   CONTINUE WITH Q.2
   Single   _____ (2)   SKIP TO Q.3
2. How long have you been married? FILL IN YEARS BELOW.
   YEARS MARRIED   _____
3. Have you ever been married?
   Yes _____ (1)   No _____ (2)
4. INTERVIEW CONTINUES

In spite of their advantages, care must be taken when using dichotomous questions. First, the choices presented to the respondent must be reasonable. Consider the following question:

Think about the advertising for Budweiser Light and Miller Lite beers. Which brand's advertising do you prefer?
Budweiser Light   _____ (1)
Miller Lite   _____ (2)

It would be unreasonable to ask this question unless it was determined *prior* to asking the question that the respondent had, in fact, seen both brands' advertising. Remember, respondents are quite willing to express an opinion on issues or topics they know nothing about. A study by Schuman and Presser found that about 30 percent of respondents

volunteered opinions about a fictitious law they could have known nothing about.[1] Thus, it is your responsibility to make certain that the question is reasonable given what you know about the respondent's level of knowledge or attitude. Second, dichotomous questions should not be used as a substitute for more detailed questions. It would be inappropriate, for example, to classify levels of brand usage through a dichotomous question which asks; "Have you used three or more tubes of toothpaste in the past month?" A question of the form "How many tubes of toothpaste have you used in the past month?" would be more appropriate.

Multiple-Choice Questions   *Multiple-choice questions* are nominal measures that present three or more exclusive and exhaustive categories of response. These questions are used when the need is to categorize the characteristics or attributes of respondents or responses into smaller, more focused categories than are permitted by dichotomous questions. The collection of demographic information is a common use of this type of question. For example:

Into which of the following groups does your total, annual household income fall?

Under $15,000	_____ (1)
$15,000–$24,999	_____ (2)
$25,000–$34,999	_____ (3)
$35,000–$44,999	_____ (4)
$45,000–$54,999	_____ (5)
$55,000 and over	_____ (6)

When writing multiple-choice questions make certain that the categories are exhaustive and exclusive. The following two questions show the types of problems that arise when these conditions are not met. The category options in the following first example lack both exhaustiveness (what about respondents with no children?) and exclusivity (a respondent with six children fits into two categories). The second example also lacks exhaustiveness and exclusivity. Here, the absence of an "other" option prohibits the classification of respondents whose last purchase was not one of the listed brands (exhaustiveness) while the question fails to account for the potential for a respondent who bought two different brands the last time he or she was shopping (exclusivity).

How many children under the age of 18 are currently living full-time in your household?

1	_____ (1)
2	_____ (2)
3	_____ (3)
4	_____ (4)
5	_____ (5)
6	_____ (6)
6 or more	_____ (7)

Think about the last time you purchased laundry detergent? Which brand did you buy?

All	_____ (1)
Cheer	_____ (2)
Tide	_____ (3)

---

[1] Howard Schuman and Stanley Presser, *Questions and Answers in Attitude Surveys: Experiments in Question Form, Wording and Context* (New York, NY: Academic Press, 1981).

Multiple-choice questions are not restricted to the collection of demographic or behavioral information. This type of question can be used to probe attitudes and motivations as long as responses are constrained to *one* of the listed options (including "other"), for example:

What is the one most important reason why you purchased a Toyota automobile?

Price	_____ (1)	
Warranty	_____ (2)	
Word of mouth	_____ (3)	
Other	_____ (4)	SPECIFY: _____

Do you plan to purchase a new automobile in the next twelve months?

Definitely yes	_____ (1)
Probably yes	_____ (2)
Probably no	_____ (3)
Definitely no	_____ (4)

Multiple-choice questions have several advantages: (1) the format is very flexible and appropriate to a wide range of situations; (2) they provide much of the same flexibility as open-ended questions, but without the reliance upon the ability of respondents to verbalize their thoughts and express themselves; and (3) versus open-ended questions, they are easier to code, edit, tabulate, and analyze.

There are important considerations associated with the use of multiple-choice questions. First, you must make certain the list of alternative answers is exhaustive. Second, when the question presents a long list of response options there is the potential for position bias. In these situations there is a general tendency for respondents to choose the first item on the list of response options.[2] For example, if you were to ask respondents to choose their favorite laundry detergent from among a list of sixteen, all other things being equal, the chances of a brand being selected would increase as it moves from the bottom to the top of the list.[3] The negative effect of order on data integrity may, however, be reduced in one of two ways.

- *Use a check procedure.* When the survey is administered by an interviewer, a "check" procedure can be used to start the list at a different point for each respondent. This requires that the questionnaires be coded for a "start point" before being used for interviews. When this is done the question takes the following form:

  What is the one most important reason why you purchased a Toyota automobile?
  READ LIST BEGINNING WITH CHECKED ITEM. RECORD RESPONSE.

Price	_____ (1)	
Warranty	_____ (2)	
√ Dependability	_____ (3)	
Word of mouth	_____ (4)	
Incentives	_____ (5)	
Advertising	_____ (6)	
Other	_____ (7)	(SPECIFY) _____

---

[2] See Schuman and Presser, *Questions and Answers,* 56–76.

[3] This example is based on the empirical work of S. L. Becker who manipulated presentation order when asking respondents to select their favorite radio station from among a set of sixteen. See S. L. Becker, "Why An Order Effect?" *Public Opinion Quarterly* 18 (1954): 271–8.

- *Use a "split-ballot" procedure.* When either a self-administered questionnaire or one administered by an interviewer is used, a "split-ballot" approach may be utilized. Here, equal numbers of different forms of the questionnaire are produced. For example, if 300 total interviews were needed three forms of the questionnaire (100 copies of each form) would be produced with response options appearing on each questionnaire as follows:

Questionnaire A	*Questionnaire B*	*Questionnaire C*
Price	Warranty	Dependability
Warranty	Word of mouth	Price
Dependability	Dependability	Word of mouth
Word of mouth	Price	Warranty
Other	Other	Other

Third, you must make certain that the response alternatives for behaviorally related multiple-choice questions reflect reasonable ranges and that typical behaviors appear in the middle of the list of choices. This is because respondents will interpret the response categories to be what is typical or normal behavior, and consequently their answers can be distorted by the very nature of the response options.[4] Schwarz, Hippler, Deutch, and Strank asked "How many hours a day do you spend watching TV?" They had half the sample select their response from Set A while the remaining half of the sample selected from Set B.

Set A	*Set B*
up to ½ hour	up to 2½ hours
½–1 hour	2½–3 hours
1–1½ hours	3–3½ hours
1½–2 hours	3½–4 hours
2–2½ hours	4–4½ hours
more than 2½ hours	more than 4½ hours

Reported TV viewing was significantly different between the two halves of the sample, for example, 16 percent of those using response Set A said that they watched two and one-half or more hours while 38 percent of those using Set B reported that they watched for more than two and one-half hours.[5]

Checklist A *checklist* is a nominal measure that combines a series of related dichotomous questions into a single question. This combination results in a less time-consuming and tedious method of data collection. Two examples of checklist questions are

---

[4] Herbert H. Clark and Michael F. Schober, "Asking Questions and Influencing Answers," In Judith M. Tanur ed., *Questions About Questions: Inquiries Into the Cognitive Basis of Surveys* (New York, NY: Russell Sage Foundation, 1992), 15–48.

[5] N. Schwarz et al., "Response Categories: Effects on Behavioral Reports and Comparative Judgments," *Public Opinion Quarterly* 49 (1985): 388–95.

Think about all the beer advertising that you have seen in the past month. Which of the following brands of beer have you seen advertised. Check as many or as few (or even no items) as apply.

Budweiser	_____ (1)
Hamms	_____ (1)
Miller	_____ (1)
Old Style	_____ (1)
.	_____ (1)
etc.	_____ (1)

Think about the commercial that you just saw. Which of the following words or phrases describe how you felt about the commercial. Check as many or as few (or even no items) as apply.

Entertaining	_____ (1)
Confusing	_____ (1)
Silly	_____ (1)
Believable	_____ (1)
.	_____ (1)
.	_____ (1)
etc.	_____ (1)

These questions illustrate several important characteristics of checklist questions. First, the question must explicitly define the criteria on which items in the checklist are to be selected. Second, the question must not assume that the respondent will check any specific number of items. The instructions must make it clear that it is up to the respondent to check as many or as few items (or even no items) as he or she feels is appropriate. Third, the checklist itself must be constructed to reduce bias. Thus, lists of brand names or reasons for purchase, for example, should be in alphabetical order. Words and phrases, as in the second checklist, should contain equal numbers of positive and negative items placed in a randomized order. Fourth, note how numbers are assigned to responses. Each item on the checklist is treated as an independent dichotomous question. In the prior examples, those who select a particular item are assigned a '1' for that item while those who do not select the item are (by default) assigned a '0'. Each item on the checklist is therefore mutually exhaustive and exclusive.

Ordinal Level Questions

Questions at the ordinal level of measurement order responses in terms of a predefined characteristic. Responses to these questions inform the researcher as to the *ordering* of items although no inferences as to the *distances* between items can be drawn. The most common question at this level of measurement is rank order scaling.

Rank order scaling presents a respondent with several characteristics, objects, or attributes and then requests the respondent to order or rank them with respect to a specific characteristic. The following rank order question might be asked of individuals who had just been exposed to examples of four electronic stores' advertising:

You have just seen advertising for four electronic stores: The Good Guys, Circuit City, Electric Avenue, and Silo. Please rank the advertising to reflect how you feel about their

believability. Place a '1' next to the store that you feel had the most believable advertising, a '2' next to the next believable, through '4' which you would place next to the store that you felt had the least believable advertising. There can be no ties and please use each number only once.

The Good Guys   _____
Circuit City   _____
Electric Avenue   _____
Silo   _____

Notice how the question is worded to state the respondent's task (ranking) explicitly, the characteristic to be used (believability), and the method used (a '1' for the most believable, etc.).

Interval Level Questions

Questions at the interval level of measurement provide information on the rank order of items and provide an estimate of the relative distance between items.

Rating scales are one of the most common types of interval measures. These questions require a respondent to place an attribute of the person or object being rated along an explicit, well-defined continuum. A rating scale may or may not provide a frame of reference for the rating and may be presented in either graphic or itemized format.

Frame of Reference   *Noncomparative rating scales* ask a respondent to assign a rating without an explicit frame of reference. For example, a scale designed to assess overall reactions to a specific commercial might ask: "Think about the commercial that you just saw. How believable or unbelievable would you say that the commercial was?" Each respondent answers this question using whatever frame of reference he or she prefers. Some respondents might compare the test commercial to other commercials in the same category, while others might compare it to "the last ads I saw," "the average ad," or "ads I like."

The lack of an explicit frame of reference in noncomparative rating scales makes data interpretation "unclear" and difficult. The tendency for different respondents to provide different frames of reference creates ambiguity in a research study. Therefore, advertising researchers typically use *comparative rating scales* that provide an explicit frame of reference for the respondent. For example:

> Think about beer advertising that you have seen in the past month. How believable or unbelievable would you say the commercial you just saw is when compared to beer advertising that you have seen in the past month?

The specific frame of reference reflects how the concept "commercial believability" is operationally defined. When using a frame of reference make certain before administering the rating, that the frame of reference is relevant and appropriate to the respondent. If a respondent is asked to "Use the following scale to indicate how much you like or dislike Dr. Pepper advertising compared to Diet Coke advertising," it is important that you confirm that the respondent has some awareness of Diet Coke advertising.

Graphic and Itemized Scales   Noncomparative and comparative rating scales may

be presented in either a graphic (sometimes called continuous) or an itemized format.

A *graphic rating scale* asks a respondent to indicate his or her rating by placing a mark (a check or an 'x') at the appropriate point on a line that runs from one extreme of the rating scale to the other. This line may be presented without (Question A) or with scale points (Question B) to help the respondent more clearly identify the appropriate place to make a response, as follows:

A. Place a mark on the line below to indicate how you would rate the believability of the commercial you just saw when compared to other beer advertising. You may place a check anywhere on the line. The closer to one end of the line you place your mark, the more the descriptor on that end describes your rating of the commercial's believability.

Extremely   Extremely
Believable _____Unbelievable

B. Place a mark on the line below to indicate how you would rate the believability of the commercial you just saw when compared to other beer advertising. You may place a check anywhere on the line. The closer to one end of the line you place your mark, the more the descriptor on that end describes your rating of the commercial's believability.

Extremely   Extremely
Believable _____Unbelievable
     0   10   20   30   40   50   60   70   80   90   100

Note how in both cases the line is not divided into distinct categories before use. You divide the line into categories and then assign a respondent's rating after the research is completed.

Graphic rating scales are uncommon in advertising and marketing research. Respondent directions are cumbersome and data preparation is time-consuming. Advertising and marketing researchers generally rely on itemized rating scales. An *itemized rating scale* requires a respondent to select one of a limited number of categories that are ordered in terms of their scale positions. Figure 13.1 presents several examples of itemized scales.

The questions shown in Figure 13.1 illustrate three characteristics of well-written itemized rating scales: (1) the questions are unbiased. Both ends of the rating scale are explicitly mentioned in the question itself; (2) the scales are constructed so that there are equal spaces or intervals between scale points; and (3) there is correspondence between the information requested in the question itself and the scales used to gather the information. The following question illustrates what happens when this correspondence does not occur:

How much would you agree or disagree with the statement "I liked the commercial I just saw." Would you say that you . . .

Strongly liked the commercial   _____ (1)
Slightly liked the commercial   _____ (2)
Slightly disliked the commercial   _____ (3)
Strongly disliked the commercial   _____ (4)

The prior question would need to take the following form for there to be proper correspondence between the question itself and the scale:

A. Think about the commercial that you just saw. Select the one choice from the scale below that best reflects how believable or unbelievable you feel that the commercial is when compared to other shampoo advertising.

Very Believable ⎯⎯ (1)

Slightly Believable ⎯⎯ (2)

Slightly Unbelievable ⎯⎯ (3)

Very Unbelievable ⎯⎯ (4)

B. Think about the commercial that you just saw. Select the one choice from the scale below that best reflects how believable or unbelievable you feel that the commercial is when compared to other shampoo advertising.

Very Believable (1)	Slightly Believable (2)	Neither More or Less Believable (3)	Slightly Unbelievable (4)	Very Unbelievable (5)

C. Think about the various reasons why you purchased your current brand of shampoo. How important or unimportant was price in your purchase decision? Place an 'x' on the scale below to indicate the importance of price.

Extremely Important ⎯⎯ ⎯⎯ ⎯⎯ ⎯⎯ ⎯⎯ Not At All Important
  (1)   (2)   (3)   (4)   (5)

D. Think about the quality of men's clothes sold at K-Mart. How would you rate the quality of these clothes compared to the quality of clothes sold at similar types of stores, for example, Target, Venture, and Wal-Mart? Select the option below that best reflects your opinion.

Excellent ⎯⎯ (1)

Very Good ⎯⎯ (2)

Good ⎯⎯ (3)

Fair ⎯⎯ (4)

Poor ⎯⎯ (5)

FIGURE 13.1
Forms of itemized rating scales.

How much would you agree or disagree with the statement "I liked the commercial I just saw." Would you say that you . . .

Strongly agree ⎯⎯⎯⎯ (1)
Slightly agree ⎯⎯⎯⎯ (2)
Slightly disagree ⎯⎯⎯⎯ (3)
Strongly disagree ⎯⎯⎯⎯ (4)

Itemized Scales—Special Considerations Itemized rating scales have the potential to provide important insights and information. You must make explicit decisions regarding three aspects of the scale portion of the question for them to be most useful.

First, because there is no set number of categories for scale questions, you must determine the number of categories to use. Any number of categories may be created depending on the nature of the attitude or behavior being investigated. A general rule of thumb is that between five and ten response categories provide sufficient discrimination. However, you should be certain that the finer distinctions represented in scales with more categories (such as the nine-item set below) are relevant and meaningful to the respondent. Consider, the following two rating scales:

Strongly agree	Very strongly agree
Slightly agree	Strongly agree
Neither agree nor disagree	Somewhat agree
Slightly disagree	Slightly agree
Strongly disagree	Neither agree nor disagree
	Slightly disagree
	Somewhat disagree
	Strongly disagree
	Very strongly disagree

The five-point scale assumes that respondents are able to evaluate the general direction (agree and disagree) and general strength (strongly and slightly) of their opinion. The nine-point scale assumes that respondents are able to make extremely fine distinctions.

Second, you must determine whether the scale should be balanced or unbalanced. A balanced scale provides an equal number of response categories on both ends of the continuum. This is the most common form of rating scale and satisfies all of the requirements of interval measurement. An unbalanced scale, on the other hand, should only be used in circumstances where the direction of response is generally known and finer distinctions on one end of the continuum are desired. The following question presents an unbalanced scale:

To what extent are you pleased or displeased with the ability of Prell shampoo to leave your hair tangle-free?

Pleased	_____	(1)
Slightly displeased	_____	(2)
Somewhat displeased	_____	(3)
Strongly displeased	_____	(4)
Very strongly displeased	_____	(5)

While unbalanced scales are sometimes used by marketing and advertising researchers, we recommend against their use for two reasons.

- *Bias.* The question has the potential to bias the respondent. The appearance of four negative options and only one positive response option (as in the prior example) may lead respondents to believe that they should be displeased with the product.

- *Problems with data analysis and interpretation.* Data analysis is more complex versus balanced scales. An unbalanced scale is not a true interval measure because there are not equal distances between all scale options.

Third, when balanced scales are used you must decide if the scale should contain an odd or even number of scale categories. Question A in Figure 13.1 uses an even number of categories while Question B seeks to acquire the same information using an odd number of categories. Note that when an odd number of categories is used the

middle category is generally designated as "neutral." The decision to use odd numbers versus even numbers of response categories generally reflects your assumptions regarding the respondent's state of mind. Advocates of even-numbered categories avoid neutral points because they believe that attitudes cannot be neutral and that respondents should be forced to indicate some degree of attitude or opinion. Others argue that in many cases consumers may indeed be neutral and should be allowed to express that state of opinion.

Special Types of Rating Scales   There are three special types of itemized rating scales commonly used in advertising research. These scales are: semantic differential, Stapel, and Likert scales.

The *semantic differential scale*[6] is commonly used in advertising and marketing research. In its most common form the semantic differential asks a respondent to rate an object on a number of itemized, seven-point rating scales bounded on each end by one of two bipolar adjectives. The following scales used to evaluate reactions to a product spokesperson are examples of semantic differential scales.

The celebrity was . . .

	(1)	(2)	(3)	(4)	(5)	(6)	(7)	
Attractive								Unattractive
Not classy								Classy
Beautiful								Ugly
Elegant								Plain
Not sexy								Sexy

Two considerations are important in the use of semantic differential scales. First, the semantic differential may be unfamiliar to many respondents. Consequently, instructions must explicitly explain how to mark the scales. Second, care must be taken as to the placement of the bipolar adjectives. As seen in the prior example, adjectives appearing on the right side of the scale are both positive and negative. This increases the likelihood that the respondent will read each set of adjectives and thus reduces the likelihood that the respondent will read only a few items and then, when discovering a pattern, mark the remainder in a similar way. Once the questionnaire has been administered, for purposes of data analysis and ease of presentation, all positive adjectives can be numbered similarly and placed on the same side of the continuum.

The prior approach works well when you require measurements related to one object. However, this approach becomes quite time-consuming when multiple objects need to be rated. As a consequence, two modifications to the traditional semantic differential technique have been proposed for cases where multiple objects must be rated. The upgraded semantic differential, or graphic positioning scale,[7] permits respondents to rate two or more objects simultaneously on one set of semantic differential scales by

---

[6] Charles E. Osgood, George J. Suci, and Percy H. Tannenbaum, *The Measurement of Meaning* (Urbana, IL: University of Illinois Press, 1957).

[7] R. H. Evans, "The Upgraded Semantic Differential: A Further Test," *Journal of the Market Research Society* 22 (1980): 143–7.

placing the initials of the rated objects on the continuum between the bipolar adjectives. The numerical comparative scale[8] takes the opposite approach. Here, a respondent records the number representing the appropriate point on the continuum beneath each object. Examples of these two approaches are shown in Figure 13.2.

Stapel scales are simplified versions of the semantic differential. The standard Stapel scale is a unipolar, eleven-interval rating scale with values ranging from '+5' to '−5'. However, unlike the semantic differential, on a Stapel scale the scale values indicate how accurately one adjective describes the object being rated. Figure 13.2 shows how semantic differential scales can measure consumers' perceptions of cereal manufacturers. The following scale illustrates how comparable information can be obtained by using Stapel scales.

> Think about General Mills. Then read each word or phrase shown below. Next to each word or phrase are numbers ranging from −5 to +5. Think about how accurately or inaccurately each word or phrase describes General Mills. The more a word or phrase describes General Mills, the larger the positive number you should circle. The less a word or phrase describes General Mills the larger the negative number you should circle.

	+5		+5
	+4		+4
	+3		+3
	+2		+2
	+1		+1
Trustworthy	0	Only interested in profit	0
	−1		−1
	−2		−2
	−3		−3
	−4		−4
	−5		−5

Stapel scales have three advantages over the traditional semantic differential scale. First, they are easier to construct. There is no need to pretest the adjectives or phrases to ensure that true bipolarity exists. Second, they are easy to administer. Respondents have little difficulty understanding the task of how to indicate their response. Third, they can be administered over the telephone where semantic differential scales cannot.

A *Likert scale* asks a respondent to indicate his or her degree of agreement or disagreement with a series of specific statements. Likert scales could also be used to evaluate consumers' perceptions of cereal manufacturers, as follows:

> Read each of the following statements. Then, place a check on each scale to indicate the extent to which you agree or disagree, if at all, with that statement.
> As a company, General Mills . . .

---

[8] L. L. Golden, G. Albaum, and M. Zimmer, "The Numerical Comparative Scale," *Journal of Retailing* 32 (Winter 1987): 393–410.

Upgraded Semantic Differential

Think about three manufacturers of cereal: General Mills, Kellogg's, and Post. We are interested in your attitudes toward each manufacturer. For each scale shown below, (1) decide where, in your opinion, each manufacturer falls on the scale and then (2) place the letter representing that manufacturer on that spot. The closer to one end of the scale you place a manufacturer, the more the word on that end of the scale describes that manufacturer. The codes to use are

General Mills	G
Kellogg's	K
Post	P

The code for each manufacturer should appear once on each scale.

Trustworthy __ __ __ __ __ __ __ Not Trustworthy
     (1) (2) (3) (4) (5) (6) (7)

Only Interested __ __ __ __ __ __ __ Not Only Interested
in Profit   (7) (6) (5) (4) (3) (2) (1)   in Profit

Not Interested __ __ __ __ __ __ __ Interested in
in the Environment (7) (6) (5) (4) (3) (2) (1) the Environment

Makes Healthy Foods __ __ __ __ __ __ __ Makes Unhealthy Foods
      (1) (2) (3) (4) (5) (6) (7)

Good Corporate Citizen __ __ __ __ __ __ __ Poor Corporate Citizen
       (1) (2) (3) (4) (5) (6) (7)

Numerical Comparative Semantic Differential

Think about three manufacturers of cereal: General Mills, Kellogg's, and Post. We are interested in your attitudes toward each manufacturer. For each scale shown below do the following: (1) decide where, in your opinion, each manufacturer falls on the scale and then (2) place the number representing that manufacturer on the line beneath that manufacturer's name. The closer a number is to one end of the scale, the more the word on that end of the scale describes that manufacturer.

			General Mills	Kellogg's	Post
Trustworthy	1 2 3 4 5 6 7	Not Trustworthy	__	__	__
Only Interested in Profit	7 6 5 4 3 2 1	Not Only Interested in Profit	__	__	__
Not Interested in the Environment	7 6 5 4 3 2 1	Interested in the Environment	__	__	__
Makes Healthy Foods	1 2 3 4 5 6 7	Makes Unhealthy Foods	__	__	__
Good Corporate Citizen	1 2 3 4 5 6 7	Poor Corporate Citizen	__	__	__

FIGURE 13.2
Upgraded and numerical comparative semantic differential scales.

	Strongly Agree	Slightly Agree	Neither Agree Nor Disagree	Slightly Disagree	Strongly Disagree
Is trustworthy	(1)	(2)	(3)	(4)	(5)
Is only interested in profit	(1)	(2)	(3)	(4)	(5)
Is interested in the environment	(1)	(2)	(3)	(4)	(5)
Makes healthy foods	(1)	(2)	(3)	(4)	(5)
Is a good corporate citizen	(1)	(2)	(3)	(4)	(5)

Note how the scale choices represent a continuum and how the instructions for the question state both ends of the continuum. Additionally, note how the use of the phrase "if at all" in the instructions reduces bias by explicitly allowing a neutral response.

Likert scales are widely used in marketing research and offer a number of advantages. They are relatively easy to construct and administer. The instructions that provide the lead-in to the scales are easily understood making the use of Likert scales appropriate for mail and telephone surveys.

Ratio Level Questions

Questions at the ratio level measure objects, behaviors, and beliefs on a continuum with a fixed, zero origin. Placement on this continuum reflects the degree to which the object, behavior, or belief measured possesses more, less, or even none of the characteristic represented in the continuum. The most common form of a ratio measure is the constant sum scale.

A *constant sum scale* is a ratio measure that requires a respondent to divide a preset quantity (the constant sum) among two or more objects or attributes in a way that reflects the respondent's relative preference for each object, the relative importance of each attribute or the degree to which the target object possesses each attribute. The most common constant sums used in research are ten and one hundred. The general form of a constant sum question is as follows.

Think about the reasons why you purchase a particular children's cereal. Many potential reasons are in the following list. We are interested in knowing the relative importance of these reasons in your purchase decision. Assume that you have 100 points. Divide the points among the following reasons to indicate the relative importance of each reason. The more points you give something, the more important it is. You can give as many or as few points as you wish to each reason. Please make certain that your total equals 100 points.

All natural	_____
Children like it	_____
Contains fruit	_____
Low price	_____
Low/no fat	_____
Low/no cholesterol	_____
Low/no sugar	_____
TOTAL	_____

The form of this question illustrates the characteristics of a well-written constant sum question: the target object is identified, the respondent's task is clearly described, and the criteria for point allocation is explicit.

DEVELOPING OPEN-ENDED SURVEY QUESTIONS

Quantitative research studies do not exclusively utilize closed-ended questions. Open-ended questions are also used to measure attitudes, beliefs, perceptions, and behaviors. The information collected through open-ended questions is analyzed as nominal data.

Care must be taken in the construction of open-ended questions. In addition to the considerations relevant to all question construction discussed in the next section, the writing of open-ended questions entails the following three special considerations.

The question must be truly open-ended. Open-ended questions are used to minimize or eliminate the constraints of presenting a respondent with predetermined sets of responses. Thus, open-ended questions must be worded so that the respondent is permitted to respond in his or her own words without bias from the interviewer. Consider the question: "How satisfied are you with the product?" While this may appear to be an open-ended question, it is not. The interviewer has identified the dimension along which the respondent must answer. A truly open-ended question does not presume which dimension of feelings, analysis or thought will be salient or meaningful for the respondent. Thus, a better open-ended question would ask: "What are your thoughts and feelings toward the product?"

The question must explicitly probe responses. Initial responses to an open-ended question generally lack depth. Respondents may give the easiest, most top-of-mind answer to an open-ended question. Additionally, respondents may not provide a response because they think it is obvious. For these reasons probes must be used to determine if there are additional attitudes, perceptions, etc. Common probes include: "Is there anything else?" "Do you have any additional thoughts or opinions?" and " Does anything else come to mind?" Following is an example of the use of probes in open-ended questions:

> What thoughts or feelings did you have as you watched the commercial? PROBE: Did you have any other thoughts or feelings? PROBE: "Anything else?" CONTINUE PROBING UNTIL NO FURTHER RESPONSE.

The question should be single-minded. Each open-ended request for information should be asked as a separate question. The independence of questions makes it easier for the respondent to focus on the specific request for information and facilitates question coding, analysis, and interpretation. For example, the question "Do any strengths and weaknesses of Suave shampoo come to mind?" should be divided into two separate questions: "Do any strengths of Suave shampoo come to mind?" and "Do any weaknesses of Suave shampoo come to mind?"

CONSIDERATIONS IN QUESTION DEVELOPMENT

Thus far we have seen that you have many options for the form of a particular measurement question. Different levels of measurement and types of measures within a

level are often appropriate and available. However, regardless of the specific type of question or scale selected, *all* questions must satisfy a core set of requirements. This section describes these requirements.

Explicitly state the respondents' task in simple language. The question should clearly state what respondents must do to adequately answer the question. Respondents must be told whether they should state their opinion in their own words, how and where to place a mark to indicate their opinion, or order objects to represent relative rank. Do not assume that a respondent intuitively knows how to answer a specific type of survey question.

Use simple, active sentences and commonly used language. Questionnaires should communicate and facilitate response. They are not a device for impressing a respondent with the question-writer's literary skills. Additionally, avoid the use of industry or specialized jargon. If such jargon must be used, make certain that it is defined as part of the question. The following question illustrates what not to do.

> Think about the times that you were watching television and saw a commercial for which you had either a positive or negative reaction, that is, for which you felt good or bad during or after seeing the commercial. In these instances what in the commercial, that is, what visual or oral element, was the underlying stimulus for the causation of these feelings?

Avoid bias. Biased or leading questions implicitly communicate your point of view as part of the question, for example:

> Is it true that you still purchase white bread?

> Many people are engaged in activities to improve the environment. Which of the activities shown in the following list are you doing to improve the environment?

When respondents hear these questions there is an increased probability that they will state what they think you want to hear as opposed to their own attitude or opinion. Questions can also be biased in a more subtle manner. For example, instructing a respondent to "Use the following scale to indicate how much you like the advertisement." implies that the respondent is expected to have liked versus disliked the commercial. To avoid this type of bias a question should present both alternatives, for example, "Use the following scale to indicate how much you liked or disliked the commercial." Finally, leading a respondent also biases the question and response. Questions should not begin with phrases such as "Don't you think . . ." or "Wouldn't you agree that . . ."

Avoid multiple informational requests in a single question. Similar to considerations for writing an open-ended question, each question should have a single-minded focus. Instead of asking "What is your favorite brand of shampoo and how often do you use it?" ask two questions. First ask "What is your favorite brand of shampoo?" and then ask "How often do you use it?" The separation of questions makes it easier for a respondent to answer and facilitates data coding and analysis. Moreover, the elimination of multiple informational requests greatly reduces problems in data interpretation. For example, a "yes" response to the question "Are you aware of cigarette advertising and do you approve?" may be in response to either the first part (awareness), the second part (approval) or both parts. You have no means of determining to which part of the question the "yes" refers.

Avoid ambiguity. Ambiguous words are words that are open to multiple interpretations. All words used in a question should be unambiguous in their interpretation.

Thus, a question that takes the form "Is it fair that . . ." is ambiguous because there are multiple interpretations of the word "fair." Similarly, problems may arise when you ask questions that appear on their face to be extremely simple, for example, "What kind of shampoo do you use?" Some respondents may interpret "kind" to refer to the brand name while others may interpret "kind" to mean form (gel or liquid) or type (dandruff, conditioning, or regular).

The problem of ambiguity is especially pronounced when one attempts to measure quantities and time. Consider the following scales:

Very long ago	Infrequently
Long ago	Sometimes
Recently	Often
Very recently	

Both scales are ambiguous because respondents can provide multiple, idiosyncratic interpretations to the descriptors used in the scale. One respondent might interpret "recently" to mean "yesterday" while another might interpret the same term to mean "within the past month." Similarly, respondents can provide multiple interpretations to words such as "often" and "sometimes." Ambiguity in the measurement of time and quantities can be eliminated through the use of specific numeric descriptions.

Avoid assumptions. Well written questions do not presume or assume a particular respondent's state of mind. For example, asking "What did you like about the commercial?" presumes that the respondent did, in fact, like something. A better form of the question is: "What, if anything, did you like about the commercial?"

Questions should also avoid assuming knowledge on the part of a respondent. For example, asking "What was the price of the last brand of toothpaste you purchased?" assumes that the respondent remembers the price. It would be better to first ask, "Do you recall the price of the last brand of toothpaste you purchased?" If the answer is "yes" then ask, "What was the price?"

Justify requests for personal information. Respondents are typically quite cooperative when asked for information on behaviors and attitudes as long as these requests are seen as legitimate and nonpersonal. However, respondents are often reluctant to provide personal information such as age, education, income, or information on sensitive topics, for example, the use of personal hygiene products. In these latter instances the probability of obtaining information is increased when you justify and explain the need for the requested information. A request for demographic and related types of information can be prefaced by a statement such as "The following questions will be used only to help us classify your responses." A request for sensitive information may be prefaced by a statement such as, "Now I'd like to ask you a few questions related to . . . . I know that these questions probe personal and perhaps sensitive areas, but I would really appreciate your cooperation. All of your answers, of course, are strictly confidential."

Summary

Researchers ask questions to obtain the needed information for advertising decision making. Better written questions obtain better, more reliable, and insightful information.

Questions may be written at one of four levels of measurement: nominal, ordinal, interval, and ratio. When using closed-ended questions a researcher may use the fol-

lowing question formats at each level of measurement:

Nominal level: dichotomous, multiple-choice, checklist
Ordinal level: rank order scaling
Interval level: rating scales, semantic differential, Stapel scales, Likert scales
Ratio level: constant sum, scales with a zero point

The quality of open- and closed-ended questions can also be improved by adhering to several "rules of thumb" for question development: use simple language and active sentence structure, avoid bias and multiple informational requests in the same question, avoid ambiguity, and assumptions regarding respondent knowledge or state of mind. Finally, justify all requests for sensitive information.

Review Questions

1. What level of measurement are *dichotomous*, *multiple-choice*, and *checklist* questions?
2. What are the characteristics of a dichotomous question?
3. How does a dichotomous question differ from a multiple choice question? What characteristics do they have in common?
4. What are three important considerations in the development of a checklist question?
5. What level of measurement is *rank order* scaling?
6. What are three important components of the directions in a rank order question?
7. What is the definition of a *rating scale*?
8. What level of measurement is a rating scale?
9. What are the four characteristics of all well-written rating questions?
10. What is the difference between *comparative* and *noncomparative* rating scales?
11. What is the difference between *graphic* and *itemized* rating scales?
12. What are three special considerations in the writing of itemized rating scales?
13. What are the drawbacks to the use of *unbalanced rating scales*?
14. What is a *semantic differential* scale?
15. What is a *Stapel* scale?
16. What is a *Likert* scale?
17. What level of measurement is represented by *constant sum* scales?
18. What are the three important elements in the directions of a constant sum scale?
19. What are the special considerations in the writing of open-ended questions?
20. What are the general guidelines for the writing of all survey questions?

Application Exercises

1. Each of the following questions has at least one problem with style or form. Identify the problem(s) associated with each question and then rewrite the question so that it is a well-written survey question.
   a. How many pets do you currently own and what are their ages?
   b. What kind of car do you currently own?

c. Everyone whom we talk to needs to tell us their income so that we can classify their answers. Into which of the following categories does your total annual after tax income fall?

under $10,000	_____ (x)
$10,000–$25,000	_____ (1)
$25,000–$28,000	_____ (2)
$28,000–$30,000	_____ (3)
Over $30,000	_____ (y)

d. Which of the following best reflects the extent to which you agree or disagree with this statement: Most corporations in America are concerned about the environment.

Strongly agree	_____ (1)
Agree	_____ (2)
Neither agree or disagree	_____ (3)
Slightly disagree	_____ (4)
Strongly disagree	_____ (5)

e. To what extent do you plan on purchasing a new car within the next twelve months?

Yes _____ (1)   No _____ (2)

f. Most parents are very concerned about how they will pay for their child's college education and as a result try to save some money every year for this purpose. How much money, on average, would you say that you save per year for your children's education. READ LIST. CHECK ONE RESPONSE.

$1,000 or less	_____ (1)
$1,000–$2,500	_____ (2)
$2,500–$5,000	_____ (3)
$5,000–$7,500	_____ (4)
$7,500 or more	_____ (5)

g. To what extent do you agree or disagree with the following statement: "Beer advertising portrays women in socially unacceptable ways." READ LIST. PLACE CHECK IN APPROPRIATE SPACE.

Strongly agree	_____ (5)
Slightly agree	_____ (4)
Neither agree nor disagree	_____ (3)
Slightly disagree	_____ (2)
Strongly disagree	_____ (1)

h. How often do you shampoo your hair? (READ LIST, CHECK ONE RESPONSE)

Very frequently	_____
Frequently	_____
Occasionally	_____
Infrequently	_____
Very infrequently	_____

i. Think about the five brands of soft drinks shown below. Please place them in order to indicate your preference.

Coca Cola	_____
Dr. Pepper	_____
Pepsi Cola	_____
Seven-Up	_____
Sunny Delight	_____

2. The Quicko Baking Company[9] has used past research to identify four important attributes in a cake mix: ease of preparation, consistency, color, and aroma. Quicko must now decide which of these four attributes is *the most* important to the target consumer when he or she decides on the purchase of a cake mix. Use each of the following types of questions to identify the most important cake mix attribute.

   a. rank order

   b. itemized rating scale

   c. graphic rating scale

   d. semantic differential

   e. Stapel scale

   f. Likert scale

   g. constant sum

3. Miles Laboratories has just introduced a new dog flea collar called Prescription Flea Control.[10] They now wish to measure consumers' reactions to and perceptions of this flea collar before developing their new advertising campaign.

   Miles developed a sampling plan and screened potential respondents for desired target audience characteristics and awareness of the Prescription Flea Control Collar as well as the flea collars marketed by Hartz and Pet-Pro. Questions 1–10, which follow, are some of the questions asked of respondents.

   Review this questionnaire and then address the following:

   (a) Evaluate the form and style of each question. Is each acceptable as written? If not, how would you rewrite or revise the question?

   (b) What types of questions are represented on the questionnaire? What level of measurement does each represent? Are the level of measurement and type of question appropriate for the type of information desired?

   (c) There is a great deal of redundancy in this questionnaire. What other types of questions or scales could have been used to collect the desired information in a more efficient manner? Would there have been any sacrifice in the depth of information acquired by using these alternative approaches? Specifically address how forms of the semantic differential scale, Stapel and Likert scales could have been used in this questionnaire?

   (d) Rewrite the questionnaire to reflect your views as to the best means for obtaining the desired information.

   1. We are interested in your overall opinion of the effectiveness of three flea collars. These collars are manufactured by Hartz, Miles Labs, and Pet-Pro. Please rank the flea collars marketed by these three companies by placing a '1' by the company with the most effective flea collar, a '2' by the next most effective and a '3' by the least effective.

Hartz	_____
Miles Labs	_____
Pet-Pro	_____

---

[9] Quicko is a fictitious company.

[10] The company and product in this exercise are real. However, the situation and questionnaire are fictitious.

2. Now I would like to have your opinion on a few statements that could be used to describe the flea collars manufactured by Hartz. If you agree completely with the statement then give it a '10'. If you disagree completely then give it a '0'. You can use any number between '0' and '10' to indicate the extent to which you agree or disagree. READ LIST BEGINNING WITH CHECKED STATEMENT. RECORD RESPONSE WHERE INDICATED.

> Are safe for my pet   _____
> Are made without pesticides   _____
> Are FDA approved   _____
> Work for at least 90 days   _____
> Are a good value for the money   _____

3. Now I would like to have your opinion on a few statements that could be used to describe the flea collars manufactured by Miles Labs. As before, if you agree completely with the statement then give it a '10'. If you disagree completely then give it a '0'. You can use any number between '0' and '10' to indicate the extent to which you agree or disagree. READ LIST BEGINNING WITH CHECKED STATEMENT. RECORD RESPONSE WHERE INDICATED.

> Are safe for my pet   _____
> Are made without pesticides   _____
> Are FDA approved   _____
> Work for at least 90 days   _____
> Are a good value for the money   _____

4. Lastly, I would like to have your opinion on a few statements that could be used to describe the flea collars manufactured by Pet-Pro. Again, if you agree completely with the statement then give it a '10'. If you disagree completely then give it a '0'. You can use any number between '0' and '10' to indicate the extent to which you agree or disagree. READ LIST BEGINNING WITH CHECKED STATEMENT. RECORD RESPONSE WHERE INDICATED.

> Are safe for my pet   _____
> Are made without pesticides   _____
> Are FDA approved   _____
> Work for at least 90 days   _____
> Are a good value for the money   _____

5. Think about your last five purchases of dog flea protection collars. How many were of each of the following brands?

> Hartz   _____
> Miles Labs   _____
> Pet-Pro   _____
> Store brand/generic   _____
> TOTAL   _____

6. Think about your next five purchases of dog flea protection collars. How many will be of each of the following brands?

> Hartz   _____
> Miles Labs   _____
> Pet-Pro   _____
> Other   _____
> TOTAL   _____

7. When deciding on a dog flea collar, how important or unimportant is it to you that the collar has FDA approval?

Extremely important	_____ (1)
Slightly important	_____ (2)
Neither important nor unimportant	_____ (3)
Slightly unimportant	_____ (4)
Extremely unimportant	_____ (5)

8. When deciding on a dog flea collar, how important or unimportant is it to you that the collar is pesticide free?

Extremely important	_____ (1)
Slightly important	_____ (2)
Neither important nor unimportant	_____ (3)
Slightly unimportant	_____ (4)
Extremely unimportant	_____ (5)

9. Finally, I would like to ask you a few questions to help us classify your answers. Into which of the following age groups does your age fall?

Under 25	_____ (1)
25–34	_____ (2)
35–44	_____ (3)
45–54	_____ (4)
55 and older	_____ (5)

10. Which of the following describes your highest level of education?

Not a high school graduate	_____ (1)
High school graduate	_____ (2)
Some college	_____ (3)
College graduate	_____ (4)
Advanced degree	_____ (5)

CHAPTER

14

QUESTIONNAIRE DESIGN

The creation of well-written survey questions is a critical step in the research process. But, your set of questions can not be asked haphazardly. They must be organized in a way that elicits the appropriate responses from each participant in the research study. The most commonly used method for organizing questions is, not surprisingly, the questionnaire, which can be thought of as the conduit between interviewer and interviewee. In this chapter you'll learn a systematic approach to questionnaire construction.

After reading this chapter you, will be able to

■ Determine the type of questionnaire to use in different research situations.

■ Describe the parts of a questionnaire and write and organize each part.

■ Prepare and lay out the questionnaire.

■ Identify creative techniques for question presentation.

■ Explain how pretesting can dramatically improve the quality of the questionnaire and the information that it collects.

The quality of the information gathered by a questionnaire is dependent on how carefully the questionnaire is constructed. Not all questionnaires successfully collect the desired information. Some questionnaires are organized in a confusing manner and, consequently, respondents are unable to devote full attention to answering the survey questions, instead devoting considerable energy to trying to figure out what is being asked. Some questionnaires bias responses to questions asked toward the end of the interview with earlier questions. Some questionnaires are incomplete and, as a result, the researcher is left without the data to answer many of the questions that motivated the research in the first place. Careful and precise preparation of the questionnaire is needed to overcome these and other difficulties.

The best way to avoid errors when preparing the questionnaire is to take a systematic approach to design and construction. The key issues that should be addressed

in preparing the questionnaire are shown in Figure 14.1. The remainder of this chapter discusses each of these issues.

DECISIONS TO MAKE BEFORE CONSTRUCTION OF THE QUESTIONNAIRE

You must resolve two issues before constructing the questionnaire. You must determine (1) the type of information required to provide the desired insights into the research problem and (2) the context in which the information will be collected. The decisions you reach with regard to each issue affect the characteristics of your questionnaire.

Determine the Type of Information Required

Earlier chapters discussed qualitative and quantitative approaches to data collection. You will recall that quantitative research is numeric and extensive. It generally uses large sample sizes and seeks to determine numerically quantifiable levels, trends, and differences within the total sample and between important subgroups. Qualitative research, however, is nonnumeric and intensive. Qualitative research is typically conducted with small sample sizes and seeks to provide deep insights into individuals' attitudes, beliefs, and behaviors. As might be expected given the differences in goals and desired insights, the questionnaires used in each type of research differ with regard to their structure and approach to data collection.

Quantitative research typically uses a structured questionnaire (see the example questionnaire in Figure 14.2, page 300). A *structured questionnaire* follows a prescribed pattern of questioning and all responses are assigned to predetermined response categories. Structured questionnaires are the most common form of quantitative questionnaire format for several reasons including the following:

- *Versatility*. The structured approach can be used for self-administered interviews and those conducted by an interviewer. This approach is also appropriate for face-to-face, telephone, and mail data collection methods.
- *Ease of administration*. The structured format makes the questionnaire appropriate for both professional and nonprofessional interviewers.
- *Reduction in interviewer bias and influence*. All respondents are asked the same questions with identical wording in the same order. The opportunity for the interviewer to bias the interview through the addition of biased or leading questions is greatly reduced.
- *Ease in data entry and analysis*. The heavy reliance on precoded closed-ended questions facilitates data entry and statistical analysis of responses.

Determine the Context in Which the Information Will Be Collected

Different data collection methods require different types of questionnaires. Questionnaires written for face-to-face interviews look and read differently than questionnaires written for telephone or self-administered mail studies. An absence of face-to-face contact generally requires a less complex questionnaire. Additionally, self-administered questionnaires and questionnaires administered by an interviewer are written for the "eye" and can use pictures or a variety of manipulatives. Telephone questionnaires

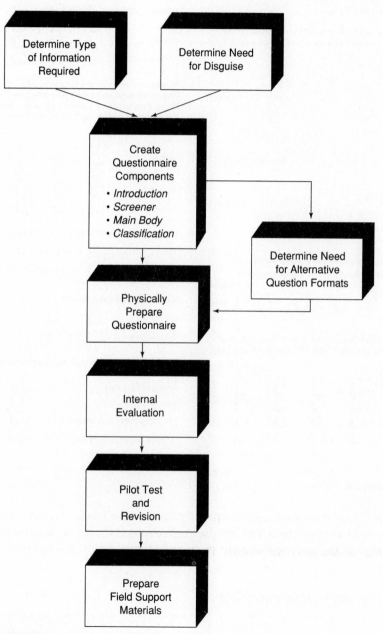

FIGURE 14.1
Steps in questionnaire construction.

Aztec American Airlines

Dear Aztec American Passenger:

Aztec American is very pleased that you have decided to fly Aztec American Air. We need you to tell us how we are doing.

Please take just a moment to complete this short survey. Your flight attendant will pick up your survey shortly before landing.

Thank you for your help.

Max Light
Max Light
Director, Operations

1. Please tell us your...

Flight number ________________ 5-9

Today's date ________________ 10-15

2. How would you rate your overall satisfaction with this flight? Please check one of the boxes below.

	Very Satisfied	Satisfied	Dissatisfied	Very Dissatisfied	
Overall satisfaction	☐ 1	☐ 2	☐ 3	☐ 4	16

3. Please rate each of the following with regard to your service on this specific flight. Please check one box for each item.

	Excellent	Good	Fair	Poor	
Courtesy	☐ 1	☐ 2	☐ 3	☐ 4	17
Attentiveness	☐ 1	☐ 2	☐ 3	☐ 4	18
Friendliness	☐ 1	☐ 2	☐ 3	☐ 4	19
Promptness	☐ 1	☐ 2	☐ 3	☐ 4	20

4. Please rate each of the following with regard to your meal on this specific flight. Please check one box for each item.

	Excellent	Good	Fair	Poor	
Appearance	☐ 1	☐ 2	☐ 3	☐ 4	21
Taste	☐ 1	☐ 2	☐ 3	☐ 4	22
Freshness	☐ 1	☐ 2	☐ 3	☐ 4	23
Variety	☐ 1	☐ 2	☐ 3	☐ 4	24

5. Please rate each of the following with regard to your check-in and boarding experience on this specific flight. Please check one box for each item to indicate the extent to which each word or phrase describes your experience.

	Strongly Agree	Agree	Disagree	Strongly Disagree	
On-time	☐ 1	☐ 2	☐ 3	☐ 4	25
Chaotic	☐ 1	☐ 2	☐ 3	☐ 4	26
Pleasant	☐ 1	☐ 2	☐ 3	☐ 4	27
Difficult	☐ 1	☐ 2	☐ 3	☐ 4	28

6. Did you check any luggage for this flight?

Yes ☐ 1 Please answer Question 7.

No ☐ 2 Please skip to Question 8. 29

7. Was your luggage checked...

	Yes	No	
Efficiently	☐ 1	☐ 2	30
Courteously	☐ 1	☐ 2	31

8. For what reason are you traveling? Please check one response.

Primarily personal ☐ 1

Primarily business ☐ 2

Mix of personal and business ☐ 3 32

Please continue with Question 9 on the following page.

FIGURE 14.2
Structured questionnaire.

are typically written more conversationally for the "ear" and, obviously, cannot use pictures or other visual aids. The specific implications of the data collection method for the design of the questionnaire are discussed at appropriate points throughout this chapter.

DETERMINE THE NEED FOR DISGUISE

Disguise refers to the extent to which the purpose of the research is hidden from the respondent. *Undisguised questionnaires* make the purpose of the research explicit to the respondent, often through the questionnaire's introduction or the wording and focus of specific questions. *Disguised questionnaires* provide a general overview of the research but hide more detailed information on research goals and sponsor from the re-

spondent. The decision whether to disguise your specific questionnaire depends on the extent to which you feel that a respondent's knowledge of the purpose and/or sponsor of the research will influence his or her responses. The greater the likelihood of influence or bias, the more appropriate it becomes to disguise the questionnaire. (Review, however, the discussion of the ethics of disguise in Chapter 3.)

When you decide to disguise your questionnaire you must make certain that there are no clues as to the specific purpose and/or sponsor of the research. Consider Exxon Corporation, which may want to obtain consumers' perceptions of their company and its products compared with other oil companies. An undisguised questionnaire might use the following introduction:

> Thank you for agreeing to participate in this study of consumer opinions. In this study we will ask you about your opinions toward a number of oil and gasoline companies and their products and services. Remember, there are no right or wrong answers to any questions. Just tell me your honest opinion.

This introduction leaves little doubt as to the focus of the interview. However, consumers' responses might be biased by knowing that the research is sponsored by an oil company. Consequently, it might be wise to disguise the questionnaire as follows:

> Thank you for agreeing to participate in this study of consumer opinions. In this study we will ask you about your opinions toward a number of different companies and their products and services. Remember, there are no right or wrong answers to any questions. Just tell me your honest opinion.

Finally, there are times that you might decide that a mixed approach is best. In these cases you begin the survey in the disguised mode and then move to a series of undisguised questions.

When thinking about the use of disguise, keep in mind that disguised and undisguised questionnaires provide different perspectives on the same set of information. This is because each type of questionnaire provides a different *frame of reference* for the respondent. A disguised questionnaire implicitly compares Exxon to a number of consumer product companies, some of which are oil companies and some of which are not. The undisguised questionnaire only compares Exxon to other oil companies. It is entirely possible that the ratings of Exxon obtained in these two formats will be different. Neither is correct nor incorrect. It is just important that you keep the frame of reference in mind when evaluating the strengths and weaknesses of a disguised versus undisguised format for a particular research problem.

CREATE QUESTIONNAIRE COMPONENTS

Once you choose the type of questionnaire to use, you then create each of the four main components of the questionnaire: introduction, screener, main body of informational questions, and classification questions.

Introduction

The *introduction* is a statement that explains the purpose and goals of the research and asks for the respondent's cooperation and participation in the research study. The in-

troduction's specific wording is dependent on the need for disguise, the complexity of the study, and the sensitive nature (if any) of the type of data collected. The goal of the introduction is to motivate the respondent to participate, thereby reducing nonresponse error (see Chapter 6). While the specific wording of the introduction for the questionnaire will vary among research studies, there are some common elements that most introductions contain. These are

- *an explicit or implicit reference to importance.* The introduction should communicate that the study itself is important (and is therefore worthy of the respondent's investment of time to complete the questionnaire) and that the respondent's own opinions are important (thereby increasing the likelihood of participation).
- *general information on the rationale and goals of the research.* The amount of detail will depend on the extent of disguise.
- *an explicit request for participation.* The introduction might say, "We would greatly appreciate you sharing your thoughts and opinions . . ."
- *reassurance that the task of participating is not too burdensome or time-consuming.* You might say that "Most of the questions are easy and quick to answer. We anticipate that you can complete the survey in no more than ten minutes."
- *the need for truthful answers*, for example: "We are interested in *your* opinions. There are no right or wrong answers . . . "
- *the promise of confidentiality.* For example: "Your responses will be kept completely confidential. No one will see your individual answers . . . "
- *the reassurance that this is real, legitimate research.* For example: "We are conducting this research to find out the opinions of people like you. This is not a sales pitch. We are not trying to sell you anything and no salesperson will call."

The extensivness of the explanation presented in the introduction of the questionnaire varies among data collection methods. Introductions in face-to-face and telephone research tend to be relatively short. These introductions quickly explain the reason for the research, assure confidentiality and the absence of a "sales pitch" and invite the potential respondent to participate, for example:

> Good morning. My name is Elyse McKenna and I am calling from Elyse McKenna Marketing Research, an independent marketing research company. I am not a salesperson and this is not a sales call. Instead, we are talking to a number of individuals like yourself to better understand their attitudes toward San Diego radio stations. The executives at these stations are very interested in the opinions of people like you. They will consider your opinions when deciding on their musical selections, radio personalities, promotions, and advertising. I have just a few questions to ask you and the entire survey will take ten minutes or less. Most of the questions are easy and quick to answer and, of course, there are no right or wrong answers. We just need your truthful opinions. Naturally, all of your answers will be strictly confidential. No one outside our company will see your name.

The introduction to a mail or other forms of self-administered questionnaires tends to be longer and more detailed because in these situations there is no interviewer present to answer any of the potential respondent's questions, especially with regard to the study's purpose and use of the data. Additionally, the introduction to self-administered questionnaires (especially those administered through the mail) must contain directions for returning the completed questionnaire. The introduction to self-administered mail questionnaires is typically communicated on the cover page of the

questionnaire or in a cover letter. Figure 14.3 presents the cover letter to the mail version of the radio station study.

Screener

A *screener* works like a gate: it admits into the study all individuals who possess all of the target characteristics and eliminates all the individuals who lack at least one of the identified sample characteristics. The use and characteristics of a screener, therefore, depends on the specifics of the research study's sample population.

Elyse McKenna Marketing Research
13654 Ridge Terrace
San Diego, CA 92559
(619) 555-3387

February 13, 1996

Mr. Johnathan Harding
13458 South Middle Trace Terrace
San Diego, CA 92128

Dear Mr. Harding:

Elyse McKenna Research is an independent marketing research company. We have been commissioned by a number of San Diego radio stations to find out what people like you think about radio in San Diego.

If you listen to the radio, it is important to let us know what you think. Your opinions can make a real difference. The executives at our client radio stations will consider your opinions when deciding on their musical selections, radio personalities, promotions, and advertising.

You can use the enclosed questionnaire to let us know what you think. Just read each question carefully and then answer it honestly. There are no right or wrong answers. We want to know what you think. The entire questionnaire can be completed in less than ten minutes.

When you've completed the questionnaire, please return it to us in the enclosed postage paid envelope. If you have any questions about either completing the questionnaire or returning it, please do not hesitate to call.

I look forward to receiving your questionnaire. And, of course, all your answers are strictly confidential. You don't even have to put your name on the questionnaire.

Won't you take a few moments now to let us know what you think?

Sincerely,

Elyse McKenna
Elyse McKenna

FIGURE 14.3
Cover letter for mail survey.

Some studies are conducted among a random sample of the adult population. In these cases, no screener is typically necessary. More often, however, advertising research is conducted among the subsets of the total population that possesses a specific combination of demographics and category- or product-related characteristics. In these cases, the introduction is followed by a screener, a short series of questions that identifies those respondents who should be included in the study. Screener complexity is dependent on the detail in the sample definition (see Chapters 2 and 8). Figure 14.4 presents a screener that can be used in a mall-intercept study. Note the importance of explicit instructions for following the screener flow and for determining whether the individual meets the research target audience characteristics. In this screener, the initial set of questions (Questions 1–3) screen for common characteristics, Question 4 permits a jump to the appropriate set of diet-related questions. Question 5 screens current dieters. Question 6 screens past dieters.

Main Body

The main body of the questionnaire contains the questions that address the research study's informational needs. The prior chapter provided detailed instruction for writing these questions.

Once the questions have been written they must be sequenced, that is, placed into a logical order on the questionnaire. When performing this task, keep the following guidelines in mind:

- *Begin with simple, nonthreatening, interesting, easy to answer questions.* Simple questions ease the respondent into the interview. They show that the task of participation is not difficult. The more comfortable the respondents are, the more likely they are to participate in and complete the survey.

- *Group questions on the same topic together; complete one topic before moving on to another.* Interviews typically ask respondents to answer questions that they had not given much thought to before the survey. As a result, respondents must give some thought to each question before answering it. Once they are thinking about a particular area it is important to stay focused on this area. This increases the potential for obtaining meaningful answers. Moving from topic to topic without a logical flow increases the potential for shallow, top-of-mind responses.

- *Within a topic move from the most general questions to the most specific.* More general questions provide a means of introducing the topic and focusing the respondent's thoughts on the topic. Once the respondent is focused, it is much easier for him or her to answer questions of greater detail or specificity.

- *Place difficult or sensitive questions at the end of the questionnaire.* Hopefully, by the end of the questionnaire the interviewer will have established some rapport with the respondent increasing the respondent's comfort level in answering these types of questions. While no rapport is established in mail surveys, it is hoped that the investment in time to complete the questionnaire up to this point will motivate the respondent to invest a little additional time to answer these questions.

- *Avoid biasing questions appearing later in the questionnaire with questions asked earlier in the questionnaire.* You must be very careful that questions asked early in the interview do not provide the information required for the answering of later questions. For example, asking the question: "How would you rate the cleaning ability of each of these detergents . . . " will bias answers to this question when asked later in the interview: "What aspect of your detergent would you like to see improved?"

Target Audience Definition: All respondents must be women between the ages of 25 and 49 who are employed full-time outside the home. All must have dieted at least once within the past twelve months. Those who are currently on a diet must have purchased for personal consumption a reduced calorie or reduced fat frozen dinner within the past week. Those who are not currently dieting may not have purchased for personal consumption a reduced calorie or reduced fat frozen dinner within the past month.

APPROACH WOMEN WHO APPEAR TO BE BETWEEN THE AGES OF 25 AND 49.

Hello. My name is _____ of _____ . Today we are talking with a number of women to help us better understand their opinions and attitudes. We are trying to talk to a number of different types of women so, before we begin, I have just a few short questions to ask you.

1. Into which of the following categories does your age fall?

under 25	[	]	.... THANK AND DISCONTINUE
25–35	[	](1)	.... CONTINUE WITH Q. 2
36–49	[	](2)	.... CONTINUE WITH Q. 2
50 and older	[	]	.... THANK AND DISCONTINUE

2. Are you currently employed full-time outside the home?

no	[	]	.... THANK AND DISCONTINUE
yes	[	](1)	.... CONTINUE WITH Q. 3

3. Have you dieted, that is, regulated the type and amount of food consumption, in order to maintain a desired weight or reduce your weight in the last twelve months?

no	[	]	.... THANK AND DISCONTINUE
yes	[	](1)	.... CONTINUE WITH Q. 4

4. Are you currently on a diet?

no	[	](1)	.... CONTINUE WITH Q. 6
yes	[	](2)	.... CONTINUE WITH Q. 5

5. Which of the following products have you purchased for your own personal consumption within the past week?

reduced calorie or reduced fat canned food product	[	]
reduced calorie soft drink	[	]
reduced calorie or reduced fat frozen dinner	[	](1)—IF YES, INVITE TO INTERVIEW IF NO, THANK AND DISCONTINUE

6. Which of the following products have you purchased for your own personal consumption within the past month?

reduced calorie or reduced fat canned food product	[	]
reduced calorie soft drink	[	]
reduced calorie or reduced fat frozen dinner	[	](1)—IF NO, INVITE TO INTERVIEW IF YES, THANK AND DISCONTINUE

FIGURE 14.4
Screener questions.

- *Address the most important topics first.* There is some evidence to suggest that the quality of responses declines as the respondent becomes fatigued. Thus, questions probing the most critical informational areas should appear earlier in the questionnaire.

Classification

Questionnaires typically conclude with a series of questions that collect relevant demographic, brand usage, or behavioral information not collected as part of the screener or in the main body of the questionnaire. Demographic questions may address, age, gender, education, income, ethnicity, and family/marital status. Brand usage and behavioral questions may also be included in the classification questions if the information collected by these questions is important for the analysis of different subgroups within the total sample. Remember, the purpose of *all* classification questions is to provide a means for examining important subgroups within the larger sample.

PHYSICALLY PREPARE THE QUESTIONNAIRE

The next step is to take all of the written, sequenced survey questions and construct the questionnaire that will be used for data collection. Four areas must be addressed as you begin a layout and prepare the questionnaire: (1) visual appearance, (2) transitions between major topic areas and between individual questions, (3) interviewer/respondent instructions, and (4) response column coding. Each of these areas is implemented differently in self-administered versus questionnaires administered by an interviewer.

Visual Appearance

Good visual appearance and organization are important in self-administered questionnaires and those administered by an interviewer.

An individual who receives a self-administered questionnaire will take a quick look at the questionnaire and then decide whether to spend some of his or her precious time to complete it. Any indication that the questionnaire will be too difficult or time-consuming to complete will generally cause a respondent to not answer the questionnaire. As a result, it is very important that a self-administered questionnaire be uncluttered, easy to follow, and typed in an easy to read typeface. Visual appearance and layout are also important in questionnaires administered by an interviewer. Here, good visual appearance and layout helps to ensure that the interviewer will conduct the interview in the proper manner.

The questionnaire shown in Figure 14.2 has good visual layout and appeal. The questionnaire is uncluttered, easy to read, and demonstrates several other aspects of good preparation and layout.

- *Questions are distinguished from responses.* Questions are shown in bold type, responses in normal type. This arrangement helps reduce the likelihood that a question will inadvertently be skipped.
- *Response coding is unobtrusive.* The numeric codes used to represent specific responses are small and are placed so they do not interfere with the text of either the question or response options.
- *Questions do not continue across pages.* Questions that continue across pages have a tendency to confuse respondents and interviewers.

> • *Columns (as in Question 4) are used to help maintain the respondent's focus, save space, and simplify response.*

Transitions

Transitions are the conversational, connective material that provide a sense of flow and continuity to the questionnaire. Transitions help respondents maintain their focus during a long series of questions, give warning that a change in topic or focus is imminent, and provide justification for sensitive information. While the wording of transitions among questionnaires will vary, there are some general rules for transitions. These are presented and discussed in Figure 14.5 (page 308).[1]

Interviewer and Respondent Instructions

Two types of instructions are provided in a questionnaire: (1) instructions for completing an individual question and (2) instructions for moving from one question to another.

Questions written for self-administered questionnaires generally provide all the information a respondent needs to answer the question. Consequently, question-specific instructions are rare in self-administered surveys. However, there are times in surveys conducted by an interviewer when you want to communicate instructions to the interviewer. In these cases, instructions for the interviewer are generally distinguished from the questions themselves by using all capital letters.

Beyond question-specific instructions, instructions are also needed to help respondents or interviewers move between questions. This is because questionnaires often use skip patterns. A *skip pattern* is a series of questions asked of some respondents but not others. The use of one or more skip patterns is common in advertising research and is illustrated in the following series of questions.

1. Now, I would like to focus on advertising for children's toy stores. Think about any advertising that you might have seen over the past week for a children's toy store. Do you recall seeing any advertising for this type of store?

   Yes   [   ] (1) ⟶ GO TO Q.2
   No   [   ] (2) ⟶ GO TO Q.5

2. For which children's toy store or stores do you recall seeing any advertising? CHECK ALL MENTIONS. DO NOT READ LIST.

   Children's Toy House   [   ] (1) ⟶ GO TO Q.3
   Kay-Bee   [   ] (2) ⟶ GO TO Q.5
   PlayCo   [   ] (3) ⟶ GO TO Q.5
   Toynation   [   ] (4) ⟶ GO TO Q.5
   Toys-R-US   [   ] (5) ⟶ GO TO Q.5
   Other   [   ] (6) ⟶ GO TO Q.5
   SPECIFY _____

3. You mentioned that you saw some advertising for Children's Toy House. Would you say that this advertising was primarily directed toward parents, primarily directed toward children, or directed equally toward parents and children?

   Parents   [   ] (1)
   Children   [   ] (2)
   Equal   [   ] (3)

---

[1] Don A. Dillman, *Mail and Telephone Surveys* (New York, NY: John Wiley & Sons, 1978).

Poorly Written Transitions

Potential to bias response.

Now I'd like to talk to you about advertising. There's so much of it I know that you must have seen some.

Too long; too detailed. Increases difficulty level of the questionnaire.

Now I would like to ask you some questions about how you feel toward various advertisers, in particular, those advertisers who have made some environmentally related claim for their product. In this context, for this discussion, an environmental claim is an explicit or implicit communication that promises that the use of a particular product will be beneficial to the environment. An environmental claim, for example, may make reference to biodegradability, ozone, the elimination of CFCs and HCFCs, recylability, or compostability.

Too demanding; damages rapport.

Now, tell us how you feel about automotive parts advertisers.

Well-Written Transitions

Lends conversational tone; helps to maintain rapport.

Next, I'd like to ask your opinions about …

There is certainly a range of opinions with regard to --------. I'd like to find out what your opinions are.

Alerts respondent to the introduction of a new topic.

Thank you for sharing your opinions with regard to --------. Now, I'd like to move to another topic. Let's discuss --------.

A second goal of this survey is to better understand people's opinions about --------. Let's discuss this topic for a moment.

Alerts respondent to more detailed questions within a topic.

Let's explore your reactions toward -------- in more detail.

Now, I'd like to ask you some questions to help me better understand your opinions about --------.

Provides a reason for collection of sensitive or personal information.

Finally, there are just a few more questions I'd like to ask you. These questions are important because they let us combine your answers with those of others similar to you.

This last set of questions is very important to us. These questions help us to understand who we talked to and the similarities and differences in opinions held by different individuals.

FIGURE 14.5
Characteristics of poorly and well-written transitions.

4. Still thinking about the advertising for Children's Toy House, would you say that the advertising stressed toys for boys, stressed toys for girls, or stressed toys for boys and girls equally?

Boys	[ ]	(1)
Girls	[ ]	(2)
Equal	[ ]	(3)

5. Questionnaire continues . . .

Question 1 probes overall advertising awareness for children's toy stores while Question 2 probes advertising awareness for specific stores. It would be inappropriate to ask awareness of specific stores unless overall awareness was present. Thus, a "Yes" to Question 1 leads to Question 2 while a "NO" skips the entire series of advertising awareness questions and sends the interviewer to a new series of questions beginning with Question 5. A similar logic underlies the skip pattern shown in Question 2.

Skip patterns make certain that appropriate questions are asked of the correct individuals. The complexity of skip patterns makes them a common source of error in construction of the questionnaire. When developing and preparing your skip patterns make certain that

- *all responses are accounted for.* Examine Questions 1 and 2 in the prior series of questions. All responses are assigned a destination. This greatly reduces the potential for incorrect or inappropriate movement between questions.

- *all skip directions send the respondent somewhere appropriate.* Make certain that when you send a respondent to a particular question (for example, "GO TO QUESTION 6") that a question with that number appears on the questionnaire and is the appropriate question to ask next.

Column Coding

Data input and analysis are greatly facilitated when column coding appears on the questionnaires themselves. *Column coding* refers to the process by which you assign (for the benefit of the computer that processes the data) each *unique response* a *unique place* in the overall group of data collected. Consider the next two questions.

11. Are you aged . . .

18–29	[　　]	(1)
30–39	[　　]	(2)
40–49	[　　]	(3)
50 and older	[　　]	(4)

  (32)

12. RECORD GENDER OF RESPONDENT.

Male	[　　]	(1)
Female	[　　]	(2)

  (33)

The numbers '32' and '33' are column codes. They tell the computer that the number appearing in column 32 of the data input is the code for respondents' age (a coded value of 1–4) while the code appearing in column 33 is the code for respondents' gender (a value of 1–2).

Open-ended questions also need to be coded. A true open-ended question, for example, "What did you like about the commercial?" is typically given a range of column values to permit data entry of responses once these responses are coded. Thus, the column codes for this question might be 34–44. Other types of open-ended questions, such as "How many children do you have?" or "How long have you lived in your current home or apartment?" have an upper limit of acceptable or anticipated responses. It would not be expected that any respondent would answer over '99' to either of the prior questions, although a two-digit number such as ten might be given. Consequently, given that no response greater than '99' is expected, but that other two-digit numbers might be given, two columns would be assigned to each of these questions. Thus, if columns 48 and 49 were assigned to the question "How many children do you have?" and a respondent answers '10' then a '1' would appear in column 48 and a '0' would appear in column 49.

DETERMINE NEED FOR ALTERNATIVE QUESTION FORMATS

The majority of data collection needs are satisfied by the types of questions and formats discussed earlier in this chapter and in Chapter 13. These traditional ways to prepare survey questions and structure the questionnaire work well when surveys are conducted by an interviewer and, in most cases, for self-administered surveys. There are times when alternative formats, especially for self-administered surveys, improve the quality of the information collected.

Alternative Forms for Questions on Self-Administered Surveys

Multiple, Sequential Scale Questions   Figure 14.6 shows two traditional ways in which a series of scale questions can be administered. Example A places the scale after each question while Example B uses a column format to record responses. Either of these approaches works well when the series of questions is short. The column format (Example B) works better than the question-scale format (Example A) when the series of questions is of moderate length (about four or five questions). However, when more than five questions all using the same scale are asked in sequence, problems may arise with both of the prior two approaches. First, a respondent wears out. It becomes mind-numbing to read the same type of scale, question after question. Consequently, responses to questions asked later in the sequence may be given less consideration than those asked earlier. Second, as the number of similar types of questions increases, respondents may fall into a response pattern. If the answer to the first seven (of say fourteen) questions is "strongly agree," then a respondent may indicate "strong agreement" with the remaining questions without even reading them. The quality of collected information is greatly reduced whenever wear out and response patterns occur. The need for innovation and creativity in survey research requires that you structure your questionnaire in a way that reduces the likelihood of these occurrences.

One approach to reducing problems with multiple, sequential scale questions is to write and present questions from both the positive and negative perspective. The questions shown in Figure 14.6 could be written as

16. My children would like the cereal.
17. I would not feel comfortable serving my children the cereal.
18. The cereal is healthier than other children's cereals.

An individual who believes that the advertised cereal is healthier than other children's cereals and who would (presumably) feel comfortable serving the cereal would have to strongly disagree with Question 17 *and* strongly agree with Question 18. The mixing of response options (i.e., agree with some questions, disagree with others) as an indicator of consistent beliefs increases the likelihood that each statement will be considered and reduces the likelihood of a pattern of response being established.[2]

---

[2] The mixing of positive and negative statements works well from a data collection perspective but slightly complicates data analysis. When presenting data from a series of scale questions it is important that you maintain consistency in what each response value represents, for example, you may decide that smaller numbers represent more positive beliefs or attitudes. To maintain consistency when positive and negative statements are mixed, before data analysis it is necessary to (1) rewrite each negative statement into its positive format and (2) reverse the coding of responses to each negative statement, for example responses of '5' become a '1', responses of '4' become a '2' etc.

Example A

Now I would like you to think about the product shown in the commercial. Please read each statement below and then indicate the extent to which you may agree or disagree with the statement.

16. My children would like the cereal. (CHECK ONE ANSWER BELOW)

Strongly agree	_____ (1)
Slightly agree	_____ (2)
Neither agree nor disagree	_____ (3)
Slightly disagree	_____ (4)
Strongly disagree	_____ (5)

17. I would feel comfortable serving my children the cereal. (CHECK ONE ANSWER BELOW)

Strongly agree	_____ (1)
Slightly agree	_____ (2)
Neither agree nor disagree	_____ (3)
Slightly disagree	_____ (4)
Strongly disagree	_____ (5)

18. The cereal is healthier than most children's cereals. (CHECK ONE ANSWER BELOW)

Strongly agree	_____ (1)
Slightly agree	_____ (2)
Neither agree nor disagree	_____ (3)
Slightly disagree	_____ (4)
Strongly disagree	_____ (5)

19. Etc.

Example B

Now I would like you to think about the product shown in the commercial. Please read each statement below and then place a check in the column that indicates the extent to which you may agree or disagree with the statement.

(CHECK ONE COLUMN FOR EACH STATEMENT)

	Strongly Agree (1)	Slightly Agree (2)	Neither Agree Nor Disagree (3)	Slightly Disagree (4)	Strongly Disagree (5)
16. My children would like the cereal.	____	____	____	____	____
17. I would feel comfortable serving my children the cereal.	____	____	____	____	____
18. The cereal is healthier than other children's cereals.	____	____	____	____	____
19. Etc.	____	____	____	____	____

FIGURE 14.6
Traditional formats for multiple, sequential scale questions.

A second approach to reducing problems with multiple, sequential scale questions uses a format where the scale is shown on the top of the series of questions and the respondent places a number after each individual question to indicate the extent of agreement or disagreement, for example:

> Now I would like you to think about the product shown in the commercial. I would like you to tell me how much you may agree or disagree with each statement. You can tell me your opinion by writing the number from the following scale after each question.

If you	**strongly agree**	write 1
If you	**slightly agree**	write 2
If you	**neither agree nor disagree**	write 3
If you	**slightly disagree**	write 4
If you	**strongly disagree**	write 5

> 16. My children would like the cereal.   ____
> 17. I would not feel comfortable serving my children the cereal.   ____
> 18. The cereal is healthier than other children's cereals.   ____
> 19. Etc.   ____

The mix of questions written from both the positive and negative perspective coupled with the demand that the respondent read the scale and find and record the appropriate number after reading each question increases the likelihood that each statement will be read and considered and reduces the likelihood that a pattern of response will be established.

Paired-Choice Questions Advertising and creative strategies are, in part, based on an understanding of the target consumer's attitudes and beliefs. In survey research, insights into attitudes and beliefs are often obtained by having a respondent select the one statement from a pair of statements that he or she feels best represents his or her own belief or attitude. A politician planning a communications program, for example, might use the following paired-choice question to determine the prevailing perspective of individuals in the target audience:

> The following question presents two statements. Read the pair of statements and then place a check by the one statement in the pair that best describes your own thoughts or feelings.
>
> 16. I am most concerned about community—about local problems and issues.   ____
>   or
> I am most concerned about the world community—about international problems and issues.   ____

This approach works well when the total number of paired statements is small. However, similar to multiple, sequential scale questions, the likelihood of response problems increases as the number of pairs increases. These problems can be reduced by using a less traditional, more visual, format for presenting the paired options. An example of an alternative format is shown in Figure 14.7. The novelty of this alternative format helps to ensure that each pair is read and considered.

Purchase Intent The measurement of a consumer's intention to purchase a product or service is an important measure in many types of advertising research. For most packaged goods, a traditional purchase intent question is an appropriate and effective way to assess a respondent's interest in or intent to purchase a product, for example:

Each question below presents two statements. Read each pair of statements and then place a check by the statement in each pair that best describes your own thoughts or feelings. Just place your check in the empty box in the statement that you prefer.

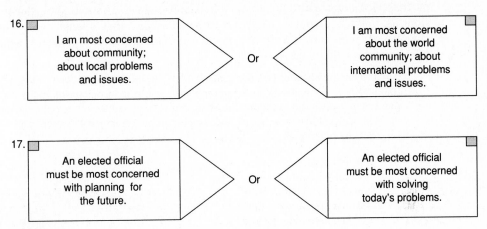

16.
I am most concerned about community; about local problems and issues.

Or

I am most concerned about the world community; about international problems and issues.

17.
An elected official must be most concerned with planning for the future.

Or

An elected official must be most concerned with solving today's problems.

FIGURE 14.7
Nontraditional format for presenting paired-choice questions.

Think about the product that you just saw advertised. What is the likelihood that you would purchase this product if it were available at your local store and were priced comparably to the leading brands?

I would definitely buy it	_____ (1)
I would probably buy it	_____ (2)
I would probably not buy it	_____ (3)
I would definitely not buy it	_____ (4)

This type of purchase intent question works well because it contains all the information a respondent needs to evaluate the product, specifically, the situation where it will be found and the product's price.

Purchase intent questions become more difficult to write as the context for the purchase decision becomes more complex, that is, as environmental and nonbrand influences begin to exert a greater role on influencing the purchase decision. Gasoline is a good example. The decision to purchase a particular brand of gasoline is influenced not only by the brand name and current brand perceptions, but also by the price differential between brands and the location or availability of specific brands at the time of purchase. Given all these influences, the following *written* purchase intent question is too simplistic to generate the desired information as well as too divorced from the reality of product selection and purchase.

Think about the brand of gasoline that you just saw advertised. What is the likelihood that you would purchase this brand of gasoline the next time that you needed gasoline for your car?

I would definitely buy it	_____ (1)
I would probably buy it	_____ (2)
I might or might not buy it	_____ (3)
I would probably not buy it	_____ (4)
I would definitely not buy it	_____ (5)

Revisions to the standard purchase intent question that reflect the complexity of the purchase decision are also not acceptable. The following questions show that the revisions are verbally complex. Moreover, the requirement that a respondent visualize a complex situation may exceed the cognitive abilities of many respondents, negatively affecting the quality of response.

> Think about the brand of gasoline, Shell, which you just saw advertised. What is the likelihood that you would purchase Shell the next time you needed gasoline for your car if you had to make a right turn into the Shell station and there was an Amoco station across the street that could be reached by making a left turn? Assume that Amoco is priced about two cents more per gallon than Shell.

I would definitely buy it	_____ (1)
I would probably buy it	_____ (2)
I might or might not buy it	_____ (3)
I would probably not buy it	_____ (4)
I would definitely not buy it	_____ (5)

> Think about the brand of gasoline, Shell, which you just saw advertised. What is the likelihood that you would purchase Shell the next time you needed gasoline for your car if you had to make a right turn into an Amoco station and there was a Shell station across the street that could be reached by making a left turn? Assume that Amoco is priced about two cents more per gallon than Shell.

I would definitely buy it	_____ (1)
I would probably buy it	_____ (2)
I might or might not buy it	_____ (3)
I would probably not buy it	_____ (4)
I would definitely not buy it	_____ (5)

An alternative to the written purchase intent question is the *visual* purchase intent question. Here, the purchase context is represented visually, permitting a respondent to use his or energy to consider the proper response to the question as opposed to simply trying to understand the question itself. An example of the visual approach to the measurement of purchase intent for brands of gasoline is shown in Figure 14.8.

Alternative Forms for Questions on Surveys Administered By an Interviewer

Ranking and constant sum questions are easy for respondents to answer when the number of items to be ranked or evaluated via a constant sum are relatively few (typically three to five). However, as with other types of questions, increasing the number of items to be considered by the respondent increases the difficulty level of the question.

One way to increase the number of items in a questions without increasing the difficulty level is to restructure the question to incorporate manipulatives such as index

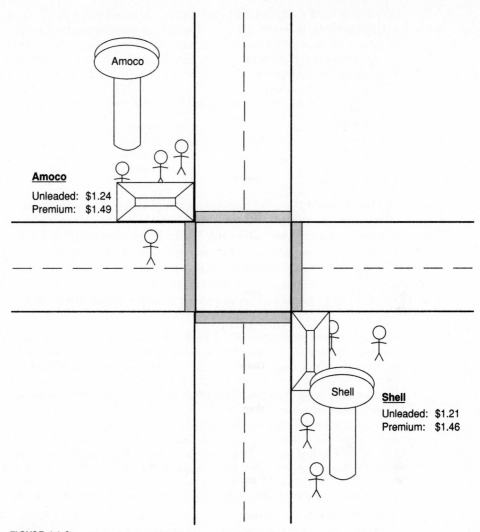

FIGURE 14.8
Visual format for purchase intent question. (Visual courtesy of Kyle Davis.)

cards and poker chips. Manipulatives not only make the task of responding easier, but they also allow respondents the utmost flexibility to change their mind while answering the question. Additionally, because items are placed on index cards and shuffled for each respondent, order bias is greatly reduced.

Index cards work well for ranking questions. The name of each item to be ranked is typed on a separate index card, the cards are shuffled and given to the respondent, directions for performing the ranking are read, and the final ordering is recorded by the interviewer. The following question illustrates how the actual question is written:

> There are many different manufacturers of automobiles. I am interested in your perceptions of the relative *overall quality* of cars made by ten specific manufacturers. I have written the name of each manufacturer on an index card. SHUFFLE CARDS AND

HAND DECK OF CARDS TO RESPONDENT. On the table in front of you line up the cards from highest to lowest quality. Put the manufacturer that you feel has the best quality cars on the top of the line, the manufacturer with the next best quality cars next in line, etc. As you begin to rank quality of each manufacturer's cars, feel free to move the cards about and change their positions. Tell me when you are done. WHEN RESPONDENT IS DONE RECORD RANKING NEXT TO EACH MANUFACTURER SHOWN BELOW. TAKE BACK CARDS AND CONTINUE INTERVIEW.

Cadillac	_____	Lexus	_____
Chevrolet	_____	Nissan	_____
Ford	_____	Pontiac	_____
Honda	_____	Saturn	_____
Kia	_____	Toyota	_____

The combination of poker chips and index cards work well in constant sum questions. The name of each item that may be given chips (the equivalent of allocating points) is typed on a separate index card. The cards are then shuffled and placed on a table in front of the respondent. (The randomization of order tends to reduce order bias.) The respondent is then given the poker chips and asked to allocate them according to the specified criterion. The interviewer records the number of chips given to each item. The following question illustrates how a constant sum question using manipulatives is written:

Many things may be important to you when you are considering and evaluating different brands of automobiles. I would like you to tell me the relative importance of ten features or characteristics of cars in your evaluation and purchase decision. SHUFFLE CARDS. Here are the ten features. PLACE CARDS ON TABLE IN FROM OF RESPONDENT. Here are thirty poker chips. HAND CHIPS TO RESPONDENT. Divide the chips among the features to show each feature's relative importance to you. The more chips you give a particular feature, the more important that feature is to you. You can give as many or as few chips as you wish to each feature. If a feature is not at all important to you, you may give no chips to that feature. Please use all the chips. Please feel free to move the chips around and change the amount given to any particular feature. Tell me when you are done. WHEN RESPONDENT IS DONE, RECORD CHIP ALLOCATION NEXT TO EACH FEATURE SHOWN BELOW. REMOVE CARDS AND CHIPS AND CONTINUE INTERVIEW.

Air bags	_____	Leather seats	_____
Antilock brakes	_____	Price	_____
Color	_____	Responsiveness	_____
Cost of Repairs	_____	Styling	_____
Gasoline Mileage	_____	Warranty	_____

INTERNAL EVALUATION

Prior to pretesting the questionnaire, you and others associated with the project within the agency and with the client should review the questionnaire. You and your research team should review the questionnaire prior to review by others within the agency or with the client. Prior to review by nonresearchers you should make very certain that

- *the questionnaire is complete and concise*. Research objectives and informational needs should be cross-referenced to the numbers of all questions contained in the questionnaire. The key to completeness is that the questions contained in the questionnaire all correspond to identified informational needs and that there are no questions that do not correspond.
- *questions themselves are clear, unambiguous, and appropriate for the type of information needed*.
- *the layout is clear and easy to follow*. You must make certain that there are no vague or ambiguous instructions and that all skip patterns do, in fact, lead the respondent to the proper place on the questionnaire.

Once you and your research team have decided that the questionnaire satisfies each of these requirements, you then submit the questionnaire for internal agency and client review. It is extremely important that those who will ultimately use the information collected as a basis for decision making "buy-into" the instrument used to collect the information. This helps to ensure that the discussion of the research results focuses on what is learned rather than how the information was collected.

PILOT TEST THE QUESTIONNAIRE

Pilot testing is a crucial step in the development process of the questionnaire. It is however, the step that is most often skipped when there are time or financial constraints. The pilot test is important because it offers the insights needed for improving the questionnaire's wording, structure, format, and organization. *No* questionnaire is ever perfect after the initial draft and review. Remember, if the questionnaire used in the actual research is faulty then the quality of the information collected will be significantly diminished.

Pilot testing involves the administration of the questionnaire to a small group of target audience individuals. Since the goal of the pilot test is to assess the manner in which the questionnaire collects the information, the data from the pilot test is not included with the data collected in the main research study. With regard to pretesting we recommend an active versus a passive pretest. Individuals in a *passive pretest* are asked the questions on the questionnaire after which the interviewer assesses the quality of response and adequacy of the questionnaire's construction. In an *active pretest* the interviewer administers the questionnaire, takes notes on potential problem areas, and then discusses each problem area with the respondent. Here, the insights into problem areas come from both the interviewee and the interviewer. In most cases, the active approach tends to provide better insights for revising the questionnaire.

Regardless of the approach selected for the pretest, a debriefing should follow the administration of all pretests. The debriefing should systematically discuss potential problems with the questionnaire. One way to structure the debriefing is to organize comments concerning the problem areas, such as[3]

---

[3] For an extended discussion of these areas and approaches to pretesting the questionnaire see Stanley Presser and Johnny Blair, "Survey Pretesting: Do Different Methods Produce Different Results?" *Sociological Methodology* 24 (1994): 73–104.

- *problems with the administration.* Did the questionnaire take as long as expected to administer? Did it take longer? If it is too long, what can be done to shorten the questionnaire without sacrificing important questions?

- *problems related to question comprehension.* Were there any questions that were hard for the respondent to understand? Was this difficulty due to the amount of information contained in the question? Was this difficulty due to the question's length? Were any questions ambiguous? How can problem questions be rewritten to make the information needed explicit and unambiguous?

- *problems related to question demands.* Were technical terms used without definition? How might these be explained to reduce confusion? Were common words used in unusual ways or contexts? How can the use of these terms be clarified? Were there any questions that asked for difficult pieces of information (for example, "What percent of the time would you say that price is an important factor in the brands of shampoo you purchase?")? Were there any questions that asked for information that is not likely to be known (for example, "How many miles did you drive last year?"; "How much beer advertising have you seen in the past three months?")? How can these questions be rewritten to collect better the desired information?

- *problems related to response options.* Are there any questions for which "Don't Know" or "No Answer" is the most common response? Are there any questions that "Other" gathers a significant percentage of responses? Are there some scales that do not provide enough levels of distinction (for example, an agree–neutral–disagree scale)? Are there some scales that provide too great a level of distinction (for example, "Use the following scale of 1 to 100 to . . .)? How can these problems be addressed through question revision?

- *problems related to organization and question sequencing.* Did the questionnaire flow as well as expected? How well did transitions and interviewer/respondent instructions work? Do any transitions or instructions need to be rewritten? Do any transitions need to be added or deleted? Did all skip patterns work as expected? Do any skip patterns needs to be revised? Were any questions asked later in the questionnaire biased by earlier questions?

PREPARE FIELD SUPPORT MATERIALS

Once the questionnaire has been pretested and revised, it is ready for use as a data collection instrument. As discussed in Chapter 1, field services are often used to collect the data. In these cases, the questionnaire and appropriate supporting materials are sent to the field service, interviews are conducted and the questionnaires are returned for data coding and analysis. Potential problems with field service data collection are minimized when the questionnaire is accompanied by three types of support materials:

1. A cover letter that (a) identifies the study, (b) itemizes materials sent to the field service, (c) discusses data collection techniques, (d) presents a detailed description of the sample and any special quotas, (e) identifies any special material or equipment requirements, and (f) confirms study cost, timing, and procedures for return of the questionnaires and any other test-related materials,

2. A memo describing the questionnaire and any particular administrative details of which interviewers should be aware,

3. A memo presenting acceptable interviewer responses to respondent concerns and questions (see Figure 14.9, page 320).

Summary

A well-constructed questionnaire is a vital component of successful advertising research. The likelihood that the questionnaire *is* well-constructed increases when a systematic approach to the construction of the questionnaire is followed.

Before constructing the questionnaire, you must answer two questions: "Is qualitative or quantitative information the best suited for satisfying my informational needs?" and "What method will I use for data collection?" Next, you must determine if the questionnaire needs to be disguised. The answers to these questions provide the direction for how you approach the development process of the questionnaire.

The questionnaire itself consists of four components. The introduction explains the purpose and goals of the research and asks for the respondent's cooperation and participation in the research. The screener makes certain that the information is collected only from appropriate individuals. The main body of the questionnaire contains the questions that explore the areas of interest. Classification questions collect any relevant demographic, brand usage, or behavioral information not collected as part of the screener or in the main body of the questionnaire.

The questions appearing in the questionnaire must be sequenced so that they facilitate data collection. Additionally, the sequenced questions must be presented with appropriate transitions and directions for the respondent and interviewer. The final result must be a clean, visually appealing questionnaire.

Before using the questionnaire in the field, it must be evaluated by others at the agency and by the client. Once these individuals approve the questionnaire (and any appropriate revisions based on their comments are made), it must be pilot tested.

The final, revised version of the questionnaire, with supporting materials, is then sent to the field service for data collection.

Review Questions

1. What are the key steps in the development process of the questionnaire?

2. How does the type of information collected affect the types of questions asked on the questionnaire?

3. What is a *structured* questionnaire? What are its primary advantages?

4. What is an *unstructured* questionnaire? In what situations is it most commonly used?

5. How does the context in which the information will be collected affect the structure of the questionnaire?

6. What is *disguise*? In what situations is a disguised questionnaire most appropriate?

7. How might *frame of reference* affect an individual's responses to a question? Provide an example.

8. What are the four main components of a questionnaire?

Who's conducting this survey?

I am employed by _____ , an independent market research company. We have been hired to conduct this survey by one of the country's leading national advertisers. I am not at liberty to name that company because I don't want to influence any of your responses to my questions.

Why are you doing this?

Our client uses the information we gather to design and develop new products and to better respond to their customers' needs.

Isn't this just a disguised sales pitch?

No, not at all. No one will ever call you about your participation in this research.

But I don't want anyone to know what I personally think. Is this confidential?

This survey is strictly confidential. You will never be identified by name or telephone number. By keeping the survey confidential we hope that you will feel free to share your honest thoughts and opinions with us.

I haven't got the time.

I realize that you're busy. But, our client relies on people like you sharing your honest ideas and opinions. This is your opportunity to represent others like you in an important research study. The entire survey should take less than fifteen minutes.

How did you get my telephone number?

Everyone who lives in San Diego had an equal opportunity to be called. We select individuals to call by chance.

How about interviewing my husband/wife/son/daughter? He's/she's more opinionated than I am.

We can't do that. If we did, it would affect the representativeness of the final group of individuals who we interviewed.

I probably don't qualify.

You may or may not qualify. I have a short series of questions to ask you that will let us know if you qualify. (BEGIN SCREENER)

FIGURE 14.9
Responses to common respondent questions.

9. What is the purpose of the *introduction*?
10. What are the primary characteristics of the introduction?
11. What is the purpose of the *screener*?
12. What are the key considerations for sequencing questions in the main body of the questionnaire?
13. What are *classification* questions? What is their purpose?
14. What are the primary considerations when evaluating the *visual appearance* of a questionnaire?
15. What are *transitions*? What is their primary purpose?

16. What is a *skip pattern*?

17. How do you indicate instructions directed toward the respondent or interviewer?

18. What are *column codes*?

19. Name and describe two traditional formats for presenting multiple, sequential scale questions. Which format works better for short lists? Which format works better for lists of four to five items?

20. Describe two ways to improve the presentation of long lists of multiple, sequential scale questions?

21. Describe how a visual approach can improve the presentation of paired-choice questions.

22. Describe how a visual approach can improve the presentation of checklist questions.

23. In what circumstances can problems arise with traditional purchase intent questions? How can a visual approach to the measurement of purchase intent reduce these problems?

24. What is a *manipulative*?

25. How can the use of manipulatives improve the collection of ranking and constant sum questions?

26. Describe nontextual or nonverbal approaches to data collection. In what circumstances are these approaches most useful?

27. Why is *internal evaluation* of the questionnaire important?

28. Why is *pilot testing* important?

29. What are the common types of problems pretesting helps to uncover?

30. What types of materials are sent to field services? What is the purpose of each?

Application Exercises

1. The William Pace Advertising Company wishes to determine consumers' awareness of and reactions to its current advertising campaign for the NorthWest Consolidated Banking Corporation (NWCBC).[4] Quantitative research will be conducted. The campaign target, and therefore the research sample, consists of adults aged 50 and older who live in Detroit and currently carry an ATM card. The campaign is designed to communicate the benefits of NWCBC's redesigned ATM machine.

   Your client at NWCBC asks you whether you intend to disguise the research. What questions would you ask NWCBC and/or what types of information would you like to see to make this determination? What factors might lead you to disguise the NWCBC questionnaire? What are the relative advantages and disadvantages of disguise for this specific research project?

2. Anheuser-Busch has developed a program to help parents discuss drinking with their younger children. This program is advertised in a number of women's and family-oriented magazines. One ad in this campaign is specifically directed toward mothers who have younger female daughters (i.e., those between the ages of 8 and 14). Assume that Anheuser-Busch wishes to determine their target mothers' awareness of and (among those who remember seeing the ad) reactions to the ad.[5]

---

[4] The company and situation in this exercise are fictitious.

[5] Advertising described is real. However, the research situation is fictitious.

You are unsure, however, whether the research will be conducted over the telephone or through the mail. As a result, (a) write the introduction and screener for a telephone study and (b) write the introduction and screener for a mail study. What special considerations do you need to keep in mind as you prepare each introduction and screener? When you are done, examine the telephone and mail versions. What are their common elements? How were these elements expressed in both versions? What information does one version have that is missing in the other version? Why do these differences occur? How are the screeners handled in both versions? How does each version provide instructions and direction for qualifying or disqualifying a respondent from participating in the study?

3. Your agency has just been awarded the advertising assignment for the National Photographic Industries Trade and Promotion Association.[6] The Association's goal is to develop and sponsor an advertising campaign that encourages individuals to buy more film and take more pictures. The Association's research department suggests that research be conducted before to the start of the campaign and after the campaign has run for six months as a way of assessing the effects of the campaign on the number of rolls of film purchased (overall, by type of film, by brand of film). You agree that this makes sense. The research, appropriately, will be conducted among a random sample of the adult population.

   The Association's research department drafts a questionnaire and then sends it to you for your comments and insights. The questionnaire, designed for a mail survey, is shown in Figure 14.10. Write a memo to the client expressing (a) your beliefs as to the strengths and weaknesses of the questionnaire and (b) your specific recommendations for revising and improving the questionnaire. Make certain that your memo and suggestions for revision address the appropriateness (given study objectives) of questions asked and the layout of the questionnaire. If you feel that this questionnaire is "beyond help," attach your own version of what you believe the questionnaire should look like.

4. The San Ystero Regional Blood Center is conducting research to determine donor and nondonor awareness and perceptions of the Regional Blood Center, past donor behaviors, influences on donor and nondonor behavior, and attitudes toward blood donation.[7] The questionnaire drafted by their *pro bono* agency's research department is shown in Figure 14.11 (pages 324–326). The survey is designed to be used for telephone interviews and is targeted to take from five to seven minutes to complete.

   As an initial step in the evaluation process, you make certain that all key areas relevant to research goals are addressed in the questionnaire. You construct the following chart:

Area of Research Focus	Questionnaire Items
Donor behavior classification	1, 2, 3, 5, 19
Awareness and perceptions	4, 6, 7, 8, 18
Donor behaviors in San Ystero County	9, 10, 15, 16
Influences on donors and nondonors	11, 12, 13, 14, 20, 21, 22, 23
Attitudes toward donating	17
General classification	24, 25, 26, 27, 28, 29

---

[6] The company and situation in this exercise are fictitious.

[7] The company and questionnaire shown in this exercise are fictitious.

Film Log: April

Please fill out one line in the grid below for each roll or package of film that you or any other household member purchased or had developed during April.

Use the codes in the side boxes to help you provide all required information.

1. Gift	4. Holiday	7. To have
2. Birthday	5. Special occasion	on hand
3. Christmas	6. Gift	8. Other

NOTE: The top grid continues on the bottom of the page. Fill out both grids for each roll or package purchased or developed during April.

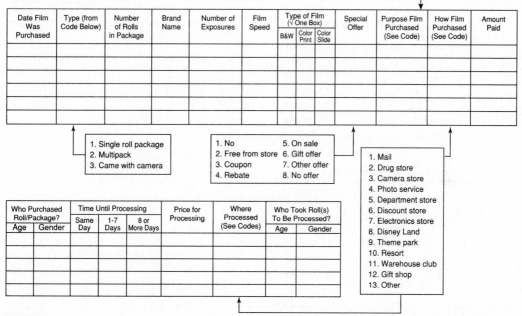

Date Film Was Purchased	Type (from Code Below)	Number of Rolls in Package	Brand Name	Number of Exposures	Film Speed	Type of Film (√ One Box) B&W	Color Print	Color Slide	Special Offer	Purpose Film Purchased (See Code)	How Film Purchased (See Code)	Amount Paid

| 1. Single roll package |
| 2. Multipack |
| 3. Came with camera |

1. No	5. On sale
2. Free from store	6. Gift offer
3. Coupon	7. Other offer
4. Rebate	8. No offer

| 1. Mail |
| 2. Drug store |
| 3. Camera store |
| 4. Photo service |
| 5. Department store |
| 6. Discount store |
| 7. Electronics store |
| 8. Disney Land |
| 9. Theme park |
| 10. Resort |
| 11. Warehouse club |
| 12. Gift shop |
| 13. Other |

Who Purchased Roll/Package? Age	Gender	Time Until Processing Same Day	1-7 Days	8 or More Days	Price for Processing	Where Processed (See Codes)	Who Took Roll(s) To Be Processed? Age	Gender

FIGURE 14.10
Film research mail questionnaire.

On the basis of this table and your examination of the questionnaire, are all areas adequately addressed? If not, what specific questions would you add?

Once you are certain that the questionnaire addresses all appropriate areas, examine the questionnaire itself. With your knowledge gained from the prior chapter on question writing and from this chapter on the design of the questionnaire, what suggestions do you have for improving the questionnaire? Revise the questionnaire as needed. Then, pilot test the questionnaire. What additional insights into questionnaire form and structure did the pilot test provide? How would you revise the questionnaire based on the results of the pilot test?

San Ystero Regional Blood Center Survey

ID_ _ _ _ (1-4)

Hello, my name is _____ . I am a student at San Ystero State University. The university is helping the San Ystero Regional Blood Center with an important piece of research. Would you be willing to answer a few questions about donating blood? The survey will only take a few minutes and your participation would be a great help. We need to understand the attitudes and opinions of people like you. This is not a call to donate blood. Of course, all your answers will be strictly confidential.

1. **First of all, what is your age? FILL IN BELOW.**

   _____ IF BETWEEN 17 AND 59 CONTINUE WITH Q. 2

          IF OVER AGE 60 TERMINATE INTERVIEW   (5-6)

2. **Have you ever donated blood before?**

   Yes   ☐ (1) ⇨ SKIP TO Q. 5

   No   ☐ (2) ⇨ SKIP TO Q. 4   (7-8)

3. **At what age did you first donate blood? RECORD AGE BELOW.**

   _____   (8-9)

4. **If you wanted to donate blood would you know where to go?**

   Yes   ☐ (1)

   No   ☐ (2)   (10)

5. **How many times have you donated blood? RECORD NUMBER BELOW.**

   _____   (14-12)

6. **Have you ever heard of the San Ystero Blood Center?**

   Yes   ☐ (1) ⇨ CONTINUE WITH Q. 7

   No   ☐ (2) ⇨ SKIP TO Q. 9   (13)

7. **Do you know where the nearest branch of the San Ystero Blood Center is located?**

   Yes   ☐ (1) ⇨ CONTINUE WITH Q. 8

   No   ☐ (2) ⇨ SKIP TO Q. 9   (14-15)

8. **How did you find out about this location? READ LIST. CHECK ONE RESPONSE.**

Driven by the center	[ ]	(1)
Asked center for directions	[ ]	(2)
Friend or relative	[ ]	(3)
Someone took me to the center	[ ]	(4)
Yellow Pages	[ ]	(5)
Other	[ ]	(6)
Don't know or can't remember	[ ]	(7) (16)

9. **Have you ever given blood through the San Ystero Regional Blood Center?**

   Yes   ☐ (1)

   No   ☐ (2)

10. **At which center did you donate? READ LIST. CHECK ONE RESPONSE.**

The East City location	[ ]	(1)
The North City location	[ ]	(2)
The North Suburban location	[ ]	(3)
Don't know or can't remember	[ ]	(4) (19)

11. **Have you ever been asked through the media to donate blood?**

    Yes   ☐ (1)

    No   ☐ (2)   (20-22)

12. **How did you feel about these appeals? READ CHOICES BELOW. CHECK RESPONSE. Did you feel...**

Very pressured	[ ]	(1)
Somewhat pressured	[ ]	(2)
Not at all pressured	[ ]	(3) (19)

(continued)

FIGURE 14.11
Draft questionnaire for blood donor/nondonor survey.

13. **Have you ever been personally asked to donate blood?**

Yes ☐ (1) ⇨ CONTINUE WITH Q. 14

No ☐ (2) ⇨ SKIP TO Q. 15   (20)

14. **How did you feel about these appeals? READ CHOICES BELOW. CHECK RESPONSE. Did you feel…**

Very pressured   [   ] (1)
Somewhat pressured   [   ] (2)
Not at all pressured   [   ] (3)   (21)

15. **Have you donated blood in San Ystero County within the last five years?**

Yes ☐ (1) ⇨ CONTINUE WITH Q. 16

No ☐ (2) ⇨ SKIP TO Q. 17   (22)

16. **Where did you donate? RECORD LOCATION BELOW.**

_____ (24-25)

17. **Here are some reasons others have given for donating blood. For each reason that I read to you, please tell me, using a scale 0 to 100, how much you agree or disagree that the statement that I've just read is true of your own personal feelings, thoughts, or opinions. A '0' means that you absolutely agree that the statement is not true of you and a 100 means that you absolutely agree that the statement is true of you. You can pick any number between 0 and and 100 but the number that you pick must fall within the range of 0 to 100. Remember, pick a number to indicate how much you agree or disagree that the statement is true of you. Record number in appropriate space.**

I give because I enjoy participating in community service
_____ (26-29)

I give because it is the right thing to do
_____ (30-31)

I gave because I was asked to
_____ (32-34)

I gave because there was a community shortage
_____ (35-37)

18. **Now I'd like to get your impressions of the San Ystero Regional Blood Center. For each statement that I read to you, please tell me if you agree or disagree. Specifically, tell me if you strongly agree, slightly agree, slightly disagree, or strongly disagree. READ EACH STATEMENT AND CHECK RESPONSE IN APPROPRIATE COLUMN.**

Strongly agree (1)	Slightly agree (2)	Slightly disagree (3)	Strongly disagree (4)
The centers are clean and neat			
_____	_____	_____	_____
The centers are convenient			
_____	_____	_____	_____
My experience was positive			
_____	_____	_____	_____
The staff was friendly			
_____	_____	_____	_____

19. **Have you ever donated blood?**

Yes ☐ (1) ⇨ SKIP TO Q. 23

No ☐ (2) ⇨ SKIP TO Q. 23   (38)

20. **Has a friend or relative ever asked you to donate blood?**

Yes ☐ (1) ⇨ SKIP TO Q. 23

No ☐ (2) ⇨ SKIP TO Q. 23   (39)

21. **Please listen to each statement that I read and tell me whether or not that statement describes you.**

I am afraid of needles
Describes   [   ] (1)
Does not describe   [   ] (2)

How afraid of needles are you?   (40)
Very afraid   [   ] (1)
Somewhat afraid   [   ] (2)
Just a little afraid   [   ] (3) (41)

I am certain that if I gave blood I would faint
Describes   [   ] (1)
Does not describe   [   ] (2) (42)

How certain are you?
Very certain   [   ] (1)
Somewhat certain   [   ] (2)
A little certain   [   ] (3) (43)

(continued)

22. **Have you ever heard an appeal on the radio or television to give blood?**

    Yes   ☐ (1)

    No   ☐ (2)   (44)

23. **Have you ever received any phone calls from San Ystero Regional Blood Center asking you to donate blood?**

    Yes   ☐ (1)

    No   ☐ (2)   (45)

    How long ago was this call? _____   (46)

    Did you fulfill your civic duty and give blood?   (47)

24. **Now, I'd like to end with just a few more very important questions.**   (49)

25. **What is your current marital status?**

    Married   ☐ (1)   ⇨ SKIP TO Q. 26

    Single   ☐ (2)   ⇨ SKIP TO Q. 27   (38)

26. **How many children do you have?**

    _____   (50)

27. **What is your approximate household annual income, before taxes, in thousands?**

    _____   (50-52)

28. **What is your highest level of education completed?**

Less than high school diploma	[ ] (1)
College graduate	[ ] (4)
High school	[ ] (2)
Master's degree	[ ] (5)
Some college	[ ] (3)
Advanced degree	[ ] (6) (53)

    Thank you for your time. AFTER INTERVIEW RECORD GENDER.

Male	[ ] (1)
Female	[ ] (2) (54)

FIGURE 14.11 (continued)

15

ANALYSIS OF QUANTITATIVE DATA: DESCRIPTIVE APPROACHES

Chapters 13 and 14 showed you how to write well-written survey questions and how to turn these questions into a well-constructed questionnaire. The questionnaire is then used to collect the data.

Data analysis, the organization, examination, and statistical testing of the collected information begins after all data is collected. This chapter introduces you to the fundamentals of data analysis.

After reading this chapter, you will be able to

■ Describe types of analyses appropriate for nominal, ordinal, interval, and ratio level data.

■ Identify methods for summarizing and presenting data collected by special types of questions: checklists and semantic differential.

■ Define the meaning and usage of measures of central tendency—means, medians, and modes—for summarizing the characteristics of a data set.

■ Define the meaning and usage of measures of dispersion—variance and standard deviation—for summarizing the range of responses in a data set.

Chapters 12 and 13 discussed the four levels of measurement: nominal, ordinal, interval, and ratio. Table 15.1 (page 328) summarizes the types of descriptive statistics that are appropriate to each level of measurement and, in doing so, illustrates two important aspects of the relationship between level of measurement and data analysis.

• Fewer data analysis techniques are appropriate for lower levels of measurement.

• Higher levels of measurement can be analyzed using all techniques appropriate for lower levels of measurement.

TABLE 15.1   Levels of Measurement and Appropriate Statistical Techniques

Descriptive Data Analysis Technique	*Level of Measurement*			
	Nominal	*Ordinal*	*Interval*	*Ratio*
Frequency distribution	X	X	X	X
Proportion	X	X	X	X
Percentage	X	X	X	X
Ratio	X	X	X	X
Mode	X	X	X	X
Median		X	X	X
Mean or average			X	X

The reminder of this chapter discusses the descriptive data analysis techniques shown in Table 15.1. The next two sections explore the techniques that are appropriate for data at all levels of measurement. This section is followed by a discussion of techniques appropriate only for interval and ratio level data.

DESCRIPTIVE TECHNIQUES FOR ALL LEVELS OF MEASUREMENT

Data at all levels of measurement can be described in terms of frequencies, proportions, percents, and ratios.

Frequency Distributions

Consider a basic demographic survey question, for example:

Which of the following describes your current marital status (READ LIST)?

Single, never married	_____	(1)
Single, separated	_____	(2)
Single, divorced	_____	(3)
Single, widowed	_____	(4)
Married	_____	(5)

The first step in the creation of a frequency distribution for this (or any other question) is the assignment of responses to each category used in the scale. The assignment of each response to the appropriate category creates a tally. The final count of the number of responses falling into each category is called a *frequency distribution*. A tally and frequency distribution can be conducted manually or by computer. The frequency distribution for the data collected by this question might be

Response Category	*Number of Responses*
Single, never married	5
Single, separated	10
Single, divorced	6
Single, widowed	1
Married	28
Total	**50**

As the table illustrates, an initial frequency distribution should always present the data in the form collected by the survey question, that is, there should be a one-to-one match between the response categories used in the survey question and the response categories shown in the frequency distribution. Once this is done, you can then summarize the data in ways that do not directly correspond to the original response categories. In these cases, the original response categories are grouped together in some logical fashion and the cumulative frequency for the new categories is presented. The marital status question divides currently "single" individuals into four classes: never married, separated, divorced, widowed. You might want to group all of the "single" classifications together to more easily see how many individuals in the sample are currently *either* single or married. In this case, your frequency distribution would be

Current Marital Status	Number of Responses
Single	22
Married	28
Total	**50**

Similarly, you might want to regroup the sample to determine how many individuals were *ever* married versus those who were *never* married. In this case, your frequency distribution would be

Current Marital Status	Number of Responses
Ever married	45
Never married	5
Total	**50**

A different perspective on the marital characteristics of the sample is provided by each regrouping.

Proportions, Percentages, and Ratios

Once you have constructed a frequency distribution you can then select any of three types of analyses to help you better understand the characteristics of the data that you have collected. These analyses are: proportions, percentage distributions, and ratios.

Proportions *Proportions* report the relative frequency of responses falling into each response category. Proportions are computed by dividing the total number of responses in a particular response category by the total number of responses among all categories. Consider the frequency distribution to the marital status question. There are fifty responses to the question, each response representing one individual in the sample. Twenty-eight individuals indicated that they are currently married. The proportion of married individuals among the total sample would be .56, calculated as follows:

$$\text{Proportion of married individuals} = \frac{\text{Number of married individuals}}{\text{Total number of individuals in the study sample}}$$

Proportion of married individuals = 28/50 = .56

The following table presents the proportions for the marital status frequency distribution. Each column in the table presents a necessary table component: the response categories are clearly labeled, the raw count (frequency) for each category and proportion of the total sample falling into each category have been computed and reported. Note how the sum of the proportion column adds to '1' indicating that the sum of all the parts adds to a unified whole.

Current Marital Status	*Frequency*	*Proportion*
Single, never married	5	.10
Single, separated	10	.20
Single, divorced	6	.12
Single, widowed	1	.02
Married	28	.56
Total	**50**	**1.00**

As both a user and communicator of research you should be aware that end users of research information, such as your associates at the advertising agency and your clients, generally find proportions a difficult method for acquiring insights into data trends and implications. Proportions are a valid but not a common way for thinking about the relative sizes of groups.

Percentages   A more common way to summarize data is with *percentage distributions*. You create a percentage distribution by dividing the total number of responses in a particular category by the total number of responses among all categories and then multiplying the quotient by 100. (This is the same as multiplying the proportion by 100.) Thus, the percentage of married individuals among the total sample would be 56 percent, calculated as follows:

$$\text{Percentage of married individuals} = \frac{\text{Number of married individuals}}{\text{Total number of individuals in the study sample}}$$

$$
\begin{aligned}
\text{Percentage of married individuals} &= 28/50 \times 100 \\
&= .56 \times 100 \\
&= 56\%
\end{aligned}
$$

The following table shows the frequency and percentage distributions for marital status. Similar to the table reporting proportions, the table reporting the frequency distribution contains three essential elements: the category labels, the frequency for each category, and percentage of the total sample falling into each category. Note how the sum of the percentage column adds to '100'.

Current Marital Status	Frequency	Percent of Responses
Single, never married	5	10%
Single, separated	10	20%
Single, divorced	6	12%
Single, widowed	1	2%
Married	28	56%
Total	**50**	**100%**

The calculation of percentages from nominal, interval, and ratio level data is straightforward. The percentage represents the frequency in a particular category divided by the sum of all categories. This approach to the calculation of percentages applies slightly differently to ordinal data. When calculating percentage distributions for ordinal data, each ranked item is considered an independent unit. Ordinal scales, such as rank order scaling, present a respondent with several characteristics, objects, or attributes and then request that the respondent rank them with respect to a specific characteristic. The following is a typical rank order question:

Think about the three commercials that you just viewed. Each commercial was named before you saw it. The following lists the names of the commercials in the order in which you viewed them. Please rank the commercials to indicate how well you believed each commercial. Place a '1' next to the commercial that you felt was most believable, a '2' next to the commercial that you felt was next most believable, and a '3' next to the commercial that you felt was least believable. Use each number from 1 to 3 only once. There can be no ties.

New Century Scientist   _____
New Century Mom   _____
New Century Environment   _____

The first step in the analysis of ranking data is the creation of a frequency distribution that reflects the number of each ranking assigned to each ranked item. A frequency distribution for the fifty respondents who ranked these three commercials might be:

Frequency of Each Commercial's Rankings at Level:	Scientist	Mom	Environment
1	38	10	2
2	8	24	18
3	4	16	30
Total Rankings	**50**	**50**	**50**

The table shows, for example, that thirty-eight people gave 'Scientist' a ranking of '1', eight gave it a ranking of '2', and four individuals gave it a rank of '3'.

The next step in the analysis and presentation of the ranking data is the translation of each frequency distribution into a percentage distribution for each ranked item. For each commercial in this case, it is as follows:

Percentage of Each Commercial's Rankings at Level:	Scientist	Mom	Environment
1	76%	20%	4%
2	16%	48%	36%
3	8%	32%	60%
Total	**100%**	**100%**	**100%**

The data in each column (from top to bottom) indicates that the majority of rankings for

- 'Scientist' were '1' (76%) while the remainder were '2' (16%).
- 'Mom' were '2' (48%) while the majority of rankings for 'Environment' were '3' (60%).

Ordinal percentage distributions should also be read across the columns. The data across the columns in the prior table indicates that 'Scientist' received the greatest number of '1' rankings (76%), far exceeding the number of '1' rankings given to 'Mom' (20%) and 'Environment' (4%).

In sum, the calculation and presentation of proportion and percentage distribution tables and charts are straightforward. However, two guidelines must be observed. First, always report the total number of cases in each table or chart. This permits your audience to evaluate the size of the sample summarized in the distribution. Second, avoid computing a proportion or percentage when the total number of cases or observations is less then fifty. When samples sizes are much smaller than this, random fluctuations in the data can cause large changes in the proportions or percentages reported for an individual response category.

Ratios   A third way to summarize data at all levels of measurement is by using *ratios*. A ratio of one number X in relation to another number Y is defined as X divided by Y. The important term in the definition is *in relation to*. Whatever quantity precedes *in relation to* (in this case X) is placed in the numerator of the fraction while the number following *in relation to* is placed in the denominator. Ratios, as expressed in this mathematical formula, permit you to see clearly the relationship between the relative size of two of the response categories used in the survey question. Referring to the marital status data, we can see that the ratio of single to married individuals in the sample is nearly equivalent at 22/28 or 22:28. However, ratios are often more easily understood if the smaller term is reduced to one. In these cases, the ratio represents two numbers X and Y both divided by the smaller of X and Y. Thus, the ratio of the single to married individuals can also be expressed as 1:1.27. Note how the use of ratios makes the *relative* size of these groups immediately apparent.

THE ANALYSIS OF INTERVAL AND RATIO DATA

Interval and ratio scales possess all of the characteristics of nominal and ordinal scales plus additional characteristics not possessed by these latter, less powerful levels of measurement. Consequently, all of the numerical and pictorial methods used to describe and present nominal and ordinal data can be used to describe and present interval and ratio data. However, the power of interval and ratio level data permits additional analyses not appropriate to nominal and ordinal level data. The type and number of steps that must be performed before the application of these additional analyses depends on whether the data collected is discrete or continuous.

Discrete Data

Consider the following rating question:

Please think about the commercial you just saw. Please use the following scale to indicate your agreement or disagreement, if any, with the statement "This commercial is for people like me."

Strongly agree	_____ (1)
Slightly agree	_____ (2)
Neither agree nor disagree	_____ (3)
Slightly disagree	_____ (4)
Strongly disagree	_____ (5)

The data collected by this question is discrete. *Discrete* data reflects responses constrained to a specific set of numbers and separated by finite and uniform steps. This question collects discrete data because the respondent must select one of the response options (constrained set) that will be coded a '1', '2', etc. (finite and uniform steps between levels of response). Descriptive summaries and analyses may be performed on discrete data without any intermediary steps.

Continuous Data

Continuous data, on the other hand, represents a response option where any numeric response is possible and where values may, at least in theory, be infinitely close together. The question "How old are you?", for example, collects continuous data.
It is possible for an individual to tell us that his or her age is 40, $40\frac{1}{2}$, $40\frac{5}{12}$, 41, $41\frac{3}{4}$, etc. Because questions that collect continuous data do not have any predefined and precoded categories, the data must be organized before the computation of a percentage distribution and the translation of the data into bar or pie charts. The organization of continuous data is called *grouping* and involves the following steps:

- Order the data
- Determine the number and size of category intervals
- Construct a frequency distribution

Order the Data   Imagine 100 individuals reporting their age in response to the prior question. The first step in the grouping of continuous data requires that you put the responses in numeric order. This arrangement is called an array, and is equivalent to lining up a classroom of children by height or arranging olives according to size. The array of the 100 responses to the age question is shown in Figure 15.1.

Determine the Number and Size of Class Intervals   The next step requires you to determine the number and size of category intervals that will govern how the data will be grouped. Should we group the age data into five or twenty-five categories?

The determination of number and size of category intervals is an essential step but, unfortunately, there are no fixed guidelines for the selection of category boundaries. However, when determining group size and boundaries keep in mind that

- the groupings should reflect the nature of the data. If the range of the data (that is, the distance from smallest to the largest value) is large, then the size of the groups will also likely be large. However, data limited in range may be best summarized by using relatively smaller categories;
- the number of groupings should not be so large as to obscure important characteristics of the data nor so small as to make the grouping virtually meaningless;
- the size of the interval should be a whole number and whenever possible, should be divisible by a common divisor such as 2, 10, 25, 100, etc.;
- the groupings should, whenever possible, be of uniform width.

With these considerations in mind you can mathematically try out different grouping schemes. The age data, for example, can be grouped in any of the following ways by manipulating the interval covered by each group:

Five Categories	*Eight Categories*	*Sixteen Categories*
1–15	1–9	1–4
16–30	10–19	5–9
31–45	20–29	10–14
46–60	30–39	15–19
70–79	40–49	20–24
	50–59	25–29
	60–69	30–34
	70–79	35–39
		40–44
		45–49
		50–54
		55–59
		60–64
		65–69
		70–74
		75–79

7	28	39	53
9	28	39	53
9	33	39	54
12	34	41	54
12	34	41	54
13	34	41	54
13	34	41	55
13	34	41	57
13	35	41	58
14	36	41	58
16	36	43	58
16	36	43	63
17	36	43	64
19	37	43	64
19	37	44	64
20	37	44	64
21	37	44	68
21	37	44	69
21	37	44	69
21	37	44	73
21	37	44	73
21	37	47	73
26	39	47	75
27	39	52	75
27	39	53	75

FIGURE 15.1
Array of responses to the question: "How old are you?"

Intuitively the middle grouping seems correct. While all three grouping schemes satisfy the third and fourth grouping criteria discussed earlier, the eight-category approach appears to satisfy best the first two criteria. The group interval range in the eight-group approach is reasonable given the full range of the data. Additionally, the groups are not so large that respondents of vastly different characteristics are grouped together (for example, the grouping of sixteen- and thirty-year-olds) nor are they so small that grouping provides little advantage over examination of the raw data.

Descriptive Statistics

As stated earlier, the characteristics of interval and ratio level data permit the use of statistical analyses not appropriate for data on the nominal and ordinal level of measurement. The remainder of this chapter discusses two fundamental statistics: measures of central tendency and measures of dispersion. The next chapter discusses how these measures are used in more advanced statistical techniques.

Means and Measures of Dispersion   The *mean*, or *average*, is probably the most common summary measure of a set of interval or ratio data. The concept of mean scores should be familiar. You calculate and use this statistic often, for example, in calculating your average for the last three tests that you have taken or in determining your

TABLE 15.2   Calculation of the Mean from Grouped Data

Age Group	Step 1: Calculate Midpoint Midpoint	Frequency	Step 2: Multiply Midpoint By Frequency Midpoint · Frequency
0–9	4.5	3	13.5
10–19	14.5	12	174.0
20–29	24.5	12	294.0
30–39	34.5	26	897.0
40–49	44.5	20	890.0
50–59	54.5	13	708.5
60–69	64.5	8	516.0
70–79	74.5	6	447.0
Total		**100**	**3,940.0**

Step 3: Add Products

Step 4: Divide Sum of Products By Total Number in Sample
   = 3,940/100
   = 39.4 = $\overline{X}$

overall grade point average. In these and similar cases you calculate the mean by adding up the value of all scores in the set and then dividing this sum by the total number of scores. For example, the mean of 2,3,7,8,10 would be 6 (30 ÷ 5). This approach is expressed mathematically in the formula[1]

$$\text{Mean} = \overline{X} = \frac{\sum_{i=1}^{n} X_i}{N}$$

When the number of responses is small or when the data is ungrouped, means are easily computed by summing raw scores and then dividing by the total number of scores. However, larger data sets and grouped data require a different technique for calculating the mean of the data set. Here, the approach is the same but the mathematical computation is different.

When calculating the mean for a set of grouped data you assume that all responses within a grouping are concentrated at the midpoint of their group. (Note, that one result of this assumption is that a mean calculated from grouped data will be different from the mean calculated from the ungrouped, original data set.) With this assumption in mind, calculating the mean from a set of grouped data requires four steps (see Table 15.2).

- First, calculate the midpoint of each grouping by subtracting the lower value from the higher value and then dividing the result by two. For example, the midpoint of the 20- to 29-year-old age category would be 24.5 (20 + 29 ÷ 2).

[1] In this and other statistical formulas, symbols are often used to represent mathematical concepts and computations. The symbol $\overline{X}$ represents the sample mean or average. The symbol N represents the total number of scores or responses in the data set. The symbol Σ means "sum of all items from the first ($i = 1$) to the last (n)." X_i represents an individual score in the sample. Thus, the formula means "The mean score is calculated by adding all scores in the set from the first to the last and then dividing this sum by the total number of scores."

- Second, multiply the midpoint of each group by the group frequency (that is, the number of instances in that group).
- Third, add all the products from the prior step.
- Fourth, divide the sum obtained in the prior step by the total number of responses.[2]

The mean of a data set can be integrated into a table that presents the frequency and percentage distributions and can also be integrated into pictorial representations of the data as discussed in Chapter 4.

Means are very powerful. They provide a single numeric summary of the entire set of responses to a survey question. However, when using means you must be certain that the mean score does represent the set of responses from which it was calculated.

The following table shows a hypothetical set of consumers' purchase intent after seeing one of three commercials.

I Would Purchase the Advertised Product	Commercial 1: Ultra	Commercial 2: Power	Commercial 3: Kids
Strongly agree (1)	20%	50%	5%
Slightly agree (2)	20	0	15
Neither agree nor disagree (3)	20	0	60
Slightly disagree (4)	20	0	15
Strongly disagree (5)	20	50	5
Mean	**3.0**	**3.0**	**3.0**

The mean purchase intent for each commercial is identical in spite of the fact the underlying distributions of response are quite different. Responses to Commercial 1, Ultra, are evenly spread out among the five response categories while responses to Commercial 2, Power, fall exclusively at the ends of scales. Responses to Commercial 3, Kids, resemble what is commonly called a normal distribution or bell curve—most of the responses are in the center of the distribution and the percentage of responses declines as you move to the extremes of the scale. An examination of these distributions illustrates an important aspect of means: means become less representative of the distribution from which they were calculated the more the distribution moves away from the normal curve. While all three commercials have a mean purchase intent of 3.0, this mean is more representative of the distribution of responses to Commercial 3 versus the responses to Commercial 1 and 2. It is misleading to say that the average response to Commercial 2 is 3.0 or neutral for in fact *no* respondent provided this rating.

---

[2] Mathematically, these steps are expressed in the formula:

$$\bar{X} = \frac{\sum_{i=1}^{l} m_i f_i}{N}$$

that means "the mean ($\bar{X}$) is computed by taking each grouping from the first ($i = 1$) to the last (l), in each case multiplying the group midpoint (m_i) by its frequency (f_i) and then dividing the sum (Σ) of these products by the total number of observations, N.

Thus, when you use and report mean scores it is important to determine how well the mean represents the distribution of responses from which it is calculated. You can do this by visually examining the distribution of scores and subjectively deciding that the mean is or is not representative *or* you can use statistics to identify the range of response and the appropriateness of the mean in describing this range. In this latter case, you would calculate and examine each distribution's variance and standard deviation. Variance and standard deviation, which may be calculated from both grouped and ungrouped data, are calculated numbers that provide insights into the range or dispersion of scores in relation to the mean score.

Variance (denoted by the symbol s^2) is calculated by taking the sum of the squared differences between each item in the data set (X_i) and the mean of the data set ($\bar{X}$) and then dividing this sum by the total number of items in the data set minus one ($N - 1$). Mathematically this is expressed in the formula:

$$s^2 = \frac{\sum_{i=1}^{m}(X_i - \bar{X})^2}{N - 1}$$

The step-by-step procedures for calculating the variance of a data set is shown in Table 15.3 for both ungrouped and grouped data.

While variance is a good measure of the degree of the dispersion in a set of data there is one drawback to using this measure. Variance is expressed in units of squared deviations rather than in the same units as the original measurements. For example, the variance for the data shown in Table 15.3 represents squared ratings. Consequently, it is difficult to relate the numeric value of the variance to the numeric value of the mean.

This problem is solved through use of the standard deviation. The *standard deviation* is the square root of the variance as expressed in the following formula:

$$s = \sqrt{\frac{\sum_{i=1}^{m}(X_i - \bar{X})^2}{N - 1}}$$

The standard deviation, as the square root of the variance is thus expressed in the same units as the original measurement scale. The use of a square root eliminates the drawback of the variance representing squared units rather than the original units of measurement. As a result, it is easy to relate the magnitude of the standard deviation to the mean.

Intuitively, it should be clear that the greater the dispersion in a set of data the greater are the variance and standard deviation. If there is no dispersion, if every observation equals the mean score, then all deviations will equal zero and the variance and standard deviation, the sum of the squares of these deviations, will also be zero. (You can prove this to yourself. Calculate the variance and standard deviation for a set of ten identical scores. The value of the score does not matter.) As the dispersion in the data set increases, the deviations from the sample mean will also tend to increase as will the squared sum of these deviations. Therefore, if two samples of individuals respond to the same question, greater standard deviations will indicate greater dispersion of scores.

TABLE 15.3 Calculation of the Variance and Standard Deviation from Ungrouped and Grouped Data

Grouped Data

Step 1: Calculate Mean = (15·1) + (45·2) + (40·3) + (30·4) + (70·5) ÷ 200
= 695 ÷ 200 = 3.48

Number of Respondents (Frequency)	Response Value	Difference from Mean	Squared Difference	Squared Difference · Frequency
15	1	−2.48	6.15	92.25
45	2	−1.48	2.19	98.55
40	3	−0.48	0.23	9.20
30	4	+0.52	0.27	8.10
70	5	+1.52	2.31	161.70
Total = 200				Total = 369.8
		Step 2: Calculate Difference from Mean	Step 3: Square Differences from Mean	Step 4: Sum of the Squared Differences · Frequency

Step 5: Variance = Total Squared Differences ÷ (Number of Respondents −1)
= 369.8 ÷ 199 = 1.86

Step 6: Standard Deviation = $\sqrt{\text{Variance}}$ = $\sqrt{1.86}$ = 1.36

Ungrouped Data

Step 1: Calculate Mean = (2 + 1 + 4 + 5 + 5 + 4 + 4 + 5 + 5 + 5) ÷ 10
= 40 ÷ 10 = 4.0

Respondent Number	Response Value	Step 2: Calculate Difference from Mean *Difference from Mean*	Step 3: Square Differences *Difference Squared*
1	2	−2	4
2	1	−3	9
3	4	0	0
4	5	+1	1
5	5	+1	1
6	4	0	0
7	4	0	0
8	5	+1	1
9	5	+1	1
10	5	+1	1
			Total = 18
			Step 4: Sum Squared Differences

Step 5: Variance = Total Squared Differences ÷ (Number of Respondents −1)
= 18 ÷ 9 = 2.0

Step 6: Standard Deviation = $\sqrt{\text{Variance}}$ = $\sqrt{2.0}$ = 1.42

The Median   A mean is a common descriptor of the central tendency of a set of data. The variance and standard deviation provide insights into the dispersion of scores around the mean and, thus by inference, how well the mean describes the set of data. Beyond the mean, there are two additional descriptors of central tendency: the median and the mode.[3]

Given an ordered set of data (that is, an array) a *median* is the middle value. The median divides the set of data in half so that 50 percent of the measurements are equal to or above the median and 50 percent of the measurements are equal to or below the median. In those circumstances where there is an odd number of cases, the median will be the measure that falls in the exact center of the distribution, located by visual inspection or through the following formula:

$$\text{Position of the median} = \frac{\text{Total number of measurements} + 1}{2}$$

If the number of cases is even, the median is the average of the two middle cases.

Which to Use: Mean or Median?   The mean and the median of a set of scores are important and useful for obtaining insights into the characteristics of the data set. In general, the mean is the preferred descriptor because of the ability to manipulate mathematically this measure and the ability to better estimate the population mean from the sample mean. There are, however, two instances in which the median is preferred to the mean.

One instance of median preference occurs when there are one or more extreme values in a data set. The median in these circumstances is the preferred measure because the value of the mean is extremely sensitive to extreme values while the value of the median is not. When extreme values are present, the mean may provide a very distorted picture. For example, assume that you are attempting to describe the income level of the target audience for a new product. You show the new product concept to a representative sample of the population and note the income levels of those who express strong or slight interest in the product. Imagine that the income levels of those expressing a strong or slight interest were as follows:

Income ($)	Frequency
10,000	9
12,000	10
17,000	7
20,000	8
747,000	1

The mean income of the sample expressing an interest in the new product is $35,314. This mean is not a very good description of the sample. It is artificially high because of the one extreme value and can lead to misleading decisions. The median of $12,000 is a much better descriptor.

---

[3] Note the use of means, medians, and modes varies as a function of the data's level of measurement. Means can only be calculated for interval and ratio data. Medians can be calculated for ordinal, interval, and ratio data. Modes can be used to summarize data at all levels of measurement.

The second instance of median preference occurs when open-ended categories appear in a data grouping. The grouping of "age" presented earlier in this chapter contained all closed-ended groups, that is, there were both lower and upper values to each age category. However, some groupings utilize open-ended categories. For example, one category for the grouping of income data might be "over $100,000." It is impossible to estimate the midpoint of this group because no upper limit is specified. Consequently, the median must be used because without a midpoint, no mean may be calculated from this grouped data.

The Mode Another measure of central tendency is the *mode*. The mode is defined as the most frequently observed value in a set of data. The purchase intent scales shown earlier have different modes. The distribution for Commercial 1, "Ultra," is multimodal because there are more than two values tied for the most frequently occurring value. Commercial 2, "Power," is bimodal because there are two values tied for the most frequently occurring value. Commercial 3, "Kids," has one mode, value three, as this is the most frequently occurring value.

Relationship of Mean, Median, and Mode The mean, median, and mode each provide a different insight into the characteristics of the distribution of a set of scores. A distribution is symmetrical when the mean, median, and mode are identical (see the top portion of Figure 15.2, page 342). In these cases (a) the distribution to the right of the mean, median, and mode is a mirror image of the distribution to the left of these measures and (b) the majority of scores fall into the center of the distribution. In these cases the mean is an accurate and preferred descriptor of the distribution. Many distributions are not symmetrical. A distribution in which the value of the mode falls below the median that subsequently falls below the mean is said to skew left. This distribution has a number of values at low frequencies at the *upper* end of the distribution (see the middle portion of Figure 15.2). A distribution in which the value of the mode falls above the median that subsequently falls above the mean is said to skew right. This distribution has a number of values at low frequencies at the *lower* end of the distribution (see the bottom portion of Figure 15.2). Depending on the skewed distribution and range of values either the median or the mode is often the preferred descriptor.

SIMPLIFYING MULTIPLE DESCRIPTIVE MEASURES

Descriptive measures summarize trends in the underlying data. There are times, however, when the presentation of multiple descriptive measures becomes overwhelming for end users of the research. When this occurs, the value of the research significantly declines because the end user is unable to see the broader pattern of the findings and is, therefore, unable to identify the implications of the research for the decisions that need to be made.

This situation can be avoided. Several different analytical techniques can be used to simplify the presentation of multiple-related measures. The approach selected depends upon the data's level of measurement.

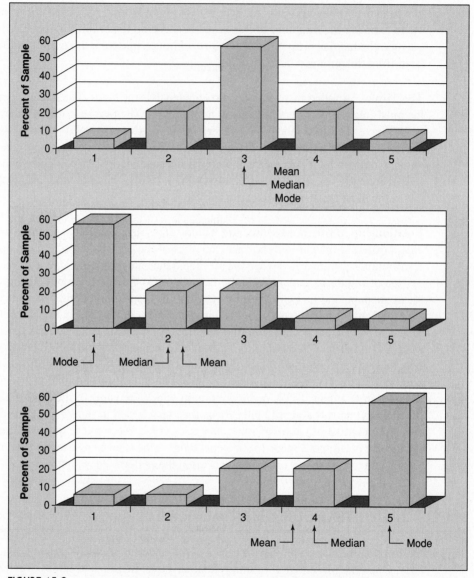

FIGURE 15.2
The effects of distribution characteristics on the mean, median, and mode.

Nominal Data: Organizing Measures and Calculating "Net" Percents

Consider the following checklist question:

> Please think about the commercial you just saw. Place a check after each statement that you agree with—that is—that reflects how you feel about the commercial. You may check as many or as few (or even no) statements depending on your feelings toward the commercial.

	I agree
The commercial was dull	_____
The commercial told me something new	_____
The commercial was for people like me	_____
I have seen this type of commercial before	_____
The people in the commercial were believable	_____
The commercial confused me	_____
I would tell my friends to "keep an eye out" for this commercial	_____
The music was appropriate	_____
The spokesperson was believable	_____
The commercial was not interesting	_____
I do not like this type of commercial	_____
The spokesperson was irritating	_____
I would like to see this commercial again	_____

Responses to this question can be presented as shown in Table 15.4 (page 344). The individual items can be shown in the order presented in the questionnaire (Example A) or in descending order of percent agreement (Example B). Unfortunately, both formats have a difficult time communicating the overall pattern of response.

The pattern of response to this question can be made clearer if several steps are taken.

- First, determine the analytical area that the data will address. For example, will the presentation of responses to the checklist focus on overall positive or negative responses or focus on reactions to the execution versus reactions to the message? (In this example we focus on overall positive versus negative responses.)
- Second, group statements in accordance with the presentation focus. Given our focus, we group all positive statements together and all negative statements together.
- Third, prepare a group label. In this example, our labels are "Positive Responses" and "Negative Responses."
- Fourth, calculate a *net percentage* for each group of items. A net percent represents the unduplicated percentage of respondents selecting at least one item in the grouping.[4]

---

[4] The "net," and the unduplicated percentage that it respresents, reflect the fact that each respondent is counted only once in the calculation of the net percentage. Assume, for example, that four statements are grouped together. These statements are labeled Statement 1, Statement 2, Statement 3, and Statement 4. Each respondent's agreement with each statement, as indicated by a check on the checklist, is as follows:

	Statement 1	*Statement 2*	*Statement 3*	*Statement 4*	*"Net" (Any)*
Respondent 1	x	x	x	x	x
Respondent 2	x				x
Respondent 3					
Respondent 4					
Respondent 5	x	x			x
Total	3	2	1	1	3
Percent	60%	40%	20%	20%	60%

The "net" for this group of respondents for this group of statements is 60 percent, which means that 60 percent of the respondents (3 out of 5) agreed with *at least one* of the four statements.

TABLE 15.4 Methods for Presenting Responses to a Checklist

	Percent Agreeing
Example A: Order Corresponding to Questionnaire Order	
The commercial was dull	23%
The commercial told me something new	74
The commercial was for people like me	87
I've seen this type of commercial before	25
The people in the commercial were believable	31
The commercial confused me	26
I would tell my friends to "keep an eye out" for this commercial	24
The music was appropriate	83
The spokesperson was believable	84
The commercial was not interesting	28
I don't like this type of commercial	22
The spokesperson was irritating	26
I would like to see this commercial again	78

	Percent Agreeing
Example B: Ordered By Descending Level of Agreement	
The commercial was for people like me	87%
The spokesperson was believable	84
The music was appropriate	83
I would like to see this commercial again	78
The commercial told me something new	74
The people in the commercial were believable	31
The commercial was not interesting	28
The commercial confused me	26
The spokesperson was irritating	26
I've seen this type of commercial before	25
I would tell my friends to "keep an eye out" for this commercial	24
The commercial was dull	23
I don't like this type of commercial	22

A table representing this approach to the manipulation of nominal data is shown in Table 15.5. When the data is organized in this manner, the following conclusions become immediately apparent:

- Almost all respondents liked at least one thing about the commercial (based on high "Positive" net);
- Most consumers agreed that the commercial was relevant ("for people like me") and that the spokesperson was believable, although irritating;
- Negative ratings reflect the opinions of few respondents (based on low "Negative" net) each of whom disliked many things (almost all negative opinion statements checked).

TABLE 15.5 Presenting Responses to a Checklist: Grouped Items

	Percent Agreeing
Positive Responses—Net	**97%**
The commercial was for people like me	87
The spokesperson was believable	84
The music was appropriate	83
I would like to see this commercial again	78
The commercial told me something new	74
The people in the commercial were believable	31
I would tell my friends to "keep an eye out" for this commercial	24
Negative Responses—Net	**31%**
The commercial was not interesting	28
The commercial confused me	26
The spokesperson was irritating	26
I've seen this type of commercial before	25
The commercial was dull	23
I don't like this type of commercial	22

Interval and Ratio Data: Combining Related Scales   It is common to use multiple scales to assess individual attitudes or behaviors. The use of multiple scales tends to provide multifaceted insights into the area of inquiry. For example, an advertiser who is considering repositioning a product to emphasize the product's health benefits might want to first assess the target audience's views toward health-themed advertising and the company who sponsors it. The following questions might be presented:

1. A product advertised as "lite" or "reduced fat" really is better for your health.
2. Ads promoting a product's health benefits are generally deceptive.
3. Corporations who advertise the health benefits of their products genuinely care about the consumer.
4. Health-related ads are very exploitive.
5. Most health-related advertising is believable.
6. Corporations use health claims to make more money.
7. Most corporations intentionally exaggerate the health benefits of their products.

In this set of questions, Questions 1, 2, 4, and 5 assess consumers' views of health-themed product advertising while Questions 3, 6, and 7 assess the views of the company that sponsors the advertising.

The results of responses to these seven questions can be presented as shown in Table 15.6 (page 346). While this approach presents all relevant data for important study subsamples, the audience viewing this table is immersed in data. Important conclusions and implications are lost.

Important insights can be better communicated by first organizing and then manipulating the responses to the scales shown in Table 15.6. First, similar to checklist responses, related items are grouped and a group label is created. Next, a mean for each

TABLE 15.6   Responses to Attitude Statements

Statement*	Total Sample	Adults 18–25	Men 26–54	Women 26–54
Products advertised as "lite" are not better for your health	3.3	3.2	2.9	3.7
Ads promoting a product's health benefits are generally deceptive	4.4	4.6	4.2	4.4
Corporations who advertise their product's health benefits do not genuinely care about the consumer	4.1	4.3	3.9	4.1
Health-related ads are very exploitive	4.5	4.7	4.0	4.8
Most health-related ads are not believable	4.3	4.7	3.9	4.3
Corporations use health claims to make more money	4.3	4.4	4.2	4.3
Corporations exaggerate their product's health claims	4.5	4.7	4.2	4.6

* Core idea of statement. Some statements reversed for numeric consistency in interpretation of response. Higher values indicate stronger agreement and more negative attitudes.

set of scales is calculated. This summary information, when added to the original table (see Table 15.7), makes the differences of the subgroups in perceptions of health-themed advertising and advertisers readily apparent.

The averaging of responses to related scales is an intuitively reasonable way to summarize information. However, to maintain the integrity of the data, you must make certain that the scales are related before you compute and present the group average. Then make certain that it is appropriate to average the set of scales by evaluating a calculated number, the coefficient alpha,[5] which represents the internal consistency in the responses to the items in the group. (See Table 15.8 for an illustration of the calculation process.) It is recommended that you only average a set of questions when the coefficient alpha for that set is .80 or greater.[6]

DATA ANALYSIS AND COMPUTERS

The descriptive statistics discussed in this chapter are not computationally complex and can be arrived at using a calculator. The use of inferential statistics, described in the next chapter, requires considerably more complex computations. In both chapters, formulas and computations are presented to help you clearly understand the logic of various measures and analyses.

Fortunately, the availability of statistical programs for the personal computer reduces (and often eliminates) the need for manual computations. These programs, such

---

[5] See Lee J. Cronbach, "Coefficient Alpha and the Internal Structure of Tests," *Psychometrika* 16 (1951): 297–334, Edward G. Carmines and Richard A. Zeller, *Reliability and Validity Assessment* (Beverly Hills, CA: Sage Publications, 1979), 43–47.

[6] See Carmines and Zeller, *Reliability and Validity,* 51.

TABLE 15.7 Responses to Attitude Statements: Grouped and Summarized

Statement*	Total Sample	Adults 18–25	Men 26–54	Women 26–54
Attitudes Toward Product Advertising				
Overall Attitude	**4.1**	**4.3**	**3.8**	**4.2**
Products advertised as "lite" are not better for your health	3.3	3.2	2.9	3.7
Ads promoting a product's health benefits are generally deceptive	4.4	4.6	4.2	4.4
Health-related ads are very exploitive	4.5	4.7	4.0	4.8
Most health-related ads are not believable	4.3	4.7	3.9	4.3
Attitudes Toward Corporations				
Overall Attitude	**4.3**	**4.5**	**4.1**	**4.3**
Corporations who advertise their product's health benefits do not genuinely care about the consumer	4.1	4.3	3.9	4.1
Corporations use health claims to make more money	4.3	4.4	4.2	4.3
Corporations exaggerate their product's health claims	4.5	4.7	4.2	4.6

* Core idea of statement. Some statements reversed for numeric consistency in interpretation of response. Higher values indicate stronger agreement and more negative attitudes.

TABLE 15.8 Calculation of Coefficient Alpha

Step 1: Obtain the Correlation Matrix for Variables in the Proposed Set

	Var 1	Var 2	Var 3	Var 4
Var 1	–	–	–	–
Var 2	.876	–	–	–
Var 3	.768	.769	–	–
Var 4	.963	.976	.787	–

Step 2: Find the Average Intercorrelation

Average of correlations = (.876 + .768 + .963 + .769 + .976 + .787) ÷ 6
= 5.139 ÷ 6
= .857

Step 3: Place Numbers in the Formula

$$\text{alpha} = \frac{N \cdot p}{1 + [(p)(N - 1)]}$$

where N is the number of items and p is the average of the correlations.
Coefficient alpha for this example would be .960 calculated as

$$\text{alpha} = \frac{4 \cdot .857}{1 + [(.857)(4 - 1)]}$$

as Minitab or SPSS permit quick and efficient data exploration and analysis. Appendix A presents a basic workbook to help you begin using computers for data analysis. The workbook is best read after you have acquired an understanding of the material in Chapters 15 and 16.

Summary

Data analysis helps you to see patterns and trends in response to survey questions. The types of analyses appropriate for a specific question are determined by the question's level of measurement.

All data, regardless of its level of measurement, can be analyzed with frequencies, proportions, percentages, and ratios. These summary measures can be presented in either tabular or pictorial format. Additional statistical techniques can be used with interval and ratio level data.

Means (or averages), variance, standard deviation, medians, and modes can be calculated for interval and ratio level data. A mean is the computed average of a distribution of scores. The variance and standard deviation, computed measures of the distribution's dispersion, provide direction for determining how well the mean represents the distribution. The median, the middle response in the distribution, and the mode, the most common response, provide additional insights into the characteristics of the distribution and for determining how well the mean represents the distribution.

Review Questions

1. What is a *tally* of responses?
2. What is a *frequency distribution*?
3. What is the relationship between a tally and a frequency distribution?
4. What does a *proportion* represent? How is it calculated?
5. What is a *percentage distribution*? How is it calculated?
6. What is the relationship between a frequency distribution, a proportion, and a percentage distribution?
7. Which is easier for most individuals to understand: a proportion or a percentage? Why do you think this is the case?
8. Which of the following should be used when sample sizes are small: frequency, proportion, or percent? Why?
9. What is a *ratio*? How is it calculated?
10. What does a frequency distribution for ranking data represent? How is this similar to and different from a frequency distribution for nominal data?
11. What does a percentage distribution for ranking data represent? How is this similar to and different from a frequency distribution for nominal data?
12. What is *discrete* data? How does discrete data differ from *continuous* data?
13. What is *grouping* and in what circumstances is it used?
14. What are the three steps for grouping data? Briefly describe each step.
15. What are the guidelines for creating categories from continuous data?

16. What does the mean, or average, of a set of numbers represent?

17. What circumstances affect the extent to which a mean represents the set of values from which it is calculated?

18. What is *variance*? How is it calculated?

19. What is *standard deviation*? How is it calculated?

20. What is the relationship between variance and standard deviation?

21. What is a *median*? How is it identified?

22. In what circumstances is the median versus the mean the preferred descriptor of the data set?

23. What is the *mode*?

24. What is the relationship between the mean, median, and mode for bell-shaped and skewed distributions?

25. What three steps are involved in the simplification of nominal data?

26. What is a *net* and how is it calculated?

27. What three steps are involved in the simplification of interval and ratio data?

28. What is a *coefficient alpha* and what does it tell you about the set of grouped items?

29. How is a *coefficient alpha* calculated?

Application Exercise

The Tastee-Yummy Dog Bone Company has developed four new commercials for their line of flavored dog cookies.[7] Before selecting one of the commercials for production, they conducted research to assess the target audience's reactions to each commercial as well as their reactions to specific product claims communicated by the commercials.

Mall-intercept interviews were used to collect the data. Individuals walking through the mall were screened and those in the target audience who agreed to participate in the research were taken to an interviewing area and shown the three commercials. After viewing all three commercials a twenty minute interview was conducted by a trained interviewer.

The interview was extensive. Some key questions asked of each respondent were

Q1. Gender
RECORD FROM VISUAL INSPECTION.   Male   _____ (1)
                                        Female   _____ (2)

Q2. Age
What is your age to the nearest whole year?   _____

Q7. Product Appeal
Now that you have seen the commercials for Tastee-Yummy Dog Cookies, I would like you to think about how much your dog may or may not like these cookies. Please listen to each statement that I am about to read you. After each statement, use the scale on this card (CARD CONTAINS FIVE-POINT STRONGLY AGREE (1) TO STRONGLY

---

[7] The company, situation, questionnaire, and data in this exercise are fictitious.

DISAGREE (5) SCALE) to indicate how much you agree or disagree with each statement.

    a. My dog would like the advertised treats better than the brand I am currently buying. _____

    b. My dog would be better behaved if I used the advertised treats as a reward for good behavior. _____

Q9. Product Benefits

The commercials discussed several benefits of Tastee-Yummy Dog Cookies. I would like you to indicate the relative importance of these benefits to you and your dog by assigning points to each benefit. You have 100 points to distribute among the following four benefits listed. You can give as many or as few points, or even no points, to each benefit. The more points that you give to a specific benefit the more important you feel that benefit is. Fewer points indicate less importance. Please make sure that you use all 100 points. HAND QUESTIONNAIRE TO RESPONDENT. TAKE BACK WHEN FINISHED. MAKE CERTAIN THAT TOTAL ADDS TO 100.

Cleans teeth	_____
Prevents tooth decay	_____
Freshens breath	_____
Provides added nutrition	_____
Total	**100**

Q13. Commercial Liking

The names of the four commercials are shown next. I would like you to rank the commercials to reflect how well you liked them. Place a '1' next to the commercial that you liked the best, a '2' next to the commercial that you liked the next best, a '3' next to the commercial that you liked the next best, and finally a '4' next to the commercial that you liked the least. Please use each number only once. HAND QUESTIONNAIRE TO RESPONDENT. TAKE BACK WHEN FINISHED. MAKE CERTAIN THAT EACH RANKING IS USED ONLY ONCE.

Dog's Day Out	_____
Nine Yards	_____
Couch Dog	_____
Teeth of My Dreams	_____

Q16. Purchase Intent—High Price

Please indicate how likely or unlikely you would be to purchase Tastee-Yummy Dog Cookies if they were available at your local grocery store and were priced comparably to the *leading* brand of dog cookies.

Extremely likely	_____	(1)
Somewhat likely	_____	(2)
Neither likely nor unlikely	_____	(3)
Somewhat unlikely	_____	(4)
Extremely unlikely	_____	(5)

Q17. Purchase Intent—Low Price

Please indicate how likely or unlikely you would be to purchase Tastee-Yummy Dog Cookies if they were available at your local grocery store and were priced comparably to the *store* brand of dog cookies.

Extremely likely	_____	(1)
Somewhat likely	_____	(2)
Neither likely nor unlikely	_____	(3)
Somewhat unlikely	_____	(4)
Extremely unlikely	_____	(5)

The responses of the fifty individuals in the sample are shown in Table 15.9 (pages 352–353). Use this data and your knowledge of the relationship between levels of measurement and levels of analysis to address the following issues.

Q1. Gender

At what level of measurement is this question?

What are the characteristics of the sample in terms of gender? Which measure of central tendency (mean, median, or mode) best describes this characteristic? Why is that measure the most appropriate? Is it appropriate to calculate variance and standard deviation? Why or why not? Present the results of your analysis in both tabular and pictorial formats.

Q2. Age

At what level of measurement is this question?

Group the data to determine the characteristics of the sample in terms of age? Which measure of central tendency (mean, median, or mode) best describes this characteristic? Why is that measure the most appropriate given the distribution of age in the sample? Is it appropriate to calculate variance and standard deviation? Why or why not? Present the results of your analysis in both tabular and pictorial formats.

Q7. Product Appeal

At what level of measurement are these two questions?

Using the data from Q7a, determine the extent to which the product appeals to the target audience. How does each measure of central tendency help you to understand the characteristics of the distribution? What measure do you believe is the most appropriate for illustrating the level of product appeal? Is the calculation of variance or standard deviation appropriate? Why or why not?

Using the data from Q7b, determine the extent to which the target audience believes that the cookie will help their dog to become better behaved. As with Q7a, determine how each measure of central tendency helps you understand the characteristics of the distribution? What measure do you believe is the most appropriate for illustrating the audience's belief that the cookie will help their dog become better behaved? Is the calculation of variance or standard deviation appropriate? Why or why not?

Present your analysis of Q7a and 7b in both tabular and pictorial formats.

Q9. Product Benefits

At what level of measurement is this question?

When you present the results of the research, your client at Tastee-Yummy will ask for your recommendation as to which product benefit should receive the most emphasis in the advertising campaign. Which benefit would you recommend? On what basis do you make this recommendation? What descriptive measures are most appropriate for describing the characteristics of the distribution and for helping you to identify the most important benefit? Present your findings in both tabular and pictorial format and provide a narrative explanation to show how you reached your recommendation.

Q13. Commercial Liking

At what level of measurement is this question?

The client at Tastee-Yummy loves the fourth commercial, "Teeth of My Dreams." The client has every expectation that others in the target audience will love this commercial also and that, at least in part due to this very high liking, the agency will recommend "Teeth of My Dreams" for production. Is the client correct? Does the target audience love this commercial? Do they even like this commercial? Which commercial would you recommend for production? On what basis did you select this commercial? What descriptive measures are most appropriate for describing the characteristics of the distribution and for

TABLE 15.9 Data for Tastee-Yummy Dog Cookie Research

| Respondent Number | Gender | Age | Q7a | Q7b | Q9: Benefits | | | | Q13: Liking | | | | Q16 | Q17 |
					Cleans	Decay	Breath	Nutrition	Day Out	Nine Yards	Couch	Teeth		
1	1	20	1	1	30	30	30	10	1	2	3	4	5	1
2	2	24	2	2	34	33	27	6	1	3	4	2	4	2
3	1	23	1	5	50	25	15	10	1	2	3	4	5	3
4	2	41	3	4	45	35	15	5	2	1	3	4	3	4
5	2	43	1	2	5	5	5	85	2	1	3	4	5	2
6	2	37	2	1	1	1	1	97	1	2	3	4	4	1
7	2	34	2	4	30	30	30	10	2	1	4	3	3	2
8	1	57	1	4	40	30	20	10	1	2	3	4	2	1
9	1	42	3	5	2	3	1	94	3	1	2	4	4	3
10	2	41	4	1	30	40	20	10	3	2	1	4	5	2
11	1	22	5	4	1	0	1	98	1	2	3	4	4	1
12	1	19	3	2	42	37	20	1	1	3	2	4	5	2
13	2	17	2	5	46	34	18	2	2	1	3	4	4	1
14	2	23	2	2	33	33	33	1	1	2	3	4	1	1
15	1	37	1	1	47	40	10	3	1	2	3	4	5	2
16	1	41	2	4	5	1	2	92	4	1	2	3	3	4
17	2	58	2	5	40	40	15	5	1	2	4	3	3	3
18	1	42	3	1	0	0	1	99	2	1	3	4	4	3
19	1	33	4	4	35	35	20	10	1	2	3	4	4	5
20	2	29	2	5	40	30	18	12	1	2	4	3	5	2
21	1	22	2	2	31	31	31	7	1	2	3	4	5	1
22	2	25	1	2	34	35	30	5	1	3	4	2	5	1
23	1	21	2	4	55	20	15	10	1	2	3	4	5	3

Respondent Number	Gender	Age	Q7a	Q7b	Q9: Benefits				Q13: Liking				Q16	Q17
					Cleans	Decay	Breath	Nutrition	Day Out	Nine Yards	Couch	Teeth		
24	2	43	3	3	47	33	17	3	2	1	3	4	4	3
25	2	40	1	2	2	2	2	94	2	1	3	4	4	1
26	2	36	2	1	30	30	30	10	2	1	4	3	3	3
27	2	32	1	5	1	0	5	94	1	2	3	4	5	2
28	1	59	1	4	40	30	25	5	2	1	3	4	4	2
29	1	44	3	5	43	20	20	7	1	2	4	3	3	3
30	2	49	1	1	58	32	5	5	1	3	2	4	5	2
31	2	29	2	5	40	25	25	10	1	2	3	4	5	1
32	1	35	2	4	1	0	1	98	1	3	2	4	4	2
33	2	43	3	3	47	33	17	3	2	1	3	4	4	3
34	2	40	1	2	2	2	2	94	2	1	3	4	4	1
35	2	36	2	1	30	30	30	10	2	1	4	3	3	3
36	2	32	1	5	1	0	5	94	1	2	3	4	5	2
37	2	34	2	4	30	30	30	10	2	1	4	3	3	2
38	1	22	5	4	1	0	4	95	1	2	3	4	4	1
39	1	19	3	2	42	37	20	1	1	3	2	4	5	2
40	2	17	2	5	46	34	18	2	2	1	3	4	4	1
41	1	57	1	4	40	30	20	10	1	2	3	4	2	1
42	1	42	3	5	3	6	1	90	3	1	2	4	4	3
43	2	41	4	1	30	40	20	10	1	3	2	4	4	1
44	2	33	5	2	50	35	15	0	1	2	3	4	5	2
45	1	37	4	3	42	30	20	5	1	3	2	4	1	2
46	1	41	2	4	0	1	2	97	4	1	2	3	3	4
47	1	33	4	4	35	35	20	10	1	2	3	4	4	2
48	2	29	2	5	40	30	18	12	1	2	4	3	5	1
49	1	42	3	1	0	1	0	99	2	1	3	4	4	5
50	2	58	2	5	38	38	20	4	1	2	4	3	3	3

helping you identify the commercial that is best liked by the target audience? Present your findings in both tabular and pictorial format and provide a narrative explanation to show how you reached your recommendation.

Q16. and Q17. Purchase Intent
At what levels of measurement are these two questions?

Your client is in the process of reevaluating product pricing. What is the purchase intent of the target audience at the two levels of pricing? What descriptive measures are most appropriate for describing the characteristics of each distribution and for helping you to understand the purchase intent at each pricing level? Based on the data, which pricing level would you recommend? Why? Present your findings in both tabular and pictorial format. Provide a narrative explanation to show how you reached your recommendation.

CHAPTER

16

ANALYSIS OF QUANTITATIVE DATA: INFERENTIAL STATISTICS

Descriptive statistics help you to understand the data you have collected so that you can draw appropriate conclusions from the research. In some cases data analysis stops at this point. Percent distributions and means may provide all the information required for decision making. In many cases additional analyses are needed so that decision making is accurate. Here, there is a need to determine the relationship between observed measures and the statistical differences between measures.

This chapter will show you how to examine the relationship between different measures to determine whether observed differences are due to real differences in the groups' attitudes, beliefs, and behaviors or whether observed differences are simply due to random fluctuations or error in the data.

After reading this chapter, you will be able to

■ Understand how the normal curve and hypothesis testing provide a foundation for examining relationships and differences among measures.

■ Statistically evaluate levels of response from a single group of individuals.

■ Statistically evaluate the meaningfulness of differences in level of response among two or more groups of individuals.

■ Determine the relationship between two or more measures.

Researchers need to be confident in conclusions that they draw from research studies. When researchers compare two mean scores and then decide that one is in fact higher or better then the other they want to be certain that the differences between the mean scores reflect *real* differences as opposed to random error in the data. They want to have confidence that the marketing and advertising decisions based on inferences

355

and conclusions drawn from the data are the right decisions. Because few data-based decisions can be made with absolute certainty, confidence in decision making is typically expressed in terms of a probability. A researcher might say, "I have just tested two commercials. In examining the scores that represent responses to these commercials I want to be confident that any observed differences are meaningful and that decisions I reach based on the data reflect the proper interpretation of the data. The data primarily involves a mean level of response. I want to be 95 percent certain that the difference between the means of the two commercials is real and not due to error."

To understand how levels of confidence are determined it is necessary to understand the relationship among the normal curve, standard deviation, and probability.

THE NORMAL CURVE

Chapter 15 showed how a frequency and percentage distribution of responses to a particular research question can take a variety of shapes. Some distributions are symmetrical where the mean, median, and mode are identical; some distributions are skewed to the left or right where the mean, median, and mode assume different values; some are bimodal or multimodal where the distribution begins to resemble a range of mountains and valleys. While distributions can assume any of these forms, the first type of distribution is of the most interest and importance to researchers. This distribution, called the bell-shaped curve, has three defining characteristics:

- *Symmetrical*—If we divide the curve at its exact center the left hand half would be an exact mirror image of the right hand half.
- *Unimodal*—There is only one mode, which appears in the exact center of the bell-shaped curve.
- *Unskewed*—The mean, median, and mode have identical values.

There are an infinite number of bell-shaped curves that satisfy these criteria, differing in the extent to how sharply the curve rises toward the central peak. Statisticians are interested in one unique member of the set of bell-shaped curves: the standard normal distribution or normal curve (see normal distribution on the top of Figure 16.1) that has a mean of zero and a standard deviation of one (see distribution on bottom of Figure 16.1). The standard normal distribution is important because it provides a basis for (1) describing distributions of responses to a particular survey question, (2) interpreting the magnitude of a standard deviation, and (3) determining the probability of observing any particular level of response. Each of these factors is an important component of statistical tests and analyses.

The Standard Normal Curve, Standard Deviation, and Area Under the Curve

The characteristics of the standard normal curve let you determine the area under any particular segment of the curve. The boundaries of a segment under the curve are defined in terms of standard deviations from the mean, expressed as a Z score. The normal curve shown on the bottom of Figure 16.1 illustrates the relationship between area and standard deviation.

The Standard Normal Curve

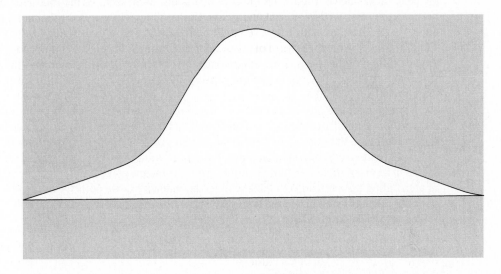

Area Under the Standard Normal Curve

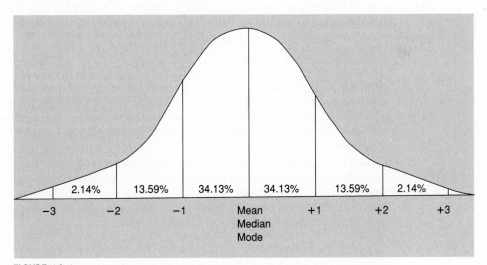

FIGURE 16.1
The standard normal distribution.

The majority of the area of a standard normal distribution lies within one standard deviation on either side of the mean. The fact that the majority of the area under the curve lies close to the mean is reasonable considering that the mean is at the highest peak of the curve. Figure 16.1 shows that about 34 percent of the total area of the normal curve lies within one standard deviation to the positive side of the mean while about 34 percent lies within one standard deviation to the negative side of the mean. Thus, about 68 percent of the total area under the normal curve lies within ± one standard deviation of the mean. Two standard deviations from the mean contains almost all the area under the curve, 95.44 percent, while very little area lies outside the three standard deviations (.28%).

Area under the curve is therefore related to standard deviation. If you know the standard deviation from the mean of any point on the normal curve, you can determine the area beneath the curve from the mean to that point or the percent of the total area of the curve up to and beyond that point. Further, if you know the placement of any two points in terms of their standard deviation from the mean, you can calculate the percent of area falling between and outside the range bounded by those points. Fortunately, you need not manually calculate area under the curve, the results of the calculations are presented in Appendix B, Table B.2.

Area Under the Curve and Probability

A *probability* can be thought of as the likelihood of a particular event occurring. A probability of 50 percent means that the event should occur, on average, fifty times out of every hundred or one out of every two. A probability of 1 percent indicates that the event should occur, on average, one time out of every hundred. The area under the normal curve plays an important role in statistical analysis and subsequent decision making because the area under the curve can be translated into a probability. This probability reflects the likelihood of obtaining any particular value given its distance from the mean.

The relationship between area under the curve and probability can be seen by examining each of the examples presented in Figure 16.2:

- *Example A illustrates the probability of obtaining a value below and beyond a certain point on the normal curve.* In Example A, since 84.13 percent of the area of curve falls below one positive standard deviation from the mean (the shaded area of the distribution) then the probability of obtaining a score equal to or less than this value is 84.13 percent. The probability of obtaining a score greater than one positive standard deviation from the mean (the unshaded portion of the distribution) is 15.87 percent (100%–84.13%).

- *Examples B and C illustrate the probability of obtaining a value below and beyond the range identified by two points on the normal curve.* In Example B the area between the mean and one positive standard deviation is 34.13 percent. This percentage represents the probability of obtaining a score between the mean and one positive standard deviation. The probability of obtaining a score outside this range is 65.87 percent (100%–34.13%). In Example C the area between negative one and positive one standard deviation from the mean is 68.26 percent. This percentage represents the probability of obtaining a score within this range. The probability of obtaining a score outside this range is 31.74 percent (100%–68.26%).

As you will see in the next section, probabilities are used to determine the importance and significance of observed differences in the attitudes, beliefs, and characteristics of groups of respondents.

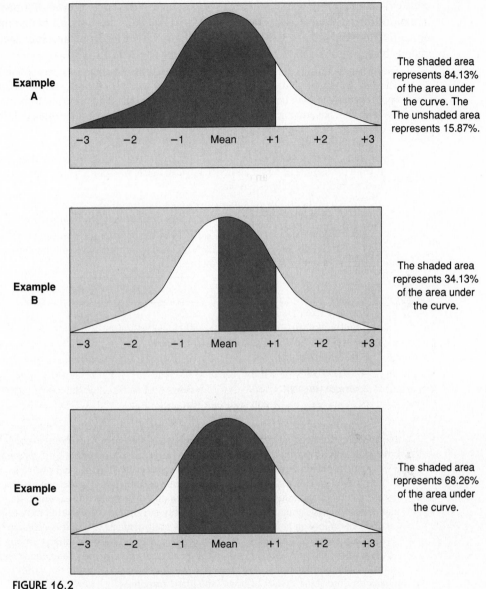

FIGURE 16.2
Determining area under the normal curve.

HYPOTHESIS TESTING

Advertising research that ends with the presentation of measures such as percentages and means is descriptive. A researcher performs the appropriate calculations and then presents the characteristics of the sample in terms of the descriptive measures. Judgment is used to assess whether levels of response are high or low. Other more powerful research analyses use inferential statistics. Inferential statistics let you mathemati-

cally evaluate levels of response and the importance of differences in levels of response among different groups. In doing so, inferential statistics lets you determine the *level of confidence* that you can have in the conclusions you draw from, and subsequent decisions based on, the data. Consider the following scenario:

Pace Manufacturing Company has developed a new line of children's play action figures. They are particularly interested in one figure, Shamantweto, because they feel that it will appeal equally to both boys and girls. The Shamantweto brand manager, Roberta Harris, has asked her advertising agency to help her evaluate the toy's appeal before development of the advertising campaign.

Kelly Gifford is the research associate at Pace's agency. Kelly designed the research and created a questionnaire that collected a broad range of information and reactions from the sample of target audience boys and girls who participated in the study. One of the key questions Kelly asked was:

"Which of the following faces shows how much you like this toy. Put a check next to the one that best shows how much you liked or disliked Shamantweto."

After all the data was collected Kelly used the appropriate descriptive statistics to provide insights into the distribution of boys' and girls' response to Shamantweto. She summarized her analysis with the following chart:

	Boys	Girls
Strongly like (5)	20%	10%
Slightly like (4)	40	20
Neutral (3)	25	35
Slightly dislike (2)	10	30
Strongly dislike (1)	5	5
Average (mean)	**3.6**	**3.0**

(Sample consists of 100 boys and 100 girls)

Kelly then presented her conclusion to Roberta: "As you can see the mean or average appeal of the product was higher among boys versus girls. The mean response among boys was slightly positive at 3.6 while the average response among girls was neutral at 3.0. The distribution of responses in both cases was quite similar. There were few scores at the extreme ends of either distribution and most scores fell near the center. Given similar distributions and a higher mean appeal among boys versus girls, I would have to say that our initial assessment was wrong. Shamantweto should be marketed only to boys."

Roberta looked at Kelly and said: "How confident are you in this decision?"

Kelly replied: "I think the decision is right, after all, the mean rating among boys is nearly a whole rating point higher than the mean rating among girls. And, there are no odd skews in the distributions of responses that would lead us to question the validity of these means for describing the set of boys' and girls' responses."

Kelly used descriptive statistics and judgment to decide that appeal was higher among boys versus girls. However, given the importance and consequences of many research-based decisions, such as target audience selection in Kelly's case, researchers often go beyond visual observation of the data and instead use inferential statistics to inform their judgment after the descriptive analyses are concluded.

Inferential statistics use hypotheses. A *hypothesis* is an unproven belief about the nature of the world. For example, an advertising manager for a laundry detergent might hypothesize that if the new advertising campaign changes consumers' attitudes toward the product's cleaning ability then the brand's share will increase. A media planner might hypothesize that a proposed media plan will generate higher levels of awareness

among older versus younger brand users. A creative might hypothesize that the new campaign will be better liked and be better believed among current users of the product versus those who use competitive products. Kelly and Roberta's hypothesis was that Shamantweto would appeal equally to both boys and girls.

Researchers translate verbal hypothesis into formal mathematical statements. In fact, every verbal hypothesis is expressed as two or more formal hypotheses: one null hypothesis and one or more alternative hypotheses. A null hypothesis (represented by the symbol H_0) is a statement about the status quo. A null hypothesis expresses the belief that there are no real, meaningful differences between groups and that any observed differences are insignificant and can be attributed to random error. Researchers typically develop null hypotheses so that they can (hopefully) disprove them in favor of the alternative hypothesis or hypotheses. An alternative hypothesis or hypotheses (represented by the symbol H_1, H_2 etc.) express the belief that any observed differences between the groups are in fact real and attributable to some difference in the characteristics of the groups. The process of translating verbal hypotheses into null and alternative hypotheses is illustrated in Figure 16.3 (page 362). Note that while Examples A and B show how the preferred outcome is often rejection of the null hypothesis, Example C, reflecting the anticipated appeal of Shamantweto, illustrates how the acceptance of the null hypothesis can in certain circumstances be the preferred outcome.

Figure 16.3 also illustrates the concept of "tails." A tail refers to the directionality of the anticipated differences as expressed in the alternative hypotheses. A one-tailed test specifies the direction of difference between the two groups and thus utilizes only one alternative hypothesis. Example A is a one-tailed test. A two-tailed test merely specifies that there will be differences between the groups without specifying the direction of difference. Therefore, a two-tailed test requires two alternative hypotheses. Example B is a two-tailed test.

Once you have expressed your beliefs regarding research outcomes as null and alternative hypotheses you must then decide how stringent you will be in determining the circumstances in which the null hypothesis is rejected in favor of an alternative hypothesis. This is your confidence in the decision reached and requires you to set a level of significance.

A *level of significance* (represented by the symbol alpha, α) represents the probability of rejecting the null hypothesis as false when it is in fact true, in other words, in concluding that meaningful differences exist when in fact they do not. You may adopt whatever level of significance appears to be appropriate to the purposes and potential consequences of decisions based on the research. Generally, the greater the consequences of the decision the higher you would set the level of significance, thereby reducing the chances of rejecting the null hypothesis when it is in fact true. Common levels of significance are .05 and .01, meaning that there is a 5 percent or 1 percent chance, respectively, of rejecting the null hypothesis when it is in fact true.

Levels of significance (and thus levels of confidence) are evaluated in light of the probabilities derived from areas under the normal curve. With a one-tailed test at the .05 level of significance the null hypothesis is rejected when probability of the observation is equal to or below 5 percent. This is the point approximately 1.6 standard deviations from the mean. With a two-tailed test at the .05 level of significance, the .05 is divided by two and the null hypothesis is rejected when the probability of the obser-

Example A: A One-Tailed Test in Which the Alternative Hypothesis Is the Preferred Outcome

The Quincy Agency has developed a media plan specifically targeted toward men and women who are aged 55 and older. It is therefore hoped that advertising awareness among those who are aged 55 and older (A_{55+}) exceeds the awareness of those aged under 55 (A_{55-}).

$$H_0: A_{55+} = A_{55-}$$
$$H_1: A_{55+} > A_{55-}$$

Example B: A Two-Tailed Test in Which the Direction of Difference Is Not Specified— Preferred Outcome Is One of the Alternative Hypothesis

A new children's cereal has been created. It is expected (and hoped) that the cereal will appeal (*A*) more to one gender so that media and creative efforts can be specifically targeted to the needs and appeals of that gender of child.

$$H_0: A_{boys} = A_{girls}$$
$$H_1: A_{boys} > A_{girls}$$
$$H_2: A_{boys} < A_{girls}$$

Example C: A Two-Tailed Test in Which the Direction of Difference Is Not Specified— Preferred Outcome Is Acceptance of the Null Hypothesis

The advertising campaign for Dandy Detergent has just begun to air. The campaign is designed to increase positive attitudes toward the brand (*IPA*) among both infrequent users and among trier-rejectors of the brand.

$$H_0: IPA_{infrequent} = IPA_{rejectors}$$
$$H_1: IPA_{infrequent} > IPA_{rejectors}$$
$$H_2: IPA_{infrequent} < IPA_{rejectors}$$

FIGURE 16.3
Translating beliefs into hypotheses.

vation is equal to or below 2.5 percent. This is the point approximately ± 2 standard deviations from the mean. Critical values for determining levels of significance for any point on the normal curve can be obtained from Appendix B, Table B.2. Critical values for the most common levels of significance for one- and two-tailed tests are

Significance Level	One-Tailed Test	Two-Tailed Test
.05	1.65	1.96
.01	2.33	2.58
.001	3.10	3.30

With this in mind, we can now explore ways in which inferential statistics can help you better understand the nature of the results obtained from a particular research study.

MAKING JUDGMENTS ABOUT A SINGLE MEASURE FROM ONE SAMPLE

Two types of analyses may be conducted when a single sample is available. The first type of analysis compares a sample mean or percentage to the corresponding mean or percentage in a larger population. An advertiser, for example, may have a data base of scores obtained from past evaluations of his commercials. This advertiser might want to compare the tested performance of each proposed new commercial to the scores in the data base to see whether a new commercial meets or exceeds the performance of past efforts.

The second type of analysis examines the internal characteristics of a single sample. An advertiser may show a group of consumers four commercials and ask them to select the one that they feel best communicates a particular message. Each commercial is selected by a certain percentage of the sample. The advertiser must then determine if the pattern of preferences within this sample reflects a significant preference of one commercial over the others.

The next section explains the procedures that can be used to analyze data in each of these types of circumstances.[1]

Comparing a Sample Mean to a Population Mean

The statistical test used to compare a sample mean to a population mean is determined by sample size and assumptions of the normality of the distribution of scores.

Large Sample Size or Normal Distribution—Interval or Ratio Level of Measurement Imagine that McDonald's tests each proposed commercial before it is produced. Over time, several hundred of these tests are conducted. Given this large number of tests, many key measures, purchase intent, for example, show a range of response. Some commercials strongly increase purchase intent, some diminish purchase intent while most commercials fall in the slightly negative to slightly positive range. In other words, the distribution of scores obtained from prior tests closely resembles the normal distribution. McDonald's can use the population of prior tests to evaluate the performance of proposed commercials.

Null and alternative hypotheses are formulated to describe the relationship of the sample to the population. In this example, the comparison of a test commercial to the population of prior commercials requires that McDonald's formulate null and alternative hypotheses with regard to purchase intent. The null hypothesis would state the belief that the new test commercial is drawn from the same population as all prior test commercials and as a result there is no difference in mean level of purchase intent generated by the test commercial and past commercials. Acceptance of this null hypothesis indicates that the test commercial is as good as (neither better nor poorer than) the average of all prior commercials in the level of purchase intent generated. But, McDonald's does not want to settle for average. They want each test commercial to be better than prior commercials. Therefore, the alternative hypothesis would state that lev-

---

[1] All data is hypothetical. Brand and company names are used for illustrative purposes only.

els of purchase intent generated by the test commercial will be higher than the average of past commercials. This is a one-tailed test because McDonald's is specifying the direction of difference between the test commercial and the population of past commercials. They do not want to reject the null hypothesis in favor of a commercial that is poorer than the population of commercials. Mathematically, these hypotheses are expressed as

$$H_0: \quad \bar{x} = \mu$$
$$H_1: \quad \bar{x} > \mu$$

where $\bar{x}$ represents the mean purchase intent score for the test commercial and μ represents the mean of the population of commercials to which the test commercial is being compared. Finally, assume that McDonald's is strict in their decision making and wants to be very confident in the decisions they make based on the analysis. As a result, the level of significance is set to .05; they will be 95 percent certain that they do not reject H_0 when it is in fact true.

McDonald's tests their new commercial. The data needed to calculate whether or not to accept or reject H_0 is the following:

	Test Commercial	*Population*
Mean purchase intent (on a scale of 1 to 5 where 5 is the most positive)	4.3	3.1
Standard deviation	not required	1.1
Number in sample	100	not required

A comparison of the test commercial to the population of commercials is carried out through the formula:

$$Z = \frac{\bar{X} - \mu}{\frac{\sigma}{\sqrt{N}}}$$

where:

Z   represents the Z statistic used to determine area under the curve and the probability of the observed differences between means,

$\bar{X}$ represents the mean of the sample (in this case the test commercial),

μ represents the population mean (in this case the mean of all past commercials contained in the population data base of commercials),

σ represents the population standard deviation,

N   represents the number of observations in the sample.

The calculations involved in using this formula, in this example, are

$$Z = \frac{4.3 - 3.1}{\frac{1.1}{\sqrt{100}}} = \frac{1.2}{\frac{1.1}{10}} = \frac{1.2}{.11} = 10.91$$

The value obtained, 10.91, is compared to the values presented in Appendix B, Table B.2 and the critical values shown on page 362 (where it is seen that the critical

value for Z for a one-tailed test at the .05 level of significance is 1.65.) Since the value obtained in our comparison of means is greater than 1.65 the null hypothesis is rejected. McDonald's can conclude that the new commercial is better than prior commercials in the level of purchase intent generated. In fact, an examination of critical levels shows that a Z score of 10.91 exceeds the .001 level of confidence. McDonald's can be certain that there is less than one chance in 1,000 that rejecting the null hypothesis is incorrect.[2] H_1 can be accepted with a high level of confidence. The test commercial's mean level of purchase intent clearly exceeds the mean purchase intent of the population of prior test commercials.

Small Sample Sizes—Interval or Ratio Level of Measurement   A Z test lets you determine the statistical difference between the mean of any sample and the mean of a relevant population. There are, however, limitations to the use of this test. As stated earlier, a Z test may only be used when the sample is large (typically defined as thirty or more respondents) or when the population distribution is (or is assumed to be) normally distributed. When either of these assumptions are violated a different test must be used to compare a sample mean to a population mean. This alternative test, called the t test, takes into account the fact that the shape of a distribution for smaller sample sizes is not bell-shaped. These distributions, while still symmetrical, tend to be lower in the central peak and higher on the tails versus the standardized normal or bell curve. Because the shape of the curve is a reflection of sample size, curves for smaller samples are described in terms of their degrees of freedom that are equal to one less than the total number of individuals or observations in the sample.

Because the t test, similar to the Z test, compares the sample mean to the population mean the numerators of both equations are identical. However, while the denominator of the Z test uses the *population* standard deviation in the denominator of its equation the t test utilizes the *sample* standard deviation. The formula for conducting a t test that compares a sample mean to the mean of a population mean is therefore:

$$ t = \frac{\overline{X} - \mu}{\dfrac{s}{\sqrt{N}}} $$

The symbols used in this equation are the same as in the Z test except that s represents the sample standard deviation.

Imagine that McDonald's tested a new commercial among twenty-five individuals and obtained the following data:

	Test Commercial	*Population*
Mean purchase intent (on a scale of 1 to 5 where 5 is the most positive)	3.6	3.1
Standard deviation	1.5	not required
Number in sample	25	not required

---

[2] The outcome of a statistical test is typically written in terms of *p*, the final probability. In this example, the outcome would be written as $p < .001$ which means that the probability of this outcome (*p*) is less than (<) one in one thousand (.001).

As with the calculation of the Z score the null hypothesis predicts no difference in the mean level of purchase intent (H_0: $\bar{x} = \mu$) while the alternative hypothesis would state that the mean purchase intent score for the test commercial is higher than the mean purchase intent of the population of commercials (H_1: $\bar{x} > \mu$).

The calculation would be

$$t = \frac{3.6 - 3.1}{\frac{1.5}{\sqrt{25}}} = \frac{.5}{\frac{1.5}{.5}} = \frac{.5}{.3} = 1.66$$

The value obtained, 1.66, is compared to the values presented in Appendix B, Table B.3. The critical value of t for a one-tailed test at the .05 level of significance with twenty-four degrees of freedom is 1.711.[3] Since the value obtained in our comparison of commercials is less than 1.711 the null hypothesis cannot be rejected and must be accepted. In this test, McDonald's cannot conclude that the new commercial is better than prior commercials in the level of purchase intent generated.

Comparing a Sample Proportion to a Population Proportion

The prior Z and t tests used interval data to compare the mean level of response in a sample to the mean level of response among the population of relevant scores. A similar approach can be used to compare the distribution of responses on a nominal measure (where, as indicated in Chapter 15, no means are calculated) to the distribution of scores among the relevant population. This is a test of proportions.

Think about McDonald's trying to assess the impact of proposed commercials on consumers' intention to eat at McDonald's. In addition to asking a five-point purchase intent question they might also ask: "The next time you go to a fast food restaurant will you go to McDonald's or some other fast food restaurant?" Respondents answer "McDonald's" or "other." The percentage of respondents selecting each response option is calculated. McDonald's can compare the proportion of respondents saying "McDonald's" after seeing a test commercial to the percentage saying "McDonald's" within their population of prior tests. The formula they would use is

$$Z = \frac{p - P_u}{\sqrt{\frac{P_u Q_u}{N}}}$$

where

Z represents the Z statistic used to determine area under the curve and the probability of the observed difference between proportions,

p represents the sample proportion selecting the target response option (in this case "McDonald's"),

P_u represents the population proportion selecting the target response option (in this case "McDonald's"),

Q_u represents the population proportion selecting the alternative response option (in this case "other" fast food restaurant),

N represents the number of observations in the sample.

---

[3] The critical value is determined by locating the degrees of freedom in the first column (labeled *df*) and then reading across to the number in the appropriate significance column (in this case .05 one-tailed test).

Note how this formula is similar to the Z and t test formulas. The numerator calculates the difference between the proportions while the denominator reflects population distribution.

McDonald's tests their commercial among fifty individuals and obtains the following data:

	Test Commercial	*Population*
Percent saying "McDonald's"	75%	57%
Percent saying "other"	not required	43
Number in sample	50	not required

As with the calculation of the Z and t scores, the null hypothesis predicts no difference in the proportion of individuals who say that they will try McDonald's ($H_0: p = P_u$) while the alternative hypothesis would state that the proportion of individuals saying "McDonald's" after viewing the test commercial is higher than the percent saying "McDonald's" in the population of commercials ($H_1: p > P_u$). The level of significance is very stringent and is set at .01. The calculation would be

$$Z = \frac{.75 - .57}{\sqrt{\frac{.47 \cdot .53}{50}}} = \frac{.18}{\sqrt{.0049}} = \frac{.18}{.07} = 2.57$$

The value obtained, 2.57, is compared to the values presented in Appendix B, Table B.2 and the values of statistical significance shown on page 362 (where the critical value for Z for a one-tailed test at the .01 level of significance is 2.33). Since the Z value obtained in this comparison of the commercial proportions exceeds the critical value McDonald's can conclude that the proportion of respondents who say they intend to try McDonald's after seeing the test commercial is higher than the proportion of individuals saying "McDonald's" in the population of test commercials.

Examining the Internal Characteristics of a Single Sample

The prior tests took a single measure, a mean or proportion, from a single sample of respondents and compared the level of this measure to the level of the same measure within the relevant population. There are times, however, when an advertiser needs to examine the overall pattern of response to a single measure without worrying about its distribution within the population. The most common approach to examining the internal characteristics of responses to a single measure is chi-square.

The *chi-square test* (represented by the symbol x^2) allows you to examine the frequency distribution within a single sample and then determine if the pattern is significant. As a result, the chi-square test is appropriate for all ordinal, interval, and ratio level data.

Imagine that an advertiser has four commercials and wishes to determine which commercial best communicates the target message. All four commercials are shown to a sample of consumers and, after all are seen, each respondent selects the commercial

he or she thinks was the best communicator. Chi-square lets the advertiser examine the pattern of response to determine whether, from a statistical perspective, one commercial is seen as better than the others.

The chi-square test examines a trend in actual sample frequencies in light of the trend that would be obtained if there were no deviations from chance. In other words, the chi-square test compares observed frequencies (O) with expected frequencies (E) thereby testing the "goodness of fit" of the observed distribution with the expected distribution. The logic is that the greater the extent to which the observed frequencies depart from expected frequencies the greater the likelihood that there are *real* differences among the levels of response. Consequently, the null hypothesis in the chi-square test is that observed frequencies are equivalent to expected frequencies while the alternative hypothesis states that the two sets of frequencies are not equal.

The formula used to calculate the chi-square statistic is

$$x^2 = \sum \frac{(O_i - E_i)^2}{E_i}$$

where

x^2 represents the value of the chi-square statistic,

O_i represents the observed frequency in the ith cell,

E_i represents the expected frequency in the ith cell.

The use of this formula is shown in the following example.

Assume that 112 individuals participated in a commercial test. Each respondent was shown four commercials and then asked to indicate which commercial best communicated the desired essential message. The preferences of this sample of individuals were as follows:

Commercial	Frequency of Respondents Selecting Commercial As Best Communicator
1	49
2	20
3	32
4	11
Total	**112**

An analysis of this data begins with a formulation of the null and alternative hypothesis. The null hypothesis states that the number of respondents selecting each commercial will be equal among the cells, in this case equal to an expected frequency of 28.[4] The alternative hypothesis states that the pattern of observed frequencies will significantly deviate from the expected frequencies. A level of significance is then se-

---

[4] The expected frequency is calculated by dividing the total number of observations by the number of cells, in this case $112 \div 4 = 28$.

lected. In this example, significance is set to .05. The computation of the chi-square statistic using the prior formula would be

$$x^2 = \frac{(49-28)^2}{28} + \frac{(20-28)^2}{28} + \frac{(32-28)^2}{28} + \frac{(11-28)^2}{28}$$

$$x^2 = \frac{(21)^2}{28} + \frac{(-8)^2}{28} + \frac{(4)^2}{28} + \frac{(-17)^2}{28}$$

$$x^2 = \frac{441}{28} + \frac{64}{28} + \frac{16}{28} + \frac{289}{28}$$

$$x^2 = 15.75 + 2.29 + .57 + 10.32$$

$$x^2 = 28.93$$

The x^2 distribution is a family of curves that vary according to the underlying number of degrees of freedom. Degrees of freedom for this type of x^2 distribution (that is, for examining the internal characteristics of a single measure) is the number of cells in the analysis minus one. Since there were four cells in this example there are three degrees of freedom. Levels of significance for the x^2 distribution are shown in Appendix B, Table B.4. The value obtained, 28.93, is compared to the critical value of x^2 at the .05 level of significance with 3 degrees of freedom. The critical value is 7.82.[5] Since the value obtained in the analysis of commercial preferences is more than 7.82 the null hypothesis is rejected and the alternative hypothesis is accepted. In fact, the level obtained even exceeds the critical value at the .01 level of confidence. As a result, the advertiser can be *very* certain that the distribution of preferences are not equal and that one or more of the commercials were preferred over the others.

MAKING JUDGMENTS ABOUT A SINGLE MEASURE FROM TWO INDEPENDENT SAMPLES

Often the population mean and standard deviation are unknown or the required analysis involves comparing two groups to each other rather than one group to the relevant population. This is the situation faced by Mary and Roberta earlier in this chapter. Fortunately, comparing the mean or proportion from two independent samples follows the same logic and procedures as when comparing a sample mean to a population mean. As with the prior tests, the specific test used reflects sample size and level of measurement used.

As in the prior sections, we will examine the specific statistical techniques within the context of hypothetical examples.

Comparing Two Means From Independent Samples

Large Sample Sizes—Interval or Ratio Level of Measurement Advertisers are often interested in comparing groups of individuals. They may be interested in groups

---

[5] This table is read similarly to Table B.3. To read the chi-square table find the degrees of freedom in the first column and read across until the column with the appropriate level of significance is found. The number at the intersection is the critical value of chi-square.

that differ in terms of an advertising-related variable such as advertising awareness, advertising exposure, or exposure to different forms of advertising. Additionally, they may want to compare groups that differ on specific characteristics, for example, they may want to compare the attitudes of brand users versus nonusers or younger versus older consumers.

Imagine that Amoco Oil is interested in comparing motorists' reactions to their commercials versus motorists' reactions to Shell Oil commercials. Specifically, Amoco wants to determine whether their commercials are more, less, or equivalent in believability to the Shell commercials. The research that explores this question is two-tailed (the directionality of the difference is not specified) and there are one null and two alternative hypotheses. The null hypothesis states that the mean believability of the Amoco (A) commercials is equal to the mean believability of the Shell (S) commercials ($H_0: \overline{x}_A = \overline{x}_S$). The first alternative hypothesis states that the mean of Amoco commercials is higher than the mean of the Shell commercials ($H_1: \overline{x}_A > \overline{x}_S$) while the second alternative hypothesis states that the mean of the Amoco commercials is less than the mean of the Shell commercials ($H_2: \overline{x}_A < \overline{x}_S$). The level of significance is set to .05.

Amoco selects two groups of gasoline purchasers and exposes one group of fifty respondents to three Amoco commercials and a different group of forty respondents to three Shell commercials. After all three commercials, in addition to other measures, they ask respondents to assess believability using a five-point scale. The relevant data from the research is

	Amoco Commercials	Shell Commercials
Mean believability (on a scale of 1 to 5 where 5 is the most believable)	4.2	3.6
Variance	1.7	1.5
Number in sample	50	40

The formula needed to compute the level of significance of the difference between the two means drawn from these two samples is

$$Z = \frac{\overline{X}_1 - \overline{X}_2}{\sqrt{\dfrac{s_1^2}{N_1} + \dfrac{s_2^2}{N_2}}}$$

where

Z represents the Z statistic used to determine area under the curve and the probability of the observed difference between means,

$\overline{X}_1$ represents the mean of the first group (in this case those who saw the Amoco commercials),

$\overline{X}_2$ represents the mean of the first group (in this case those who saw the Shell commercials),

s_1^2 represents the variance of the first group,

s_2^2 represents the variance of the second group,

N_1 represents the number of observations in the first group,

N_2 represents the number of observations in the second group.

The calculation of the Z statistic would be

$$Z = \frac{4.2 - 3.6}{\sqrt{\dfrac{1.7}{50} + \dfrac{1.5}{40}}} = \frac{.6}{\sqrt{.034 + .0375}} = \frac{.6}{.267} = 2.25$$

The value obtained, 2.25, is compared to the values presented in Appendix B, Table B.2 and the list of critical values shown on page 362 (where the critical value of Z for a two-tailed test at the .05 level of significance is 1.96). Since the value obtained in our comparison is greater than 1.96 the null hypothesis is rejected and one of the alternative hypotheses can be accepted. Given the directionality of the difference in means between the two commercials, Amoco can accept the second alternative hypothesis (H_2) and conclude that their commercials are more believable than Shell's commercials with a 95 percent level of confidence.

Small Sample Sizes   Similar to the comparison of the sample mean to population mean for small sample sizes, if the size of one or both samples is small (typically defined as thirty or fewer respondents) then the t test rather than the Z test is used. The formula used to calculate the t statistic for two independent groups is

$$t = \frac{\overline{X}_1 - \overline{X}_2}{\sqrt{\dfrac{(n-1)s_1^2 + (n_2 - 1)s_2^2}{(n_1 + n_2 - 2)}\left(\dfrac{1}{n_1} + \dfrac{1}{n_2}\right)}}$$

The two terms in the numerator represent the same values as in the Z test for two independent samples. They are the means of group 1 and group 2, respectively. The sample size of each group is represented by n_1 and n_2 while the variance of each group is represented by s_1^2 and s_2^2.

Assume the same circumstances and levels of response as in the prior example except that the sample sizes are smaller. There are twenty-five respondents in the Amoco group and there are twenty respondents in the Shell group. Given the means and variances from the prior case along with the revised smaller sample sizes the t statistic would be calculated as

$$t = \frac{4.2 - 3.6}{\sqrt{\dfrac{(24)(1.7) + (19)(1.5)}{(25 + 20 - 2)}\left(\dfrac{1}{25} + \dfrac{1}{20}\right)}} = \frac{.6}{\sqrt{\dfrac{40.8 + 28.5}{43}}(.04 + .05)}$$

$$= \frac{.6}{\sqrt{\dfrac{69.3}{43}}(.09)} = \frac{.6}{\sqrt{.145}} = \frac{.6}{.38} = 1.58$$

The value obtained, 1.58, is compared to the values presented in Appendix B, Table B.3. The critical value of t for a two-tailed test at the .05 level of significance with 43 degrees of freedom (sample size one + sample size two minus 2) is approximately 2.02. Since the value obtained in this comparison is less than 2.02 the null hypothesis cannot be rejected. Amoco cannot conclude, based on the difference in the means between the two small groups of respondents that their commercials are more believable than Shell commercials.

Determining the Difference Between Two Proportions

As you have seen, advertisers have many occasions for comparing the mean level of response between two groups. Beyond comparisons of means, advertisers often need to assess the difference in the proportion of two groups that differ in terms of an important behavior or characteristic.

Imagine that Toys "Я" Us has developed a media plan that is targeted toward both boys and girls. After the media plan has run for four months Toys "Я" Us conducts research to determine if awareness of the campaign is in fact at equivalent levels among boys and girls. The null hypothesis (which in this case Toys "Я" Us hopes to confirm) is that the proportion of boys aware of the advertising (P_{boys}) is equivalent to the proportion of girls aware (P_{girls}). The alternative hypotheses state that the proportion of boys aware is either greater than or less than the proportion of girls aware, as follows:

$$H_0: \qquad P_{boys} = P_{girls}$$
$$H_1: \qquad P_{boys} > P_{girls}$$
$$H_2: \qquad P_{boys} < P_{girls}$$

The level of significance for this research is set to .05.

A test of these hypotheses, or any hypothesis describing the relationship between two proportions, involves the same procedures used to test the difference between means. A test of proportions, however, uses the standard error of the difference between the two proportions instead of the standard error of the difference between the means. The formula used to determine the significance of the observed difference between two proportions is

$$Z = \frac{p_1 - p_2}{\sqrt{\left(\dfrac{n_1 p_1 + n_2 p_2}{n_1 + n_2}\right)\left[1 - \left(\dfrac{n_1 p_1 + n_2 p_2}{n_1 + n_2}\right)\right]\left(\dfrac{1}{n_1} + \dfrac{1}{n_2}\right)}}$$

where

p_1 represents the proportion in group 1 (in this case boys aware),

p_2 represents the proportion in group 2 (in this case girls aware),

n_1 represents the size of group 1,

n_2 represents the size of group 2.

Toys "Я" Us interviews a sample of 150 boys and 110 girls. Awareness of Toys "Я" Us advertising is 87 percent and 55 percent respectively. The calculation of the significance of the difference between these two proportions would be

$$Z = \frac{.87 - .55}{\sqrt{\left(\dfrac{(150 \times .87) + (110 \times .55)}{(150 + 110)}\right)\left[1 - \left(\dfrac{(150 \times .87) + (110 \times .55)}{(150 + 110)}\right)\right]\left(\dfrac{1}{150} + \dfrac{1}{110}\right)}}$$

$$= \frac{.87 - .55}{\sqrt{\left(\dfrac{(130.5) + (60.5)}{(260)}\right)\left[1 - \left(\dfrac{(130.5) + (60.5)}{(260)}\right)\right](.067 + .091)}}$$

$$= \frac{.87 - .55}{\sqrt{(.74)[1 - .74](.158)}} = \frac{.32}{\sqrt{.03}} = 1.85$$

The value obtained, 1.85, is compared to the values presented in Appendix B, Table B.2 and the list of critical values shown on page 362 (where it is seen that the critical value of Z at the .05 level of significance is approximately 1.68). Since the value obtained in our comparison is greater than 1.68 the null hypothesis must be rejected. Given the directionality of the difference between the proportion of boys and girls aware of the advertising, Toys "Я" Us must accept H_1 which states the proportion of boys aware of the advertising is greater than the proportion of girls aware.

MAKING JUDGMENTS ABOUT THE RELATIONSHIPS BETWEEN MEASURES

Contingency Tables and Chi-Square

One of the simplest techniques for examining the relationships between two or more variables is cross-tabulation. A cross-tabulation or contingency table lets you see how respondents with a given value on one variable responded to one or more other variables. Figure 16.4 illustrates a cross-tabulation, in this case, the relationship between product preference and education.

You construct this type of cross-tabulation in the following steps:

- First, on the horizontal axis list the name and value for each category of the first variable. In Figure 16.4 this is the name of the preferred product.

- Second, on the vertical axis, list the value or name for each category of the second variable. In Figure 16.4 this is the level of education.

KEY: COUNT COL % ROW % TOTAL %	**Brand of Cleaner**			
Level of Education	SUDZ	SHINZ	CLEANZ	
High School or Less	75 50% 60% 23%	30 24% 24% 8%	20 20% 16% 5%	125 33.3%
Some College	45 30% 36% 12%	70 56% 56% 19%	10 10% 8% 2%	125 33.3%
College Graduate or Beyond	30 20% 24% 8%	25 20% 20% 7%	70 70% 56% 19%	125 33.3%
	150 40%	125 33%	100 27%	

FIGURE 16.4
Contingency table.

- Third, for each respondent, locate the category or value on the horizontal axis that corresponds to his or her response on that variable.
- Fourth, for that same respondent, find the category or value on the vertical axis that corresponds to his or her response on that variable.
- Fifth, place a slash mark in the cell where the horizontal and vertical axis intersect.
- Sixth, tally all slash marks in each cell. Use these tallies to calculate the percentages for each row and column as well as for each individual cell.

Figure 16.4 is the end result of this process. The calculations presented in each table cell provide several insights into the pattern of response. The marginal totals provide insights into the overall pattern of response.

- Each table cell contains four pieces of data. First, the tally or frequency (COUNT) for each cell is presented. Thus, seventy-five individuals with a high school education selected SUDZ as their preferred brand. Second, the column percent (COL %) is presented. This figure represents the percentage of the total column falling into a particular cell. Thus, 50 percent of all those who preferred SUDZ had a high school education or less. Third, the row percent (ROW %) represents the percent of the total row falling into a particular cell. Thus, 60 percent of all those with a high school education or less preferred SUDZ. Finally, the percent of the total sample falling into a particular cell is reported (TOTAL%). Thus, 23 percent of the total sample had a high school education or less and preferred SUDZ.
- The marginal totals and percents describe the overall trend. Thus, from the horizontal margin we see that 40 percent of the total sample preferred SUDZ while 33 percent preferred SHINZ and 27 percent preferred CLEANZ. The data in the vertical margin tells us that one-third of the sample fell into each of the educational categories.

The overall trend in the data suggests that SUDZ is the preferred brand. However, a visual examination of the row totals indicates that it might be dangerous to assume that the preference for SUDZ is universal and constant among the three educational groups. From visual inspection, it appears that there may be a relationship between education and product preference. Those with lower levels of education appear to prefer SUDZ while those with higher levels of education appear to prefer CLEANZ. We can statistically evaluate the significance of the relationship between product preference and educational level using the chi-square test.

The chi-square test for two or more variables follows the same logic as the chi-square test for a single variable. The test compares the number of observations in each cell to the number of expected observations for that cell to determine if the pattern of response is affected by the relationship between the variables being examined. In this example, the chi-square test will answer the question: "Is product preference independent of educational level?"

To compute the chi-square statistic for a contingency table you must determine the frequency of observed and expected responses for each cell. The observed frequencies are obtained from the tally of responses. The expected frequencies for each cell are computed from the marginal totals through the formula

$$E_{ij} = \frac{R_i C_j}{n}$$

where

R_i represents the observed frequency in the ith row,

C_j represents the observed frequency in the jth column,

n represents sample size.

Figure 16.5 (page 376) revises the table shown in Figure 16.4 to illustrate the comparison of observed and expected frequencies and the method for computing expected frequencies. The chi-square statistic itself is calculated through the same formula as before:

$$x^2 = \sum \frac{(O_i - E_i)^2}{E_i}$$

In this case the degrees of freedom are calculated as the number of rows minus one $(R - 1)$ times the number of columns minus one $(C - 1)$. The chi-square statistic for the data shown in Figures 16.4 and 16.5 would be as follows:

$$x^2 = \frac{(75 - 50)^2}{50} + \frac{(45 - 50)^2}{50} + \frac{(30 - 50)^2}{50} + \frac{(30 - 41.7)^2}{41.7} + \frac{(70 - 41.7)^2}{41.7}$$

$$+ \frac{(25 - 41.7)^2}{41.7} + \frac{(20 - 33.3)^2}{33.3} + \frac{(10 - 33.3)^2}{33.3} + \frac{(70 - 33.3)^2}{33.3}$$

$$= \frac{(25)^2}{50} + \frac{(5)^2}{50} + \frac{(20)^2}{50} + \frac{(-11.7)^2}{41.7} + \frac{(28.3)^2}{41.7} + \frac{(-16.7)^2}{41.7}$$

$$+ \frac{(-13.3)^2}{33.3} + \frac{(-23.3)^2}{33.3} + \frac{(36.7)^2}{33.3}$$

$$= \frac{(625)}{50} + \frac{(25)}{50} + \frac{(400)}{50} + \frac{(136.9)}{41.7} + \frac{(800.9)}{41.7} + \frac{(278.9)}{41.7}$$

$$+ \frac{(176.9)}{33.3} + \frac{(542.9)}{33.3} + \frac{(1346.9)}{33.3}$$

$$= 12.5 + .5 + 8 + 3.3 + 19.2 + 6.7 + 5.3 + 16.3 + 40.4$$

$$= 112.2$$

Degrees of freedom for this x^2 distribution are calculated by multiplying the number of rows minus one by the number of columns minus one. In this example $(3 - 1) \times (3 - 1)$ or 4. Levels of significance for the x^2 distribution are shown in Appendix B, Table B.4. The value obtained in this example, 112.2, is compared to the critical value of x^2 at the .05 level of significance with 4 degrees of freedom which is 9.49. Since the value obtained in our example is greater than the critical value shown in the table, the null hypothesis is rejected and the alternative hypothesis is accepted. The advertiser can conclude that there is a meaningful relationship between respondents' educational level and product preference. Given the trend in the pattern of preferences it can be concluded that those with greater levels of education prefer CLEANZ while those with lower levels of education prefer SUDZ. Those with some college education appear to prefer SHINZ.

Correlation

A second technique for determining the relationship between two variables is correlation, a statistical measure of the covariation or association between two variables. A

Brand of Cleaner

Level of Education	SUDZ	SHINZ	CLEANZ	
High School or Less	O: 75 E: 50	O: 75 E: 41.7	O: 20 E: 33.3	125 33.3%
Some College	O: 45 E: 50	O: 70 E: 41.7	O: 10 E: 33.3	125 33.3%
College Graduate or Beyond	O: 30 E: 50	O: 25 E: 41.7	O: 70 E: 33.3	125 33.3%
	150 40%	125 33%	100 27%	

FIGURE 16.5
Observed and expected frequencies.
O = observed; E = expected.

correlation coefficient (noted by the symbol r) consists of two parts ranging in value from -1 to $+1$. The sign of the correlation coefficient, either $+$ or $-$, indicates the directionality of the association. The numeric component indicates the magnitude of the association. If the value of r equals $+1.0$ then there is a perfect positive correlation between the two variables. All of the observations fall on a straight line and as one variable increases so does the other. If the value of r equals -1.0 then there is a perfect negative correlation. Here, all of the observations fall on a straight line but as one variable increases the other decreases. The total absence of a relationship between two variables occurs when $r = 0$ (see Figure 16.6).

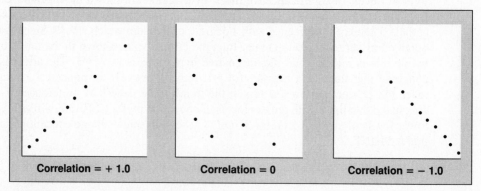

Correlation = + 1.0   Correlation = 0   Correlation = − 1.0

FIGURE 16.6
The range of the correlation coefficient.

	Believ	Like	Sex	Age
Believ	–	–	–	–
Like	.87	–	–	–
Sex	−.65	.02	–	–
Age	−.88	.06	.55	–

FIGURE 16.7
Correlation matrix.
Believ Commercial believability on a scale of 1 (very unbelievable) to 5 (very believable)
Like Commercial liking on a scale of 1 (not at all liked) to 5 (extremely well liked)
Sex Gender of respondent (1 represents males; 2 represents females)
Age Age of respondent

Correlation tells you about the simultaneous movement of two variables. Imagine that after viewing a commercial each respondent in the study was asked to use a five-point scale to indicate how well they liked the commercial and a different five-point scale to indicate how believable they felt the commercial was. In both cases '5' was the most favorable response. The correlation between the two variables is +.89. This would be interpreted to mean that those respondents who provided a high liking score also tended to provide a high believability score while those who provided a low liking score also tended to provide a low believability score. The +.89 correlation indicates that there is a strong relationship and that the two sets of scores move together in the same direction.

The manual calculation of a correlation coefficient is tedious. Statistical programs, however, can quickly calculate the interrelationships among one or more pairs of variables. When correlation coefficients for multiple pairs of variables are calculated, the set of correlations is reported in the form of a correlation matrix, as shown in Figure 16.7. The correlation between any two variables is found by locating the value at the intersection of the column specifying the first variable and the row specifying the second variable. Figure 16.7 shows that the correlation between commercial believability and commercial liking is .87 while the correlation between age and believability is −.88.

The statistical significance of a specific correlation between two variables can be determined by referring to Appendix B, Table B.5.

MAKING JUDGMENTS ABOUT A SINGLE MEASURE FROM THREE OR MORE INDEPENDENT SAMPLES

The Z and *t* tests described earlier are appropriate when you need to draw conclusions about the differences between two means representing two independent groups. However, Z and *t* tests are not appropriate when there are three or more means to compare. First, they are inefficient. The comparison of five sample means would require ten Z or *t* tests. Second, they may lead to the wrong conclusions. Increasing the number of comparisons increases the likelihood that a statistically significant difference will appear but will be due to sampling error as opposed to real, meaningful differences. Analysis of variance (ANOVA) eliminates these problems when multiple means are compared.

A *one-way ANOVA* looks at a single measure, such as purchase intent, and compares the mean score on this measure among three or more independent groups. The

null hypothesis in a one-way ANOVA assumes that all means are equivalent while the alternative hypothesis states that the variability or differences in the means being compared is greater than would be expected due to sampling error, that is, that at least one of the means is significantly different from the others in the test.

The conduct of an analysis of variance requires a significant amount of computation. As a result, most researchers use computerized statistical programs to conduct the analysis (see Appendix A). However, while the computer can "do the math" it is nevertheless important for you to understand the logic underlying ANOVA. The remainder of this section leads you through the logic and computations underlying ANOVA.

Consider the Amoco case discussed earlier in this chapter (pages 370 to 371) where Amoco wished to compare the believability of their commercials to that of Shell commercials. Assume now that Amoco wishes to compare the believability of their commercials not only to Shell but to those of Arco and Mobil as well. The null hypothesis states that the mean believability of the Amoco (A) commercials is equal to the mean believability of the other commercials [Shell (S), Arco (Ar), and Mobil (M)]:

$$H_0: \overline{x}_A = \overline{x}_S = \overline{x}_{Ar} = \overline{x}_M$$

The alternative hypothesis states that the variability among groups is greater than the variability within groups, indicating that at least one of the four means is not equivalent to one of the remaining means. The level of significance is set to .05.

Amoco selects four groups of gasoline purchasers and exposes each group of respondents to three of one company's commercials. After each set of commercials is viewed, they use a five-point scale to assess believability. The relevant data from the research is

	Amoco	Shell	Arco	Mobil
Mean believability	4.3	3.6	4.9	3.5
(on a scale of 1 to 5 where 5 is the most believable)				
Number in sample	50	60	55	65

The ANOVA is conducted through the following steps.

Step 1. Calculate the overall mean. This is accomplished by taking the sum of the products of each individual mean and the sample size on which that mean is based and then dividing by the overall sample size. In this example, the overall treatment mean (X_T) is calculated as

$$X_T = \frac{(50 \times 4.3) + (60 \times 3.6) + (55 \times 4.9) + (65 \times 3.5)}{230}$$
$$= \frac{215 + 216 + 269.5 + 227.5}{230}$$
$$= 4.03$$

Step 2. Calculate the sum of squares among groups (*SSA*). The *SSA* equals the sum of the products of each individual mean minus the overall treatment mean squared and then weighted by that mean's underlying sample size. In this example *SSA* would be calculated as

$$SSA = [50 \times (4.3 - 4.03)^2] + [60 \times (3.6 - 4.03)^2] + [55 \times (4.9 - 4.03)^2]$$
$$+ [65 \times (3.5 - 4.03)^2]$$
$$= 3.65 + 11.09 + 41.63 + 18.26$$
$$= 74.63$$

Step 3. Calculate the degrees of freedom (*df*) for the *SSA*. This is calculated by subtracting one from the total number of groups, in this case, $4 - 1$ or 3.

Step 4. Calculate the mean sum of squares among groups (*MSA*). This figure represents the variation across the sample means. The *MSA* increases in direct proportion to increases in differences among the individual group means. The *MSA* is calculated by dividing the *SSA* by the degrees of freedom for the *SSA*. In this example, the *MSA* would be calculated as

$$MSA = \frac{SSA}{df}$$
$$= \frac{74.63}{3}$$
$$= 24.88$$

Step 5. Calculate the sum of squared error (*SSE*). The procedure for calculating the *SSE* is similar to that of calculating variance and standard deviation. The *SSE* represents the sum of the squared differences of each observation in the sample and that observation's group mean. Thus, in this example *SSE* would be the sum of the square of each observation in the Amoco group minus 4.3 plus the sum of the square of each observation in the Shell group minus 3.6 plus the sum of the square of each observation in the Arco group minus 4.9 plus the sum of the square of each observation in the Mobil group minus 3.5. In this example, this sum equals 1,236.

Step 6. Calculate the degrees of freedom for the *SSE*. This is calculated by subtracting one from the total number individuals in the sample minus the number of groups, in this case, $230 - 3$ or 227.

Step 7. Calculate the amount of the variation within the groups. This number, mean square error (*MSE*) is calculated by dividing the *SSE* by the degrees of freedom for the *SSE*. In this example, the *MSE* would be calculated as

$$MSE = \frac{SSE}{df}$$
$$= \frac{1236}{227}$$
$$= 5.44$$

Step 8. Calculate the F statistic. The F statistic equals the *MSA* divided by the *MSE*. In this case the F statistic $= 24.88 \div 5.44$ or 4.57.

The F statistic represents the ratio of between group variance to within group variance. An F statistic greater than one indicates that between group variance is greater than within group variance. An F statistic less than one indicates that within group variance is greater than between group variance. Therefore, in order for the null hypothesis to be rejected the F statistic must be some amount greater than one. The exact amount needed for an F statistic to be significant is determined by the F distribution. Computer programs use the number of degrees of freedom in the numerator and

denominator of the F statistic to determine the level of significance.[6] In this example, the F statistic is significant at $p < .01$.

The results of a one-way ANOVA are typically presented in the following format:

Source of Variation	Sum of Squares	Degrees of Freedom	Mean Square	F Statistic	Significance
Groups	74.63	3	24.88	4.57	$p < .01$
Error	1,236.00	227	5.44		

SOME CAUTIONS

Statistical tests are powerful tools that help researchers determine how confident they can be in the conclusions that they draw from survey data. However, the power of these tools means that they must be used with care. Three cautions are particularly noteworthy.

Let statistical tests inform your judgment, not replace it. A statistically significant difference between means tells you that the observed difference between two means is due to underlying differences in the populations and not due to random error. In most advertising research situations (that use moderate sample sizes) statistically significant differences are also meaningful differences. However, statistical tests of mean differences, such as the Z and t tests, are greatly affected by sample size. Consider the test of the Amoco and Shell commercials discussed earlier in this chapter (pages 370 to 371). While the scores in the two tests were identical, the means were only statistically different in the test involving a large sample size. Given these statistical tests' sensitivity to sample size you should never blindly follow the results of your statistical tests. Use judgment and common sense in addition to statistical tests to interpret all differences between means and proportions.

Be aware of the sensitivity of the chi-square test to sample size. Sample size and distribution characteristics also affect the types of insights provided by the chi-square test. Examine the two distributions shown in Figure 16.8. Each distribution is identical in terms of the percent of the sample falling into each cell of the contingency table. And yet, because of its sensitivity to sample size, the chi-square statistic is significant only in the distribution shown on the right of Figure 16.8. Thus, you should always interpret the findings of your chi-square test in the context of *both* the distribution of scores and the sample size underlying the distribution. It may be misleading to interpret a nonsignificant chi-square statistic as indicative of no relationship if that finding is solely due to the presence of a small sample size. Additionally, the distribution itself affects the calculation of the chi-square statistic. A chi-square should not be computed if there are less than five observations in any cell of the contingency table.

Correlation is not predictive. Correlation indicates the relationship between two variables. A strong positive correlation indicates that the two variables generally move together in the same direction. Correlation, however, does indicate causation; it does not indicate that one variable *causes* the movement in the other or that a change in one will result in a change in the other. For example, it would be erroneous to conclude from a +.89 correlation between commercial liking and purchase intent that causing

---

[6] Statistical tables are also available to determine the significance level of an F-value.

	Aware	Not aware
Male	O: 16 E: 13	O: 10 E: 16
Female	O: 10 E: 13	O: 16 E: 13

	Aware	Not aware
Male	O: 160 E: 130	O: 100 E: 160
Female	O: 100 E: 130	O: 160 E: 130

FIGURE 16.8
Sensitivity of the chi-square to sample size.
O = observed; E = expected.

people to like the commercial more will cause people to have higher levels of purchase intent.

Summary

Researchers need to have confidence in the decisions that they make. When decisions are based on research data, statistical tests are used to determine if observed differences between groups of individuals or if observed relationships between two measures are meaningful and important (and thus should be a factor in decision making) or if the observations imply reflect random fluctuation or error in the data (and thus should be ignored).

Statistical testing uses hypothesis testing to determine levels of confidence. A null hypothesis states that there are no differences between the groups being compared while alternative hypotheses state that there are meaningful differences. The circumstances in which the null hypothesis is accepted or rejected in favor of an alternative hypothesis depends on the level of significance set by the researcher.

The specific type of statistical test used to evaluate group differences and relationships between measures is determined by the nature and size of the sample and the data's level of measurement. The appropriate test to use in various circumstances is summarized below:

Comparison	*Sample Size*	*Level of Measurement*	*Statistical Test*
Sample mean to population mean	Large	Interval or ratio	Z test
Sample mean to population mean	Small	Interval or ratio	*t* test
Sample proportion to population proportion	N/A	Nominal	Z test of proportion
Two sample means	Large	Interval or ratio	Z test
Two sample means	Small	Interval or ratio	*t* test
Two sample proportions	N/A	Nominal	Z test of proportions
Frequency of observations:			
One or more variables	N/A	Nominal, interval, or ratio	Chi-square
Association of two variables	N/A	Nominal, interval, or ratio	Correlation
Three or more sample means	N/A	Interval or ratio	ANOVA

N/A = not applicable.

The formulas used in each of these situations are shown in Figure 16.9.

Sample Mean to Population Mean: Z test of Means

$$Z = \frac{\overline{X} - \mu}{\frac{\sigma}{\sqrt{N}}}$$

where

Z represents the Z statistic used to determine the area under the curve and the probability of the observed differences between means,

$\overline{X}$ represents the sample mean,

μ represents the population mean,

σ represents the population standard deviation,

N represents the number of observations in the sample.

Sample Mean to Population Mean: *t* test of Means

$$t = \frac{\overline{X} - \mu}{\frac{s}{\sqrt{N}}}$$

where

t represents the t statistic used to determine the area under the curve and the probability of the observed differences between means,

$\overline{X}$ represents the sample mean,

μ represents the population mean,

s represents the population standard deviation,

N represents the number of observations in the sample.

Sample Proportion to Population Proportion: Z test of Proportions

$$Z = \frac{p - P_u}{\sqrt{\frac{P_u Q_u}{N}}}$$

where

Z represents the Z statistic used to determine the area under the curve and the probability of the observed difference between proportions,

p represents the sample proportion selecting the target response option,

P_u represents the population proportion selecting the target response option,

Q_u represents the population proportion selecting the alternative response option,

N represents the number of observations in the sample.

(*continued*)

FIGURE 16.9
Statistical formulas.

Two Sample Means: Z test

$$Z = \frac{\overline{X}_1 - \overline{X}_2}{\sqrt{\frac{s_1^2}{N_1} + \frac{s_2^2}{N_2}}}$$

where

Z represents the Z statistic used to determine the area under the curve and the probability of the observed differences between means,

$\overline{X}_1$ represents the mean of the first group,

$\overline{X}_2$ represents the mean of the second group,

s_1^2 represents the variance of the first group,

s_2^2 represents the variance of the second group,

N_1 represents the number of observations in the first group,

N_2 represents the number of observations in the second group.

Two Sample Means: t test

$$t = \frac{\overline{X}_1 - \overline{X}_2}{\sqrt{\frac{(n-1)s_1^2 + (n_2-1)s_2^2}{(n_1 + n_2 - 2)}\left(\frac{1}{n_1} + \frac{1}{n_2}\right)}}$$

where

t represents the t statistic used to determine the area under the curve and the probability of the observed differences between means,

$\overline{X}_1$ represents the mean of the first group,

$\overline{X}_2$ represents the mean of the second group,

s_1^2 represents the variance of the first group,

s_2^2 represents the variance of the second group,

n_1 represents the number of observations in the first group,

n_2 represents the number of observations in the second group.

Two Sample Proportions: Z test of Proportions

$$Z = \frac{p_1 - p_2}{\sqrt{\left(\frac{n_1 p_1 + n_2 p_2}{n_1 + n_2}\right)\left[1 - \left(\frac{n_1 p_1 + n_2 p_2}{n_1 + n_2}\right)\right]\left(\frac{1}{n_1} + \frac{1}{n_2}\right)}}$$

where

p_1 represents the proportion in group 1,

p_2 represents the proportion in group 2,

n_1 represents the size of group 1,

n_2 represents the size of group 2.

(*continued*)

Frequency of Observations with One Variable: Chi-square

$$x^2 = \sum \frac{(O_i - E_i)^2}{E_i}$$

where

x^2 represents the value of the chi-square statistic,

O_i represents the observed frequency in the ith cell,

E_i represents the expected frequency in the ith cell.

FIGURE 16.9 (continued)

Finally, statistical tests must be conducted and interpreted with care and an understanding of their limitations. The results of statistical tests should inform your judgment, not replace it.

Review Questions

1. What are the three characteristics of the *bell-shaped* curve? How is the *standard normal distribution* a special case of this type of distribution?
2. What is the relationship between standard deviation and area under the normal curve?
3. What is a *probability*?
4. How do standard deviation and area under the normal curve determine probability?
5. What is the probability of obtaining a score at least $+1.5$ standard deviation from the mean of the normal curve?
6. What area of the normal curve falls between -1.5 and $+1.5$ standard deviations from the mean of the normal curve?
7. What is a *hypothesis*?
8. What is a *null hypothesis*? What does it represent?
9. What is an *alternative hypothesis*? What does an alternative hypothesis represent?
10. What does the term *tails* refer to in the context of hypothesis testing?
11. What is the difference between a *one-tailed* and *two-tailed* test? In what situations is each type of test most appropriate?
12. What is a *level of significance*? What is the role of level of significance in hypothesis testing?
13. Two common levels of significance are .01 and .05. What do these numbers represent? How can they be explained to a nonstatistician?
14. In what two types of comparisons is a *Z test* appropriate? What types of data are needed to conduct a *Z* test in each circumstance?
15. What does it mean when we say that the computed *Z* statistic exceeds the critical value? How can you explain implications of this situation to a nonstatistician?

16. In what two types of circumstances is a *t test* appropriate? What types of data are needed to conduct a *t* test in each?

17. What does it mean when we say that the computed *t* statistic exceeds the critical value? How can you explain implications of this situation to a nonstatistician?

18. In what two circumstances is a *test of proportions* appropriate? What types of data are needed to conduct a test of proportions in each circumstance?

19. In what circumstances is a *chi-square test* appropriate? What types of data are needed to conduct a chi-square test in each circumstance?

20. What does it mean when we say that the computed chi-square-statistic exceeds the critical value? How can you explain implications of this situation to a nonstatistician?

21. What is a *cross-tabulation* or *contingency table*?

22. What do *row counts* and *column counts* represent in a contingency table?

23. In what circumstances is *correlation* appropriate?

24. What is the range or numeric values that the correlation coefficient can take? Interpret what the extreme and central values of the correlation coefficient represent.

25. Explain the relationship between a strong correlation coefficient and causation.

26. How do you tell if a correlation is statistically significant?

27. What is a one-way ANOVA? In what circumstances is it used?

28. What are the null and alternative hypotheses in a one-way ANOVA?

29. What does the F statistic represent? How is the significance of the F statistic determined?

30. Describe the cautions associated with the use and interpretation of statistical tests.

Application Exercises[7]

1. Each of the following situations represents a researchable circumstance an advertiser and his or her agency might encounter. Read each hypothetical situation and then (a) translate each situation into a null and alternative hypotheses or hypotheses, (b) explain why you decided to make the comparison one-tailed or two-tailed, (c) state whether the preferred outcome is acceptance or rejection of the null hypothesis, and (d) set an appropriate probability level for acceptance or rejection of the null hypothesis.

   • KXXC is a local radio station. In March they measured awareness of their new morning format. Between March and August they spent $100,000 advertising their new format. In August they again measured awareness. KXXC wants to compare awareness at these two points in time to determine the extent to which awareness has increased.

   • David Palmer is running for a seat on the city council. His friends, who are helping with his advertising, have suggested two slogans: "Put Palmer on the Council" and "Palmer: The Citizen's Choice." David's staff conducts research to determine which slogan should be selected.

   • The San Diego Union-Tribune has just redesigned their business section. The paper wants to determine readers' reaction to the new design versus the prior design. It is hoped that the redesigned business section is more appealing than the prior format.

---

[7] All application exercises are hypothetical. Actual organizations are used for illustrative purposes only.

2. Each of the following situations represents a circumstance in which an advertiser needs to rely on research data to aid in decision making. For each hypothetical situation do the following: (1) read the question or questions posed, (2) conduct the statistical test or tests that will provide you with the insights to answer the question(s), and (3) use the data and the results of your statistical test to answer the question(s).

- *Based on ratings of believability and purchase intent, which of two tested commercials should be recommended for production?* The research was conducted among a sample of the commercials' target audience. A hundred (100) respondents saw Commercial A and 100 different respondents saw Commercial B. Believability and purchase intent were both measured through the use of five-point scales where '1' was the least positive (i.e., extremely unbelievable; would definitely not buy) and '5' was the most positive (i.e., extremely believable; would definitely buy) response option.

		Commercial A	Commercial B
Believability:	Mean	4.2	3.7
	Variance	1.3	1.1
Purchase:	Mean	4.0	3.3
	Variance	1.2	1.4

- Over the years, the AAbCo Corporation has used a number of celebrities as corporate spokespeople. This year, AAbCO is considering three individuals who, for security reasons, have been identified as Persons X, Y, and Z. The appeal of each was assessed by showing a group of twenty-five target audience individuals the person's picture and then asking for a rating of appeal. Appeal was measured through the use of seven-point scale where '1' was the least positive (i.e., extremely unappealing) and '7' was the most positive (i.e., extremely appealing) response option. The appeal of Persons X, Y, and Z were then compared to the appeal of past spokespeople. *Which, if any, person would you recommend?*

	Person X	Person Y	Person Z	Past Spokespeople
Appeal (mean)	4.3	5.9	6.3	5.5
Standard deviation	1.5	1.2	1.1	not required
Number in sample	25	25	25	not required

- San Diego University has initiated a communication program designed to enhance the University's image among graduating high school seniors in cities greater than 100 miles from the university. This was done to recruit seniors from beyond the immediate San Diego area. The university has tracked attitudes of these target individuals over time and has an extensive base of past survey results. After the communication program has run for a year the university surveys the attitudes of 200 target individuals: 100 men and 100 women. The key measure used to evaluate the program is "consideration of San Diego University" measured on a seven-point scale of '1' (would not at all consider) to '7' (would definitely consider). *Overall has the campaign been successful? Is the campaign more successful among women or men or does it affect the attitudes of each gender group equally?*

	Men	*Women*	*Past Surveys*
Consideration (mean)	4.1	4.5	3.2
Standard deviation	1.1	1.2	1.2

- The Becker Brewing Company has reformulated their no-alcohol beer. It is hoped that no-alcohol beer drinkers, especially those aged 25–39, will prefer the reformulated product to both the Old Becker product and their major competitor. Taste tests are conducted. Target audience individuals are given a sample of the Old Becker formulation, the New Becker formulation, and O'Doul's (Becker's major competitor). After tasting all three brands each respondent is asked to name the one brand that he or she prefers. *Overall, is the new Becker formulation preferred to the old formulation and O'Doul's? Has Becker accomplished its goal by fostering preference among the target audience of individuals aged 25–39?*

	Number of Individuals in Sample		
Brand Preferred	*Total Sample*	*Aged 25–32*	*Age 32–39*
Becker old formulation	72	36	36
Becker new formulation	97	32	75
O'Doul's	86	37	49

- The North Coast Environmental Action Committee is planning a communications program designed to increase the public's recycling behaviors. Specifically, it is designed to increase individuals' stated inclination to recycle aluminum cans. Two versions of the campaign are developed. One version uses fear of negative consequences to motivate recycling (i.e., more garbage, more landfills, etc.) while another version uses positive appeals (i.e., a better world for all of us). Each campaign is shown to 100 individuals. After viewing each campaign a respondent is asked: "After viewing this advertisement, would you say that you are now more or less likely to recycle aluminum cans?" *Which campaign, if any, would you recommend?*

	Fear	*Positive Appeals*
Percent saying "more likely"	82%	92%
Percent saying "less likely"	18	8

3. Refer to the application exercise at the end of Chapter 12. Use the data shown in the figure to answer the following questions:

   - Question 16 measures purchase intent. What statistical test can be used to determine if responses to this question differ as a function of respondents' gender?

   - The sample is divided into three groups: aged 18–34, 35–49, and 50 and older. What statistical test can be used to determine if responses to Question 17, the second purchase intent question, differ as a function of respondents' age?

   - What technique or techniques can you use to determine the association between responses to Questions 7a and 7b?

- Can ANOVA be used to determine which product benefit (Question 9) is the most preferred? Explain your decision.
- Which statistical test can be used to determine if any of the commercials are better liked versus the others? Explain your decision and how the test would be conducted.

4. Cynthia Howard is a political consultant. She is planning the new advertising program for Lee Ann Vasquez who is running for a seat in the Illinois State Senate. Lee Ann and Cynthia have a fundamental disagreement over the tone the advertising campaign should take. Cynthia wants a to use a hardhitting "negative" campaign to attack their opponent while Lee Ann wants to use a more positive, issues-oriented approach. They decide to settle their disagreement through research.

Two test ads are created. One ad, labeled "OH NO" is extremely negative and unrelenting in its attack on Lee Ann's opponent. The second ad, "Let Lee Ann," is positive in tone and focuses on Lee Ann's past accomplishments and plans for her role as state senator.

Three hundred adults of voting age residing in Lee Ann's district are randomly selected via mall-intercept interviews. While this number is relatively high for a communications test, they decided the extra expense to increase the sample was necessary so that they could be assured that there would be sufficient numbers of individuals in key subgroups of the total sample. One hundred fifty (150) adults see each commercial. After viewing the commercial each respondent is interviewed to determine his or her reactions to the commercial and the commercial's influence on his or her attitudes and anticipated voting behavior. Demographic information and information on past voting behaviors are collected at the end of the interview.

Cynthia analyzes the data and presents the following verbal report on the results to Lee Ann. Critique this report. What are the strengths of the report? What are the specific weaknesses of the report? How would you recommend addressing and eliminating the weaknesses? Do you agree with Cynthia's conclusion? Why or why not?

The Presentation

A full write-up of the results of the research is in front of you. The written report contains the full analysis and responses to all of the survey questions that we asked those individuals who saw the two commercials. Right now, I'd just like to highlight some of the most important findings.

As you know, one of the key questions we asked the respondents was: "Based on what you have just seen, if the election were held today would you say that you would be most likely to vote for Todd Andrews, Lee Ann Vasquez, or some other candidate?" The percent of respondents saying Lee Ann is shown on this chart.

	Commercial	
	"OH NO"	*"Let Lee Ann"*
Percent Likely to Vote for "Lee Ann"	60%	44%
(Base: All respondents)	(n = 150)	(n = 150)

On first glance it appeared that I was right and that the negative ad was more effective. Clearly, more people said that they would vote for Lee Ann after seeing "OH NO." Importantly, the 60 percent level is also higher than the average (55%) of all the other commercials that we have tested so far. It seemed that this was a really good commercial. But,

as I looked deeper into the data I saw that the results were not that simple. In fact, the reverse is true. Based on my analysis of the data I would recommend the positive ad. Here is why.

First, it occurred to me that the question we asked assumed that everyone would vote. We know this is not so. As a result, I eliminated from our analytical sample those individuals who said that they were unlikely to vote for any candidate for the district's state senate seat. When I did this, I found the following:

	Commercial	
	"OH NO"	*"Let Lee Ann"*
Percent Likely to Vote for "Lee Ann"	50%	55%
(Base: Likely voters)	(n = 120)	(n = 120)

As you can see, including nonvoters in our analysis really skewed the findings. When we eliminate these individuals from our analytical sample, more people said that they would vote for you after seeing "Let Lee Ann." It is comforting to know that after seeing either commercial, a majority of those we interviewed said that they would vote for you.

Next, I looked at attitude shift. That is, I looked at who the people supported before they saw "OH NO" and the candidate they supported after they saw the commercial. The trend was startling. Here is the shift after seeing "OH NO":

		Candidate Likely to Vote for	
		Lee Ann	*Other*
		Before Seeing "OH NO" Commercial	
Candidate Likely to Vote for	Lee Ann	50%	50%
After Seeing 'OH NO' Commercial	Other	50	50
(Base: Likely voters)		(n = 120)	(n = 120)

Your support in terms of the total percentage of the sample stayed the same. But, note where your support came from. You lost half of your supporters (the first column of data) after they saw "OH NO," but this was made up for by converting half of those who did not initially support you (the second column of data). This pattern is dangerous. While it is good that nonsupporters are converted it is very risky to run advertising that "turns-off" those who initially like you.

Here is the shift after seeing "Let Lee Ann":

		Candidate Likely to Vote for	
		Lee Ann	*Other*
		Before Seeing "OH NO" Commercial	
Candidate Likely to Vote for	Lee Ann	100%	10%
After Seeing "Let Lee Ann" Commercial	Other	0	90
(Base: Likely voters)		(n = 120)	(n = 120)

All of those who initially supported you stayed with you after seeing "LET LEE ANN" (the first column of data). Moreover, 10 percent of those who did not support you switched after seeing the commercial (the second column of data). I think that this pattern of response is much more positive and holds much more potential for long-term success.

Some questions we asked on the survey explain why this commercial was more effective and provide some direction for how we might revise the commercial to more powerfully affect those who do not currently support you.

We asked each respondent a number of attitude statements after the commercial was seen. I have grouped these statements into three groups: Would Make a Good Representative, The Kind of Person I Want in Office, and Just Another Politician. Obviously, we want more agreement with the first two statements and more disagreement with the last statement. Stronger levels of agreement are reflected in larger numbers on this chart:

	Commercial	
	"OH NO"	*"Let Lee Ann"*
Would be a good representative	1.4	3.9
Kind I want in office	1.6	4.1
Just another politician	4.5	2.1
(Base: Likely voters)	(n = 120)	(n = 120)

"Let Lee Ann" fosters much higher levels of agreement with positive statements and much lower levels of agreement with negative statements. Importantly, the positive attitudes displayed after seeing this commercial were true for both initial supporters and nonsupporters, but more so for initial supporters versus initial nonsupporters, as shown in this table:

	Commercial: "Let Lee Ann"	
	Initial Supporters	*Initial Nonsupporters*
Would be a good representative	4.0	3.8
Kind I want in office	4.1	4.1
Just another politican	2.0	2.2
(Base: Likely voters)	(n = 120)	(n = 120)

Clearly the potential to move current nonsupporters exists.

The commercial reaction checklist provides some clues for how we might revise "LET LEE ANN" to better appeal to nonsupporters. Overall, current nonsupporters versus supporters found the commercial less relevant and more confusing.

	Commercial: "Let Lee Ann"	
	Initial Supporters	*Initial Nonsuporters*
For people like me	78%	23%
Confusing	21	63
(Base: Likely voters)	(n = 120)	(n = 120)

Both issues can be addressed as we take the commercials into production.

17

ADVERTISING CONTENT ANALYSIS

Content analysis is a quantitative research technique that helps us better understand advertisers' practices, specific brand's advertising strategies, and the effects of advertising.

An understanding of advertisers' practices is important. This understanding, typically the result of nonbrand specific content analyses such as examinations of racial and gender roles in advertising, the uses of different types of selling propositions, and international differences in advertising tone and content, provides a detailed, multifaceted picture of advertising's current characteristics and uses.

Advertising agencies require an understanding of specific brands' advertising practices. Decisions regarding advertising tone, manner, and strategy are not made in a vacuum. Options in each of these areas are best enumerated and evaluated when there is an understanding of competitors' advertising practice. An understanding of competitive brands' advertising strategies, learned using content analysis, helps an advertiser determine the best way to structure his or her own brand's advertising program in light of what the competitors are showing and saying in their advertising.

Advertising content analysis can also be used with other quantitative research. In these instances, content analysis helps increase our understanding of the relationship between advertising characteristics and advertising effects. This understanding extends the theory of advertising and provides direction for advertisers who are evaluating their own strategic and creative options. This chapter discusses the characteristics and use of content analysis.

After reading this chapter, you will be able to

- Describe the characteristics of content analysis and the settings in which advertising content analysis is most commonly used.

- Plan and conduct an advertising content analysis.

- Analyze the information collected in a content analysis.

CONTENT ANALYSIS: CHARACTERISTICS AND USES

Advertising content analysis is the systematic, objective, and quantitative analysis of advertising conducted to infer a pattern of advertising practice or the elements of

brands' advertising strategies such as brand positioning, selling proposition, and creative tone.[1] This definition specifies both the characteristics of content analysis and its primary uses in advertising research.

The Characteristics of Content Analysis[2]

Advertising content analysis is systematic, objective, and quantitative.

Systematic   Advertising content analysis must be systematic and not haphazard. The degree to which one has confidence in the outcome of a content analysis is directly related to the extent to which the analysis is conducted in a systematic, planned manner. This means that the sampling and selection of the advertising examined in the content analysis proceeds in accordance with explicit and defensible rules and that the advertising is treated and examined in exactly the same way throughout the content analysis. A systematic approach to content analysis is presented in the next section.

Objective   Advertising content analysis must be objective. The validity of conclusions drawn from a content analysis is greatly reduced if personal idiosyncrasies and biases are allowed to influence the selection and examination of the advertising. As you will see in the next section, objectivity in content analysis is enhanced when

- there are clear and objective rules for advertising selection and examination,
- coding categories are well-defined,
- coders or examiners are well-trained and work independently of each other,
- data analysis is appropriate to the measurement level of data collected.

Quantitative   Advertising content analysis is a quantitative endeavor. Quantification is important because it increases precision in conclusions drawn and permits a more accurate description of results and the relationships between themes and elements observed in the advertising. It is, for example, more precise and meaningful to say that "ninety percent of all competitive advertising mentions the dual product benefits 'no fat and no cholesterol'" versus "most of our competitors' advertising discusses health benefits." Finally, the quantification of findings allows researchers to use statistical techniques to summarize and investigate the findings, increasing the potential for uncovering underlying relationships in the data.

The Uses of Content Analysis

Content analysis is used in academic and applied settings. Content analyses conducted in the former setting are generally concerned with identifying trends in advertising practices or in relating advertising characteristics to advertising effects. Applied content analysis, generally conducted by advertising agencies, is concerned with identifying the product positioning and advertising strategies of competitive brands.

---

[1] This definition is based on more general definitions of content analysis presented by B. Berelson, *Content Analysis in Communication Research* (New York, NY: Hafner, 1952) and F. Kerlinger, *Foundations of Behavioral Research* (New York, NY: Holt, Rinehart & Winston, 1973).

[2] The discussion in this section is adapted from Roger D. Wimmer and Jospeh Dominick, *Mass Media Research: An Introduction* (Belmont, CA: Wadsworth Publishing Co., 1987), 166–7.

Academic Content Analysis   Content analysis in this setting increases our understanding of advertising practices and the relationship between advertising characteristics and advertising effects. "Content analysis can assess the effects of environmental variables (e.g., regulatory, economic, and cultural) and source characteristics (such as attractiveness, credibility, and likeability) on message content in addition to the effects (cognitive, affective, and behavioral) of kinds of message content on receiver responses."[3] Descriptions of content analyses that address advertising practices are presented in Figure 17.1.

Research conducted by Stewart and Furse[4] provides an example of how content analysis can further our understanding of advertising effects. Stewart and Furse explored how television commercial characteristics influence commercial effectiveness by (1) performing an extensive content analysis of more than 1,000 commercials, (2) obtaining related recall, main message comprehension, and persuasion scores for this set of commercials, and then (3) statistically exploring how specific commercial characteristics identified by the content analysis predict or relate to recall, comprehension, and persuasion. One conclusion of the research was that the presence of a brand-differentiating message is the single most important executional determinant of recall and persuasion.[5]

Applied Content Analysis   Applied content analysis is typically conducted by advertising agencies and marketing research companies on behalf of advertisers and their agencies. The goal of this type of content analysis is to provide insights into competitive brands' product positioning, advertising tone and manner, advertising target audience, and other elements of advertising strategy. Information in these areas is extremely useful as an advertiser evaluates his or her own brand's advertising options.

CONDUCTING A CONTENT ANALYSIS

Applied and academic advertising content analyses follow the same sequence of steps. Figure 17.2 (page 396) shows these steps to be similar to the steps underlying the conduct of any quantitative research study (see Chapter 2). The process begins with the formulation of research questions or hypotheses; then the development of data collection instruments, data collection, and analysis of raw data, and ends with conclusions and application to decision making. The remainder of this section discusses each step in content analysis.

Specify the Research Hypotheses or Questions

Content analysis begins with a specification of the research hypotheses or questions (that is, what needs to be learned from the content analysis). The specification of hypotheses and questions is important because it helps focus the content analysis and influences decisions made at each of the succeeding planning steps.

---

[3] Richard H. Kolbe and Melissa S. Burnett, "Content-Analysis Research: An Examination of Applications with Directives for Improving Research Reliability and Objectivity," *Journal of Consumer Research* 18 (September 1991): 243–50.

[4] David Stewart and David Furse, *Effective Television Advertising* (Lexington, MA: Lexington Books, 1986).

[5] Ibid., 120.

Content analysis of the information content in television commercials. Stern and Resnick found that while the *overall* informativeness of television advertising had not changed between 1975 and 1986, there was a significant decline in the informativeness of weekday afternoon ads and institutional ads.[a]

A content analysis of animation and animated spokes-characters in television commercials. This study found that (1) the majority of spokes-characters in television commercials were human, animal personifications, or product personifications, (2) there were significantly more noncelebrity than celebrity spokes-characters, (3) the majority of spokes-characters were male, and (4) animated spokes-persons are increasingly being used to present high involvement products to adult audiences.[b]

An examination of the use of figures of speech in print and headlines. This content analysis found that certain figures of speech such as alliteration, assonance, and puns are more likely to be used in headlines than are nearly forty other types of figures of speech. Moreover, a relationship was found between executional aspects of a print ad and the type of figure of speech selected for the headline.[c]

An examination of how advertisers modify their print advertising for use in foreign countries. The research found that Japanese advertisers are much more likely than German advertisers to modify their home country advertising to respond to the specific cultural and social norms of a foreign country.[d]

An examination of the communication styles of female political candidates. The content analysis of thirty-nine ads prepared by female senatorial candidates found that female candidates primarily focused on issues and avoided negative messages in their ads. These ads also tended to highlight the candidates' competency as political figures and their past accomplishments.[e]

As examination of Black and White models and their activities in cigarette and alcohol ads. Similarities and differences were found in the portrayal of Black and White models in these types of ads. Both groups were shown with sexual suggestiveness and involvement in erotic or romantic activities. Black models, however, were more often shown in leisure activities while White models were more commonly shown at work. In addition, femininity is a more dominant theme in the representation of Black models while masculinity is the more dominant theme in the representation of White models.[f]

FIGURE 17.1
Examples of academic content analysis.
[a] Bruce L. Stern and Alan J. Resnick, "Information Content in Television Advertising: A Replication and Extension," *Journal of Advertising Research* 30 (June/July 1991): 36–46.
[b] Margaret F. Callcott and Wei-Na Lee, "A Content Analysis of Animation and Animated Spokes-Characters in Television Commercials," *Journal of Advertising* 23 (December 1994): 1–13.
[c] James H. Leigh, "The Use of Figures of Speech in Print Ad Headlines," *Journal of Advertising* 23 (June 1994): 17–33.
[d] John L. Graham, Michael Kamins, and Djoko Oetomo, "Content Analysis of German and Japanese Advertising in Print Media from Indonesia, Spain and the United States," *Journal of Advertising* 22 (June 1993): 5–15.
[e] Anne Johnston and Anne B. White, "Communication Styles and Female Candidates: A Study of the Political Advertising During the 1986 Senate Elections", *Journalism Quarterly* 71 (Summer 1994): 321–29.
[f] Leonard N. Reid, Karen W. King, and Peggy J. Kresher, "Black and White Models and Their Activities in Modern Cigarette and Alcohol Ads," *Journalism Quarterly* 71 (Winter 1994): 873–86.

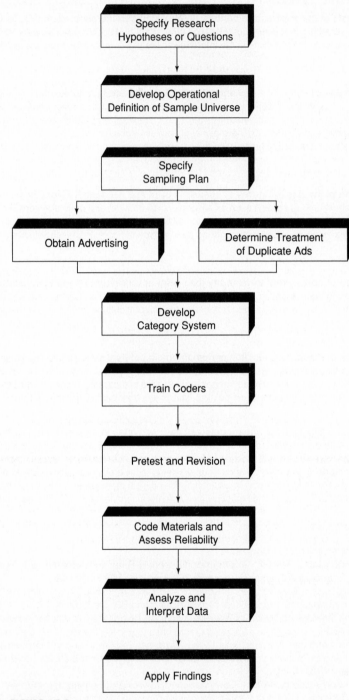

FIGURE 17.2
Steps in content analysis.

Some research hypotheses in content analysis typically flow from existing theory, prior research or changes in social conditions and/or perspectives. These hypotheses often suggest a relationship between two or more variables, for example:

- Prior research suggests that women use a style of interpersonal communication that is less aggressive, less assertive, more prosocial, and more supportive than the interpersonal style commonly used by men.[6] A content analysis will be conducted to determine if these aspects of interpersonal communication are reflected in each gender's political advertising. It is hypothesized that women candidates' political advertising will contain fewer aggressive and assertive elements and more prosocial and supportive elements versus male candidates' political advertising.

- Societal perceptions of male and female roles have changed over the past twenty years. A content analysis will be conducted to determine the extent to which these societal attitudes are reflected in advertising. It is hypothesized that print advertising published in 1975 will contain more instances of male and female role stereotyping versus advertising published in 1995.

Other content analyses raise and seek to answer questions that are implied or unanswered by prior research. A study of the portrayal of African-American and White models in cigarette and alcohol ads,[7] for example, reviewed prior research in these product categories and the portrayal of African American and White models in advertising and then asked these four questions:

1. Are model-associated *themes* featured in cigarette and alcohol ads with African American models different from those with White models?
2. Are *characteristics* of models featured in cigarette and alcohol ads with African American models different from those with White models?
3. Are *contextual elements* associated with model depictions in cigarette and alcohol ads with African American models different from those with White models?
4. Are model-associated *activities* featured in cigarette and alcohol ads with African American models different from those with White models?

Finally, other content analyses address planning- and business-related questions. The answer to questions raised in this type of applied content analysis helps individuals at advertising agencies and their clients better understand the advertising practices of specific competitors. This understanding helps them formulate stronger and more competitive advertising strategies for their own brand. An applied content analysis of competitive advertising might ask questions such as the following:

- What benefits are our competitors communicating in their advertising?
- What visual devices are being used?
- What types of promises, appeals, or selling propositions are being used?
- What tone or approaches are being used?
- Do different messages or selling propositions appear in different advertising media?

---

[6] See, Michael Burgoon, James P. Dillard, and Noel E. Doran, "Friendly or Unfriendly Persuasion: The Effects of Violation of Expectations of Males and Females," *Human Communication Research* 10 (1983): 283–94; Barbara Montgomery and Robert W. Norton, "Sex Differences and Similarities in Communicator Style," *Communication Monographs* 48 (1981): 121–32.

[7] Leonard N. Reid, Karen W. King, and Peggy J. Kresher, "Black and White Models and Their Activities in Modern Cigarette and Alcohol Ads," *Journalism Quarterly* 71 (Winter 1994): 873–86.

Develop an Operational Definition of the Sample Universe

An operational definition of the universe of materials to be studied is the outcome of this second step in content analysis. The operational definition responds to issues raised in the research questions or hypotheses and, similar to a population definition in survey sampling (see text pages 169, 172), precisely defines the population of interest, in this case the population of advertising that will be examined. A well-constructed operational definition eliminates all ambiguity and clearly defines all terminology.

Consider an operational definition that states: "The content analysis will examine instances of competitive advertising." This operational definition is unsatisfactory because it fails to clearly define or specify the following:

- What is meant by "competitors?" Do we mean any advertiser that sells a product in our product category? Or do we mean just national brands? Or just leading brands? Or those brands that advertise at the same budget level as our brand?
- What is meant by "advertising?" Do we mean advertising in all media? Or do we mean just television advertising? Or just electronic advertising? Or just print advertising? What about direct mail and promotional materials?
- What is the appropriate time period? Will we examine the last decade's worth of advertising? Or will we only examine the prior year? Or the prior six months?

In this example, a much better operational definition would be:

> The content analysis will examine the toothpaste advertising of Crest, Colgate, Arm & Hammer, Mentadent, and Aqua Fresh. The sample universe consists of ads appearing between January 1 and December 31, 1995 in the following media: television, radio, newspapers, and magazines.

Note how brands, media and dates of interest are all explicitly specified.

Specify a Sampling Plan and Obtain the Advertising

The sample plan determines how specific advertising from the operationally defined sample universe will be selected. Some content analyses use a census, that is, *all* exemplars of the sample universe are examined. A census is feasible whenever the advertising and the advertising context (that is, where the advertising appears) are small, manageable, and finite in nature, for example:

> The content analysis will examine advertising for all brands of motor oil appearing in *Car and Driver, Hot Rod,* and *Road & Track* magazines in issues dated January 1995 to December 1995.

As might be expected, a census is common in applied content analyses. There are three reasons for this. First, the amount of competitive advertising to be sampled and examined is generally limited to a small number of ads. Second, the business decisions that will be based on the content analysis require a high degree of confidence. Sampling from a small population of advertising increases the chances that "outlier" or nonrepresentative ads will be selected, resulting in the formation of inaccurate generalizations about the total population of ads. Third, a nearly complete census of radio, television, and print ads can be purchased from commercial companies such as Radio-TV Reports. The availability of nearly all competitive radio and television ads significantly

reduces the amount of search time and lets the researcher focus his or her efforts on data analysis rather than data collection.

Academic or theory-based content analyses are generally concerned with broad issues and large sets of advertising. In these cases, samples of the advertising are selected because it is simply not practical or even possible to conduct a complete census. It would be nearly impossible, for example, to examine all print advertising appearing in a given month or year. When sampling is used, researchers make certain that the sample of advertising selected for inclusion in the research is both representative of the universe from which it is drawn (and to which generalizations will be made) and sufficiently large to represent that universe. These criteria can be usually satisfied by the random, systematic, or stratified sampling techniques discussed earlier in the text (see pages 172–180). Examples of sampling techniques used in content analyses are shown in Figure 17.3.

Samples for more complicated or broader research questions can be obtained from multistage sampling. Here, decisions are made in a sequential fashion with regard to key parameters of advertising context and sample selection. A research question such as "Have there been changes in the types of products advertised in women's

---

Example 1

Commercials were selected using a computer program so that each day of the week received four randomly chosen combinations of seven possible television stations and five possible dayparts. The stations included in the study were ABC, CBS, NBC, Fox, and three cable stations CNN2, MTV, and Nickelodeon. They were chosen in an attempt to obtain programming representative of a diverse television audience. The television dayparts were 7:00 A.M.–11:00 A.M., 11:00 A.M.–4:00 P.M., 4:00 P.M.–7:00 P.M., 7:00 P.M.–10:00 P.M., and 10:00 P.M.–12:00 P.M. Taping took place during September 1990. All commercials appearing during a designated program-daypart combination were included in the content analysis.[a]

Example 2

Spot and network television advertisements were selected during a two-week period in February 1987. Three-hour time periods (9:00 A.M.–12:00 A.M., 1:00 P.M.–4:00 P.M., and 8:00 P.M.–11:00 P.M.) were sampled across all three networks. All commercials appearing during these time periods were included in the content analysis.[b]

Example 3

Eleven consumer magazines were selected. These magazines (*Atlantic, Esquire, Essence, Jet, Life, Newsweek, People, Rolling Stone, Sports Illustrated, Time,* and *Vanity Fair*) were selected because they all accepted cigarette and alcohol advertising and were targeted to five distinct target audiences. All cigarette and alcohol ads appearing in these magazines between June 1990 and June 1991 were included in the content analysis.[c]

FIGURE 17.3
Sampling in content analysis.
[a] Margaret F. Callcott and Wei-Na Lee, "A Content Analysis of Animation and Animated Spokes-Characters in Television Commercials," *Journal of Advertising* 23 (December 1994): 1–13.
[b] Lynette S. Unger, Diane M. McConocha, and John A. Faier, "The Use of Nostalgia in Television Advertising: A Content Analysis," *Journalism Quarterly* 68 (Fall 1991): 345–53.
[c] Leonard N. Reid, Karen W. King, and Peggy J. Kresher, "Black and White Models and Their Activities in Modern Cigarette and Alcohol Ads," *Journalism Quarterly* 71 (Winter 1994): 873–86.

magazines between 1975 and 1995?" might use the following multistage sampling method:

Stage 1—*Delineation of women's magazines.* A magazine is considered a woman's magazine if 85 percent of its paid circulation consists of women.

Stage 2—*Selection of titles.* A list of all women's magazines from 1975 and 1995 will be created from magazines listed in Simmons Market Research Bureau, Mediamark Research, Inc., and Standard Rate and Data Service. Magazines from each year will be kept separate. Within each year, magazine titles will be assigned to one of four groups:

- circulation more than 5,000,000,
- circulation between 2,500,000–4,999,999,
- circulation between 500,000–2,499,999, and
- circulation less than 500,000.

A total of twenty-four magazines will be selected, twelve from 1975 and twelve from 1995. The twelve magazines from each year will consist of three magazines randomly selected from each circulation group.

Stage 3—*Selection of dates.* Each year will be divided into four quarters (January–March, April–June, July–September, and October–December). Two issues of each magazine (selected in the prior step) from each quarter will be randomly selected.

Stage 4—*Selection of ads.* Every third display ad of one-fourth page or larger will be included in the content analysis.

Determine How Duplicate Ads Will Be Treated

Many ads appear more than once in any given time period. An ad may appear several times in the same month in different magazines, in consecutive issues of the same magazine, or even several times in the same television program. It is therefore possible that several instances of "duplicate" ads will appear in the set of sample ads. The decision to code all ads in the sample (treating each instance of the duplicate ad as a separate ad) or code only each unique instance of an ad (eliminating duplicate occurrences) is guided by the underlying motivation for the content analysis.

Some content analyses ignore duplication and code all sampled ads. This approach is appropriate when the content analysis seeks to understand aspects of the "total number of ads." For example, a content analysis designed to determine the use of sexual themes in men's magazine ads would use this approach since duplicate ads are an important component of advertising weight and audience exposure. However, when the focus is on specific advertiser or brand strategies duplication is often eliminated. In these instances the emphasis is on *messages* rather than total exposure or weight. Conclusions drawn about advertising approach and content can be distorted by coding multiple occurrences of the same ad.

Develop a Category System

Development of a category system consists of two steps: (1) identification of categories of interest and (2) enumeration of the specific dimensions of each category.

Identification of Categories   Categories represent the universe of information that will be extracted during the content analysis. Great care must be taken in their identi-

fication and selection. First, it is important that the set of identified categories is comprehensive. The omission of important categories prevents the collection of important data limiting the insights provided by the content analysis. Second, categories must be clearly labeled and have a direct relationship to the research questions and hypotheses motivating the content analysis. Berelson points out that the eventual success of a content analysis is dependent on the extent to which the categories are clearly formulated and well-adapted to the research problem and content under examination.[8] The specific categories developed for the content analysis reflect the analysis' goals and orientation, as illustrated in the two examples shown next. The categories in Set A reflect what an advertiser conducting a content analysis will want to know about competitive advertising. The categories in Set B were used in a content analysis of female senatorial candidates' advertising. Here, the categories flow from prior research and represent the specific dimensions of the political advertising that will be examined during the content analysis.[9]

Set A	*Set B*
Commercial format	Commercial format
Commercial structure	Rhetorical style
Primary product benefit	Commercial length
Additional, secondary product benefits	Production technique
Type of selling proposition	Ad setting
Commercial tone	Type of speaker
Types of claim substantiation	Type of voice-over
Types of disclaimers	Type of dress
Type of brand identification	Type of issues mentioned
Commercial tone	Ad emphasis
Musical elements	Use of content appeals
Commercial characters	Dominant content appeal
Commercial setting	
Use of competitive claims	
Types of competitive claims	
Elements of product display	
Elements of production techniques	

Enumerate Specific Dimensions of Each Category   This step identifies the specific dimensions of each category and determines how these dimensions will be measured once categories are identified and labeled. The identification of specific dimensions can come from prior research, theory, or personal knowledge of advertisers' practices within a product category. However, regardless of their source, category dimensions must be relevant to the goals and objectives of the content analysis. Dimensions can represent a type of characteristic, the amount of a characteristic, or the presence or absence of a characteristic, for example:

---

[8] B. Berelson, *Content Analysis.*

[9] Anne Johnston and Anne B. White, "Communication Styles and Female Candidates: A Study of the Political Advertising During the 1986 Senate Elections," *Journalism Quarterly* 71 (Summer 1994): 321–29.

Category	*Dimension*
Commercial format	Announcer alone
	Lifestyle
	Testimonial
	Slice-of-life
	Celebrity endorser
	Lifestyle
Sexual suggestiveness	Present
	Absent
Product introduction	Time in seconds until the product is shown or named

Measurement in content analysis typically takes place at one of three levels: nominal, interval, and ratio. The specific dimensions selected for a particular category generally determine the appropriate level of measurement.

Nominal Level   Measuring a category at the nominal level entails listing the dimensions of the category and then counting the number of occurrences falling into each dimension. For example, the category system "Gender of Principal Character" would contain two dimensions: male and female. Coders conducting the content analysis would examine the advertising and then count the number of occurrences of each gender. Similarly, as shown in the prior example, the category "Commercial Format" assigns the ad to one of six dimensions.

Similar to nominal level survey questions, content analysis categories measured at the nominal level must contain dimensions that are mutually exclusive and exhaustive. Categories contain mutually exclusive dimensions if an ad or an ad element can be placed into one and only one dimension. Imagine that we are conducting a content analysis of commercials that make either an explicit or implicit comparison to another product. One category system in the content analysis might address "type of comparison" as follows:

Explicit claim:	The criteria for comparison are stated.
Implicit claim:	The criteria for comparison are not stated.
Direct comparison:	Competitive products are named.
Indirect comparison:	Competitive products are not named.

This category system and specific categories are unacceptable because the categories are not mutually exclusive. A particular commercial may present both an implicit claim and a direct comparison. Mutually exclusive categories in this example could be created by separating the category into two smaller, mutually exclusive categories: type of claim (implicit and explicit) and type of comparison (direct and indirect).

Mutual exclusivity, as just discussed, is accomplished when and ad or ad element can be assigned to one and only one category. However, for convenience, some category systems use checklists in which each item on the checklist is one nominal level measure. For example, measurement for the category system "Major and minor characters in the advertising" might use the following checklist:

No principal character	_____
Male adult principal character	_____
Male adult in minor role	_____
Female adult principal character	_____
Female adult in minor role	_____
Male child principal character	_____
Male child in minor role	_____
Female child principal character	_____
Female child in minor role	_____

For purposes of data analysis, each item on the checklist is treated as a separate nominal level measure.

A category system with exhaustive categories is one where there is a place to code each unit of analysis, that is, there is an existing slot into which every ad or ad element can be placed. Similar to the construction of nominal level survey questions, exhaustivity can often be accomplished by adding an "other" category.

Interval Level   Measurement at the interval level uses some form of rating scale to evaluate each identified dimension. Seven-point Likert-type scales might be used, for example, to record the "friendliness" of commercial characters or the "dominance" of men and women shown in print and television advertising. It is the researcher's responsibility to weigh the advantages and disadvantages of measurement at the interval versus nominal level. Disadvantages of interval level measures in content analysis are their difficulty to administer, the amount of time necessary to form and record an evaluation, and the generally lower level of intercoder agreement. These disadvantages are often outweighed by the added depth and insights these measures provide. Consider the category "Sexual Suggestiveness" shown earlier. In this example, the category was given two dimensions at the nominal level: present or absent. This category could also be measured at the interval level where a coder uses a scale to assess the relative amount of sexual suggestiveness in the ad. The researcher developing the categories and dimensions must determine which level of measurement provides the required insights into advertising content.

Ratio Level   Ratio level measures are most commonly used for examining advertising elements, advertising time, and space. This level of measurement could be used, for example, when recording commercial length, print ad size, the number of words in a disclaimer, or the amount of time a disclaimer appears on the television screen.

Number of Dimensions Within a Category   The number of category dimensions is an issue relevant to all levels of measurement.

There is no absolute correct number of dimensions. In any particular content analysis, the number of dimensions will vary as a function of the complexity of the category and the need for detail. Generally, there should be enough dimensions within a category so that meaningful differences across dimensions can be maintained. Imagine that you were developing the dimensions for a category that focused on health-related

Category: Commercial Structure

Refers to the use of surprise or unexpected elements in the commercial. Five demensions:

1. Front-end surprise   The first ten seconds of the commercial uses suspense, implicit or explicit questions, surprise, tension, mood, music, or something else that otherwise gains attention.

2. Middle surprise   The middle portion of the commercial (11 to 20 seconds in a :30 or 20 to 40 seconds in a :60) uses suspense, implicit or explicit questions, surprise, tension, mood, music, or something else that otherwise gains attention.

3. End surprise   The last ten seconds of the commercial uses suspense, implicit or explicit questions, surprise, tension, mood, music, or something else that otherwise gains attention.

4. Unexpected setting   The product is shown in an unusual way or in a way that is unexpected for the product category.

5. Humorous intro   The first ten seconds of the commercial uses a joke, pun, slapstick, or other humorous devise.

Category: Primary and Secondary Selling Benefits

Primary selling benefit receives the greatest amount of emphasis in the ad. Secondary selling benefit is the benefit mentioned in addition to the principal selling benefit. Eight dimensions:

1. Price   The product is sold at a low or lowest price for the product category.

2. Value   The product is the best value (price/benefit relationship) for the product category.

3. Hypo-allergenic   The product contains no perfumes or dyes, safe for those sensitive to perfumes or dyes, safe for those with allergies or sensitive skin.

4. Cleaning ability   The ability of the product to remove dirt and stains.

5. Color fastness   The product does not fade colors.

6. Concentration   Results are obtained by using a lesser quantity of the product.

7. Fabric softener   Contains fabric softener, no supplemental fabric softener is required.

8. Other   Any selling benefit not mentioned above.

Category: Product Introduction

Amount of *elapsed time* from the beginning of the commercial to the first visual or oral introduction of the product name or product package. Recorded in seconds.

Category: Commercial Approach

The extent to which (1) the commercial stressed rationality over emotion and (2) the commercial adapted a positive versus a negative approach. A straightforward logical presentation is typically rational. An emotional approach appeals to feelings rather than logic. A positive approach is one where the commercial tells the consumer how he or she will be better off if the product is used. A negative approach is one where the commercial tells the consumer how he or she will be worse off if the product is not used.

FIGURE 17.4
Excerpt from a hypothetical content analysis code book.

benefits communicated in advertising. The creation of three dimensions, such as "good for heart," "good for cholesterol," "other health benefits" lacks the specificity needed to understand fully the differences among various types of health-related claims. On the other hand, the creation of eleven, extremely small dimensions may not improve insights and accuracy. Common sense, pretesting, and practice with the coding system are valuable guides to determining the appropriate number of dimensions. However, when it doubt, many researchers suggest erring on the side of more specific, rather than broader, dimensions. Smaller dimensions can always be combined during data analysis but larger categories cannot be divided.

Prepare Code Book and Code Sheets

A code book, the dictionary of content analysis, contains the definitions of all important terms. Code books are important because they provide a common frame of reference for all coders, thus increasing the likelihood independent coders will view and respond to the same stimulus in the same way. An excerpt from a hypothetical code book is shown in Figure 17.4.[10]

A code sheet is similar to a survey questionnaire. It is where coders (individuals who examine and evaluate the advertising) record their observations. Code sheets are prepared following the specification of categories, dimensions, levels of measurement, and specific measures. A sample hypothetical code sheet (reflecting the definitions shown in Figure 17.4) is shown in Figure 17.5 (pages 406–407). Note how the code sheet is clearly laid out and provides clear directions for stimulus observation and data recording.

Train Coders

Coders are selected and trained after code book and code sheet development. As might be expected, the accuracy and dependability of the coding process are greatly influenced by coder selection and training. With regard to coder selection, two or more independent individuals of similar background and training should be selected. Additionally, coder independence, to each other and to the principal researchers, is of critical importance. Individuals involved in research design and data analysis of the *should not* code the advertising content themselves. "Probably the worst practice in content analysis is when the investigator develops his recording instructions and applies them all by himself or with the help of a few close colleagues and thus prevents independent reliability checks."[11]

Once selected, coders are trained in the coding procedure. The training process begins with an explanation of the categories, category definitions and dimensions shown in the code book. This verbal instruction is followed by practice in actual coding where (1) examples of sampled advertising are shown to the coders, (2) coders code the advertising according to their understanding of category definitions, and (3) at the conclusion of coding, coders' problems and experiences are discussed and additional training, if needed, is provided.

---

[10] Several of the items on this code sheet are adapted from Stewart and Furse, *Effective Television Advertising*.

[11] K. Krippendorff, *Content Analysis: An Introduction to its Methodology* (Beverly Hills, CA: Sage Publishers, 1980), 74.

Commercial ID# _____

Brand code _____

Product category code _____

Category: Commercial Structure

Directions: Reset time to zero. Rewind tape to beginning of commercial. View the entire commercial. Note the time codes on the television screen. Place a check mark next to *each* commercial structure category shown below that you observe in the commercial. If none appear in the commercial, check the "NONE" code at the conclusion of the commercial.

_____ Front-end surprise

_____ Middle surprise

_____ End surprise

_____ Unexpected setting

_____ Humorous intro

_____ None of the above appeared in the commercial

Category: Primary Selling Benefits

Directions: View the entire commercial. Place a check mark next to the *one* selling benefit that is the primary focus of the advertising.

_____ Price

_____ Value

_____ Hypo-allergenic

_____ Cleaning ability

_____ Color fastness

_____ Concentration

_____ Fabric softener

_____ Other

Category: Secondary Selling Benefits

Directions: View the entire commercial. Place a check mark next to *each* selling benefit mentioned at any point in the advertising other than that identified as the primary selling benefit.

_____ Price

_____ Value

_____ Hypo-allergenic

_____ Cleaning ability

_____ Color fastness

_____ Concentration

_____ Fabric softener

_____ Other

Category: Product Introduction

Directions: Reset time to zero. Rewind tape to beginning of commercial. View the entire commercial. Note the time codes on the television screen. Use the space below to record the *elapsed time* to the first visual or oral introduction of the product name or product package.

_____ Elapsed time to first product introduction

Category: Commercial Approach
Directions: After viewing the commercial record your impressions of the commercial approach using the scales below. Circle one answer on each scale.

To what extent did the commercial use a rational versus emotional approach? The commercial was ...

Entirely rational	_____	(1)
Mostly rational with some emotional elements	_____	(2)
Both rational and emotional, equally	_____	(3)
Mostly emotional with some rational elements	_____	(4)
Entirely emotional	_____	(5)

To what extent did the commercial use a positive versus negative approach? The commercial was...

Entirely positive	_____	(1)
Mostly positive with some negative elements	_____	(2)
Both positive and negative, equally	_____	(3)
Mostly negative with some positive elements	_____	(4)
Entirely negative	_____	(5)

FIGURE 17.5
Hypothetical code sheet for advertising content analysis.

Pretest Coding System, Revise Coding and Training If Necessary

Every content analysis, similar to every survey research study, can be improved by pretesting and subsequent revision of the research materials. Pretesting in content analysis helps to improve category system structure, category definitions, and coding instruments and procedures.

Pretesting begins with each coder independently coding a small, representative sample of the advertising stimuli. (This exercise is different from and follows coder training.) The responses of each coder are then examined and used to evaluate category definitions, dimensions, and measurement instruments. Consider, for example, the hypothetical coding data from three coders shown in the following table:

Judge	Dimension A	Dimension B	Dimension C	Dimension D
1	1,5,7,8	2,3,4	6,9,10	11,12,13
2	1,5,7,8	2,3,4	9,11,12	6,10,13
3	1,5,7,8	2,3,4	13	6,9,10,11,12
4	1,5,7,8	2,3,4	6,10,12	9,11,13

The definitions for Dimensions A and B appear to be well defined. All four coders placed ads 1, 5, 7, and 8 in Dimension A and ads 2, 3, and 4 in Dimension B. Dimensions C and D appear to have some confusion in their definitions. Coders cannot agree

on which ads should be placed in each category. As a result, the definitions of these two dimensions would be reexamined and revised before the start of the actual study.

A pretest also provides an initial opportunity to evaluate the relative "goodness" of the coders themselves. Coders who do not understand their task can be retrained. Additionally, those coders who are chronic disagreers can be eliminated from study participation. (Chronic disagreers are those coders that consistently provide codes contrary to the other coders in the study.)

Code the Materials

The coding process is straightforward and is done after pretesting and revision. Coders work independently to observe the advertising and record their observations on the code sheet.

Assess Reliability

Reliability is a critical part of any research study. (See text pages 269–270 for a review of the concept of reliability.) Reliability in coding is evidenced by two coders independently assigning the same code to the same stimulus. This type of reliability, known as intercoder reliability, can be calculated by any of several methods but *must* be calculated before the data analysis. Low levels of intercoder reliability indicate that one cannot have a great deal of confidence in the data.

Holsti[12] recommends that intercoder reliability for nominal data be calculated to reflect the overall percentage of agreement, that is, the percentage of times when both coders independently assign the same code to the same object. This measure of reliability is calculated using the formula:

$$\text{Reliability} = \frac{2M}{N_1 + N_2}$$

where:

M is the total number of coding decisions on which the two coders agree,

N_1 and N_2 are the total number of coding decisions made by coders one and two.

For example, if the coders each judge 100 stimuli and agree on eighty of them, the estimate of reliability is 80 percent, calculated as

$$\text{Reliability} = \frac{2(80)}{100 + 100} = \frac{160}{200} = 80\%$$

Holsti's method is simple, straightforward, and easy to use. However, some statisticians have criticized this approach because it may overestimate reliability by not controlling for coder matches that occur strictly by chance. For example, in a two-category coding system we would expect a level of 50 percent "reliability" strictly by chance. Two additional formulas correct for chance matches in the calculation of intercoder reliability. In doing so, each formula increases the sensitivity to other parameters in the coding process.

---

[12] Ole Hosti, *Content Analysis for the Social Sciences and Humanities* (Reading, MA: Addison-Wesley Publishing Co., 1969).

The pi index of intercoder reliability[13] corrects for chance matches in the formula:

$$pi = \frac{\% \text{ observed agreement} - \% \text{ expected agreement}}{1 - \% \text{ expected agreement}}$$

This formula is sensitive to the *percentage distribution* of coded responses. For example, assume that as part of a content analysis of gasoline advertising, primary benefits were found to be

Benefit	Percent of All Ads
Better acceleration	30%
Better mileage	25
Cleans engine	15
Best value	10
Easy/quick to fill up/pay for	10
Good for environment	10

The first step in the calculation of pi determines the percentage of expected agreement, calculated as the sum of the squared percentages across all dimensions. In this example, the percent expected agreement equals .205 (calculated as $[.30]^2 + [.25]^2 + [.15]^2 + [.10]^2 + [.10]^2 + [.10]^2$). Next, the actual percent of agreement is calculated using Holsti's formula. Assume that, as in the prior example, this figure is 80 percent. Substituting these two figures into the formula results in an estimate of reliability of .79, calculated as

$$pi = \frac{\% \text{ observed agreement} - \% \text{ expected agreement}}{1 - \% \text{ expected agreement}}$$

$$= \frac{.80 - .205}{1 - .205}$$

$$= \frac{.595}{.75}$$

$$= .79$$

Perreault and Leigh have developed a second approach to a corrected calculation of intercoder reliability.[14] Their formula, sensitive to reliability differences that arise as the *number of classification dimensions* increases, calculates I_r (intercoder reliability) as

$$I_r = \{[(F_0 \div N) - (1 \div k)][k \div (k-1)]\}^{.5}$$

where:

F_0 is the number of coded items on which the coders agree,

---

[13] W. Scott, "Reliability of Content Analysis: The Case of Nominal Scale Coding," *Public Opinion Quarterly* 61 (1955): 483–92.

[14] Willaim D. Perreault and Laurence E. Leigh, "Reliability of Nominal Data Based on Qualitative Judgments," *Journal of Marketing Research* 26 (May 1989): 135–48.

N is the total number of codings,

k is the number of coding dimensions.

For example, if two coders agree on 80 of 100 items that coded in a category with six dimensions (as in the gasoline benefit example), the intercoder reliability would be .87, calculated as

$$I_r = \{[(80 \div 100) - (1 \div 6)][6 \div (6 - 1)]\}^{.5}$$
$$= \{[.8 - .167][6 \div 5]\}^{.5}$$
$$= \{[.633][1.2]\}^{.5}$$
$$= \{.76\}^{.5}$$
$$= .87$$

All three formulas are appropriate for nominal level data and the research literature reports usage of each. However, regardless of the formula used, it is generally recommended that the calculated measure of intercoder reliability be at least .80, representing intercoder agreement of 80 percent.

The reliability of data coded at the interval level of measurement can be determined using correlation (see pages 375–377). Care must be taken when using the correlation coefficient in this context. A strong, positive correlation merely indicates that the correlated scores are associated and move in the same direction. It is therefore possible to obtain an intercoder correlation of 1.0 and have complete *absence* of intercoder agreement. Examine the two sets of codes shown in Table 17.1. The data represents the coders' assessment of an ads' "hard sell" on a scale of '1' (not at all a hard sell) to '10' (extremely hard sell). Table 17.1A presents the codes of two coders for ten ads. The correlation is perfect, *r* = 1.0. Both coders agreed all of the time. Table 17.1B also presents the "hard sell" codes of two coders for a second set of ten ads. Here, there is *no* intercoder agreement. Coder two is always two rating points higher than coder one. But the correlation coefficient is still perfect, *r* = 1.0. This is because there is a perfect correspondence between the movement of the two coders. Clearly, the interpretation of the correlation coefficient as an estimate of intercoder reliability must be made in light of a visual examination of the data and data trends. Given a reasonable set of underlying data, it is generally recommended that the correlation of intercoder reliability be at least .80.

Analyze and Interpret the Data[15]

Data analysis typically begins with descriptive statistics such as percentages, means, medians, and modes (see Chapter 15). Descriptive statistics can be calculated for the categories that appear on the code sheet and for calculated variables.

The reporting and descriptive analyses of categories shown on the code sheet are straightforward. (Refer to the code sheet shown in Figure 17.5). Table 17.2 (page 412) shows the descriptive analyses of the categories within the "Commercial Structure,"

---

[15] All data presented in this section are fictitious. Brand names shown in Table 17.4C and 17.4D are used for illustrative purposes only.

TABLE 17.1 Use of Correlation to Estimate Intercoder Reliability

Situation A: Correlation = 1.0

Commercial	Rating By Coder 1	Rating By Coder 2
1	1	1
2	2	2
3	3	3
4	4	4
5	5	5
6	4	4
7	5	5
8	6	6
9	5	5
10	2	2

Situation B: Correlation = 1.0

Commercial	Rating By Coder 1	Rating By Coder 2
1	1	3
2	2	4
3	3	5
4	4	6
5	5	7
6	4	6
7	5	7
8	6	8
9	5	7
10	2	4

"Primary Selling Benefits," and "Product Introduction" category systems. Tables such as these provide a starting point for data analysis.

The analysis of calculated measures typically follows the analysis of coded variables. Calculated measures are variables formed using a combination of existing variables. These variables, therefore, do not exist on the original code sheet. The two tables in Table 17.3 (page 413) illustrate the use and value of calculated variables. Table 17.3A reports the frequency distribution of "Total Selling Benefits in the Commercial" that was computed by adding the number of items coded in the "Primary Selling Benefits" and "Secondary Selling Benefits" sections of the code sheet for each commercial. Table 17.3B examines "Commercial Structure." Here, the percent of commercials using *any* form of surprise is calculated. The calculated variables developed in any particular content analysis reflect the researcher's creativity and analytical needs.

The next step in data analysis typically involves cross-tabulation. Cross-tabulations can be conducted among categories within a single category system, categories among two or more category systems, and among categories and a computed measure. Each of these approaches is illustrated in the tables shown in Table 17.4 (page 414).

TABLE 17.2   Descriptive Analysis of Category Data

Percentage Distribution of Commercial Structure Category

Commercial Structure Dimensions	Percent of Commercials*
End surprise	51%
Front-end surprise	43
Middle surprise	21
Unexpected setting	15
Humorous intro	6
NONE	11

Base is 100 commercials.

* Percentages do not add to 100 percent due to multiple codings.

Percentage Distribution of Principal Selling Benefits Category

Dimensions of the Primary Selling Benefit	Percent of Commercials
Cleaning ability	36%
Price	22
Hypo-allergenic	18
Value	13
Fabric softener	5
Color fastness	4
Concentration	2
Other	0
Total	**100%**

Base is 100 commercials.

Frequency Distribution and Descriptive Statistics of Product Introduction Category (:30 commercials)

Elapsed Time to Product ID (sec)	Percent of Commercials
less than 2	25%
2.0 to 3.9	11
4.0 to 5.9	3
6.0 to 7.9	12
8.0 to 9.9	6
10.0 to 14.9	4
15.0 to 19.9	3
20.0 to 24.9	23
25.0 to 29.9	13
Total	**100%**
Mean	*12.0*
Median	*7.0*
Mode	*1.0*

Base is 100 commercials.

TABLE 17.3 Use and Value of Calculated Variables

A. Total Selling Benefits in the Commercial

Total Number of Selling Benefits	Percent of Commercials
0	5%
1	45
2	21
3	14
4	6
5	5
6 or more	4
Total	**100%**

Base is 100 commercials

B. Commercial Use of Multiple "Surprise" in Commercial Structure

Uses of "Surprise" (Net)	Percent of Commercials*
Commercial uses one type	82%
Commercial uses any two types	63
Commercial uses all three types	2

Base is 100 commercials.

* Percentages do not add to 100% due to multiple codings

- Table 17.4A cross-tabulates the items *within* the "Commercial Structure" category. This table indicates that most commercials with front-end impact also use unexpected settings (59 percent) while most commercials with an end surprise have humorous introductions (52 percent).

- Table 17.4B cross-tabulates items *across* category systems. Here, "Primary Selling Benefits" are cross-tabulated with "Secondary Selling Benefits." This table indicates that the secondary product benefit appearing in a commercial varies as a function of the primary benefit. There is a consistent pattern of association between primary and secondary benefits. The table indicates, for example, that "price" as a primary benefit is typically associated with a secondary benefit of "value," and that "cleaning ability" as a primary benefit is typically associated with "color fastness" as a secondary benefit.

- Table 17.4C cross-tabulates the mean of the commercial approach measures with specific brands. This table indicates that while all brands have taken a positive approach, specific brands have taken different approaches to the rationality of benefit presentation. Some brands use a very rational approach, some use a very emotional approach, and some balance the two approaches.

- Table 17.4D cross-tabulates category system and calculated variables. This table presents the total number of product benefits in each brand's commercials and indicates that there are wide differences among brands in terms of the number of benefits communicated per commercial. The vast majority of All, Tide, and Woolite commercials tend to have only one or two selling benefits while most Cheer commercials have five or six benefits.

TABLE 17.4 Content Analysis Cross-Tabulations

A: Cross-Tabulation of "Commercial Structure" Categories: Percent Dual Elements

	Front End	Middle Surprise	End Surprise	Unexpected Setting	Humorous Introduction
Front end	–	–	–	–	–
Middle surprise	7	–	–	–	–
End surprise	12	5	–	–	–
Unexpected setting	59	10	5	–	–
Humorous introduction	0	10	52	2	–
Base	(43)	(21)	(51)	(15)	(6)

B: Cross-tabulation of Principal and Secondary Selling Benefits: Percent Dual Elements

Primary Selling Benefit

	Price	Value	Hypo-allergenic	Cleaning Ability	Color Fastness*	Concentration*	Fabric Softner*
Price	–	0	0	7	–	–	–
Value	91	–	0	5	–	–	–
Hypoallergenic	0	0	–	0	–	–	–
Cleaning ability	0	0	0	–	–	–	–
Color fastness	0	0	0	72	–	–	–
Concentration	0	77	0	0	–	–	–
Fabric softener	0	8	95	–	–	–	–
Base	(22)	(13)	(18)	(36)	(4)	(2)	(5)

* Base of commercials is too small for analysis.

C: Commercial Approach of Specific Brands

	All	Cheer	Tide	Wisk	Woolite
Rational/emotional	1.2	1.4	4.7	3.2	4.9
Positive/Negative	1.5	1.6	1.6	1.4	1.1
Base	(13)	(10)	(10)	(10)	(13)

D: Total Number of Selling Benefits By Brand As Percent of All Brand Commercials

Number of Selling Benefits	All	Cheer	Tide	Wisk	Woolite
1–2	84	0	90	10	93
3–4	8	10	10	80	7
5–6	8	90	0	10	0
Base	(13)	(10)	(10)	(10)	(13)

Finally, where appropriate, more sophisticated data analyses and tests of hypotheses can be performed using significance testing (see Chapter 16). One could, for example, determine whether there was (1) a significant difference among brands in the average elapsed time to product introduction, (2) a significant difference among primary benefits in terms of rational/emotional and positive/negative ratings, or (3) any deviation from expectations in the distribution of primary benefits.

Apply the Findings

The goal of content analysis is to help us better understand advertisers' practices, the relationship between advertising form and effects, and specific competitors' advertising strategies. This final step in the process makes this improved understanding explicit. The result of a content analysis of advertisers' practices is a deeper understanding of how advertising is structured and utilized. The result of an exploration of the relationship between advertising form and content is an increased understanding of how changes in the characteristics of advertising affect consumer response to the advertising. In both cases, the deeper understanding often leads to extensions or modification of existing theory. Finally, the result of an applied content analysis is deeper insights into competitors' advertising strategy and practices, allowing for improved brand advertising strategic planning. The tables shown in Table 17.4 illustrate the types of insights an advertiser might acquire about competitive brand and overall category advertising practices and strategies.

Summary

Advertising content analysis is the systematic, objective, and quantitative analysis of advertising conducted to infer a pattern of advertising practice or the elements of brands' advertising strategies such as brand positioning, selling proposition, and creative tone and manner. Content analysis is used in both academic and applied settings. Content analyses conducted in the former setting, which flow from existing theory, prior research, or changes in social conditions or perspectives, are generally concerned with identifying trends in advertising practices or in relating advertising characteristics to advertising effects. Applied content analysis, generally conducted by advertising agencies or marketing research companies on behalf of agencies and their clients, is concerned with identifying the positioning and advertising strategies of product categories and competitive brands.

Both applied and academic advertising content analyses follow the same sequence of steps. The process begins with the specification of research question(s) or hypotheses that make explicit what needs to be learned from the content analysis. The research question(s) and hypotheses lead to operational definitions of the universe of interest and the sampling plan. These two steps specify the types of advertising that will be examined and how the advertising will be selected.

After the advertising is selected logistical issues are addressed. Categories and their dimensions are created and techniques for measurement within each system are developed. Coding materials are prepared and coders are selected and trained. Finally, before the actual content analysis begins, pretesting is conducted to improve category system structure, category definitions and coding instruments and procedures. The ac-

tual data is then collected and examined. Judges code their observations, intercoder reliability is evaluated, and the data is analyzed by both descriptive and inferential statistics.

The result of a content analysis of advertisers' practices is a deeper understanding of how advertising is structured and utilized. The result of an exploration of the relationship between advertising form and content is an increased understanding of how the characteristics of advertising affect consumer response to the advertising. In both cases, this deeper understanding often leads to extensions or modification of existing theory. Finally, the results of a product category or brand-specific content analysis are deeper insights into competitors' advertising strategy and practices, allowing for improved brand advertising strategic planning.

Review Questions

1. What is content analysis?
2. What are the three characteristics of content analysis?
3. What are the purposes of academic or theory-based content analysis?
4. What are the purposes of applied content analysis?
5. What are the steps in conducting a content analysis?
6. What is the process by which the research questions(s) or hypotheses are developed?
7. What are typical questions asked in applied content analysis?
8. What are the characteristics of a well-written operational definition of the sample universe?
9. What is the difference between a census and a sample in content analysis? In what circumstances is each approach appropriate?
10. What is the role of categories and dimensions in content analysis?
11. How are different levels of measurement used in content analysis? Provide an example of the use of each level of measurement appropriate to a content analysis.
12. How does one determine the correct number of categories within a specific category system?
13. What is a code book? What is the role of a code book in content analysis?
14. What is a code sheet and what are its characteristics?
15. What are important considerations in coder selection and training?
16. Why is pretesting in content analysis important?
17. What are three methods for estimating intercoder reliability? What are the relative advantages and disadvantages of each approach?
18. What are approaches to the analysis of content analysis data?

Application Exercises

1. Your agency has just been awarded the Ford Windstar advertising account. Ford has asked that you conduct an analysis of competitive minivan advertising to prepare for the upcoming year's strategic discussions. Prepare a memo for the agency account

team that describes the approach you will take in conducting the content analysis. Be certain to *specifically* address issues related to (1) the operational definitions of the sample universe, (2) your sampling plan, and (3) the treatment of duplicate advertising. Provide support and justification for all recommendations.

2. You are interested in exploring age-related stereotypes in television advertising. Specifically, you want to know if the portrayal of individuals aged 50 and older is different on programs with high youth audiences (defined as those aged 18–34) versus high older audiences (defined as those aged 50 and older). Prepare and support an operational definition of the sample universe and a sampling plan.

3. You have been asked to conduct a content analysis of beer advertising. The content analysis will be used by the agency and client to understand better the beer category and specific beer brand's advertising practices. You are specifically interested in the types of benefits communicated in beer advertising, the use and portrayal of individuals in the advertising, and advertising tone and manner.

First, address the issues of categories and category dimensions by (1) preparing a list of *specific* categories that will be examined during the content analysis, (2) identifying the dimensions within each category, and (3) selecting the appropriate level of measurement for each category.

Second, prepare a code book that explains and defines the categories and dimensions you identified. Once the code book is completed prepare code sheets.

Third, video tape several examples of television beer advertising and find several examples of print beer advertising.

Fourth, select two individuals to act as your coders. Train the coders, provide them with practice coding exercises and then have the coders pretest your code sheets. What insights did you obtain from the pretest? Revise category definitions and code sheets as necessary. Compare the original category definitions and code sheets to their revisions. In what ways are the revised versions an improvement over the originals.

Fifth, present a plan for the analysis of the data collected in the content analysis. Based on your revised code sheet, what are the key descriptive statistics, computed variables, and cross-tabulations? What inferential statistics can be used to analyze the data?

4. Select one of the content analyses discussed in this chapter or another of your own choosing from an academic journal. Read the entire article and then provide a point of view on (1) sampling procedures, (2) category definitions, (3) category dimensions and their level of measurement, (4) evaluation of intercoder reliability, and (5) data analysis. Evaluate the author's strengths and weaknesses in each of these areas. Provide recommendations for improvement where weaknesses are identified.

5. Johnston and White conducted a content analysis of women's political advertising.[16] The categories and dimensions of each category examined during the content analysis are shown in Figure 17.6 (pages 418–419). All measurement is at the nominal level. Do you believe that this level of measurement is appropriate and useful for all measures? Could any of the categories and dimensions be measured at the interval or ratio level? If so, provide examples. How do measures of the same category at different levels provide different insights?

---

[16] Johnston and White, "Communication Styles."

Commercial format:
documentary
bandwagon/excitement
testimonial
introspection
opposition focused
issue dramatization

Rhetorical style:
exhortive
bureaucratic
emotional
informative

Production technique:
cinema verite
slides with print and voice-over
candidate head-on
someone other than candidate head-on
combination

Setting of ad:
inside–general
inside–home or family setting
inside–classroom or other educational setting
inside–office or other professional setting
inside–store setting
outside–general
outside–family setting
outside–factory setting
combination
other

Speaker:
candidate
government official
anonymous announcer
combination
other

Voice-over:
male
female
none

Dress:	formal suit
	soft feminine suit
	dress
	casual
	combination
	not applicable

Emphasis of ad:	issues
	image

Use of content appeals in ads: (checklist)

        partisanship

        issue concerns

        policy preference

        policy proposals

        personality characteristics

        group affiliations

Dominant content of appeal in ad:

        partisanship

        issue concerns

        policy preference

        policy proposals

        personality characteristics

        group affiliations

FIGURE 17.6
Categories and dimensions from content analysis of womens' political advertising.

18 PERCEPTUAL MAPPING

The development of successful advertising strategy requires that an advertiser address multiple issues related to the competitive marketplace, the product, and the consumer. One specific set of issues that contributes to strategy development relates to consumer evaluation of brands and products, specifically, the value consumers' place on various product attributes and the extent to which they believe various brands in the product category possess these attributes. Perceptual mapping is a means of obtaining the information required to understand these aspects of consumer brand and product evaluation. This chapter introduces you to perceptual mapping.

After reading this chapter, you will be able to

■ Explain what perceptual mapping accomplishes and how it helps advertisers make better strategic decisions.

■ Describe the two approaches to perceptual mapping and the appropriate use of each approach.

■ Construct and interpret perceptual maps.

Perceptual mapping has been used to satisfy marketing and advertising informational needs related to product positioning,[1] competitive market structure,[2] consumer preferences, and brand perceptions.[3] Perceptual maps satisfy these types of in-

[1] Wayne S. DeSarbo and Vithala R. Rao, "GENFOLD@: A Set of Models and Algorithms for the GENeral inFOLDING Analysis of Preference/Dominance Data," *Journal and Classification* 1 (Winter 1984): 147–86; Yoram Wind, *Product Policy: Concepts, Methods and Strategy* (Reading, MA: Addison-Wesley Publishing, 1982).

[2] Rajendra K. Srivastava, Mark I. Alpert, and Allan D. Shocker, "A Consumer Oriented Approach for Determining Market Structures," *Journal of Marketing* 48 (Spring 1984): 32–45; Allan D. Shocker and David W. Stewart, "Strategic Marketing Decision Making and Perceptual Mapping," In F. S. Zufyden ed., *Advances and Practices of Marketing Science—1983 Proceedings* (Providence, RI: Institute of Management Science, 1983), 224–39.

[3] For a review of research in these areas see Lee G. Cooper, "A Review of Multidimensional Scaling in Marketing Research," *Applied Psychological Measurement* 7 (1983): 427–50. For specific applications see C. Carl Pegels and Chandra Sekar, "Determining Strategic Groups Using Multidimensional Scaling," *Interfaces* 19 (May/June 1989): 47–57; Grahame R. Dowling, "Measuring Corporate Images: A Review of Alternative Approaches," *Journal of Business Research* 17 (1989): 27–34; George S. Day, Allan D. Shocker, and Rajendra K. Srivastava, "Consumer-Oriented Approaches to Identifying Product Markets," *Journal of Marketing* 43 (Fall 1979): 8–20.

formational needs by analyzing and then translating consumers' numeric ratings, brand similarity data, and brand preference data into a *visual* representation of how those consumers view the set of brands and products.[4] There are two approaches to perceptual mapping: attribute-based and nonattribute-based. Attribute-based approaches require a respondent to evaluate a set of brands on a large number of specific attributes, typically those attributes felt to influence how consumers perceive, evaluate, and distinguish between brands and products. Attribute-based perceptual maps can be created using one of three mathematical techniques: factor analysis, discriminant analysis, and correspondence analysis. These approaches to attribute-based perceptual mapping are discussed in the next section. Nonattribute-based approaches require a respondent to rate brands in terms of similarities or preferences rather than attributes. A discussion of nonattribute-based perceptual mapping is presented later in this chapter. While attribute- and nonattribute-based approaches to perceptual mapping differ in terms of the types of data collected, both approaches share the fundamental assumption of perceptual maps: that consumers use broad dimensions to evaluate brands and products.

The Nature of Dimensions

Research indicates that consumers in most product categories try to evaluate brands using the least amount of time and energy. Consumers accomplish this goal by first identifying and then using a few broad dimensions to compare brands or products. Consumers evaluate brands and products in terms of broad dimensions because, in doing so, they save time and energy. They can refer to and use a small number of broad dimensions instead of having to perform much more complex evaluations based on a larger set of narrower individual attributes. It is easier to remember and act on two or three broader dimensions rather than twenty or thirty individual attributes. Perceptual mapping attempts to make these dimensions explicit.

The approach to dimension creation differs according to the type of perceptual map and the corresponding differences in underlying data. Attribute-based perceptual mapping creates dimensions from an analysis of the underlying brand and product attributes. For example, in the context of "gasoline," two dimensions that consumers might use to evaluate alternative brands of gasoline are "performance" and "convenience." Each dimension, in turn, is made up of a number of individual brand or product attributes. The dimension of gasoline "performance," for example, might contain the attributes: no knock, no run-on, smooth acceleration, and quick acceleration. The dimension for "convenience" might contain the attributes: many locations; locations have many pumps; can pay by cash, charge, or ATM; easy to pull in and out. Nonattribute-based perceptual maps create dimensions from an analysis of consumers' evaluations of brand and product similarities or preferences. Here, dimensions reflect the implicit criteria consumers use to determine similarities and differences among brands or overall brand preference.

---

[4] The most common use of perceptual mapping in advertising and marketing research relates to brand perceptions. However, perceptual mapping is appropriate for exploring perceptions of any set of objects, for example, types of television programs or political candidates. Perceptual maps can also be used to determine similarities and differences among groups of consumers.

The Contribution of Dimensions and Mapping to Decision Making

Perceptual maps make an important contribution to advertising strategic planning. The visual presentation and underlying analysis represented in a perceptual map helps an advertiser to understand the following:

- *The number of dimensions consumers use to distinguish between brands or products.* The complexity of the product category from the consumer's perspective is made explicit. Highly complex categories are those where consumers use a large number of dimensions to evaluate brands and products; less complex categories are typically those where fewer dimensions are used.
- *The nature and characteristics of these dimensions.* This information reveals the specific attributes or dimensions that consumers use to distinguish among products.
- *The location of actual brands, as well as the ideal brand, on these dimensions.* This information reveals consumers' evaluations of the advertiser's product versus other products and versus the ideal product on dimensions of importance. Further, it makes clear *from the consumers' perspective,* a brand's most direct competitors and provides a basis for deciding whether future advertising should reinforce or seek to change the brand's current positioning.

The types of insights provided by perceptual mapping are illustrated in the hypothetical perceptual map of the beer category shown in Figure 18.1.[5] First, the perceptual map indicates the two primary dimensions used by consumers to evaluate brands of beer. The horizontal dimension relates to quality while the vertical dimension relates to strength and taste. Second, the map identifies the specific characteristics of each dimension. The horizontal dimension is anchored by expensive, fine beers consumed when drinking out and low-quality beers drunk when alone. The second dimension is anchored by pale, sweet beers and full-bodied, malty beers. Third, it appears that consumers use these dimensions to separate beer brands into the following six distinct groups:

1. Brands A, B, and D are perceived similarly. These brands are all seen as low in price and quality and are appropriate only for drinking alone. Their taste falls in the center of the continuum, neither too sweet nor too malty.
2. Brands G and H are also seen as low in price and quality and are appropriate only for drinking alone. These brands are felt to have a full-bodied, malty taste.
3. Brands C and E are felt to be of average quality and expense and are appropriate for drinking alone or dining out. These brands are felt to be pale and sweet.
4. Brands K and L are also felt to be of average quality and expense and are appropriate for drinking alone or dining out. These brands are also felt to have a taste that falls in the center of the continuum, neither too sweet nor too malty. The perceived characteristics of these brands places them closest to the "ideal" beer.
5. Brand J has no direct competitors. It is seen as high quality, expensive, and only appropriate for dining out. It is also felt to be pale and sweet.
6. Brands F and I are also seen as being high quality, expensive, and are only appropriate for dining out. These brands are felt to have a taste that falls in the center of the continuum, neither too sweet nor too malty.

---

[5] This perceptual map is based on research conducted by Market Facts. The dimensions reflect the actual dimensions consumers use to evaluate beer brands. See Richard M. Johnson, "Market Segmentation: A Strategic Management Tool," *Journal of Marketing Research* 8 (February 1971):13–18. The placement of brands on the map, however, is not based on research and is for illustrative purposes only.

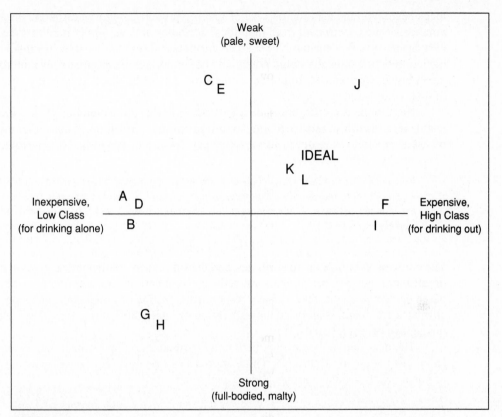

FIGURE 18.1
Hypothetical perceptual map of twelve beer brands.

Fourth, the groupings of beer brands along the two dimensions provide important insights into brand positioning, both with regard to the "ideal" brand and competitive products. Brand G, for example, is seen as an inexpensive, low-quality, full-bodied, malty beer that is primarily consumed when drinking alone. It is a beer that most directly competes with Brand H and is considered far from the "ideal beer." Finally, the perceptual map provides a starting point for discussion of advertising strategy. Brand G, or any other beer brand, can examine the perceptual map and then decide if their brand's position and competitive sets are acceptable (and thus should be supported in the advertising) or unacceptable (and thus should be addressed by advertising designed to alter brand perceptions).

The remainder of this chapter describes the procedures by which perceptual maps such as the prior example are constructed and used to inform advertisers' strategic planning.

ATTRIBUTE-BASED PERCEPTUAL MAPS

Attribute-based perceptual maps make explicit the broader dimensions consumers use to evaluate and distinguish among brands and products. Attribute-based perceptual

maps begin with the creation of a list of specific product category attributes. Because dimensions are constructed from individual attributes, it is very important that the list of brand and product attributes contain *all* attributes that are known to be (or that judgment or research indicates could potentially be) important in consumers' evaluation of target brands or products. Important dimensions cannot be discovered in the absence of their component attributes.

Next, semantic differential or Likert rating scales are developed. These scales enable respondents to rate each brand or product on each attribute. A consumer might be asked the following question to assess perceptions of brands on the attribute of "expense":

> Rate each brand of beer shown below on the basis of expense. Place a number after each brand of beer to indicate how *expensive or inexpensive* you feel that brand is. You can use any number between '1' (to represent "not at all expensive") and '10' (to represent "extremely expensive").

(Brand list appears here)

The rating of all brands on all attributes, and the subsequent mathematical combination of attributes into broader dimensions, reflects the underlying assumption of attribute-based perceptual maps, that is, that a respondent's "rating or judgments about specific attributes are manifestations of the underlying or latent dimensions that [they] use to distinguish between brands."[6]

The next step in the development of an attribute-based perceptual map is the selection of a mapping technique. Three approaches may be used: factor analysis, discriminant analysis, and correspondence analysis.

Factor Analysis

Chapter 16 presented the concept of correlation and the correlation coefficient, a computed number that indicates the simultaneous movement of two measures. A positive correlation coefficient indicates that two measures move together in the same direction, both measures tend to receive either a high or a low rating. A negative correlation coefficient indicates that two measures move in opposite directions, one measure tends to receive high ratings at the same time the second measure tends to receive low ratings.

Examining and interpreting the correlation of one pair of measures is straightforward. You note the direction and magnitude of the correlation coefficient. Examining and determining the meaning of the pattern of correlation coefficients for multiple measures is more difficult because of the large number of correlation coefficients that need to be examined. The intercorrelations of fifteen measures, for example, result in 105 pairs of correlations. Factor analysis responds to and solves this problem. Factor analysis is a statistical technique that "identifies the small number of factors or dimensions that represent the relationships among a large number of interrelated variables."[7]

The process of factor analysis begins after consumers rate each of the target brands or products on each individual attribute. A factor analysis computer program

---

[6] Donald S. Tull and Del I. Hawkins, *Marketing Research, Fifth ed.* (New York, NY: Macmillian Publishing Company 1990), 372.

[7] Marija J. Norusis, *SPSS Introductory Statistics Student Guide* (Chicago, IL: SPSS Inc. 1990), 321.

TABLE 18.1	Initial Factor Characteristics for Big Screen/Projection Television Perceptual Map

Factor	Eigenvalue	Percent of Variance
1	6.71	48.0%
2	4.51	32.2
3	.64	4.6
4	.54	3.9
5	.46	3.3
6	.42	3.0
7	.21	1.5
8	.17	1.2
9	.11	.8
10	.07	.5
11	.06	.4
12	.06	.4
13	.02	.1
14	.02	.1
Total	14.00	100.0%

examines the set of ratings data and calculates the correlation coefficient for each pair of variables. These correlations are the basis of the factor analysis. "The basic assumption of factor analysis is that underlying dimensions, or factors, can be used to explain complex phenomena. Observed correlations between variables result from their sharing these factors."[8] After correlation coefficients have been calculated for each pair of variables, factor analysis proceeds as follows:

1. The factor analysis computer program examines all pairs of correlation coefficients and then creates enough factors (typically equivalent to the number of variables) to account for 100 percent of sample variance (for a discussion of variance see text pages 338–340).

2. The program calculates three important pieces of data for each factor. This data is illustrated in Table 18.1 displays fourteen factors formed from the hypothetical ratings of eleven brands of big screen/projection television sets on fourteen attributes.[9]

   The first column in Table 18.1 reports the factor number. The number of factors reported is equal to the number of variables in the analysis. The second column reports eigenvalue, the total variance explained by each factor. Eigenvalues greater than one typically indicate important factors while eigenvalues less than one typically indicate factors that are less important. Factor importance increases as eigenvalues increase.

   The third column translates eigenvalues into percentages. The total of the eigenvalue column is equal to the number of variables. Thus, Factor 1, with an eigenvalue of 6.71, accounts for 47.9 percent of total sample variance (calculated as 6.71 ÷ 14). The percent of variance is a very important calculation and indicates a factor's contri-

[8] Ibid., 322.

[9] The data presented in this section is hypothetical and for illustrative purposes only. Brand names are represented by capital letters.

bution to an understanding of the underlying pattern of response. Larger percentages indicate a greater contribution.

3. The researcher examines eigenvalues and percent of variance explained by each factor and selects the number of factors to be used in subsequent analyses. Typically, a researcher tries to select the least number of factors that explain the highest amount of sample variance. (Obviously, "high" is a relative term that will vary from study to study.) In this example, Factor 1 and Factor 2 would most likely be selected. These two factors together account for 80.1 percent of the total variance. Including additional factors results in little gains in explanation of total variance.

4. The factor analysis computer program reanalyzes the data restricting the number of factors to that specified in the prior step.

5. A factor loading for each measure is computed and examined. A factor loading is an indicator of the degree of association between an individual measure and a factor. Similar to a correlation coefficient, a positive factor loading indicates a positive association between the measure and a factor, while a negative loading indicates a negative association.

   The factor analysis program then examines the patterns of factor loadings and generates a table in which variables are ordered to reflect their factor loadings, as shown in Table 18.2. This reordering permits the underlying pattern of association between measures and factors to be clearly seen.

6. The researcher examines the attributes comprising each factor and then creates a name for each factor. Remember, the factor analysis computer program uses mathematical computations to identify the factors. The researcher must determine what the factors represent. Factor 1 contains attributes that directly relate to the viewing experience. This factor is labeled "Viewing Experience." Factor 2 contains attributes related to the setup and usage. This factor is labeled "Get Going." (It is interesting to note that Factor 1 contains attributes that relate to both audio and video. The factor would be quite different and would be given a different name if audio and video attributes were associated with different factors.)

TABLE 18.2 Factor Loadings for Big Screen/Projection Television Perceptual Map

Attribute	Factor 1	Factor 2
Audio response	+.876	−.025
Stereo separation	+.775	+.122
Color accuracy	+.712	−.122
High-light viewing	+.698	+.130
Low-light viewing	+.651	−.252
High-sound reproduction	+.599	−.197
Low-sound reproduction	+.489	+.058
Pictures sharpness	+.477	+.139
Ease of setup	−.199	+.854
Quality of instructions	−.258	+.721
Programming ease	−.158	+.699
Remote control ease	+.025	+.571
Picture-in-picture ease	+.066	+.542
Visual displays	−.258	+.426

TABLE 18.3	Average Factor Scores for Big Screen/Projection Television Perceptual Map	
Brand Code	**Factor 1**	**Factor 2**
A	− 1.3	− 1.8
B	− 1.7	+ 1.1
C	− 1.6	− 1.6
D	+ 1.4	− 1.5
E	− 1.6	− 1.2
F	+ 1.4	− 1.4
G	+ 1.6	− 0.7
H	− 1.5	+ 1.5
I	− 1.3	+ 1.7
J	− 0.3	+ 0.3
K	+ 0.1	− 0.1
IDEAL	+ 1.5	+ 1.6

7. The factor analysis program calculates an average factor score for each brand. This score represents the average rating of each brand across the measures comprising an individual factor. The average factor scores for the eleven brands of big screen/projection televisions are shown in Table 18.3.

8. The average factor score is used to plot the brands on the perceptual map (see Figure 18.2, page 428). Note how the brands tend to cluster into four groups and the absence of brands from the area that indicates the brand is both "Easy to Get Going" and provides an "Excellent Viewing Experience." The absence of brands from this important area, which contains the ideal brand, indicates an unmet niche and a marketing and advertising opportunity.

The prior example presented on analysis in which two dimensions were sufficient to explain consumers' perceptions. There are often times, however, when more than two factors are identified or when more detail on the perceptual map is required for a true understanding of consumers' perceptions. Each of these situations is handled in the following manner.

The presence of three or more factors requires that a perceptual map be formed for each pair of factors. Thus, in a case in which there are three factors (Factor A, Factor B, and Factor C), three perceptual maps must be created (Map 1: Factors A and B; Map 2: Factors A and C; Map 3: Factors B and C). Examining brand positions and competitive sets among multiple, related perceptual maps provides a comprehensive view of how consumers use important dimensions to evaluate and distinguish among brands and products.

The need for additional detail is accomplished by adding vectors to the perceptual map. Vectors are represented as arrows that indicate the influence and directionality of specific underlying attributes. These attributes may or may not be associated with the dimensions shown on the perceptual map. An example of this approach is shown in Figure 18.3 (page 429), a revision of the perceptual map shown in Figure 18.1. In this case, the specific attributes sweet, color, expensive, and drinking when

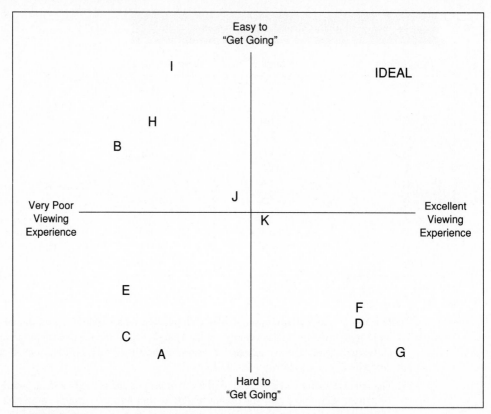

FIGURE 18.2
Perceptual map for big screen/projection television perceptual map.

alone are highly associated with their respective factors. These attributes are important because they help to provide the characteristics of their respective dimensions. However, additional attributes (those that leave the center of the map at 45° angles) are not highly associated with the dimensions used to create the map. These attributes provide additional insights; for example, Brand J is considered to be a beer that is popular with women.

Discriminant Analysis

As discussed in the prior section, factor analysis reduces a set of brand attribute ratings to several dimensions and then plots the positions of the brands on these dimensions. The result of the factor analysis is a grouping of brands where consumers perceive a brand to be more like other brands within its group and less like brands in different groups. The greater the distance between groups of brands the greater the perceived dissimilarity among brands in those groups.

Discriminant analysis also uses mathematical computations to identify dimensions and place brands and products on the perceptual map displaying these dimensions. However, in the case of discriminant analysis, dimensions are developed to minimize overlap between brand groupings. Discriminant analysis seeks to discriminate among brands and products by identifying and using dimensions that permit the great-

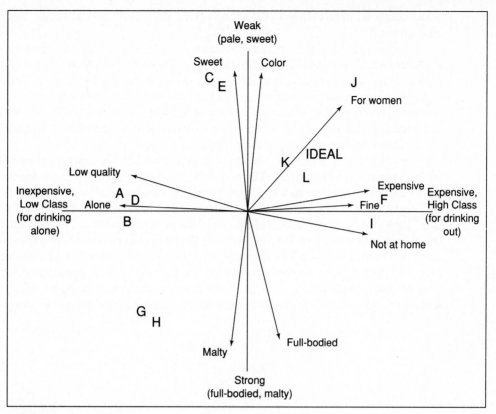

FIGURE 18.3
Perceptual map for beer brands with vectors.

est level of brand and product group separation.[10] While this approach has the potential to provide important insights, factor analysis generally produces more readily interpretable and useful perceptual maps.[11] As a result, discriminant analysis is used less frequently than factor analysis.[12]

Correspondence Analysis

Factor analysis and discriminant analysis require that brand perceptions and evaluations be at the interval level of measurement. This is the reason for the use of semantic differential and Likert scales to collect brand ratings on the set of attributes. However, not all data need to (or can) be measured on the interval level. Many product attributes can only be measured on the nominal or ordinal level, for example, an airline serves meals or it does not (nominal), American Airlines flies to more cities in the South than United, which flies to more than Continental (ordinal). Correspon-

[10] See Norusis, *SPSS Introductory Statistics,* 309.

[11] See J. F. Hair, Jr., R. E. Anderson, and R. L. Tatham, *Multivariate Data Analysis* (New York, NY: Macmillian Publishing Company 1987), 73–144 and D. R. Lehmann, *Market Research and Analysis* (Homewood, IL: Iwrin 1989), 691–95.

[12] J. R. Hauser and F. S. Koppelman, "Alternative Perceptual Mapping Techniques," *Journal of Marketing Research* 16 (November 1979): 495–506.

dence analysis creates perceptual maps from data collected at these levels of measurement.

The differences in levels of measurement between factor and discriminant analysis versus correspondence analysis require different types of underlying computations. However, while the computations are different, the process is quite similar to that of factor analysis: dimensions (or factors) are identified, the amount of variance accounted for by each dimension is calculated, the number of dimensions are selected and named, brand and product scores for each dimension are calculated, and individual attributes, brands, and products are plotted.

An example of a hypothetical study of department stores using correspondence analysis is shown in Figure 18.4. The map indicates that consumers believe department stores differ in the extent to which they genuinely care for their customers (anchored by "Real Customer Concern" and "Just In It For The Money") and the value of goods sold (anchored by "Excellent Service" and "Inadequate Service"). The placement of the individual attributes on the map indicate the component attributes of each dimension. "Real Customer Care," for example, is characterized by friendly and attentive. Finally, the placement of the department stores on the map indicate consumers' perceptions of how each dimension describes each department store. Store A, for example, is seen as providing both real customer care and excellent service (placing it close to the

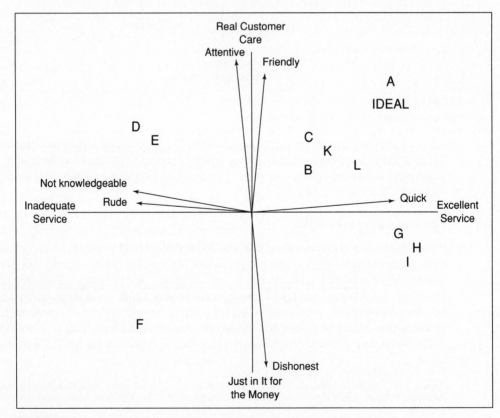

FIGURE 18.4
Perceptual map of department stores from correspondence analysis.

ideal department store). Store F, on the other hand, is far from the ideal department store. It is perceived to provide neither real customer care nor excellent service.

AN EXAMPLE: USING ATTRIBUTE-BASED PERCEPTUAL MAPPING TO MEASURE ADVERTISING IMPACT

A study conducted by the advertising agency D'Arcy Masius Benton & Bowles[13] demonstrates how perceptual mapping can help to determine

- the dimensions by which consumers differentiate between brands in a product category,
- how consumers perceive specific brands on these dimensions before advertising exposure,
- the effect of advertising on dimensions used to differentiate between brands, and
- the effect of advertising on consumers' brand perceptions.

The study began by asking respondents to rate twelve automobile manufacturers on fifteen attributes (such as quality, sporty, technologically advanced, etc.). The results of these initial ratings are shown on the preexposure perceptual map in Figure 18.5A (page 432). The perceptual map shows that, before advertising exposure, consumers use two dimensions to distinguish among car manufacturers. One dimension relates to age of driver and affordability. This dimension is anchored by "affordable, young person's car" (exemplified by manufacturer M) and "luxurious, comfortable, older person's car" (exemplified by manufacturers F and G). The second dimension relates to car characteristics and is anchored by "a family car" (exemplified by manufacturer B) and "high-quality, technologically advanced car" (exemplified by manufacturer I).

Following this initial rating, respondents were exposed to multiple advertising campaigns. Each respondent viewed six television commercials and read two print ads for each automobile manufacturer evaluated in the initial ratings. Next, respondents again rated each manufacturer on the same attributes used in the preexposure ratings.

The perceptual map that resulted from this second set of ratings was different from the preexposure map (see postexposure perceptual map Figure 18.5B). The postexposure map showed four ways by which the advertising affected consumers' perceptions of both the automotive category and individual automotive brands:

1. The advertising appears to have changed the dimensions with which consumers evaluate and distinguish among automobile manufacturers. The dimension displayed on the vertical axis changed from "family car—a high-quality, technologically advanced car" to "family car—exciting powerful fun car." This suggests that the advertisers changed the criteria by which consumers distinguish among car brands.
2. It is this new dimension, "family car—exciting powerful fun car," that most differentiates car manufacturers. Manufacturers on the preexposure perceptual map were dispersed along both dimensions with many manufacturers at the extremes. The postexposure perceptual map shows less differentiation along the horizontal axis (more

---

[13] The discussion in this section is based on Charles I. Stannard, "Perceptual Mapping and Cluster Analysis: Some Problems and Solutions," *Quirk's Marketing Research Review* (March 1990):12–22.

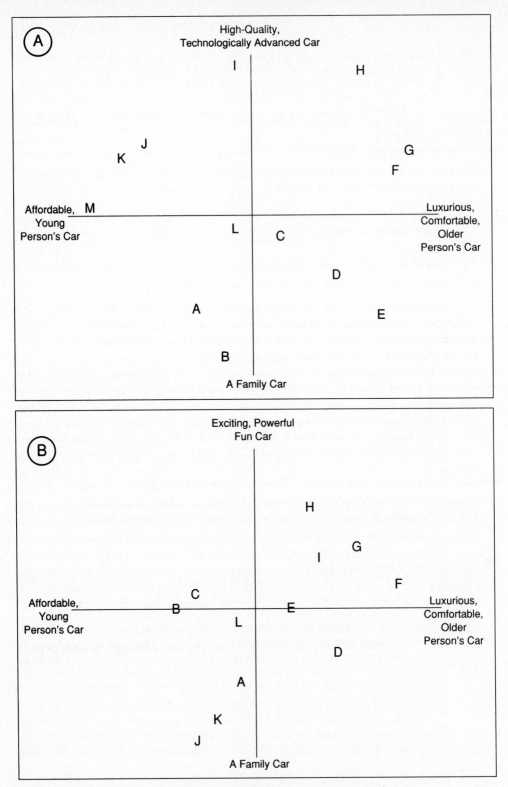

FIGURE 18.5 A. Preexposure perceptual map. B. Postexposure perceptual map.

brands now appear near the center) and more differentiation on the vertical axis.

3. Advertising does appear to affect manufacturer image. While some manufacturers' images (such as A, D, F, G, H) were constant (either as a result of the advertising purposively reinforcing that image or failing to change that image, if needed), other manufacturers showed great change in image. Consumers changed their perceptions of manufacturers J and K, for example, from a "high-quality, technologically advanced car" to "a family car."

4. Competitive sets appear to have changed for some manufacturers. Brand I, for example, which had no close competitors on the preexposure map, appears to compete with a number of manufacturers on the postexposure map. Similarly, manufacturers B and C, which were far apart on the preexposure map, are seen as very close competitors on the postexposure map.

Summary: Attribute-Based Perceptual Maps

The prior two sections discussed attribute-based perceptual maps. This type of map is constructed from consumers' ratings of multiple brands on multiple attributes. The quality and value of the insights derived from an attribute-based perceptual map are directly dependent on the list of attributes used. The more thorough the list of *important* attributes, the better the quality and value of the map.

There are several strengths of attribute-based perceptual mapping. Data collection is easy (although time-consuming), many computer programs are able to process and analyze the data, dimensions are easily interpreted and named, and brand placement provides visual evidence of consumers' perceptions and competitive set.

The one drawback to attribute-based perceptual mapping is the requirement that the full list of attributes be known in advance. Often, significant additional research is required to generate this list. The need for a complete list of important attributes often prevents researchers from using attribute-based perceptual mapping. However, there is an alternative mapping procedure appropriate to these situations. This alternative approach, nonattribute-based perceptual mapping, is discussed in the next section.

NONATTRIBUTE-BASED PERCEPTUAL MAPS

Nonattribute-based perceptual maps do not require a list of brand, product, or category attributes. Rather, the underlying data in this approach are consumers' judgments of brand and product similarities or preferences. Consumers determine brand similarities and preferences using whatever criteria they normally use. Attributes or other explicit criteria are not supplied by the researcher. The following example illustrates how this is accomplished.

Step 1: Selection of Type of Consumer Evaluation

Nonattribute-based perceptual maps can reflect one of two types of consumer evaluations. Similarity and dissimilarity evaluations present the consumer with pairs of

brands and then asks that consumer to rank order the pairs from most similar to least similar (similarity) or from least similar to most similar (dissimilarity). Preference evaluations present a consumer with a list of individual brands and asks that consumer to rank the brands from most to least preferred. Both forms of consumer brand evaluation are frequently used. To illustrate nonattribute-based perceptual mapping, we will develop a preference-based perceptual map for airlines.[14]

Step 2: Identification of Brands or Products

The next step requires selection of the brands and products that will appear on the perceptual map. Thus, for this example we need to determine the number of airlines that will be mapped and which specific airlines those are to be. While there is no computational limit to the number of brands or products that can be selected, there are mathematical and practical considerations.

First, for both similarity and preference approaches, there is a relationship between the number of brands or products evaluated and the number of dimensions one expects to result from the analysis. It is recommended that a ratio of at least 3:1 be used. That is, one should evaluate at lease three brands for every dimension one expects to uncover. Thus, six or more brands are required for a two-dimensional solution, nine brands for a three-dimensional solution, etc.

Second, there are practical limits on the number of brand pairs that can be rank ordered as part of similarity and dissimilarity data collection. Respondent task demands dramatically increase as the number of brands increase:

Number of Brands	Required Number of Pairs
4	6
6	15
8	28
10	45

Thus, the goal is to select a sufficient number of brands to satisfy mathematical considerations without overburdening the respondent. In the airline example we anticipate two dimensions will form and have selected ten airlines.

Step 3: Write the Survey Question

The question used to collect the data closely resembles traditional rank order questions. However, in this case, the criteria for performing the ranking are not specified and are left up to the respondent. A similarities or dissimilarities question may take the following form:

> SHUFFLE INDEX CARDS. HAND DECK OF CARDS TO RESPONDENT. Each of these cards contains the names of two airlines. Look at the names shown on each card and think about how similar or dissimilar you feel the two airlines are. On the table I have placed numbers from one to forty-five. The card with the two brands you feel are the *most similar* to each other should go in place #1. POINT TO SPACE #1. The card with the two airlines that you feel are the *most dissimilar* from each other should go in place # 45.

---

[14] Data is fictitious and for illustrative purposes only.

POINT TO SPACE # 45. You can move the cards once you have placed them on the table. Here are the cards. HAND DECK OF INDEX CARDS TO RESPONDENT. Let me know when you are satisfied with your placement of all the cards. Remember, each card must go in a separate place. There cannot be any ties. RECORD CARD PLACEMENT BEFORE REMOVING CARDS.

A preferences question may take the following form:

SHUFFLE INDEX CARDS. HAND DECK OF CARDS TO RESPONDENT. Each of these cards contains the name of one airline. Look at the name shown on each card and think about how much you prefer or do not prefer that airline. On the table I have placed numbers from one to ten. The card with the name of the airline that you *most prefer* should go in place #1. POINT TO SPACE #1. The card with the airline that you *least prefer* should go in place #10. POINT TO SPACE #10. You can move the cards once you have placed them on the table. Here are the cards. HAND DECK OF INDEX CARDS TO RESPONDENT. Let me know when you are satisfied with your placement of all the cards. Remember, each card must go in a separate place. There cannot be any ties. RECORD CARD PLACEMENT BEFORE REMOVING CARDS.

This latter question is the type of question that would be used in the airline example, given that we are creating a preference-based perceptual map.

Step 4: Collect and Analyze the Data and Create the Map

Data collection is straightforward. Consumers in the target audience are sampled and data is obtained. In this example, the sample might consist of frequent business travelers.

Data analysis is similar in approach to factor analysis, although the underlying mathematical computations are different. First, eigenvalues for each dimension in the solution are calculated and those dimensions with the largest eigenvalues are selected. Next, using the number of specified dimensions, a score for each object on each dimension is calculated. These scores are used to create the perceptual map.

In this example, the preference ratings result in a two-dimensional solution. The map representing the plot of the ten airlines on these two dimensions is shown in Figure 18.6 (page 436). Note how the airlines cluster into groups in four distinct areas of the map.

Interpreting Dimensions

One drawback of nonattribute-based perceptual mapping is the difficulty in interpreting and naming dimensions. The absence of brand and product attributes makes this a difficult task. What, for example, do the two dimensions in Figure 18.6 actually represent? Is an airline's inclusion in a particular group good or bad?

The difficulty in interpreting dimensions in nonattribute-based perceptual mapping is reduced when rating data is also collected as part of the survey and incorporated into the perceptual map. Consumers can be asked to provide ratings to indicate the extent to which various product attributes are related to their determination of brand preference or affect their determination of brand similarities and differences. The incorporation of this additional data into the perceptual map is illustrated in Figure 18.7 (page 437). As it can now be seen, preference appears strongly related to honesty and on-time performance and somewhat related to number of flights available.

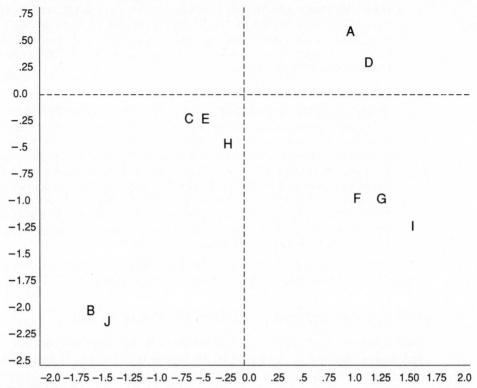

FIGURE 18.6
Preference-based perceptual map of airlines.

Summary

Perceptual maps translate consumers' brand and product perceptions into visual displays that provide data to marketers and advertisers as to

- the number of dimensions consumers use to distinguish between brands and products,
- the nature and characteristics of these dimensions, and
- the location of actual brands, as well as the ideal brand, on these dimensions.

There are two approaches to perceptual mapping: attribute-based and nonattribute-based. Attribute-based approaches require consumers to evaluate a set of brands on all attributes believed to contribute to brand and product evaluation and differentiation. One of three mathematical approaches (factor analysis, discriminant analysis, or correspondence analysis) is then used to isolate relevant dimensions and place evaluated brands or products on the perceptual map. Nonattribute-based perceptual mapping does not require a list of brand, product, or category attributes. Rather, the underlying data in this approach are consumers' judgments of brand and product similarities or preferences. Consumers determine brand similarities and preferences using whatever criteria they normally use. As with attribute-based perceptual mapping, mathematical procedures are used to isolate dimensions and place brands and products along those dimensions.

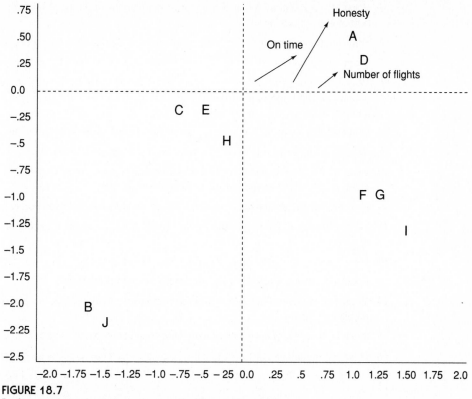

FIGURE 18.7
Preference-based perceptual map of airlines with vectors.

The two approaches to perceptual mapping have complementary strengths and weaknesses. Attribute-based approaches create maps in which the meaning of dimensions is easily discerned. Moreover, the statistical procedures underlying the creation of these types of maps are straightforward and readily available in most personal computer statistical programs. The drawback to this approach is the heavy dependence on a complete list of attributes. The insights provided by an attribute-based perceptual map are greatly diminished if the list of attributes is incomplete. Nonattribute-based perceptual maps rely on the implicit evaluative criteria provided by each respondent. As a result, no list of attributes is required, greatly simplifying data preparation and collection procedures. However, the dimensions created in nonattribute perceptual mapping are often difficult to interpret and personal computer statistical programs for these analyses are not readily available.

Review Questions

1. How have marketers and advertisers used perceptual mapping?
2. What are the two approaches to perceptual mapping? What are the distinguishing characteristics of each approach?

3. What is a *dimension?* What is the role of dimensions in the creation and interpretation of a perceptual map?

4. What are the contributions to strategic planning provided by a perceptual map?

5. What are the steps underlying the creation of an attribute-based perceptual map?

6. Why is it important that the list of attributes for an attribute-based perceptual map contain all the important attributes that consumers use to distinguish among brands and products?

7. What is the goal of *factor analysis?* How does factor analysis achieve this goal?

8. What is an *eigenvalue?* What is its relationship to *sample variance?*

9. How are the dimensions identified by factor analysis selected for inclusion in subsequent analyses and construction of the perceptual map?

10. How are specific brands and products placed on an attribute-based perceptual map?

11. What is a vector? How does the use of vectors help clarify the meaning of a perceptual map?

12. How does *discriminant analysis* differ from factor analysis?

13. How does *correspondence analysis* differ from factor analysis?

14. What is the nature of the data underlying similarity and preference nonattribute-based perceptual maps?

15. What is the process by which nonattribute-based perceptual maps are created?

16. How can the interpretation of nonattribute-based perceptual maps be made clearer?

Application Exercises[15]

1. Your client, Sony, wishes to determine the dimensions consumers use to evaluate CD players and its position versus the competition on these dimensions. You decide that the construction of an attribute-based perceptual map is an appropriate response to this informational need. Sony agrees. Prepare a questionnaire that permits you to collect the appropriate data. Evaluate your questionnaire for thoroughness and completeness.

2. Exchange the questionnaire you developed for the prior exercise with two others in your class. Compare the questionnaires' wording and the lists of product attributes shown in each questionnaire. To what extent are the differences in content significant? How will these differences affect the types of information provided by the perceptual map? Address these two questions and then revise your questionnaire to reflect your conclusions.

3. You have just received the printout for the initial factor analysis of a study of fast food restaurants. The eigenvalues, as well as other data, for each factor are shown in the following table. Which factors would you select for subsequent analyses and construction of the perceptual map? Explain your decision.

[15] All situations and data are fictitious. Brand names are used for illustrative purposes only.

Factor	Eigenvalue	Percent of Variance
1	4.29	39.0
2	3.41	31.0
3	2.99	27.2
4	.13	1.2
5	.06	.5
6	.04	.4
7	.03	.2
8	.02	.2
9	.01	.1
10	.01	.1
11	.01	.1
	11.00	100.0%

4. Your client, CompuDesign, is a company that makes business-oriented microcomputer software. CompuDesign believes that its software suffers from an image problem in the marketplace and, to determine if this is in fact the case, has just completed an attribute based perceptual mapping study. The study was conducted among individuals who use their microcomputer for business at least 50 percent of the time. CompuDesign sends you the following printout of the factor loadings of each attribute measured in the research.

Attribute	Factor 1	Factor 2	Factor 3
Clarity of mannuals	+.589	−.025	+.026
Program expense	−.001	+.879	−.111
Programs are advanced	+.002	−.111	+.895
Programs take advantage of new hardware developments	+.211	+.111	+.789
Company is continually revising programs	−.112	−.058	+.766
Ease of program installation	+.788	−.022	+.111
Quality of in-program help	+.669	−.011	+.025
Quality of 800-number support	+.789	−.069	−.222
Company is continually improving programs	+.222	+.125	+.879
Ease of program use	+.795	−.022	−.158
Company is industry leader	+.111	−.210	+.758
Ease of program customization	−.105	+.102	+.689
Technical support expense	−.022	+.799	+.068
Upgrade expense	−.100	+.879	+.125

CompuDesign asks for your point of view on what the dimensions mean. Write a short memo that names each dimension and explains what each dimension represents. Be certain to fully explain and provide support for your decision.

5. As you are preparing your memo on dimension characteristics for CompuDesign, the client sends you the average factor scores for each competitive software company studied on the research and the average factor scores for the "ideal" company (see the following).

Brand	Factor 1	Factor 2	Factor 3
A	+1.6	+1.7	+1.8
B	+0.2	+0.3	+0.1
CompuDesign	−1.4	−1.6	−1.5
D	−1.6	+1.4	+1.3
E	−0.3	−0.2	−0.1
F	−0.2	−0.1	+0.2
G	+1.2	+1.3	+0.9
H	−1.2	+0.5	+1.7
I	−1.2	+1.5	−1.1
J	+1.5	−1.1	+1.6
Ideal	+1.8	+1.8	+1.9

Use this data to construct the appropriate perceptual maps, using average factor loadings to place individual software companies on the appropriate map or maps. Then, write a memo to CompuDesign explaining the key findings and implications of the perceptual maps that you constructed. Enclose and refer to the appropriate map or maps in the memo.

CHAPTER

19 SEGMENTATION

Very few products are marketed or advertised to a target audience defined as "all adults" or "all consumers." Marketers have learned that "universal" products produced to meet the needs of the "average consumer" are rarely successful, in great part because in today's marketplace there is no such thing as an "average consumer." Today's marketplace is fragmented, consisting of small, distinct groups of consumers that have different attitudes, personal characteristics, product needs, and media habits. To successfully develop and market a product to one of these groups, marketers and advertisers must first identify and understand the unique characteristics of that group. Advertising target audience selection, product positioning, creative strategy, advertising essential message, and media selection are all influenced by group characteristics.

Marketers and advertisers use consumer segmentation research to identify and understand the groups of consumers that comprise the marketplace for a particular product or service. The segmentation research that provides the required marketplace insights may either be conducted by the marketers and advertisers themselves (resulting in customized, proprietary segmentation data) or it may be an adaptation of consumer segmentation research developed and syndicated by others. This chapter introduces you to both forms of consumer segmentation.

After reading this chapter, you will be able to

■ Explain the reasons marketers and advertisers segment markets.

■ Identify the criteria that can be used to define consumer segments.

■ Describe how segmentation research influences advertising planning.

■ Plan and conduct proprietary segmentation research.

■ Identify the most common forms of syndicated segmentation research.

■ Evaluate and select segments for communications targeting.

A great deal of advertising research aggregates the data collected by a research study. The findings summarize and describe relevant aspects of the *sample* of individuals who participated in the research. Consumer segmentation research is just the opposite. A consumer segmentation study seeks to *break down* a population of individu-

als into smaller subgroups where individuals in a specific subgroup are similar to each other in terms of important characteristics and possess characteristics different from individuals in other groups

The outcome of a segmentation of the United States adult population is shown in Table 19.1 (page 444). The segmentation divides the population into six generational cohorts or segments that reflect both an individual's age (his or her generation) and important external events that took place during his or her formative years (the cohort).[1] The cohorts or segments satisfy the two characteristics of a well-conceived segmentation. First, segments are homogeneous with respect to the criteria underlying the segmentation. Each group in this segmentation represents a unique generational cohort and individuals within each group share important characteristics. Second, there is heterogeneity among groups. Each segment is distinct and has its own profile and identity.

WHY ADVERTISERS USE SEGMENTATION

The generational cohort segmentation illustrates how a segmentation divides a population into smaller distinct groups. The unique characteristics of each group formed during a segmentation provide advertisers with important guidance for communications planning.[2]

First, segmentation permits advertisers to consider differences within the potential consumer audience for a particular product or service. As the segment characteristics in the generational cohort segmentation illustrate, it is unlikely that all individuals in the broader adult population will see all brands within a product category as equally acceptable or all advertising messages for brands within a category as equally relevant or persuasive. Different segments are likely to respond differently to the same product or advertising message. Thus, segmentation provides the information required for the planning and presentation of an advertising campaign that exactly fits and responds to the characteristics, needs, and lifestyles of a unique segment of the market, increasing the relevance and potential impact of the advertising. Consumer segmentation thus helps an advertiser to realize that no brand positioning or advertising message can be expected to appeal to all people. As a result, segmentation helps an advertiser understand the need to target a specific group of people with a specific message.

Second, segmentation permits an advertiser to respond to the current structure and realities of the marketplace. Halley, in this regard, points out that it is usually easier to take advantage of market segments that already exist than to try to create new segments. Segmentation, therefore, improves the communication planning process by helping an advertiser understand the consumer segments that comprise the marketplace and how brands are positioned against each other within and among these segments. This understanding makes explicit the range of available positioning, target audience, and message options.

---

[1] Faye Rice, "Making Generational Marketing Come of Age," *Fortune* (June 25, 1995): 110–113.

[2] This discussion is adapted from Richard I. Haley, *Developing Effective Communications Strategy* (New York, NY: John Wiley & Sons, 1985), 231–9; Art Weinstein, *Market Segmentation* (Chicago, IL: Probus Publishing Company, 1994), 8–9.

Third, segmentation helps multibrand advertisers avoid brand cannibalization and maintain distinct brand images. The positioning of different brands against different consumer segments increases a multibrand advertiser's potential to control more of a market by becoming the dominant brand in multiple segments rather than having multiple brands fight each other for a share of the same segment.

Fourth, segmentation helps refine and increase the efficiency of media and promotional plans. Different segments often have different media habits and receptivity to different types of promotional efforts. The identification of a specific segment's media preferences helps a media planner better match media selection with target audience media habits.

Finally, segmentation helps an advertiser uncover new opportunities in secondary smaller or fringe segments. Jello, for example, used segmentation to discover and target a group of mothers who were concerned about the fat and cholesterol in their children's snacks. This group, traditionally not Jello users, was targeted in a special print advertising campaign that communicated the fat-free, cholesterol-free character of Jello.[3]

In sum, marketers and advertisers conduct and use consumer segmentation research because it makes them more efficient and increases their chances for marketplace success.

THE BASIS OF SEGMENTATION

The generational cohort segmentation shown in Table 19.1 (pages 444–445) divided the adult U. S. population based on age and external events. However, these are not the only bases for consumer segmentation. A segmentation can be performed using any of a number of criteria.

Consumer segmentation research typically defines segments by characteristics that fall into four broad areas:

- demographics
- geography
- psychographics (personal attitudes, values, motivations, and lifestyle)
- brand/category-related attitudes and behaviors

Specific characteristics within each of these areas can be used individually as a basis for population segmentation (for example, age or gender) or multiple characteristics can be used simultaneously (for example, age, gender, and psychographics). The remainder of this section discusses the most common criteria and characteristics used for consumer segmentation.

Demographic Characteristics

A *demographic segmentation* of the marketplace defines groups of individuals in terms of demographic characteristics such as age, gender, race, ethnicity, household charac-

---

[3] American Association of Advertising Agencies, *Behind the Scenes: The Advertising Process at Work* (1990), videotape.

TABLE 19.1 Generational Cohort Segmentation

Cohort Name	Born	Age in 1995	Money Motto	Sex Mindset	Favorite Music	Description
The Depression Cohort (the GI generation)	1912–1921	74–83	Save for a rainy day	Intolerant	Big band	Were scarred in ways that persist through today–especially in terms of financial matters such as spending, saving, and debt. The first to be truly influenced by contemporary media: radio and especially television.
The World War II Cohort (the Depression generation)	1922–1927	68–73	Save a lot, spend a little	Ambivalent	Swing	Came of age in the 1940s and are unified by the shared experience of a common enemy and a common goal. A sense of self-denial stemming from and outliving the war is very strong among the cohort's 16 million veterans and their families.
The Postwar Cohort (the silent generation)	1928–1945	50–67	Save some, spend some	Repressive	Sinatra	These war babies benefited from a long period of economic growth and relative social tranquility. However, global unrest and the fear of nuclear war sparked a need to reduce uncertainty in everyday life.

Cohort Name	Born	Age in 1995	Money Motto	Sex Mindset	Favorite Music	Description
The Boomers I Cohort (the Woodstock generation)	1946–1954	41–49	Spend, borrow, spend	Permissive	Rock & roll	Vietnam is the dividing point between younger and older boomers. The Kennedy and King assassinations signaled an end to the status quo and galvanized this vast cohort. These early boomers, however, continued to enjoy economic good times and want a lifestyle at least as good as their parents.
The Boomers II Cohort (zoomers)	1955–1965	30–40	Spend, borrow, spend	Permissive	Rock & roll	Things changed after Watergate. The idealism of youth disappeared. In its place this cohort exhibited a narcissistic preoccupation that manifested itself in things like the self-help movement. In this cohort's dawning age of downward mobility, debt as a means of maintaining a lifestyle had appeal and made sense.
The Generation X Cohort (baby-busters)	1966–1976	19–29	Spend? Save? What?	Confused	Grunge, rap, retro	This cohort has little to hang on to. The latchkey kids of divorce and day care are searching for anchors with their seemingly contradictory "retro" behavior: the resurgence of proms, coming-out parties, fraternities, and sororities. Their political conservatism is motivated by a "What's in it for me?" cynicism.

Source: Fay Rice, "Making Generational Marketing Come of Age, *Fortune* (June 25, 1995): 110–130.

teristics, and social class. These characteristics may be used alone or in combination with other characteristics.

Age   Within any product category, consumers of different ages are likely to have different product needs and product perceptions. College aged men and women, for example, are likely to seek different benefits in audio speakers versus those aged 50 and older. Thus, when age serves as a basis for segmentation, advertisers customize their advertising messages to respond better to differences in needs, perceptions, and behaviors among different age groups.

While age has the potential to form meaningful segments, this potential is only realized when appropriate age ranges are used to define the segments. Defining age segments too broadly tends to blur the differences between age segments. Defining age segments too narrowly results in too many small segments. The presence of either condition significantly reduces a segmentation's usefulness. Thus, age segments must be defined with care. Gibson, for example, points out that it is misleading to treat the nation's 77 million baby boomers as if they were one homogeneous consumer market. His analysis of individuals born between 1946 and 1966 revealed four distinct age segments within the baby boom population. The four segments (defined by age) differed with regard to characteristics such as marriage, childbearing, household income, and home ownership.[4]

Shifts in the size of various age groups are also an important consideration in age-based segmentation. The shrinking teenage market, coupled with the large and growing size of the "aging boomer" market, for example, has prompted jeans marketers and advertisers to shift their target audience focus from the former to the latter group and alter the focus of the product's key benefit from "tight fit style" to "relaxed comfort." Similarly, Maybelline has developed and advertised a line of beauty products for "aging boomers" that wish to look younger.[5]

Gender   Social and cultural forces, as well as physiological and psychological factors, contribute to differences between men and women in product perceptions and product usage. As with age, an understanding of the differences between men and women in a product category provides advertisers with a basis for customizing product positionings and advertising messages. Marlboro, Virginia Slims, and Eve cigarettes are examples of a broad-based consumer product targeted to consumer segments defined by gender.

Household   A household can consist of a single individual, two individuals (friends or married), a nuclear family (with or without two parents, with or without the two biological parents), an extended family, or another combination of adults with or without children. Additionally, when present, the children in a household can be of any age. Marketers and advertisers often segment the population based on household characteristics to identify product needs and advertising opportunities. The marketing and advertising of single serving size food products, for example, responded to the rise in single person households.

[4] Campbell Gibson, "The Four Baby Boomers," *American Demographics* (November 1993): 36–40.
[5] Gabriella Stern, "Aging Boomers Are New Target For Maybelline," *Wall Street Journal* (April 13, 1993): B1.

Life Stage Age, gender, and household size are often combined to form multidimensional life-stage or family life cycle segments. The following is an approach to life-stage segmentation:[6]

1. Young, single
2. Young, married without children
3. Other young
   a. Young divorced without children
   b. Young married with children
      (1) Infant
      (2) Young child (4–12 years old)
      (3) Adolescent
   c. Young divorced with children
      (1) Infant
      (2) Young child (4–12 years old)
      (3) Adolescent
4. Middle-aged
   a. Middle-aged married without children
   b. Middle-aged divorced without children
   c. Middle-aged married with children
      (1) Young
      (2) Adolescent
   d. Middle-aged divorced with children
      (1) Young
      (2) Adolescent
   e. Middle-aged married without dependent children
   f. Middle-aged divorced without dependent children
5. Older
   a. Older married
   b. Older unmarried
      (1) Divorced
      (2) Widowed
6. Others

The relationship between life stage, interests, and behaviors can be seen when you compare the demographics, interests and activities of life-stage segments that differ on only one dimension, for example, dual income households *without* children and dual income households *with at least one child under the age of 13*. Not surprisingly, dual income households without a child are more likely to participate in activities that require a greater commitment of time and disposable income (such as attendance at cultural/arts events and domestic/foreign travel). Dual income households with a child under age 13 are far less likely to participate in these types of activities and are more likely to participate in home-centered activities that require less of a time or financial commitment.[7] Clearly, different types and products and advertising messages would appeal to each segment.

Life-stage segmentation often results in a more useful and powerful segmenta-

[6] Patrick E. Murphy and William A. Staples, "A Modernized Family Life Cycle," *Journal of Consumer Research* 6 (June, 1979): 12–22.

[7] Standard Rate and Data Service, *The Lifestyle Market Analyst*™ (Wilmette: IL: Standard Rate and Data Service, 1994).

tion of the marketplace versus segmentations based on individual demographic characteristics. This is because life-stage segmentation acknowledges that consumers in the same life stage are likely to have similar needs *regardless* of differences in one or two underlying demographic characteristics. A diaper advertiser, for example, knows that new mothers will likely need (and seek similar benefits from) diapers regardless of whether that new mother is aged 24 or 44.

Race and Ethnicity   Many marketers and advertisers have segmented their total target audience to increase the relevance and appeal of their advertising to specific racial or ethnic groups, for example:

- Cadillac has initiated an advertising campaign specifically targeted to African Americans.[8]
- The John H. Harland Company has developed and advertised a bank check series specifically targeted to African Americans.[9]
- Scott Paper, General Foods, and Metropolitan Life have developed ads in Chinese, Japanese, Spanish, and Korean.[10]

The impact of racial segmentation on communications planning can be seen in advertising developed by the Burrell Communications Group for Stove Top Stuffing Mix. The ad responded to the perceptions and lifestyle of the target segment of African American women by

- using the more common term (for this target audience) "dressing" instead of "stuffing,"
- featuring the target audience's formulation preference (cornbread) rather than the company's best selling formulation (turkey),
- discarding the traditional positioning of "instead of potatoes." This reflected the fact that traditional African American meals include both stuffing and potatoes,
- shifting the visual scene from a suburban to an urban setting.[11]

Social Class   Similar to life-stage segmentation, social class segmentation reflects the combined influence of several related demographic characteristics: education, occupation, and income. Social class segmentation reflects the assumption that individuals in different social classes may have different attitudes, product needs, and different amounts of available funds for product purchase. As a result, different advertising messages and product positionings (for example, "lowest price" versus "value" or "highest quality") may be more appropriate for different groups. The product lines, store positionings, and advertising messages of mass marketers such as Wal-Mart, Target, Sears, and Nieman-Marcus clearly reflect social class segmentation.

---

[8] Cyndee Miller, "Cadillac Promo Targets African-Americans," *Advertising Age* (May 21, 1994): 12–13.

[9] Karen Holliday, "Reaching Ethnic Markets," *Bank Marketing* (February 1993): 35–37.

[10] See Gail B. Woods, *Advertising and Marketing to the New Majority* (New York, NY: Wadsworth Publishing Company, 1994), Holliday "Reaching Ethnic Markets."

[11] This example is taken from Gail B. Woods, *Advertising and Marketing to the New Majority*, 69–78.

Geographic Segmentation

Geographic location provides clues about how individuals live, think, and relate to various brands and product benefits. It is a common belief that different geographic areas, formed by different patterns of population dispersion, reflect different types of cultural development, behavioral patterns, attitudes, and perceptions.[12] Consequently, marketers and advertisers often use *geographic segmentation* to identify consumer segments based on geographic boundaries and population characteristics.

The most common criteria used in geographic segmentation research are: region, population size, population density, and climate.

Region   Several approaches have been used to divide the United States into regions. These approaches differ with respect to the size and number of divisions presented, for example:

- East, North, West, South
- East, West Central, East Central, West, South
- Pacific, Mountain, West North Central, West South Central, East North Central, East South Central, South Atlantic, Middle Atlantic, and New England

Population Size   The U. S. census defines population size in terms of metropolitan statistical areas.[13] The three types of areas are

- *Metropolitan Statistical Area (MSA)*—A geographic area that contains at least one city of 50,000 or more people or urban areas of at least 50,000 people in a region with a total population of 100,000 or more.
- *Primary Metropolitan Statistical Areas (PMSAs)*—Geographic areas with 1 million or more residents that are associated with one or more urbanized counties.
- *Consolidated Metropolitan Statistical Areas (CMSAs)*—Geographic areas containing more than one PMSA.

The A. C. Nielsen Company, as well as other leading research organizations, also classify counties by population, as follows:

County Size A: All counties belonging to the largest MSAs.

County Size B: All counties not included under A that are either over 150,000 population or in MSAs over 150,000.

County Size C: All counties not included under A or B that are either over 40,000 population of in MSAs over 40,000

County Size D: All remaining counties

Population density refers to the concentration of people within a specific area, for example, number of people per square mile. Urban areas tend to have the highest population density, followed by suburban and rural areas.

---

[12] Ronald D. Michman, *Lifestyle Market Segmentation* (New York, NY: Praeger, 1991), 27.

[13] For information on the classification of specific geographic areas see the current edition of the *Statistical Abstract of the United States* (Washington, D.C.: United States Government Printing Office).

Climate is generally described in terms of seasonality and temperature. Southern California tends to have a consistent (dry, 60°F–80°F) climate throughout the year while the Midwest has four distinct seasons, each displaying a different weather pattern.

Geographic segmentation can contribute to several areas of marketing and advertising planning. Marketers who understand regional differences in product preferences can make certain that the characteristics of their products respond to the needs and desires of a particular region. Campbell's, for example, has introduced spicier versions of their soups to better satisfy consumers' preference for spicier food in the West and South. Advertisers who understand regional variance in product usage can also create better, more efficient media plans.

- Different purchase patterns in different geographic areas imply different media schedules. Barbeque sauce is purchased all year in warmer climates, and thus may require a different advertising schedule than cooler markets where product purchase is concentrated in the summer months.

- Different levels of product purchase in different geographic areas often imply the need for different levels of media allocation, since many advertisers wish to concentrate their advertising spending in those geographic areas that show higher levels of consumption. Sparkling water, for example, shows higher consumption in urban areas in the Northeast and West while powdered soft drinks show higher consumption in the Midwest.

Psychographic Segmentation

The term "psychographic" is used to describe measures of an individual's attitudes, values, motivations, and lifestyle. A *psychographic segmentation*, therefore, divides the population into groups based on characteristics in one or more of these areas. Psychographic segmentation assumes that what people think, how they are motivated, and how they lead their lives are often strong determinants or predictors of their use of specific types of goods and services.

Attitudes and Values   Individuals who are in the same demographic category often have different attitudes and values. Consequently, consumers' attitudes and values often provide a useful basis for market segmentation. Attitudes and values can be generalized attitudes toward life, career, self-image, the importance of status and recognition *or* they can be attitudes and values specific to a product category.

The use of *general* attitudes and values as a basis for segmentation helps advertisers better understand important differences within individuals of the same age group and among individuals of different age groups. Attitudes toward oneself and the future was an effective way of distinguishing different attitudinal segments within the demographic segment of "mature individuals" (defined as those who are aged 50 and older). Morgan and Levy[14] identified four attitudinal segments within this market:

- *Upbeat Enjoyer*—Individuals who are most likely to feel that their best years are now and in the future. High priorities are looking good and staying active. They feel financially secure.

---

[14] Carol M. Morgan and Doran J. Levy, *Segmenting the Mature Market,* (Chicago, IL: Probus Publishing Company, 1993).

- *Insecure*—Individuals who feel that they have not been successful in life and that the best years of their lives lie in the past. They are afraid they will not have enough money for the future, they invest conservatively, shop for value, and are generally uncomfortable with their appearance.
- *Threatened Active*—Individuals who have a positive outlook on life, although the outlook is tempered by worries about crime. Very resistant to change, they want to keep living in their own homes and working at their current job. These individuals do not worry about "looking young."
- *Financial Positives*—Individuals who are more open to change and more concerned about looking good. They feel financially secure, successful, and optimistic.

Thus, while the age composition of all four groups is similar, the attitudes within each group are very different, indicating that one single advertising message is unlikely to be effective in reaching the entire "mature market."

Different attitudinal segments indicate the need for different advertising messages. Additionally, it is often the case that different attitudinal segments (even within the same age group) also have different media habits, indicating the need for different media plans for different attitudinal segments. The four "mature market" segments formed by Morgan and Levy illustrate this occurrence. There was considerable variance among the four segments in terms of network and cable television viewing, radio listening, and newspaper readership. Morgan and Levy found that the *Insecure* were more likely than the other groups to watch network television, the *Threatened Actives* were more likely to watch cable television and listen to the radio and the *Financial Positives* were more likely to read the newspaper.[15]

Category specific attitudes, rather then general attitudes, can also be used as the basis of a psychographic segmentation. Here, the segmentation reflects differences in individuals' attitudes toward the product category, his or her relationship to the product category, and how the product category fits into his or her lifestyle. Nissan, for example, used attitudes toward cars to segment consumers in the automotive market. Nissan discovered six attitudinal groups of car owners and purchasers:

- *gearheads,* who enjoy driving and working on their cars;
- *epicures,* who prefer stylish, elegant sports cars;
- *purists,* who like cars and enjoy driving, but who are skeptical about ad claims;
- *functionalists,* who prefer sensible, conservative cars;
- *road-haters,* who do not like driving and who do value safety features;
- *negatives,* who view cars as a necessary evil.[16]

Clearly, the types of cars featured and the messages communicated by Nissan would vary among the six attitudinal segments.

Motivations   Brand perceptions and consumer buying behavior are often influenced by underlying motivations. Consequently, the motivations that underlie consumer behavior often provide an insightful basis for segmenting a product category and advertising audience. Motivational segmentation assumes that if you understand an individ-

---

[15] Ibid.

[16] Marc B. Rubner, "The Hearts of New Car Buyers," *American Demographics* (August, 1991): 14–15.

ual's motivations for buying (or not buying) a product then you can tailor your advertising message to capitalize on (or counter) those motivations.

Quidel Corporation provides an excellent example of motivational segmentation and the tailoring of communications (in this case, package design) for different motivationally defined consumer segments. Quidel is a manufacturer of home pregnancy tests, ovulation tests, and other home-based medical products. The company markets two different home pregnancy tests: Conceive and RapidVue. The package of Conceive brand pregnancy test features an adorable baby smiling at the potential purchaser from a pink box. The package exudes warmth and friendliness. The package of Rapid-Vue brand pregnancy test is much starker. There are no warm, happy colors. There is no smiling baby. The product name is printed in brick-red lettering against a mauve background. However, while the packaging of the two brands are very different *the product inside each package is identical*. Each package is nevertheless designed to appeal to a different motivational segment. Conceive is marketed to those who desire to conceive, RapidVue is marketed to those who do not.[17]

Lifestyle   Lifestyle segmentation divides the population based on interests, activities, hobbies, participation in various forms of social events, sports, and other activities. Segmentation based on these and related measures helps marketers understand the relationship between how consumers spend their time and lead their lives and the types and brands of products that they use.[18] Lifestyle segmentation has proven to be a useful way of segmenting the market for "badge" products (i.e., products that are conspicuously consumed or displayed) such as liquor, automobiles, cigarettes, and clothing.

Category and Brand-Related Attitudes and Behaviors

Segmentation based on category and brand-related attitudes and behaviors is an extremely common form of consumer segmentation. This form of segmentation divides a population of consumers by product usage, brand loyalty, or desired benefits.

Product Usage Segmentation   Product usage segmentation is straightforward. The population is divided to reflect patterns in brand and product usage, quantity of consumption, or the situation in which the product is used. These characteristics may be used independently or in combination with other brand or product related characteristics. When used independently the population is divided as follows:

- Segmentation based on *brand usage* divides the population into groups that differ with respect to *patterns* of brand usage, typically the brand used most often. Beer drinkers, for example, could be segmented to reflect the beer brand that had the greatest consumption within the prior month.
- Segmentation based on *product usage* divides the population into groups based on the *types* of products consumed. Beer drinkers could be segmented to reflect the type of

---

[17] Rita Koselka, "Hope and Fear as Marketing Tools," *Forbes* (August 29, 1994): 78–79.

[18] See, for example, Anne B. Fisher, "What Consumers Want in the 1990s," *Fortune* (January 29, 1990): 108–12; Joseph T. Plummer, "The Concept and Application of Lifestyle Segmentation," *Journal of Marketing* 38 (January, 1974): 33–37.

beer (import, domestic; premium, super-premium) that had the greatest consumption within the prior month.

- Segmentation based on *quantity of consumption* divides the population on the basis of *amount* of product consumed. Beer drinkers could be segmented to reflect the total amount of beer consumed within the prior month.

- Segmentation based on *situation of consumption* divides the population to reflect the *circumstances* in which the product is used. Beer drinkers could be segmented to reflect where the product is primarily consumed, for example, at restaurants, at home, at a bar, etc.

Brand Loyalty   Brand loyalty is a measure of consumer attachment to a particular brand. Loyalty can range from absolute commitment to a total lack of preference. Segmentation based on brand loyalty divides the population to reflect loyalty to a particular brand. An understanding of the attitudes, demographics, and motivations of different loyalty groups helps an advertiser to identify the creative approach and essential message that is most likely to reinforce loyalty among their own users and reduce loyalty among the competitors' users.

Benefit Segmentation   Benefit segmentation divides a consumer population to reflect the benefits sought from products in the target product category. Consumers who want similar product benefits are placed in the same segment, resulting in as many segments as there are major benefits in the product category. Advertisers can examine the internal characteristics of each benefit segment and then determine the segment they wish to address and the appropriate advertising message to communicate to that specific segment.

The two ads shown in Figure 19.1 (pages 454–455) demonstrate the results of a benefit segmentation and the implications of this segmentation for advertising communications. Both Chase Manhattan Bank and Great Eastern Savings Bank are offering the same product: personal banking and related financial services via personal computer. The Great Eastern ad is directed toward a "cost-conscious" segment of consumers. The ad's headlines and copy stress the free aspects of the service. The Chase Manhattan Bank ad is directed toward a different benefit segment of consumers—those for whom banking is not a priority and who seek the benefits of time savings and convenience.

CONDUCTING CUSTOMIZED, PROPRIETARY SEGMENTATION RESEARCH

The planning and conduct of customized, proprietary segmentation research begins similarly to other quantitative research (see Chapter 2). The need for the research is identified, segmentation is selected as an appropriate response to informational needs and sample and sampling issues are addressed. The actual segmentation research follows eleven steps (see Figure 19.2, page 456). This section discusses the major events and decisions that take place at each step. A segmentation study of baby boomer shoppers conducted by Swinyard and Rinne[19] is used to illustrate the process "in action."

---

[19] Tom R. Swinyard and Heikki J. Rinne, "The Six Shopping Worlds of Baby Boomers," *American Demographics* (September/October, 1994): 64–69.

ME & MY TIME

"First comes my family, then my job. Banking is somewhere down the list."

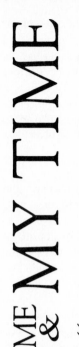

CHASE has created a new way of banking for people who no longer have time for banking. It's called ChaseDirect℠ and it lets you manage your money by computer, fax, ATM or phone, whenever you have the time, from any place you happen to be. At ten p.m. after the kids are already asleep. At two a.m. when you can't get to sleep. From the office, car - even when you're out of town.

It's more personal because you can always speak to a well-informed banking specialist. It's more convenient because almost all your financial activity can be linked through one core ChaseDirect account. And it's more rewarding because there is no charge

INTRODUCING

CHASE DIRECT

for PC Banking, ATM transactions and paying bills by phone. And now only ChaseDirect lets you manage your money with PC Banking and your choice of free Microsoft® Money for Windows®95 or Quicken® 5.0 software. After three months, we'll even credit your account with a $50 bonus. Call now for full details. ChaseDirect. It's banking for the 21st Century and only Chase has it.

Get free Quicken 5.0 or Microsoft Money and $50 to boot.

1 - 8 0 0 - C H A S E - 2 4

FAX: 1-800-881-9475 · **E-MAIL:** ChaseOnLine@DELPHI.COM · 24 HOURS A DAY, 7 DAYS A WEEK

CHASE MANHATTAN. PROFIT FROM THE EXPERIENCE.

FIGURE 19.1

Chase Manhattan (above) and Great Eastern Savings Bank (page 455) ads.
Sources: The Chase Manhattan Bank ad reprinted with permission. The Great Eastern ad courtesy of K&MD.

Your Personal Computer.
Great Eastern's free services.
Your new fee free bank!

Free
Banking via PC

Free
Technical support

Free
Banking software

Free
Data access

Free
Bill payment services

Call Great Eastern today. Start using our free banking services tomorrow.

Now with your personal computer and modem and Great Eastern's free on-line banking services you can bank from your office or home. Anytime night or day. Free of all charges.

Everything you need. Free.

Some banks charge you for access. And some charge you for software. Even others charge you for technical support. But not Great Eastern. Everything you need, and everything that you need to do, is free.

Great Eastern offers a full range of services:
    Free stock quotes, 24 hours a day
    Free support, 24 hours a day
    Free bill payment services
    Free account access
    Free money transfers

And perhaps most importantly, a free and easy way to get started.

To enroll or for more information call:
1-800-FREE-PCS Ext. 9937

FIGURE 19.1 (continued)

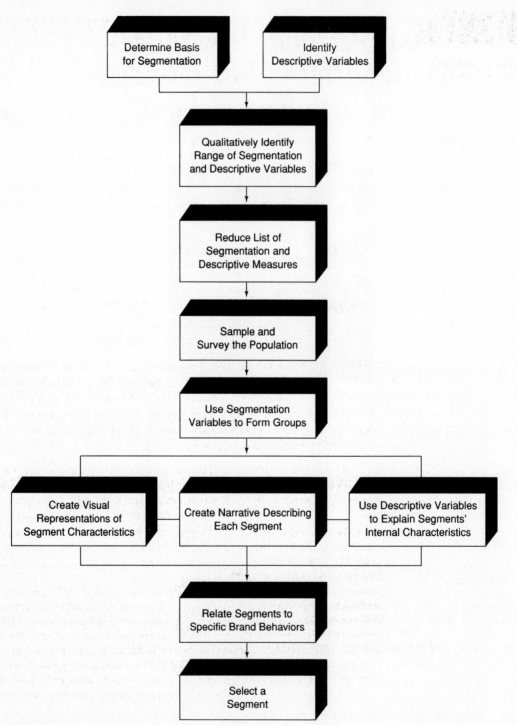

FIGURE 19.2
Steps in the conduct of customized, proprietary segmentation research.

Determine Basis for Segmentation

The prior sections presented examples of four ways to segment a market: (1) demographics, (2) geography, (3) psychographics, and (4) category- and brand-related characteristics. In each segmentation, one or more criteria were selected to serve as the basis of the segmentation. The generational cohort segmentation used age and external events, for example, while Quidel used consumer motivations.

The first step in the conduct of customized, proprietary segmentation research is the identification of the variable(s) that will be used to segment the market. The variable(s) used to segment the market are labeled the *segmentation variable(s)* and is the equivalent of the independent variable(s) in experimental research. The variable(s) selected as the basis for population segmentation should be

- relevant to the product category,
- related to category, product or brand-related perceptions and behaviors,
- have a high likelihood of being causal factors of category, product, or brand choice and usage.

The key to meaningful segmentation research rests on the relevance and completeness of the set of segmentation variables used in the research. The inclusion of extraneous variables or the exclusion of important variables greatly reduces the contribution of the segmentation research to a better understanding of marketplace structure and dynamics.

Swinyard and Rinne's goal was to provide an understanding of how baby boomers decide at which discount store to shop. They began their research by identifying the basis for the segmentation—the attributes baby boomers sought in a discount store.

Qualitatively Identify the Range of Segmentation and Descriptive Variables

Segmentation variables are the dimensions or characteristics that individuals within a group share and that differ among individuals in different groups. *Descriptive variables,* additional measures of each consumer, provide the basis for understanding the characteristics of each segment once they have been formed based on the segmentation variables. (Descriptive variables are the equivalent of dependent variables in experimental research.) The extent of insights provided by descriptive variables are directly related to the care with which they are selected, their relevance to the segmentation and most importantly their ability to provide an understanding of the internal characteristics of each segment.

Swinyard and Rinne decided to use lifestyle and attitudinal measures to explain the internal characteristics of discount store shopper segments. Their descriptive variables assessed attitudes toward shopping, factors that might affect shopping behaviors such as financial and time resources, attitudes toward one's self and one's lifestyle, values and personal priorities, money spent shopping, and demographics.

After the range of measures are identified, most consumer segmentation studies utilize qualitative research *before* the quantitative portion of the study is finalized and sent "into the field." As discussed earlier, the success of any segmentation study rests on the successful identification of segmentation and descriptive variables. Qualitative

research, in conjunction with any secondary research already conducted, assists in the identification of these variables by helping a researcher develop and explore

- intuitions, hypotheses, and beliefs about the specific dimensions of the segmentation and descriptive variables relevant to the proposed segmentation,
- the language used by consumers to describe these specific dimensions.[20]

These insights guide the content and form of attitude scales and other measuring instruments that will be used in the quantitative phase of the research.

The initial list of discount store attributes and descriptive measures in the Swinyard and Rinne research was compiled from focus groups, a specialized repertory grid technique, and a comprehensive search of secondary research sources. These procedures produced a list of approximately 200 discount store attributes.

Reduce the List of Segmentation and Descriptive Measures

Qualitative research produces a large initial list of items. Many items on the initial list measure similar characteristics. As a result, the initial list of segmentation and descriptive measures is often reduced via a pilot study and factor analysis to a smaller list of items each of which measures unique characteristics, attitudes, and behaviors.

This is the approach that Swinyard and Rinne used to reduce their initial set of measures. The list of 200 store attributes was reduced via factor analysis to a set of twenty-two discount store attributes. These attributes measured attitudes toward discount stores in eight areas:

- prices and consistency
- style and quality of clothing
- store layout
- merchandise assortment
- advertising
- salespeople
- customer service
- location

The large set of lifestyle measures was reduced via factor analysis to a set of forty items that measured attitudes in nine areas:

- style and service awareness
- shopping as recreation
- stress
- price sensitivity
- traditional values
- modern values
- financial optimism
- promotion sensitivity
- time sensitivity

---

[20] Tony Lunn, "Segmenting and Constructing Markets," In Robert M. Worcester and John Downham eds., *Consumer Market Research Handbook, Third Edition* (Amsterdam: North-Holland, 1986), 387–424.

Sample and Survey the Population

Once the segmentation and descriptive variables have been identified the question-naire is developed, pilot tested, revised, and quantitative research is used to survey the target population. Typically, random or stratified random sampling is used to select the sample. Interviews are generally conducted by mail or telephone and typically consist of closed-ended Likert-type scales. Swinyard and Rinne utilized the following methodology:

> The study was conducted among 1,003 adult shoppers in six geographic markets saturated with discount stores . . . We sent 3,300 questionnaires to a probability sample of female shoppers with the mailout divided equally among the cities. Each mailing included a cover letter, a six-page questionnaire, a $2 bill and a business return envelope. The questionnaire included measures of the importance of store attributes in choosing a discounter, respondent lifestyle measures, store use patterns and demographics. By the cut off date, 1,003 responses had been received for a return rate of 30.4%. The 544 respondents who are baby boomers became the focus of the study.[21]

Use the Segmentation Variables to Form Groups

Data analysis follows data collection. Segments are formed via cluster analysis. Here, respondents with similar patterns of response to the segmentation variables are placed in the same group.[22] Swinyard and Rinne found six segments of baby boomer discount store shoppers.

Cluster analysis forms the groups. It is a researcher's responsibility to determine how the groups differ from each other in terms of the segmentation variables. This is commonly accomplished by cross-tabulating the segmentation variables with each segment. Depending on the level of measurement, percentages or means may be used to summarize the differences in segmentation measures among individual segments.

The pattern of response underlying segment structure is then examined. This pattern is used to name each group, where the name is intended to provide a quick identifier of the most salient aspects of group structure. Swinyard and Rinne named their six shopper segments:

- Discount Hobbyists
- Discounter Dodgers
- Tough Nuts
- Creative Shopping Avoiders
- Time-Poor Shoppers
- Price-Mobilized Shoppers

---

[21] Swinyard and Rinne, "The Six Shopping Worlds of Baby Boomers," 64–69.

[22] The most common form of cluster analysis is the "nearest neighbor approach." Here, each respondent's pattern of response is examined. The first two cases combined into a cluster are those that have the smallest distance (or largest similarity) between them. The distance between a new cluster and each succeeding new case is then computed as the minimum distance between an individual case and a case in the cluster. "The distances between cases that have not been joined do not change. At every step, the distance between two clusters is the distance between their two closest points." This process forms segments such that cases within a segment are very similar to each other and very different from cases in other clusters. See Marija J. Norusis, *SPSS Introductory Statistics Student Guide,* (Chicago, IL: SPSS Inc., 1990), 344–61.

	Discount Hobbyists	Tough Nuts	Discounter Dodgers	Creative Shopping Avoiders	Price-Mobilized Shoppers	Time-Poor Shoppers
Prices and consistency	0.4	0.7	−1.0	0.1	0.8	0.8
Clothing style and quality	0.7	0.4	0.0	0.2	0.7	−2.2
Store layout	0.2	0.7	0.0	0.2	−0.1	−0.3
Assortment	0.7	0.0	−0.2	−0.6	0.5	0.7
Advertising	0.3	0.0	0.5	−1.4	−0.4	−0.1
Salespeople	0.7	0.3	−0.2	0.6	−1.6	0.5
Customer service	0.3	0.6	−0.4	0.8	0.1	−0.3
Location	0.8	−0.9	0.2	0.2	0.3	−0.4

TABLE 19.2 Swinyard and Rinne Segments and Discount Store Importance Ratings

Note: Importance–unimportance ratings range from +0.8 to −2.4.

Source: Tom R. Swinyard and Heikki J. Rinne, "The Six Shopping Worlds of Baby Boomers," *American Demographics* (September/October 1994): 64–69.

The underlying patterns of response that led to these names is reflected in each segment's importance ratings of the eight discount store attributes. Table 19.2 shows the results of the cross-tabulation that led these group names.

Create Visual Representation of Segment Characteristics

The format used in Table 19.2 is one way to present the data underlying various segments. While this format is complete, it may not be the best means of presenting the data to nonresearchers at the agency and client. The many rows of columns and numbers make it difficult for nonresearchers to see the underlying pattern of response and to compare the similarities and differences among groups.

An alternative format for presenting the data underlying a segmentation is the "radar chart" (see Figure 19.3). Here, concentric circles are used to communicate the magnitude of a segment's response on a particular segmentation variable. The smaller inner circles represent high negative response while the larger outer circles represent high positive response. Each radius represents one segmentation variable or factor. The radar charts shown in Figure 19.3 present the importance ratings of the *Discount Dodgers* and *Creative Shopping Avoiders* segments in the Swinyard and Rinne study. Notice how the radar charts immediately communicate the differences between the two segments.

Create A Narrative Describing Each Segment

The next step in analysis of segmentation variables is the creation of a narrative. This narrative describes in words, rather than numbers, the characteristics of each segment

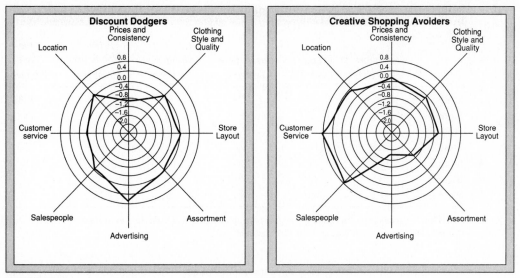

FIGURE 19.3
Radar charts of *Discount Dodgers* and *Creative Shopping Avoiders.*
Source: Data is from Tom R. Swinyard and Heikki J. Rinne, "The Six Shopping Worlds of Baby Boomers," *American Demographics* (September/October 1994): 64–69. Radar charts constructed by the author.

with respect to the segmentation variables. Swinyard and Rinne's narrative description of *Discount Hobbyists* was as follows:

> Discount Hobbyists want the best of everything. They want high-quality merchandise on sale or at a low price. They scan ads looking for bargains and are offended when sale items are out of stock. They look for quality clothing of the latest styles. Uniquely attracted to stores and departments having immense assortments of merchandise, they want to be served by friendly and speedy clerks, do not want to wait in line at checkout and insist on a conveniently located outlet.[23]

Use Descriptive Variables to Explain Each Segment's Internal Characteristics

A second cross-tabulation typically follows the formation of segments. Here, the individual descriptive measures (or the factors formed from the descriptive measures) are cross-tabulated with each segment. The goal of this cross-tabulation is the identification and description of each segment's internal characteristics so that similarities and differences among groups on descriptive measures can be easily seen.

The outcome of the analysis of descriptive measures is similar to that of the segmentation variables. A verbal description of the unique characteristics of each segment is created. Swinyard and Rinne used the cross-tabulation of psychographic and demographic information to create this description of the *Discount Hobbyist:*

> *Psychographics.* Shopping is a leisurely hobby for members of this segment, who are big coupon users. They like stores that give them the royal treatment. They like buying presents. They feel the stress of life, can't live with clutter, are style and fashion conscious,

---

[23] Swinyard and Rinne, "The Six Shopping Worlds of Baby Boomers," 64–69.

TABLE 19.3 Discount Store Usage Within Shopper Segments					
	Discount Hobbyists	*Tough Nuts*	*Discounter Dodgers*	*Creative Shopping Avoiders*	*Price-Mobilized Shoppers*	*Time-Poor Shoppers*
Store A	26%	10%	11%	9%	20%	13%
Store B	8	8	31	5	14	15
Store C	11	32	3	7	11	16
Store D	15	11	9	36	12	17
Store E	5	11	16	13	19	17
Store F	32	22	22	25	19	19
Store G	3	6	8	5	5	3

Note: Data is hypothetical. The numbers in each column represent that segment's estimate of the percent of its total discount store expenditures spent at each discount store.

and feel self-confident. They have traditional values. They like to listen to the radio and have no real interest in the arts.

Demographics. Discount Hobbyists spend an intermediate amount ($657 per family) for Christmas. It is the youngest group, currently having among the lowest education (perhaps because many are still studying for another degree), personal income, and family size. It is the second lowest segment in the proportion holding white-collar jobs.[24]

Relate Segments to Specific Brand Behaviors

Once the segments are understood in terms of the segmentation and descriptive variables, it is then necessary to determine the brand specific behaviors of each segment. This analysis, typically based on additional cross-tabulations, permits marketers and advertisers to determine areas of strength and weakness among the segments comprising the broader target population. This information provides critical insights into the final step in segmentation research, selection of a segment to be the brand's marketing, and advertising target audience.

Hypothetical data relating discount store shopping behaviors by shopper segment is shown in Table 19.3.[25] The data illustrates that Discount Stores A though D each have different mixes of strengths and weaknesses as each is dominant within a different discount shopper segment. Discount Store F appears to be the strongest of all stores, accounting for a high share of expenditures within each segment. Discount Store G appears to be the weakest store, accounting for few expenditures within any of the discount shopper segments.

Select A Segment

The final step in segmentation research is the selection of a segment for marketing and advertising focus. Because not all segments within a population have equal appeal

---

[24] Ibid.

[25] Swinyard and Rinne did not present the results of this step in their study, perhaps because their study was academically rather than marketing oriented. This is the reason why hypothetical data is presented.

from a marketing or advertising perspective, marketers and advertisers must examine the internal characteristics of the segments to evaluate each segment's appeal as a potential target audience. Marketers and advertisers evaluate the potential appeal and appropriateness of a segment to be a target audience in terms of several criteria.

First, and perhaps most important, the segment must be of sufficient size to be profitable, that is, it must be large enough to support the cost of marketing and advertising efforts directed toward that segment. This does not mean that small segments are, by definition, unattractive. It simply means that segment size must be evaluated in light of a marketer's ability to balance sales and marketing/advertising expenditures.

Second, the segment must show growth potential. Clearly, segments that show growth potential are more attractive to advertisers than segments that are stable or declining.

Third, the segment must be accessible. Accessibility is related to profitability. As just discussed, one underlying rational of segmentation is that the increased cost of reaching distinct segments of consumers can be justified by higher sales and market share in those segments. However, there are limits to increased costs that advertisers are willing to bear. If extraordinary efforts (and associated funds) are required to reach and communicate a message to a segment then that segment may not be a reasonable one to select.

Fourth, there should be reasonable confidence that the segment will respond to advertising or other communication programs. An identified market segment that can be efficiently reached, is growing and is potentially profitable may still be eliminated if it is believed that there are barriers that prevent the segment from positively responding to marketing and advertising initiatives. Thus, many segments are eliminated from consideration because of the belief that the advertising will have little effect or other barriers exist that would prevent the advertiser's success in that segment.

These considerations in segment selection also apply to syndicated segmentation research, as illustrated in the next section's discussion of syndicated approaches to consumer segmentation.

SYNDICATED APPROACHES TO CONSUMER SEGMENTATION

The prior sections discussed how marketers and advertisers conduct and use segmentation research as well as the procedures that underlie the conduct of customized, proprietary population segmentation. There are times when proprietary segmentation research is too costly or time consuming. In these cases, marketers and advertisers might use one of the syndicated approaches to segmentation. Syndicated approaches generally fall into one of three categories:

- psychographic segmentation
- product usage segmentation
- geodemographic segmentation

The remainder of this chapter discusses each of these syndicated approaches to segmentation.

Psychographic Segmentation

Values and Lifestyle Segmentation 2 (commonly known as VALS2) is the most commonly used syndicated psychographic segmentation. VALS2 is a segmentation of the adult population that reflects differences in individuals' attitudes, motivations, lifestyles, and resources. The underlying philosophy of the VALS2 segmentation is that individuals' receptivity to products and advertising messages can be predicted by their attitudes and motivations as represented in the VALS2 typology.[26]

VALS2 divides the adult population into eight groups (see Figure 19.4). The groups are stacked vertically to reflect the amount of *resources* available to each group, where resources include income, education, self-confidence, health, eagerness to buy, intelligence, and energy level. Most resources tend to increase from young adulthood to middle age and then decline between middle and old age. The groups are spread horizontally to reflect differences in *self-orientation*. VALS2 posits the existence of three self-orientation groups. Principle-oriented individuals are guided by their view of the ideal world and by how people in this ideal world should treat and interact with others. Status-oriented individuals are most influenced by the actions and opinions of others while action-oriented individuals are motivated by a desire for social or physical activity, variety, and risk-taking.

Two groups fall at the extreme vertical ends of the VALS2 typology. *Actualizers,* who represent about 8 percent of adults, enjoy the "finer things" in life and value personal growth and challenges. Image is important to these individuals, not as evidence of status or power but as a means for expressing their taste, independence, and character. Actualizers have the highest income of all groups. Moreover, they have such high self-esteem and resources that they can indulge in all three self-orientations. Actualizers are very receptive to new products, new technologies, and new forms of product and message distribution. *Strugglers* (about 12 percent of adults) fall on the opposite end of the resource continuum. Strugglers are the oldest, poorest, and least well educated of all segments. Individuals in this group are so focused on immediate health and safety needs (they are heavy users of coupons and watch for sales) that the self-orientation principles do not really apply.

The Principle-oriented group consists of the Fulfilleds and Believers segments. *Fulfilleds* are well-educated, professional, mature individuals. (Half of this group is aged 50 or older.) They are content with their families, social position, and careers and, perhaps as a result, a great deal of their leisure activities center around their homes and family. In spite of this close-to-home orientation, however, Fulfilleds are well informed about what goes on in the world and they are open to new ideas and social change. Fulfilleds have little interest in image or prestige, and despite their high incomes, they are practical, value-oriented consumers. *Believers* (16 percent of adults) share the principle-orientation of Fulfilleds but have fewer resources. (More than one-third of Believers are retired.) Believers are conservative, follow established norms and patterns, are slow to change habits, buy American, and look for bargains. Believers' lives tend to be centered on their families, church, community, and the nation.

---

[26] This discussion is based on Courtland L. Bovee, et al., *Advertising Excellence* (New York, NY: McGraw-Hill, 1994), 123; Judith Waldrop, "Markets With an Attitude," *American Demographics* (July, 1994): 22–32; Martha Riche, "Psychographics for the 1990s," *American Demographics* (July, 1989), 24–26.

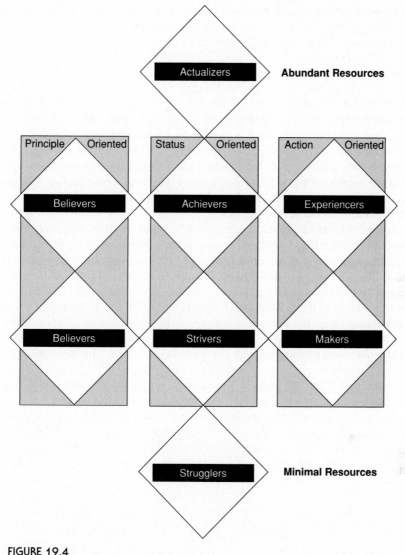

FIGURE 19.4
VALS2 segmentation.
Source: Adapted from SRI International (Menlo Park, CA) and Judith Waldrop, "Markets With an Attitude," *American Demographics* (July 1994): 22–32.

The Status-oriented group consists of Achievers and Strivers. *Achievers* (13 percent of adults) are committed to their families and their work. They are politically conservative and respect authority and the status quo. Image is very important to these individuals, and consequently, they are attracted to and tend to purchase premium, name-brand, and image-oriented products that show off their success to their friends and associates. *Strivers* (13 percent of adults) are also image-conscious but they have fewer resources with which to achieve their desired image and status. Style is very im-

portant to Strivers as they attempt to emulate the people they wish they were or aspire to become. Strivers are dominated by younger blue-collar workers.

The action-oriented group consists of Experiencers and Makers. Both groups like to affect their environment in meaningful and observable ways. *Experiencers* (12 percent of adults, the youngest of all eight segments) are enthusiastic about their life and career, rebellious, and politically ambivalent. They follow fashion and fads, spend much of their disposable income on socializing, clothing, fast food, music, and other youth-oriented pastimes. They tend to be impulse shoppers and are particularly prone to place particular value on what is "new." *Makers* (13 percent of adults) are also action-oriented but with fewer personal resources. These individuals value self-sufficiency and like working with their hands. Moreover, they are very practical and tend to only be impressed by material possessions that have a practical or functional purpose. They shop for comfort, durability, and value. They are unimpressed by appeals to status, image, or the luxury lifestyle.

Marketers and advertisers use the VALS2 typology in several ways. First, the typology can contribute to target audience selection and message planning. The specific types of products used by individuals in each group can be identified and those groups with the highest usage can be targeted. Luxury items, for example, sell best to Actualizers and Achievers; sports equipment sells best to Experiencers and hunting equipment sells best to Makers. Transport Canada (the equivalent of the U.S. Department of Transportation) provides a concrete example of this type of VALS2 application to marketing and advertising planning. Transport Canada conducted a VALS2 survey of 850 travelers who were passing through the Vancouver airport. The majority of those surveyed were either Actualizers (37 percent) or Experiencers (20 percent). The high levels of these two groups, especially Actualizers, suggested that stores like Sharper Image or Nature Company had strong potential to do well at the airport.[27]

Second, when used with product purchase data, the VALS2 typology helps identify product opportunities. A marketer can compare the usage of his or her brand within a VALS2 segment to that segment's overall use of the product category. Discrepancies between brand and category usage may indicate untapped brand opportunities. Actualizers, for example, are heavy users of ibuprofen pain relievers. Nuprin (which contains ibuprofen), however, had a very low share within this segment. Thus, it was reasonable for Nuprin to attempt to increase its share among this group of individuals that were predisposed to buy the product category but not Nuprin as a specific brand within the category.

Third, the typology can make a contribution to media and promotional planning. VALS2 can be used to determine the relative incidence of VALS2 groups in a specific metropolitan area. Media planners can use this information to increase the efficiency of media plans by better matching spot media purchases to VALS2 target audience locations. Marketers, in a similar way, can use the geographic concentration of VALS2 groups to determine where promotional activities should take place.

Category and Brand Usage Behaviors

Simmons Market Research Bureau (SMRB) and Mediamark Research Inc. (MRI) are two marketing research companies that provide an extensive data base on the demo-

---

[27] Rebecca Piirto, "VALS the Second Time," *American Demographics* (July, 1991): 6.

graphic, self-concept, media habits, and product usage of a nationally representative sample of adults. Advertisers can use either the SMRB or MRI data base to segment the population into groups that reflect differences in behaviors within a specific product category.[28]

The core of the SMRB or MRI database is an extensive questionnaire that collects information on a respondent's demographics, attitudes, media habits, and usage of more than 3,000 brands and products. An excerpt from the SMRB questionnaire, which collects information on shampoo and related hair care product usage, is shown in Figure 19.5 (page 468). Notice how the questionnaire collects information on the kinds of shampoo purchased, shampooing frequency, and specific brand usage.

SMRB and MRI take this core information and publish the results in a set of printed volumes, each of which contains reports for a specific product category. Within each volume, there are detailed reports for the specific brands and products measured by SMRB or MRI in the volume's product category. The SMRB volume *Hair Care and Shaving Products*, for example, contains data related to aftershave, colognes, perfumes, depilatories, shavers, hair coloring products, creme rinse and conditioners, styling creams, hair sprays, hair loss products, home permanents, razor blades, shampoos, and shaving creams and gels.

Each detailed report presents information on demographics and media usage. An excerpt from the SMRB demographic report for the shampoo category is shown in Figure 19.6 (page 470). MRI reports use a nearly identical format and are interpreted in the same way as SMRB reports. The printed report is interpreted as follows:

- Centered on the top of the page is the product category and audience for whom the data is reported. Figure 19.6 reports home shampoo usage by females.

- The far left-hand column contains demographic classifications. The sample (female shampoo users) can be described in terms of age, education, employment, ethnicity, geography, and income.

- The next column (labeled TOTAL U.S. '000) presents an estimate of the size of each demographic group in the total United States. As seen in Figure 19.6, it is estimated that there are 96,866,000 adult women in the United States. (This estimate is obtained by looking at the number that is at the intersection of the "TOTAL FEMALES" row and the "TOTAL U.S." column and then adding three zeros.) Similarly, it is estimated that there are 12,307,000 women aged 18–24 in the United States.

- As you move right, there are sets of four columns. Above each set of four columns is a label for that set of columns. In Figure 19.6, the first set of columns represents all female shampoo users, the second set of four columns relates to women who are heavy users of shampoo (defined as eight or more shampoos in the past seven days) while the remaining two sets of columns relate to the kind of shampoo used.

- The individual columns in each set of columns are labeled A though D. Each column presents a different way of examining segment composition.

    Column A always presents the absolute number of people falling into a particular category within the group specified in the column label. For example, Column A in the "HEAVY USERS" set of columns (Figure 19.6) informs us that

---

[28] Both SMRB and MRI use complex sampling procedures to ensure that their samples of about 20,000 adults is representative of and generalizable to the overall U.S. population. Data is collected from personal diaries, self-administered surveys, and in-home interviews. For additional information on data collection procedures see the technical guide that accompanies each company's printed reports.

SHAMPOO (For use at home)

1a. Do you yourself use it? Yes ☐ No ☐

IF YOU DO

1b. Who decides which brands you use? (Mark as many as apply)
Yourself ☐ Other Male ☐
Your Husband/Wife ☐ Other Female ☐

1c. What forms do you use?

	Most Often	Others
Bottle	☐	☐
Pump	☐	☐
Tube	☐	☐
Jar	☐	☐

1d. What kinds do you use?

For color-treated or permed hair	☐	☐
For silver/gray hair	☐	☐
For damaged hair	☐	☐
For dandruff	☐	☐
For dry hair	☐	☐
For extra body	☐	☐
For oily hair	☐	☐
For normal hair	☐	☐
Combination shampoo/ conditioner	☐	☐
All-purpose	☐	☐

1e. About how many times did you use shampoo in the LAST 7 DAYS?

12 or more	☐	4	☐
10-11	☐	3	☐
8-9	☐	2	☐
7	☐	1	☐
6	☐	NONE	☐
5	☐		

1f. For each of the BRANDS YOU USE, about how many times did you use each in the LAST 7 DAYS?

	8 or More	4-7	1-3	None
Agree	☐	☐	☐	☐
Aqua Net	☐	☐	☐	☐
Attractions	☐	☐	☐	☐
Aussie Mega	☐	☐	☐	☐
Aveda	☐	☐	☐	☐
Avon Dandruff Shampoo	☐	☐	☐	☐
• Naturally Gentle	☐	☐	☐	☐
• Other Avon	☐	☐	☐	☐
Breck	☐	☐	☐	☐
Care Free Curl	☐	☐	☐	☐
Chaps	☐	☐	☐	☐
Condition by Clairol	☐	☐	☐	☐
Clairol Herbal Essence	☐	☐	☐	☐
• Other Clairol	☐	☐	☐	☐
Clinique	☐	☐	☐	☐
Consort	☐	☐	☐	☐
Dark & Lovely	☐	☐	☐	☐
Denorex	☐	☐	☐	☐
Dep	☐	☐	☐	☐
Estee Lauder	☐	☐	☐	☐
Faberge Organics	☐	☐	☐	☐
Finesse	☐	☐	☐	☐
• Shampoo & Conditioner	☐	☐	☐	☐
Freeman	☐	☐	☐	☐
Halsa	☐	☐	☐	☐
Head & Shoulders	☐	☐	☐	☐
• Dry Scalp	☐	☐	☐	☐

Continued at top of next column →

SHAMPOO (Continued)

1f. For each of the BRANDS YOU USE, about how many times did you use each in the LAST 7 DAYS?

	8 or More	4-7	1-3	None
Infusium 23	☐	☐	☐	☐
Ivory	☐	☐	☐	☐
Jheri Redding	☐	☐	☐	☐
Jhirmack Silver	☐	☐	☐	☐
• Reviving System	☐	☐	☐	☐
Johnson's Baby Shampoo-Gentle Conditioning	☐	☐	☐	☐
• Baby Shampoo	☐	☐	☐	☐
L'Oreal Colorvive	☐	☐	☐	☐
• Ultra Rich	☐	☐	☐	☐
• Other L'Oreal	☐	☐	☐	☐
Lustrasilk	☐	☐	☐	☐
Matrix	☐	☐	☐	☐
Neutrogena Perm or Color Treated	☐	☐	☐	☐
• Regular	☐	☐	☐	☐
• T-Gel	☐	☐	☐	☐
Nexxus	☐	☐	☐	☐
Pantene	☐	☐	☐	☐
Paul Mitchell	☐	☐	☐	☐
Perma Soft	☐	☐	☐	☐
Pert Plus	☐	☐	☐	☐
• Dandruff Control	☐	☐	☐	☐
Prell Concentrate				
• Liquid	☐	☐	☐	☐
Proline	☐	☐	☐	☐
R&C	☐	☐	☐	☐
Rave	☐	☐	☐	☐
• All-In-One	☐	☐	☐	☐
Raveen	☐	☐	☐	☐
Redken	☐	☐	☐	☐
Regis	☐	☐	☐	☐
Revlon Aquamarine	☐	☐	☐	☐
• Clean & Clear	☐	☐	☐	☐
• Cream of Nature	☐	☐	☐	☐
• Flex	☐	☐	☐	☐
• Flex & Go	☐	☐	☐	☐
• Internationals	☐	☐	☐	☐
St. Ives	☐	☐	☐	☐
Salon Selectives	☐	☐	☐	☐
Sebastian	☐	☐	☐	☐
Selsun - Blue	☐	☐	☐	☐
Silkience	☐	☐	☐	☐
Style	☐	☐	☐	☐
• Plus	☐	☐	☐	☐
Studio (L'Oreal)	☐	☐	☐	☐
Suave	☐	☐	☐	☐
• Shampoo & Conditioner	☐	☐	☐	☐
TCB	☐	☐	☐	☐
Tegrin	☐	☐	☐	☐
Tresemmé	☐	☐	☐	☐
Vidal Sassoon D	☐	☐	☐	☐
• Ultra Care	☐	☐	☐	☐
• Other Vidal Sassoon	☐	☐	☐	☐
Vio Pure	☐	☐	☐	☐
VO5	☐	☐	☐	☐
Wella Balsam	☐	☐	☐	☐
White Rain Baby Shampoo	☐	☐	☐	☐
• Plus	☐	☐	☐	☐
• Other White Rain	☐	☐	☐	☐
Zotos	☐	☐	☐	☐
Store Brand	☐	☐	☐	☐
Other Brands	☐	☐	☐	☐

Continued at top of next column →

CREME RINSE & HAIR CONDITIONER (For use at home)

2a. Do you yourself use it? Yes ☐ No ☐

IF YOU DO

2b. What types do you use?

	Most Often	Others
Creme Rinse	☐	☐
Hair Conditioner	☐	☐
Intensive Hair Conditioner	☐	☐
Combination Rinse/ Conditioner	☐	☐

2c. What forms do you use?

	Most Often	Others
Bottle	☐	☐
Jar	☐	☐
Packet	☐	☐
Spray	☐	☐
Tube	☐	☐

2d. What kinds do you use?

Regular	☐	☐
Extra Body	☐	☐
For Dry Hair	☐	☐
For Color-Treated or Permed Hair	☐	☐
For Normal Hair	☐	☐
For Oily Hair	☐	☐
Deep Conditioning	☐	☐

2e. About how many times did you use creme rinses or hair conditioners in the LAST 7 DAYS?

TEN or more	☐	FOUR	☐
EIGHT or NINE	☐	THREE	☐
SEVEN	☐	TWO	☐
SIX	☐	ONE	☐
FIVE	☐	NONE	☐

2f. For each of the BRANDS YOU USE, about how many times did you use each in the LAST 7 DAYS?

	7 or More	3-6	1-2	None
Agree	☐	☐	☐	☐
Aquamarine	☐	☐	☐	☐
Aqua Net	☐	☐	☐	☐
Attractions	☐	☐	☐	☐
Australian 3 Minute	☐	☐	☐	☐
Aveda	☐	☐	☐	☐
Avon	☐	☐	☐	☐
Breck	☐	☐	☐	☐
Care Free Curl	☐	☐	☐	☐
Condition by Clairol Treatment	☐	☐	☐	☐
• Beauty Pack Treatment	☐	☐	☐	☐
• Hot Oil Treatment	☐	☐	☐	☐
• Pro Vitamin Treatment Spray	☐	☐	☐	☐
Clean & Clear	☐	☐	☐	☐
Dark & Lovely	☐	☐	☐	☐
Dep	☐	☐	☐	☐
Faberge Organics	☐	☐	☐	☐
Finesse	☐	☐	☐	☐
Halsa	☐	☐	☐	☐
Infusium 23	☐	☐	☐	☐
Ivory	☐	☐	☐	☐
Jhirmack	☐	☐	☐	☐
Johnson's Baby Conditioner	☐	☐	☐	☐

FIGURE 19.5 Excerpt from SMRB questionnaire.
Source: Simmons Market Research Bureau. Reprinted with permission.

- 3,124,000 female heavy users of shampoo are aged 18–24; 4,145,000 are aged 25–34,
- 2,507,000 female heavy users of shampoo graduated from college,
- 4,349,000 female heavy users of shampoo are single.

Absolute numbers are often difficult to conceptualize. As a result, Column B translates the absolute numbers into percentages. The 3,124,000 female heavy users of shampoo who are aged 18–24 represent 22.8 percent of all female heavy shampoo users while the 2,507,000 female heavy users of shampoo who graduated from college represent 18.3 percent of all female heavy shampoo users.

Column B information is important because it allows you to see the demographic composition of specific brand, type or consumption segments, noting the size of each demographic group.

Column C looks at brand or category usage within a specific classification. Thus, 14.2 percent of all women are heavy users of shampoo. (This is the number at the intersection of the TOTAL FEMALE ROW and COLUMN C.) Similarly, the data indicates that 25.4 percent of all 18–24 females are heavy users of shampoo and 15 percent of all female college graduates are heavy users of shampoo.

Column C information is important because it lets you determine the percent of particular demographic groups displaying specific category or brand behaviors.

Column D is an index of usage. This index, when used to analyze demographic characteristics, indicates the extent to which a particular demographic segment is more or less likely than the average category user to participate in a particular product category or use of particular brand.

The index reported by SMRB and MRI compares two percents: the percent of a particular demographic group in a segment (taken from the intersection of the demographic row and Column C) and the overall percent of the population in a segment (taken from the intersection of the very top row and Column C). For example, in Figure 19.6, females in the 18–24 age group show an index of 179 beneath the heading HEAVY USERS. (This index number is at the intersection of the 18–24 row and Column D beneath HEAVY USERS.) The index is calculated by comparing the percent of 18- to 24-years-olds who are heavy users to the overall percent of the sample population that are heavy users ($25.4\% \div 14.2\% \times 100 = 179$).

Higher indices of usage (those over 100) indicate that a group is more likely to fall into a particular segment while lower indices of usage (those under 100) indicate a below average likelihood of falling into a segment. Thus, the index of 179 indicates that 18–24 years olds are 79 percent more likely than the average female to be a heavy shampoo user.

Advertisers use the information in Columns B and D to better understand the demographic characteristics of a particular product or brand user segment. The demographic characteristics that are most meaningful for defining segment characteristics are those that show a high or low percentage in Column B (indicating that the group comprises a high or low proportion of all users) *and* a high (typically more than 115, indicating that the group shows an above average rate of usage) or low (typically less than 85, indicating that the group shows a below average rate of usage) index in Column D.

The information provided by indices makes a significant contribution to target audience definition and selection. For most product categories, SMRB and MRI present information on the users of specific brands. Based on the pattern of high indices, for example, the demographics of Agree Shampoo users appear to be women who are

SHAMPOO (FOR USE AT HOME): ALL USERS, USERS IN LAST 7 DAYS AND KINDS USE
(FEMALES)

	TOTAL U.S. '000	ALL USERS A '000	B % DOWN	C % ACROSS	D % INDX	HEAVY USERS EIGHT OR MORE TIMES A '000	B % DOWN	C % ACROSS	D % INDX	KIND: FOR DAMAGED HAIR A '000	B % DOWN	C % ACROSS	D % INDX	FOR SILVER/ GREY HAIR A '000	B % DOWN	C % ACROSS	D % INDX
TOTAL FEMALES	96866	91429	100.0	94.4	100	13725	100.0	14.2	100	11561	100.0	11.9	100	4675	100.0	4.8	100
MOTHERS	35509	34450	37.7	97.0	103	6228	45.4	17.5	124	5396	46.7	15.2	127	648	13.9	1.8	38
EMPLOYED MOTHERS	23928	23228	25.4	97.1	103	4118	30.0	17.2	121	3658	31.6	15.3	128	*413	8.8	1.7	36
18-24	12307	11840	12.9	96.2	102	3124	22.8	25.4	179	2639	22.8	21.4	180	*404	8.6	3.3	68
25-34	21696	21262	23.3	98.0	104	4145	30.2	19.1	135	3258	28.2	15.0	126	*543	11.6	2.5	52
35-44	20222	19742	21.6	97.6	103	3272	23.8	16.2	114	2667	23.1	13.2	110	*443	9.5	2.2	45
45-54	13905	13479	14.7	96.9	103	1423	10.4	10.2	72	1723	14.9	12.4	104	*515	11.0	3.7	77
55-64	11106	10067	11.0	90.6	96	847	6.2	7.6	54	675	5.8	6.1	51	865	18.5	7.8	161
65 OR OLDER	17630	15040	16.4	85.3	90	914	6.7	5.2	37	599	5.2	3.4	28	1905	40.8	10.8	224
18-34	34003	33101	36.2	97.3	103	7269	53.0	21.4	151	5897	51.0	17.3	145	947	20.2	2.8	58
18-49	61887	60284	65.9	97.4	103	11509	83.9	18.6	131	9633	83.3	15.6	130	1566	33.5	2.5	52
25-54	55823	54483	59.6	97.6	103	8841	64.4	15.8	112	7648	66.2	13.7	115	1501	32.1	2.7	56
35-49	27884	27183	29.7	97.5	103	4240	30.9	15.2	107	3736	32.3	13.4	112	620	13.3	2.2	46
50 OR OLDER	34979	31145	34.1	89.0	94	2217	16.1	6.3	45	1928	16.7	5.5	46	3108	66.5	8.9	184
GRADUATED COLLEGE	16741	15837	17.3	94.6	100	2507	18.3	15.0	106	1245	10.8	7.4	62	766	16.4	4.6	95
ATTENDED COLLEGE	23486	22492	24.6	95.8	101	3684	26.8	15.7	111	3210	27.8	13.7	115	1003	21.5	4.3	88
GRADUATED HIGH SCHOOL	36396	34227	37.4	94.0	100	5011	36.5	13.8	97	4373	37.8	12.0	101	1525	32.6	4.2	87
DID NOT GRADUATE HIGH SCHOOL	20244	18873	20.6	93.2	9:	2522	18.4	12.5	88	2733	23.6	13.5	113	1381	29.5	6.8	141
EMPLOYED FULL-TIME	47326	45832	50.1	96.8	103	7989	58.2	16.9	119	6548	56.6	13.8	116	1669	35.7	3.5	73
EMPLOYED PART-TIME	8584	8196	9.0	95.5	101	1314	9.6	15.3	108	1199	10.4	14.0	117	*259	5.5	3.0	63
NOT EMPLOYED	40956	37401	40.9	91.3	97	4422	32.2	10.8	76	3814	33.0	9.3	78	2747	58.8	6.7	139
PROFESSIONAL/MANAGER	14873	14186	15.5	95.4	101	2469	18.0	16.6	117	1820	15.7	12.2	103	*533	11.4	3.6	74
TECHNICAL/CLERICAL/SALES	24672	23955	26.2	97.1	103	3977	29.0	16.1	114	3703	32.0	15.0	126	896	19.2	3.6	75
PRECISION/CRAFT	1290	1275	1.4	98.8	105	**206	1.5	15.9	112	**186	1.6	14.4	121	**8	0.2	0.6	13
OTHER EMPLOYED	15076	14612	16.0	96.9	103	2651	19.3	17.6	124	2039	17.6	13.5	113	*490	10.5	3.3	67
SINGLE	18843	17797	19.5	96.3	102	4349	31.7	23.5	166	3183	27.5	17.2	144	678	14.5	3.7	76
MARRIED	54215	51666	56.5	95.3	101	7150	52.1	13.2	93	6089	52.7	11.2	94	2329	49.8	4.3	89
DIVORCED/SEPARATED/WIDOWED	24168	21967	24.0	90.9	96	2226	16.2	9.2	65	2289	19.8	9.5	79	1667	35.7	6.9	143
PARENTS	35509	34450	37.7	97.0	103	6228	45.4	17.5	124	5396	46.7	15.2	127	648	13.9	1.8	38
WHITE	82244	77767	85.1	94.6	100	12215	89.0	14.9	105	9393	81.2	11.4	96	4095	87.6	5.0	103
BLACK	11668	10868	11.9	93.1	99	1138	8.3	9.8	69	1655	14.3	14.2	119	529	11.3	4.5	94
OTHER	2952	2794	3.1	94.7	100	*372	2.7	12.6	89	*513	4.4	17.4	145	**51	1.1	1.7	36
NORTHEAST-CENSUS	20171	19050	20.8	94.4	100	2468	18.0	12.2	86	2107	18.2	10.4	88	1005	21.5	5.0	103
MIDWEST	23318	21836	23.9	93.6	99	3561	25.9	15.3	108	2870	24.8	12.3	103	1044	22.3	4.5	93
SOUTH	33761	31842	34.8	94.3	100	4662	34.0	13.8	97	4169	36.1	12.3	103	1728	37.0	5.1	106
WEST	19617	18701	20.5	95.3	101	3033	22.1	15.5	109	2415	20.9	12.3	103	899	19.2	4.6	95
COUNTY SIZE A	39922	37853	41.4	94.8	100	5667	41.3	14.2	100	4137	35.8	10.4	87	1884	40.3	4.7	98
COUNTY SIZE B	29220	27260	29.8	93.3	99	4370	31.8	15.0	106	3715	32.1	12.7	107	1339	28.6	4.6	95
COUNTY SIZE C	14716	14092	15.4	95.8	101	1925	14.0	13.1	92	2240	19.4	15.2	128	853	18.2	5.8	120
COUNTY SIZE D	13009	12223	13.4	94.0	100	1762	12.8	13.5	96	1469	12.7	11.3	95	*598	12.8	4.6	95
METRO CENTRAL CITY	30326	28462	31.1	93.9	99	4301	31.3	14.2	100	3224	27.9	10.6	89	1362	29.1	4.5	93
METRO SUBURBAN	45921	43494	47.6	94.7	100	6563	47.8	14.3	101	5666	49.0	12.3	103	2245	48.0	4.9	101
NON METRO	20819	19473	21.3	94.4	100	2862	20.9	13.9	98	2670	23.1	13.0	109	1068	22.8	5.2	107
TOP 5 ADI'S	21629	20372	22.3	94.2	100	2930	21.3	13.5	96	2177	18.8	10.1	84	1161	24.8	5.4	111
TOP 10 ADI'S	30618	29039	31.8	94.8	100	4121	30.0	13.5	95	3249	28.1	10.6	89	1417	30.3	4.6	96
TOP 20 ADI'S	42333	40197	44.0	95.0	101	5839	42.5	13.8	97	4564	39.5	10.8	90	1931	41.3	4.6	95
HSHLD. INC. $75,000 OR MORE	11373	10726	11.7	94.3	100	1544	11.3	13.6	96	1427	12.3	12.5	105	*374	8.0	3.3	68
$60,000 OR MORE	19663	18621	20.4	94.7	100	2792	20.3	14.2	100	2237	19.4	11.4	95	617	13.2	3.1	65
$50,000 OR MORE	27941	26564	29.1	95.1	101	3995	29.1	14.3	101	3289	28.5	11.8	99	917	19.6	3.3	68
$40,000 OR MORE	38924	36905	40.4	94.8	100	5732	41.8	14.7	104	4550	39.4	11.7	98	1481	31.7	3.8	79
$30,000 OR MORE	52156	49629	54.3	95.2	101	7956	58.0	15.3	108	6238	54.0	12.0	100	2066	44.2	4.0	82
$30,000 - $39,000	13232	12724	13.9	96.2	102	2224	16.2	16.8	119	1688	14.6	12.8	107	585	12.5	4.4	92
$20,000 - $29,000	15773	14961	16.4	94.9	100	2049	14.9	13.0	92	2058	17.8	13.0	109	681	14.6	4.3	89
$10,000 - $19,999	16127	15135	16.6	93.8	99	2192	16.0	13.6	96	1942	16.8	12.0	101	1058	22.6	6.6	136
UNDER .$10,000	12811	11704	12.8	91.4	97	1529	11.1	11.9	84	1323	11.4	10.3	87	870	18.6	6.8	141
HOUSEHOLD OF 1 PERSON	14572	13083	14.3	89.8	95	1311	9.5	9.0	63	949	8.2	6.5	55	1117	23.9	7.7	159
2 PEOPLE	31078	28973	31.7	93.2	99	3420	24.9	11.0	78	2924	25.3	9.4	79	2128	45.5	6.8	142
3 OR 4 PEOPLE	37626	36116	39.5	96.0	102	6307	46.0	16.8	118	4905	42.4	13.0	109	965	20.6	2.6	53
5 OR MORE PEOPLE	13590	13257	14.5	97.8	103	2688	19.6	19.8	140	2783	24.1	20.5	172	**464	9.9	3.4	71
NO CHILD IN HOUSEHOLD	56046	51955	56.8	92.7	98	6471†	47.1	11.5	81	5186	44.9	9.3	78	3769	80.6	6.7	139
CHILD(REN) UNDER 2 YEARS	8013	7796	8.5	97.3	103	1366	9.9	17.0	120	1281	11.1	16.0	134	*301	6.4	3.8	78
2 - 5 YEARS	14863	14331	15.7	96.4	102	2711	19.8	18.2	129	2501	21.6	16.8	141	**362	7.7	2.4	50
6 - 11 YEARS	18898	18372	20.1	97.2	103	3067	22.3	16.2	115	2762	23.9	14.6	122	*383	8.2	2.0	42
12 - 17 YEARS	18412	17840	19.5	96.9	103	3803	27.7	20.7	146	3129	27.1	17.0	142	*268	5.7	1.5	30
RESIDENCE OWNED	65134	60939	66.7	93.6	99	7957	58.0	12.2	86	7354	63.6	11.3	95	3473	74.3	5.3	110
VALUE: $70,000 OR MORE	38655	36430	39.8	94.2	100	5055	36.8	13.1	92	3772	32.6	9.8	82	1865	39.9	4.8	100
VALUE: UNDER $70,000	26479	24509	26.8	92.6	98	2902	21.1	11.0	77	3581	31.0	13.5	113	1607	34.4	6.1	126
RESIDENCE RENTED	29775	28681	31.4	96.3	102	5252	38.3	17.6	124	3869	33.5	13.0	109	1088	23.3	3.7	76
DAILY NEWSPAPERS																	
NET ONE DAY REACH	57578	53895	58.9	93.6	99	7641	55.7	13.3	94	6267	54.2	10.9	91	2939	62.9	5.1	106
READ ONLY ONE	48818	45776	50.1	93.8	99	6590	48.0	13.5	95	5426	46.9	11.1	93	2432	52.0	5.0	103
READ TWO OR MORE	8759	8119	8.9	92.7	98	1051	7.7	12.0	85	841	7.3	9.6	80	507	10.8	5.8	120
WEEKEND/SUNDAY NEWSPAPERS																	
NET ONE DAY REACH	66366	62600	68.5	94.3	100	9175	66.9	13.8	98	7665	66.3	11.5	97	3286	70.3	5.0	103
READ ONLY ONE	59935	56526	61.8	94.3	100	8293	60.4	13.8	98	6863	59.4	11.5	96	2973	63.6	5.0	103
READ TWO OR MORE	6430	6074	6.6	94.5	100	883	6.4	13.7	97	802	6.9	12.5	104	312	6.7	4.9	101

SIMMONS MARKET RESEARCH BUREAU, INC. 1993

*PROJECTION RELATIVELY UNSTABLE BECAUSE OF SAMPLE BASE-USE WITH CAUTION
**NUMBER OF CASES TOO SMALL FOR RELIABILITY-SHOWN FOR CONSISTENCY ONLY

FIGURE 19.6 Excerpt from SMRB printed report: Consumption level and type of product.
Source: Simmons Market Research Bureau. Reprinted with permission.

- aged 18–34, particularly 18–24,
- less well educated (neither high school nor college graduates),
- employed in a precision/craft occupation when employed (but there is a greater likelihood for individuals in this group to not be employed),
- all races, with a somewhat greater likelihood to be African American,
- live in the Northeast (and not the Midwest),
- have low household incomes.

Finesse users show a very different profile. Finesse users appear to women who are

- aged 18–34, particularly aged 18–24,
- of all levels of education,
- employed, often in a professional occupation and not in a technical/sales or precision/craft occupation,
- single,
- living in all areas of the country,
- with higher incomes.

The printed information provided by SMRB and MRI is where an advertiser *begins* to develop an understanding of the characteristics of a particular product category or brand usage segment. However, because each data base can be accessed electronically, it is possible to conduct supplemental analyses that provide richer, deeper information on identified segments. The data shown in Figure 19.7 illustrate how these analyses cross-tabulate information in related categories with a product category or brand usage segment. Figure 19.7 identifies the places where Agree and Finesse users purchase their hair care products.

Cross-tabulations of related category data with category or brand user segments helps an advertiser to understand better the characteristics of these segments. The information provided in the SHAMPOO section of the questionnaire shown in Figure 19.5 could be used in the following ways to provide deeper insights into the segment of Agree shampoo users:

- A cross-tabulation of Q1c with Agree users would tell an advertiser which shampoo *packaging* is used most often by these brand users. This information can inform decisions related to the form of the product package shown in advertising.

- A cross-tabulation of Q1d with Agree users would provide information on the *types* of shampoo these consumers use. This information can inform decisions related to promotions, the types of products featured in the advertising and potential line extensions.

- A cross-tabulation of Q1f with Agree users would provide important insights into Agree's competitive set by identifying other brands of shampoo frequently used by Agree consumers. This information can inform decisions related to competitive initiatives such as which brands might be featured in competitive advertising.

The information contained in the remaining section of the questionnaire shown in Figure 19.5, though not directly related to shampoo use, can also provide insights into the characteristics of Agree users. A researcher could examine the pattern of product and brand usage to determine, for example:

- The extent to which Agree users "pamper" themselves in this area of personal care. Do they use lower priced, "value-oriented" products or do they use products that are more

costly, image- and salon-oriented? This insight can help the creative team better understand the creative tone and manner that might best appeal to these women.

- The extent to which Agree users are brand loyal. Do Agree users also use Agree Creme Rinse or are they more likely to use a competitive brand? This insight can provide data related to cross-brand promotions, cross-brand couponing and the need (or lack of need) to feature both Agree Shampoo and Agree Creme Rinse in one advertising communication.

In sum, SMRB and MRI provide a wealth of information on the characteristics of segments of category and brand users. This extent to which this information can be used by marketers and advertisers is limited only by a researcher's inquisitiveness and creativity.

Geodemographic Segmentation[29]

Geodemographic segmentation segments the population on dimensions related to demographics (such as income, age, household type), media usage, lifestyle choices, possessions and purchase behaviors. Geodemographic segmentation uses these variables as follows:

- Information is obtained from the latest United States census, automobile registration records, magazine subscriber lists, buying clubs, consumer product usage surveys, and other sources of consumer information.
- The information from these sources is aggregated on the census block level. A census block (about 340 households) is selected as the basic unit of geography because it typically represents an actual neighborhood. An underlying assumption of geodemographic clustering is that individuals within a neighborhood are fairly homogeneous with respect to attitudes, lifestyle, and behaviors.
- The characteristics of each census block in the United States are identified and examined. Then, based on this analysis, each census block is assigned to a segment (also known as a cluster) so that census blocks within a cluster are similar to each other and dissimilar to census blocks in other clusters.

There are similarities and differences in the outcomes of these procedures among geodemographic research companies. Companies are similar in that the final segmentation reflects a continuum of economic/life-stage/lifestyle characteristics. The clusters range from very wealthy individuals living in exclusive areas leading "the good life" to very poor, inner-city individuals existing at barest level.

Geodemographic research companies differ, however, in the specific types of information used to form their clusters, the total number of clusters formed and how the clusters are labeled and described. Claritas' PRIZM system and Strategic Mapping's Cluster PLUS 2000, for example, have segmented U.S. neighborhoods into sixty-two

---

[29] The discussion in this section is primarily based on Susan Mitchell, "Birds of a Feather," *American Demographics* (February 1995): 40–48.

FIGURE 19.7
Cross-tabulation of SMRB data: Brand usage by place of purchase.
Source: Simmons Market Research Bureau. Reprinted with permission.

Choices System

Source: SMM 1994 Wgt: POP
Table Base: TOTAL

Row	CELL	TOTAL	USE SHAMPOO- (FOR USE AT HOME)? - YES	SHAMPOO- BRAND SUMMARY - AGREE	SHAMPOO- BRAND SUMMARY - FINESSE
HAIR CARE PRODUCTS - PURCHASE?- DID NOT PURCHASE ANY	Resps	8890	8006	488	727
	(000)	73352	67232	3699	6984
	Vert%	39.07	37.93	42.66	39.13
	Horz%	100.0	91.66	5.04	9.52
	Index	100	97	109	100
HAIR CARE PRODUCTS - WHERE PURCHASE - DRUG STORES	Resps	5086	4950	211	510
	(000)	44096	43141	1769	4773
	Vert%	23.49	24.34	20.4	26.74
	Horz%	100.0	97.83	4.01	10.82
	Index	100	104	87	114
HAIR CARE PRODUCTS - WHERE PURCHASE - DEPARTMENT STORES	Resps	2194	2163	115	254
	(000)	21173	20950	1006	2634
	Vert%	11.28	11.82	11.61	14.75
	Horz%	100.0	98.95	4.75	12.44
	Index	100	105	103	131
HAIR CARE PRODUCTS - WHERE PURCHASE - DISCOUNT STORES	Resps	3924	3846	164	402
	(000)	36604	35955	1471	3774
	Vert%	19.5	20.28	16.96	21.14
	Horz%	100.0	98.23	4.02	10.31
	Index	100	104	87	108
HAIR CARE PRODUCTS - WHERE PURCHASE - SUPERMARKETS	Resps	3402	3347	166	365
	(000)	30506	30064	1495	3681
	Vert%	16.25	16.96	17.25	20.62
	Horz%	100.0	98.55	4.9	12.07
	Index	100	104	106	127
HAIR CARE PRODUCTS - WHERE PURCHASE - HAIR/BEAUTY SALONS	Resps	2380	2327	68	212
	(000)	21056	20720	618	2241
	Vert%	11.21	11.69	7.12	12.56
	Horz%	100.0	98.4	2.93	10.65
	Index	100	104	64	112
HAIR CARE PRODUCTS - WHERE PURCHASE - COSMETIC BOUTIQUES	Resps	282	278	**30	*47
	(000)	2397	2376	235	601
	Vert%	1.28	1.34	2.71	3.37
	Horz%	100.0	99.11	9.8	25.09
	Index	100	105	212	264
HAIR CARE PRODUCTS - WHERE PURCHASE - OTHER BOUTIQUES	Resps	81	76	**4	**14
	(000)	650	638	24	200
	Vert%	0.35	0.36	0.27	1.12
	Horz%	100.0	98.12	3.66	30.71
	Index	100	104	79	323
HAIR CARE PRODUCTS - WHERE PURCHASE - DOOR TO DOOR	Resps	303	297	**14	*31
	(000)	3260	3215	112	456
	Vert%	1.74	1.81	1.3	2.55
	Horz%	100.0	98.61	3.44	13.98
	Index	100	104	75	147
HAIR CARE PRODUCTS - WHERE PURCHASE - MAIL ORDER	Resps	175	171	**21	*33
	(000)	1675	1663	136	259
	Vert%	0.89	0.94	1.56	1.45
	Horz%	100.0	99.26	8.09	15.46
	Index	100	105	175	163
HAIR CARE PRODUCTS - WHERE PURCHASE - COSMETIC PARTIES	Resps	85	83	**8	**12
	(000)	814	794	64	121
	Vert%	0.43	0.45	0.74	0.68
	Horz%	100.0	97.59	7.91	14.9
	Index	100	103	171	157

* Projection relatively unstable because of sample base - use with caution.
** Number of cases too small for reliability - shown for consistency only.

and sixty clusters, respectively. Moreover, PRIZM gives each of its clusters a catchy name that it believes captures the essence of the cluster such as "Blue Blood Estates" and "Single City Blues" while ClusterPLUS provides a descriptive title such as "Urban New Families, New Homes." The descriptions provided in Figure 19.8 (page 476) illustrate the range of clusters and the types of cluster descriptions provided by the various geodemographic research companies.

Geodemographic clustering provides important insights into where certain types of individuals live. Moreover, the ability to describe individuals on the neighborhood level provides insights into areas that appear to be homogeneous but in fact, are not. Mitchell provides the following example:

> On a PRIZM-coded map of downtown Jackson, Mississippi, for example, some areas are predominantly populated by "Southside City" residents. This cluster is dominated by young and old African Americans who are employed primarily in low-paying blue-collar service jobs. They have little education, rent apartments and eat instant grits. But in the middle of this low-income area are a couple of "Towns & Gowns" neighborhoods. People in this cluster also rent apartments, but they are college graduates with better-paying white-collar service jobs. They like to ski, read beauty and fitness magazines and use ATM cards.[30]

Marketers and advertisers use geodemographic cluster systems to locate new customers, evaluate alternative retail store sites, select print and broadcast media vehicles, target direct mail, and develop new products. For example, imagine a direct mail campaign that receives a positive response from one zip code or cluster. A geodemographic cluster system can be used to identify other zip codes or clusters that display similar characteristics.

The creation of geodemographic clusters based on information aggregated on the census block level is a common and accepted procedure. However, one drawback of the use of aggregated data is the assumption that individuals within a census block are homogeneous. A new generation of geodemographic clustering may make this assumption unnecessary. Several research companies[31] have used databases of up to 180 million individuals to develop clusters built up from individual rather then census block characteristics. In these systems next door neighbors, even spouses, can be assigned to different clusters. These individual-based cluster systems would provide several advantages over traditional approaches to geodemographic segmentation. First, as the direct broadcast of television signals becomes more commonplace, advertisers will have the opportunity to send their advertising only to those individuals that are their best prospects. (The same is true for direct mail.) Consequently, the efficiency of advertising media plans will be greatly increased. Second, clusters based on individuals rather than households will better identify the characteristics of diverse neighborhoods, for example, well-educated professionals scattered throughout primarily blue-collar neighborhoods. Third, marketers and advertisers can seize opportunities quicker. Individuals who move frequently, for example, would show up faster than they would in census block approaches. The data bases must be constantly updated and reflect only

---

[30] Ibid.

[31] These companies and their products are Trans Union Corporation (SOLO), Metromail (DNA), National Demographics and Lifestyles (Cohorts).

the latest information for these approaches to realize their potential. As might be expected, keeping track of every adult in the United States is no small task.

Summary

Consumer segmentation is the process of dividing a population into distinct smaller subgroups where individuals in a specific group are similar to each other in terms of important characteristics and possess characteristics different from individuals in other groups. Marketers and advertisers segment populations because it makes them more efficient and increases their chances for marketplace success. Segmentation accomplishes this by helping marketers and advertisers take into account and respond to differences within the consumer's audience.

Consumer segmentation research defines segments using characteristics that fall into one or more of the following areas:

- demographics (age, gender, household, life stage, race, ethnicity, social class, lifestyle),
- geographics (region, population size, population density, climate),
- psychographics (attitudes, values, motivations, and lifestyle),
- category and brand-related attitudes and behaviors (product usage, brand loyalty and benefits).

The segmentation research used by a marketer or advertiser can either be customized and proprietary or it can be an adaptation of consumer segmentation research developed and syndicated by others.

Customized, proprietary segmentation research begins similarly to other quantitative research. The need for the research is identified, segmentation is selected as an appropriate response to the informational need, and sample and sampling issues are addressed. The actual segmentation research then proceeds through eleven steps:

1. Determine the basis for the segmentation.
2. Identify descriptive variables.
3. Use qualitative research to explore the range of segmentation and descriptive variables.
4. Reduce the list of segmentation and descriptive measures.
5. Sample and survey the population.
6. Use segmentation variables to form groups.
7. Create visual representation of segment characteristics.
8. Create a narrative describing each segment.
9. Use descriptive variables to explain each segment's internal characteristics.
10. Relate segments to specific brand behaviors.
11. Select a segment.

There are three major syndicated approaches to segmentation: psychographic, product usage, and geodemographic.

ClusterPlus Categories

Group 1: Highest socioeconomic status, highest income, prime real estate areas, highest educational level, professionally employed, low mobility, homeowners, children in private schools.

Group 10: High education level, average income, professionally employed, younger mobile, apartment dwellers, above average rents.

Group 30: Low income, lowest educational level, families with one worker, farms, rural areas.

Group 35: Older housing, low income, average education, younger, mobile, fewer children, apartment dwellers, small towns.

Group 47: Urban Blacks, very low income, low educational level, very high unemployment, female householders with children, older housing.

PRIZM Clusters

"Shotguns and Pickles": Many small, outlying townships and crossroad villages that provide the nation's breadbasket and other rural areas. Large families, school-aged children headed by a blue-collar craftsman, equipment operators, and transport workers with high school education.

"Bohemian Mix": America's Bohemia, a largely integrated, singles-dominated, high-rise hodge-podge of white collars, students, divorced persons, actors, writers, artists, aging hippies and races. While it is only a $5 cab ride from Manhattan's "East Side" to "The Village," the shift in income and perspective is dramatic.

"Pools and Patios": Upscale areas in a greenbelt surrounding a major city. The children have mostly grown and departed, leaving aging couples in empty nests too costly for young homemakers. The "good life" is assured by good education, high white-collar employment levels, and double incomes.

VISION Clusters

"The Good Life": Eight of ten in this group are in white-collar careers, most often in management/professional or technical/service work. Almost one-fourth have incomes of $50,000 or more and 93 percent have homes valued at $150,000 or more. They are concentrated in areas such as San Clemente and other parts of California, Hawaii, Washington, D.C., Nevada, and Connecticut.

"Metro Hispanic Mix": This group is mainly comprised of poor, low-income Hispanics who live in rented apartments and duplexes in urban areas. Most are blue-collar workers. Half have graduated from high school. Individuals in this group often eat at McDonald's and at family steak restaurants, occasionally at Denny's or Coco's. They enjoy rock music and go to movies. They listen to Spanish radio stations, watch little television, and do not read daily newspapers. In terms of finances, these individuals carry credit card balances that average $1,800 and typically do not use checking accounts or mutual funds

FIGURE 19.8
Descriptions of demogeographic clusters.

VALS2 (the Values and Lifestyle Segmentation 2) is the most widely used psychographic segmentation. VALS2 divides the adult population into eight groups. The groups are formed in a way that reflects the resources available to each group and differences in the groups' self-orientation. Resources include income, education, self-confidence, health, eagerness to buy, intelligence, and energy level. Self-orientation reflects an individual's world view and lifestyles. Three types of self-orientation are used to form segments. Principle-oriented individuals are guided by their view of how the world should be and by how people, in the best of worlds, should treat and interact with others. Status-oriented individuals are most influenced by the actions and opinions of others while action-oriented individuals are motivated by a desire for social or physical activity, variety, and risk-taking.

The data provided by Simmons Market Research Bureau and Mediamark Research Inc. provide the basis for brand usage segmentation. The printed reports provided by these companies, in addition to the ability to manipulate the data electronically, provide marketers and advertisers with the ability to understand the demographic, attitudinal, and brand usage characteristics of segments defined in terms of category and brand-specific behaviors.

Geodemographic segmentation segments the population on dimensions related to demographics, media usage, lifestyle choices, possessions, and purchase behaviors. These characteristics are used to classify each census block in the United States into a cluster so that census blocks within a cluster are similar to each other and dissimilar to census blocks in other clusters. While there is a variance among geodemographic research companies in terms of the number of clusters formed the final segmentation of each company typically reflects a continuum of economic, life-stage, and lifestyle characteristics.

Review Questions

1. What is *consumer segmentation*? What are the two characteristics of a good consumer segmentation?

2. What are the six specific reasons why marketers and advertisers use segmentation as part of the strategic and communications planning process?

3. What are the four general types of characteristics that can be used to segment a population?

4. What is a *demographic* segmentation?

5. What specific types of characteristics can be used to perform a demographic segmentation? Provide an example of how the use of each characteristic has influenced a marketing or advertising decision.

6. Why are demographic segmentations based on combined characteristics (such as life stage and social class) often more useful that demographic segmentations based on a single variable?

7. What is a *geographic* segmentation?

8. What specific types of characteristics can be used to perform a geographic segmentation? Provide an example of how the use of each characteristic has influenced a marketing or advertising decision.

9. What is a *psychographic* segmentation?

10. What specific types of characteristics can be used to perform a psychographic segmentation? Provide an example of how the use of each characteristic has influenced a marketing or advertising decision.

11. What is a segmentation based on *product category or brand* characteristics?

12. What specific types of characteristics can be used to perform a product category or brand based segmentation? Provide an example of how the use of each characteristic has influenced a marketing or advertising decision.

13. What is the difference between a *proprietary* and a *syndicated* segmentation?

14. What is a *segmentation* variable? What is a *descriptive* variable?

15. What are the eleven steps underlying a proprietary segmentation. Briefly describe the primary activity conducted at each step.

16. Why is it necessary to reduce the initial list of segmentation and descriptive variables?

17. Why is it necessary to describe the outcome of a segmentation in tabular, pictorial, and narrative forms?

18. What are the three primary syndicated approaches to consumer segmentation? What are the underlying segmentation variables of each approach?

19. What are the two primary dimensions through which VALS2 segments the population? Briefly explain the characteristics of each dimension.

20. What are the characteristics of each of eight segments proposed by VALS2?

21. How can VALS2 contribute to the advertising planning process?

22. What types of information are provided by Simmons Market Research Bureau (SMRB) and Mediamark Research Inc. (MRI)?

23. How does the information provided by SMRB and MRI contribute to the advertising planning process?

24. What is *geodemographic* segmentation?

25. How does the information provided by a geodemographic segmentation contribute to the advertising planning process?

Application Exercises[32]

1. Your agency has just acquired the Health Nation account. Health Nation is a holding company that owns Health Maintenance Organizations (HMOs) in eleven cities (Atlanta, Boise, Boston, Chicago, Denver, Los Angeles, New Orleans, New York, Phoenix, Spokane, and Tulsa). Health Nation has requested the agency to develop one

---

[32] All situations are fictitious. Actual brand names are used for illustrative purposes only.

advertising campaign that can be used in all cities in which they do business. They suggest a 30-second commercial targeted to all adults. They suggest further that the commercial should have a five-second donut in the center where the names of their specific hospitals in each city can be inserted.

As the agency researcher, you suggest that the development of a single commercial targeted to all adults may not be the best approach. You feel that this target definition may be too broad and that there may be important differences among the eleven cities in which the advertising is scheduled to appear. You believe that segmentation research may be a necessary prerequisite to the advertising planning process. Others at the agency are not convinced of the importance of segmentation in this instance after you informally propose the idea.

Write a memo to others on the agency brand team (consisting of account management, creative, and media) that attempts to convince them that segmentation research is necessary in this instance. Your memo should, at minimum, address the following issues:

- The reasons why segmentation is necessary.
- The manner in which the segmentation will contribute to better, more successful advertising.
- The characteristics that you propose using to segment and describe the population (with a justification for their selection).
- The potential outcomes and application to advertising planning process.

When writing your memo, remember that your audience is not interested in a theoretical discussion. Be certain to present your argument, examples, and recommendations within the context of your client, Health Nation. Feel free to incorporate relevant information from secondary sources that supports your argument.

2. Congratulations. Your memo was successful. The agency and Health Nation have agreed to conduct segmentation research before the development of the advertising campaign. Health Nation, however, is still unclear on the details. Write a letter to Mary Ford, Health Nation's Director of Advertising, that describes the specific steps you will take to conduct the research and the outcomes that she can expect from each step. Be certain to

- focus the discussion on Health Nation,
- provide detailed, relevant examples of actions, decisions, and potential outcomes,
- inform Mary of your expectations of her (that is, at what stages will she need to be involved and what types of decisions will she have to make?).

3. Consider each of the following product categories:

- wine coolers
- home computers
- low fat snack foods
- children's cereal
- laundry detergent
- coffee
- prepackaged ice cream
- pain relievers

Select three of the categories. Then, for each selected category: (1) determine which broad type of segmentation (demographic, geographic, psychographic, or brand/category) is the most likely to provide key insights into the relevant population of category consumers and (2) identify the most appropriate segmentation and descriptive measures. Be certain to explain fully and justify your answers.

4. Consider each of the following advertisers:

 • Chic jeans

 • Apple Computer

 • Niemen-Marcus

 • Blockbuster Video

 • BASF audio tapes

 • Jeep

 • Salon Selectives

Select four of the advertisers. Then, for each selected advertiser, identify the VALS2 group that you feel would make the most appropriate target. Be certain to fully explain and justify your answers.

5. Fournier, Antes, and Beaumier[33] used U.S. government data to segment the adult United States population. The segmentation, which reflected how individuals spent their money on a broad array of products and services, was conducted as follows:

Data were obtained from the 1986 Consumer Expenditure Survey (CES), a "public domain data set that contains a rich collection of household expenditure and demographic information . . . The BLS (Bureau of Labor Statistics) estimates that 90%–95% of total yearly household expenditures are captured in survey panel member diaries."

The sample for this study consisted of 6,868 interviews conducted within 1,717 households.

Expenditures were grouped into eighteen broad classes (see Table 19.4, page 482). Each household's pattern of expenditures among these classes was examined, after which clustering was used to form nine distinct groups of consumers. Nine consumer groups were formed where each consumer group represented a different pattern of expenditures.

The spending patterns of each of the nine groups are shown in Table 19.5 (page 483). The demographic characteristics of each group are shown in Table 19.6 (page 484).

Examine the information shown in Tables 19.4–19.6. Based on this data, name each group. Provide a brief explanation and justification for each name you selected.[34] Then, select two groups for more detailed analysis. For each group selected, provide a detailed narrative that describes the group, paying particular attention to the expenditure and demographic characteristics that define the group and that distinguish the group from the other groups. Finally, for each of the two selected groups, construct a radar chart that effectively communicates each group's unique characteristics.

---

[33] Susan Fournier, David Antes, and Glenn Beaumier, "Nine Consumption Lifestyles," *Advances in Consumer Research* 19 (1992): 329–37. The tables from this study are reproduced with the permission of the Association for Consumer Research. All rights reserved.

[34] Fournier, Antes, and Beaumier named each group. Their names have been deleted for the purposes of this exercise.

6. Go to your library and select a product category for which SMRB or MRI reports the demographic characteristics of specific brand users. Prepare a memo that summarizes the similarities and differences of two different brand usage groups.

7. You are the researcher on the Johnson's baby account. Johnson's strategic planning unit has asked you to prepare a report that describes purchasers of baby products with specific emphasis on the purchase and purchasers of Johnson baby products. The data collected by MRI relevant to this assignment is shown in Figure 19.9 (pages 485–486). Prepare a memo to your research supervisor, Noel Smith, that describes the types of analyses you will conduct using the information provided by MRI. Be certain to fully explain, for each proposed analysis, the specific data that will be used, the types of information that will be provided and why the provided information is important.

TABLE 19.4 Expenditure Categories from Fournier, Antes and Beaumier

Category	Exemplar Products and Services
Appearance	Clothing, jewelry, wigs, hair care products/services, personal care appliances, health club memberships
Beauty/aesthetics	Artwork, paint and paper, curtains, rugs, china, aesthetic home improvements
Belonging	Monthly telephone charges, campers, trailers, outdoor camping/hunting/fishing gear, country/tennis/social clubs, wine and liquor
Cleanliness/orderliness	Garbage collection fees, cleaning equipment/supplies/charges, closet and storage organizers, dry cleaning, maid/cleaning services
Comfort	Bed and other linens, air conditioning, cigarettes, jackets and coats, blankets
Conformity	Uniforms, car registration/licensing/inspection fees
Control/power	Power tools, insect and pest control, answering machines
Convenience	Dishwashers, disposals, washers and dryers, microwaves, record and book clubs, calculators, convenience store purchases
Creativity	Sewing materials and supplies, sewing machines, landscaping supplies, musical instruments, camera equipment, and photo supplies
Fun/entertainment	Cable television, movies, movie rentals, VCRs, video cameras, stereos, sports equipment, toys and games, tickets to sporting events, dining out
Functionality	Transportation expenses, general maintenance charges, luggage, dinner- and glassware, towels, roofing and gutters, clocks, lamps, stoves, refrigerators, tools
Housing	Rent, taxes, mortgage
Knowledge	Radios, newspapers, magazines, books, tuition, computers
Morality	Contributions to church/charity/educational institutions, alimony, child support
Nurturance	Plants, babysitting services, care for elderly/invalids, children's clothing, pets and pet services
Security	Personal/fire/homeowner's insurance, safe deposit boxes, smoke alarms
Status	Vacation homes and related expenses, silver serving pieces, housekeeping/gardening services
Survival	Food and beverages, plumbing/heating/electrical services, water and sewage

Adapted from: Susan Fournier, David Antes, and Glenn Beaumier, ''Nine Consumption Lifestyles,'' *Advances in Consumer Research,* 19(1992): 329–37.

TABLE 19.5   Expenditures of Nine Consumption Lifestyles

| Percent of Total | \|—— *Expenditure Patterns of the Clusters* ——\| | | | | | | | | | Total Sample |
	12.7	4.8	8.1	23.8	5.2	5.5	3.2	22.5	14.2	
	Percentage Allocation									
Survival	19.0	26.5	14.3	21.4	18.6	22.4	26.2	44.6	29.0	27.1
Housing	9.6	13.6	9.6	15.6	13.1	12.9	12.3	6.9	36.4	14.9
Functionality	39.0	8.7	8.8	12.6	14.0	15.3	11.6	12.1	7.7	14.8
Entertainment	4.6	5.2	5.0	9.2	7.1	5.2	6.1	4.1	4.3	5.8
Security	3.7	3.7	3.4	5.1	3.8	4.9	6.5	5.6	1.5	4.3
Status	0.6	0.9	34.6	1.4	3.5	3.1	2.3	0.7	0.8	4.1
Belonging	2.9	3.7	2.3	3.9	3.8	3.7	3.3	4.5	4.0	3.7
Nurturance	2.5	18.3	1.7	2.3	3.3	1.9	3.5	1.6	1.8	2.9
Appearance	1.7	2.1	2.3	3.3	3.8	3.0	2.9	2.6	1.6	2.6
Aesthetics	1.5	1.5	1.7	1.9	1.6	2.0	20.0	1.7	0.6	2.1
Comfort	1.2	1.3	1.3	1.7	0.7	1.2	1.9	3.4	2.1	2.0
Convenience	1.3	1.4	1.2	3.1	1.7	1.9	2.3	0.9	0.9	1.7
Morality	1.4	1.0	0.9	1.1	0.8	12.8	2.1	1.0	0.5	1.7
Knowledge	1.0	0.7	0.9	1.2	7.6	1.3	1.3	1.0	0.8	1.4
Creativity	0.2	0.3	0.1	0.6	0.5	0.5	0.2	0.2	0.1	0.3
	Dollar Allocation									
Survival	5,052	4,942	5,292	4,706	6,195	4,623	5,791	5,657	3,196	4,916
Housing	2,912	3,123	3,689	3,629	4,029	3,730	3,909	971	4,387	3,064
Functionality	11,770	1,844	3,337	3,085	5,147	4,041	3,503	1,737	1,177	3,747
Entertainment	1,445	1,076	1,876	1,976	2,105	1,366	1,895	597	578	1,319
Security	1,126	867	1,308	1,203	1,453	1,365	1,552	792	265	993
Status	314	195	12,823	507	1,839	975	972	129	211	1,452
Belonging	829	785	890	856	1,195	878	905	563	473	752
Nurturance	874	3,473	668	679	1,427	631	1,104	261	292	739
Appearance	524	420	932	844	1,407	818	790	388	214	624
Aesthetics	480	394	642	556	593	507	5,518	255	109	571
Comfort	319	286	494	353	294	299	595	441	238	362
Convenience	428	305	495	732	602	555	602	130	116	410
Morality	426	183	395	279	360	3,158	640	153	55	415
Knowledge	360	172	344	285	2,511	331	382	136	106	356
Creativity	65	48	58	146	168	151	48	22	17	76
Total $ Expenditure	26,924	18,113	33,243	19,836	29,325	23,428	28,206	12,232	11,434	19,796
CES Total Expenditure	27,117	18,276	33,422	20,036	29,566	23,668	28,460	12,356	11,504	22,712
# of Categories Purchased	49	48	52	51	61	52	54	31	22	43

Source: Susan Fournier, David Antes, and Glenn Beaumier, ''Nine Consumption Lifestyles,'' *Advances in Consumer Research* 19(1992): 329–37. Reprinted by permission of the Association of Consumer Research.

TABLE 19.6 Demographic Characteristics of Nine Consumption Lifestyles

Sociodemographic Characteristics of the Clusters

	28,632	19,569	35,946	32,048	42,779	39,558	38,129	14,909	12,573	Total Sample 25,875
Income before Tax										
% under $7,000	14	11	3	11	7	5	4	27	38	17
$7,000 - $14,999	12	18	9	13	10	19	4	32	23	18
$15,000 - $34,999	40	40	31	32	20	23	40	25	22	29
$35,000 - $54,999	22	18	31	25	20	28	20	6	6	18
over $55,000	11	3	19	15	42	23	28	3	2	12
One earner	27	34	29	43	19	42	20	21	31	31
Two earner	65	50	65	45	74	44	44	38	31	47
No earner	8	16	6	11	7	14	36	41	38	22
Average Age	46	44	45	46	45	54	54	59	50	50
18 - 34	33	52	33	25	20	9	20	10	26	23
35 - 54	37	24	41	45	59	38	32	26	35	37
55 - 64	14	5	13	16	15	30	12	20	15	16
65 +	16	18	14	14	7	23	36	44	24	23
Ave. Household Size	3.22	3.21	2.81	2.59	3.32	2.32	2.76	2.78	2.41	2.80
% H/W only	23	18	28	22	12	30	36	29	11	23
H/W w/kids	50	48	44	37	58	31	44	32	19	37
Single parents	6	13	5	5	0	0	0	4	13	6
Singles	14	16	16	32	21	30	16	19	41	25
% Married	78	66	75	61	73	63	80	63	31	62
Div/Sep/Wid	14	22	12	21	7	18	16	31	46	24
Never Married	8	13	13	19	20	19	4	6	22	14
% Lower Class	14	13	3	12	7	5	8	30	38	19
Working Class	36	26	13	22	12	33	36	45	31	30
Middle Class	31	45	48	39	24	30	20	18	19	30
Upper Middle Class	12	16	33	20	37	19	20	5	10	16
Upper Class	7	0	3	8	20	14	16	2	2	6
% Bachelors	6	11	8	16	20	2	4	3	18	10
Newly Married	10	0	11	7	7	5	8	2	1	5
Full Nest	45	47	28	31	39	18	40	22	17	29
Empty Nest	20	14	36	20	24	37	32	31	9	23
Sole Survivor	6	8	6	7	4	7	12	15	19	10
% White	90	84	86	90	90	93	96	80	71	85
% White Collar	40	47	63	52	56	49	36	16	28	39
Blue Collar	31	24	25	21	17	26	20	23	22	23
Retired	13	11	8	14	5	16	40	36	22	20
% Less than HS	23	29	11	20	2	12	32	47	38	28
HS Graduate	55	39	48	46	32	63	40	40	51	46
College	22	32	41	34	66	26	28	12	11	26

Source: Susan Fournier, David Antes, and Glenn Beaumier, "Nine Consumption Lifestyles," *Advances in Consumer Research* 19(1992): 329–37. Reprinted with permission of the Association of Consumer Research.

BABY/CHILDREN'S PRODUCTS

BABY FOODS

	Your Household:	
	Used in last 6 months	Containers/ last 7 days

982
TOTAL: ☐ _____ 00

TYPES:
- Baby Juice .... ☐ _____ 01
- Baby Meats .... ☐ _____ 02
- First Foods/ Baby's First ☐ _____ 03
- Second Foods/ Stages 1, 2 .... ☐ _____ 04
- Third Foods/Stage 3 ..... ☐ _____ 05

BRANDS:
- Beech-Nut .... ☐ _____ 06
- Gerber .... ☐ _____ 07
- Heinz .... ☐ _____ 08
- ☐ _____ 999

OTHER (Write In)

INFANT CEREAL

	Your Household:	
	Used in last 6 months	Packages/ last 30 days

983
TOTAL: ☐ _____ 00

BRANDS:
- Beech-Nut .... ☐ _____ 01
- Gerber .... ☐ _____ 02
- ☐ _____ 999

OTHER (Write In)

PREPARED INFANT FORMULA

	Your Household:	
	Used in last 6 months	Times/ last 7 days

984
TOTAL: ☐ _____ 00

TYPES:
- Ready-to-feed .... ☐ _____ 01
- Concentrated liquid (dilute with water) ...... ☐ _____ 02
- Concentrated powder (dilute with water) ...... ☐ _____ 03

BRANDS:
- ☐ _____ 04
- Enfamil .... ☐ _____ 05
- Gerber .... ☐ _____ 06
- Isomil .... ☐ _____ 07
- Similac .... ☐ _____ 999

OTHER (Write In)

BABY NURSERS

	Your Household:	
	Used in last 6 months	Number bought last 30 days

985
TOTAL: ☐ _____ 00

TYPES:
- Firm plastic .... ☐ _____ 01
- Disposable .... ☐ _____ 02

BRANDS:
- Cherubs .... ☐ _____ 03
- Evenflo .... ☐ _____ 04
- Gerber .... ☐ _____ 05
- Luv 'N' Care .... ☐ _____ 06
- Playtex .... ☐ _____ 07
- ☐ _____ 999

OTHER (Write In)

TEETHING REMEDIES

	Your Household:	
	Used in last 6 months	Times/ last 7 days

986
TOTAL: ☐ _____ 00

BRANDS:
- Anbesol, Jr. .... ☐ _____ 01
- Ora-Jel .... ☐ _____ 02
- ☐ _____ 999

OTHER (Write In)

LIQUID BABY BATH

	Your Household:	
	Used in last 6 months	Times/ last 7 days

987
TOTAL: ☐ _____ 00

BRANDS:
- Fisher-Price .... ☐ _____ 01
- Johnson's Baby Bath ..... ☐ _____ 02
- Mennen Baby Magic ..... ☐ _____ 03
- Store's Own Brand ...... ☐ _____ 04
- ☐ _____ 999

OTHER (Write In)

SOAP FOR BABY

	Your Household:	
	Used in last 6 months	Times/ last 7 days

988
TOTAL: ☐ _____ 00

TYPES:
- Bar .... ☐ _____ 01
- Liquid .... ☐ _____ 02

BRANDS:
- Dove .... ☐ _____ 03
- Ivory .... ☐ _____ 04
- Johnson's Baby Bar ...... ☐ _____ 05
- Johnson's No More Germies .... ☐ _____ 06
- ☐ _____ 999

OTHER (Write In)

BABY SHAMPOO

	Your Household:	
	Used in last 6 months	Times/ last 7 days

989
TOTAL: ☐ _____ 00

BRANDS:
- Baby Don't Cry .... ☐ _____ 01
- Fisher-Price .... ☐ _____ 02
- Johnson's .... ☐ _____ 03
- Johnson's Baby Conditioning .... ☐ _____ 04
- Johnson's Pooh .... ☐ _____ 05
- Mennen Baby Magic ..... ☐ _____ 06
- Suave .... ☐ _____ 07
- White Rain .... ☐ _____ 08
- ☐ _____ 999

OTHER (Write In)

BABY OIL

	Your Household:	
	Used in last 6 months	Times/ last 7 days

990
TOTAL: ☐ _____ 00

BRANDS:
- Johnson's Baby Oil .... ☐ _____ 01
- Johnson's Creamy Baby Oil .... ☐ _____ 02
- Mennen Baby Magic ...... ☐ _____ 03

- Mennen Baby Magic Rich 'N' Creamy ...... ☐ _____ 04
- Generic (No Label) ...... ☐ _____ 05
- Store's Own Brand ...... ☐ _____ 06
- ☐ _____ 999

OTHER (Write In)

BABY OINTMENTS

	Your Household:	
	Used in last 6 months	Times/ last 7 days

991
TOTAL: ☐ _____ 00

BRANDS:
- A & D .... ☐ _____ 01
- Desitin .... ☐ _____ 02
- Diaparene Diaper Rash Ointment .... ☐ _____ 03
- Dyprotex .... ☐ _____ 04
- Johnson's Baby Diaper Rash Relief .... ☐ _____ 05
- Swan .... ☐ _____ 06
- Vaseline Petroleum Jelly ☐ _____ 07
- Store's Own Brand ...... ☐ _____ 08
- ☐ _____ 999

OTHER (Write In)

BABY LOTION

	Your Household:	
	Used in last 6 months	Times/ last 7 days

992
TOTAL: ☐ _____ 00

BRANDS:
- Johnson's .... ☐ _____ 01
- Mennen Baby Magic ..... ☐ _____ 02
- Mennen Baby Magic with Aloe .... ☐ _____ 03
- Vaseline Intensive Care. ☐ _____ 04
- Store's Own Brand ...... ☐ _____ 05
- ☐ _____ 999

OTHER (Write In)

DISPOSABLE DIAPERS

	Your Household:	
	Used in last 6 months	Packages/ last 30 days

993
TOTAL: ☐ _____ 00

BRANDS:
- Huggies (Regular) .... ☐ _____ 01
- Huggies Baby Steps ...... ☐ _____ 02
- Huggies Pull-ups .... ☐ _____ 03
- Huggies Ultratrim .... ☐ _____ 04
- Luvs Phases with Prints - Boys .... ☐ _____ 05
- Luvs Phases with Prints - Girls .... ☐ _____ 06
- Pampers (Regular) .... ☐ _____ 07
- Pampers Phases - Boys/Girls .... ☐ _____ 08
- Generic (No Label) .... ☐ _____ 09
- Store's Own Brand ...... ☐ _____ 10
- ☐ _____ 999

OTHER (Write In)

COTTON SWABS

	Your Household:	
	Used in last 6 months	Times/ last 7 days

994
TOTAL: ☐ _____ 00

BRANDS:
- Johnson's .... ☐ _____ 01
- Q-Tips .... ☐ _____ 02
- Generic (No Label) .... ☐ _____ 03
- Store's Own Brand ...... ☐ _____ 04
- ☐ _____ 999

OTHER (Write In)

FIGURE 19.9
Excerpt from MRI questionnaire.
Source: Mediamark Research, Inc. Reprinted with permission.

(continued on next page)

PRE-MOISTENED BABY WIPES

	Your Household:	
	Used in last 6 months	Times/ last 7 days

995

TOTAL:	☐	00

BRANDS:

Baby Fresh (Original)	☐	01
Baby Fresh - Unscented	☐	02
Chubs		03
Diaparene/Baby Wash	☐	04
Cloths	☐	05
Huggies		
Johnson's Baby Wash Cloths............	☐	06
Kidfresh Flushable Wipes	☐	07
Wash-A-Bye Baby	☐	08
Wet Ones..................	☐	09
Store's Own Brand	☐	10
	☐	999

OTHER (Write In)

BABY POWDER

	Your Household:	
	Used in last 6 months	Times/ last 7 days

996

TOTAL:	☐	00

TYPES:

Corn Starch.................	☐	01
Talcum	☐	02

BRANDS:

Baby Magic Baby Powder....................	☐	03
Baby Magic Cornstarch..	☐	04
Diaparene Cornstarch Baby Powder............	☐	05
Johnson's Baby Powder	☐	06
Johnson's Baby Powder Pure Cornstarch	☐	07
Store's Own Brand	☐	08
	☐	999

OTHER (Write In)

BABY FURNITURE & EQUIPMENT

	Your Household:	
	Now owns	Bought in last 6 months

997

	1	2
Baby carrier-back pack	☐	☐ 01
Baby car bed	☐	☐ 02
Baby car seat	☐	☐ 03
Bathing/dressing table	☐	☐ 04
Baby bath tub.................	☐	☐ 05
Baby mobiles.................	☐	☐ 06
Baby rattles	☐	☐ 07
Cradle gym...................	☐	☐ 08
Crib mattress................	☐	☐ 09
High chair	☐	☐ 10
Infant crib	☐	☐ 11
Jump seat	☐	☐ 12
Juvenile bed	☐	☐ 13
Playpen	☐	☐ 14
Stroller	☐	☐ 15
Stuffed toys	☐	☐ 16
Toilet chair....................	☐	☐ 17
Walker........................	☐	☐ 18
	☐	☐ 19

OTHER (Write In)

PAIN RELIEVERS & FEVER REDUCERS FOR CHILDREN

	Your Household:	
	Used in last 6 months	Times/ last 30 days

998

TOTAL:	☐	00

BRANDS:

Bayer Children's Aspirin.	☐	01
Liquipin	☐	02
Panadol Drops/Liquid ...	☐	03
Panadol Tablets	☐	04
St. Joseph Aspirin (Children).................	☐	05
Tempra Drops/Liquid	☐	06
.....	☐	07
Tylenol Drops/Liquid	☐	08
Tylenol Tablets	☐	09
	☐	999

OTHER (Write In)

CHILDREN'S COUGH SYRUP

	Your Household:	
	Used in last 6 months	Times/ last 30 days

999

TOTAL:	☐	00

BRANDS:

Benylin	☐	01
Pediacare	☐	02
Robitussin	☐	03
St. Joseph	☐	04
Triaminic	☐	05
Vick's Pediatric 44	☐	06
	☐	999

OTHER (Write In)

CHILDREN'S COLD TABLETS & LIQUIDS

	Your Household:	
	Used in last 6 months	Times/ last 30 days

99A

TOTAL:	☐	00

TYPES:

Liquid......................	☐	01
Tablet	☐	02

BRANDS:

Benadryl	☐	03
Dimetapp	☐	04
Children's Nyquil..........	☐	05
Pediacare	☐	06
Robitussin	☐	07
St. Joseph	☐	08
Sudafed	☐	09
Triaminic....................	☐	10
Children's Tylenol Cold..	☐	11
Vick's	☐	12
	☐	999

OTHER (Write In)

VITAMINS FOR CHILDREN

	Your Household:	
	Used in last 6 months	Times/ last 7 days

99E

TOTAL:	☐	00

TYPES:

Chewable..................	☐	01
Liquid	☐	02

BRANDS:

Bugs Bunny	☐	03
Centrum Jr.	☐	04
Flintstones Complete.....	☐	05
Flintstones with Extra C..	☐	06

Continued on next column

Garfield	☐	04
Poly Vi Flors	☐	05
Poly Vi Sol	☐	06
Sesame Street	☐	07
Sunkist Chewable.........	☐	08
	☐	999

OTHER (Write In)

CHILDREN'S CLOTHING

	Your Household:	
	Bought in the last 6 months	Number bought/last 6 months

99F

For Baby Under 1 Year:

Outerwear	☐	01
Sleepwear	☐	02
Stretchies	☐	03
Underwear (excluding diapers)	☐	04
Waterproof Pants	☐	05

Children 1-5 Years:

Jeans or Slacks...........	☐	06
Outerwear	☐	07
Shorts	☐	08
Sleepwear	☐	09
Suits or Dresses...........	☐	10
Sweatpants................	☐	11
Sweatshirts	☐	12
Tops/Shirts	☐	13
Underwear (excluding diapers)	☐	14
Waterproof Pants	☐	15

Children 6-12 Years:

Jeans	☐	16
Outerwear	☐	17
Shorts	☐	18
Slacks......................	☐	19
Sleepwear	☐	20
Suits & Dresses	☐	21
Sweatpants................	☐	22
Sweatshirts	☐	23
Sweaters	☐	24
Tops/Shirts	☐	25
Underwear.................	☐	26

Amount Spent Last 6 Months: 99H-O

Less than $25	☐ 1
$25-$50	☐ 2
$51-$99	☐ 3
$100-$199	☐ 4
$200 +........................	☐ 5

CHILDREN'S SHOES

	Your Household:	
	Used in last 6 months	Pairs bought/last 6 months

TOTAL: 99J	☐	00

TYPES:

Athletic	☐	01
Canvas	☐	02
Casual/leisure	☐	03
Dress	☐	04
Leather	☐	05
Rain or Snow Boots	☐	06
Sandals	☐	07
Slippers	☐	08
Western Boots	☐	09
Other	☐	999

Bought For: 99K-0

Child under 1 year	☐ 1
Child 1-5 years	☐ 2
Child 6-12 years	☐ 3

Amount Spent Last 6 Months: 99L-0

$1-$25	☐ 1
$26-$50	☐ 2
$51-$99	☐ 3
$100 + ...	☐ 4

FIGURE 19.9 (continued)

CHAPTER

20 Q-METHODOLOGY

As discussed throughout this text, one component of the advertising development process is a comprehensive understanding of the target consumers' attitudes and beliefs. Advertising researchers may select from among several research techniques when they need to understand these attitudes and beliefs. Researchers may use qualitative techniques such as focus groups or cognitive mapping or quantitative survey techniques. One research technique that falls in the center of the qualitative-quantitative research continuum is Q-methodology, a research technique whose sole purpose is to make explicit the internal structure of consumers' attitudes and beliefs. Q-methodology is qualitative in the sense that it uses small sample sizes and quantitative in the sense that the data is analyzed using sophisticated statistical techniques. This chapter describes Q-methodology.

After reading this chapter, you will be able to

■ Identify the characteristics of Q-methodology.

■ Describe the steps involved in the planning, conduct and analysis of a Q-methodology research study.

■ Explain how Q-methodology helps to foster a better understanding of consumers' attitudes and beliefs.

Q-methodology[1] is a simple, yet remarkably powerful means for acquiring insights into consumers' attitudes and beliefs toward themselves, brand and product users, brand and product categories, advertisers, and advertising practice. Q-methodology, in its most basic form, presents an individual with a set of statements (theQ-sample) that he or she sorts along a continuum (the Q-sort) according to a specified criterion (for example, "sort the statements to reflect how much you think each is *most*

---

[1] Q-methodology has its roots in personality and developmental psychology. For seminal readings on the development and refinement of Q-methodology see W. Stephenson, "Correlating Persons Instead of Tests," *Character and Personality* 6 (1935):17–34; W. Stephenson, *The Study of Behavior: Q-Technique and Its Methodology* (Chicago, IL: University of Chicago Press, 1953); J. A. Block, *The Q-Sort Method in Personality Assessment and Psychiatric Research* (Springfield, IL: Charles C. Thomas, 1961). For a review of Q-methodology see Bruce McKeown and Dan Thomas, *Q Methodology* (Beverly Hills, CA: Sage Publications, 1988).

like your point of view or *most unlike* your point of view"). The distribution of statements among respondents is then analyzed to determine the similarities and differences in how each respondent assigns statements to places on the continuum. Different patterns of statement assignment reveal differences in the underlying structure of consumers' attitudes and beliefs.

The quality of the data and insights provided by Q-methodology reflects the rigor applied to the development and selection of statements, the characteristics of the sorting technique used, and the application of appropriate statistical techniques. Each of these considerations in a Q-methodology study is discussed in the next section.

STEPS IN CONDUCTING Q-METHODOLOGY RESEARCH

Q-methodology research begins similarly to other types of quantitative advertising research (see Chapter 2). Initial decisions relate to the identification of informational needs and the acknowledgment that Q-methodology is an appropriate means of providing the required information. These decisions lead to the identification of the research concept(s) of interest and the detailed, explicit operational definition of each concept.

Once decisions in these areas are made, planning for the Q-methodology research begins. The planning and conduct of Q-methodology research requires eight steps, as shown in Figure 20.1.

Develop and Edit Statements

The first step in Q-methodology research is the development and editing of statements. Statements may be developed in any number of ways using a variety of sources as "raw material." Statements can, for example, be generated or obtained from

- prior Q-methodology research projects,
- prior survey research,
- responses to open-ended, in-depth interview questions,
- volunteered comments in focus groups,
- responses to projective stimuli such as sentence completion and picture projection,
- brainstorming or idea-generation sessions.

The goal at this stage in the Q-methodology planning process is to develop as many statements as possible disregarding duplication or grammatical form. Figure 20.2 (page 490) illustrates how statements are created from a portion of an in-depth interview. Note how the set of statements generated from the interview expresses ideas that are mentioned both explicitly and implicitly by the interviewee.

Once statement development is complete, all statements (regardless of their source) are merged into a single set that represents the total population of statements. Once formed, the population of statements is examined and edited with regard to item appropriateness, item clarity, item independence, range of statements represented in the total population, and grammatical form.

- *Item appropriateness* refers to the relationship between the statement and the operationally defined concept to which it relates. Only those statements that have face valid-

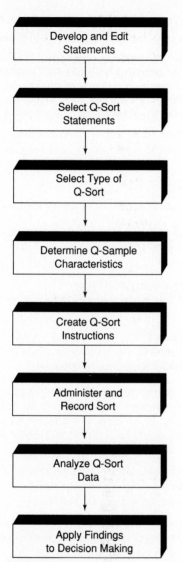

FIGURE 20.1

Steps in the design and conduct of Q-methodology research.

ity (see text pages 270–271) remain in the population. Statements without face validity, that is statements that are not felt to have a strong and direct relationship to the operationally defined concept(s), are eliminated from the population.

- *Item clarity* refers to statement comprehensibility. Statements that are vague, hard to understand, or ambiguous are eliminated from the population. Additionally, statements that express more than one idea are either split into two statements or are removed from the population.

- *Item independence* relates to the thought expressed by each statement in the population. Statements with nearly identical wording, sentiment, and/or ideas are paired and only one exemplar is selected to remain in the population. Statements expressing an identical thought are then eliminated from the population.

Segment of In-depth Interview

I really don't know what to think about VCRs these days. They are just so complicated. They have so many features and buttons and things to turn that the only thing I'm sure about is that I'm sure that I don't know how to use it all. Do you really need all those features? Do they really make the VCR better? Who knows? Maybe they do. And the VCRs without all the features, they look and feel so cheap that I think they wouldn't last for more than a few months. What's a person supposed to do? Maybe you really do need all the extra features.

Q-sort Statements

Buying a VCR is very confusing.
VCRs are too complicated to use.
Most VCRs have features that you don't really need.
It's better to invest in VCRs with more features when you don't really know what you will need.
The number of features is an indication of how long a VCR will last.
The number of features is an indication of VCR quality.
I wish the buying process for VCRs was easier.
You have to be an electronics expert in order to know what type of VCR to buy.

FIGURE 20.2
Example of Q-statement creation.

- *Range of statements* relates to the characteristics of statements remaining in the population. It is important that the final population of statements be unbiased.

  - If all statements in the population are to relate to only one operationally defined concept, then it is recommended that there be an equal number of positive statements, negative statements, and neutral statements.[2] If this range of statements does not exist in the population, additional statements should be generated and subjected to the review process just described.

  - If there are several operationally defined concepts in the population, then there should be an equal number of statements for each concept and within each concept there should be an equal number of positive, negative, and neutral statements.[3]

- All statements should be written in the same grammatical format. The most common format is the simple declarative sentence. Statements not written in this format are revised.

Select Q-Sort Statements

Once a population of statements has been carefully reviewed and edited, statements from that population are selected for use in the Q-sort. As might be expected, the number of statements required for any particular Q-methodology varies as a function of the complexity of the attitudes being examined and the number of operationally defined concepts. While more complex areas of investigation typically require more statements, most Q-methodology research utilizes between 50 and 100 statements.

---

[2] M. Sherif and C. I. Hovland, "Judgmental Phenomena and Scales of Attitude Measurement: Placement of Items With Individual Choice of Numbers and Categories," *Journal of Abnormal and Social Psychology* 48 (1953): 135–41.

[3] A. Goldberg, "The Q sort in Speech and Hearing Research," *ASHA* 4 (1962): 255–7.

The set of statements used in the research is called the *Q-sample*. If we view the Q-sample as representative of a larger population, then traditional sampling techniques can be used to select statements from the population. The selection of a sampling technique reflects the underlying structure of the population of statements, just as the selection of a survey sampling technique reflects the characteristics of the larger population (see pages 172–180). Three approaches to statement selection can be used:

- A census can be used when the population of statements is small and when it is felt that the entire population of statements should be examined during the Q-sort.

- Random sampling is appropriate when the population is homogeneous with respect to the nature and focus of the statements. When all of the statements in the population are related to one operationally defined concept then random sampling should result in a set of statements representative of the total population of statements.

- Stratified random sampling is appropriate when the population of statements is heterogeneous and therefore reflects a number of related but different operationally defined concepts. Random sampling within each strata (in this case each concept of interest) should result in a set of statements reflective of the broader population.

This selection of Q-sort statements ends with each selected statement being transferred to a numbered index card.

Select Type of Q-Sort

A respondent's distribution of Q-sample statements may be either forced or unforced.

A *forced sort procedure* requires a respondent to place a predetermined number of index cards (each card containing one statement) at each point on the continuum. Thus, in this approach the researcher specifies the shape and scatter of the distribution curve, which typically resembles a normal (bell-shaped) curve. The forced Q-sort distribution shown next asks a respondent to place ninety statements on the continuum of "Most like me" to "Least like me."

Most like me										Least like me
3	4	7	10	13	16	13	10	7	4	3

There are eleven points or spaces in this distribution. The forced nature of the distribution dictates that a respondent place three statements on the extreme ends of the continuum, four statements on the next two inner points, etc. The three statements placed at the extreme left are the statements the respondent believes to be most like him or herself, while the three statements or items in the space at the extreme right are the statements the respondent believes to be least like him- or herself. The center pile with sixteen cards is neutral. Other examples of forced choice distributions are

9 categories, 70 items:	4	6	9	10	12	10	9	6	4	
9 categories, 100 items:	5	8	12	16	18	16	12	8	5	
10 categories, 72 items:	2	5	7	10	12	12	10	7	5	2
11 categories, 90 items:	3	5	8	10	12	14	12	10	8	5	3

An *unforced sort procedure* also specifies the number of points on the continuum. However, unlike the forced sort, an unforced sort allows a respondent to place statements at any point in the continuum regardless of the number of items already assigned to that point. Thus, a respondent is free to assign any number of statements to any point on the distribution.

Researchers and statisticians have argued for and against each type of sorting procedure.[4] Research has shown, however, that generally equivalent information is obtained from both methods. Block, for example, asked a group of respondents to use both forced and unforced sorts for the same set of fifty-five statements. He found that the overall mean correlation was .94 with only two correlations falling below .90.[5] After conducting similar analyses, Hess and Hink concluded that forced and unforced sorts do not give strikingly different results.[6] Thus, given the general equivalence of sorting procedures, researchers have relied on personal preference (typically forced choice) when selecting the sorting technique.

Both the forced and unforced sorting procedures used in Q-methodology are related to other rating and ranking procedures (see pages 263–281). However, the unique demands of the Q-sort provide insights different from traditional rating and ranking data. These differences become explicit when you consider the respondent's task in each approach to data collection.[7] Imagine presenting a respondent with a list of forty or fifty statements, asking that respondent to read each statement on the list and then providing a rating of '1' (very much like me) to '7' (not at all like me). Most respondents will read each statement in sequence, provide a rating, and move onto the next statement. Few, if any, respondents will reexamine the ratings once the task is completed even if their standard of how much "like me" a rating of '5', '6', or '7' changes during the course of the task. Moreover, the rating or ranking of a large number of statements is very demanding and respondent performance and item discrimination tends to diminish during the task. Finally, in the context of standard rating and ranking techniques, some respondents may be reluctant to use any extreme ratings while others may use all extreme ratings. In both cases, discrimination between statements is re-

---

[4] Proponents of the forced choice approach believe that free choice artificially increases variability between respondents. One respondent, for example, may evaluate more statements as extremely characteristic or extremely uncharacteristic than a second respondent. Moreover, some respondents may be less assertive about their beliefs and perceptions and thus may place fewer items in the extreme positions, while others may place more items in the extreme positions and thus tend to dominate the consensus (average) judgment through the disproportionate weighting caused by the larger variance of their responses. Finally, it is argued that the unforced Q-sorting procedure provides data that is more difficult to analyze versus forced Q-sort data. Proponents of free or unconstrained sorting techniques argue that forcing is of dubious value. They believe that while forcing does insure variance in the responses and eliminate response sets, it discards possibly important information about differences in scatter and restricts the types of statistical tests that can be applied to the data. Additionally, some researchers have criticized the forced sort on statistical grounds; the forced sort, they argue, violates the assumption of independence. The opportunity for a statement to be placed in any space on the continuum is reduced each time another card is assigned to a space, that is, in a forced choice sort the response and placement of one item is affected by responses to and placement of other items. (This latter objection is addressed by making explicit the permissibility of taking any item from the pile into which it has been sorted and placing it in any other pile.)

[5] Block, *The Q-Sort Method.*

[6] R. D. Hess and D. L. Hink, "A Comparison of Forced Vs. Free Q-Sort Procedure," *Journal of Educational Research* 53 (1959): 83–90.

[7] This discussion is based on Daniel J. Ozer, "The Q-Sort Method and the Study of Personality Development," In David C. Funder, eds., *Studying Lives Through Time* (Washington, DC: American Psychological Association, 1993), 147–68.

TABLE 20.1 Example of Q-Methodology Sample Size Determination			

Population Characteristic	*Levels*		*Level Description*
Gender	2	(a)	male
		(b)	female
Employment status	3	(c)	employed full-time outside home
		(d)	employed part-time outside home
		(e)	not employed outside home
Category usage	2	(f)	used any brand in category at least once in past 30 days
		(g)	did not use any brand in category within past 30 days

Total number of combinations $= 2 \times 3 \times 2 = 12$

Combinations   acf   acg   adf
               adg   aef   aeg
               bcf   bcg   bdf
               bdg   bef   beg

Number of replications per combination $= 4$

Sample size $=$ Combinations $\times$ Replications $= 12 \times 4 = 48$

duced. These problems with the rating or ranking of large sets of statements are all eliminated in Q-methodology.

Determine Q-Sample Characteristics

The determination of sample characteristics for Q-methodology research, as well as the procedures for sample selection, are similar to those used in survey research. The sample for Q-methodology research consists of a group of individuals who are representative of the larger population from which they were drawn.

Sample sizes in Q-methodology research tend to be small and typically reflect

- the number of population variables believed to be important and influential,
- the number of required replications per combination of identified variables. Most Q-methodology research utilizes between three and five replications per combination of variables[8]

Consider the information shown in Table 20.1. Three population variables (gender, employment status, and product category usage) are identified as potentially important and influential on the structure of an individual's attitudes. There are twelve combinations of these variables. Given the desire for four replications per combination, the required sample size is forty-eight.

Create Appropriate Q-Sort Instructions

Q-sort instructions explain the task that each respondent needs to perform. Instructions generally consist of two parts: sorting criteria and sorting procedures.

---

[8] See McKeown and Thomas, *Q-Methodology*, 37–41.

Sorting criteria, a respondent's guide for sorting Q-sample statements, can either be a simple request for agreement or disagreement or a more elaborate scenario. The following are examples of each type of sorting criteria:

Simple Requests
Sort the statements to reflect how much you think each is "most like my point of view" or "most unlike my point of view."

Sort the statements to reflect the extent to which each you believe each represents the "most ideal children's cereal" to the "least ideal children's cereal."

Scenario
Imagine that you are in charge of developing a new children's ready-to-eat packaged lunch. You can develop a product that has any combination of characteristics. Sort these statements to indicate how likely or unlikely you would be to include each characteristic in the new children's ready to eat packaged lunch. Sort the statements from "most likely to include" to "least likely to include."

The sorting criteria are presented within the context of more general instructions that explain the sorting procedures. These instructions explain the characteristics of the statements in the Q-sample, the nature of the sorting task, and any special conditions that control the sort. For example, the directions for a forced sort of sixty-three items using a 3–4–4–7–8–11–8–7–4–4–3 distribution might be

Here is a deck of sixty-three index cards. Each card contains a statement which, to a greater or lesser extent, might reflect your own point of view. I would like you to sort the statements according to those that are most like your point of view to those that are most unlike your point of view.

You can sort the statements using the board I have placed on the table. (POINT TO BOARD) The ends of the board are labeled "most unlike my point of view" and "most like my point of view." You can see that there are eleven spaces on this board between the labels "most unlike my point of view" and "most like my point of view." The closer a space is to an extreme end of the board the more the descriptor on that end applies to that space. For example, the statements that you place in this space (POINT TO SPACE ON EXTREME RIGHT END OF BOARD) are those which you feel are the very most like your own point of view.

(POINT TO NUMBERS IN EACH SPACE ON BOARD.) The number written in each space indicates the number of cards that you can place in that space. You can, for example, place only three statements in this space. (POINT TO SPACE ON EXTREME LEFT END OF BOARD)

Please begin by reading the statements on each card. (SHUFFLE CARDS AND HAND TO RESPONDENT. WHEN RESPONDENT IS DONE READING CARDS CONTINUE.)

Now, please sort the cards into two piles: those that to any extent reflect your point of view, and those that to any extent do not reflect your point of view. Each card should be placed in one pile. When you are done, tell me which pile is which.

(POINT TO PILE WITH "MOST LIKE POINT OF VIEW" STATEMENTS.) Please reread the statements in this pile and then select the *three* statements that are the *very most like* your point of view. Place those three cards in the space on the extreme right on this board. (POINT TO SPACE ON EXTREME RIGHT END OF BOARD.)

(WHEN RESPONDENT HAS FINISHED, POINT TO PILE WITH "MOST UNLIKE MY POINT OF VIEW" STATEMENTS.) Now, please reread the statements in this pile and select the *three* statements that are the *very most unlike* your own point of view. Place those three cards in the extreme left space on this board.

(CONTINUE ALTERNATING PILES OF CARDS, NOTING NUMBER OF CARDS TO BE PLACED INTO EACH SPACE ON THE BOARD. WHEN ONE PILE OF CARDS IS COMPLETELY ASSIGNED CONTINUE WITH REMAINING PILE OF CARDS. BE CERTAIN TO INDICATE TO RESPONDENT THAT CARDS CAN BE MOVED FROM PILE TO PILE AT ANY TIME.)

(WHEN RESPONDENT HAS FINISHED THE Q-SORT OF ALL CARDS, COUNT THE NUMBER OF CARDS IN EACH SPACE ON THE BOARD. MAKE CERTAIN THAT EACH SPACE CONTAINS THE PROPER NUMBER OF STATEMENTS. IF SPACE TOTALS ARE INCORRECT, START Q-SORT OVER.)

Administer and Record Sort

The interviewer, at the completion of a successful Q-sort, records the placement of each statement using a form of the type shown in Figure 20.3. The item number of each card is recorded in the appropriate column to represent its assignment to a particular place on the continuum. The values shown beneath the continuum are assigned to each card for data analysis. For example, the three cards placed in the far left pile are each assigned a value of -5.

Analyze Q-Sort Data

Q-sort data is analyzed differently than traditional survey data. In Q-methodology, the variables are the individuals performing the Q-sort, not the individual Q-sample statements. With this in mind, the first step in data analysis uses factor analysis to identify similarities and differences in respondents' patterns of statement distribution. The factor analysis calculates each respondent's loading on identified factors, where a "loading" indicates the degree of association between a person's individual Q-sort and the

MOST UNLIKE MY POINT OF VIEW										MOST LIKE MY POINT OF VIEW
3	4	4	7	8	11	8	7	4	4	3
(-5)	(-4)	(-3)	(-2)	(-1)	(0)	($+1$)	($+2$)	($+3$)	($+4$)	($+5$)
card#	card#	card#	card#	card#	card#	card#	card#	card#	card#	card#
card#	card#	card#	card#	card#	card#	card#	card#	card#	card#	card#
card#	card#	card#	card#	card#	card#	card#	card#	card#	card#	card#
	card#	card#	card#	card#	card#	card#	card#	card#	card#	
			card#	card#	card#	card#	card#			
			card#	card#	card#	card#	card#			
			card#	card#	card#	card#	card#			
				card#	card#	card#				
					card#					
					card#					
					card#					

FIGURE 20.3
Form for recording results of Q-sort.

underlying composite attitude or perspective of that factor. (Factor loading in the context of Q-methodology is interpreted similarly to factor loading within the context of perceptual mapping and multidimensional scaling, see page 426.) Thus, in Q-methodology the presence of several independent factors is evidence of different points of view or underlying attitudes within the sample. An individual's positive loading on a factor indicates his or her shared attitudes and beliefs with others who have high loading on that factor, while a negative loading is a sign that an individual rejects or does not share a factor's perspective or attitudes.

The results of Q-methodology data analysis are best illustrated by example. Imagine an advertiser who wishes to introduce a new line of healthy packaged sandwich meats. These meats are low in fat, sodium, cholesterol, calories, and even contain a good amount of fiber. The advertiser wishes to understand consumers' attitudes toward health and dieting in preparation for internal discussions of the product's positioning, targeting, and advertising essential message. Table 20.2 presents the hypothetical results of respondents' Q-sort of statements related to health and dieting. A factor analysis of these individuals' distribution of statements identified three factors. Respondents one through nine "define" Factor A by their shared common attitudes toward health and dieting. Each individual has a statistically significant loading on Factor A and statistically insignificant loading on the remaining two factors (the level of statistical significance at $p \le .05$ is a factor loading $\pm .35$). Respondents ten through twenty-four are clearly associated with Factor B while respondents twenty-five through twenty-eight are clearly associated with Factor C. Moreover, most respondents in Factor B explicitly reject the underlying attitudes expressed in Factor A (as reflected in significant negative loading on Factor A). Respondents twenty-nine and thirty are difficult to classify. Respondent twenty-nine shares some beliefs with all three factors while respondent thirty shares few attitudes with any of the factors.

Once individuals are assigned to factors, the next step in data analysis identifies the distinguishing characteristics of each factor. Attitudinal characteristics are examined first, by comparing the mean scores of individual Q-sample items among the factors. Statements with similar means among the factors indicate shared attitudes while statements with statistically significant different means among the factors define differences in the attitudes and perceptions underlying each factor.

Hypothetical mean scores for a subset of the health and diet statements in the Q-sample are shown in Table 20.3 (page 498). The scores reflect continuum values of -5, "not at all like me," to $+5$, "very much like me." The mean scores of two statements are consistently high among all three factors, indicating that all respondents feel that they are participating in some healthy eating behaviors by avoiding foods with fat and cholesterol (statements 3 and 24). However, beyond these shared beliefs, individuals in the three factors view themselves differently.

- Individuals in Factor A appear to believe that avoiding fat and cholesterol is sufficient. These individuals are pleased with their current weight (statement 4) and believe that they have little need to diet (statement 25). Additionally (and perhaps as a result of these attitudes) they indicate that they do not actively participate in other diet related behaviors (see statements 7, 11, 17, 23, 8, and 2).

- Individuals in Factors B and C share some attitudes (although these attitudes are quite different from those of individuals in Factor A). Individuals in Factors B and C believe that dieting is an important part of their life (statement 7) and that, in addition to moni-

TABLE 20.2 Hypothetical Factor Loading for Q-Sort Respondents

Respondent #	Loading On:		
	Factor A	*Factor B*	*Factor C*
1	**+.81**	+.22	−.21
2	**+.78**	−.11	+.03
3	**+.79**	+.06	−.08
4	**+.84**	+.23	+.11
5	**+.79**	+.17	−.17
6	**+.80**	−.08	−.05
7	**+.81**	−.21	−.01
8	**+.78**	+.17	+.19
9	**+.79**	−.05	−.06
10	**−.39**	**+.87**	−.05
11	+.10	**+.91**	−.01
12	**−.37**	**+.74**	+.05
13	**−.36**	**+.55**	+.21
14	−.22	**+.62**	−.18
15	**−.57**	**+.76**	+.11
16	+.13	**+.49**	+.01
17	+.00	**+.64**	+.14
18	+.01	**+.81**	−.08
19	**−.71**	**+.73**	−.07
20	**−.62**	**+.77**	−.14
21	**−.41**	**+.47**	−.01
22	**−.37**	**+.63**	−.17
23	−.23	**+.42**	−.10
24	**−.41**	**+.55**	+.25
25	−.21	−.21	**+.58**
26	+.01	−.01	**+.89**
27	−.11	−.21	**+.79**
28	+.22	+.21	**+.56**
29	+.23	+.33	+.32
30	−.23	−.32	−.29

Note: A bold item indicates a loading significant at $p \leq .05$.

toring fat and cholesterol, they try to avoid foods with sugar (statement 9) and try to eat enough fiber every day (statement 11). At this point the underlying attitudes of Factors B and C diverge.

• Individuals in Factor B perceive themselves to be *actively involved* in health and diet related behaviors. These individuals alone (versus those in the other two factors) see themselves actively and consciously monitoring many aspects of what they eat (statements 5, 17, 23 and 16, and 8) and actively seeking out relevant diet-related information (statements 21 and 2).

• Individuals in Factor C appear to be *less active* and *less positive* than those in Factor B. Factor C individuals feel that dieting is hard work (statements 10, 22, and 20) and, perhaps as a result, tend to move from diet to diet (statement 12).

Once group attitudes are identified, the demographics, brand-related behaviors, or other salient characteristics of individuals in each group are compared to determine the correlates of each set of attitudes represented in the individual factors. Hypothetical information in these areas is presented in Table 20.4. (Note, because of small sample sizes this type of information if often used as directional rather than definitive.)

• Factor A primarily consists of men of a wide range of ages. These men, both married and single, are less likely than the other two groups to purchase "low/no fat" or "low/no cholesterol" foods. They do not purchase a great deal of packaged sandwich meats.

• Factor B is primarily composed of single, younger women. These women are the most likely to purchase "low/no fat" and "low/no cholesterol" foods. They do not, however, purchase a great deal of packaged sandwich meats, primarily because they feel that there are no healthy packaged sandwich meats.

TABLE 20.3   Hypothetical Q-Statement Factor Loading

Statement	*Mean Score Within:*		
	Factor A	*Factor B*	*Factor C*
3. I consistently avoid foods with fat	+3	+4	+4
24. I consistently try to avoid foods with high cholesterol	+4	+5	+4
4. I am pleased with my weight	+5	+1	−3
25. I really don't need to watch my weight	+4	−3	−4
7. Dieting is an important part of my life	−4	+5	+4
9. I consistently avoid foods with sugar	−2	+4	+3
11. I try to get enough fiber each day	−4	+3	+4
5. I consistently try to avoid foods that are high in fat	−3	+4	+1
17. I carefully monitor my daily caloric intake	−4	+4	+1
23. I carefully monitor my daily calcium intake	−4	+4	+1
16. I carefully monitor my daily fat intake	−3	+4	+1
21. I always read food labels	−3	+3	0
8. I always try to eat balanced meals	−4	+4	+1
2. I tend to pay attention to health or nutrition claims in advertising	−4	+3	0
10. It is really hard for me to stay on a diet	0	−2	+4
12. I tend to go from diet to diet	0	−3	+4
22. I have difficulty determining just what is a "healthy food"	−3	−3	+4
20. It takes too much time to keep track of what I eat	0	−3	+3

Note: For each statement, a difference of 3 points is statistically significant at $p \le .05$.

TABLE 20.4 Hypothetical Demographic and Product Usage Data By Q-Sort

Characteristic	*Factor A*	*Factor B*	*Factor C*
Gender			
Male	89%	20%	30%
Female	11	80	70
Marital status (%)			
Married	50%	25%	85%
Not married	50	75	15
Age range	25–64	25–34	35–49
Mean age	42	28	43
Number of low-/no-fat products purchased in past 14 days	2	14	5
Number of low-/no-cholesterol products purchased in past 14 days	3	16	7
Number of packages of sandwich meat purchased in past 14 days	1	1	6
Ratings of ''healthiness'' of packaged sandwich meats (1–5 scale; 5 is 'very healthy')	3.0	1.2	2.7

- Factor C is primarily composed of married, mid-aged women. These women are likely to purchase "low/no fat" or "low/no cholesterol" foods. They purchase the highest amount of packaged sandwich meats of all three groups. However, in spite of this high level of category purchase, these women also believe that there are no *really* healthy packaged sandwich meats.

Apply Findings to Decision Making

The final step in Q-methodology research, similar to all other advertising research, is the application of the results to the decision-making process. The hypothetical sandwich meat advertiser might draw the following conclusions from this research:

- The target audience for the new product is most likely women. Women, versus men, are more likely to purchase sandwich meats and are much more likely to be concerned about the health benefits of their food and the quality of their diet.

- There are two potential groups of individuals within the larger female target. Each group displays a different combination of strengths and weaknesses.

    The subgroup represented by Factor B appears larger than the group represented by Factor C. Attitudinally, Factor B women appear to be the most receptive to healthy products and to health- and diet-related advertising messages. They actively seek out these products and they pay attention to messages that help them to evaluate and find appropriate products. Unfortunately, they are light users of packaged sandwich meats, apparently due to the perception that there are no healthy sandwich meats currently available. Thus, while these women are likely to pay attention to the advertising (assuming it stresses the health benefits of the product), the advertising faces a significant challenge: it must change these womens' category purchase behaviors.

The subgroup represented by Factor C mirrors the strengths and weaknesses of Factor B. On the positive side, those in Factor C feel that dieting and eating healthy is quite hard, and so they are likely to respond positively to a product that makes healthy eating easy, especially (as in the case of packaged sandwiched meats) in a product category that they already use. On the negative side, these women are a small group and they say that they are unlikely to pay attention to health-related messages or advertising that stresses a product's health benefits. Consequently, these women are an easier "sell" *only* if the advertising successfully attracts their attention.

Summary

Q-methodology uncovers underlying attitudes and beliefs by having individuals sort a series of statements related to one or more operationally defined concepts into a prescribed number of piles along a descriptive continuum. The conduct of a Q-methodology study contains eight steps.

The research begins with the development and editing of potential Q-sample statements. First, statements are collected or generated from secondary or primary research sources. Then, this set of statements is edited, paying particular attention to item appropriateness, item clarity, item independence, range of ideas covered, and grammatical consistency. Statements that survive the editing and revision process comprise the population of Q-statements. Second, the Q-sample is created by sampling statements from the total population of statements. Third, a distribution method (either forced or unforced) is selected. Fourth, decisions related to sample characteristics and sample size are made. Fifth, instructions that explain sorting criteria and sorting procedures are created, after which (sixth) the Q-sort is administered to the sample. The seventh step, data analysis, uses factor analysis to determine similarities and differences in attitudes and perceptions among subgroups of the total sample. The eighth step applies the results to decision making.

Review Questions

1. What is the goal of Q-methodology research?

2. What are the basic characteristics of Q-methodology research?

3. How are statements for the Q-sample generated?

4. What criteria are used to evaluate and edit potential Q-sample statements?

5. What sampling options are available for selecting Q-sample statements? In what type of circumstance is each sampling option most appropriate?

6. What is the difference between a *forced* and *unforced* Q-sort? Is one approach better than the other?

7. How is sample size determined in Q-methodology research?

8. What are the two components of Q-sort instructions? What is the role or intention of each component?

9. How are the results of a Q-sort recorded? How is each Q-statement coded for data analysis?

10. How is the analysis of Q-methodology data different from traditional survey data?

11. What do factors in Q-methodology research represent?

12. What procedure is used to determine attitudinal similarities and differences among the factors?

13. Beyond factor loading, what additional types of information provide insights into similarities and differences among factors?

Application Exercises[9]

1. The Northwest Regional Healthcare System (NRHS) has lost several thousand patients to competitive HMOs over the past year. NRHS believes that patients are leaving due to higher costs and dissatisfaction with their primary care doctor. NRHS is planning to air an advertising campaign directed toward current patients in an effort to reverse this trend. As part of the advertising planning process, NRHS seeks to determine current perceptions of their primary care doctors so that it may change doctors' behaviors in these areas and publicize these changes in its advertising campaign.

   Patients' perceptions of NRHS primary care doctors will be probed via Q-methodology. You have decided to conduct in-depth interviews to assist in the development of Q-statements. Portions of the interview responses are shown next. Prepare a memo to the client that presents the full set of Q-sort statements generated from these interviews.

   You call and call and then a machine answers. Then you have to push a lot of buttons. And then another machine answers. Then, if you are really lucky, your doctor's office answers. But, you never get to speak with the doctor. You leave a message with the nurse or the receptionist who says that the doctor will get back to you. But he never does.

   My doctor has absolutely no idea who I am. And you know what, he really doesn't want to know. I come in, he reads my chart in front of me, he asks me some questions and then he's gone. His nurse gives me my prescription that the doctor has written. I probably see the doctor for less than ten minutes. It's like a factory. I'm just a cog in the system. You know, I think my doctor would be happiest if he didn't have any patients at all.

   A bother, that's what they make me feel like. They make me feel like I'm distracting them from something more important. What could be more important than my health and my problems. They just don't care.

   Every time I went in I saw a different doctor. My personal doctor changed every time. I think that I must have had three or four doctors by now. They just come and go.

   I think that I've been very lucky. My friends all tell me their horror stories. If only part of their stories are true, then it's really scary. But I love my doctor. She's always there when I need her. And when I go in I don't feel rushed or hurried. She takes the time to talk with me. She seems to really care about me. And, she's a really good listener.

---

[9] All application exercises and data are hypothetical. The use of actual brand and company names is for illustrative purposes only.

My doctor is really smart. And she always figures out what's wrong with me and fixes me right up. But something's missing. Personality. My doctor has the personality of a slug.

My doctor is so, so old. I think that he's been around forever. And it seems to me that he has his way of doing things. I'm always wondering. Does he know the latest advances? Has he kept up? I can only hope so.

2. Exchange the set of statements you generated for the prior exercise with four other individuals in your class. Combine their statements with yours to form a population of statements. Then, review and edit the population of statements to create your Q-sample. Prepare a memo that presents your recommendation and describes the process by which the final Q-sample was developed.

3. Assume that you wish to use a forced sort procedure. Specify the characteristics of the distribution for Q-samples consisting of 43, 55, 63, 80, and 97 statements.

4. You have been asked for a sample size recommendation for an upcoming Q-methodology research study. The most important characteristics of the sample are gender, age (three dimensions: 18–29, 30–49, and 50 and older), and political orientation (two dimensions: liberal or conservative). Present, explain, and justify your sample size recommendation?

5. Coors Brewing has asked you to conduct a Q-methodology study to probe perceptions of the drinkers of Coors, Miller, and Budweiser regular beers. You have already developed the set of Q-statements. Assume that you have decided to use an unforced sort procedure. Prepare the Q-sort directions.

6. Gourmet Foods Inc. has developed a new line of no fat, no cholesterol gourmet frozen dinners. These dinners will present unique dishes priced 25 percent higher than the closest competitor. In preparation for advertising planning, Gourmet Foods has asked the agency to probe consumers' current perceptions of frozen dinners and the contribution of no fat, no cholesterol to these perceptions. The agency decides to probe these perceptions using Q-methodology.

   The results of the research are summarized in Table 20.5A–20.5C. Table 20.5A presents the factor loadings of the thirty individuals who participated in the study. The sample consists of women aged 20–39 who purchased and personally consumed at least two diet-related (i.e., reduced calorie, no fat, no cholesterol) frozen dinners within the past two weeks. Table 20.5B (page 504) summarizes demographic, brand, and category information for each factor while Table 20.5C (page 504) presents a subset of the Q-sample, noting each statement's average score for each factor. The scale is −5 to +5, where a higher number indicates the statement is more "what I think".

   Write a memo to the client describing the insights obtained by this research.

| TABLE 20.5A | Hypothetical Factor Loading for Q-Sort Respondents | | |

| | Loading On: | | |
Respondent #	Factor A	Factor B	Factor C
1	+.76	+.22	−.21
2	+.28	−.11	+.73
3	+.29	+.06	+.68
4	+.24	+.63	+.11
5	+.79	+.26	+.17
6	+.67	−.26	−.05
7	+.11	+.71	−.01
8	−.28	−.17	+.69
9	−.29	−.05	+.86
10	−.29	+.87	−.05
11	−.22	+.58	−.24
12	−.27	+.74	+.05
13	−.33	+.55	+.21
14	−.22	+.22	+.48
15	−.27	+.66	−.01
16	+.13	+.49	+.01
17	+.70	+.24	+.14
18	−.22	+.56	−.01
19	+.61	+.03	−.07
20	−.22	+.77	−.14
21	−.11	+.57	−.01
22	−.17	+.43	−.17
23	+.63	−.12	−.10
24	+.21	+.55	−.25
25	−.21	−.21	+.58
26	+.01	+.89	−.19
27	−.11	−.21	+.29
28	+.22	+.21	+.16
29	+.23	+.33	+.32
30	−.23	+.62	−.29

Note: A significant loading at $p \leq .05$ is $\pm .35$.

TABLE 20.5B   Hypothetical Demographic and Product Usage Data By Q-Sort Factor

Characteristic	Factor A	Factor B	Factor C
Age range	25 to 39	22 to 34	24 to 39
Mean age	34	36	35
Employment (%)			
Full-time outside home	45%	62%	55%
Part-time outside home	20	19	23
Not employed outside home	35	19	22
Mean household income	$35,292	$47,463	$37,727
Total number of low-/no-fat products purchased in past 14 days	8	24	14
Total number of low-/no-cholesterol products purchased in past 14 days	5	26	11
Total number of frozen dinners purchased in past 14 days	5	11	10
Total number of "diet" frozen dinners purchased in past 14 days	3	10	6

TABLE 20.5C   Hypothetical Q-Statement Factor Loading

Statement	Mean Score Within: Factor A	Factor B	Factor C
1. I am pleased with my weight	+1	+5	+4
11. I really don't need to watch my weight	+1	−2	−2
27. I carefully monitor my daily caloric intake	−1	+4	+3
8. I always try to eat balanced meals	−4	+4	+3
6. I carefully monitor my daily fat intake	0	+4	+1
5. I consistently try to avoid foods that are high in salt	−1	+3	0
2. I have difficulty determining just what is a "healthy food"	+2	−2	0
3. I rely on convenience foods to simplify my life	+3	+4	+3
15. When I eat convenience foods, I sacrifice taste and quality	+1	+4	0
18. I enjoy eating frozen dinners	0	+2	+2
19. I enjoy eating "diet" frozen dinners	−1	−4	0
23. I often feel hungry after eating a "nondiet" frozen dinner	0	1	1
29. I often feel hungry after eating a "diet" frozen dinner	1	4	1
16. When I eat a "nondiet" frozen dinner, I feel like I sacrifice taste	1	−1	1
8. When I eat a "diet" frozen dinner, I feel like I sacrifice taste	1	4	−1

Note: For each statement, a difference of 3 points between factors is statistically significant at $p \leq .05$.

CHAPTER

21

CONCEPT AND
BENEFIT TESTING

Advertising is most effective when it is benefit oriented, that is, when it communicates a benefit that the target audience views as unique, relevant, and important. Thus, it is critically important that an advertiser select the right benefits for the advertising's focus. Concept tests help an advertiser identify the single benefit, from among the array of product benefits, that should serve as the focus of the product's advertising.

Advertisers and marketers are also faced with the task of introducing new products and repositioning existing products. Concept tests help determine the appeal of new product ideas and product positionings in the early stages of product planning and development. This chapter introduces you to concept tests.

After reading this chapter, you will be able to

■ Define the term "concept" and explain how it differs from an advertisement.

■ Explain two types of concept tests and the role of each in advertising and marketing decision making.

■ Prepare written concepts for use in concept tests.

■ Identify the areas addressed in a concept test questionnaire and the options for writing questions to assess consumers' reactions in each area.

■ Plan, administer, and analyze a concept test.

WHAT IS A CONCEPT?

A *concept* is a simple, written expression of a product's positioning, benefit, reason for being, or unique selling proposition. A concept clearly and realistically communicates one or more of these core product characteristics without exaggeration, salesmanship, or advertising puffery.

A concept is therefore distinct from an advertisement. An advertisement is designed to sell and, consequently, must accomplish multiple goals. An ad must: break

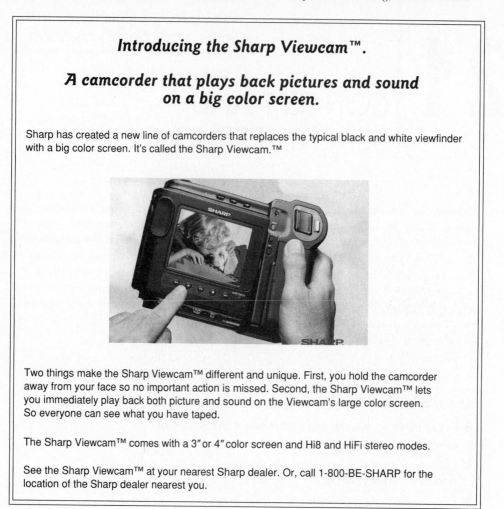

FIGURE 21.1
Concept for the Sharp Viewcam™.

through clutter and attract attention, be memorable and remembered by the target audience, and persuasively communicate the selling proposition. A concept, on the other hand, is designed to communicate. The most important task of a concept is to present the core idea simply and realistically so that consumers' comprehension is maximized and response to the core idea can be confidently assessed.

The differences between a concept and a product advertisement are illustrated in Figures 21.1 and 21.2. Figure 21.1 presents a concept for the Sharp Viewcam™ while Figure 21.2 presents the concept's core idea translated into an advertisement. Note how the concept is constructed and written. It is designed to directly and without embellishment inform the reader of the product's characteristics and principal benefits. The product advertisement, on the other hand, contains visual elements to help it break through the competitive clutter, headlines to draw the reader into the ad, and copy written to appeal to the emotions of the target (i.e., "imagine," "relive the

FIGURE 21.2
Advertisement for the Sharp Viewcam™.
Source: Sharp Electronic Corp./Griffin Bacal, Ive., with permission.

excitement," "magic of those moments"). The ad is designed to attract attention and sell the product.

TYPES OF CONCEPT TESTS

There are two different types of concept tests. *New product concept tests* determine the appeal of a potential new product. *Benefit positioning concept tests* identify the one product benefit that leads to the most advantageous product positioning and, consequently, the benefit that should be emphasized in product advertising.

New Product Concept Tests

Marketers may have a number of ideas for new products. These ideas may come from their own internal brand and research/development staff or from consumer research. A new product idea may develop a completely new product category (such as PERT, the first shampoo with conditioner), reflect a line extension (such as Diet Coke extended to Caffeine-free Diet Coke), or describe an entry into an existing product category (such as PERT for permed or colored hair, PERT with dandruff control).

All new product ideas are not equally appealing to the target consumer. Simply because a marketer can make a product or consumers indicate in prior research that they *might* have a need or desire for the product does not necessarily mean that consumers will want to buy the product should it become available and/or once they fully understand the product's characteristics. Marketers and advertisers need to systematically screen new product ideas to identify those that have the greatest potential for marketplace success. It is much more cost-efficient to find out that consumers reject the *idea* of a new product rather than the manufactured product itself. A marketer administers a concept test to identify, from the consumer's perspective, the new product ideas that have merit and therefore should be produced and supported with development, marketing, and advertising dollars. Thus, a new product concept test is conducted early in the product development cycle.

The goal of a new product concept test is to assess consumer response to an individual new product idea. As a result, one or more new product ideas may be tested at the same time and, based on consumer response, one or more may be selected for further development and market introduction.

Benefit Positioning Concept Tests

A product's positioning represents its "niche" in the consumer's mind. This niche, in turn, reflects the product's emphasized benefits. Alternative benefit positionings can be identified through judgment, analysis of secondary research, and/or primary consumer research such as paired comparison scaling, conjoint analysis, cognitive mapping, and focus groups. At this stage of the advertising development process, advertisers use benefit positioning concept tests to identify the strongest product benefit and subsequent product positioning. Thus, this type of concept test is conducted early in advertising strategic planning process.

Given that the goal of a benefit positioning concept test is the identification of the strongest product benefit positioning, advertisers typically test multiple positioning

---

Version A: "Lasts longer, saves you money"

Dansk Hair Treatments presents PermaPerm. A shampoo that helps your perm last longer, saving you money.

PermaPerm is specially formulated for permed hair. Its formula is so unique that it is patented. PermaPerm's enhancing shampoo for permed hair is formulated with coconut oil, nettle extract, panthenol, and other natural and organic ingredients for mild, gentle cleaning.

PermaPerm washes out dirt but leaves your perm intact. Independent, clinical tests have shown that, on average, perms shampooed with PermaPerm last three weeks longer than perms shampooed with other leading shampoo brands.

When your perm lasts longer you need to visit your stylist less often. So PermaPerm actually saves you time and money.

A 16-ounce bottle of PermaPerm retails for $3.99 and is available at leading grocery and drug stores.

Version B: "Healthy perm"

Dansk Hair Treatments presents PermaPerm. A shampoo that helps keep your perm healthy.

PermaPerm is specially formulated for permed hair. Its formula is so unique that it is patented. PermaPerm's enhancing shampoo for permed hair is formulated with coconut oil, nettle extract, panthenol, and other natural and organic ingredients for mild, gentle cleaning.

PermaPerm washes out dirt but leaves your perm healthy and manageable. PermaPerm makes permed hair look and feel healthy. Its unique formula fights frizz and dryness. It helps curls stay curly and bouncy. It makes permed hair feel silky and soft. Independent clinical tests show that women prefer the feel and look of their hair after a PermaPerm shampoo, versus the leading brands, by a margin of nearly 2 to 1.

A 16-ounce bottle of PermaPerm retails for $3.99 and is available at leading grocery and drug stores.

FIGURE 21.3
Two versions of benefit positioning concepts.

concepts at the same time and, based on consumer response, select the strongest benefit from among those tested for the product's positioning and advertising emphasis. Examples of alternative benefit positionings for a woman's perm-sensitive shampoo are shown in Figure 21.3. The body copy in both benefit positionings contains identical introductions and descriptions of product formulation. Beyond these shared elements the headline and benefit-specific body copy shown in Version A presents the shampoo's benefit as "makes your perm last longer, saving you time and money," while the copy in Version B presents the shampoo's benefit as "keeps your perm healthy."

PREPARING FOR A CONCEPT TEST

Preparation for a concept test entails the generation of concepts and the construction of a concept test questionnaire.

Generate Concepts

Concept tests are also known as "white card" tests because concepts are typically presented on sheets of 8 ½" × 11" white cardboard. Most concepts contain three elements: a headline, body copy, and an illustration.

Headlines   A concept headline succinctly summarizes the main selling proposition or product benefit and provides an explicit lead-in to body copy. Well-written headlines provide a clear understanding of the ideas that will be discussed later in the concept.

Concept headlines are not advertising headlines. As opposed to advertising headlines that may use sentence fragments, questions, or catchy phrases, concept headlines are best presented as simple declarative statements. This is because simple, straightforward declarative statements generally best communicate (a concept's goal) by being very easy to understand. The headline for the camcorder concept shown in Figure 21.1, for example, reads "Instant playback with sound on a big color screen" as opposed to the advertising headline shown in Figure 21.2 that reads "Imagine a camcorder that instantly plays back sounds on a big color screen."

Body Copy—General Considerations   Concept body copy should be direct and clear. Short paragraphs consisting of active, declarative statements communicate better than paragraphs composed of passive sentences or sentence fragments.

Concept body copy should avoid "advertisingese." It is important to communicate the product's unique benefits or features without embellishment or puffery. Thus, (assuming that they are true) words such as "first," "introducing," and "only" are acceptable. However, uninformative superlatives and advertising puffery often get in the way of communication and should be avoided. Additionally, body copy should avoid jargon or industry terminology that is unfamiliar and likely to confuse the reader.

Finally, the overall length of concept body copy should be short. Overwritten or overly long concepts have the potential to affect consumer response negatively by boring respondents or causing them to lose focus on the core idea. When this occurs responses to the core idea may be distorted. A negative response to the concept may reflect the influence of body copy characteristics as opposed to negative responses to the core idea or benefit itself.

Body Copy—Special Considerations for New Product Concepts   The body copy in a new product concept must clearly describe the product described in the concept by

- identifying the category the product or service is a member (i.e., an aspirin or laundry detergent) and communicating in straightforward language the characteristics of the product or service that make it a *new* product;
- listing the set of primary product benefits. The description and selection of these benefits must be realistic. The presentation of benefits should avoid overpromise and should not include any benefits that cannot be substantiated or are likely to be rejected by regulatory agencies;
- identifying the specific areas that distinguish the described product from others in the product category.

Body Copy—Special Considerations for Benefit Positioning Concepts   A new product concept test assesses overall reaction to the product idea and, consequently,

presents multiple product benefits. Benefit positioning concept tests, on the other hand, are designed to isolate the single most important product benefit. Thus, in a benefit positioning concept test one concept is written for each benefit. The body copy used among these individual concepts contains shared and unique elements. As illustrated in Figure 21.3, shared body copy generally provides product background, a general introduction, and a product description. Unique body copy in each concept single-mindedly focuses on one and only one product benefit.

The rule of "one benefit-one concept" is important because it reduces ambiguity in data interpretation. Successful concept test research allows one to determine clearly the relationship between the core idea expressed in the concept and consumer response. When the concept body copy single-mindedly focuses on one core idea, positive or negative consumer response can reasonably be attributed to the relative appeal of the concept's core idea and expressed product benefit. On the other hand, placing multiple ideas or benefits in body copy confuses the interpretation of the results. An overall neutral response to the concept might reflect an overall blasé consumer response or it might reflect the average of two extremes—a strong positive response to one core idea and a strong negative response to a second core idea in the same concept.

Body Copy—Branding and Price Information   There is some controversy regarding two aspects of the product description expressed in concept test body copy.

First, there is the issue of branding. Some recommend expressing the core idea without brand identification. This recommendation reflects the belief that it is the innate appeal of the product that must be evaluated and that branding biases this evaluation. Others argue that a product idea cannot be evaluated in the absence of brand and manufacturer identification. The latter group would argue, for example, that reactions to a concept for a new chocolate candy would be very different when it is presented as a nonbranded concept than when it is presented with the Hershey's brand-name. Recent research tends to support this latter perspective. Brand perceptions do appear to play an important role in product evaluation and preference. As a result, we recommend that product descriptions include brand-name identification.

Second, there is the issue of price. In some instances price may be irrelevant; for example, in a concept test that investigates various ways to position a retail store. Price however, is a consideration in most all concept tests for goods and services. An important part of most product decisions is the evaluation of the product's price-value relationship. A concept test can address pricing in one of three ways:

1. The concept can be presented without any indication of the product's price. When this occurs pricing information must be integrated into the research questionnaire.

2. The concept can mention price comparability without explicitly mentioning a specific price. In this instance, while no specific price is communicated, the body copy notes that the product described in the concept is priced comparably (or similarly) to other leading brands.

3. The concept can mention a specific price. This should only be done, however, if the marketer is certain of the product's eventual retail price.

Illustrations and Format Among Concepts   Advertisers may test multiple concepts at the same time (as in the case of benefit positioning concept tests and some new prod-

uct concept tests) seeking to determine which concept is the best from among those tested. Or, they may wish to compare reactions to concepts tested at different points in time. A fair and unbiased comparison of multiple concepts requires that the research avoid any extraneous factors that can differentially influence consumers' reactions to the concepts and, as a result, the outcome of the concept test. When multiple concepts are tested and comparisons among concepts are required then all concepts should be the same format and visual style. Layout of the copy, placement of the copy, headline, and type style should all be identical for all concepts. Beyond layout and visual appearance, visual elements and illustrations (if they are used) should also be identical for all concepts.

Finally, care should be taken in the selection of visuals regardless of whether multiple or single concepts are tested. Visuals and other illustrations play an important role in influencing response to both concepts and advertising. Consequently the researcher must not allow the visual to overwhelm the copy. Simple illustrations reinforcing brand name or package identification should be used.

Generate Questionnaire

Questions asked on concept tests fall into one of three sets. First, there is a set of questions that contains information on brand usage, respondent demographics, etc. These questions may be asked as part of the screener or at the very end of the concept test questionnaire. Second, there is a core set of questions that are asked on almost all concept tests. These questions pertain to

- communication of the main idea
- believability of the main idea
- uniqueness of the main idea
- personal relevance of the main idea
- purchase intent
- purchase frequency
- reasons for purchase intent and frequency of purchase

The third set of questions, diagnostic in nature, pertain to the specific characteristics of the individual concept. The following sections describe the core and diagnostic sets of questions.

Core Questions—Communication of the Main Idea   The concept must clearly communicate its core idea in order for the true value of a concept to be assessed. Consumers cannot fairly assess and respond to a concept that is confusing or that they do not fully understand.

Communication questions provide a basis for interpreting other measures on the concept test. When levels of communication are high, that is, when consumers understand key communication elements, then positive and negative reactions on other measures can be interpreted as accurate reactions to the ideas expressed in the concept. When levels of communication are low, data interpretation becomes more ambiguous. Here, positive or negative responses to other measures may or may not reflect reactions to the actual information presented in the concept.

The need to assess communication requires that the concept test questionnaire provides each respondent with the opportunity to state his or her interpretation of the main idea(s) communicated by the concept. Main idea communication is typically assessed using one or two open-ended questions. This format lets each respondent, without bias or direction from the interviewer, state his or her interpretation of the concept's main points and ideas. Communication question(s), typically asked first in the questionnaire, may use any of the following or similar forms:

> What was the one main idea in the description that you just read? That is, what was the one main thing they were trying to tell you about the product? PROBE: Were there any other ideas?

> What information was presented in the description that you just read? PROBE: Was there any other information?

> Suppose you needed to tell a friend what this description just told you about the product. What would you tell this friend? PROBE: Was there any other information you would tell your friend?

Core Questions—Believability of the Main Idea The clear communication of a concept's main idea is a necessary but not sufficient condition for concept success. Consumers must understand the main idea expressed in the concept and also find the communicated idea believable before the marketer or advertiser can have confidence in the product or benefit described in the concept.

A measure of believability assesses the extent to which consumers believe that the product or benefit described in the concept will appear or perform as described. One way that this can be accomplished is by measuring consumers' global feelings of the concept's believability. When this approach is selected the believability question refers to the concept itself and scale options reflect the believable/unbelievable continuum, for example:

> Think about the description you just read. Which option best describes how believable or unbelievable you feel the description is? Would you say that it is . . .

Very believable	_____ (1)
Slightly believable	_____ (2)
Neither believable nor unbelievable	_____ (3)
Slightly unbelievable	_____ (4)
Very unbelievable	_____ (5)

A second approach to measuring consumers' perceptions of believability assesses the probability of the product performing as described in the concept. Here, the question refers to product performance and the scale options reflect a likely/unlikely continuum, as follows:

> Think about the product description you just read. In your opinion, which option best describes how likely or unlikely it is that the product will act or perform as described?

Very likely	_____ (1)
Somewhat likely	_____ (2)
Neither likely nor unlikely	_____ (3)
Somewhat unlikely	_____ (4)
Very unlikely	_____ (5)

Core Questions—Uniqueness of the Main Idea A concept may clearly and believably present its core idea and yet still describe a product that has little chance of success. The potential for a product's marketplace success depends on the extent to which it is viewed as unique or as an improvement over existing products. A product seen as a "me-too" product is unlikely to succeed. Consumers are unlikely to try a new product when their needs are already met by a set of existing products.

Assessment of perceived uniqueness is similar to the second approach to the assessment of believability. The uniqueness question focuses on the product description while the scale reflects the unique/not unique continuum. However, because uniqueness is a relative measure (that is, uniqueness cannot be assessed without a frame of reference) this question must provide an explicit frame of reference to the appropriate product class or category. Considering this requirement, the uniqueness question can take the following form:

Think about the product description you just read. Which option best describes how unique or not unique you feel this product is when compared to other (INSERT CATEGORY OF PRODUCT)?

Very unique	_____ (1)
Somewhat unique	_____ (2)
Slightly unique	_____ (3)
Not at all unique	_____ (4)

In addition to explicitly evaluating consumers' perceptions of uniqueness, a product's uniqueness can also be assessed by asking consumers to state their perceptions of the *difference* between the product described in the concept and other products in the category. Here, the question itself parallels the prior approach but scale options provide the opportunity to rate the described product's similarity to other category products, as follows:

Think about the product description you just read. Which option best describes how similar or different you feel this product is when compared to other (INSERT CATEGORY OF PRODUCT)?

Very similar	_____ (1)
Somewhat similar	_____ (2)
Somewhat different	_____ (3)
Very different	_____ (4)

Think about the product description you just read. Which option best describes how new and different you feel this product is when compared to other (INSERT CATEGORY OF PRODUCT)?

Very new and different	_____ (1)
Somewhat new and different	_____ (2)
Slightly new and different	_____ (3)
Not at all new and different	_____ (4)

Think about the product description you just read. Place a check in the scale shown to indicate how you feel this product compares to other (INSERT CATEGORY OF PRODUCT).

This is a product
with a point
of difference   ___   ___   ___   ___   ___   ___   ___
                      (1)   (2)   (3)   (4)   (5)   (6)   (7)

This product
is the same as
other products

Core Questions—Personal Relevance   Concept tests are conducted among consumers who are in the product's current or potential target audience. If these consumers do not feel that the product is relevant and appropriate to them personally then, given the role of selective perception, they are unlikely to notice and pay attention to the product's advertising. Further, it is unlikely they will seek out and purchase the product should it become available in the marketplace. Thus, assessment of personal relevance is important. It provides an opportunity to determine consumers' perceived personal value of the product's positioning or benefit.

Personal relevance can be measured several ways. The specific manner selected will reflect the operational definition selected by the researcher. The question can directly assess perceptions of personal relevance (Questions A and B next) or assess how well the product fulfills a perceived need (Questions C and D next).

A. Think about the product description you just read. Which option best describes how relevant this product is to your particular needs? Use a scale of one to ten, where '1' represents 'extremely relevant' and '10' represents 'not at all relevant' to indicate how relevant or not relevant you feel this product is. Select any number between 1 and 10.

      NUMBER SELECTED   _____

B. Think about the product description you just read. Place a check in the scale shown to indicate how you feel about this product.

This is a product
for people
like me   ___   ___   ___   ___   ___   ___   ___
                (1)   (2)   (3)   (4)   (5)   (6)   (7)

This is not a
product for
people like me

C. Think about the product description you just read. How well do you think the product will or will not fulfill a personal need of yours?

Would definitely fulfill a need   _____ (1)

Would probably fulfill a need   _____ (2)

Would probably not fulfill a need   _____ (3)

Would definitely not fulfill a need   _____ (4)

D. Think about the product description you just read. Which of the statements would you say best describes how well the described product would meet your needs in comparison to other. . . (INSERT CATEGORY OF PRODUCT)?

Better than other (INSERT CATEGORY OF PRODUCT)   _____ (1)

About the same as other (INSERT CATEGORY OF PRODUCT)   _____ (2)

Not as well as other (INSERT CATEGORY OF PRODUCT)   _____ (3)

Core Questions—Purchase Intent A consumer's intent to purchase a product after reading a concept represents a "bottom-line" assessment of a product's likelihood (as described in the concept) of marketplace success. Consequently, a purchase intent question almost always appears on a concept test and is considered a key measure for evaluating the consumer's response. The wording of a purchase intent question uses the following general form:

> Think about the product description you just read. What is the likelihood that you would purchase this product if it were available at your local store?

> I would definitely buy it   _____ (1)
>
> I would probably buy it   _____ (2)
>
> I might or might not buy it   _____ (3)
>
> I would probably not buy it   _____ (4)
>
> I would definitely not buy it   _____ (5)

When the price of the product or service is not relevant to the consumer's evaluation or when the price is explicitly stated in the concept than the prior purchase intent question can be used without modification. However, if price is relevant and is not explicitly stated in the concept, then the purchase intent question must be modified.

The simplest modification occurs when the concept itself provides a frame of comparison, for example, stating that the product or service will be priced "comparable to the leading brands." In these situations the purchase intent question incorporates the wording used in the concept, as follows:

> Think about the product description you just read. What is the likelihood that you would purchase this product if it were available at your local store and were priced comparably to the leading brands?

> I would definitely buy it   _____ (1)
>
> I would probably buy it   _____ (2)
>
> I might or might not buy it   _____ (3)
>
> I would probably not buy it   _____ (4)
>
> I would definitely not buy it   _____ (5)

More extensive modification to the purchase intent question is required when price is an important component of the purchase decision but no explicit or implicit pricing information is provided in the concept. In these cases the purchase intent question must assess consumers' likelihood to purchase the product at various pricing levels. This may be done by providing a frame of reference in the question and then assessing purchase interest as the relationship between the product price and frame of reference varies, as follows:

Think about the product description you just read. Please indicate how likely or unlikely you would be to purchase the product in each of the following situations. Indicate your likelihood to purchase the product described on the card by placing a check mark at the point on each line that best reflects your opinion.

If the product were priced $.25 below the average leading brand, I would . . .

Definitely   Definitely
buy   ___   ___   ___   ___   ___   ___   ___   not buy
          (1)   (2)   (3)   (4)   (5)   (6)   (7)

If the product were priced the same as the average leading brand, I would . . .

Definitely   Definitely
buy   ___   ___   ___   ___   ___   ___   ___   not buy
          (1)   (2)   (3)   (4)   (5)   (6)   (7)

If the product were priced $.25 above the average leading brand, I would . . .

Definitely   Definitely
buy   ___   ___   ___   ___   ___   ___   ___   not buy
          (1)   (2)   (3)   (4)   (5)   (6)   (7)

Core Questions—Purchase Frequency A consumer's positive desire to purchase a product described in a concept indicates that the product has cleared one hurdle. It has sparked consumer interest. However, intent to purchase is not all that is required for marketplace success. Successful products are those which consumers integrate into their set of preferred products. For many packaged food products, product success requires that the consumer integrate the product into their daily routine and regularly purchase the product. Thus, to understand clearly the potential for the product described in the concept, measures of purchase frequency and estimates of product usage are typically incorporated into the concept test questionnaire. These questions are reached using a skip pattern and are only asked if the consumer indicates at least modest intent on the purchase intent measure.

Purchase frequency may be assessed in one of two ways. Each approach provides different insights into purchase frequency. As with the purchase intent questions, these questions would be modified to reflect the need for pricing information. Consumers cannot estimate purchase frequency if they do not understand how much the product will cost. One approach assesses anticipated purchase frequency in absolute terms. When this approach is selected the range shown on the scale reflects the range and frequency appropriate to the specific product, as follows:

Think about the product description you just read. Using the following scale, please indicate how frequently or infrequently you think you would purchase this product.

Less than once a week   _____ (1)

Once a week   _____ (2)

Two to three times a week   _____ (3)

Four to six times a week   _____ (4)

Seven to nine times a week   _____ (5)

Ten or more times a week   _____ (6)

Second, purchase frequency can be assessed relative to the consumer's currently preferred brand within the product category. This approach may take the following form:

Think about the product description you just read. Also, think about the brand of (INSERT NAME OF PRODUCT CATEGORY) that you use most frequently. Select the one choice that indicates how frequently or infrequently you think you would purchase the described product versus your most frequently used brand.

I would purchase the described product . . .

More frequently then my current brand	_____	(1)
About the same as my current brand	_____	(2)
Less than my current brand	_____	(3)

Reasons for Purchase Intent   Marketers and advertisers are pleased and encouraged when consumers express high levels of purchase intent. Such responses show that the product or service has real potential in the marketplace. However, if this potential is to be realized the marketer must fully understand the specific reasons underlying high intent. Similarly, while low purchase intent may be discouraging, a low purchase intent score does not necessarily imply low product potential. If low purchase intent reflects a small, correctable flaw in the product or its description then the product or its positioning might be modified and then successfully introduced into the marketplace. Open-ended questions that probe reasons underlying level of purchase intent provide insights as to why a consumer might or might not be interested in purchasing the product described in the concept.

One or two questions may be used to probe reasons for level of purchase intent. These questions are asked immediately following the purchase intent question. The questions are cued to the level of purchase intent expressed and skip patterns are used to make certain that the proper open-ended questions are asked. The question sequence would take the following form:

13. Think about the product description you just read. How likely or unlikely would you be to buy this product if it were available at your local store?

Very likely to purchase	_____	(1) CONTINUE WITH Q14
Somewhat likely to purchase	_____	(2) SKIP TO Q15a
Slightly likely to purchase	_____	(3) SKIP TO Q15a
Not at all likely to purchase	_____	(4) SKIP TO Q16

14. You indicated that you would be very likely to purchase the product. Why did you say that? PROBE: What other reasons, if any, do you have for feeling this way? AFTER RESPONSE SKIP TO Q17.

15a. You indicated that you would be (INSERT RESPONSE FROM Q13) the product. What specific aspects of the product made you (somewhat/slightly) likely to purchase the product? PROBE: What other reasons, if any, do you have for feeling this way?

15b. What specific aspects of the product prevented you from being more likely to purchase the described product? PROBE: What other reasons, if any, do you have for feeling this way? AFTER RESPONSE SKIP TO Q17.

16. You indicated that you would not be at all likely to purchase the product. Why did you say that? PROBE: What other reasons, if any, do you have for feeling this way?

17. (Questionnaire continues)

Concept-Specific Diagnostic Questions   Questions that probe main idea communication, believability, perceptions of the product's uniqueness, personal relevance, and reasons for purchase intent comprise the core set of concept test questions. These questions should be asked on all concept tests. Because these questions may not cover the full range of potential issues or questions associated with a specific concept, the core set of questions should be followed by customized, specific diagnostic questions that probe consumers' responses to important, specific aspects of the individual concept. A diagnostic question for the concept shown in Figure 21.1 might be

What would you anticipate the sound quality to be on the Sharp Camcorder?

Excellent	_____ (1)
Good	_____ (2)
Fair	_____ (3)
Poor	_____ (4)

ADMINISTERING A CONCEPT TEST

The administration of a concept test entails four steps. First, a target definition is constructed and, if appropriate, target subgroups are identified and quota requirements are established. As with other advertising research, members of each quota subgroup represent an important yet distinct target for the product or service described in the concept. Subgroups may include current brand users, current category users, users of competitive brands/products, or potential category users. While total sample and subgroup sample sizes may be set to reflect required levels of statistical confidence, industry rules-of-thumb generally require the selection of between 150 and 200 respondents per concept (when there are no quota subgroups) or minimum of about seventy-five people per analytical subgroup when two or more subgroups are identified.

Second, a research methodology is selected. Concept tests can be administered either by mail or by individual personal interviews. (Refer to Chapter 6 for a discussion of the relative advantages and disadvantages of these two approaches.)

Third, the questionnaire is constructed. The questionnaire addresses the areas discussed earlier in this chapter. The content of the questionnaire will be identical for mail and mall-intercept methodologies. However, the format of the questionnaire will vary to reflect the specific methodology selected. Mail panel questionnaires are self-administered while mall-intercept questionnaires are typically administered by an interviewer.

Fourth, a procedure for exposing the concept is determined. Almost all concept tests are monadic, that is, each individual respondent views only one concept. When the concept test is administered by mail the concept is enclosed with the questionnaire. When mall-intercept interviews are used the concept is typically given to the respondent at the start of the interview and then removed before questioning. The removal of the concept prevents a respondent from reading and repeating the concept verbatim when responding to communication questions.

DATA ORGANIZATION, ANALYSIS, AND INTERPRETATION

The examination of concept test data consists of two types of data organization procedures:

1. Presentation and analysis of total sample responses, noting (where applicable) similarities and differences in responses among quota groups.
2. Presentation and analysis of total sample responses, noting similarities and differences in response among distinct attitudinal, brand usage, or demographic groups.

Differences Among Quota Groups

Quota groups are not specified in every concept test. However, when quota groups are specified, data analysis must always acknowledge the existence of those groups. It is very important to determine whether levels of response to the concept were consistent among quota groups or whether levels of response varied as a function of the defining characteristics of individual quota groups. To determine consistency of response, descriptive statistics such as means and/or frequency distributions, depending on scale level of measurement, are reported for each measure for each quota group as well as for the sample as a whole.

Table organization and data analysis are straightforward when a single concept is tested or when one concept is examined independently of other concepts. The following table, for example, provides detailed information on response to a single measure, in this case consumers' ratings of the concept's believability.

		Women With:	
	Total Sample *(n = 200)*	*Children Aged 3–7* *(n = 100)*	*Children Aged 8–12* *(n = 100)*
Very believable (1)	50%	75%	25%
Slightly believable (2)	20	20	20
Slightly unbelievable (3)	10	5	15
Very unbelievable (4)	20	0	40
Mean	**2.0**	**1.3***	**2.7***

* *t* test is significant at $p < .01$.

Note how the measure's frequency distribution and overall mean as well as quota group distributions, means, and tests of significance have been integrated into a single table.

When several concepts are tested at the same time or when an advertiser wishes to compare concepts tested at different points in time, analyses require that multiple comparisons be conducted. Multiple comparisons require two approaches to data organization and analysis. First, the data must be organized and presented so that responses to each individual concept can be clearly seen and understood. *Here, data presentation and analysis hold the concept constant and determine if individuals in different quota groups reacted similarly or differently to that specific concept.* De-

pending on the number of concepts tested, tables can present each concept independently or a single table can simultaneously present data relevant to two or more concepts, as shown in the following table.

	Concept A			Concept B		
		Women With:			*Women With:*	
	Total Sample (n = 200)	*Children Aged 3–7 (n = 100)*	*Children Aged 8–12 (n = 100)*	*Total Sample (n = 200)*	*Children Aged 3–7 (n = 100)*	*Children Aged 8–12 (n = 100)*
Very believable (1)	50%	25%	75%	50%	70%	30%
Slightly believable (2)	20	40	0	20	30	10
Slightly unbelievable (3)	20	30	10	20	0	40
Very unbelievable (4)	10	5	15	10	0	20
Mean	**1.9**	**2.2***	**1.6***	**1.9**	**1.8†**	**2.8†**

* t test is significant at $p < .05$; † t test is significant at $p < .01$.

Second, the data must be organized so that any differences in response within a quota group among the concepts can be explored. *Here, data presentation and analysis hold the quota group constant and determine the extent to which a specific quota group's reactions were similar or different among concepts.* The organization of data for this type of analysis is shown in the following table.

	Women With Children Aged 3–7		Women With Children Aged 8–12	
	Concept A (n = 100)	*Concept B (n = 100)*	*Concept A (n = 100)*	*Concept B (n = 100)*
Very believable (1)	25%	70%	75%	30%
Slightly believable (2)	40	30	0	10
Slightly unbelievable (3)	30	0	10	40
Very unbelievable (4)	5	0	15	20
Mean	**2.2***	**1.0***	**1.6†**	**2.8†**

* t test significantly different at $p < .001$; † t test significantly different at $p < .001$.

Differences Among Attitudinal, Brand Usage, and Demographic Groups

Data analyses among quota groups provide insights into a concept's appeal and potential for success among preidentified target audiences. To obtain additional insights into consumer response to a concept, quota group analyses are often supplemented by analyses that probe differences in response among attitudinal, brand usage, or demographic groups. These latter analyses provide the diagnostic information required to more completely understand concept strengths and weaknesses. There are two different types of these latter analyses: standard and concept-specific.

Standard Analyses There is a core set of analyses appropriate to all concept tests. Analyses in this set entail (1) cross-tabulation of response to primary study measures by purchase intent, brand usage, and communication; and (2) determination of the relationship between believability, uniqueness, and relevance.

Analysis of primary study measures by level of purchase intent provides important insights into why consumers reacted to the concept as they did. This analysis permits one to determine if high or low purchase intent is related, for example, to concept believability, uniqueness, or the presence/absence of elements communicated to the consumer. To perform this type of analysis respondents are divided into two or three "Level of Purchase Intent" groups based on their response to the purchase intent question. The number of groups formed reflects the purchase intent scale used in the research. Group 1 typically consists of those with high or positive purchase intent, Group 2 typically consists of those with neutral purchase intent (assuming that a neutral response was a scale option) and Group 3 typically consists of those respondents with low or negative purchase intent.

Table 21.1 illustrates this type of analysis and displays the results of the open-ended reason for purchase intent question cross-tabulated by level of purchase intent. This table indicates that the belief that the product was "better for their child's health" was the primary reason for high purchase intent. The claim of "no alcohol" was the most frequently mentioned reason for this belief and high purchase intent. Consumers who were not interested in purchasing the product felt this way because they saw the product as "too expensive" and/or "just another gimmick." The cross-tabulation of other study variables, such as believability and uniqueness, by purchase intent is accomplished in a similar manner and provides additional insights into why respondents were or were not interested in purchasing the product described in the concept.

Analysis of key measures by brand usage (taken from the demographics section of the questionnaire) indicates the level of product acceptance among brand-specific target audiences and indicates the source of the product's likely user base. This analysis is especially important when testing alternative benefit positionings of an existing product as it allows one to determine the extent to which each benefit positioning is likely to "hold on to" current brand users while simultaneously appealing to users of competitive brands. Tables presenting this type of analysis are developed identically to

Table 21.1 Reasons for Purchase Intent Cross-Tabulated By Level of Purchase Intent

	Level of Purchase Intent		
Reason for Purchase Intent	*High (n = 40)*	*Neutral (n = 10)*	*Low (n = 100)*
Better for children's health (net)	75%	30%	10%
No alcohol	75	20	5
No aspirin	25	10	0
Better for health (unspecified)	20	10	10
Just another gimmick	5	40	75
Kids won't like it	5	10	20
Probably too expensive	0	10	65

TABLE 21.2 Ratings of Purchase Intent (Response to Concepts A and B By Brand Usage Group)

	Concept A			Concept B		
	Brand Usage			Brand Usage		
	Total Sample (n = 200)	Current (n = 100)	Competitive (n = 100)	Total Sample (n = 200)	Current (n = 100)	Competitive (n = 100)
Highly likely (1)	25%	27%	23%	25%	10%	40%
Somewhat likely (2)	35	33	37	35	20	50
Slightly likely (3)	20	20	20	20	30	10
Not at all likely (4)	20	20	20	20	40	0
Mean	**2.4**	**2.4**	**2.4**	**2.4**	**3.0***	**1.8***

* t test is significantly different at $p < .01$.

those for purchase intent. An example is shown in Table 21.2. Here, two benefit positionings (labeled A and B) were tested. Assume that each benefit positioning was designed to (1) primarily reinforce loyalty among current brand users while (2) secondarily stimulating purchase intent among users of competitive brands. Note that the overall means for purchase intent for both concepts are identical. However, the cross-tabulation shows that the underlying pattern of response is very different among concepts. Concept A shows modest appeal to current brand users as well as users of competitive brands. Concept B, on the other hand, strongly appeals only to users of competitive brands; current brand users react negatively. The cross-tabulation shows the failure of Concept B to achieve its primary objective of reinforcing loyalty among current brand users.

Finally, insights are obtained when the relationships between believability, uniqueness, and relevance are made explicit. A presentation of the individual frequency distribution of each of these measures indicates the range and frequency of that measure's scale ratings. However, an examination of the individual frequency distributions does not indicate how each individual respondent simultaneously perceived the product along these three dimensions. A correlation matrix is constructed to determine the relationship among these three measures (see Chapter 16). Concepts with the greatest probability of success are those that generate feelings that the product is both unique and will deliver its promise (that is, is believable) and is relevant to consumers' specific needs (relevance). A product seen as unique but not relevant, for example, has little hope of acceptance among the target holding these perceptions. Thus, the most successful concepts are those that show strong, positive intercorrelations among these three measures.

Concept-Specific Analyses Beyond the prior core set of data analysis tables, additional tables generated after a concept test reflect concept-specific measures, concerns,

and hypotheses. Any measure in the research can be utilized in a cross-tabulation. However, one should not mindlessly attempt to examine the relationships among all possible sets of measures. Rather, one should formulate specific questions and then prepare a table that specifically addresses these questions.

Data Interpretation and Recommendations

The final step in concept test research, similar to other research, is data interpretation and the formulation of recommendations. Interpretation requires the researcher to not simply report what trends and differences are, but additionally to determine and report the underlying reasons for observed trends and differences. This latter task typically requires the synthesis of information from multiple cross-tabulations of the data.

Summary

A *concept* is a simple, written expression of a product's positioning, benefit, reason for being, or unique selling proposition. A concept clearly and realistically communicates one or more of these core product characteristics without exaggeration, salesmanship, or advertising puffery. Advertisers use concept and benefit tests to assess consumers' reactions to new product ideas and to identify the product benefits that should be the focus of the advertising campaign.

Questions asked on concept tests fall into one of three sets. First, there is a set of questions that contains information on brand usage, respondent demographics, etc. These questions may be asked as part of the screener or at the very end of the concept test questionnaire. Second, there is a core set of questions asked on almost all concept tests. These questions pertain to

- communication of the main idea
- believability of the main idea
- uniqueness of the main idea
- personal relevance of the main idea
- purchase intent
- purchase frequency
- reasons for purchase intent and frequency of purchase

The third set of questions, diagnostic in nature, pertain to the specific characteristics of the individual concept.

The administration of a concept test entails four steps. First, a target definition is constructed and, if appropriate, target subgroups are identified and quota requirements are established. Second, a research methodology is selected. Concept tests can be administered either by mail or by individual personal interviews. Third, the questionnaire is constructed. Fourth, a procedure for exposing the concept is determined. Almost all concept tests are monadic, that is, each individual respondent views only one concept. When the concept test is administered by mail the concept is enclosed with the questionnaire. When mall-intercept interviews are used the concept is typically given to the respondent at the start of the interview and then removed before questioning.

The examination of concept test data consists of two types of data organization procedures:

1. Presentation and analysis of total sample responses, noting (where applicable) similarities and differences in responses among quota groups.
2. Presentation and analysis of total sample responses, noting similarities and differences in response across distinct attitudinal, brand usage, or demographic groups.

Review Questions

1. What is a *"concept?"*
2. In what ways does a concept differ from an advertisement?
3. What are the two different types of concept tests? What is the goal of each?
4. What are the two steps researchers take in preparing for a concept test?
5. Most concepts contain three elements. What are these elements?
6. What is the role of a headline in a concept?
7. What advice would you give to creatives for the writing of concept headlines and body copy?
8. What are three specific areas that must be addressed in the body copy of new product concepts?
9. What are the options for presenting pricing information within a concept?
10. What advice would you give to creatives for the selection of concept visuals?
11. What three broad types of questions are typically asked on a concept test?
12. What seven specific areas are addressed in the core set of concept test questions?
13. There are four considerations related to the administration of a concept test. What are these considerations?
14. What are the role and importance of *quota groups* in concept testing?
15. What are the differences in test administration and questionnaire design when mail panels versus mall-intercept interviews are selected as a means of collecting consumers' responses to a concept?
16. What are the two required approaches to concept test data organization and analysis?
17. What two types of core analyses are appropriate to all concept tests?
18. Describe two approaches to data analysis when two or more concepts, each with quota groups, are tested at the same time.

Application Exercises[1]

1. Your client, Reebok, has developed the technology for a new type of running shoe. The client and your agency both agree that a concept test be conducted to assess consumers' reactions to this new shoe before committing funds for manufacturing, distribution, and advertising. Reebok has provided the agency with following briefing on this shoe:

   • Combines technologies of GraphLite™, THE PUMP™, and HEXALITE™.
   • Shoe is named THE PUMP GraphLite™.

---

[1] All application exercises are hypothetical. Data are fictitious. The names of real products and data are used for illustrative purposes only.

- Graphite makes things light-weight while permanently retaining shape.
- THE PUMP GraphLite™ has a radically designed underfoot arch bridge that offers exceptional support to the serious runner.
- The bridge retains shape no matter how much one pronates or supinates and dramatically reduces weight of sole (by 20%) without sacrificing support.
- Incorporation of THE PUMP™ technology in the collar of the shoe provides each wearer with customized heel fit. Just four or five pumps completely cradles the heel in a cushion of air, allowing each individual runner to adapt their shoe to their own personal foot profile and thus, giving each foot a superior, unsurpassed fit.
- For years runners have looked for a way to overcome the contradiction of a well-cushioned, lightweight shoe. Now they can stop looking. HEXALITE™ is one of the first foot protection systems that successfully incorporates lightweight technology with superior cushioning. Located in the midsole, HEXALITE™ gives THE PUMP GraphLite™ all the critical cushioning and support necessary to protect runners' feet from the severe shocks their body endures while running.
- THE PUMP GraphLite™ carries a suggested retail price of $209 and is available wherever fine running shoes are sold.
- The target audience for this shoe consists of men and women who consider themselves a serious runner.

Take this information and prepare a concept that can be used to assess target audience consumers' reactions to this new shoe (do not worry about visual elements of the concept).

2. Agency creatives have been given the assignment to prepare two benefit positioning concepts for the Fuji THRILL all terrain bicycle (ATB). One concept should communicate the principal benefit of "durability without sacrificing responsiveness" while the second concept should communicate "best value for the money." The target audience consists of serious riders who are sophisticated, informed purchasers of mountain bikes. The creatives prepare the headline and body copy for the "durability without sacrificing responsiveness" concept. They show you the copy (shown next). Do you approve the copy as written? If not, what suggestions would you recommend for copy revision?

Headline: There is only one place you won't want to take Your Fuji THRILL: Back in the garage.

Copy: No matter how far off the road you go (or even if you never leave the street) the Fuji THRILL ATB not only endures punishment, but its superior performance and handling inspire you to bring it back for more.

From Chrome-moly tubing and Araya silver alloy rims to competition style thumbshifters and 21-speed Shimano Hyperglide components, the THRILL comes equipped with full-fledged mountain bike features at less than a mountainous price. In fact, you can comparison shop from now until the mountains freeze over and you won't find a better value. And like all Fuji ATBs, the THRILL is engineered for optimum durability on the trail—without sacrificing responsiveness and lightness of weight.

3. Select a product category. Think of a new product that might be introduced into that category. Identify the new product's specific characteristics and point(s) of difference from existing products in the category. Once you have identified these characteristics (a) develop a white card concept statement for the product, (b) construct a questionnaire to assess the target audience's reaction to the concept, (c) interview ten individuals in the target audience, and (d) prepare a memo that describes your findings. Be certain to address the marketability of your product concept.

4. Six focus groups were held to determine consumers' perceptions of and attitudes toward packaged spaghetti/pasta side-dishes and dinners. Leading brands in this category are Rice-A-Roni, Noodle Roni, and Lipton Golden Saute.

Three focus groups were held with current, regular users of these products (where regular was defined as usage of at least once a week). A principal goal of these groups was the identification of problems and dissatisfactions with currently available packaged spaghetti/pasta side-dishes and dinners. Consumers in these groups indicated a broad range of problems with packaged pasta side-dishes and dinners. Frequently mentioned problems included poor pasta quality, not enough pasta, and too expensive. One problem area, however, was consensually identified as the *most* significant: a lack of flexibility in preparing the pasta. Each packaged product provides only one sauce flavor. Moreover, directions need to be followed exactly and cannot be customized. As a result, variety in flavors can only be obtained if multiple boxes of different flavors were purchased.

Three focus groups were held with category nonusers, defined as individuals who have not used these products within the past twelve months. An important goal of these groups was the identification of barriers preventing these consumers from purchasing and using these products. While a wide range of barriers were mentioned (for example, too expensive, poor value, "boxy"/artificial taste), the most significant barrier related to preparation. Consumers did not buy these products because of a perceived lack of flexibility. They like to prepare their own recipes and, whenever possible, customize the preparation of prepared foods.

With the responses of category users and nonusers in mind, Katery Kitchens has developed the technology to produce a new line of packaged pasta side-dishes and dinners. These dinners, it is believed, respond to the concerns of these two consumer segments (both users and nonusers) by providing a great deal of flexibility and customization in sauce preparation.

The agency and client concurred that consumer response to this new product line should be quantitatively assessed before initiating production. As a result, a concept test was conducted to determine consumer response to Katery Kitchen's new product idea. This idea, as expressed in the concept used in the research, is shown in Figure 21.4 (page 528).

Following is a description of target definition and a description of sampling.

Target Definition

Versagetti was developed to appeal to two groups of consumers. Group membership reflected extent of category usage. One group consisted of consumers who currently purchase and use packaged pasta side-dishes and dinners at least once per week (labeled current, regular users). The second group consisted of those consumers who never use these products (labeled noncategory users). The following sample specifications and quota requirements were used to obtain an analytical sample of both groups:

- All study participants (200 in total), regardless of category usage, were the primary or shared decision maker within their household for main course and side-dish selection. Further, all participants had to eat pasta or spaghetti at home at least occasionally (defined as at least once per month). Since the study was interested in the reactions of the decision maker, no quotas were established for sex, age, income, or other demographics.

  - Of the total study sample, 100 individuals were current category users. These individuals, in addition to satisfying the prior requirements, purchased and used a packaged pasta side-dish or main course at least once per week (on average).

Introducing *Versagetti*.
A new line of versatile pasta side-dishes and dinners.

There is a problem with typical packaged pasta side-dishes and dinners like Noodle Roni and Golden Saute. You have no flexibility.

When you make these dishes you must exactly follow the manufacturer's recommendations.

Any attempt to customize the sauce may ruin the outcome. So, you can't make it exactly the way you like it.

This lack of flexibility also means a lack of variety. You can only get different sauces and flavors if you buy multiple boxes of several different flavors.

Versagetti ends these flexibility problems.

Versagetti is a dried pasta sauce and comes in a 22-ounce container. *Versagetti* contains only the freshest, most natural, ingredients.

Each canister of *Versagetti* makes ten servings. Each serving makes enough sauce to cover 16 ounces of pasta. But what makes *Versagetti* different is that you can customize the flavorings so that one package can produce ten of the same dish or ten different dishes. You can customize the flavoring using your own preferences or by following the manufacturer's recommendations. Different flavors. Different ways to customize. The choice is yours.

Versagetti comes in two basic flavors: **Versagetti Italian** and **Versagetti American**.

Versagetti is available at all leading grocery stores and is priced at $2.29 per container.

Versagetti
Maximum flexibility

FIGURE 21.4
Versagetti new product concept.

TABLE 21.3 Data Tables for Versagetti Concept Test

A. Main Idea Communication (Multiple Mentions)

	Total Sample (n = 200)	Category Users (n = 100)	Category Nonusers (n = 100)
Product flexibility (net)	<u>74%</u>	<u>76%</u>	<u>72%</u>
More flavors	50	49	51
Can customize taste	45	47	43
Can use own pasta	12	11	13
Improved better taste (net)	72	77	67
Fresher taste	45	42	48
Better taste because of fresh ingredients	40	43	37
More economical	20	20	20
Longer shelf-life	15	14	16

B. Believability

	Total Sample (n = 200)	Category User (n = 100)	Category Nonusers (n = 100)
Very believable (1)	65%	67%	63%
Slightly believable (2)	23	20	26
Slightly unbelievable (3)	12	13	11
Very unbelievable (4)	0	0	0
Mean	**1.5**	**1.5**	**1.5**

C. Uniqueness

	Total Sample (n = 200)	Category Users (n = 100)	Category Nonusers (n = 100)
Very unique (1)	36%	72%	0%
Somewhat unique (2)	13	22	4
Slightly unique (3)	18	6	30
Not at all unique (4)	33	0	66
Mean	**2.5**	**1.3***	**3.7***

D. Relevance

	Total Sample (n = 200)	Category Users (n = 100)	Category Nonusers (n = 100)
Would fulfill a need . . .			
Definitely (1)	39%	72%	6%
Probably (2)	13	16	10
Probably not (3)	10	10	10
Definitely not (4)	38	2	74
Mean	**2.4**	**1.4***	**3.5***

* t test is significant at $p < .001$.

(continued)

TABLE 21.3 *(continued)*

E. *Relationship of Believability, Uniqueness, and Personal Relevance: Correlation Matrix for Category Users*

	Believability	Uniqueness	Relevance
Believability	–	–	–
Uniqueness	.78*	–	–
Relevance	.67*	.81*	–

* Significant at $p < .01$.

F. *Relationship of Believability, Uniqueness, and Personal Relevance: Correlation Matrix for Noncategory Users*

	Believability	Uniqueness	Relevance
Believability	–	–	–
Uniqueness	− .65*	–	–
Relevance	− .72*	− .73*	–

* Significant at $p < .01$.

G. *Purchase Intent*

	Total Sample (n = 200)	Category Users (n = 100)	Category Nonusers (n = 100)
Very likely (1)	40%	76%	4%
Somewhat likely (2)	10	14	6
Slightly likely (3)	40	5	75
Not at all likely (4)	10	5	15
Mean	**2.2**	**1.4***	**3.0***

* *t* test is significant at $p < .01$.

H. *Purchase Intent Cross-tabulated by Brand Usage*

	Total Category Users (n = 100)	Noodle Roni Users (n = 25)	Golden Grain Users (n = 25)
Very likely (1)	76%	80%	72%
Somewhat likely (2)	14	10	18
Slightly likely (3)	5	5	5
Not at all likely (4)	5	5	5
Mean	**1.4**	**1.4**	**1.4**

I. *Purchase Intent Cross-tabulated by Category Usage*

	Heavy Users (n = 25)	Medium Users (n = 50)	Light Users (n = 25)
Very likely (1)	88%	80%	50%
Somewhat likely (2)	12	4	18
Slightly likely (3)	0	4	22
Not at all likely (4)	0	12	10
Mean	**1.1**	**1.4**	**1.6**

(continued)

TABLE 21.3 *(continued)*

J. Reasons for Purchase Intent Among Consumers With Positive Purchase Intent

	Consumer With Positive Purchase Intent (n = 100)
Flexibility/versatility (net)	<u>95%</u>
Can customize taste	76
Can customize	24
More flexible recipes	24
Makes for more meal variety	12
Improved/better taste	23
More convenient	15
Better value	12

K. Reasons for Purchase Intent Among Consumers With Negative Purchase Intent

	Consumers With Negative Purchase Intent (n = 100)
Poor taste (net)	<u>77%</u>
Taste bad	42
Taste artificial	24
Poor taste due to fake ingredients	24
Poor value for the money	57
Same as other boxed mixes	33
Too difficult to prepare	12

L. Ratings of Product Taste

	Total Sample (n = 200)	Category Users (n = 100)	Category Nonusers (n = 100)
One a scale of 1 (extremely good) to 10 (extremely poor) anticipated product taste was rated . . .			
1–3	35%	70%	0%
4–6	35	20	50
7–10	30	10	50
Mean	**5.0**	**2.1***	**7.9***

* *t* test is significantly different at $p < .001$.

M. Ratings of Product Value

	Total Sample (n = 200)	Category Users (n = 100)	Category Nonusers (n = 100)
On a scale of 1 (extremely good) to 10 (extremely poor) product value was rated . . .			
1–3	33%	60%	5%
4–6	30	40	20
7–10	37	0	75
Mean	**5.0**	**1.7***	**8.1***

* *t* test is significantly different at $p < .001$.

(continued)

TABLE 21.3   *(continued)*

N. Purchase Frequency

	Category Users (n = 100)
Would purchase Versagetti . . .	
More frequently than current brand	82%
About the same as current brand	18
Less than my current brand	0

O. Formulation Appeal Among Consumers With Positive Purchase Intent

	Consumers With Positive Purchase Intent, Rating of	
	Italian (n = 100)	American (n = 100)
On a scale of 1 (extremely appealing) to 10 (not at all appealing) formulation was rated...		
1–3	83%	20%
4–6	16	55
7–10	1	25
Mean	**1.2***	**5.4***

* t test is significantly different at $p < .001$.

P. Sample demographic

		Category Users (n = 100)	Category Nonusers (n = 100)
Gender:	Male	23%	25%
	Female	77	75
Age:	18 to 24	21	23
	25 to 34	24	25
	35 to 44	45	50
	45 to 54	5	2
	55 and older	5	0
Education:	High school or less	44	39
	Some college	24	25
	College graduate	32	36
Household income:	Less than $20	18	15
(in $ thousands)	$20 to $29.9	17	19
	$30 to $39.9	15	18
	$40 to $49.9	22	20
	$50 and over	28	28
Marital status:	Married	48	52
	Single	52	48

- Of the total study sample, 100 individuals were noncategory participants. These individuals, in addition to satisfying general study requirements, had not used any packaged pasta side-dish or main course in the past year.

Sampling

Mall-intercept personal interviews were utilized. Four geographically dispersed cities were selected to avoid bias due to geography: New York, Chicago, Houston, and San Diego. Fifty interviews were held in each city (half among category users; half among noncategory participants). Within each city three malls, dispersed in different parts of the city, were utilized. An equal number of interviews was conducted at each mall.

Analysis

Data preparation has been completed and key data tables are shown in Table 21.3 (pages 529–532). Examine the tables and then answer the following questions. Support your answer to each question with the appropriate data.

1. Do you recommend the introduction of Versagetti into the marketplace?
2. If Versagetti is introduced into the marketplace should it be targeted toward current category users, category nonusers, or both groups simultaneously?
3. If Versagetti is introduced into the marketplace what key product benefit do you recommend be selected as the focus of the advertising?
4. If Versagetti is introduced into the marketplace is there evidence to support a recommendation that specific competitive brands be mentioned in the advertising?

22

COMMUNICATION RESEARCH: EXPLORING THE STRENGTHS AND WEAKNESSES OF THE ADVERTISING CREATIVE

Positioning research, benefit tests, focus groups, and other research techniques help advertisers determine which product benefit should be the focus of the advertising. Once the focal benefit is identified, the creative team then attempts to translate the benefit into compelling, motivating advertising.

A benefit can be communicated in any number of different ways. The benefit of "removes all types of dirt while being gentle on your clothes," for example, can be communicated in the context of a slice-of-life, testimonial, celebrity spokesperson, demonstration or other creative approach. It can be communicated with humor, pathos, or in serious earnest. When faced with several creative alternatives, advertising agencies use communication research to identify the strengths and weaknesses of each alternative. The information gathered by communication research is used to determine how proposed advertising should be altered before it is either taken into production or evaluated at a more finished stage of development. This chapter explains communication research.

After reading this chapter, you will be able to

■ Explain why advertising agencies conduct communication research.

■ Plan and conduct a communication test of the advertising creative.

■ Identify the areas addressed in a communication test questionnaire and the types of questions commonly used to probe these areas.

■ Analyze and present communication test data.

The Association of National Advertisers estimates that most national advertisers test their advertising creative before production and media placement. These advertisers use communication testing, copy testing, or both forms of testing.

Communication testing (also known as copy development research), the subject of this chapter, is conducted in the early stages of creative development. Its purpose is to aid in the development of executional approaches and elements by identifying the strengths and weaknesses of a proposed advertisement before production.[1] The results of a communication or copy development test help the agency better understand how to revise an advertisement so that the finished ad maximizes strengths and minimizes weaknesses. Thus, communication testing is diagnostic in nature. Communication testing is typically conducted by the advertising agency. Copy testing, which can be performed on both rough and finished advertisements, is evaluative and is designed to help advertisers make a "go–no go" decision about an advertisement, that is, to help them decide whether to produce and/or run an ad in the marketplace.[2] Copy testing, which can be conducted by the agency or by a specialized third-party research company, is addressed in the next chapter.

REASONS FOR COMMUNICATION RESEARCH

Creative judgment and skill are wonderful gifts. Talented creatives have the ability to translate an advertising plan's essential message and benefit statement into compelling, distinctive, motivating advertising. However, advertisers know that there is considerable risk in relying *entirely* on creative judgment and taking a proposed advertisement directly into production without any indication of how consumers (as opposed to the agency and client) respond to the ad. Once an ad is produced the potential for alternation—either to increase strengths or minimize weaknesses—is greatly reduced. Advertisers therefore use communication research to reduce their risk. Communication research permits advertisers, early in the development process, to examine proposed advertising *from the consumers' perspective* and to make appropriate changes before production, thus increasing the potential success of the finished advertisement.

The goal of communication research is to complement not replace creative judgment. The design and presentation of communication research must therefore make certain that information collected during the research contributes to an understanding of the advertising creative. The research should help individuals at the agency understand *how consumers are reacting to the advertising* and *why these reactions are taking place*. With this understanding, the creative team can then determine how an advertisement can be revised and strengthened before production.[3]

---

[1] PACT, "Positioning Advertising Copy Testing: A Consensus of Leading American Advertising Agencies," *Journal of Advertising* 11 (1982): 3–29.

[2] Ibid. 8.

[3] The purpose of diagnostic pretesting is the identification of advertisement strengths and weaknesses. It is not designed to be evaluative, that is, the basis for a "go–no go" decision. However, it is possible that as a result of a diagnostic pretest, the account and creative team may decide that the problems associated with an ad are so great and unsolvable that the commercial should be eliminated from further consideration.

PREPARING FOR COMMUNICATION RESEARCH

Preparation for a communication test entails four steps: (1) the creation of test advertisements, (2) specification of respondent characteristics, (3) selection of a research methodology, and (4) construction of the communication test questionnaire.

Create Test Advertisements

Advertisements in communication research are tested in "rough" stages of development. Production values need only give the respondent a reasonably good idea of what the final advertisement will look like.

The physical characteristics and level of finish of the test advertisements depend on the advertising medium for which an ad is intended, for example:

- Print ads should be actual size, that is, the size that they will be when placed in magazines and newspapers. In terms of level of finish, communication testing only requires that the test print ad resemble the finished ad. It is entirely permissible to use drawings instead of photographs and to use simple type styles rather than the intended style that will be used in the final ad. An example of a print ad at the appropriate level of finish for communication research is shown in Figure 22.1.
- Radio ads can be "scratch" tracks.
- Television ads can be tested in one of three formats: storyboards, animatics, or photomatics. Storyboards are the easiest and least expensive form in which to test a proposed television ad. However, in spite of their efficiency, we recommend against their use. Most consumers have difficulty visualizing a finished commercial from a storyboard. As a result, we recommend that proposed television ads be tested in either animatic or photomatic form. An *animatic* is a storyboard on film or tape accompanied by a rough soundtrack. A *photomatic* is similar to an animatic except that photographs are used instead of drawings. (Photomatics are most appropriate when a drawing is an inadequate visual representation, for example, when showing an appetizing food shot.) Both animatics and photomatics use camera movement to simulate movements and actions that will appear in the finished commercial.

Finally, regardless of the advertising medium, the written or verbal copy in all tests ads should be identical to the copy that is proposed for the finished ad. The results of a communication test are irrelevant and misleading if this is not the case. Remember, the goal of communication testing is to provide a reliable estimate of how consumers will respond to the finished ad. Thus, it is important that the tested ad reflect the appearance and contain the content of the proposed finished ad.

Specify Respondent Characteristics

Communication research must be conducted among those individuals who comprise the advertising's target audience.[4] For example, it is uninformative, uninsightful, and misleading to use the reactions of individuals aged 35 and older to assess the strengths and weaknesses of a commercial targeted to 18- to 24-year-olds. While the need to con-

---

[4] PACT, 25.

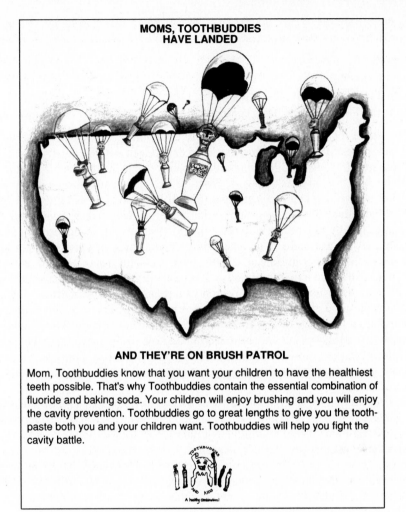

MOMS, TOOTHBUDDIES HAVE LANDED

AND THEY'RE ON BRUSH PATROL

Mom, Toothbuddies know that you want your children to have the healthiest teeth possible. That's why Toothbuddies contain the essential combination of fluoride and baking soda. Your children will enjoy brushing and you will enjoy the cavity prevention. Toothbuddies go to great lengths to give you the toothpaste both you and your children want. Toothbuddies will help you fight the cavity battle.

FIGURE 22.1
Appropriate level of finish for a print ad in a communication test.
Source: Courtesy of the Creative Juices Advertising Agency.

duct the research among the appropriate target audience seems intuitively reasonable, it is, nevertheless, not an accepted practice.[5]

Once defined, the appropriate target audience for a communication test can be identified via a screener.

Select Research Methodology

Advertising agencies use both qualitative and quantitative approaches to communication research.

Qualitative approaches generally use focus groups. Focus group participants typically see each of the proposed advertisements (one at a time) commenting on and dis-

---

[5] Don E. Schultz and Beth E. Barnes, *Strategic Advertising Campaigns, Fourth Edition* (Lincolnwood, IL: NTC Business Books, 1995).

cussing their reactions to each ad after it is shown. Many advertisers prefer a qualitative approach to communication testing because it is

- quick,
- inexpensive,
- possible to show multiple executions,
- the best means for listening to consumers describe their reactions in their own words.

In spite of these advantages, particularly the ability to personally observe consumers' responses to the advertising, our own experience with conducting communication research in focus groups leads us to believe that these advantages are outweighed by three crucial disadvantages. First, we have constantly observed an inherent bias against advertising in a focus group setting. It is fashionable and often the "group norm" for individuals in a focus group setting to deride advertising. This perspective, which can be greatly reduced in individual interviews, prevents an advertiser from obtaining an accurate and realistic understanding of consumer response to the proposed advertising. Second, peer influence, quite high in focus groups in general, is particularly high in terms of advertising response. It is unlikely that others with contrary views will express their opinions if the first person who speaks says, "This advertising is terrible and insulting." This phenomenon also prevents advertisers from obtaining a clear understanding of the range of consumer response to the advertising. Third, only reactions to the first ad shown are unbiased. No matter how many disclaimers the moderator uses (for example, "Now I am going to show you a second ad. Think just about this ad.") focus group participants cannot help but evaluate later ads in light of their reactions to earlier ads.[6]

Our recommended alternative to focus groups is quantitative, individual interviews conducted among the brand's target audience who are selected as a convenience sample. This approach, using mall intercept interviews, for example, provides consistent and reliable insights when each execution is seen by about fifty to seventy-five target audience consumers (each consumer seeing only one execution). In spite of the small sample size, this approach generally provides the *diagnostic* insights needed to evaluate an advertisement's strengths and weaknesses among the total target audience and within key target audience subgroups.

Generate Questionnaire

Similar to a concept test, questions asked on a communication test fall into one of three sets.[7] First, there is a set of questions that collects information on brand usage, respondent demographics, etc. These questions may be asked as part of the screener or at the end of the communication test questionnaire. Second, there is a core set of questions that are asked on almost all communication tests. The areas of consumer response ad-

---

[6] Obviously, this last objection to focus group communications research is eliminated if only one ad is shown to the group. However, this is almost never done, primarily because the cost-efficiency of the focus group approach is eliminated if multiple groups are required for multiple ads. Also, even if one ad is shown, the first two reasons remain and argue against focus group communications research.

[7] This discussion assumes that each respondent will see only one test ad and, consequently, the questionnaire probes responses to that single ad. We recommend against the use of multiple exposures, that is, showing more than one test ad to a respondent. While the multiple exposure approach may save some time and money, the data obtained is biased. Responses to the second or third test ad seen will always be influenced by reactions to the first test ad viewed.

dressed in this section of the questionnaire reflect our understanding of how advertising affects consumers' attitudes and behaviors.

- *The content of an advertisement must be processed by the consumer.* A consumer must be aware of and understand the advertisement's essential message and sales points. Research has demonstrated a significant positive relationship between message playback and communication effectiveness.[8] Commercial effectiveness increases as message playback increases. Thus, a central communication test measure probes respondents' memory for, and understanding of, the commercial message and key sales points.

- *The message must be positively received.* Comprehension and recall of an advertisement's message and sales points are important contributors to commercial effectiveness. However, comprehension alone is generally not enough. Research has shown that attitudes toward the message are an important component of attitude and behavioral change.[9] As with main message communication, commercial effectiveness increases as positive attitudes toward the message increase. Thus, a communication test should contain questions that probe rational and emotional responses to the advertisement's message.

- *The advertisement itself must be positively received.* An extensive body of research has clearly demonstrated the role of attitudes toward the advertisement in attitude and behavioral change. The more positive an individual is toward an advertisement, especially in terms of general affect such as 'liking,' the greater the likelihood that the commercial will positively influence that individual.[10] Thus, a communication test should contain questions that probe the consumer's subjective responses to the execution.

The third set of questions on a communication test probe consumer response to execution-specific issues and concerns.

We recommend against the inclusion of persuasion or purchase intent measures on a communication test. The information collected by these types of measures runs counter to the goals of a communication test. Persuasion and purchase intent measures are evaluative and not diagnostic in nature and have the potential to shift the focus away from and tend to overwhelm diagnostic measures.

Figure 22.2 (pages 540–543) presents a hypothetical questionnaire that could be used for a communications test of a dandruff shampoo television commercial.[11] The remainder of this section examines and discusses each section of this questionnaire.

---

[8] Russell I. Haley and Allan L. Baldinger, "The ARF Copy Research Validity Project," *Journal of Advertising Research* 31 (1991): 11–32.

[9] Ibid.

[10] Gabriel Biehal, Debra Stevens, and Eleonora Curlo, "Attitude Toward the Ad and Brand Choice," *Journal of Advertising* 21 (1992): 19–36; Haley and Baldinger, "ARF Copy Research"; David A. Aaker and David M. Stayman, "Measuring Audience Commercials and Relating Them To Advertising Impact," *Journal of Advertising Research* 30 (July–August, 1990): 7–17; Pamela M. Homer, "The Mediating Role of Attitude Toward the Ad: Some Additional Evidence," *Journal of Marketing Research* 27 (February, 1990): 78–86; Scott B. Mackenzie, Richard J. Lutz, and George E. Belch, "The Role of Attitude Toward the Ad as a Mediator of Advertising Effectiveness: A Test of Competing Explanations," *Journal of Marketing Research* 23 (May, 1986): 130–43.

[11] The questions used on the questionnaire are taken from our own experience with communications tests and from the following sources: Haley and Baldinger, "ARF Copy Research"; Christopher P. Puto and William D. Wells, "Informational and Transformational Advertising: The Different Effects of Time," In Thomas C. Kinnear ed., *Advances in Consumer Research*, Vol 11 (Provo Utah: Association for Consumer Research, 1984): 638–43; David A. Aaker and Donald Bruzzone, "Viewer Perceptions of Prime-Time Television Advertising," *Journal of Advertising Research* 21 (October, 1981): 15–23; Clark Leavitt, "A Multidimensional Set of Rating Scales for Television Commercials," *Journal of Applied Psychology* 54 (September, 1970): 427–29.

K&M ADVERTISING

DIAGNOSTIC COMMUNICATION TEST

JOB #559-2

MAIN QUESTIONNAIRE

RESPONDENT SHOULD BE SEATED IN PRIVATE INTERVIEW AREA. MAKE CERTAIN THAT THE VIDEO LABELED "A" IS REWOUND AND IN THE VCR. CHECK BELOW TO CONFIRM THAT TAPE "A" IS THE TAPE IN THE VCR. THE TAPE IN THE VCR IS TAPE ...

A	[	]1	C	[	]3
B	[	]2	D	[	]4

[10]

MAKE CERTAIN THAT RESPONDENT HAS A CLEAR VIEW OF THE VCR AND THEN SAY: Today we are talking to different people in order to get their reactions to some ideas for dandruff shampoo advertising. I would like to show you one idea for a commercial and then talk to you about your reactions. What I am about to show you is called an animatic. It uses rough drawings instead of live action to show what the commercial will look like. When you watch the animatic you'll have to use your imagination to see what the finished commercial will look like. The finished commercial will look like other commercials you are used to seeing—it will have real people. It will not be animated. Ready? PLAY TAPE. STOP TAPE WHEN COMMERCIAL IS DONE.

1. What thoughts or feelings went through your mind as you watched this commercial? PROBE: Anything else?

[11-14]

2. Aside from trying to get you to buy the product, what do you think was the main idea of this commercial? PROBE: Anything else?

[15-17]

3. What brand of dandruff shampoo was advertised? DO NOT READ LIST. CHECK RESPONSE.

Avon	_____ (1)		Jenkins	_____ (6)
Agree	_____ (2)		Revlon	_____ (7)
Breck	_____ (3)		Other	_____ (8)
Clairol	_____ (4)		DK/NA	_____ (9)
Finesse	_____ (5)			

[18]

4. Think about what the commercial said or showed about the advertised product. How important or unimportant *to you* was this information? Would you say that it was (READ LIST) ...

Extremely important	[	]1
Important	[	]2
Neither important nor unimportant	[	]3
Unimportant	[	]4
Extremely unimportant	[	]5

[19]

(continued)

FIGURE 22.2
Questionnaire for a dandruff shampoo communication test.

5. Why was what the commercial said or showed [INSERT RESPONSE FROM Q4] to you?
PROBE: Anything else?

[20-21]

6. How believable or unbelievable to you was what the commercial said or showed about the product?
Would you say that it was (READ LIST) ...

Extremely believable	[ ]1	.... SKIP TO Q8
Believable	[ ]2	.... SKIP TO Q8
Neither believable nor unbelievable	[ ]3	.... SKIP TO Q8
Unbelievable	[ ]4	.... CONTINUE WITH Q7
Extremely unbelievable	[ ]5	.... CONTINUE WITH Q7 [22]

7. What in particular did you find hard to believe? PROBE: Anything else?

[22-24]

8. Which of the following best describes how you feel about the commercial. The commercial was
(READ LIST) ...

Not at all confusing	[ ]1	.... SKIP TO Q10
Slightly confusing	[ ]2	.... CONTINUE WITH Q9
Very confusing	[ ]3	.... CONTINUE WITH Q9 [25]

9. What in particular did you find confusing? PROBE: Anything else?

10. Overall, how would you rate how much you liked or disliked the commercial. Would you say that you
(READ LIST) ...

Liked the commercial very much	[ ]1	.... CONTINUE WITH Q11
Liked the commercial	[ ]2	.... CONTINUE WITH Q11
Neither liked or disliked the commercial	[ ]3	.... SKIP TO Q15
Disliked the commercial	[ ]4	.... SKIP TO Q13
Disliked the commercial very much	[ ]5	.... SKIP TO Q13 [28]

11. What in particular did you like about the commercial. PROBE: Anything else?

[29-30]

12. Was there anything that you disliked about the commercial? PROBE: Anything else?

[31-32]

CONTINUE WITH QUESTION 15

(continued)

13. What in particular did you dislike about the commercial? PROBE: Anything else?

[33-34]

14. Was there anything that you liked about the commercial? PROBE: Anything else?

[35-36]

15. READ THE FOLLOWING TO RESPONDENT

The lists I'm about to show you contain phrases that might be used to describe your reactions to the commercial and the commercial message. Please read and follow the directions shown at the top of each list. You can hand the questionnaire back to me when you are done.

HAND QUESTIONNAIRE AND PENCIL TO RESPONDENT. TAKE BACK WHEN RESPONDENT IS FINISHED. MAKE CERTAIN BOTH PAGES HAVE BEEN COMPLETED.

The phrases shown below might describe how you feel about *the commercial* you just saw. Place a check next to each phrase that *does* describe *your* thoughts, feelings, or reactions to the commercial. You may check as many or as few (or even no) phrases as needed.

The ad was appealing to me	_____	[37]
The ad was uninteresting	_____	[38]
The kind of ad that I would easily forget	_____	[39]
The ad was fascinating	_____	[40]
The ad left me cold	_____	[41]
The ad was a fresh approach to shampoo advertising	_____	[42]
The ad was fun to listen to	_____	[43]
The ad was too complicated	_____	[44]
The ad was too unrealistic	_____	[45]
The ad was fun to watch	_____	[46]
The ad was pointless	_____	[47]
The ad was irritating	_____	[48]
The ad held my attention	_____	[49]
The ad was clever	_____	[50]
The ad was for people like me	_____	[51]

(continued)

FIGURE 22.2 (continued)

16. The phrases shown below might describe how you feel about what the commercial said *about the product*. Place a check next to each phrase that *does* describe *your* thoughts, feelings, or reactions to what the commercial said about the product. You may check as many or as few (or even no) phrases as needed.

The ad's message was interesting	_____	[52]
I learned something new from the ad	_____	[53]
The ad's message is worth remembering	_____	[54]
The ad's message was not informative	_____	[55]
The ad's message was exaggerated	_____	[56]
The ad's message was important to me	_____	[57]
The ad's message was the same old thing	_____	[58]
The ad's message was silly	_____	[59]
The ad's message was for people like me	_____	[60]

PLEASE RETURN THIS BOOKLET TO YOUR INTERVIEWER

17. I'd like to ask you just a few more questions about this commercial. What, if any, were your reactions to the background music? PROBE: Do you have any other reactions?

[61-62]

18. The commercial ended with the phrase "Don't flake out!" What is your reaction to this phrase? PROBE: Do you have any other reactions?

[63-64]

(Questionnaire would continue with additional brand usage and demographic questions, if needed.)

FIGURE 22.2 (continued)

Introduction The first page of the questionnaire, the introduction, serves two purposes. First, it makes certain that the proper commercial is shown to each respondent. In this example, four commercials (labeled A, B, C, and D) are being tested at the same time. Each respondent will see only one commercial. Directing the interviewer to check the appropriate commercial code on the questionnaire confirms that the correct video tape will be shown to the respondent and provides a basis for cross-tabulating responses during data analysis. Second, the introduction explains the nature and characteristics of an animatic. This helps the respondent understand that the commercial that he or she is about to view is a rough, drawn version of the finished commercial.

Question 1—Spontaneous Initial Reactions   The interview begins immediately after the respondent views the commercial. The questionnaire begins with a broad, open-ended question that permits the respondent to describe his or her reactions to the commercial without direction from the interviewer. Initiating the interview with this type of question works well for two reasons: (1) it begins the interview in a nonthreatening way and (2) it provides a respondent with the opportunity to describe *in his or her own words* how he or she feels about the execution, the message, and specific executional and message elements before the interviewer more narrowly focuses the interview.

It is important that a respondent answer this and other questions from memory. The ability to review the advertising during the interview has the potential to bias measures of brand recall and main idea communication. These areas are not fairly assessed if the respondent if permitted to "look up the answer" by reexamining the advertising. Consequently, a respondent must not be able to review or reexamine the advertising during the course of the interview. This is why, in this example, the video is shown only once. If this were a communication test of print advertising, the questionnaire would direct the interviewer to remove the print ad and place it out of sight before the start of the interview.

Questions 2 and 3—Essential Message and Brand-Name Communication   Questions 2 and 3 probe communication, specifically, the extent to which the advertising communicates its intended message and the name of the advertised product. Similar to a concept test, main idea communication is assessed with an open-ended question. Note that Question 2 asks "What was the main idea?" as opposed to "What did the commercial say?" This distinction is important. Communications research is not interested in simply testing the consumer's memory (as is done when you ask "What did it say?") but seeks to determine how the consumer has interpreted and internalized the commercial message (as is done when you ask "What was main idea?").

Brand-name communication is also asked in an open-ended manner, although a list is provided in which the interviewer will check the response. Similar to the prior question, having a respondent volunteer the advertised brand's name provides a measure of comprehension and recall versus simple recognition, as would happen if a list of brands were read to the respondent.

Questions 4 through 9—Specific Reactions to the Message and Execution   Questions 4 through 9 provide an opportunity to probe reactions to specific aspects of the message and execution.

- Questions 4 and 5 ask the respondent to evaluate (and explain his or her evaluation) of the importance of the message. A benefit test, other research, or judgment was the basis for selecting the focal benefit of the advertising. The advertising execution was developed with the belief that in an *absolute sense* the focal benefit is important to the target audience. Questions 4 and 5 assess the extent to which the target audience sees the message as important *within the context* of a specific creative execution.
- Questions 6 and 7 probe message believability. An advertisement has little chance of

persuading a consumer if its message is not believed. Question 6 uses a scale to assess perceptions of message believability. To facilitate an understanding of the advertising's weaknesses (if any) those consumers who feel the message was not believable are asked to explain their feelings in Question 7.

- Questions 8 and 9 follow a similar pattern in probing a respondent's perceptions of the advertisement's clarity. A respondent is first asked to use a rating scale to indicate his or her view of the advertisement's clarity (Question 8) and then, if problems are noted, he or she is asked to identify the cause of the problem in Question 9.

The sequence of a scale followed by an open-ended question provides important diagnostic information and helps advertisers better understand the underlying reasons of consumer response to the advertising.

Questions 10 through 14—Spontaneous Likes and Dislikes   This series of questions provides a respondent with the opportunity to volunteer what he or she might have liked or disliked about the commercial. The like/dislike questions are sequenced so that Question 10, the scale question, serves as the basis for a skip pattern appropriate to the respondent's attitude toward the ad. A respondent who indicates that he or she liked the commercial is immediately asked what he or she liked, and is then given the opportunity to state what, if anything, he or she did not like. Similarly, a respondent who indicates that he or she disliked the commercial is immediately asked what he or she disliked, and is then given the opportunity to state what, if anything, he or she liked. The pattern of relating the first open-ended question to the respondent's attitude makes the question sequence intuitively reasonable and makes it easier for the respondent to answer.

Questions 15 and 16—Execution and Message Diagnostics   Two different checklists are used to further probe reactions to the execution and message. The first checklist, presented in Question 15, probes reactions to the execution while the second checklist, presented in Question 16, probes reactions to the message. The checklists are kept separate to make certain that the respondent focuses on and evaluates the desired aspect of the commercial. Each checklist adheres to the recommendations for checklist construction discussed earlier in the text, specifically:

- the directions clearly explain the respondent's task
- checklist items were placed in random order
- there is an even mix of positive and negative checklist items

Questions 17 and 18—Execution-Specific Issues   The main body of the questionnaire ends with execution-specific questions. These questions ensure that important execution-specific concerns and issues are explored. Open-ended questions are used so that respondents' answers are not constrained or biased by predetermined response categories.

ANALYSIS AND PRESENTATION OF COMMUNICATIONS TEST DATA

There are two tasks associated with the analysis of communication test data: summarization of the findings and the uncovering of underlying relationships among measures.

- Data summarization is the easiest of the two tasks. Descriptive statistics are commonly used to describe the pattern of response. Statistical tests such as chi-square and *t* tests are used to provide greater confidence in conclusions drawn from the data.

- The uncovering of underlying relationships between measures tends to be the more difficult of the two tasks. However, while often difficult and time consuming, is well worth the effort and is a crucial part of the research. The extent to which individuals at the agency will understand how to strengthen an advertisement is directly related to the *depth* of data analysis. Creativity on the part of the data analyst is needed to help the agency team understand not only the *what* of consumer response but the *why*.

The presentation of communication test data should follow a logical flow, moving from the analysis and discussion of one principal area to another. The presentation should be organized by topic area rather than strictly adhering to the sequence of questions as presented on the questionnaire. The remainder of this section illustrates both analysis and presentation of communication test data. This portion of a larger oral presentation illustrates how the data from a communication test provides direction for the modification and improvement of the advertising creative.[12]

Background

Background information is an important part of any research presentation (see Chapter 4). Thus, a presentation of communication test findings generally begins with a review of essential background information, specifically a description of the research methodology, a statement of study purpose, and the viewing of tested advertising, for example:

We are here today to discuss the results of a communication test of four proposed commercials for Jenkins Dandruff Shampoo. We will discuss, one at a time, consumers' reactions to each commercial.

Each commercial was viewed by individuals in the brand's target audience, specifically: twenty-five men and twenty-five women between the ages of 35 and 64 who use a dandruff shampoo for the majority of their shampooing and who are primarily responsible or share equally in the decision as to which brand of dandruff shampoo they personally use. These individuals were screened, taken to a private interview room, shown the commercial animatic and then interviewed. The interview lasted about fifteen minutes. Each respondent saw only one test commercial.

Respondent's were selected using mall-intercept interviews in three Jenkins markets: Denver, Chicago, and Tampa. These markets provide geographic dispersion and are representative markets for Jenkins. Jenkins has average brand development in each market.

Before we begin the presentation of findings, let me remind you of the purpose of

---

[12] The data shown is fictitious.

the test. We designed the test to help us better understand the strengths and weaknesses of each commercial, not to make "go-no go" decisions.

Here is the commercial that we will discuss first. (Animatic would be shown here.)

Reactions to the Execution

The presentation of communication test findings typically begins with the most significant findings. The pattern of consumer response to a specific advertising execution typically dictates whether the presentation begins with attitudes toward the advertisement or attitudes toward the message. In this example, we believe that the data indicates that presentation should begin with reactions to the execution.

The first table in this portion of the sample presentation reveals consumers' spontaneous, open-ended responses to the advertising execution and message and provides the reason why the presentation initially focuses on reactions to the execution. The basis for the initial set of insights comes from the simultaneous coding of responses to Questions 1, 2, 3, and 11–14. Responses to these questions are coded as if they were a single question. There are two advantages to this combined coding as opposed to coding and presenting each question individually. First, redundancy is reduced. There is little point in presenting three individual tables that present responses to Question 1, Question 12, and Question 13 if the content of responses are identical (for example, a respondent mentions not liking the music in each case). Second, the combined coding better focuses your audience on important findings. The pattern of consumer response appears in a single table. The responses to the individual questions can be presented where appropriate later in the presentation.

The presentation of spontaneous reactions is followed by additional execution-related information. This additional information provides deeper insights into respondent's feelings about the execution and the causes of these feelings. Sequencing and presenting information in this manner, that is, by topic rather than in questionnaire order, keeps the audience focused on one specific aspect of target audience response, thus facilitating their understanding of response in this area. In this example, the presentation of spontaneous execution-related reactions would be followed by data collected by questions 8, 9, 15, and 17.

With this in mind, the presentation continues as follows:

After respondents saw the animatic, they were given several opportunities to describe in their own words their reactions to the execution and commercial message. They were asked to share their thoughts, feelings, likes, and dislikes.

Most respondents took this opportunity to comment on the execution. This first table shows the percent of respondents who mentioned either the execution or the message and the percent who expressed positive or negative attitudes:

Spontaneous Reactions to the Execution and Message

Reactions to the execution (supernet)	*94%*
Positive (net)	84
Negative (net)	78
Reactions to the message (supernet)	*46%*
Positive (net)	22
Negative (net)	28

(Base is 50 respondents; Responses do not add to 100% due to multiple mentions.)

As you can see, nearly all respondents commented on the execution while fewer, about half, commented on the message. The pattern of execution-related comments is interesting. The high number of respondents shown in the positive and negative nets indicates that most respondents volunteered *both* positive and negative comments. Thus, we believe that we can increase the effectiveness of the finished execution if we can capitalize on the target audiences' perceived strengths and eliminate or reduce perceived problems.

What were the executional strengths and weaknesses?

One insight into strengths and weaknesses comes from the specifics of respondent's spontaneous comments as shown in this table:

Specific Positive and Negative Reactions to the Execution

Positive (net)	*84%*
Different	66
Better	64
Pacing/fast moving	18
Music	16
Characters/actors	10
Voice-over	10
Negative (net)	*78%*
Pacing/fast moving	64
Music	60
Characters	10
Product-shot	10
Voice-over	10

(Base is 50 respondents; Responses do not add to 100% due to multiple mentions.)

The target reacted very positively to the basic execution. Nearly two-thirds felt that it was different (in a good sense) *and* better than other shampoo advertising. Specific words respondents used to express their feelings of "different" were novel, distinct, and unique. Specific words respondents used to express their feelings that the execution was better than other shampoo ads were exciting, distinctive, and fun. Thus, it appears that the basic executional approach is sound. This is a very positive pattern of response.

A few respondents said that they liked the pacing and music. But, given the small sample size, these levels are low and represent few respondents.

Respondents who said that they liked the pacing and music were far outnumbered by those who had problems in these areas. Nearly two-thirds of the respondents felt that the pacing was too fast moving and that the music was inappropriate. Respondents felt that the music was too loud and too fast. Many said that the music was "not for me, but for my kids." Mentions of other areas, such as characters, product-shot, and voice-over, are at such low levels that we do not perceive any problems in these areas.

In sum, this pattern of response indicates that the executional approach appears sound but the pacing and music appear to be problematic. Responses to additional questions confirm this assessment of the execution.

We presented respondents with a checklist and asked them to check those phrases that described how they felt about the execution. Some phrases were positive and some were negative. First, let us look at the strengths of the commercial. Strengths are reflected in positive statements with high levels of agreement and negative statements with low levels of agreement. Here are the statements that show this pattern of response:

Viewer Response to Execution Checklist—Execution Strengths

Positive phrases—high agreement	*Percent Checked*
Fascinating	76%
Would not easily forget	74
Fresh approach to shampoo advertising	74
Fun to watch	68
Held my attention	68
Clever	66
Unrealistic	10

Negative phrases—low agreement	
The ad was uninteresting	16%
The ad left me cold	14
The ad was pointless	10
The ad was irritating	10

(Base is 50 respondents; Responses do not add to 100% due to multiple selections.)

Viewers responded very positively to the execution; over two-thirds agreed that it was fascinating, fresh, fun, clever, and worth remembering. Additionally, few felt that the ad was uninteresting, pointless, or irritating. This is a very strong profile.

Interestingly (and importantly) this strong profile was obtained in spite of respondent concerns. These concerns are reflected in positive statements with low agreement and negative statements with high agreement:

Viewer Response to Execution Checklist—Execution Weaknesses

Positive phrases—weak agreement	
Fun to listen to	10%
For people like me	10

Negative phrases—strong agreement	
Not appealing to me	66%
Too complicated	60

(Base is 50 respondents; Responses do not add to 100% due to multiple selections.)

Almost two-thirds of the respondents felt that the ad was too complicated and not appealing. Further, few agreed that the ad was fun to listen to or for people like me. This last measure is troubling, for the advertising to be noticed, attended to, and acted on it is important that the execution be seen as relevant by the target audience.

Let us look more closely at each of the problem areas. Confusion first.

Given the high number of respondents who said the ad was too complicated, it is not surprising that many also felt that the execution was confusing. Confusion was, in fact, high. About three-quarters of those who saw the commercial said that they were confused and half said that they were *very* confused.

Consumers' Rating of Confusion

Very confused	50%
Slightly confused	26
Not at all confused	24
Total	100%

(Base is 50 respondents.)

Confusion appears to be related to commercial pacing. Nearly all of those who said that they were confused mentioned the fast pacing, while pacing was not a factor among those not confused. The relationship between pacing and confusion is statistically significant at a 95 percent confidence level.

Relationship between Respondent Confusion and Commercial Pacing

Percent of confused respondents who mentioned fast pacing as reason for confusion	80%
Percent of confused respondents who did not mention fast pacing as reason for confusion	20%

(Base is 50 respondents.)

We can isolate the specific portion of the commercial that is causing respondent problems with pacing. When we examine reactions to the questions "What thoughts or feelings did you have as you watched the commercial?" and "What did you find confusing?" we see similar responses. Problems with pacing are almost always associated with the second vignette, the one with the mother and daughter, as shown in the following table:

Reasons Mentioned for Problems with Commercial Pacing

	Commercial confusing or complicated
Mentioned any problem with pacing (net)	*64%*
Mother and daughter	56
Father and son	12
Two brothers	8
Two sisters	6

(Base is 50 respondents.)

Now let us look at the music. Because we thought that the music might be a problem, we asked a music-specific question at the end of the interview.

Negative reactions to the music appear to underlie lack of commercial appeal, lack of listening pleasure, and lack of relevance. The following table shows the reactions to the music among those with negative feelings in these three areas:

Relationship Between Measures of Commercial Appeal and Reactions to the Music

	Respondents who felt that the ad was		
	"Not appealing to me" (Base = 30)	*"Not fun to listen to"* (Base = 45)	*"Not for people like me"* (Base = 45)
Spontaneous Reactions to the Music			
Positive reactions (net)	*17%*	*9%*	*7%*
Negative reactions (net)	*83%*	*91%*	*93%*
Too loud	67	82	89
Too fast	67	76	87
Too noisy	50	47	44
For younger people	47	40	33
My kids' music	44	33	22
Trashy	41	33	22
Gives me a headache	41	11	11

(Responses do not add to 100% due to multiple mentions.)

A clear relationship, statistically significant at the 99 percent level of confidence can be seen. Lack of appeal, fun to listen to, and personal relevance are highly associated with negative reactions to the music. Specifically, as we saw in prior measures, the music was felt to be too loud, fast, noisy, and for younger people.

In sum, a consistent picture of response to the execution can be seen. The basic executional approach appears to be quite strong. However, problems with the pacing in the mother and daughter vignette and music should be addressed before production.

Communication and Reactions to the Message

As stated earlier, main message communication is an important area explored in a communication test. Thus, a presentation of results must include an assessment of how well the advertising communicated its essential message and the advertised product's brand name. The information that addresses these areas, in this example, is collected from Questions 1, 2, 3, and 18. Additionally, if appropriate, this section of the presentation may also relate communication to other measures on the questionnaire, for example, respondents' assessment of the commercial's appeal. With this in mind, the presentation might continue as follows:

We all know how important is for an advertisement to clearly communicate the product's brand name and essential message identified in the strategy statement. The brand name, Jenkins Dandruff, was clearly communicated. Almost all respondents were able to name Jerkins as the advertised brand.

Brand Name Identification	Percent of respondents
Jerkins Dandruff Shampoo	82%
Jerkins Shampoo	8
Other/ no response	10
Total	100%

(Base is 50 respondents.)

We asked each respondent to tell us in his or her own words the main idea of the commercial. Before I show you their responses, let me refresh your memory of the thinking that let to the commercial's essential message. A dual benefit message was adapted: "Jerkins Dandruff shampoo gets rid of your dandruff in one washing at a cost less than that of the leading brands." Some at the agency felt that this dual-benefit message should be extremely motivating while others felt that the message should be a single benefit, specifically "Jerkins Dandruff shampoo get rid of your dandruff in one washing."

In terms of message playback, few respondents played back both aspects of the message. About half said the main idea was "gets rid of dandruff in one washing" while about one-quarter said the message was "costs less than the leading brands." Few respondents, only about one in ten, played back both messages.

Message Playback	Percent of respondents
One washing	52%
Lowest cost	24
One washing and lowest cost	10
Other/no response	14
Total	100%

(Base is 50 respondents.)

Given this split in message playback, it is interesting to see how respondents reacted to each part of the message.

First, we examine believability and importance. As the following table shows, the "gets rid of dandruff in one washing" message was seen as much more important and believable versus the "lowest cost" message. These differences were statistically significant at the 95 percent level of confidence, in spite of the low sample sizes.

Message Importance and Believability As a Function of Message Playback

	Playback of "one washing" only (Base =26)	Playback of "lowest cost" only (Base =12)
Percent rating commercial		
Extremely important	54%	25%
Extremely believable	81%	33%
Average commercial rating*		
Importance	2.1	3.4
Believability	1.6	3.1

* Lower numbers indicate a more positive rating.

Second, responses to the message-specific adjective checklist showed that individuals who saw the message as "gets rid of dandruff in one washing" were much more likely to agree with positive statements about the message and disagree with negative statements about the message versus those who saw the message as "lowest cost." Again, all differences are statistically significant.

Reactions to the Message As a Function of Message Playback

	Playback of "one washing" only (Base =26)	Playback of "lowest cost" only (Base =12)
Agreement with positive message statements		
Learned something new	76%	54%
Worth remembering	74	32
Interesting	66	32
For people like me	64	12
Agreement with negative message statements		
Not informative	10%	44%
Exaggerated	12	42
Same old thing	8	38
Silly	6	38

We believe that this pattern of response indicates that the "lowest price" component of the essential message provides little positive contribution. Few respondents can playback this message and, among those that do, reactions to the commercial are far less positive than the reactions of those who playback "gets rid of dandruff in one washing."

Finally, as you will recall, there was some concern that respondents would not understand or respond favorably to the tag line "Don't flake out!" These concerns appear to be unfounded. Respondents reacted very positively to this line in terms of both affect and interpretation. First, there were significantly more positive versus negative responses to the line. Second, the line was felt to be memorable, unique, different, and clever. Third, most respondents understood the line to mean "Don't worry. Jenkins gets rid of your dandruff right away (in one washing)."

Spontaneous Reactions to Tag Line "Don't Flake Out."

Reactions to the tagline	
Positive (net)	*86%*
Memorable	68
Unique	66
Different	36
Clever	18
Intriguing	14

Negative (net)	26%
Silly	10
Inappropriate	8
Confusing	8
Interpretation of the tag line	
Correct interpretation (net)	90%
Don't worry	52
Works right away	30
Works in one washing	30
Works better than others	10
Incorrect interpretation/no response	10%

(Base is 50 respondents.)

Summary, Conclusions, and Next Steps

As discussed in Chapter 4, research presentations end with a summary of the findings, conclusions, and implications of the findings for next steps. In this example, the summary and conclusions would include the following points:

- Reactions to the execution were very positive. Responses to both closed- and open-ended questions were consistent and quite favorable. The execution was felt to be fun to watch, clever, memorable, different, and better than other commercials. We recommend maintaining the overall approach of the execution.

- Positive reactions to the commercial might be increased if modifications are made to two aspects of the internal structure of the commercial. First, respondents feel that the mother and daughter vignette is too complicated and confusing. A decision should be made as to whether this vignette can be successfully modified or should be dropped from the final version of the commercial. Second, the music is a problem. The music generates high levels of viewer discomfort, primarily because it is felt to be too loud, too fast, and too young. We recommend that a new music track be considered for the finished commercial.

- Communication playback of the brand name is strong. No changes in this area appear to be warranted.

- Main message communication is single-minded. Respondents playback either "gets rid of your dandruff in a single washing" or "the lowest cost." The pattern of response associated with each portion of the message indicates that the former message, which was played-back by the majority of respondents, is the stronger of the two benefits. It is rated higher in importance and believability versus "lowest cost." We recommend more strongly focusing the message on this one product benefit.

- The tag line "Don't flake out!" is well received and communicates well within the context of the commercial. The tag line should be used without alteration.

Summary

Advertisers conduct communication or copy development research to better understand how consumers are reacting to a proposed advertisement and why these reactions are taking place. This information helps the agency determine methods by which the advertisement can be revised and strengthened before production.

Preparation for a communication test entails four steps:

1. Test advertisements are prepared in rough stages of finish. Print ads may use drawings, radio ads may use scratch tracks, and television commercials may use animatic or photomatic formats.

2. Important characteristics of the advertising's target audience are identified and a screener is written.

3. A qualitative or quantitative methodology is selected. We recommend the latter approach.

4. A questionnaire is written. The questionnaire addresses message and brand-name communication, reactions to the message, reactions to the advertisement and advertisement-specific concerns, if any.

The presentation of communication test results entails two tasks: summarization of the findings and the uncovering of underlying relationships among measures. Data summarization describes target audience response. The uncovering of underlying relationships between measures explains why the target audience responded as they did.

Review Questions

1. What is the difference between a *communication* test and a *copy* test? How does each type of test contribute to the process of creative development?

2. Why is there a risk in not conducting a communication test?

3. What are the four steps to preparing for a communication test?

4. In what form or format should advertisements be tested in a communication test?

5. What is an *animatic*? What is a *photomatic*?

6. Why is it important to conduct a communication test among the brand's advertising target audience?

7. What are the relative advantages of qualitative versus quantitative approaches to communication research?

8. What are the three sets of questions asked on a communication test?

9. What are the three advertising-related areas of target audience response explored on a communication test? Why is each area important?

10. What two tasks need to be performed in the analysis and presentation of communication test data?

11. What types of information are presented in the presentation background section?

12. When presenting the results of a communication test, what considerations affect how you sequence the findings?

Application Exercises[13]

1. A communication test has been proposed for the Yard Nine Dog Food ad (shown in Figure 22.3, page 556). The target audience for the ad consists of men and women aged 18 and older who own a dog and who

---

[13] The companies, brands, and data in all application exercises are fictitious.

> # Is Your Mutt In A Rut?
>
> If your dog acts unmotivated and lacks energy to even fetch a stick, then he needs new Yard Nine. Yard Nine is specially formulated for the athletic dog. It is full of vital nutrients that give your dog the energy he needs to stay athletic.
>
> Importantly, Yard Nine is corn free. Research has shown that corn can cause digestive problems and skin and coat allergies. Yard Nine replaces corn with poultry, rice, and cheleated minerals to give your athletic dog the protein he needs.
>
> Yard Nine is available at your grocery store priced comparably to the leading brands.
>
> ## *FEED HIM YARD NINE*
>
> K9

FIGURE 22.3
Yard Nine Dog Food ad.
Source: Courtesy of JJD Advertising.

- share in or are responsible for the brand of dog food purchased,
- primarily purchase dry dog food,
- do *not* typically purchase a store or generic brand of dog food.

Your client is unsure whether to use a qualitative or quantitative methodology for the test and asks you to provide an unbiased assessment of the strengths and weaknesses of each approach. Do the following to respond to this request:

- First, prepare a screener that can be used to identify individuals in the advertising target audience.
- Second, prepare one questionnaire that can be used to explore reactions to the advertising in a quantitative setting (you can modify the questionnaire shown in Figure 22.3) and a discussion guide that can be used to explore reactions to the advertising in a focus group setting.
- Third, identify fifteen individuals who fit the target audience description.

THE TWO TASTES YOU LOVE, COMBINED INTO ONE.

Irish Mocha Mint

Coffee House Creations

Irish Mocha Mint

Coffee House Creations has taken the two tastes you love the most and combined them to make one unique taste. Coffee House Creations has united your favorite gourmet coffeehouse flavors with rich, creamy gourmet ice cream made from the finest ingredients available. Available now in your local grocery store in Irish Mocha Mint, Vanilla Nut, and Chocolate Caramel.

IF EVERY COMBINATION IN LIFE COULD BE THIS GOOD.

Coffee House Creations containers are made of 100% recyclable, biodegradable plastic. We support our environment.

FIGURE 22.4
Coffee House Creations print ad.
Source: Courtesy of Ad Ventures.

TABLE 22.1 Responses to Coffee House Creations Communications Test Rating and Checklist Questions

Respondent #	Q1	Q2	Q3	Q4	Q5a	Q5b	Q5c	Q5d	Q5e	Q5f	Q5g	Q5h	Q5i	Q6a	Q6b	Q6c	Q6d	Q6e	Q6f	Q6g
1	1	2	1	2	+		+				+	+	+	+	+	+			+	
2	1	1	2	1	+						+		+							
3	2	1	2	1	+		+						+	+	+	+			+	
4	1	2	1	1			+				+	+	+	+	+	+			+	
5	1	2	4	5			+		+	+		+	+							
6	1	1	4	4					+	+		+	+							
7	2	2	5	5					+											
8	1	2	5	4					+											
9	1	4	4	2		+		+	+	+			+	+						
10	2	5	5	1		+		+	+	+			+	+					+	
11	1	5	5	1		+			+	+			+						+	
12	1	4	4	1		+		+		+										
13	5	4	4	5		+		+		+							+	+	+	+
14	5	5	5	4		+		+	+	+							+	+	+	+
15	4	5	4	4		+			+	+	+	+					+	+	+	+
16	5	4	5	4		+		+	+		+		+	+	+					
17	2	1	1	2	+	+	+		+		+	+	+	+	+	+			+	
18	2	1	2	1	+	+	+					+	+	+	+	+			+	
19	1	2	1	2	+	+	+						+	+	+	+			+	
20	1	2	1	1		+	+						+							
21	1	2	5	4					+	+										
22	1	2	4	5					+	+				+						
23	1	1	5	5					+											
24	1	2	4	5																

Respondent

#	Q1	Q2	Q3	Q4	Q5a	Q5b	Q5c	Q5d	Q5e	Q5f	Q5g	Q5h	Q5i	Q6a	Q6b	Q6c	Q6d	Q6e	Q6f	Q6g
25	1	5	5	1		+		+	+	+			+	+					+	
26	2	5	5	2		+		+	+	+				+					+	
27	1	4	5	1		+		+	+	+			+	+						
28	1	4	4	1		+		+	+	+			+	+					+	
29	4	5	4	5		+		+	+	+							+	+		+
30	5	4	4	4		+		+		+							+	+		+
31	5	5	4	4		+		+	+	+							+	+		+
32	5	4	5	4		+		+	+	+							+	+		+
33	2	1	2	1	+		+					+	+	+	+	+			+	
34	1	2	1	1			+					+	+	+	+	+			+	
35	1	2	4	5			+		+	+	+		+	+		+			+	
36	1	1	5	4					+	+			+							
37	2	2	5	5					+											
38	1	2	5	4					+											
39	1	4	4	2		+		+	+	+			+	+					+	
40	2	5	5	1		+		+	+	+			+	+					+	
41	1	5	5	1		+			+	+			+	+					+	
42	1	4	4	1		+		+		+										
43	5	4	4	5		+		+	+	+							+	+		+
44	5	5	5	4		+		+	+	+							+	+		+
45	4	5	4	4		+			+	+							+	+		+
46	5	4	5	4		+		+	+	+							+	+		+
47	2	1	1	2	+	+					+	+	+	+	+	+			+	
48	2	1	2	1	+	+	+				+		+	+	+	+			+	
49	1	2	1	2	+	+	+				+	+		+	+	+			+	
50	1	2	1	1		+	+					+	+	+	+				+	

Note: A '+' in Questions 5 and 6 indicates that a specific checklist item was checked.

- Fourth, conduct a quantitative communication test with five target audience individuals, seven quantitative interviews.
- Fifth, conduct a communication test in a focus group setting with eight target audience individuals.

When you have completed the quantitative and qualitative communication test research, write a memo to the client (using your knowledge and experiences in the qualitative and quantitative approaches) to provide a point of view of the relative advantages and disadvantages of each approach to communication testing. Be certain to justify all conclusions and to provide illustrative examples from your experience.

2. Coffee House Creations' agency has developed and tested a print advertisement designed to introduce the new line of coffee flavored ice cream. The ad (shown in Figure 22.4, page 557) is targeted toward individuals who purchase premium ice cream in grocery stores.

You are the agency research supervisor hired after the communication test was placed in the field. The following questions were asked on the communication test:

Question Asked	*Type of Question*
1. Rating of importance (five-point scale where '1' is extremely important and '5' is extremely unimportant)	Likert-type scale
2. Rating of believability (five-point scale where '1' is extremely believable and '5' is extremely unbelievable)	Likert-type scale
3. Rating of confusion (five-point scale where '1' is not at all confusing and '5' is extremely confusing)	Likert-type scale
4. Rating of ad liking (five-point scale where '1' is extremely liked and '5' is extremely disliked)	Likert-type scale
5. Reactions to the execution a. the ad was appealing to me b. the ad was uninteresting c. the kind of ad that I would readily notice d. the ad left me cold e. the ad was too complicated f. the ad was pointless g. the ad held my attention h. the ad was clever i. the ad was for people like me	Checklist
6. Reactions to the message a. the ad's message was interesting b. I learned something new from the ad c. the ad's message is worth remembering d. the ad's message was the same old thing e. the ad's message was silly f. the ad's message was for people like me g. the ad's message was not important	Checklist

You notice that there are no open-ended questions. (You ask about this and learn that the client does not believe in open-ended questions. The client likes "real" numbers.) Individual respondent's responses to these questions are shown in Table 22.1 (pages 558–559).

Write a memo to Coffee House Creations that (1) presents the findings of the research, (2) provides recommendations for actions to be taken before completion of the ad, and (3) provides specific examples of how future communication tests can be improved.

CHAPTER

23 | COPY TESTING

Advertisers use the procedures described in the prior chapter to identify the strengths and weaknesses of an advertisement before production. Once an advertisement is produced, advertisers often conduct additional research, commonly referred to as copy testing, to make certain that the finished advertisement successfully achieves its strategic and communication goals. Advertisements that demonstrate effectiveness in copy research are placed or remain in the appropriate advertising medium; advertisements that do not demonstrate effectiveness may be revised or, more commonly, withdrawn from future media exposure.

Advertisers have a variety of methodological options for copy testing their advertisements. The beginning sections of this chapter explain copy testing options for television and magazine advertisements. The presentation of copy testing options is followed by a discussion of how to most effectively use copy testing to identify and select advertising.

The chapter concludes by examining copy testing from a legal perspective. Advertisers whose advertising claims are challenged by the Federal Trade Commission (FTC), individual states, or other advertisers often use copy research to respond to and defend against these challenges. However, problems with research design and questionnaire construction can lead to rejection of the research findings. The final section of the chapter addresses considerations in the planning, execution, and reporting of copy testing conducted in response to an FTC or other legal challenge. This discussion highlights the characteristics of copy tests most likely to be accepted by the FTC or other regulatory or legal bodies.

After reading this chapter, you will be able to

■ Explain how copy testing differs from communication testing.

■ Determine the role of copy research in the evaluation and selection of advertising creative.

■ Evaluate the strengths and weaknesses of copy testing options for television and magazine advertising.

■ Understand the aspects of research conduct and analysis that lead to greater acceptance of copy test results by the Federal Trade Commission (FTC) and other regulatory agencies.

Advertisers use copy testing research to determine the extent to which an advertisement accomplishes its strategic and communication objectives and, as a result, whether or not the ad should appear in the marketplace. Consequently, copy testing differs from communication testing (discussed in the prior chapter) in several important ways.

First, copy testing is evaluative; communication testing is diagnostic. Copy testing research is designed to help an advertiser make a "go/no go" decision for an advertisement, that is, whether to place or keep that ad in the media rotation. As a result, copy testing occurs at the conclusion of the creative development process and is primarily concerned with measuring consumers' reactions to finished advertising (typically as it appears in the context of an advertising medium) while diagnostic communication testing generally measures consumers' responses to rough advertisements viewed in isolation.[1]

Second, copy testing is almost always conducted by independent research companies that specialize in this form of testing. This contrasts with diagnostic communication testing that is typically conducted by the advertising agency or client research department. The use of external companies for copy testing permits an advertiser to take advantage of specialized research techniques and to have the advertisement tested by a strictly objective third-party.

Third, copy testing research uses norms to evaluate advertising effectiveness. Every major research company that conducts copy test research has developed a set of norms for measurements in key areas. These norms let advertisers make their "go/no go" decisions about whether the advertising should run in the marketplace on the basis of an objective criterion or set of criteria. Advertising that scores at or above the applicable norm(s) generally remains in the media schedule; advertising that tests below norm(s) is either revised or, more commonly, eliminated from the media schedule.

The range of copy testing options available to an advertiser varies with advertising media. The greatest number of copy testing options exist for television advertising, reflecting an advertiser's need to protect the substantial media investment required to place and air television commercials. Copy testing procedures are also available for magazine, newspaper, radio, and outdoor advertising. Fewer services are available, however, to test advertising in these media. This may reflect advertisers' decreased interest in testing advertising that has lower production and placement costs. The next two sections in this chapter discuss copy testing options for television and magazine advertising.[2]

---

[1] Many of the copy testing companies discussed in this chapter have the capability to test ads in rough form and, as a result, evaluative decisions can be made on the basis of consumers' response to rough advertising. We recommend, however, that advertisers not make evaluative (i.e., "go/no-go") decisions for ads tested at this unfinished level. The copy testing guidelines developed by a consortium of advertising agencies [PACT, "Positioning Advertising Copy Testing: A Consensus of Leading American Advertising Agencies," *Journal of Advertising* 11 (1982): 3–29] specifically addresses and supports this point of view: "A good copy testing system recognizes that the more finished a piece of copy is, the more soundly it can be evaluated . . . Experience has shown that test results can often vary depending on the degree of finish of test executions. Thus, careful judgment should be used in considering the importance of what may be lost in a less than finished version. Sometimes the loss may be inconsequential; sometimes it may be critical." In other words, the decision to run or not to run an ad is best made on the basis of the finished version of the ad.

[2] Radio copy testing is not addressed in this chapter for two reasons. First, copy testing in this medium accounts for a relatively low percentage of all copy testing research. Second, the methodologies used for radio copy testing tend to parallel those used for television advertising copy testing.

COPY TESTING OPTIONS FOR TELEVISION

Copy testing options for television advertising can be characterized by four dimensions:

1. The *place* where the advertising is seen. Advertising can be viewed at home or out-of-home.

2. The *naturalness* of the viewing situation. There are three levels of naturalness. A completely natural viewing situation is one where respondents in the commercial audience are identified and interviewed *after* the ad has aired *without* any prior contact. A quasi-natural situation is one where respondents are *invited* to watch a television program in which the test ad is embedded. This viewing is not entirely natural because respondents are watching a program that they may not have ordinarily viewed *and* they are aware that they are watching the program in the context of a research study (although not a research study on advertising evaluation). An unnatural viewing condition (also known as forced exposure) directly focuses respondents' attention on the advertising. Here, respondents are asked to focus specifically on advertising presented in isolation.

3. The *number of advertising exposures*. Data collection can take place after one or more exposures to the advertising.

4. *Key measures*. Available measures vary among copy testing methodologies as do the specific measures for which norms are available. For any particular copy testing methodology, normative measures can include one or more of the following: advertising recall, message communication, attitude shift, buying intention (persuasion), and attitudes toward the advertising.

The remainder of this section presents an overview of the major copy testing methodologies available for television advertising. For purposes of discussion, copy testing companies have been grouped on the basis of place of viewing and the naturalness of the viewing situation, as follows:

Characteristics	*Representative Research Companies*
At home viewing, quasi-natural viewing situation	ASI Marketing Research Gallup & Robinson Mapes and Ross
Out-of-home viewing, quasi-natural viewing situation	Research Systems Corporation McCollum Spielman Worldwide
Out-of-home viewing, forced viewing situation	Viewfacts Ortek Data Systems Quick-Tally Systems Market Opinion Research

This chapter also focuses on copy testing *methodologies*. For *conceptual* discussions of copy testing and its role in the advertising development process see the special issue devoted to copy testing of the *Journal of Advertising Research* (May/June, 1994); Surendra N. Singh and Catherine A. Cole, "Advertising Copy Testing in Print Media," In James H. Leigh and Claude R. Martin, Jr. eds., *Current Issues & Research in Advertising* (Ann Arbor, MI: University of Michigan School of Business Administration, 1988), 215–84; David W. Stewart, et al., "Methodological and Theoretical Foundations of Advertising Copytesting: A Review," In James H. Leigh and Claude R. Martin, Jr., eds. *Current Issues & Research in Advertising* Part 2 (Ann Arbor, MI:University of Michigan School of Business Administration, 1985), 1–74; John D. Leckenby and Joseph T. Plummer, "Advertising Stimulus Measurement and Assessment Research: A Review of Advertising Testing Methods," In James H. Leigh and Claude R. Martin, Jr., eds., *Current Issues & Research in Advertising* Part 2 (Ann Arbor, MI: University of Michigan School of Business Administration, 1983), 135–66.

We begin by examining the three companies that expose the test commercial to pre-recruited respondents in their own homes.

At Home Viewing, Quasi-Natural Viewing Situation

ASI Marketing Research: Recall Plus and Apex   ASI Marketing Research offers two complementary copy testing services: Recall Plus and Apex. Recruitment and commercial exposure for both the Recall Plus and Apex services are identical. Typically, each service recruits about 200 individuals to watch a special television program under the guise of a research study designed to measure television viewing habits. Respondents reside in two geographically dispersed markets and are cable TV subscribers. The television program, typically broadcast over an unused cable channel, is a thirty-minute situation comedy into which the test commercial, four noncompeting test commercials, and one nontest filler commercial have been edited. Recall Plus and Apex differ with regard to the types of measures collected.

Recall Plus, as the name implies, measures respondents' recall of the test commercial. The day after viewing, respondents are contacted and asked (with and without prompts) to name the commercials they remember seeing in the prior day's program. The percent of the sample who can prove recall after the prior day's single exposure represent the commercials' ability to break through clutter and attract attention. Norms are available for the Recall Plus recall measure. Should an advertiser wish to collect diagnostic information, the test commercial can be shown to respondents for a second time after the standard interview has ended.

Apex adds a measure of persuasion to the Recall Plus measure. Here, a separate but comparable sample of viewers watches the television program. Within two hours of exposure, participants are questioned about their viewing, reactions to the program, and brand preferences (persuasion). Preexposure brand preferences are obtained by reading a list of brands to respondents and asking which brand they are most likely to purchase next and the brand that they use most often. Postexposure brand preferences are obtained by asking respondents, within the context of a prize drawing for a certain amount of a product in a given category, to select the brand they would most like to win. A comparison of these two pre- and postexposure levels is interpreted to indicate the commercial's persuasiveness and is evaluated in terms of Apex persuasion norms. As with Recall Plus, persuasion is assessed after a single exposure.

ASI is unique in two respects. First, it offers an advertiser the option of assessing either a commercial's recall or both recall and persuasion. Second, the use of comparable but different samples for measures of recall and persuasion helps to reduce any bias from collecting both measures from a single sample of respondents.

Gallup & Robinson: InTeleTest   InTeleTest assesses consumers' reactions to television commercials when they appear in the context of a videotaped television program. Test commercials are embedded in an actual television pilot and distributed to respondents via VCR cassettes.

The sample for a typical InTeleTest survey is typically 150 men or 150 women aged 18 and older chosen from ten geographically dispersed metropolitan areas. Respondents are personally recruited at their homes under the guise of a study to measure television viewing habits. Each respondent is given a test cassette and is told that a follow-up telephone interview will take place the following day.

Data collection in an InTeleTest copy test proceeds as follows: Before viewing the program, a respondent completes a self-administered questionnaire that probes his or her television viewing habits. The respondent then views the cassette that contains additional instructions, the pilot program and test and control commercials embedded in the program. After viewing the cassette, the respondent completes a second self-administered questionnaire about the pilot program. The next day the respondent is recontacted and is asked questions relating to commercial recall, commercial communication, and reactions to the commercial.

The InTeleTest interview yields customized diagnostic information as well as four normative measures related to recall, communication, persuasion, and commercial reactions. Some measures are collected after a single exposure while others are collected after a second commercial viewing, as follows:

- *Intrusiveness* is defined as a commercial's ability to break through the clutter and communicate an advertiser or brand name. InTeleTest measures three levels of intrusiveness: (1) *Unaided Recall—Correct Brand* is the percentage of viewers who, when prompted by the product or subject category, claim to have seen the commercial and correctly identify the sponsor or brand name; (2) *Proved Unaided Recall* is the subset of the prior group who are also able to describe accurately the commercial; and (3) *Proved Brand Aided Recall* is the percentage of viewers who, aided by a company or brand name cue, can prove recall of the commercial. Recall measures are obtained after a single commercial viewing.

- *Communication* measures identify the ideas viewers take away from the commercial. InTeleTest measures two aspects of communication. The *Idea Communication Profile* reports the ideas or messages individuals can recall seeing or hearing in the commercial from the prior day's viewing. The most commonly recalled idea is identified as the *Lead Idea. Main Point Communication* reports the ideas or messages individuals can recall seeing or hearing after a second exposure to the commercial.

- *Persuasion* measures a commercial's ability to foster favorable attitudes toward the advertised product. Similar to measures of communication, InTeleTest measures two levels of persuasion. *Favorable Buying Attitude* measures purchase intent after a single exposure and reflects the percent of the sample who said that their interest in purchasing the product increased somewhat or considerably. *Brand Rating* is the percent of the sample who, after reexposure to the commercial, rate the brand excellent or very good (on a six-point scale with end-points of excellent and poor).

- *Commercial reaction* measures two aspects of consumers' affective responses to the commercial. *Commercial Liking* is measured on a five-point scale (with end points of "I liked it very much" to "I disliked it very much"). *Commercial Excellence* uses a four-point agree—disagree scale to measure agreement with the statement: "This commercial is one of the best I've seen recently."

Norms are available for all of the previously mentioned standard InTeleTest measures.

A sample (but hypothetical) InTeleTest commercial performance summary is shown in Figure 23.1 (page 566). The summary reports the raw data for each key measure as well as the InTeleTest norm for that measure. The data shown in Figure 23.1 indicate that the test commercial performed well. Measures of intrusiveness are all above the norm, communication is strong and consumers provided above norm favorable buying attitudes and brand ratings. These strong scores may be due, in part, to consumers' positive reactions to the commercial itself. Measures of commercial liking and commercial excellence were also above the InTeleTest norms.

30" SUPER SOUND AUDIO SPEAKERS
January 11–14, 1996

PERFORMANCE SUMMARY

	Men & Women	Norms
Intrusiveness		
Unaided Recall, Correct Brand	38%	31%
Proved Unaided Recall	24%	16%
Proved Brand Aided Recall	38%	24%
Communication		
Lead Idea	77%	67%
Main Point	42%	35%
Persuasion		
Favorable Buying Attitude (FBA)	52%	43%
Brand Rating[1]	69%	45%
Commercial Reaction		
Commercial Liking[2]	78%	58%
Best Commercial Seen Recently[3]	58%	48%

[1] Excellent/Very Good (6-point scale)
[2] Liked Very Much/Liked (5-point scale)
[3] Agree Completely/Somewhat (4-point scale)

NOTE: This performance summary is identical to the format followed by Gallup & Robinson. However, the brand, data, and norms are fictitious and are presented for illustrative purposes only.

FIGURE 23.1   Hypothetical data from a Gallup & Robinson InTeleTest commercial.

Mapes and Ross: On-Air Television Commercial Evaluation System   Mapes and Ross measures commercial effectiveness and consumers' reactions to commercials within the context of an actual broadcast television program (generally a movie on a UHF or independent channel). Mapes and Ross recruits a sample of between 150 and 200 individuals to view a specific television program under the guise of television program evaluation. Respondents are told that their reactions to the program are the focus of the research.

The Mapes and Ross methodology focuses on the assessment of commercial per-

suasiveness. At the time of recruitment, Mapes and Ross obtains brand preferences in five product categories (including the category of the test commercial) using open-ended questioning. Open-ended, nondirective questions in a range of categories are used to reduce any potential respondent sensitization to the test product or test commercial. The test commercial appears during the program the respondents are instructed to watch. The day following commercial exposure, each respondent is contacted by telephone and, after confirming program viewership, postexposure brand preferences are collected. The percentage shift from pre- to postexposure levels of brand preference is interpreted to represent a commercial's persuasiveness. (Thus, persuasiveness is evaluated after a single exposure.) Greater shifts in purchase intent from pre- to postexposure indicate greater levels of persuasiveness. Following preference questions, recall levels are obtained in response to category and brand prompts. All respondents who claim recall are questioned to determine the specific content of their recall. Norms are available to help interpret levels of recall and persuasion.

Similarities and Differences Among At Home, Quasi-Natural Copy Testing Methodologies

ASI, Gallup & Robinson, and Mapes and Ross evaluate consumers' responses to a television commercial when that commercial is viewed at home in the context of a television program. Moreover, all three companies provide measures of recall and persuasiveness and permit an advertiser to customize the interview to include additional diagnostic questions. In spite of these similarities, there are important differences in the three services.

First, the *context* in which the ad is seen varies in each of the three services. ASI and Gallup & Robinson maintain a consistent commercial environment, that is, the television program is consistent in all testing. Thus, ASI and Gallup & Robinson norms are based on the performance of other commercials tested under identical conditions. Mapes and Ross, by using actual broadcast television programs, varies commercial environment from test to test. As a result, Mapes and Ross' norms represent the performance of commercials tested in similar, but not identical, program environments. This is an important difference, especially given the fact that research has demonstrated that the program environment can affect commercial recall and communication as well as influence reactions to the commercial.[3]

Second, even though all three viewing situations have been classified as quasi-natural, there are, nevertheless, important differences. Mapes and Ross provides the most realistic of the three viewing situations. Respondents are exposed to the test commercial on a regularly scheduled program broadcast over air. Thus, the Mapes and Ross methodology comes closest to replicating actual marketplace viewing conditions. ASI's methodology is the next most realistic. Although the television program is not a regularly scheduled one, the commercial is still being broadcast on television. Gallup

---

[3] See Michael A. Kamins, Lawrence J. Marks, and Deborah Skinner, "Television Commercial Evaluation in the Context of Program Induced Mood: Congruency Versus Consistency Effects," *Journal of Advertising* 20 (1991): 1–14; David Schumann and Esther Thorson, "The Influence of Viewing Context on Commercial Effectiveness," In James H. Leigh and Claude R. Martin, Jr., eds., *Current Issues & Research in Advertising* (Ann Arbor, MI: University of Michigan School of Business Administration, 1990), 1–24; Marvin E. Goldberg and Gerald J. Gorn, "Happy and Sad TV Programs: How They Affect Reactions to Commercials," *Journal of Consumer Research* 14 (December 1987): 387–403.

& Robinson's VCR methodology is the least realistic of the three approaches. Although respondents are watching the program on their television, the program is being played from a video cassette. Viewing the program on videocassette may or may not replicate actual or original program viewing.

Third, the three services differ in their *control* over commercial exposure. The broadcast methodologies of ASI and Mapes and Ross ensure that the commercial is seen the appropriate (and same) number of times. The Gallup & Robinson methodology provides less control over commercial exposure. In spite of instructions to the contrary, there is little to prevent respondents from replaying the videocassette.

Finally, while each service collects information on commercial recall and persuasiveness, the methodologies used to collect this information are quite different. Persuasion in the ASI and Mapes and Ross methodologies reflects a comparison in pre- to postexposure brand preferences while Gallup & Robinson estimates persuasion on the basis of postexposure buying attitudes and brand ratings. Additionally, the number of exposures preceding the collection of recall and persuasion measures, as well as the amount of time elapsed since commercial viewing, varies among the three companies.

Out-Of-Home-Viewing—Quasi-Natural Viewing Situation

Research Systems Corporation: ARS Persuasion System   The ARS Persuasion system invites between 400 and 600 randomly selected adults (100 to 150 people in each of four geographically dispersed markets) to attend a screening of two television pilot programs. The screening is typically held in a convention center or large hotel ballroom. The viewing room is organized so that groups of twenty-five individuals are seated around a television monitor.

The ARS methodology is primarily designed to evaluate a commercial's persuasiveness. The evening begins with an introduction from a Master of Ceremonies who explains that the purpose of the evening is to obtain reactions to two pilot television programs. Respondents are then told that a lottery will be held to reward some of those who have come to participate. Lottery winners will receive a prize basket. However, to make certain that lottery winners receive their preferred prizes, each participant is asked to indicate his or her brand preferences in a number of product categories. Several of the product categories relate to test commercials that have been embedded into the television pilots. Two pilot programs, each program containing one exposure of the test commercial, are then shown. After each program is viewed, respondents answer questions about the programs and the advertising (such as attitudes toward the advertising, communication, etc.). The evening ends with an announcement of another lottery. Once again, respondents are asked to indicate their brand preferences.

The ARS Persuasion measure reflects the shift in pre- to postadvertising exposure brand preferences. A greater percentage of individuals selecting the advertised brand at the end of the evening (versus the percentage at the beginning of evening, before exposure to the advertising) indicates that the ad was persuasive, that is, that individuals changed their brand preferences after seeing the commercial. An equal or lesser percentage of individuals selecting the advertised brand at the end of the evening indicates that the ad was not persuasive, that is, that individuals did not change their preferences or that their brand preferences moved away from the advertised brand after seeing the commercial. ARS provides norms to interpret the magnitude of pre- to postadvertising exposure brand preference shifts.

The ARS Persuasion system can also assess commercial recall, although these scores are typically used diagnostically as opposed to evaluatively. Recall data is collected three days following advertising exposure, at which time about half of the respondents who attended the screening are contacted by telephone. The ARS Related Recall Score represents the percentage of respondents claiming to have seen the commercial and who are able to provide some proof of recall by playback of commercial message or visuals.

McCollum Spielman Worldwide: Advertising Control for Television Advertising Control for Television (ACT) is McCollum Spielman's copy testing procedure. The ACT methodology is very similar to that of ARS.

ACT is primarily designed to evaluate a commercial's persuasiveness, although additional measures such as awareness, communication, and attitudes toward the advertising are also collected. ACT conducts its research in four regions in the country, generally recruiting about 100 respondents per location. Like ARS, respondents are recruited under the guise of television pilot program evaluation. Once respondents arrive at the test location, the evening proceeds similarly to that of ARS. Groups of about twenty-five individuals are seated around television monitors. An on-screen video host provides a standardized introduction and explains the agenda for the evening. Following this general introduction respondents answer demographic and brand usage questions. Then, a half-hour variety show containing the test commercial is shown. After program viewing, respondents provide written reactions to the program, unaided commercial recall, and copy recall. (Recall and communication are therefore assessed after a single exposure.) The test commercial is then shown to the group a second time, after which diagnostic and brand preference questions are asked. Similar to ARS, postadvertising exposure brand choice is determined by the brands respondents indicate that they want to win. The difference between pre- and postadvertising exposure brand choice is interpreted to be an indication of the commercial's persuasiveness. Norms are provided to help interpret shifts in pre- to postadvertising exposure brand preferences.

Similarities and Differences Between Out-of-Home, Quasi-Natural Copy Testing Methodologies

The two major out-of-home, quasi-natural television copy testing methodologies are very similar. Respondents are prerecruited to a group viewing situation under the guise of television program evaluation. Moreover, both systems are primarily designed to evaluate commercial effectiveness, which is measured by comparing pre- to postexposure brand preferences.

Although the ARS and ACT methodologies are similar, there is one important difference in terms of sample characteristics. ARS recruits a broad cross-section of respondents while ACT recruits respondents who meet the advertising's target audience definition.

Out-Of-Home-Viewing—Forced Viewing Situation

Four copy testing services evaluate advertising in an out-of-home setting using a forced viewing situation. These companies (Viewfacts, Quick-Tally Systems, Ortek

Data Systems, and Market Opinion Research) all use similar methodologies: testing is conducted at a central research facility; testing is conducted via a group interview; handheld interactive devices are used for data input; key measures relate to reactions to the advertising; responses to the advertising can be seen on a second by second basis and are available immediately after advertising exposure. The basic methodology used by these services is as follows.

A convenience sample of about 50 to 100 consumers is recruited. Respondents are told that they will spend approximately an hour viewing and discussing commercials. On arrival, each respondent is given a handheld electronic unit that he or she will use to indicate reactions to the advertising. A unit may have keys or a dial. Respondents are told to press the key or turn the dial to indicate their reactions throughout commercial viewing. Test commercials are shown after some practice exercises.

The hand-held devices send their data to a computer that computes a second by second average of the audience's reactions. After commercial viewing, these averages are superimposed over the commercial so that the audience (and the client) can instantly see the pattern of response. The playback of the commercial with the superimposed tally is used as a stimulus for further discussion. A moderator can stop the commercial at high or low points or at points in which there was a reversal in the pattern of response to probe the group for reasons underlying the observed response.

COPY TESTING OPTIONS FOR MAGAZINE ADVERTISING

Magazine advertising can be tested under the following three conditions:

1. It can be shown directly to the consumer by forced exposure.
2. It can be tested in the context of a prototype magazine before actual media placement.
3. It can be tested either before or after media placement in the context of an actual magazine.

The magazine copy testing methodologies that represent these conditions are

Characteristic	*Representative Research Company*
Forced exposure	Perception Research Services
Prototype magazine	McCollum Spielman Worldwide
Actual magazine	ASI Marketing Research
	Gallup & Robinson
	Mapes and Ross
	Roper Starch Worldwide

This section discusses the copy testing methodologies underlying each of these approaches.

Forced Exposure—Perception Research Services

Perception Research Services (PRS) measures consumers' responses to a print advertisement by using eye tracking and supplemental diagnostic questions. The procedure used by PRS for assessing reactions to a print ad is described next.[4]

---

[4] Perception Research Services has applied its methodology to a broad range of print materials, for example, print and outdoor advertisements and product packages.

Target audience respondents are recruited via mall-intercept at Perception Research Services mall-based locations across the United States. Once a respondent has been screened and qualified, he or she is taken to the PRS research facility.

An interview begins with a respondent viewing images projected on a large screen several feet away. The respondent examines each image at his or her own pace. As each image is examined, the respondent's eye movements are continuously tracked by a computer that records exactly where the respondent is looking at any given point in time and what portion of the image the respondent is viewing. After a respondent has finished looking at all images, he or she is reexposed to the test ad and is asked about his or her attitudes and opinions toward the ad and, when appropriate, product purchase intent. Responses to these questions help advertisers better understand a respondent's pattern of eye movements.

PRS eye-tracking data provides four key measures, as shown in Figure 23.2 (page 572). The measures are

1. *Percent Noting*—The percent of respondents who spent any time looking at a specific element.

2. *Percent Reading*—The percent of respondents who spent some time reading or examining a specific element.

3. *Percent Of Total Time*—The *average* percent of total viewing *time* spent reading or examining a specific element.

4. *Total Time in Seconds*—The absolute average number of seconds spent reading or examining a specific element.

The data shown in Figure 23.2 provides the following insights into consumers' response to the Feldene ad:

- There are likely to be problems with name recognition and main message communication. Few respondents noted or read the name/tag line or copy.

- The dominant focal point in the ad is the bar chart. Slightly more than half the time consumers' spent reading the ad was spent on this visual element.

PRS provides the following example of how eye-tracking measurements, combined with diagnostic verbal questions, helped to improve the effectiveness of a print advertisement.

TWBA created a print ad for Bombay Gin (see upper ad in Figure 23.3, page 573). PRS tested the ad using its eye-tracking methodology and found that readership of the ad below the visual was virtually nonexistent and that the Bombay bottle on the far right-hand side of the ad was being ignored by nine out of every ten readers. Consequently, main message communication and recall were very low. Questioning that followed ad exposure indicated that respondents found the ad to be confusing. Respondents did not understand the link between the visual, the artwork overall and the message. Based on these findings the agency made a number of major changes in the ad (see lower ad in Figure 23.3). These changes included increasing the size of the Bombay bottle and adding a headline that makes explicit the relationship between the action depicted in the artwork and the Bombay Gin bottle. A test of the revised ad showed significant increases in measures of attention-getting, memorability, motivation, and recall.

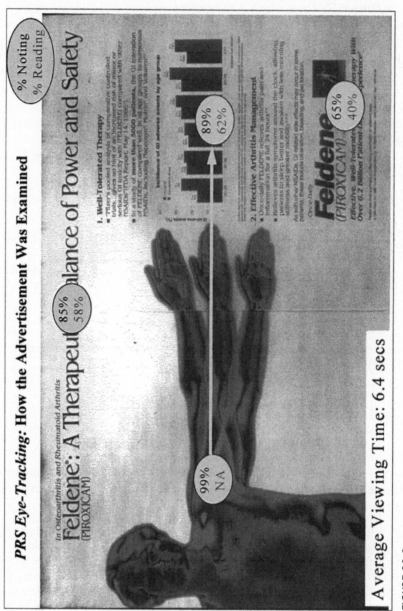

FIGURE 23.2
Presentation of PRS eye-tracking data.
Source: Perception Research Services. Reproduced with permission.

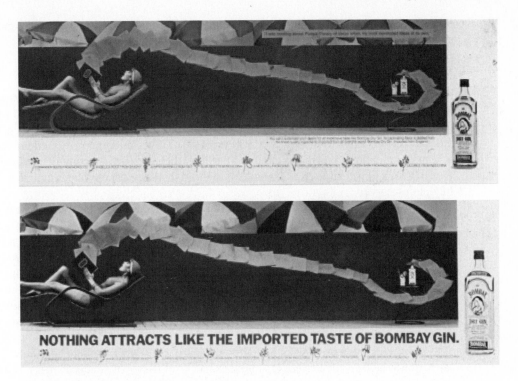

FIGURE 23.3
Initial and revised ads for Bombay Gin.
Source: Perception Research Services. Reproduced with permission.

Testing in Context of Prototype Magazine: McCollum Spielman Worldwide

AD*Vantage Print, McCollum Spielman's print testing methodology, uses a prototype issue of a magazine to test print advertising. Approximately 125 qualified respondents are recruited via mall-intercept and are invited to participate in a study exploring reactions to a new "pilot" magazine. The test ad is embedded in the magazine. Individuals agreeing to participate in the research are taken to the mall research facility for a one-to-one interview. AD*Vantage Print uses a sequence of three exposures to assess advertising effectiveness and consumers' reactions to the ad.

The interview begins with questions related to magazine readership and usage of various products and product categories. The prototype magazine is then given to the respondent, who is asked to flip quickly through the magazine and provide his or her initial reactions to the magazine. When the respondent has finished, unaided brand recall questions are asked to measure the "stopping power" of the ad, defined by AD*Vantage Print as an ad's ability to capture readers' attention and generate awareness. Respondents are then asked to look through the magazine again. After this second examination, a second unaided brand recall question, an unaided communication question and a persuasion/attitude shift question are asked. Finally, respondents are

specifically asked to read the test ad. Customized communication and diagnostic questions can be asked after this final exposure to the ad.

Testing in the Context of an Actual Magazine[5]

ASI: Print Plus   ASI Marketing Research measures consumers' reactions to magazine advertising via its Print Plus Methodology. Testing is typically conducted in five metropolitan areas with single gender samples of about 175 men or women or dual gender samples of 200 (100 men and 100 women). Target audience respondents are screened and, after qualification and recruitment, they are given a copy of the magazine in which the ad appears. Respondents are told that they are participating in a public opinion survey.

The Print Plus methodology is primarily designed to assess the persuasiveness of a print advertisement. The methodology is similar to that which ASI uses with television advertising. A short interview takes place when the magazine is given to a respondent. Within the context of a prize drawing, respondents are asked about attitudes toward and preferences for various brands. The next day each respondent is reinterviewed. Again, in the context of a prize drawing, respondents are asked about their brand preferences. As with other copy test pre- and postmeasures, a positive shift in brand preference is attributed to the persuasiveness of the advertising, in this case after a single exposure.

Print Plus' also provides a day after exposure interview to collect additional information to help an advertiser better understand an ad's level of persuasiveness. Brand cues are used to assess claimed recall and open-ended questions are used to measure communication. After these questions are asked, respondents are requested to review the test ad and complete an adjective checklist.

Gallup & Robinson: Rapid Ad Measurement (RAM)   The sample for a RAM test is typically 150 qualified readers of the magazine in which the ad appears. A qualified reader is an individual aged 18 or older who has read at least two of the last four issues of the test magazine or others in the same classification. Qualified readers are contacted at home by a continuous household canvas within five to ten SMSAs geographically dispersed across the United States.

Once a respondent is screened and selected, a magazine containing the test ad is placed in the respondent's home. Respondents are asked to read the magazine as they normally would that day or evening. No specific attention is drawn to the magazine's editorial or advertising content. The next day the respondent is recontacted and interviewed via telephone. (During this interview the respondent is not allowed to look at the magazine.) After preliminary questions to confirm issue readership, the interview focuses on advertising content. At this point, each respondent is read a roster of the ads being tested and is asked to indicate which of the ads he or she recalls seeing. For each ad a respondent claims to recall, he or she is asked a sequence of open-ended questions to determine recall of advertising content and reactions to the ad.

---

[5] Many of these companies also have the capability to test magazine ads using forced exposure or in the context of a prototype magazine.

The RAM test provides an advertiser with the following four key measures of advertising effectiveness:

1. *Proved Name Recognition* (PNR)—An index number that measures an ad's ability to break through the magazine's advertising clutter and communicate the advertiser's name. Proved Name Recognition is the percentage of readers who can provide recall, adjusted to reflect the test ad's size and color relative to a single-page four color ad.

2. *Idea Communication "Profile"*—A distribution of specific copy points recalled by the respondent and respondent's affective reactions to the ad. This measure is an indicator of the ideas communicated by the ad and feelings generated by the ad.

3. *Favorable Buying Attitude/Favorable Attitude* (FBA/FA)—A measure of purchase intent.

4. *Net Effectiveness*—The product of Proved Name Recognition (PNR) and Favorable Buying Attitude/Favorable Attitude (FBA/FA). Net Effectiveness is a summary measure of the ad's ability to intrude and persuade.

Mapes and Ross: Magazine Advertisement Evaluation System   The Mapes and Ross approach to respondent sampling and print advertising exposure is very similar to that of Gallup & Robinson. Respondents are prerecruited in person or by telephone and are screened for readership of the magazine category being tested. Qualified respondents are invited to read and give their reactions to the editorial content appearing in the current issue of the magazine. Those who agree to participate are given a copy of the magazine containing the test ad and are recontacted and interviewed the following day.

The Mapes and Ross methodology differs from that of Gallup & Robinson with respect to data collection methods and key measures. The key measure in the Mapes and Ross assessment of print advertising is persuasion. Persuasion is measured beginning at the time of recruitment when brand preference in the target and five other product categories is collected. The inclusion of additional categories is done to provide a masking effect. Questioning in this preexposure interview is nonadvertising or brand specific. Respondents are recontacted the next day and, after confirming readership, postexposure brand preference levels are obtained. The percentage shift from pre- to postexposure levels of preference is interpreted to represent an ad's persuasiveness. As with other pre- and postmethodologies, greater shifts in purchase intent from pre- to postexposure are interpreted to indicate greater levels of persuasiveness.

Roper Starch Worldwide: Roper Readership Reports   Starch Readership Reports report the extent to which consumers notice and read ads in selected issues of consumer, business, trade, and professional magazines. The research is similar to Gallup & Robinson's RAM in that Starch measures consumers' reactions to the advertising within its natural context—the magazine selected by the advertiser. Starch's methodology and key measures, however, are significantly different from those of Gallup & Robinson's RAM.

Starch assesses consumer response to nearly all advertisements appearing within a specific issue of a magazine. A Starch magazine sample consists of 100 individuals who satisfy the age, gender, and occupation requirements for a particular publication

and who have glanced at or read some part of the magazine before the start of the interview. (If there is any doubt whether the issue had been read, no interview is conducted.) Once issue readership is established the respondent is interviewed (face to face) to determine advertisement readership. The interviewer takes out a copy of the magazine and then turns the pages of the publication asking about each advertisement being studied. (Interviews are structured so that the questions asked about each advertisement appear with equal frequency toward the beginning, middle, and end of the interview. This is done to reduce any bias due to order effects.) Three key measures for each ad are obtained from the question sequence.

1. *Noted Reader*—The percent of issue readers who remember having previously seen the advertisement.
2. *Associated Reader*—The percent of issue readers who not only "Noted" the advertisement but also saw or read the parts of the ad that communicate the brand or advertiser.
3. *Read Most Reader*—The percent of issue readers who read half or more of the written material in the ad.

The interview ends with the collection of classification data.

Starch presents the results of advertising performance in several ways. First, each studied ad in the test issue is labeled to indicate overall readership levels as well as the noting or reading of the major components of the ad, for example, illustrations, headlines, signatures, and copy blocks. Second, several summary reports are constructed.

- *Ranking Reports* list the top ten ads in the issue in terms of Noted Score, Associated Score, and Read Most/Noted Ratio.
- *Category Summary Reports* show the Noted, Associated, and Read Most percentages for each ad within a particular product category. The data shown in Figure 23.4 show the performance of Computer and Data Processing ads on these measures. Arranging the ads by product category makes it convenient for advertisers to compare directly the readership levels of their ads to the ads of their competitors.
- *Readership Index Reports* are also arranged by category (see Figure 23.5, page 578). These reports compare each ad's readership performance against the issue median (where the issue median readership percentage is assigned an index of 100). Readership indices permit an advertiser to quickly compare ad performance to the average ad performance in the magazine. Indices over 100 indicate greater than average issue readership, indices below 100 indicate below average issue readership.[6]

The ability to compare consumers' reactions to ads in the same and past issues of a magazine is the core strength of Starch readership data. The types of comparisons most frequently carried out entail comparing: current ads to competitors ads in the same issue, current ads and campaigns against Starch norms, current campaigns to previous campaigns, and current campaigns to competitors' prior campaigns. With the data provided by these types of comparisons, advertisers can begin to look for recurring factors that distinguish high readership ads and campaigns from those with low readership.

---

[6] An ad with an index of 150, for example, means that ad obtained a score 50 percent above the issue median (and is, as a result, a strong ad), while an ad with an index of fifty means that ad obtained a score 50 percent below the issue median (and is, as a result, a weak ad).

[2A] **Fortune**   **STARCH READERSHIP**

October 17, 1994
Readers
Total of 84 1/2 Page or Larger Ads

PAGE	SIZE & COLOR	ADVERTISER	RANK By Noted	RANK By Associated	PERCENTAGES Noted	PERCENTAGES Assoc.	PERCENTAGES Read Some	PERCENTAGES Read Most
		COMPUTERS/DATA PROCESSING EQUIP.						
44	1S4B	IBM COMPUTERS/AS400 ADVANCED SERIES	21	10	46	41	36	20
47	1P4B	HEWLETT-PACKARD PRINTERS/ LASERJET 4V	42	42	32	24	21	11
50	1P4	COMPUTER SCIENCES CORP GP	61	62	20	15	13	5
60	1S4B	APPLE COMPUTERS/POWER MACINTOSH	10	13	52	40	23-	15-
71	1P4	ZENITH DATA SYSTEMS COMPUTERS/Z-NOTEFLEX	34	32	37	30	27	11
82	1S4B	IBM CORP GP	5	4	59	51	34	13
102	1P4	TOSHIBA COMPUTERS/ T4700C SERIES PORTABLE	47	42	30	24	20	12
118	1S4	IBM CORP GP	39	32	33	30	27	13
127	1P4	WANG LABS INC GP	68	62	17	15	10	4
131	1P4B	DIGITAL EQUIPMENT CORP GP	36	40	35	26	12	3
152	1S4B	COMPAQ COMPUTERS/DESKPRO XL	27	16	42	38	30	18
156	H1/2S4B	ADVANTIS NETWORKING SERVICES	64	69	18	11	10	3
187	1P4	UNISYS CORP GP	57	59	23	16	16	5
212	1P2	BROTHER PRINTERS/HL-600 SERIES	50	41	28	25	20	12
		ENGINEERING/PROFESSIONAL SERV.						
107	1P4	WHEELABRATOR TECHNOLOGIES INC GP	62	59	19	16	12	9

[*] Less than 0.5%   [-] Fewer than 50 Words   [**] Not Applicable   [=] Fewer than 4 Words   [#] Page/Copy Varies
[++] Not Available   [+] All Ads for Size/Color Used as Base

Roper Starch Worldwide Inc.

FIGURE 23.4
Starch Category Summary Report.
Source: Roper Starch Worldwide. Used with permission.

SUMMARY REPORT   Fortune   [2B]

October 17, 1994
Readers
Total of 84 1/2 Page or Larger Ads

	INDEX				RATIOS			ADNORM INDEX		
ADVERTISER	Noted	Assoc.	Read Some	Read Most	Assoc./ Noted	Read Some/ Noted	Read Most/ Noted	Noted	Assoc.	Read Most
COMPUTERS/DATA PROCESSING EQUIP.										
IBM COMPUTERS/AS400 ADVANCED SERIES	131	152	164	200	89	78	43	102	103	143
HEWLETT-PACKARD PRINTERS/ LASERJET 4V	91	89	95	110	75	66	34	89	77	100
COMPUTER SCIENCES CORP GP	57	56	59	50	75	65	25	56	48	45
APPLE COMPUTERS/POWER MACINTOSH	149	148	105-	150-	77	44	29	116	100	**
ZENITH DATA SYSTEMS COMPUTERS/Z-NOTEFLEX	106	111	123	110	81	73	30	103	97	100
IBM CORP GP	169	189	155	130	86	58	22	131	128	93
TOSHIBA COMPUTERS/ T4700C SERIES PORTABLE	86	89	91	120	80	67	40	83	77	109
IBM CORP GP	94	111	123	130	91	82	39	73	75	93
WANG LABS INC GP	49	56	45	40	88	59	24	47	48	36
DIGITAL EQUIPMENT CORP GP	100	96	55	30	74	34	9	97	84	27
COMPAQ COMPUTERS/DESKPRO XL	120	141	136	180	90	71	43	93	95	129
ADVANTIS NETWORKING SERVICES	51	41	45	30	61	56	17	51+	37+	21+
UNISYS CORP GP	66	59	73	50	70	70	22	64	52	45
BROTHER PRINTERS/HL-600 SERIES	80	93	91	120	89	71	43	108+	109+	150+
ENGINEERING/PROFESSIONAL SERV.										
WHEELABRATOR TECHNOLOGIES INC GP	54	59	55	90	84	63	47	46	48	75

[*] Less than 0.5%   [-] Fewer than 50 Words   [**] Not Applicable   [=] Fewer than 4 Words   [#] Page/Copy Varies
[++] Not Available   [+] All Ads for Size/Color Used as Base

Roper Starch Worldwide Inc.

FIGURE 23.5
Starch Readership Index Report.
Source: Roper Starch Worldwide. Used with permission.

EVALUATING ALTERNATIVE COPY TESTING METHODOLOGIES

Advertisers have a number of very different options for copy testing their television or print advertising. Each option has its own set of proponents and detractors and each has its own unique set of strengths and weaknesses. However, when evaluating the relative appropriateness of alternative copy testing methodologies for a particular piece of advertising, we recommend that the following be kept in mind:[7]

1. The closer a methodology is to "real world" exposure, the more accurately the results will reflect "real world" advertising performance and consumer response.

2. The ability to collect different types of information after different numbers of exposures permits an advertiser to evaluate better a commercial's long- and short-term potential.

3. Respondents are more likely to provide "real world" responses to commercials when they are not aware that they are participating in copy testing research.

4. Multiple measures and diagnostics provide a multifaceted look at commercial performance. Therefore, methodologies that provide multiple measures are generally more informative and useful to an advertiser versus those that provide a single measure.

5. Among copy testing methodologies, measures with the same name may not have the same underlying data collection methodology. Thus, it is important to be aware of the methodology underlying the collection of data for a specific measure. Different methodologies, for example, measure persuasion very differently. The preferred methodology for any particular copy test is the one whose approach to measurement best corresponds to the advertiser's view of how the commercial is intended to affect the target consumer.

6. Norms must be current and appropriate to the product and product category shown in the commercial. An advertiser should never "make do" with norms that are either outdated or not directly related to the advertised product.

7. Methodological validity and reliability are important. Only those copy testing methodologies that can empirically demonstrate acceptable levels of reliability and validity should be considered.

COPY TESTING FROM A LEGAL PERSPECTIVE[8]

The Federal Trade Commission (FTC) is taking a more active role in monitoring and challenging advertising claims believed to be legally deceptive. According to the FTC, an advertisement is legally deceptive when it displays the following three characteristics:[9]

1. The ad makes a representation, has an omission, or uses a practice that is likely to mis-

---

[7] Several of these guidelines are adapted from Joel Axelrod, *Choosing the Best Advertising Alternative: A Management Guide to Identifying the Most Effective Copy Testing Technique* (New York, NY: Association of National Advertisers, 1986); and PACT, *"Positioning Advertising Copy Testing"* (1982).

[8] For simplicity, we discuss copy test design in the context of an FTC challenge. However, the discussion applies not only to FTC challenges, but also to state advertising challenges and Lanham Act challenges (where one advertiser directly sues another advertiser.)

[9] Federal Trade Commission, "Policy Statement on Deception," 45 *ATRR* (October 27, 1983): 689–90.

lead the consumer. The representation, omission, or practice may be explicit or implied in the advertising. Additionally, the ability of an ad to mislead a consumer does not have to be directly attributable to specific elements in the ad. A consumer can be misled by the overall net impression left by an ad.

2. The representation, omission, or practice is misleading when examined from the perspective of a reasonable consumer.

3. The representation, omission or practice is "material." The FTC evaluates the extent to which the representation, omission, or practice influences consumer behavior or purchasing patterns. A representation, omission, or practice is material when behaviors or purchasing patterns are affected.

Advertising copy tests represent an important form of evidence offered in support of or in opposition to FTC claims of deceptiveness. The FTC has utilized its own copy tests to assess the validity of its challenges to particular advertisements. Advertisers have used copy tests to counter FTC challenges.[10] Both advertisers and the FTC use copy tests because copy test data responds to an FTC preference for objective, external data. The FTC has stated that

> The extrinsic evidence we prefer to use and to which we give great weight is direct evidence of what consumers actually thought upon reading the advertisement in question. Such evidence will be in the form of consumer survey research for widely distributed ads . . .[11]

However, while the FTC has shown a predisposition to rely on copy test data in support of an argument or position, it has also shown a great willingness to discard and ignore copy test findings that result from research that is deficient in methodological planning, execution, or data reporting. An FTC evaluation of the soundness of a copy test addresses the following areas:

• universe definition and sample selection

• research design and use of control groups

• questionnaire design and question formats

• interviewer qualifications, training, and techniques

• data analysis and presentation

• research project administration

The remainder of this section presents guidelines for copy test planning and administration in each of these areas. Adherence to these guidelines can substantially increase the likelihood of FTC acceptance of copy test findings.[12]

---

[10] Copy tests conducted by advertisers are generally designed to address the first and third characteristics of deceptiveness, that is, to demonstrate that the representation, omission, or practice is not misleading and/or that even if it is misleading, it is not material.

[11] *Federal Trade Commission v Thompson Medical Co. Inc.*, 104 FTC 648, Affirmed 791 F2d 189 (D.C. Circ 1986).

[12] This section discusses methodological issues in the context of copy test research. However, these methodological guidelines can be generalized to apply to all research conducted in response to regulatory or legal challenges. The discussion in this section draws from the following sources: Jacob Jacoby and George J. Szybillo, "Consumer Research in FTC Versus Kraft (1991): A Case of Heads We Win, Tails You Lose?" *Journal of Public Policy & Marketing* 14 (1995): 1–14; David W. Stewart, "Deception, Materiality, and Survey Research: Some Lessons From Kraft," *Journal of Public Policy & Marketing* 14 (1995): 15–28; J. Craig Andrews and Thomas J. Maron-

Universe Definition and Sample Selection

Copy test research findings are only acceptable when they reflect the opinions and behaviors of appropriate individuals, typically defined as individuals who are relevant to the advertising's underlying strategy, objectives, and target audience. The FTC has criticized and rejected research that included respondents who should not have been included in the sample frame and/or that failed to sample from the universe of all relevant consumers.[13] This is because "the central question in any deceptive advertising matter is: What percent of the relevant population have been misled? When members of the relevant population have been excluded and persons who are not members of that population included, this all important question cannot be answered."[14] Thus, the psychographic, demographic, and behavioral characteristics of the advertising's target definition must *all* be reflected in the definition of the copy test sample universe.

Once the sample universe has been defined, individuals from that universe must be identified and recruited in a methodologically sound and defensible manner. Care must be taken to ensure the following:

- *The sample size is reasonable given the required degree of accuracy.* Sample sizes of about 100 individuals per test condition are generally acceptable.

- *The sampling plan does not appear to be biased toward any viewpoint or opinion group.* Imagine, for example, an appropriate sample universe definition of "purchasers of Brand X within the past thirty days." It would be inappropriate to sample from a list of past thirty-day purchasers who were dissatisfied with the product and who used the product guarantee to return the product for a refund. These individuals are clearly biased against the product and are not representative of all product purchasers. A sample of these individuals would result in a biased sample that is not generalizable to the population specified in the sample universe definition and is therefore likely to be rejected.[15]

- *The sampling is reasonable and meets accepted industry practice.* While probability sampling is always preferable over convenience sampling, the FTC has shown a willingness to accept the results of copy tests conducted among individuals recruited by mall-intercept interviews[16] *provided* that the distribution and location of the malls are reasonable given product distribution and advertising scheduling. The malls must be located where the advertising has run.[17]

---

ick, "Advertising Research Issues From FTC Versus Stouffer Foods Corporation," *Journal of Public Policy & Marketing* 14 (1995): 301–27; Ivan L. Preston, "The Scandalous Record of Avoidable Errors in Expert Evidence Offered in FTC and Lanham Act Deceptiveness Cases," *Journal of Public Policy & Marketing* 11 (1992): 57–67; Thomas J. Maronick, "Copy Tests in FTC Deception Cases: Guidelines for Researchers," *Journal of Advertising Research* 31 (December 1991): 9–17; Fred Morgan, "Judicial Standards for Survey Research: An Update and Guidelines," *Journal of Marketing* 54 (1990): 59–70.

[13] See, for example, *Stouffer Foods Corp*, " Initial Decision Findings of Fact (Section 1–196) and Initial Decision Discussion," FTC Docket No. 9250 (May 21, 1993): 1–78; *Jovan, Inc. v Garan, Inc.*, No. 81-C-0347, Slip Op. (N.D. Ill, December 12, 1985); *Safeway Stores, Inc. v Safeway Insurance Co.*, 657 F. Supp 1307 (D. La 1985); *Thompson Medical Company, Inc.*, 104 FTC 648–844 (1984) and *Amstar Corp. v Domino's Pizza, Inc.*, 615 F2d 252 (5th Circuit 1980).

[14] Jacoby and Szybillo, "Consumer Research in FTC Versus Kraft," 4.

[15] This example is based on *Smith v Strum, Ruger & Co. Inc.*, 39 Washington App. 740, 695 P. 2d 600 (1985).

[16] The FTC in *Thompson Medical* (1984, CD at p. 794–795) noted that the use of mall-intercept designs are acceptable because this type of sampling is a generally accepted method for advertising copy test research. In addition, the use of forced exposure in a mall setting has also been accepted because it directly focuses consumers' attention on the advertising's explicit and implicit messages. [*Bristol-Myers Co., 85 FTC 1975*].

[17] Ibid., 688.

Research Design and Use of Control Groups

As discussed earlier, the FTC makes a determination of deception based on what consumers "take away" from an advertisement (that is, the messages consumers explicitly or implicitly receive) and the materiality of the communication. Consequently, one crucial goal of a copy test performed in the context of an FTC challenge is the accurate determination of *what* is communicated by an ad and the *importance* of that communication in affecting consumer brand preference or brand choice.

Consumers, however, are not "blank slates." They bring a broad array of pre-existing knowledge and attitudes to the advertising viewing situation. Consequently, a copy test must be designed in a way that permits one to distinguish what consumers *already* think and feel from what they *specifically learned* from an advertisement.

The FTC has responded favorably to copy test designs that use control groups to help distinguish prior knowledge from knowledge acquired as the direct result of advertising exposure. Typically, a posttest only with control group design is used (see page 149) because a pretest-posttest with control design (see text pages 149–150) has the potential to sensitize respondents and thus bias how they view the advertising and answer postexposure questions. An advertiser has several options as to the nature of the control group within the posttest only with control group design.

One option is to define the control group as a *nonexposure* group. Here, the control group does not see any advertising while the test group is exposed to the disputed advertising. Data analysis in this design assumes that given random assignment to control and experimental groups, differences in knowledge and attitudes between the control and test group can be directly related to the independent variable, the contested advertising.

The no exposure control group approach works well when the advertising has had limited marketplace exposure. However, when the disputed ad has had significant exposure, the problem of distinguishing communication *from the advertising* versus *from existing attitudes* becomes more complex. The beliefs expressed by the no exposure group may have been influenced by their having already seen the advertising. Thus, if no differences are observed between the control and exposure groups, it is unclear whether this absence of difference is due to a lack of communication by the test ad *or* due to the fact that prior exposure to the advertising has caused individuals in both the control and test groups to have acquired the same knowledge and attitudes, therefore resulting in little incremental effect from *additional* exposure to the advertising.[18]

There are three methods for distinguishing existing knowledge and attitudes from knowledge and attitudes formed after exposure to an advertisement in situations where the advertising has had substantial exposure before the copy test.

One approach uses an experimental design in which one group is exposed to the advertising with the potentially deceptive elements and a second group is exposed to the same advertising in which the potentially deceptive elements have been eliminated. Differences in outcomes between groups are attributed to the presence or absence of

---

[18] The FTC has explicitly taken the position that a 'no exposure' condition is inappropriate when the advertising has had significant exposure prior to the copy test. It has stated that the comparison of nonexposure and test group responses is impractical in cases where "a limited number of consumers in the universe [are] not . . . previously exposed to the challenged ads." See *Kraft, Inc.*, IDF 149.

the identified and manipulated commercial elements. This approach works well when the deceptive practice or claim can be attributed to only a few specific elements in the ad. However, in situations in which almost everything in the ad is part of a challenged claim, a revised "cleansed" ad would be difficult to use because it would require the deletion of almost all the ad elements. When this occurs, it could be argued that resulting executional differences between the two ads were the primary reason for observed differences.[19]

A second approach exposes a test group to the disputed advertising and a control group to a modified version of the disputed ad. Differences in outcomes between the test and control groups are attributed to the difference between exposure to the original versus modified advertising claim. Russo, Metcalf, and Stephens,[20] who proposed this design, argue that this approach works best in cases where advertisers appear to be exploiting consumers preexisting beliefs toward a particular brand or product.

A third approach exposes a test group to the disputed advertising and a control group to other similar, but nondisputed, advertising for the brand. The ideal control ad is an ad from a different campaign that displays executional similarities to the test ad. This approach is suggested whenever it is believed that significant exposure to the disputed advertising (before the copy test) has the potential to result in a "halo" effect, that is, when consumers are likely to attribute information obtained from prior viewing of the disputed ad to a modified version of that ad. As with the prior design, differences in outcomes between test and control groups are attributed to the exposure to the potentially deceptive elements.

The FTC, in a test of Kraft Singles cheese advertising, used a combination of these approaches. The FTC challenged Kraft Singles cheese advertising that stated that one slice of cheese was made from five glasses of milk. The FTC challenged the ad because it believed that the ad implied that one slice of cheese had the same calcium content as five glasses of milk, which it did not. (One slice of cheese has only 70% the calcium content of five ounces of milk.) [21] The FTC copy test used five cells and was structured to account for extensive advertising exposure before the copy test.

> Cells one and two were exposed to the TV versions of "Skimp" (the contested ad). The only difference was the presence of wording superimposed on commercial 2: "Milk amounts based on cheese content. One-¾ ounces slice has 70% of the calcium of five ounces of milk." Cell 3 (TV-control) viewed another Kraft Singles TV commercial that said nothing about milk or calcium and was not in dispute. Respondents exposed to the Skimp print advertisement (Cell 4) were contrasted to a control group (Cell 5) exposed to another Kraft print advertisement that did not mention milk or calcium. Respondents in each cell followed identical patterns of advertising exposure and responded to identical interview protocols.[22] In terms of the television commercials, a comparison of Cells 1 and 2 indicated the effects of modifying the disputed claim while a comparison of Cells 1 and 3 indicated responses to the disputed versus a nondisputed ad for the same product.

In sum, the presence of a control group greatly increases the strength of copy test

---

[19] Andrews and Maronick, "Advertising Research Issues," 306.

[20] Edward J. Russo, Barbara L. Metcalf, and Debra Stephens, "Identifying Misleading Advertising," *Journal of Consumer Research* 8 (September 1981): 119–31.

[21] Jacoby and Szybillo, "Consumer Research in FTC Versus Kraft," 2.

[22] Jacoby and Szybillo, "Consumer Research in FTC Versus Kraft," 4.

results. However, given the options for control group designs, a researcher must be able to justify clearly and explicitly the characteristics of the control group, that is, whether the control group is not exposed to any advertising, exposed to a modified version of the disputed ad, or exposed to a similar (but not disputed) ad for the same product.

Finally, it is important to note that even the use of a control group cannot redeem a copy test viewed as using a contrived or deceptive research design. Research perceived in this way, in which the results are considered an *artifact* of the research design, is not only ignored, but is often held against the individuals or company offering the research.[23]

Questionnaire Design and Question Formats

The legitimacy and acceptability of copy test data is dependent on the survey methods used to collect that data. Copy test findings that report data collected by faulty questionnaires or flawed individual survey questions are quickly rejected. A researcher must make certain that questionnaire design and question wording are beyond reproach.

Questionnaire design and content should follow the generally accepted principles of survey research discussed throughout this text. At minimum, the questionnaire should

- *avoid biasing questions asked later in the survey by earlier questions.* This can often be accomplished by grouping questions on the same topic together and by completing one topic before moving onto another.
- *proceed, within any specific topic, from the most general questions to the most specific.* This is typically accomplished by using open-ended questions to begin a topic and then moving to a series of more focused closed-ended questions. This form of question progression works well because it permits respondents to provide "top-of-mind" answers without having been sensitized by the response options contained in later closed-ended questions.
- *reflect accepted industry procedures with regard to question sequence.* The Kraft cheese copy test used by the FTC measured "claimed recall" using a generally accepted sequence of product and brand cues:

Do you remember seeing an advertisement for cheese slices?
What brand was being advertised?
Do you remember seeing an advertisement for Kraft singles?[24]

- *be complete.* A survey that narrowly focuses on isolated parts of the advertising is likely to be rejected. Numerous advertisers have conducted copy tests in which reactions to isolated portions of the advertising were probed.[25] In *Coca-Cola v. Tropicana,*[26] con-

---

[23] Preston, ("Scandalous Record," 4) provides an example of a biased research design: "Sears, Roebuck and Co., advertised that its dishwasher could clean the dirtiest dishes, and pots and pans, with no prerinsing or prescraping . . . In its tests, Sears used hotter water . . . than most home water heaters can supply. It used more detergent than its instruction book told consumers to use. It rigged wash cycles to run longer than those on units sold to the public . . . It used lighter loads . . . including laying dishes flat . . . [and it] . . . did some tests with foods that are easy to clean, although the claims had been about foods that are the most difficult to clean." The FTC found the data obtained in this research worthless. [For additional information see *Sears Roebuck*, 49 FTC 263 1980.]

[24] Stewart, "Deception," 21.

[25] *Thompson Medical.*

[26] *Coca-Cola v Tropicana Products, Inc.*, 538 F Supp 1091 (SD NY 1982).

sumers were shown a commercial and were then asked for their responses. Several questions, however, focused *only* on communication and reactions to the *audio* portion of the commercial. These questions were rejected because they did not focus on the entire commercial.

Once the design and content of the questionnaire have been determined, it is then necessary to make certain that the questions themselves are written without bias. Maronick has observed that "probably the single greatest source of conflict in copy test research for litigation is whether individual questions are properly drafted to elicit rather than suggest answers."[27] Adherence to the guidelines presented in Chapter 13 can greatly reduce or prevent wording-related bias, especially with regard to the most frequently occurring problems where

- *the question lead-in may bias the respondent by not explicitly stating alternative response options.* Asking "How much better or worse do you think that the brand . . . " is less biased than "How much better do you think that the brand . . ."[28]

- *closed-ended questions do not contain an* **appropriate** *set of response options.* A set of response options that does not permit respondents to express their true opinion is likely to be rejected. Respondents in *American Home v. Johnson & Johnson* were shown an advertisement and were asked, using a closed-ended question, to pick which of five options reflected what was communicated in the ad. The question was rejected because none of the options reflected the literal meaning of the advertisement and two of the remaining options were clearly false. Additionally, a closed-ended question is likely to be found unacceptable if the available choices do not include options that a consumer would find reasonable.[29]

- *closed-ended questions do not contain the* **full** *range of response options.* It is important that the set of response options permits respondents to state clearly their opinion, rather than have to choose arbitrarily from a restricted set of options. For example, in seeking to determine purchase intention, instead of asking if the respondent intends to "continue buying" or "stop buying," one should assess the degree of intention by using a range of options such as "stop buying completely," "continue buying, but purchase significantly less," continue buying but purchase less," etc.[30]

Interviewer Qualifications, Training, and Techniques

The professionalism of the individuals who conduct the interviews and record respondents' comments and responses affects the integrity of copy test data. Real or perceived problems with the individuals who collect the data can cause the entire copy test to be discounted. It is important to demonstrate that interviewers have properly followed reasonable data collection procedures without error or bias. The problem of error can be minimized by

- providing interviewers with formal, systematic training in the procedures underlying the collection of data for the specific copy test,

---

[27] Maronick, "Copy Tests," 14.

[28] See Seymour Sudman, "When Experts Disagree: Comments on the Articles By Jacoby and Szybillo and Stewart," *Journal of Public Policy and Marketing* 14 (Spring 1995): 29–34.

[29] *Kraft* (1991).

[30] See Jacoby and Szybillo, "Consumer Research in FTC Versus Kraft," 8

- supporting training with written documentation,
- systematically monitoring the quality of interviews, correcting problems as soon as they are noted.

Problems of bias can be eliminated by making certain that

- interviewers do not know the name of the organization sponsoring the copy test or the purpose of the research project,
- interviewers are independent of all participants involved in the case,
- interviewer discretion and independent decision making are kept to a minimum. Interviewers should be given passive roles in the data collection process. Interviewer activities initiated at their discretion (e.g., clarifying question wording or question intent, engaging in casual small talk between questions, etc.) may be seen as providing the interviewer with the opportunity to lead, mislead, or bias respondents.[31]

Data Analysis and Presentation

The procedures for data reporting discussed in Chapter 4 apply to the presentation of copy test data. Data must be analyzed and presented in a fair, objective manner where assumptions underlying analytical techniques, decisions, and interpretations are "obvious and justifiable."[32] Standards for the analysis and reporting of closed-ended questions are so well established that problems with this type of data are almost always instantly recognizable, for example, when inappropriate manipulations of the data have been performed or when data reporting is selective or incomplete.[33] More ambiguity exists in the treatment of responses to open-ended questions.

The FTC scrutinizes the treatment of responses to open-ended questions (verbatims) and is quick to reject treatments of these responses that appear inherently biased, self-serving, or arbitrary. The likelihood of these negative perceptions occurring can be reduced by

- providing an explicit description of the rules governing verbatim coding;
- developing coding categories and labels that in an unbiased manner reflect the true nature of consumers' responses;
- coding and reporting all verbatims. Any appearance of bias due to selection must be avoided;
- distinguishing between first versus subsequent responses to each open-ended question;
- providing a complete, unedited transcript of all verbatims (to facilitate a determination of the appropriateness and completeness of coding).

Research Project Administration

The value and acceptability of copy test research findings are always evaluated in light of the experience and expertise of the individuals and companies who planned, con-

---

[31] *AmBrit, Inc. v Kraft, Inc.*, 805 F2d 488 (Ind App 1986).

[32] Morgan, "Judicial Standards," 67.

[33] *Federal Trade Commission v Brown & Williamson*, 580 F Supp 981 1983; *Ragold v. Ferrero*, 506 F Supp 117 1980.

ducted, and analyzed the research. Experience and competence count in all aspects of the copy test. Thus, it is recommended that

- the individual responsible for study design and administration be recognized as an expert in survey research in general and advertising copy research in particular. This expertise should be the result of practical experience. The FTC has shown a tendency to criticize an academic witness or consultant when that individual has lacked practical experience in conducting advertising or copy research outside the classroom.
- the companies responsible for data collection have extensive experience and industry-recognized expertise in the collection of survey information in general and copy testing information in particular.
- the individuals responsible for survey administration have demonstrated experience in the collection of survey data.
- the individuals responsible for data coding and analysis have demonstrated experience and expertise in these areas.

The presence of experience and expertise is a necessary, but not sufficient basis for copy test acceptance. It must be demonstrated that this expertise was used to design and supervise a copy test that is without internal bias or error. Consequently, it is recommended that

- the individual responsible for the design and administration of the research continuously and closely monitor all steps in the research project. The case of *Toys R Us v. Canarsie* illustrates the danger of what happens when this is not done.

   The research administrator in the case "hired several other firms to assist with validation, coding, and data analysis. The administrator (later) testified that he did not know whether these forms instructed their employees properly or whether these people actually followed recommended procedures. The court concluded that the survey did not satisfy the trustworthiness criterion and (as a result) was not admissible."[34]

- the individual responsible for the design and administration of the research act without interference or direction from attorneys. The involvement of attorneys in the design of a copy test or other research study is almost always viewed with a great deal of suspicion.

Summary

Copy tests help advertisers determine whether to run an advertisement in the marketplace. As such, copy tests differ from communication tests because they are (1) evaluative rather than diagnostic, (2) typically conducted with finished advertising, (3) generally conducted by specialized research companies, and (4) have norms against which test scores can be compared.

The copy testing of television advertising is the most common form of copy testing. Approaches to television copy testing can be described in terms of four dimensions: (1) the place where the advertising is seen, (2) the naturalness of the viewing situation, (3) the number of advertising exposures, and (4) key measures.

---

[34] Morgan, "Judicial Standards," 67 discussing *Toys R Us, Inc. v Canarsie Kiddie Shop, Inc.*, 559 F Supp 1189 (SD NY 1983).

- Three research companies (ASI Marketing Research, Gallup & Robinson, and Mapes and Ross) conduct their television tests in an at home, quasi-natural viewing situation. However, although all three companies provide recall and persuasion measures derived from exposure in this context, there are nevertheless important differences in methodology and the operationalization of key measures.
- Two research companies conduct their television copy tests in an out-of-home, quasi-natural viewing situation. Sampling in these two approaches differs, although the basic methodologies and measurements are very similar.
- Four research companies (Viewfacts, Ortek Data Systems, Quick-Tally Systems, and Market Opinion Research) conduct copy tests in an out-of-home, forced viewing situation. The methodological approaches of all four companies are similar.

Magazine copy tests are conducted under three conditions. The first condition is forced exposure. The eye-tracking system used by Perception Research Services is representative of the first approach. The second condition tests the ad in the context of a prototype magazine prior to actual media placement. Ad*Vantage Print (McCollum Spielman Worldwide) is representative of this approach. The third condition tests the ad in the context of an acutal magazine. Print Plus (ASI), Rapid Ad Measurement (RAM), Magazine Advertisement Evaluation System (Mapes and Ross), and Starch (Roper Starch Worldwide) are representative of this third approach. As with television copy tests, different services collect similarly named measurements, although the underlying methodologies and operational definitions differ.

Advertisers also conduct copy tests in response to regulatory or other legal challenges. Advertisers use copy tests to defend themselves against claims of deception while regulatory bodies, such as the FTC, use copy tests to demonstrate the deceptiveness of an advertisement. Copy test data is accorded significant weight in cases of disputed claims if the copy test research meets high standards of planning, administration, and analysis. The FTC and the courts evaluate the acceptability of a copy test and the merit of that test's findings in terms of six broad areas:

- universe definition and sample selection
- research design and use of control groups
- questionnaire design and question formats
- interviewer qualifications, training, and techniques
- data analysis and presentation
- research project administration

Perceived deficiencies in any of these areas can cause the research findings to be discounted or rejected.

Review Questions

1. In what important ways does copy testing differ from communication testing?
2. What four dimensions can be used to classify approaches to television copy testing? Briefly describe each dimension.
3. What are the key measures in ASI Marketing Research Recall Plus and Apex? Briefly describe how data for each measure are collected.

4. What are the key measures in Gallup & Robinson's InTeleTest? Briefly describe how data for each measure are collected.

5. What are the key measures in Mapes and Ross On-Air Television Evaluation System? Briefly describe how data for each measure are collected.

6. In what ways can one compare and contrast the methodological approaches of at home, quasi-natural copy testing methodologies?

7. What are the key measures in the ARS Persuasion System? Briefly describe how data for each measure are collected.

8. What are the key measures in McCollum Spielman's ACT? Briefly describe how data for each measure are collected.

9. In what three formats can magazine advertising be copy tested?

10. What methodology does Perception Research Services use to evaluate consumer response to print advertising? What are the key measures in this system and how are they collected?

11. What are the key measures in McCollum Spielman's Ad*Vantage Print? Briefly describe how data for each measure are collected.

12. Compare and contrast the procedures used by ASI, Gallup & Robinson, Mapes and Ross, and Roper to copy test magazine advertising. In what ways are the key measures from each system similar or different?

13. What considerations should be noted when evaluating alternative approaches to copy testing television or print advertising?

14. What three characteristics must an ad display to be considered legally deceptive?

15. What are the key areas in which the FTC or other legal body evaluates the soundness of copy test findings?

16. How can a researcher ensure that universe definition and sample selection are appropriate?

17. Why are control groups important in copy test research conducted to meet a legal challenge? What control group options are available to a researcher? What is the most appropriate use of each option?

18. How can a researcher ensure that questionnaire design and question format are acceptable?

19. How can a researcher improve perceptions of the soundness of data collection procedures?

20. How should verbatims be treated when conducting copy test research to meet a legal challenge?

21. What are important considerations in copy test research administration?

Application Exercises

1. This exercise will help you understand how changes in commercial viewing situations and the naturalness of the viewing situation affect measures of commercial recall. You will work on this project with others in your class to facilitate the administration and analysis of sixty completed interviews conducted among college students.

   You will have four test conditions. Individuals in each condition (fifteen individuals per condition) will view the same commercial as it appears within the same television program. You must identify the program in advance of the research. The program should be one that your target audience of college students is likely to watch.

Select the program about one week in advance of its airing and then do the following:

Group 1: Recruit fifteen individuals to watch the program. Tell them that you are conducting research on their television viewing habits. You will interview these individuals the day after the program airs.

Group 2: Recruit fifteen individuals. Tell them that you are conducting research on their television viewing habits. Ask them not to watch any programs on the night the target program airs. However, request that they videotape the target program. Request individuals in this group to watch the video the following day. You will interview these individuals the day after they view the video tape.

Group 3: The day after the program airs randomly telephone college students. Identify fifteen who watched the target program. Tell them that you are conducting research on their television viewing habits and conduct your interview. Do not contact these people before the program airing.

Group 4: Tape record the target program. Recruit fifteen individuals and instruct them not to watch television the night the program airs. However, instruct them to come to a classroom to watch a television program a day or two after the program airs. Tell them that you are conducting research on their television viewing habits. Show them the video of the program and conduct the interview the following day.

You will need to select one of the commercials shown in the program to be your test commercial. You can then customize the questionnaire shown in Figure 23.6 for the commercial selected and the specific characteristics of each viewing group.

Analyze the collected data after all interviews have been completed. Pay particular attention to how you define "recall." Does the questionnaire permit you to define different types or levels of "recall?" After your analysis of the data prepare a short paper that describes

- the characteristics of each group,
- the copy testing methodology each group reflects,
- the effects of viewing situation and naturalness on advertising recall.

Conclude your paper with a discussion of the implications of your findings for the measurement and interpretation of recall measures. Be certain to provide a point of view on the strengths and weaknesses of each approach and the approach you would recommend.

2. As discussed in this chapter, different copy testing methodologies use different procedures for assessing the persuasiveness of an advertisement. This exercise is designed to help you determine how different approaches to measuring persuasion can result in different outcomes. Again, you will work with others in your class to complete sixty interviews.

Videotape a television program. Select one commercial in that program to be your test advertisement. Next, create four different ways to assess the persuasiveness of the selected commercial. You can use methods described in this chapter or you can invent new approaches. Write a short questionnaire for each method of measurement.

Recruit sixty individuals to come to a classroom and watch the program. These individuals should be scheduled so that they attend in groups of fifteen (thus resulting in four groups.) Use a different method of measuring persuasiveness for each group.

After all interviews have been completed, analyze the data collected by your interviews. Then, prepare a short paper that describes

SCREENER QUESTIONS

(Customize all screener questions to television program and test commercial. Write and include appropriate introductory material.)

SCREENER QUESTIONS FOR INDIVIDUALS IN GROUPS 1 AND 3

A. Yesterday, (NAME OF PROGRAM) was shown on Channel (NAME OF CHANNEL) between _____ and _____ P.M. Did you, yourself, see any part of this program?

        Yes   [   ]
        No   [   ]·······► DISCONTINUE

B. Do you remember seeing the part of the program where (DESCRIBE PROGRAM ACTION JUST PRIOR TO COMMERCIAL BREAK IN WHICH TEST COMMERCIAL APPEARS).

        Yes   [   ]
        No   [   ]·······► DISCONTINUE

C. Do you remember seeing the part of the program where (DESCRIBE PROGRAM ACTION JUST AFTER COMMERCIAL BREAK IN WHICH TEST COMMERCIAL APPEARS).

        Yes   [   ]·······► CONTINUE WITH MAIN QUESTIONNAIRE
        No   [   ]·······► DISCONTINUE

SCREENER QUESTIONS FOR INDIVIDUALS IN GROUP 2

A. You were asked to videotape (NAME OF PROGRAM) and watch it for the first time yesterday. (NAME OF PROGRAM) was shown on Channel (NAME OF CHANNEL) between _____ and _____ P.M. Did you video tape the program?

        Yes   [   ]
        No   [   ]·······► DISCONTINUE

B. Have you, yourself, now seen any part of this program?

        Yes   [   ]
        No   [   ]·······► DISCONTINUE

C. Do you remember seeing the part of the program where (DESCRIBE PROGRAM ACTION JUST PRIOR TO COMMERCIAL BREAK IN WHICH TEST COMMERCIAL APPEARS).

        Yes   [   ]
        No   [   ]·······► DISCONTINUE

D. Do you remember seeing the part of the program where (DESCRIBE PROGRAM ACTION JUST AFTER COMMERCIAL BREAK IN WHICH TEST COMMERCIAL APPEARS).

        Yes   [   ]·······► CONTINUE WITH MAIN QUESTIONNAIRE
        No   [   ]·······► DISCONTINUE

(continued)

FIGURE 23.6
Core questionnaire for application exercise one.

SCREENER QUESTIONS FOR INDIVIDUALS IN GROUP 4

A. Yesterday, I showed you a videotape of (NAME OF PROGRAM). Do you remember seeing the part of the program where (DESCRIBE PROGRAM ACTION JUST PRIOR TO COMMERCIAL BREAK IN WHICH TEST COMMERCIAL APPEARS).

Yes   [   ]
No   [   ]-------► DISCONTINUE

B. Do you remember seeing the part of the program where (DESCRIBE PROGRAM ACTION JUST AFTER COMMERCIAL BREAK IN WHICH TEST COMMERCIAL APPEARS).

Yes   [   ]-------► CONTINUE WITH MAIN QUESTIONNAIRE
No   [   ]-------► DISCONTINUE

MAIN QUESTIONNAIRE

1. While watching (NAME OF PROGRAM) did you happen to see any commercials?

Yes   [   ]-------► CONTINUE WITH Q2
No   [   ]-------► DISCONTINUE

2. Can you tell me the names of the products you remember seeing advertised? DO NOT READ LIST.

TARGET BRAND MENTIONED: Yes [ ]-------► SKIP TO Q4
No [ ]-------► CONTINUE WITH Q3

3. Do you recall seeing a commercial for (NAME OF PRODUCT CATEGORY)?

Yes   [   ]-------► CONTINUE WITH Q5
No   [   ]-------► DISCONTINUE

4. What was the name, or what were the names, of the brand or brands advertised in the (NAME OF PRODUCT CATEGORY)?

TARGET BRAND MENTIONED: Yes [ ]-------► SKIP TO Q6
No [ ]-------► CONTINUE WITH Q5

5. Do you recall seeing a commercial for (INSERT NAME OF BRAND)?

Yes   [   ]-------► CONTINUE WITH Q6
No   [   ]-------► DISCONTINUE

6. What, if anything, can you remember about the (NAME OF BRAND) commercial?

7. What did the commercial look like?

8. What did the commercial show?

9. What ideas were brought out in the commercial? PROBE: Any other ideas?

(CONCLUDE QUESTIONNAIRE WITH CLASSIFICATION AND APPROPRIATE BRAND USAGE QUESTIONS)

FIGURE 23.6 (continued)

- each approach to measuring persuasion and your rationale for why you feel the approach is methodologically sound,
- the effects of each approach on observed levels of persuasion.

Conclude your paper with a discussion of the implications of your findings for the measurement and interpretation of persuasion measures. Be certain to provide a point of view on the strengths and weaknesses of each approach and the approach you would recommend.

3. Your agency has just acquired a new account that is about to begin development of its first advertising campaign. The brand manager, who came up through the ranks of Research and Development, is unfamiliar with the advertising development process in general and advertising testing (i.e., communication and copy testing) in particular. The client has allocated $15,000 for advertising testing, which is enough to support *either* a communication test or a copy test.

   Write a memo to the client attempting to convince him that both forms of testing are necessary and that additional funds are required. Clearly explain how each form of testing will contribute to the advertising's creative excellence.

4. Your memo (from the prior exercise) was well received and appreciated. The client, however, was unable to obtain additional funds for advertising testing. The client has asked for your opinion as to which form of testing (communication or copy test) should be utilized. The client knows that there is only enough money to conduct one type of test and will follow your recommendation as to the specific type of test that should be used.

   Write a memo to the client that, given the circumstances, recommends either communication testing or copy testing. Clearly support and justify your recommendation.

5. Between 1985 and 1987 Kraft aired a series of cheese commercials that addressed the issue of calcium in real versus imitation cheese. Following is the disputed copy in the "Skimp" execution:

   > I admit it. I thought of skimping. Could you look into those big blue eyes and skimp on her? So I buy Kraft Singles. Imitation slices use hardly any milk. But Kraft has five ounces per slice. Five ounces. So her little bones get the calcium they need to grow. No, she doesn't know what that big Kraft means. Good thing I do. (This audio was accompanied by a visual of milk pouring into a glass until it reaches a mark labeled "five ounces." The commercial also shows milk pouring into a glass that shows the phrase "5 oz. milk slice.")

The FTC complaint against this commercial claimed two misrepresentations (both of which were implicit rather than explicit in the advertising):

1. That a slice of Kraft Singles contained the same amount of calcium as five ounces of milk.
2. That Kraft Singles contained more calcium than most imitation cheese slices.

If, in fact, these messages were communicated by the advertising they would be false because

1. a slice of Kraft cheeses contains only 70 percent the calcium of five ounces of milk, and
2. most imitation cheese slices sold in the United States contain about the same amount of calcium as is contained in Kraft Singles.

   Two copy tests were conducted to determine whether the two disputed claims were communicated and, if so, whether they were material. The survey designed and conducted on behalf of Kraft is shown in Figure 23.7(pages 594–595). The survey de-

SCREENER

The screener began by identifying individuals who (a) were the person in the household most responsible for their household's food shopping, (b) were not ineligible due to employment in a sensitive industry (i.e., employed by a food manufacturer or distributor or a store that sells food) or past research participation (i.e., participated in a research survey within the past three months). The following questions then were asked:

E.   Today I'd like to talk to you about various types of cheeses. As you know, cheese products that are sold in food stores are packaged in a number of different ways. Some cheese, like cottage cheese, is usually sold in a tub or container from which you spoon out as much as you want. Other cheeses come as solid pieces or chunks, and it's up to you to cut off as much as you want at any one time. Then there are some cheese products that come individually wrapped in cellophane as ready-to-use single slices. I'd like to know about the types of cheeses you buy. Which, if any, of the following types of cheese have you *bought* in the past three months, either for yourself or for other members of your household? Did you *buy* any . . . cheeses packaged in tubs or containers; solid pieces or chunks of cheese; cheese products that come individually wrapped in cellophane as ready-to-use single slices? IF "NO" TO CHEESE PRODUCTS THAT COME INDIVIDUALLY WRAPPED IN CELLOPHANE AS "READY-TO-USE SLICES," TERMINATE.

F.   ASK FOR EACH PRODUCT BOUGHT IN QE. Now, what about eating cheese: Over the past three months, did you eat any [of each of the three types of cheeses]?

G1. The few questions that I have deal with prepackaged sliced cheese products sold in packages of 8, 12, 16 slices, and so on, where each slice comes individually wrapped in its own sheet of cellophane. Which brand or brands of ready-to-use single cheese products have you bought within the past year?

G2. (FOR EACH BRAND NOT MENTIONED IN Q G1 ASK:) Within the past year have you bought (BRAND)? IF KRAFT IS *NOT* MENTIONED IN Qs G1 OR G2, TERMINATE.

MAIN QUESTIONNAIRE

Q1a. People buy cheese for a number of different reasons. What are the reasons that you buy cheese? Why else?

Q1b. What are the reasons for your buying individually wrapped cheese food slices?

Q1c. Now I'd like you to think only about "Kraft Singles" Cheese food slices. Please tell me all the reasons that you can think of as to why you buy Kraft Singles individually wrapped cheese food slices? (PROBE:) Any other reasons?

Q2.   Now I'm going to mention a number of things that Kraft Singles may or may not contain. For each item that I mention, please tell me if Kraft Singles *do* contain, do *not* contain, or you don't know if they contain this item. Do they or don't they contain . . .

Protein
Vitamin C
Milk
Riboflavin
Vitamin A
Vegetable oil
Calcium

(continued)

Q3. I'm going to read a short list of characteristics about cheese. As I read each one, please tell me how important that characteristic is to you in your decision to buy Kraft Singles. Let's start with . . . Would you say _____ is extremely important, very important, somewhat important, or not at all important?

Has real cheese flavor
Has consistent quality
Is good tasting
Made by a company you can trust
Is reasonably priced
Is a source of calcium
Is convenient to use
Is individually wrapped so it stays fresh
Is a source of Vitamin C

Q4a. (Asked only of respondents who gave an "extremely" or "very" response in Q3.) Since you said that calcium is important to you in your decision to buy Kraft Single Slices, I'd like to ask you a few questions about it. Do you have any idea as to how much calcium is contained in one slice of Kraft Singles?

Q4b. (For those answering yes to Q4a, ask:) How much calcium is there in one slice of Kraft Singles?

Q5a. As you may or may not know, although each slice of Kraft Singles is made from five ounces of whole milk, it does not contain as much calcium as five ounces of milk. One slice of Kraft Singles actually contains 70 percent of the calcium in five ounces of milk. Now that I've told you this, I'd like to know whether this difference in calcium matters to you. More specifically, (READ BOTH CHOICES BEFORE RESPONDENT ANSWERS) . . .

Would you buy Kraft Singles slices even though each slice contains 70% of the calcium in five ounces of milk?

Would you stop buying Kraft Singles slices because each slice doesn't contain the same amount of calcium as five ounces of milk?

Q5b. Would this difference in the amount of calcium be enough to affect the way in which you use Kraft Singles slices?

Q5c. (For those answering "yes" to Q5b, ask:) In what way or ways would it affect how you use Kraft Singles slices?

Q6a. By the way, do you have any idea as to how much calcium is contained in five ounces of milk?

Q6b. (For those answering "Yes" to Q6a, ask:) How much calcium is there in five ounces of milk?

FIGURE 23.7
Kraft copy test survey.

signed and conducted on behalf of the FTC is shown in Figure 23.8 (pages 596–597).[35] Prepare a paper that compares and contrasts the surveys with regard to the following:

- *Sample universe.* Use each questionnaire's screener to determine the characteristics of the sample in each copy test. In what ways are the two samples similar? In

[35] The Kraft and FTC questionnaires were reported in Appendix A and Appendix B of Jacoby and Szybillo, "Consumer Research in FTC Versus Kraft."

SCREENER

Q1.   Are you the principal food shopper in your household? (IF "NO," TERMINATE)

Q2.   Are you over 18 years of age? (IF "NO," TERMINATE)

Q3.   Do you have any children living at home who are under 18 years of age? (IF "NO," TERMINATE)

Q4.   Do you, or does anyone in your household, work for an advertising agency, a marketing research firm, or a company that manufactures or distributes grocery or dairy products? (IF "YES," TERMINATE)

Q5.   Have you purchased any of the following products in the past three months?

Cheese or cheese products
Deodorant (anti-perspirant)
Laundry detergent

(IF "NO," TO "CHEESE OR CHEESE PRODUCTS," TERMINATE)

MAIN QUESTIONNAIRE

(SHOW KRAFT "SKIMP" COMMERCIAL IN CLUTTER REEL WITH DEODORANT AND LAUNDRY DETERGENT COMMERCIALS")

Q1.   Do you remember seeing an advertisement for cheese slices?

Q2.   What brand was being advertised? (IF OTHER THAN "KRAFT," TERMINATE)

Q3.   Do you remember seeing an ad for Kraft Singles? (IF "DON'T KNOW," TERMINATE)

Q4a. What points does the Kraft ad make about the product? (PROBE:) Anything else?

Q4b. Is there anything else about the Kraft ad that stands out your mind? (PROBE:)
        Is there something else?

Q5.   Does the ad give you any reasons why you should buy Kraft Singles?

Q6.   Does the ad say or suggest anything about the nutritional value of Kraft Singles, or about how healthy or good they are for you?

Q7.   You said that the Kraft Singles ad mentioned (nutrition, healthy, is good for you). What does the ad say or suggest that makes you think they are _____?

Q8.   Does the ad say or suggest anything about the milk content of Kraft Singles? (If "milk" mentioned in Q8, ask Q9; otherwise skip to Q10)

Q9.   You said the ad mentioned the milk content of Kraft Singles. What does the milk content of Kraft singles mean to you?

(*continued*)

Q10. Does the ad say or suggest anything about the calcium in Kraft singles?

(SHOW "SKIMP" AD)

Q11a. Does this ad say or suggest anything about the amount of calcium in a slice of Kraft Singles compared to the amount of calcium in five ounces of milk? (If "no," skip to Q12.)

Q11b. Based on this ad, do you think that a slice of Kraft Singles has more calcium than five ounces of milk, the same amount of calcium, or less calcium than five ounces of milk?

Q12. Does this ad compare Kraft Singles to imitation cheese slices?

Q13. Does this ad make any direct comparisons between Kraft Singles and other cheese slices?

Q14. Based on this ad, do you think Kraft Singles have more calcium, the same amount of calcium, or less calcium than those cheese slices they are being compared to?

FIGURE 23.8
FTC copy test survey.

what ways are they different? Present a point of view on the acceptability of each sample for the copy test of the "Skimp" ad? Be certain to address how the responses to the main questionnaire in each test may be influenced by sample characteristics.

- *Questions asked.* Evaluate each questionnaire for specific content. To what extent do the questions on each questionnaire address similar issues? To what extent do they address different issues? To what extent (and how acceptably) does each questionnaire probe communication in the disputed areas and the materiality of the communication?

- *Question format.* Evaluate the strengths and weaknesses of the questions asked on each survey. Which questions are acceptable as written? Which questions do you find problematic? For each problematic question, identify the source of the problem (i.e., bias, leading, incomplete response options, etc.) and provide a recommendation for correcting the problem.

Finally, based on your observations and analysis, write a complete questionnaire (including a screener) that you feel best addresses the issues underlying testing of the disputed advertisement.

24

Part 8: Media Research

AUDIENCE MEASUREMENT

Appropriate media selection and advertising placement is crucial to the success of any advertising campaign. Advertising, no matter how creative or persuasive, cannot accomplish its goals if it is not seen or heard by the target audience. Consequently, media planners and buyers must make certain that they match media vehicles with audience characteristics—that they select media and media vehicles where the target audience has the greatest potential to see or hear the advertising. To accomplish this, media planners use syndicated audience research to help them identify those media placements that most efficiently reach and deliver their client's advertising to the target audience.

The proper use of syndicated audience research requires an understanding of the types of information available, how this data is collected, and how this data is interpreted and used for media evaluation and selection. These issues are addressed in this chapter.

After reading this chapter, you will be able to

■ Identify the types of audience information available.

■ Describe how each type of audience measurement is collected.

■ Explain how audience information is interpreted and applied to the process of media evaluation and selection.

TELEVISION AUDIENCE MEASUREMENT

Primary Measures and Terminology

Television programs are measured in terms of the size of their audience. Two different types of audience size measurements are calculated, share and rating:

• A *share* is a **relative** measure that reflects a program's ability to attract viewers when compared to other programs appearing during the same time period. A share, calculated

TABLE 24.1 Calculation of Program Share and Rating*

Station	Program	Number of Viewers	Share	Rating
KXRP	*Murphy Brown*	25,000	39.4	25.0
KKRI	*Special News*	8,000	12.6	8.0
KPPS	*Point of View*	3,000	4.7	3.0
KSSI	*Movie 19*	7,000	11.0	7.0
KUSU	*Matlock*	5,500	8.7	5.5
XXTV	*Cops*	4,000	6.3	4.0
KPOP	*Star Trek: TNG*	2,500	3.9	2.5
	Other broadcast	1,000	1.6	1.0
	Cable	7,500	11.8	7.5
Total Viewing Audience		**63,500**	**100.0**	

* Viewing at 9 P.M. Monday.

Total number of viewers in geographic area is 100,000.

Note: Data is for illustrative purposes only.

as the number of individuals or homes tuned in to a particular show divided by all individuals or homes tuned in at the time, indicates the *percentage of the total viewing audience* a program or station has acquired.[1]

- A *rating* is an absolute measure that reflects the percentage of *all* individuals or homes in a particular geographic area viewing a particular program. A rating, calculated as the number of individuals or homes watching a particular show divided by all individuals or homes that have the potential to watch, indicates the *percentage of the total potential audience* a program or station has acquired.

Shares and ratings are related measures. Consider the equation used to calculate each measure:

$$\text{Share} = \frac{\text{\# of individuals or homes tuned in}}{\textit{Actual} \text{ viewing audience at the time}}$$

$$\text{Rating} = \frac{\text{\# of individuals or homes tuned in}}{\text{Total } \textit{potential} \text{ viewing audience}}$$

Both measures are calculated in terms of a ratio. The numerator of both ratios is the actual number of individuals or homes viewing a program. The denominator changes for each measure. The denominator for the calculation of a share is the total *actual* viewing audience. The denominator for the calculation of rating is the total *potential* viewing audience.[2]

The relationship between a rating and a share is illustrated in Table 24.1. The table indicates that there are 100,000 individuals in the geographic area of interest. This

---

[1] Jim Surmanek, *Introduction to Advertising Media* (Lincolnwood, IL: NTC Business Books, 1994), 65.

[2] The technical terms for the total viewing audience are PUT and HUT where PUT stands for People Using Television and HUT stands for Homes Using Television. The technical terms for the total potential audience are PWT and HWT where PWT stands for People With Televisions and HWT stands for Homes With Televisions.

is the size of the potential viewing audience. At 9 P.M., 63,500 of these individuals were watching television. This is the size of the actual viewing audience. The table lists the viewing options at 9 P.M. and presents the share and rating for each viewing option. The share for each viewing option is calculated by dividing program viewership by total *actual* viewers. For example, *Murphy Brown's* share of 39.4 is obtained by dividing 25,000 (viewership) by 63,500 (total actual viewers). Note how shares add to 100 percent because each individual share reflects the percent of actual viewing audience. The rating of each viewing option is calculated by dividing program viewership by the total number of *potential* viewers. Thus, *Murphy Brown's* rating of 25 is obtained by dividing 25,000 (viewership) by 100,000 (total potential viewers).

In practice, a rating as opposed to a share is the more valuable measure of audience size. This is because the interpretation of the share is variable. An 11 percent share of audience at 3 A.M. does not represent the same number of people or households as an 11 percent share of audience at 9 P.M. due to the fact that a share reflects the percentage of the viewing audience and there are certainly fewer people watching at 3 A.M. than at 9 P.M. A rating point, however, is not variable among the viewing periods. It always stands for the same thing. One rating point always represents 1 percent of the total potential viewing audience regardless of the time the program aired.

How Television Ratings Are Collected

A. C. Nielsen is the only company that currently reports television ratings. Nielsen uses three basic methods for collecting television audience data: (1) the diary, (2) the meter, and (3) the people meter. The diary and meter are used to collect ratings on the local level while the people meter is used to collect national television ratings.

Diary The diary, the oldest method of collecting television viewing behaviors, asks each household member to keep track of his or her viewing habits. Specifically, the diary divides each day into fifteen minute periods and asks each household member who is watching television to record the station name, station number, and the name of the program or movie viewed. Nielsen selects diary households as follows:

> Multistage probability sampling is used to select target households. "A diary for up to five television sets in operating condition is mailed to households that agree to cooperate in the survey. For listed telephone households, diaries are also mailed to refusal households and to households not answering five telephone calls spread out over at least two days at different times of day and evening. A monetary incentive is included with the diary. In order reduce the incidence of non-contacts in the unlisted samples, 10 attempts are made to contact each unlisted number."[3]

Nielsen attempts to ensure high levels of diary participation by using the following procedures:

> A reminder is sent to each household asking them to begin diary entries on Thursday. In cable households with sixty or fewer channels the reminder is a letter accompanied by a list of all cable channels. The reminder for remaining households is a postcard. At the end of the diary week a postcard is sent to all homes to remind them to return the diary. In ad-

---

[3] A. C. Nielsen Company Media Research Group, *NSI Methodology, Techniques and Data Interpretation* (New York, NY: Nielsen Media Research, 1992), 11.

dition, to maintain high levels of participation among ethnic and racial groups, "all Spanish households and listed Non-Ethnic households . . . receive a telephone call during the diary keeping week to encourage them to return their diary. All Black households and Non-Ethnic households . . . receive two telephone calls during the diary keeping week; a start of week call reminds the respondent to begin diary-keeping and an end-of-week call reminds them to return the diary."[4]

Nielsen panel members use personal diaries to record their viewing behaviors during the four "sweeps" months: November, February, May, and July.

Meter A meter is a device attached to the television set that automatically records whether the set is on or off and the station being viewed. (Similar to diary households, selection of meter households is done using multistage probability sampling.) Metered recordings versus diary households are inherently free of response error in that "they require no effort, recall, or reply from persons in the sample regarding dial settings, station call letters, programs, and the like."[5] Meters therefore provide accurate ratings and share information for the household, but unlike the diary, are unable to provide a basis for calculating ratings and shares for specific demographic groups.

Meters collect local viewership information continuously throughout the year.

People Meter National television ratings are collected via a people meter. A people meter, which resembles a cable TV box with remote control, is installed on each television set in each of the approximately 4,000 households comprising the Nielsen national ratings panel. (Households are selected by a multistage, stratified-area probability sample to maximize generalizability to the total United States.) Each people meter is programmed individually to contain information on each household member's characteristics such as age, gender, and related demographics. When the television set is turned on the people meter automatically begins to record the program being watched. The household member who turned on the set, and other household members who may be in the room, press their preassigned button on the people meter's remote control. The people meter then knows to count each person (represented by a button press) as part of the program's viewing audience. When an individual leaves the room another button is pressed, indicating that he or she is no longer part of the program audience. The people meter also has the capability to monitor the presence of guests using manual entry of demographic information.[6] Viewing data are transmitted nightly over the phone lines to Nielsen's computer facility where they are tabulated. Printed analyses are sent to clients the following day.

Problems With the People Meter

Nielsen introduced the people meter in an attempt to eliminate problems associated with the diary (for example, some individuals' tendency not to record their viewing or to record their viewing several days after the fact) and the meter (for example, no demographic viewership data was available). It was hoped that the shortcomings of the

---

[4] Ibid., 12.

[5] Ibid., 86.

[6] The description of people meter methodology is taken from *Nielsen Television Index National TV Ratings Pocketpiece*, July 26–August 1, 1993.

diary and meter could be eliminated if a machine could identify *what* was being watched and *who* was watching. While this goal was laudatory, the implementation of the people meter has been problematic and controversial.

Initial people meter data showed significant losses in audience size for the national networks and large increases in audience size for cable stations. Nielsen said that the results were sound while the networks argued that the data was flawed. In an attempt to resolve this issue, the networks formed CONTAM, The Committee on Nationwide Television Audience Measurement to explore the validity and reliability of people meter data. CONTAM concluded that the people meter data was flawed because of methodological errors and "meter fatigue." [7] Following is a description of methodological errors and "meter fatigue":

- Methodological errors related to the procedures underlying household selection and participation. A true random sample was required for people meter data to be representative and generalizable to the national population. However, the combination of a low participation rate (less than half of those contacted agreed to participate) and nonrandom procedures used to replace households that declined to participate resulted in a sample that was not truly representative and that had a "high potential for distortion and bias."[8]

- As discussed earlier, individuals in people meter households must indicate via remote control when they begin and end viewing. One must, for example, press the remote many times if they watch only portions of a program, for example:

Watch beginning of program	Use remote to tell meter you are in audience
Leave at commercial break	Use remote to tell meter you are *no longer* in audience
Return two minutes later	Use remote to tell meter you are *back* in audience
Leave to answer telephone	Use remote to tell meter you are *no longer* in audience
Return after telephone call	Use remote to tell meter you are *back* in audience
Etc.	

- "Meter fatigue" relates to panel members' increasing predisposition over time not to push the buttons required for the people meter to know whether they are in the room watching television. CONTAM found that reported viewing behaviors for key demographic groups, especially younger viewers, showed substantial declines as members' length of time in the panel increased. In the absence of other evidence, CONTAM interpreted this finding to indicate that individuals in people meter households simply gave up noting their presence in the television audience.

Nielsen has taken several steps to respond to criticisms of the people meter methodology. First, they have revised the procedures by which homes are selected for participation, improving the methodological soundness of the sampling procedure. Second, they have initiated programs to increase compliance rates, especially among younger viewers. Third, they have begun work on a passive people meter, which would

---

[7] For detailed discussion of reactions to the people meter methodology see J. Ronald Milavsky, "Review: How Good Is the A. C. Nielsen People-Meter System? A Review of the Report by the Committee on Nationwide Television Audience Measurement," *Public Opinion Quarterly* 56 (Spring 1992):102–15; Lynn G. Coleman, "People Meter Rerun: Doubts About Its Accuracy Linger As TV Season Opens," *Marketing News* (September 2, 1991): 1; Wayne Walley, "Finding Nielsen Glitch: Nets Cite Sample for Disputed Ratings Shortfall," *Advertising Age* (October 22, 1990): 2.

[8] See A. B. Blankenship and George E. Breen, *State of the Art Marketing Research* (Chicago, IL: American Marketing Association, 1993), 526.

automatically scan and record the household members watching television.[9] However, in spite of Nielsen's attempts to improve the people meter methodology and to introduce a passive people meter, the television networks have begun to explore their own systems for collecting viewership information and estimating program ratings.

Nielsen Reports of Television Audiences

As discussed earlier, Nielsen reports program ratings on both the national and the local level.[10] National ratings, called the Nielsen Television Index or NTI, represent an estimate of the percentage of all individuals or households in the United States watching a particular program. Local ratings, called the Nielsen Station Index or NSI, are estimates of program audience size in individual markets.

Nielsen provides two levels of national and local television audience estimates. First, they provide total rating, share and audience size estimates for each program. Second, rating, share and audience size estimates are provided for individual demographic groups.

Figure 24.1 (page 604) shows total national audience ratings for Saturday evening, August 1, 1993. This report provides the following information:

- Across the top of the page, in fifteen minute intervals, is the percentage of all homes using TVs (HUTs), in other words, the percentage of homes in which the television is turned on. Between 7:00 P.M and 7:15 P.M about 39.3 percent of all homes in the nation had their television set on. Notice how the percent of homes using TV increases as the evening progresses.[11]

- Individual program names are noted for the four major networks. Between 8:00 P.M. and 9:00 P.M the networks presented the following: *My Brother's Wife* (ABC movie), *Dr. Quinn Medicine Woman* (CBS), *Super Bloopers* (NBC), and *Cops San Bernadino/Cops Fort Worth* (Fox).

- Audience information is provided on four lines beneath each program name. The most important data provided in this report appears in the first quarter hour column after the program begins:

  - *HHLD Audience % & (000)* reports the program's overall rating and the number of TV households represented by that rating. The overall rating for *Dr. Quinn* was 6.2. This means that, on average, 6.2 percent of all potential viewers were watching *Dr. Quinn*.

  - *Share Audience* represents the program's overall share of viewers. Fourteen percent (14%) of all viewers between 8:00 P.M and 9:00 P.M watched *Dr. Quinn*.

Additional data, shown in the remaining columns provide deeper detail:

  - *Dr. Quinn*'s overall rating of 6.2 represents 5,770,000 TV households (shown on the *HHLD Audience % & (000)* line in the second quarter hour program period).

---

[9] For further information on the passive people meter see Cheryl Heuton, "Nielsen Pitches New Meter," *Mediaweek* (July 18, 1994):10. For a discussion of these actions see Michael Freeman, "Big 4 Call Ratings Powwow," *Mediaweek* (April 4, 1994): 8; Elizabeth Jensen, "Networks Create Ratings Test System Out of Frustration with Nielsen Data," *Wall Street Journal* (February 4, 1994): B5; Steve McClellan, "Broadcasters Lash Out at Nielsen," *Broadcasting & Cable* (October 16, 1995): 18.

[10] The A.C. Nielsen Company has always been the sole provider of national television ratings. Prior to 1993, local ratings were collected by both Nielsen and Arbitron, at which time Arbitron withdrew from the local ratings business. For further information on Arbitron's withdrawal see Elizabeth Jensen, "Arbitron TV Ratings Service to End," *Wall Street Journal* (October 19, 1993): B2.

[11] The homes using the TV figure provides a basis for calculating program share, as described on page 599.

Nielsen NATIONAL TV AUDIENCE ESTIMATES

EVE. SAT. JUL. 31, 1993

TIME	7:00	7:15	7:30	7:45	8:00	8:15	8:30	8:45	9:00	9:15	9:30	9:45	10:00	10:15	10:30	10:45	11:00	11:15
HUT	39.3	40.2	39.8	40.5	41.4	42.3	43.6	45.2	46.2	47.5	48.4	48.9	48.5	48.0	47.7	47.2	46.1	43.8

ABC TV — ABC SATURDAY NIGHT MOVIE: MY BROTHER'S WIFE (R) (PAE) [8:00–10:00] → COMMISH (R) [10:00–11:15]

ABC TV	7:00	7:15	7:30	7:45	8:00	8:15	8:30	8:45	9:00	9:15	9:30	9:45	10:00	10:15	10:30	10:45	11:00	11:15
HHLD AUDIENCE% & (000)					5.5 (5,120)								7.8 (7,260)					
TA%, AVG. AUD. 1/2 HR %					11.2	5.1*		4.8*		5.6*		6.4*	10.8	7.3*		8.2*		
SHARE AUDIENCE %					12	12*		11*		12*		13*	16	15*		17*		
AVG. AUD. BY 1/4 HR %					5.2	5.0	4.9	4.7	5.4	5.7	6.5	6.4	7.2	7.5	7.9	8.6		

CBS TV — DR. QUINN MEDICINE WOMAN (R) [8:00–9:00] → CIRCUS OF THE STARS XVII (R) [9:00–11:00]

CBS TV	7:00	7:15	7:30	7:45	8:00	8:15	8:30	8:45	9:00	9:15	9:30	9:45	10:00	10:15	10:30	10:45	11:00	11:15
HHLD AUDIENCE% & (000)					6.2 (5,770)				8.2 (7,630)									
TA%, AVG. AUD. 1/2 HR %					8.7	5.8*		6.5*	17.6	7.3*		8.0*		8.9*		8.6*		
SHARE AUDIENCE %					14	14*		15*	17	16*		16*		18*		18*		
AVG. AUD. BY 1/4 HR %					5.8	5.8	6.3	6.8	7.2	7.4	7.7	8.3	9.5	8.4	8.7	8.5		

NBC TV — SUPER BLOOPERS (R) [8:00–9:00] → EMPTY NEST (R) [9:00–9:30] → NURSES (R) [9:30–10:00] → REASONABLE DOUBTS (R) [10:00–11:00]

NBC TV	7:00	7:15	7:30	7:45	8:00	8:15	8:30	8:45	9:00	9:15	9:30	9:45	10:00	10:15	10:30	10:45	11:00	11:15
HHLD AUDIENCE% & (000)					5.4 (5,030)				6.7 (6,240)		6.5 (6,050)		5.0 (4,660)					
TA%, AVG. AUD. 1/2 HR %					9.0	5.1*		5.7*	8.1		8.1		7.8	4.8*				
SHARE AUDIENCE %					13	12*		13*	14		13		10	10*				
AVG. AUD. BY 1/4 HR %					5.0	5.2	5.4	6.0	6.3	7.1	6.5	6.6	4.9	4.7	5.4			

FOX TV — COPS SAN BERNARDINO (R) [8:00–8:30] → COPS 2 FORT WORTH (R) [8:30–9:00] → FRONT PAGE [9:00–10:00] → COMIC STRIP LIVE (11:00–12:00)

FOX TV	7:00	7:15	7:30	7:45	8:00	8:15	8:30	8:45	9:00	9:15	9:30	9:45	10:00	10:15	10:30	10:45	11:00	11:15
HHLD AUDIENCE% & (000)					6.8 (6,330)		7.9 (7,350)		5.1 (4,750)								2.6 (2,420)	
TA%, AVG. AUD. 1/2 HR %					8.3		9.5		8.5	5.9*		4.3*					4.7	2.5*
SHARE AUDIENCE %					16		18		11	13*		9*					6	6*
AVG. AUD. BY 1/4 HR %					6.2	7.4	7.7	8.2	6.3	5.5	4.6	4.1					2.3	2.6

FIGURE 24.1

NTI ratings.

Source: Nielsen Media Research. Reproduced with permission.

• *Average Audience by ¼ hour* reports the program's overall rating for each fifteen minute program segment. Dr. Quinn's ratings improved during the program, where 5.8 percent of all TV households watched between 8:00 P.M. and 8:15 P.M. and 6.8 percent of all households watched between 8:45 P.M. and 9:00 P.M.

Overall ratings are important, but media buyers are interested in the demographic composition of a program's audience. Consequently, Nielsen also provides program ratings for specific demographic groups (see Figure 24.2, page 606) as follows:

• working women aged 18+ and aged 18–49
• lady of the house aged 18–49 with any child under the age of 3
• all women and women aged 18–34, 18–49, 25–54, 35–64, and 55 and older
• all men and men aged 18–34, 18–49, 25–54, 35–64 and 55 and older
• all teens aged 12–17 and female teens aged 12–17
• children aged 2–11 and 6–11

A national demographic report that covers the same time period as the report shown in Figure 24.1 is shown in Figure 24.2. This report estimates program audiences by half hour time periods, as shown by the organization of programs within time period in the first column. The second column, labeled Households, reports each program's overall ratings in each half hour time period. For example, *Dr. Quinn*'s overall rating for 8:00 P.M. to 8:30 P.M. is 5.8 and its rating from 8:30 P.M. to 9:00 P.M. is 6.5. The remaining columns report the program's ratings among individual demographic groups between 8:00 P.M. and 8:30 PM. *Dr. Quinn*'s ratings tend to be higher among women (5.2) versus men (2.5) and among older versus younger viewers (note how ratings for both men and women increase with age). *Dr. Quinn*'s highest demographic rating in this period (11.0) is among women aged 55 and older.

Nielen's local ratings contain information identical to that of the national ratings except that in these cases ratings are only relevant to a local market. Figure 24.3 (pages 608–609) shown an excerpt from a local ratings report. Notice that while the format is different than the national ratings format, overall program ratings as well as ratings among specific demographic groups are reported.

Ratings and Media Planning

Television stations and networks use total program ratings to determine advertising rates. Generally, higher ratings result in higher rates. The relationship between ratings and rates is illustrated in the following table that reports ratings and approximate advertising rates for television programs in the 1995–1996 season.[12]

Program	Rating	Cost for :30 Commercial
Seinfeld	22.7	$490,000
Caroline in the City	18.4	375,000
Coach	17.7	325,000
Hudson Street	13.6	220,000

[12] The source for advertising cost estimates is *Advertising Age* (September 18, 1995).

PROGRAM AUDIENCE ESTIMATES (By Time Periods)

JUL. 26-AUG. 1, 1993

AVERAGE MINUTE AUDIENCE %

FIGURE 24.2

DAY / TIME / NETWORK PROGRAM NAME	HOUSE-HOLDS	TOTAL PERS 2+	TOTAL PERS 18+	WORKING WOMEN 18+	WORKING WOMEN 18-49	LOH 18-49 W/CH <3	WOMEN TOTAL	WOMEN 18-34	WOMEN 18-49	WOMEN 25-54	WOMEN 35-64	WOMEN 55+	MEN TOTAL	MEN 18-34	MEN 18-49	MEN 25-54	MEN 35-64	MEN 55+	TEENS TOT 12-17	TEENS FEM 12-17	CHILDREN TOT 2-11	CHILDREN TOT 6-11
SATURDAY EVENING																						
6:00-6:30 PM TVU	34.7	19.9	17.0	16.1		18.2	21.0	15.6	16.4	17.1	19.3	30.7	21.9	18.7	18.4	19.7	21.6	30.2	16.0	14.9	14.3	14.5
A WWOS SP-HALL OF FAME GAME (S)>	5.3	2.7	1.7	1.7		.5v	2.1	1.3	1.4	1.6	2.0	3.6	4.2	4.1	3.9	3.9	4.0	5.0	2.3	2.1^	1.2	1.4^
6:30-7:00 PM TVU	35.6	20.8	18.2	17.0		17.5	22.6	16.4	17.5	17.9	21.2	33.3	22.4	19.1	18.6	19.6	21.8	31.6	16.2	14.5	14.9	15.5
A ABC WRLD NEWS TONIGHT-SAT	4.1	2.2	1.5	1.2		.6v	2.8	.9^	1.4	1.5	2.5	5.7	2.6	1.2	1.6	1.8	2.3	5.1	.6^	.7v	.6^	.3v
C CBS SAT. NEWS-SCHIEFFER	4.2	2.4	1.5	1.4		1.2^	3.1	1.0^	1.3	1.6	2.4	6.9	2.9	1.0^	1.3	1.7	2.7	7.3	.4v	.7v	.3^	.4v
N NBC NIGHTLY NEWS-SAT.	5.1	2.7	2.4	1.9		.9v	3.7	.9^	1.7	2.0	3.3	8.2	3.0	.8^	1.3	1.9	3.0	7.2	.5^	.3v	.3^	.2v
7:00-7:30 PM TVU	39.7	23.9	20.5	18.5		22.3	27.0	19.0	20.1	21.0	25.4	41.4	25.5	21.1	21.4	22.4	24.9	36.3	17.4	16.2	15.7	16.3
7:30-8:00 PM TVU	40.2	24.2	21.1	19.0		23.0	27.3	19.2	20.1	21.0	25.6	42.6	25.9	21.8	21.9	22.9	24.9	37.0	17.6	16.2	15.7	17.1
8:00-8:30 PM TVU	41.8	25.5	21.8	20.1		27.1	29.5	22.2	22.4	22.8	27.0	45.3	26.8	21.8	22.3	23.7	25.9	38.5	17.7	17.5	16.3	17.2
A ABC SATURDAY NIGHT MOVIE	5.1	2.7	3.1	2.1		1.6^	4.4	1.9	2.2	2.7	4.1	8.8	2.1	1.1	1.1	1.2	1.8	4.7	.9^	.9v	1.0	.7^
C DR. QUINN MEDICINE WOMAN	5.8	3.3	2.8	2.5		2.7^	5.2	2.2	2.6	2.8	3.9	11.0	2.5	.9^	1.4	1.5	2.4	5.5	1.6^	2.3^	1.5	1.7
N SUPER BLOOPERS	5.1	3.0	3.1	2.7		2.9^	3.5	2.8	2.6	2.7	3.8	5.0	2.9	2.4	2.5	2.7	3.0	3.7	3.1	2.9^	1.9	2.1
F COPS	6.8	4.1	3.9	3.9		7.7	4.4	5.3	4.8	4.5	3.8	4.0	4.9	6.2	5.3	5.3	4.1	4.3	2.8	2.2^	2.3	1.8
8:30-9:00 PM TVU	44.4	27.3	23.7	22.0		26.8	31.4	22.9	23.9	25.1	29.5	47.9	28.4	22.8	23.9	25.8	27.7	40.0	19.6	19.5	18.6	19.2
A ABC SATURDAY NIGHT MOVIE	4.8	2.5	3.2	2.2		.9v	4.1	1.3	2.1	2.6	4.3	8.2	1.9	1.1^	1.1	1.3	1.8	4.0	.9^	1.0^	.9^	.8^
C DR. QUINN MEDICINE WOMAN	6.5	3.7	3.4	3.1		2.7^	5.6	2.6	3.1	3.3	4.5	11.1	2.8	1.0^	1.5	1.8	2.7	6.0	1.8	2.3^	2.4	2.5
N SUPER BLOOPERS	5.7	3.4	3.3	2.9		4.1	3.9	3.6	3.0	3.3	3.4	5.4	3.3	2.7	2.9	3.2	3.5	3.8	3.1	3.0^	2.1	2.1
F COPS 2	7.9	5.0	4.4	4.2		8.6	5.1	5.8	5.3	4.4	4.4	5.1	5.8	6.8	6.1	6.0	5.1	5.1	4.2	3.5	3.3	2.7

FIGURE 24.2

NTI demographic report.

Source: Nielsen Media Research. Reproduced with permission.

TABLE 24.2 The Relationship of Ratings, Advertising Cost, Audience Characteristics, and Cost Per Thousand

Cost Per Thousand Based on Overall Program Ratings

Program	Overall Rating	Audience Size	Cost	Cost Per Thousand
Program A	17.2	16,082,000	$168,057	10.45
Program B	10.1	9,350,000	98,175	10.50
Program C	5.3	4,955,500	52,281	10.55

Cost Per Thousand Based on Ratings Among Women Aged 18–34

Program	Target Rating (Women Aged 18–34)	Target Audience Size	Cost	Cost Per Thousand for Target Audience
Program A	15.2	2,657,644	$168,057	63.23
Program B	5.1	891,710	98,175	110.10
Program C	2.2	384,659	52,281	135.90

Cost Per Thousand Based on Rating Among Men Aged 55 and Older

Program	Target Rating (Men 55 +)	Target Audience Size	Cost	Cost Per Thousand for Target Audience
Program A	5.2	850,850	$168,057	197.50
Program B	3.2	523,600	98,175	187.50
Program C	4.7	763,038	52,281	68.51

However, because different programs deliver different numbers of individuals or households (that is, the absolute size of their audience varies), advertising media planners and buyers review and evaluate program cost in a way that reflects a constant number of people or households. (This is the same principle as comparing the relative price of different sizes of laundry detergent. You make this comparison by adjusting the price of each brand so that the prices reflect a constant price per unit of size, for example, cents per ounce.) The constant in media planning is *cost per thousand*, abbreviated as CPM, which represents the cost to reach 1,000 individuals or homes.

Cost per thousand is calculated by first dividing the cost of the advertisement by the number of individuals (or households) reached and then multiplying by 1,000. The upper table in Table 24.2 illustrates the relationship between overall program rating, audience size, total advertising cost, and cost per thousand. As this example illustrates, the higher rated shows charge more in an absolute sense for commercial time, but all three programs charge the same relative cost, that is, they have nearly the same CPM. Each program charges about $10.50 to reach 1,000 individuals.[13]

---

[13] The cost per thousand is calculated by dividing the cost of the ad by the size of the audience reached and then multiplying by 1,000. For example, the $10.45 CPM for Program A is calculated by dividing $168,057 by 16,082,000 and then multiplying the quotient by 1,000.

SAN DIEGO, CA

WEDNESDAY 8:00PM–10:00PM

WK1 2/06-2/12 WK2 2/13-2/19 WK3 2/20-2/26 WK4 2/27-3/04

METRO HH		STATION	PROGRAM
RTG	SHR		
2	1		R.S.E. THRESHOLDS 25+% (1 S.E.) 4 WK AVG 50+%
			8:00 PM
17	27	KFMB	AVG. ALL WKS.
30	45		XVIOLM WTR-PRM
5	8		DAVIS RULE - CBS
13	21	KGTV	AVG. ALL WKS
9	14		DINOSAURS - ABC
26	38		IND JONES - ABC
11	17	KNSD	UNSLVD MSY - NBC
3	5	KPBS	AVG. ALL WKS
1	2		SCIENTFC - FRNTR
2	3		M RUSSELL - SPCL
6	11		NTL GRPHC SPCL
3	5		CHMPNSHP SKATE
1	2	KTTY	KTTY MOV 8
3	5	KUSI	MATLOCK
4	6	XETV	MOV
65			HUT/PUT/TOTALS*
			8:30 PM
19	28	KFMB	AVG. ALL WKS.
30	43		XVIOLM WTR-PRM
8	11		BRKLYN BRG - CBS
15	23	KGTV	AVG. ALL WKS
12	18		WONDER YRS - ABC
12	17		DOOGIE MD - ABC
26	36		IND JONES - ABC
11	16	KNSD	UNSLVD MSY - NBC
3	5	KPBS	AVG. ALL WKS
2	2		SCIENTFC - FRNTR
7	11		EVENING - POPS
3	4		NTL GRPHC SPCL
1	2		CHMPNSHP SKATE
3	4	KTTY	KTTY MOV 8
4	6	KUSI	MATLOCK
		XETV	MOV
68			HUT/PUT/TOTALS*

SAN DIEGO, CA

WEDNESDAY 8:00PM-10:00PM

METRO HH RTG	METRO HH SHR	STATION	PROGRAM	DMA HH RATINGS WK1	DMA HH RATINGS WK2	DMA HH RATINGS WK3	DMA HH RATINGS WK4	MULTI-WEEK AVG RTG	MULTI-WEEK AVG SHR	SHARE TREND NOV'91	SHARE TREND MAY'91	SHARE TREND FEB'91	PERS 2+	PERS 18+	PERS 12-24	PERS 12-34	PERS 18-34	PERS 18-49	PERS 21-49	PERS 25-54	PERS 35+	PERS 35-64	PERS 50+	WMN 18+	WMN 12-24	WMN 18-34	WMN 18-49	WMN 25-49	WMN 25-54	WMN WKG	MEN 18+	MEN 18-34	MEN 18-49	MEN 21-49	MEN 25-49	MEN 25-54	TNS 12-17	CHILD 2-11	CHILD 6-11
1	2			3	4	5	6	7	8	11	12	13	15	16	17	18	19	20	21	22	23	24	25	26	27	28	29	31	32	34	35	36	37	38	39	40	41	42	43
			9:00 PM																																				
22	34	KFMB	AVG. ALL WKS.	31	37	8	13	22	34	19	20	27	14	17	9	12	13	15	16	17	20	19	22	19	13	15	17	18	17	17	15	11	13	14	15	16	7	4	7
34	51		XVIOLM WTR-PRM	31	37			34	51				23	26	15	18	19	23	23	26	32	31	35	28	18	22	25	27	27	25	25	16	20	22	23	25	14	8	11
8	13		JAKE&FTMN - CBS			8		8	13				4	5	1	3	3	4	4	4	5	5	4	3	2	2	3	2	2	4	3	2	2	3	2	1			
13	19		MURPHY BRWN SP				13	13	19				8	10	6	8	10	11	12	11	10	10	7	12	14	12	14	12	11	15	8	8	9	11	10	3		
13	19	KGTV	AVG. ALL WKS	11	6	13	22	13	19	18	21	21	9	10	11	9	10	10	11	10	11	10	10	10	10	9	11	11	11	10	7	7	10	9	10	10	15	3	4
11	16		DOOGIE - MD - ABC	11				11	16				9	9	14	11	8	9	10	9	9	8	7	10	15	10	12	11	11	13	7	7	7	8	8	8	22	1	
6	9		ABC MOV SP WED		6			6	9				4	4	2	3	2	3	4	4	5	4	5	3	3	1	2	3	2	2	5	3	4	5	6	6	6	2	
13	21		ABC WED MOV SP			13		13	21				8	9	8	8	8	9	10	9	10	10	12	12	14	12	11	10	11	11	4	5	6	6	7	7			
22	33		IND JONES - ABC				22	22	33				17	18	19	20	19	19	17	21	18	20	16	17	8	12	17	22	22	22	20	25	21	16	19	20	25	7	
9	14	KNSD	AVG. ALL WKS	10	10	12	4	9	14	13	11	17	6	7	4	7	8	7	8	8	6	6	7	8	6	9	8	8	8	8	6	7	6	7	8	7	4	1	1
9	13		SEINFELD - WED	10		12	4	9	13				6	7	4	9	8	8	8	8	6	6	5	8	6	10	9	8	9	9	7	9	7	8	9	8	3	1	1
10	14		UNSLVD MYS - NBC		10			10	14				5	6	3	4	4	5	5	5	6	6	9	7	4	7	7	7	7	7	5	3	3	4	4	5	1	1	
1	2	KPBS	AVG. ALL WKS	1	2	2	1	1	2	6	7	5	1	1				1	1	1	1	1	1	1		1	1	1	1	1	1			1	1	1	5		
1	1		EDGE	1			1	1	1													1	1											1					
2	3		EVENING - POPS		2			2	3				1	2	1	1	1	1	2	2	2	2	2	2	2		1	1	2	1	2		1	1	2	2	2		
2	3		NEW TIJUANA			2		2	3				1	1			1	1	1	2	2	2	2	1				1	1	1	1		1	1	1	1			
1	2	KTTY	KTTY MOV 8	1	1	<<	1	1	2	2X	3	3	1	1							1	1	1	1				1			1		1	1	1	1		
4	6	KUSI	GERALDO	2	3	2	8	4	6	4X	1	2	2	3	3	3	3	3	3	3	3	3	3	4	5	6	5	4	4	5	2	1	1	2	1	1			1
4	6	XETV	MOV	3	4	5	4	4	6	8X	8	7	3	3	3	3	3	3	3	3	3	3	3	3	4	3	3	3	3	3	2	3	2	3	2	2	2	1	2
66			HUT/PUT/TOTALS*	68	67	61	67	66		55	55	61	46	53	38	46	48	51	52	54	56	55	58	57	46	54	57	57	56	54	48	43	45	47	51	52	35	19	22
			9:30 PM																																				
22	35	KFMB	AVG. ALL WKS.	30	38	8	12	22	35	20	22	30	14	17	8	12	13	15	16	17	19	18	20	18	12	15	17	18	18	16	15	11	13	14	16	16	6	3	4
34	52		XVIOLM WTR-PRM	30	38			34	52				22	26	13	19	20	23	24	27	31	30	33	27	16	23	26	28	28	24	25	17	21	23	25	27	12	5	6
8	13		JAKE&FTMN - CBS			8		8	13				4	5		2	3	3	4	4	5	5	3	6	3	4	6	5	3	2	4	3	2	2	2	2			
12	19		DESIGN WMN SPC				12	12	19				7	9	6	8	10	11	12	10	9	10	5	12	14	12	14	12	11	15	7	8	8	9	9	3		
12	18	KGTV	AVG. ALL WKS	6	6	12	22	12	18	17	16	19	8	9	10	8	9	8	9	10	10	10	10	9	9	7	9	10	10	10	9	9	9	9	9	9	13	2	3
6	9		ANYTHNG-LV-WED	6				6	9				5	5	10	7	4	5	5	5	4	4	3	9	12	5	9	9	9	11	4	4	5	5	4	4	16	
6	9		ABC MOV SP WED		6			6	9				4	4	2	3	3	3	4	4	5	4	5	3	3	1	2	3	2	2	5	3	4	5	6	6	6	2	
12	21		ABC WED MOV SP			12		12	21				8	10	6	7	8	8	11	8	11	11	13	12	11	11	10	11	10	7	4	4	6	6	7	7		
22	34		IND JONES - ABC				22	22	34				17	18	20	20	19	19	17	20	18	21	17	17	11	11	17	21	21	22	20	25	21	16	19	19	29	7	
8	12	KNSD	AVG. ALL WKS	9	10	10	2	8	12	13	10	12	4	5	3	5	5	5	5	5	5	4	6	6	4	6	6	6	6	6	5	5	4	5	5	5	2	1	1
9	14		SEINFELD - WED	9				9	14				5	7	4	10	12	9	10	8	4	3	3	8	6	13	10	10	9	11	6	4	6	6	5	5	5	1	
10	15		UNSLVD MYS - NBC		10			10	15				5	6	3	4	4	5	5	5	6	6	9	7	4	7	7	7	7	7	5	3	3	4	4	5	2	1	
6	9		NITE COURT - WED			10	2	6	9				3	4	3	3	3	3	4	3	3	4	4	5	5	4	5	4	5	4	3	3	3	4	4	5	3	
1	2	KPBS	AVG. ALL WKS	1	2	2	1	1	2	6	7	5	1	1											2	1	2		1	1	1			1					
1	1		EDGE	1			1	1	1													1	1		1						1								
2	3		CHMPNSHP - DNCNG		2			2	3				1	1							3	2	2	3	2	2	2	2			1		1	1	1	1			
2	3		NEW TIJUANA			2		2	3				1	1				1	1	1	2	2	2	2	2		1	1	1	1	1		1	1	1	1			
1	1	KTTY	KTTY MOV 8	1	1	<<	1	1	1	3X	3	3	1	1						1	1	1	1	1							1		1	1	1	1		1	
4	6	KUSI	GERALDO	2	3	3	8	4	6	4X	3	4	2	3	3	3	4	3	3	3	3	3	3	5	5	6	5	4	4	6	2	1	2	2	2	1	1		1
4	6	XETV	MOV	3	4	5	4	4	6	7X	9	7	2	3	3	3	3	3	3	3	3	3	3	3	3	4	3	3	3	3	2	3	2	3	2	2	2	1	2
63			HUT/PUT/TOTALS*	65	67	57	65	63		53	51	56	44	50	35	43	46	48	49	51	53	52	57	54	44	51	53	53	52	50	46	42	43	45	48	50	30	16	19

WEDNESDAY 8:00PM-10:00PM

1	2			3	4	5	6	7	8	11	12	13	15	16	17	18	19	20	21	22	23	24	25	26	27	28	29	31	32	34	35	36	37	38	39	40	41	42	43

FIGURE 24.3 NSI Report.

Source: Nielsen Media Research. Reproduced with permission.

Agency media planners and buyers rarely use overall program ratings to make a final determination of program cost efficiency. Because different programs attract different demographic audiences, media planners and buyers calculate the cost per thousand for their specific demographic target. The use of ratings and audience size for a specific demographic target provides a more relevant base for evaluating program cost.

The importance of evaluating program audience and cost in terms of specific target audiences is illustrated in the middle and bottom tables in Table 24.2. The middle table assumes a target of women aged 18–34, while the bottom table assumes a target of men aged 55 and older. Note how the relative cost efficiencies of each program change as the demographics of the target audience change. The demographic ratings in this example indicate that Program A is a very cost-efficient vehicle to reach younger women while Program C is a very cost-efficient vehicle to reach older men.

Manipulating Television Ratings

The "sweeps" months are periods in which it is acknowledged that the networks will present special programming designed to maximize audience size. While most in the industry recognize the artificial nature of the ratings during this period, few question the ethics of the practice.

There are practices, however, that do represent unethical attempts to manipulate the ratings in favor of a particular station. Nielsen keeps abreast of station practices and will make special notations in the ratings report or withhold the data entirely when they believe that a television station has engaged in unethical practices designed to artificially raise or otherwise manipulate the ratings. The types of practices that fall into this category of behaviors include the following:[14]

- Research surveys that "require, request, or suggest, in any fashion, that a potential respondent view a particular station(s) or program(s)" as a part of survey participation.
- Any communications that explicitly or implicitly mention the keeping and returning of Nielsen diaries.
- Contests, rewards or special promotions that (a) are concentrated during and/or just prior to a measurement period, (b) include the telecasting of code words, clues, or other information, "the knowledge of which is necessary to enter or win," (c) draw contestants winning names on-air and which require contestants to watch to see whose name is drawn, and (d) require contestants to watch specific programs to find out contest rules.

RADIO AUDIENCE MEASUREMENT

Ratings and share are also used to estimate the size of radio program audiences. These terms have the same meaning for radio as television, that is, a radio share reflects the percentage of the actual number of individuals or households listening at a particular time while a radio rating reflects the percentage of the potential number of individuals or households in the geographic area of interest.

---

[14] A. C. Nielsen Company Media Research Group, *NSI Methodology* (1992), 54–55. All quotes are from this source.

How Radio Rating Data Is Collected

Radio ratings are collected on both the national and local level. Radio's All Dimension Audience Research (RADAR) is the sole provider of national radio network ratings. A radio network, similar to a television network, is a group of affiliated stations that have agreed to simultaneously carry programs and/or commercials. RADAR uses a telephone recall methodology to measure audience delivery of radio networks. Random-digit dialing is used to contact and then recruit about 12,000 individuals per year. One randomly selected individual (over the age of 12) in each household participates for one week, during which time a daily telephone call is made to obtain his or her recall of station listening, by fifteen-minute periods, for the previous twenty-four hours. Share and rating estimates are calculated by matching respondents' reports of quarter hour listening with program and commercial clearances for each station affiliated with a specific radio network.

Local area radio ratings are provided by Arbitron. Arbitron uses diaries to collect year-round radio listening behaviors in about eighty markets. Additionally, diaries are used to measure listening behaviors during sweeps months in an additional 180 markets. Participants are contacted via random-digit dialing. Similar to the Nielsen television diary, the Arbitron radio diary provides space for participants to record day, time, and location of listening as well as the call letters of the station being listened to.

Using Radio Ratings to Match Program Audiences with Target Audiences

RADAR and Arbitron ratings provide the information that media planners and buyers need to determine how well the demographics of a particular radio network or local program audience match the demographics of their brand's or product's target audience. An example of an Arbitron radio ratings report is shown in Figure 24.4 (pages 612–613). The data is interpreted as follows.

The content of the report is noted on the top of the page. Figure 24.4 contains information on specific demographic audiences for Saturday between the hours of 10 A.M. and 3 P.M. Each demographic audience is listed in a separate column. Individual radio stations are listed in bold in the first column. Beneath each station different types of audience measures are reported. These measures are

- *MET AQH PER (00)*—The estimated number of people (reported in hundreds) in the metropolitan area (MET) listening to a station for at least five minutes during an average quarter hour (AQH). For example, 39,600, people (aged 12+) listened to station KSON–FM during the Saturday time period.

- *MET AQH RATING*—Similar to a television rating, this measure represents the percent of the population (in the metropolitan area) listening to a station in an average quarter hour divided by the total *potential* listening audience. Station KSON–FM's rating is 1.8, which means that 1.8 percent of all potential radio listeners listened to KSON–FM in this time period.

- *MET AQH SHARE*—Also similar to television share, this measure represents the percent of the population (in the metropolitan area) listening to a station in an average quarter hour divided by the total *actual* listening audience. Station KSON–FM's share is 8.7, which means that 8.7 percent of all radio listeners were tuned to KSON–FM in this time period.

Specific Audience
SATURDAY 10AM–3PM

	Persons 12+	Persons 18+	Men 18+	Men 18-24	Men 25-34	Men 35-44	Men 45-54	Men 55-64	Women 18+	Women 18-24	Women 25-34	Women 35-44	Women 45-54	Women 55-64	Teens 12-17
KSON															
MET AQH PER (00)	29	29	12				1		17		1			12	
MET AQH RATING	.1	.1	.1				.1		.2					1.2	
MET AQH SHARE	.6	.7	.6				.5		.8		.2			6.2	
MET CUME PER (00)	84	84	20				7		64		11	9		32	
MET CUME RATING	.4	.4	.2				.6		.7		.5	.4		3.3	
TSA AQH PER (00)	29	29	12				1		17		1			12	
TSA CUME PER (00)	84	84	20				7		64		11	9		32	
KSON–FM															
MET AQH PER (00)	396	388	186	18	59	54	22	19	202	22	78	51	20	7	8
MET AQH RATING	1.8	2.0	1.8	.9	2.2	2.6	1.8	2.2	2.1	1.5	3.3	2.5	1.6	.7	.4
MET AQH SHARE	8.7	9.1	8.7	3.8	10.4	11.8	10.1	11.0	9.5	6.8	14.8	11.9	7.5	3.6	2.7
MET CUME PER (00)	1074	1024	504	26	171	168	64	36	520	103	183	101	66	21	50
MET CUME RATING	4.9	5.2	5.0	1.3	6.3	8.0	5.3	4.2	5.3	7.1	7.7	5.0	5.3	2.2	2.7
TSA AQH PER (00)	396	388	186	18	59	54	22	19	202	22	78	51	20	7	8
TSA CUME PER (00)	1074	1024	504	26	171	168	64	36	520	103	183	101	66	21	50
A/F TOT															
MET AQH PER (00)	425	417	198	18	59	54	23	19	219	22	79	51	20	19	8
MET AQH RATING	2.0	2.1	2.0	.9	2.2	2.6	1.9	2.2	2.2	1.5	3.3	2.5	1.6	2.0	.4
MET AQH SHARE	9.3	9.8	9.3	3.8	10.4	11.8	10.6	11.0	10.3	6.8	15.0	11.9	7.5	9.8	2.7
MET CUME PER (00)	1148	1098	525	26	171	168	71	36	573	103	194	111	66	41	50
MET CUME RATING	5.3	5.5	5.2	1.3	6.3	8.0	5.9	4.2	5.9	7.1	8.2	5.5	5.3	4.3	2.7
TSA AQH PER (00)	425	417	198	18	59	54	23	19	219	22	79	51	20	19	8
TSA CUME PER (00)	1148	1098	525	26	171	168	71	36	573	103	194	111	66	41	50
KSPA															
MET AQH PER (00)	59	59	28	1	1			4	31				9	1	
MET AQH RATING	.3	.3	.3	.1				.5	.3				.7	.1	
MET AQH SHARE	1.3	1.4	1.3	.2	.2			2.3	1.5				3.4	.5	
MET CUME PER (00)	136	136	49	25	11			7	87				18	10	
MET CUME RATING	.6	.7	.5	1.3	.4			.8	.9				1.4	1.0	
TSA AQH PER (00)	59	59	28	1	1			4	31				9	1	
TSA CUME PER (00)	136	136	49	25	11			7	87				18	10	
KYXY															
MET AQH PER (00)	103	103	40	1	4	17	5	3	63	10	13	14	15	7	
MET AQH RATING	.5	.5	.4	.1	.1	.8	.4	.4	.6	.7	.5	.7	1.2	.7	
MET AQH SHARE	2.3	2.4	1.9	.2	.7	3.7	2.3	1.7	3.0	3.1	2.5	3.3	5.6	3.6	
MET CUME PER (00)	427	427	154	25	22	35	34	14	273	56	79	46	50	32	
MET CUME RATING	2.0	2.2	1.5	1.3	.8	1.7	2.8	1.6	2.8	3.8	3.3	2.3	4.0	3.3	
TSA AQH PER (00)	103	103	40	1	4	17	5	3	63	10	13	14	15	7	
TSA CUME PER (00)	427	427	154	25	22	35	34	14	273	56	79	46	50	32	

Specific Audience
SATURDAY 10AM-3PM

XEMO

	Persons 12+	Persons 18+	Men 18+	Men 18-24	Men 25-34	Men 35-44	Men 45-54	Men 55-64	Women 18+	Women 18-24	Women 25-34	Women 35-44	Women 45-54	Women 55-64	Teens 12-17
MET AQH PER (00)	116	108	29	6	16	5	1	1	79	42	33	3		1	8
MET AQH RATING	.5	.5	.3	.3	.6	.2	.1	.1	.8	2.9	1.4	.1		.1	.4
MET AQH SHARE	2.5	2.5	1.4	1.3	2.8	1.1	.5	.6	3.7	13.0	6.3	.7		.5	2.7
MET CUME PER (00)	284	261	111	23	46	23	13	6	150	60	72	10		8	23
MET CUME RATING	1.3	1.3	1.1	1.2	1.7	1.1	1.1	.7	1.5	4.1	3.0	.5		.8	1.2
TSA AQH PER (00)	116	108	29	6	16	5	1	1	79	42	33	3		1	8
TSA CUME PER (00)	284	261	111	23	46	23	13	6	150	60	72	10		8	23

XHKY

	Persons 12+	Persons 18+	Men 18+	Men 18-24	Men 25-34	Men 35-44	Men 45-54	Men 55-64	Women 18+	Women 18-24	Women 25-34	Women 35-44	Women 45-54	Women 55-64	Teens 12-17
MET AQH PER (00)	84	84	39	10	7	18	4		45	12	2	18	13		8
MET AQH RATING	.4	.4	.4	.5	.3	.9	.3		.5	.8	.1	.9	1.0		.4
MET AQH SHARE	1.8	2.0	1.8	2.1	1.2	3.9	1.8		2.1	3.7	.4	4.2	4.9		
MET CUME PER (00)	165	157	81	29	17	22	13		76	29	10	24	13		
MET CUME RATING	.8	.8	.8	1.5	.6	1.1	1.1		.8	2.0	.4	1.2	1.0		
TSA AQH PER (00)	84	84	39	10	7	18	4		45	12	2	18	13		8
TSA CUME PER (00)	165	157	81	29	17	22	13		76	29	10	24	13		

XHRM

	Persons 12+	Persons 18+	Men 18+	Men 18-24	Men 25-34	Men 35-44	Men 45-54	Men 55-64	Women 18+	Women 18-24	Women 25-34	Women 35-44	Women 45-54	Women 55-64	Teens 12-17
MET AQH PER (00)	74	67	41	12	17	5	7		26	5	16	2	3		7
MET AQH RATING	.3	.3	.4	.6	.6	.2	.6		.3	.3	.7	.1	.2		.4
MET AQH SHARE	1.6	1.6	1.9	2.5	3.0	1.1	3.2		1.2	1.5	3.0	.5	1.1		2.3
MET CUME PER (00)	297	258	152	73	49	12	18		106	18	52	17	19		39
MET CUME RATING	1.4	1.3	1.5	3.7	1.8	.6	1.5		1.1	1.2	2.2	.8	1.5		2.1
TSA AQH PER (00)	74	67	41	12	17	5	7		26	5	16	2	3		7
TSA CUME PER (00)	297	258	152	73	49	12	18		106	18	52	17	19		39

XHTZ

	Persons 12+	Persons 18+	Men 18+	Men 18-24	Men 25-34	Men 35-44	Men 45-54	Men 55-64	Women 18+	Women 18-24	Women 25-34	Women 35-44	Women 45-54	Women 55-64	Teens 12-17
MET AQH PER (00)	220	121	60	46	12	1	1		61	29	14	10	6	2	99
MET AQH RATING	1.0	.6	.6	2.3	.4		.1		.6	2.0	.6	.5	.5	.2	5.3
MET AQH SHARE	4.8	2.8	2.8	9.7	2.1	.2	.5		2.9	9.0	2.7	2.3	2.3	1.0	33.0
MET CUME PER (00)	705	415	236	152	63	12	9		179	79	55	25	6	10	290
MET CUME RATING	3.2	2.1	2.3	7.6	2.3	.6	.7		1.8	5.4	2.3	1.2	.5	1.0	15.4
TSA AQH PER (00)	220	121	60	46	12	1	1		61	29	14	10	6	2	99
TSA CUME PER (00)	705	415	236	152	63	12	9		179	79	55	25	6	10	290

XLTN

	Persons 12+	Persons 18+	Men 18+	Men 18-24	Men 25-34	Men 35-44	Men 45-54	Men 55-64	Women 18+	Women 18-24	Women 25-34	Women 35-44	Women 45-54	Women 55-64	Teens 12-17
MET AQH PER (00)	86	82	21	3	7	9		2	61	13	15	15	8	10	4
MET AQH RATING	.4	.4	.2	.2	.3	.4		.2	.6	.9	.6	.7	.6	1.0	.2
MET AQH SHARE	1.9	1.9	1.0	.6	1.2	2.0		1.2	2.9	4.0	2.8	3.5	3.0	5.2	1.3
MET CUME PER (00)	218	191	50	15	17	11		7	141	27	51	34	19	10	27
MET CUME RATING	1.0	1.0	.5	.8	.6	.5		.8	1.4	1.9	2.1	1.7	1.5	1.0	1.4
TSA AQH PER (00)	86	82	21	3	7	9		2	61	13	15	15	8	10	4
TSA CUME PER (00)	218	191	50	15	17	11		7	141	27	51	34	19	10	27

Footnote Symbols:
* Audience estimates adjusted for actual broadcast schedule.
+ Station(s) changed call letters since the prior survey - see page 5B.
& Both of the previous footnotes apply.

FIGURE 24.4 Arbitron radio ratings.
Source: Arbitron Co. Reproduced with permission.

Average quarter hour audience measures tell a media planner of the average audience size for a given station in a given time period and are interpreted identically to television rating and share. However, radio listenership differs from television viewership in one important respect. There is significantly more channel switching in radio versus television. Consequently, radio audience size is also reported in terms of CUME audiences, the number of *different* people who listen to a station during a specific time period. The next two measures shown in Figure 24.4 report CUME audience size (again, for those aged 12+), as follows:

- *MET CUME PER (00)*—The estimated number of *different* people (reported in hundreds) in the metropolitan area (MET) listening to a station for at least five minutes during a quarter hour during the target time period. 107,400 different people listened to station KSON–FM during the Saturday time period.

- *MET CUME RATING*—The percent of the population (in the metropolitan area) represented in the cume audience divided by the total *potential* listening audience. Station KSON–FM's cume rating is 4.9, which means that 4.9 percent of all potential radio listeners listened to KSON–FM for at least five minutes in a quarter hour during the entire time period.

The prior measures reported audience size for the San Diego metropolitan area. The metropolitan area is the standard unit of geographic coverage for Arbitron reports. However, in some markets, an audience estimate for a broader geographic area is required. This broader area, labeled Total Survey Area (TSA) is composed of the Metro area and any additional partial or whole counties that make an important contribution to audience characteristics. Arbitron therefore also reports audience size in hundreds (TSA AQH PER (00)) and CUME audience size in hundreds (TSA CUME PER (00)) for the total survey area. In the case of San Diego, however, the metropolitan area and the total survey area are identical, and consequently, station KSON–FM's metropolitan audience size is the same as its total survey audience size.

Arbitron and RADAR data, similar to Nielsen television ratings, are used in conjunction with cost of advertising time to determine the relative cost efficiency of a particular program for reaching a specific target audience.[15]

Manipulating Radio Ratings

Arbitron and RADAR ratings are not subject to the same fluctuations as television "sweeps" ratings. However, both services recognize the ability of radio stations to use practices designed to distort the ratings. Similar to Nielsen, radio rating services will note any of these practices in their report or may go so far as to eliminate suspect rat-

---

[15] As discussed in the prior sections, media planners typically use ratings to estimate the size and characteristics of a television or radio program audience. Once a program is selected, ratings are then used to determine the amount of advertising that needs to be purchased to reach the target audience at a required level of frequency and exposure. The measure of advertising amount or weight, called a gross rating point or GRP, is the product of the number of commercials placed in a program times the program's rating. For example, six commercials placed in a 16-rating program and five commercials placed in a 10-rating program result in a total of 146 GRPs, calculated as

$$6 \times 16 = 96 \text{ GRPs}$$
$$5 \times 10 = 50 \text{ GRPs}$$
$$\text{TOTAL} = 146 \text{ GRPs}$$

ings from the report. Practices considered inappropriate for a radio station include the following:[16]

- Attempts to distort diarykeepers listening behaviors by, for example, "a public or private appeal for diarykeepers to surrender their diaries or to misreport in any way (e.g., overstate, understate, or misstate) their actual listening to any station.
- Attempts to distort typical listening behaviors with contests or promotions that "may cause diarykeepers to misreport their actual listening by offering prizes based on amounts of listening recorded or claimed; might cause diarykeepers to lose their anonymity; might cause a diarykeeper to surrender a diary in trade for a prize or cash."
- Attempts to sensitize diarykeepers about recording their listening behaviors.

MAGAZINE AUDIENCE MEASUREMENT

Magazine audiences are evaluated differently from television and radio audiences. Media planners evaluate a magazine's suitability as an advertising vehicle in two different but related ways. First, they use circulation information to determine the extent to which a particular magazine's circulation base matches their target audience. Second, they use reported magazine readership to determine the incidence and concentration of their target audience among the total readers of that magazine. In both cases, a target audience cost per thousand is used to compare relative cost efficiencies.

Target Audience and Circulation Characteristics

Standard Rate and Data Service (SRDS) gathers and publishes information on the vast majority of consumer and business magazines distributed in the United States. Media planners use the information contained in SRDS to determine advertising closing dates, requirements for placing an ad, advertising space options, advertising cost, and to evaluate the size and characteristics of the magazine's circulation base. A sample SRDS listing is shown in Figure 24.5 (pages 616–617).[17]

As the SRDS listing in Figure 24.5 illustrates, Section 18 provides information on the characteristics of the magazine's circulation base.[18] In this example, each type of industry in which *CIO* readers are employed is given a numeric code while each reader's position within his or her company is given an alphabetic code. The table at the end of Section 18 cross-tablulates the *CIO* reader's job title/position with his or her company's type of business. The cross-tabulation indicates, for example, that of *CIO*'s total circulation of 53,005

---

[16] Arbitron, *Radio Market Report* (Fall 1993), 5A–5B. All quotes are from this source.

[17] An important component of a SRDS magazine listing is the Audit Bureau of Circulation (ABC) verification. Magazine and newspaper publishers submit circulation statements twice a year to the ABC. These statements are subject to external audit and verification by the ABC. Further, the ABC conducts an annual audit to substantiate or correct information reported in the prior year's statements. Audits are conducted by personal inspection of the publisher's records.

[18] Detailed circulation data do not appear for every magazine listed in SRDS. This information is, however, often available directly from the publisher. In those cases where detailed circulation information is not available, media planners and buyers must evaluate magazines based on overall CPM.

32C Computers

CIO ▽BPA

The Magazine For Information Executives
An International Data Group Publication
(This is a paid duplicate of the listing under classification No. 20.)

Location ID: 7 BLST 32C **Mid 043319-000**
Published 18 times a year by CIO Publishing, Inc., div. of International Data Group, 492 Old Connecticut Path, Framingham, MA 01701-9208. Phone 508-872-8200. Telex: 95,1518.
PUBLISHER'S EDITORIAL PROFILE
CIO is a magazine designed to address the issues vital to the success of information executives and their companies. Each CIO issue provides coverage on a variety of topics—general news, information management issues, new technologies and products, industry trends and surveys, innovative uses of information systems, legal/regulatory issues, coverage of how they impact CIOs and their companies. Special departments and columns include: Insights, Trendlines, State of the Art, Human Factors, Outlook, Working Smart and FYI. Rec'd 8/8/91.

1. PERSONNEL
Pres/Pub—Joseph L. Levy.
Editor-in-Chief—Marcia Blumenthal.
Managing Editor—Gary Hays.
Dir./Mktg.—Cathy M. Leary Hays.

2. REPRESENTATIVES and/or BRANCH OFFICES
Framingham, MA 01701—Linda Burton, New England Adv. Sales, 492 Old Connecticut Path. Phone 508-935-4039, FAX: 508-872-0618.
Fairfield, NJ 07004—Michael Masters, Eastern Reg. Dir./Adv. Sales, 30 Two Bridges Rd., Ste. 340. Phone 201-227-1140. FAX: 201-227-1555.
Rosemont, IL—Bill Mc. Donough, Midwest/Southern Reg. Dir./Adv. Sales, 10400 W. Higgins Rd., Ste. 300. Phone 708-827-4515; FAX: 708-827-9159.
San Francisco, CA 94104—Jerry Parsons, Western Reg. Dir./Adv. Sales, Richard Bastias, Western Reg Sales Mgr., 220 Montgomery St., Ste. 1120. Phone 415-398-6848; FAX: 415-398-6849.

3. COMMISSION AND CASH DISCOUNT
15% to recognized agencies.

ADVERTISING RATES
Effective September 01, 1991.
Rates received July 15, 1991.

Issue:	Closing	Issue:	Closing
Sep 1	7/28	Nov 1	9/28
Sep 15	8/11	Nov 15	10/12
Oct 1	8/27	Dec	10/27
Oct 15	9/10		

SPECIAL FEATURE ISSUES
Feb/92—EDI—Managing the Buy-In; The Emerging Telecommunications Manager; Executive Opportunities for CIOs in Medium-sized High-growth companies.
Mar/92—Annual Special Issue: Operating System Connectivity; Reusable Software; Working with Software Vendors.
Apr 1/92—Image Processing—Profiles in Re-Engineering; Manufacturing Systems—New Directions; Customer Satisfaction Measures.
Apr 15/92—Strategic Outlook: Downsizing—Economic Advantages and Improving the Corporate Competitive Posture; IT in the Non-Profit Sector.
May 1/92—Systems Integrators; Logistics—The Key to Operation Efficiency; IT in Latin America.
May 15/92—Strategic Outlook: Communications—Client/Server Strategies and LAN Opportunities; Educating Line Executives about IT.
Jun 1/92—Industry Overview: The Automotive Trade; Creating the Open Systems Environment; The Role of IT in Process Change.
Jun 15/92—Strategic Outlook: Measuring the Return on IT Investment—Techniques and Capturing the CEO's Interest; Smart Card Update.
Jul/92—Industry Overview: Broadcast and Print Media; Graphical User Interfaces; Commercial Uses of Supercomputing.
Aug/92—The 5th Annual CIO 100.
Sep 1/92—Outsourcing and ROI; Security—New Legal Issues; Decision Making with Online Information Services.
Sep 15/92—Strategic Outlook: Training—Building the Technical and Executive Programs; Innovative Techniques for Marketing IT Services.
Oct 1/92—Industry Overview: Health Care; The Decision to Downsize; Defining Best Practice Methods of IS.
Oct 15/92—Strategic Outlook: The Database Dilemma—Integrating Multiple Databases and Managing Corporate Information; Multimedia—Education and Sales Force Tools.
Nov 1/92—Client/Server User Report; CASE Implementation—Meeting the Challenge; Listening to External Customers.
Nov 15/92—Strategic Outlook: IS Personnel—Career Patterns and Re-Engineering IS Departments; Becoming a Global Competitor.
Dec/92—Industry Overview: The IT Agenda of Government; The Savvy CIO and Strategic Planning; Integrating Voice and E-mail Technologies.

17. SPECIAL SERVICES
B.P.A. Supplementary Data Report June/91.

18. CIRCULATION
Established 1987. Single copy 7.00; per year 63.00. Summary data—for detail see Publisher's Statement.
B.P.A. 6-30-91 (6 mos. aver. qualified)

	Total	Non-Pd	Paid
	53,015	53,015	

	TL	A	B	C	D	E	F
22—	1,029	56	575	66	70	25	109
23—	2,070	346	94020	96	139	59	148
TL—	53,005	6,322	24,603	3,269	2,208	1,734	4,915

	G	H	I	J	K
3—	14	488	1,014	157	25
4—	17	534	218	421	37
5—	13	38	327	191	13
6—	13	82	37	41	13
7—	5	8	17	26	8
8—	31	423	115	184	1
9—	60	48	48	909	32
10—	12	148	9	156	15
11—	10	64	29	88	4
12—	28	74	25	378	23
13—	12	40	292	160	7
14—	22	59		145	8
15—	8	1	3	88	
16—	8		13	25	4
17—	2	27	44	65	3
18—	20	134	583	234	27
19—	1	87	13	34	4
20—	5	221	39	82	7
21—	16	41	11	32	5
22—	11	53	182	155	41
23—TL	386	2,574	2,708	3,998	288

Publisher states: Effective with September 1991 issue, rates based on guaranteed non-paid circulation average of 60,000.

CIRCUIT CELLAR INK
The Computer Applications Journal

Location ID: 7 BLST 32C **Mid 049478-000**
Published bimonthly by Circuit Cellar, Inc., 4 Park St., Vernon, CT 06066. Phone 203-875-2751. FAX: 203-872-2204.
PUBLISHER'S EDITORIAL PROFILE
CIRCUIT CELLAR INK is a source of practical, technical information for designers and builders of computer hardware and software applications. Editorial content includes complete projects, practical tutorials, and useful design and construction techniques. Rec'd 2/14/89.

1. PERSONNEL
Pub—Daniel Rodrigues.
Editorial Dir—Steve Ciarcia.
Managing Editor—Ken Davidson.
Prod Mgr—Mark Vereb.

2. REPRESENTATIVES and/or BRANCH OFFICES
Norwood, MA 02062—Hajar Associates, Debra Andersen, 49 Walpole St. Phone 617-769-8950. FAX: 617-769-8982.

18. CIRCULATION
Established 1988. Single copy 3.95; per year 17.95.
SWORN 6-30-91 (6 mos. aver.)

Total	Non-Pd	Paid (Single)	(Assoc)
33,849	4,576	29,073 24,893	4,180

Unpaid Distribution (not incl. above):
  Total 245
TERRITORIAL DISTRIBUTION 6/91—35,525

N.Eng.	Mid.Atl.	E.N.Cen.	W.N.Cen.	S.Atl.	E.S.Cen.
2,480	4,579	5,215	1,972	4,682	956

W.S.Cen.	Mtn.St.	Pac.St.	Canada	Foreign	Other
2,771	2,341	8,281	998	1,284	38

COLOR PUBLISHING
A PennWell Publishing Co. Publication

Location ID: 7 BLST 32C **Mid 051105-000**
Published bimonthly by PennWell Publishing Co., One Technology Park Dr., Westford, MA 01886. Phone 508-692-0700.
For shipping info see Print Media Production Data.
PUBLISHER'S EDITORIAL PROFILE
COLOR PUBLISHING covers color publishing systems, color proofers, color monitors, high-end imagesetters, memory systems, color scanners, color-based publishing software, color graphics controllers, PC's Mac's and workstations. Rec'd 3/13/91.

1. PERSONNEL
Pub—Robert Holton.
Pub/Mktg—Alan Ventura.
Mktg Comm Dir—Hope Mascott.
Editor—Frank Romano.

2. REPRESENTATIVES and/or BRANCH OFFICES
Feasterville, PA 19053—Daniel Ferro, Reg'l Mgr, Suite 7, 1200 Bustleton Pike. Phone 215-953-6970. FAX: 215-355-4395.
Westford, MA 01886—Alan D. Ventura, Sales/Mktg. Mgr., P.O. Box 987, One Technology Park Dr. Phone 508-392-2162. FAX: 508-692-0529.
Rosemont, IL 60018—Phil Davis, Reg. Mgr, 9501 W. Devon, Ste. 300. Phone 708-696-4350. FAX: 708-696-4839.
Palo Alto, CA 94303—Bill Cooper, Reg. Mgr, 1000 Elwell Ct., Ste. 234. Phone 415-965-4334. FAX: 415-965-0255.
Santa Ana, CA 92707—Tom Boris, Reg. Mgr, 2232 S.E. Bristol, Ste. 109. Phone 714-756-0681. FAX: 714-756-0621.
Spring, TX 77388—Randy Jeter, Reg. Mgr, 19627 Interstate 45 N., Ste. 220. Phone 713-353-0309. FAX: 713-353-8550.
England—David T. Round, 69 Imperial Way, Croydon, Surrey CR0 4RR England. Phone 44-81-686-7655. FAX: 44-81-686-2134.
France—Daniel Bernard, Prominier, 247 Rue St. Jacques, 75005 Paris France. Phone 33-1-435-455-35. FAX: 33-1-563-3616.
Germany—Johann Bylek, Verlagsbuero Bylek, Stockaeckering 63, D-8011 Kirchern/Muenchen. Phone 49-89-903-8606. FAX: 49-89-904-3526.

5. BLACK/WHITE RATES

	1 ti	6 ti	9 ti	12 ti	18 ti
1 page	11,330.	11,210.	11,090.	10,970.	10,730.
				24 ti	36 ti
1 page				10,490.	10,250.

6. COLOR RATES

	1 ti	6 ti	9 ti	12 ti	18 ti
2-Color:					
1 page	13,230.	13,110.	12,990.	12,870.	12,630.
				24 ti	36 ti
1 page				12,390.	12,150.
	1 ti	3 ti	6 ti	9 ti	12 ti
3-Color:					
1 page	14,170.	14,050.	13,930.	13,810.	13,570.
				18 ti	24 ti
1 page				13,330.	13,090.
	1 ti	3 ti	6 ti	9 ti	12 ti
4-Color:					
1 page	15,125.	15,005.	14,885.	14,765.	14,525.
				18 ti	24 ti
1 page				14,285.	14,045.

Metallic:
1 page, extra .... 250. Sprd, extra .... 500.

7. COVERS

	1 ti	6 ti	9 ti	12 ti	18 ti
2nd cover	18,920.	18,800.	18,680.	18,560.	18,320.
3rd cover	17,980.	17,860.	17,740.	17,620.	17,380.
4th cover	22,710.	22,590.	22,470.	22,350.	22,110.
				24 ti	36 ti
2nd cover				18,080.	17,840.
3rd cover				17,140.	16,900.
4th cover				21870.	21,630.

8. INSERTS
Available.

9. BLEED
Extra 15%
Spread/page rate.

10. SPECIAL POSITION
Spread/page rate plus 10%

14. CONTRACT AND COPY REGULATIONS
See Contents page for location—items 1, 4, 7, 8, 9, 11, 12, 13, 14, 15, 17, 18, 19, 20, 21, 22, 24, 25, 26, 28, 29, 30, 31, 32, 35, 36.

15. GENERAL REQUIREMENTS
Also see SRDS Print Media Production Data.
Printing Process: Offset Full Run Regional Cover
Trim Size: 8-1/8 x 10-3/4; No./Cols. 3.
Binding Method: Saddle Stitched.
Colors Available: Black and white; Black and one color; 4-color process; Matched; GAA/SWOP; 5th cylinder.
Covers: 4-color process.

AD PAGE DIMENSIONS
Sprd 15-1/8 x 10 1/2 h 7 x 4-5/8
1 pg 7 x 10
1/2 sprd 15-1/8 x 4-5/8

16. ISSUE AND CLOSING DATES
Published 18 times a year.

Issue:	Closing	Issue:	Closing
Feb	12/27	May 15	4/10
Mar	1/27	Jun 1	4/27
Apr 1	2/26	Jun 15	5/11
Apr 15	3/11	Jul	5/27
May 1	3/27	Aug	6/26

Average Non-Qualified (not incl. above):
Total 14,086

TERRITORIAL DISTRIBUTION 5/91—53,005

N.Eng.	Mid.Atl.	E.N.Cen.	W.N.Cen.	S.Atl.	E.S.Cen.
4,319	9,834	9,388	3,522	9,631	1,783
W.S.Cen.	Mtn.St.	Pac.St.	Canada	Foreign	Other
4,015	2,390	7,901	20	3	199

BUSINESS ANALYSIS OF CIRCULATION

1 —Mftg. of Computers, Communications or Peripheral Equip.
2 —Mftg. of Other Products/Processes.
3 —Finance: Banking.
4 —Finance: Insurance.
5 —Finance: Securities.
6 —Finance: Real Estate, Credit or Securities.
7 —Wholesale or Retail Trade.
8 —Gov't: Federal, State or Local.
9 —Military.
10 —Transportation: Land, Sea or Air.
11 —Education: College, University, Library, Secondary, Other.
12 —Medical Services.
13 —Utility: Communications.
14 —Utility: Electric, Gas, Sanitation.
15 —Hotels or Recreation.
16 —Accounting or Legal Services.
17 —Communications: Publishing, Broadcast, Advertising, PR.
18 —Computer and Data Processing Services and Software.
19 —Business Services (other than computer).
20 —Research & Development.
21 —Aerospace / Defense Contractor.
22 —Mining / Construction / Petroleum / Refining / Agriculture.
23 —Other Businesses and Services.
TL —Total.

TL. Total. A. Pres., Owner, Partner, Gen. Mgr. B. VP / Dir. / Mgr. of Information Systems / MIS / DP C. VP / Dir. / Mgr. of Data / Voice Communications Systems. D. VP / Dir. Finance / Controller. E. CIO-Chief Information Officer. F. MIS / DP Communications Consultant. G.-VP / Dir. / Mgr. Accounting. H. VP / Dir. / Mgr. Eng. / Mftg. I. VP / Dir. / Mgr. Mktg. / Sales. J. VP / Dir. / Mgr. Operations Admin. K. Other.

	TL	A	B	C	D	E	F
1—	4,106	668	811	258	87	61	523
2—	9,727	496	5,836	462	663	238	728
3—	2,625	122	1,424	279	117	74	199
4—	2,371	89	1,495	178	61	78	208
5—	721	71	381	95	27	21	53
6—	626	118	345	43	32	16	34
7—	3,785	616	2,083	193	249	108	175
8—	6,121	217	2,741	447	166	348	725
9—	1,206	48	443	78	39	85	173
10—	1,209	66	635	124	55	35	99
11—	3,068	207	1,639	184	90	163	257
12—	2,541	145	1,528	138	135	180	142
13—	1,601	126	435	185	25	16	261
14—	1,059	26	580	79	33	27	129
15—	247	19	143	18	23	8	18
16—	459	125	170	19	20	11	73
17—	864	246	304	44	46	26	57
18—	5,083	2,054	1,253	152	60	75	502
19—	970	342	316	36	44	32	64
20—	509	78	165	33	14	21	61
21—	1,035	41	361	62	13	27	177

Hollywood, FL 33024—Hajar Associates, Christa Collins, 7640 Farragut St., Phone 305-966-3939. FAX: 305-985-8457.
Hinsdale, IL 60521—Hajar Associates, Nanette Traetow, 907 N. Elm St., Ste. 100. Phone 708-789-3080. FAX: 708-789-3082.
Fairhaven, NJ 07704—Hajar Associates, Barbara Best, 569 River Rd. Phone 908-741-7744. FAX: 908-741-6823.
Costa Mesa, CA 92626—Hajar Associates, Barbara Jones, Shelley Rainey, 3303 Harbor Blvd., Ste. G-11. Phone 714-540-3554. FAX: 714-540-7103.

3. COMMISSION AND CASH DISCOUNT
Advertisers with approved credit extended terms of net/30. 15% agency commission allowed for advertising space, color and premium position charges. No cash discount.

ADVERTISING RATES
Effective September 1, 1991.
Rates received September 10, 1991.

5. BLACK/WHITE RATES

	1 ti	3 ti	6 ti	12 ti
1 page	1575.	1495.	1415.	1355.
2/3 page	1080.	1025.	970.	930.
1/2 pg isl	1025.	975.	925.	880.
1/2 page	965.	915.	865.	830.
1/3 page	630.	600.	565.	540.
1/4 page	555.	525.	500.	475.

6. COLOR RATES
2nd color, extra .... 100.
Matched color, extra .... 175.
4-color, extra .... 250.

7. COVERS
Rates are fixed and not subject to frequency discounts.
2nd cover .... 2125. 4th cover .... 2285.
3rd cover .... 1925.

8. INSERTS
BINGO CARDS
1/9 pg with reader service .... 200.
1/9 pg without reader service .... 175.

10. SPECIAL POSITION
Extra 5%

15. GENERAL REQUIREMENTS
Also see SRDS Print Media Production Data.
Printing Process: Offset Full Run
Trim Size: 8-1/8 x 10-7/8; No./Cols. 3.
Binding Method: Saddle Stitched.
Colors Available: 4-color process; Matched.

AD PAGE DIMENSIONS

Sprd	15-1/4 x 10	1/2 v	3-3/8 x 10
1 pg	7 x 10	1/2 h	7 x 4-3/4
2/3 v	4-5/8 x 10	1/3 v	2-1/4 x 10
2/3 h	7 x 6-1/2	1/3 h	4-5/8 x 4-3/4
1/2 isl	4-1/2 x 7	1/4 v	3-3/8 x 4-3/4

16. ISSUE AND CLOSING DATES
Published bimonthly.

Issue:	— Closing — (+)	(*)	Issue:	— Closing — (+)	(*)
Feb/Mar	12/10	12/16	Aug/Sep	6/12	6/18
Apr/May	2/10	2/14	Oct/Nov	8/10	8/14
Jun/Jul	4/13	4/17	Dec/Jan	10/12	10/16

(+) Space
(*) Material

Japan—Sumio Oka, International Media Representives, Ltd., Room 100, 21 Building 2-2-22 Okusawa, Setagaya-Ku, Tokoy 158. Phone 81-3-3502-0656. FAX: 81-3-5706-7349.

ADVERTISING RATES
Effective January 1, 1992. (Card)
Rates received October 2, 1991.

5. BLACK/WHITE RATES

	1 ti	3 ti	6 ti	12 ti	18 ti	24 ti	36 ti
1 page	3675.	3381.	3197.	2903.	2683.	2462.	2315.
1/2 page	2940.	2705.	2558.	2323,	2146,	1970.	1852.

Advertisers in TypeWorld and Computer Graphics World may combine units toward additional frequency discounts.

6. COLOR RATES
2nd & 3rd colors, each additional color .... 425.
4 color process .... 1195.
4 color spread .... 1795.

7. COVERS

	3 ti	6 ti		3 ti	6 ti
2nd cover	5720.	5490.	4th cover	5950.	5710.
3rd cover	5262.	5050.			

8. INSERTS
Furnished inserts coulnt towards frequency. Inserts are billed at current contract rate for B/W full page less the following discounts:
2 pages .... 20% 6 pages 30%
4 pages .... 25% 8 pages 35%

15. GENERAL REQUIREMENTS
Also see SRDS Print Media Production Data.
Printing Process: Offset Full Run
Trim Size: 8 x 10-3/4; No./Cols. 3.
Binding Method: Saddle Stitched.
Colors Available: 4-color process.
Covers: 4-color process.

AD PAGE DIMENSIONS
1 pg 7 x 10 1/2 h 7 x 4-7/8
1/2 v 3-5/16 x 10

16. ISSUE AND CLOSING DATES
Published bimonthly.

Issue:	Closing (+)	(*)	Issue:	Closing (+)	(*)
Jan-Feb	1/2	1/8	Jul-Aug	7/1	7/8
Mar-Apr	3/1	3/8	Sep-Oct	9/1	9/8
May-Jun	5/1	5/8	Nov-Dec	11/1	11/8

(+) Space
(*) Material

SPECIAL FEATURE ISSUES
Jan/Feb/92—Color Proofing; Know Thy Printing Press.
Mar/Apr/92—Mid-Range Color Systems; Storage Media.
May/Jun/92—High-Resolution; Imagesetting.
Jul/Aug/92—Color Printer; Color-Oriented RIPS.
Sep/Oct/92—Monitors and Graphic Cards; Data Compression.
Nov/Dec/92—Scanners; Networking.

18. CIRCULATION
SWORN 12-31-91 (6 mos. aver.)

Total	Non-Pd	Paid	(Subs)	(Single)	(Assoc)
20,771	20,200	571	...	...	...

Unpaid Distribution (not included above):
Total 257

TERRITORIAL DISTRIBUTION Nov-Dec/91—20,771

N.Eng.	Mid.Atl.	E.N.Cen.	W.N.Cen.	S.Atl.	E.S.Cen.
1,563	4,132	3,851	1,542	2,684	599
W.S.Cen.	Mtn.St.	Pac.St.	Canada	Foreign	Other
1,165	984	4,007	119	106	19

continued

FIGURE 24.5
SRDS listing.
Source: Standard Rate and Data Service. Reprinted with permission.

- 4,106 are engaged in the manufacture of computers (see intersection of TL [total] and row 1); 2,625 are in banking industries (see intersection of TL and row 3)
- 668 are President/Owner/Partner etc., in a company that manufactures computers (see intersection of column A and row 1)

Media buyers use this information to determine how cost efficiently a magazine or set of magazines reaches the buyer's particular target audience. Assume that a computer-products advertiser wants to reach individuals working at companies involved in financial industries (banking, insurance, securities, etc.).

The following table provides hypothetical SRDS information for four computer magazines:

Magazine	Full Page B&W Ad	Total Circulation	Target Audience Circulation	Overall CPM	Target Audience CPM
Magazine A	$11,300	54,120	5,200	$208.80	$2,173.08
Magazine B	16,500	150,044	16,750	109.96	985.08
Magazine C	8,900	80,200	6,650	110.97	1,338.36
Magazine D	14,000	136,800	2,476	102.33	5,833.33

Given the specified target audience, each magazine's circulation characteristics, and current advertising rates, it appears that Magazine B is the better vehicle because

- its *overall* cost per thousand is among the lowest, comparable to Magazines C and D;
- its ability to reach the specific target exceeds that of the other magazines. Magazine B reaches *more* target audience individuals at a *lower* cost per target audience thousand.

The Source of Circulation Information

The circulation data reported in SRDS is of two types: audited and nonaudited. Audited circulation data is information that has been verified by an external source while nonaudited data relies on the publisher's sworn statement.

The Audit Bureau of Circulation (ABC) is the primary external source for audited circulation information. The ABC was "established in 1914 as a not-for-profit association by advertisers, advertising agencies, and publishers who came together to establish standards and rules for circulation reporting. They created ABC to verify circulation reports by audit and, as a result, to provide credible and objective information to the buyers and sellers of print advertising."[19] The ABC is a self-regulating and self-supporting independent body whose revenues come from dues paid by its members (typically advertisers and advertising agencies) and auditing fees paid by publishers who request ABC audits.

The ABC audit process involves three activities including the creation of two publisher's statements and an ABC audit:

- Publishers' statements are issued twice a year. One statement covers the period October 1 to March 31; the second statement covers the remainder of the year (April 1 to

---

[19] Audit Bureau of Circulation, "Introduction to ABC," WWW page at URL http://www.abc.org.

September 30). Publishers' statements report average paid circulation over the audit period, single issue circulation, circulation as a function of new and renewal subscriptions, paid versus nonpaid circulation, geographic analysis of paid and nonpaid circulation, and where appropriate, demographic, or trade analysis of circulation.

• The ABC audit consists of an annual independent verification of the information provided in the two publishers' reports.

Most magazines are members of the ABC because it allows them to provide advertisers with objective, externally verified (and thus highly credible) circulation information.

Not all magazines, however, are members of ABC. These magazines may, for example, be small local magazines or magazines that are targeted to narrowly defined consumer or occupational groups. SRDS reports the publisher provided (but nonaudited) circulation information for these magazines only if the magazine's publisher provides a sworn, written statement supporting the accuracy of the submitted data.

Target Audience Incidence and Concentration

A different perspective on magazine audience estimates is provided by Simmons Market Research Bureau (SMRB) and Mediamark Research Inc. (MRI). In contrast to SRDS which provides information on the characteristics of magazine *circulation*, SMRB and MRI provide information on consumers' levels of reported magazine *readership*. SMRB and MRI collect and report magazine readership in a similar manner, as follows:[20]

> Each respondent is given a deck of cards. Each card contains the logo of one of the 200+ magazines monitored by the service. The respondent is first asked to think about the magazines that he or she has read within the past six months. Then, the respondent is asked to sort the cards into one of three piles to reflect his or her reading behaviors. One pile represents magazines the respondent is sure he or she has read, one pile represents those the respondent is certain were not read, and the third pile represents magazines about which the respondent is uncertain of having read. When all the magazines have been sorted, the "certain read" pile is left in front of the respondent while the other two piles are removed. The respondent is then instructed to go through the magazines in the "certain read" pile and to indicate those that he or she is certain were read during the *most recent publication interval*. (A publication interval for magazines published weekly is seven days, the interval is thirty days for magazines published monthly, etc.)

SMRB and MRI cross-tabulate reported magazine readership by category and product usage. This cross-tabluation of media usage by target audience is important because it lets one determine the specific media habits of individuals who exhibit desired product-related behaviors. SMRB magazine readership data is shown in Figure 24.6 (pages 620–621). This example illustrates the magazine reading habits of indi-

---

[20] Before Fall, 1995 Simmons used a different magazine readership methodology than MRI. This methodology was abandoned, however, in response to criticism from the advertising and research communities. For a detailed discussion of reactions to Simmons methodology and its response see the special report in *Advertising Age* (October 24, 1994), as well as Stuart Elliot, "Simmons Market Research Bureau Changes Its Methodology," *New York Times*, (September 15, 1994): D17, and Wayne Friedman, "Simmons Research Falls Under MPA Scrutiny," *Folio: The Magazine for Magazine Management* 23, (August 1, 1994):16. For a discussion of Simmons' current methodology see *Simmons Introduces Survey of American Readership* (Simmons Market Research Bureau, Inc, undated).

PERSONAL COMPUTER: BRANDS OWN AT HOME OR USE AT WORK
(ADULTS)

	TOTAL U.S. '000	APPLE MACINTOSH A '000	B DOWN %	C ACROSS %	D INDX	OTHER APPLE A '000	B DOWN %	C ACROSS %	D INDX	IBM PS/2 A '000	B DOWN %	C ACROSS %	D INDX	OTHER IBM A '000	B DOWN %	C ACROSS %	D INDX
TOTAL ADULTS	185822	8032	100.0	4.3	100	4374	100.0	2.4	100	5782	100.0	3.1	100	5959	100.0	3.2	100
AMERICAN BABY	2979	**100	1.2	3.3	77	**38	0.9	1.3	54	**184	3.2	6.2	199	**65	1.1	2.2	68
AMERICAN HEALTH	2649	**139	1.7	5.3	122	**42	1.0	1.6	67	**78	1.3	2.9	95	**73	1.2	2.7	86
AMERICAN WAY (AMERICAN AIRLINES)	526	**40	0.5	7.7	177	**31	0.7	5.9	249	**9	0.2	1.7	55	**85	1.4	16.2	505
ARCHITECTURAL DIGEST	2771	194	2.4	7.0	162	*136	3.1	4.9	208	**96	1.7	3.4	111	*127	2.1	4.6	143
AUDUBON	1158	*121	1.5	10.5	242	**7	0.2	0.6	24	**16	0.3	1.4	45	**34	0.6	2.9	91
BABY TALK	1683	**97	1.2	5.7	133	**50	1.1	2.9	125	*107	1.8	6.3	204	**60	1.0	3.6	112
BABY TALK/PARENTING(GROSS)	4771	*220	2.7	4.6	107	**75	1.7	1.6	67	*312	5.4	6.5	210	**146	2.5	3.1	95
BARRON'S	1182	*51	0.6	4.3	100	**42	1.0	3.5	149	**35	0.6	3.0	96	**45	0.8	3.8	119
BETTER HOMES AND GARDENS	21440	803	10.0	3.7	87	591	13.5	2.8	117	916	15.8	4.3	137	984	16.5	4.6	143
BON APPETIT	4175	294	3.7	7.0	163	*185	4.2	4.4	188	*284	4.9	6.8	219	*177	3.0	4.2	132
BRIDAL GUIDE	1167	**75	0.9	6.4	148	**28	0.6	2.4	102	**17	0.3	1.5	48	**79	1.3	6.8	211
BRIDE'S & YOUR NEW HOME	1980	**92	1.1	4.6	106	**27	0.6	1.4	58	**83	1.4	4.2	134	*111	1.9	5.6	174
BUSINESS WEEK	6501	531	6.6	8.2	189	226	5.2	3.5	148	417	7.2	6.4	206	289	4.9	4.5	139
CAR & DRIVER	5447	250	3.1	4.6	106	*147	3.4	2.7	115	*197	3.4	3.6	116	*208	3.5	3.8	119
CAR CRAFT	2220	**70	0.9	3.2	73	**13	0.3	0.6	25	**87	1.5	3.9	126	**67	1.1	3.0	94
COLONIAL HOMES	1627	**139	1.7	8.6	198	**46	1.1	2.8	121	**54	0.9	3.3	106	**77	1.3	4.7	147
CONDE NAST SELECT (GROSS)	42074	2999	37.3	7.1	165	1821	41.6	4.3	184	1441	24.9	3.4	110	1546	25.9	3.7	115
CONDE NAST TRAVELER	1912	*194	2.4	10.2	235	**118	2.7	6.2	262	**65	1.1	3.4	108	*174	2.9	9.1	283
CONSUMERS DIGEST	3854	209	2.6	5.4	126	*142	3.3	3.7	157	*197	3.4	5.1	164	*156	2.6	4.1	126
COSMOPOLITAN	11211	843	10.5	7.5	174	469	10.7	4.2	178	292	5.0	2.6	84	306	5.1	2.7	85
COUNTRY HOME	3491	**104	1.3	3.0	69	**90	2.1	2.6	110	*154	2.7	4.4	142	*164	2.8	4.7	147
COUNTRY LIVING	8465	387	4.8	4.6	106	293	6.7	3.5	147	454	7.8	4.5	172	380	6.4	4.5	140
EBONY	9948	267	3.3	2.7	62	*116	2.6	1.2	49	*245	4.2	2.5	79	*235	4.0	2.4	74
ELLE	2416	*166	2.1	6.9	159	*156	3.6	6.4	274	**31	0.5	1.3	41	*111	1.9	4.6	144
ENTERTAINMENT WEEKLY	3556	*205	2.6	5.8	133	**58	1.3	1.6	69	*135	2.3	3.8	122	*224	3.8	6.3	196
ESQUIRE	2553	*177	2.2	6.9	161	**56	1.3	2.2	94	**40	0.7	1.6	51	*161	2.7	6.3	197
ESSENCE	5144	*116	1.4	2.3	52	**69	1.6	1.3	57	*167	2.9	3.2	104	*193	3.2	3.8	117
FAMILY CIRCLE	17255	515	6.4	3.0	69	432	9.9	2.5	106	757	13.1	4.4	141	493	8.3	2.9	89
FAMILY CIRCLE/MCCALL'S (GRS)	29129	938	11.7	3.2	74	912	20.9	3.1	133	1347	23.1	4.6	149	907	15.2	3.1	97
THE FAMILY HANDYMAN	2587	**55	0.7	2.1	49	**83	1.9	3.2	136	*149	2.6	5.8	185	**99	1.7	3.8	120
FIELD & STREAM/OUTDOOR	9726	430	5.3	4.4	102	*181	4.1	1.9	79	351	6.1	3.6	116	*186	3.1	1.9	60
FIELD & STREAM/OUTDOOR LIFE (GROSS)	16015	793	9.9	5.0	115	261	6.0	1.6	69	614	10.6	3.8	123	350	5.9	2.2	68
FINANCIAL WORLD	1187	**77	1.0	6.5	151	**62	1.4	3.1	222	**4	0.1	0.3	10	**36	0.6	3.0	94
FIRST FOR WOMEN	3098	*239	3.0	7.7	178	*135	3.1	4.4	185	**139	2.4	4.5	144	**89	1.5	2.9	89
FOOD & WINE	2023	*130	1.6	6.4	149	**74	1.7	3.7	156	*105	1.8	5.2	167	**71	1.2	3.5	109
FORBES	3522	247	3.1	7.0	162	*143	3.3	4.1	173	*150	2.6	4.3	143	*198	3.3	5.6	175
FORTUNE	3360	354	4.4	10.5	244	*115	2.6	3.4	145	*144	2.6	4.1	143	241	4.0	7.2	223
GQ/GENTLEMEN'S QUARTERLY	3948	268	3.3	6.8	157	**95	2.2	2.4	102	**44	0.8	1.1	36	**177	2.9	1.9	61
GLAMOUR	7401	565	7.0	7.6	177	*338	7.7	4.6	194	*156	2.7	2.1	68	*178	3.0	2.4	75
GOLF DIGEST	3649	188	2.3	5.1	119	**86	2.0	2.4	100	*167	2.9	4.6	147	*198	3.3	5.4	169

Magazine	Total	'000	Down %	Across %	Index	'000	Down %	Across %	Index	'000	Down %	Across %	Index	'000	Down %	Across %	Index
GOLF ILLUSTRATED	1367	*54	0.7	4.0	92	**32	0.7	2.3	98	**76	1.3	5.5	178	**57	1.0	4.2	131
GOLF MAGAZINE	2755	*109	1.4	4.0	92	**89	2.0	3.2	137	**156	2.7	5.7	182	*137	2.3	5.0	155
GOOD HOUSEKEEPING	18895	893	11.1	4.7	109	558	12.8	3.0	126	823	14.2	4.4	140	538	9.0	2.8	89
GOURMET	2789	180	2.2	6.4	149	*104	2.4	3.7	158	*96	1.7	3.4	110	*119	2.0	4.3	133
GUNS & AMMO	4184	**120	1.5	2.9	66	**86	2.0	2.1	88	*175	3.0	4.2	134	*168	2.8	4.0	125
HACHETTE MAG. NETWORK (GRS)	39879	1821	22.7	4.6	106	1333	30.5	3.3	142	1321	22.8	3.3	106	1614	27.1	4.0	126
HACHETTE MEN'S PACKAGE (GRS)	18490	1026	12.4	5.5	128	579	13.2	3.1	133	576	10.7	3.1	94	788	13.2	4.3	133
HARPER'S BAZAAR	2278	*192	2.4	8.4	195	**143	3.3	6.3	267	*41	0.7	1.8	61	*62	1.1	2.7	85
HEARST HOME BUY (GROSS)	16857	854	10.6	5.1	117	723	16.5	4.3	182	768	13.3	4.6	146	695	11.7	4.1	128
HOME	3510	*158	2.0	4.5	104	**60	1.4	1.7	72	**134	2.3	3.8	117	*162	2.7	4.6	144
HOME MECHANIX	1927	**46	0.6	2.4	56	**32	0.7	1.7	70	**78	1.4	4.1	130	**57	1.0	3.0	93
HOT ROD	4343	*124	1.5	2.8	66	**109	2.5	2.5	106	*162	2.8	3.7	120	*116	1.9	2.7	83
HOUSE BEAUTIFUL	4406	197	2.4	4.4	103	*230	5.3	5.2	222	*165	2.7	3.7	120	*118	2.0	2.7	83
HUNTING	3011	*79	1.0	2.6	61	*91	2.1	3.0	129	*139	2.4	4.6	149	*113	1.9	3.8	117
INC.	1182	*124	1.5	10.5	243	*45	1.0	3.8	161	*83	1.4	7.0	226	*137	2.3	11.6	360
INSIDE SPORTS	3887	*174	2.2	4.5	104	*78	1.8	2.0	85	*65	1.1	1.7	53	*111	1.9	2.9	85
JET	9282	*223	2.8	2.4	56	*67	1.5	0.7	31	*293	5.1	3.2	101	*220	3.7	2.4	74
KIPLINGER'S PERS FINANCE MAG	1920	97	1.2	5.1	117	*62	1.4	3.2	137	*93	1.6	4.8	155	**50	0.8	2.6	80
LADIES' HOME JOURNAL	14822	657	8.2	4.4	103	449	10.3	3.0	129	620	10.7	4.2	135	606	10.2	4.1	127
LIFE	11708	467	5.8	4.0	92	319	7.3	2.7	116	390	6.7	3.3	107	353	5.9	3.0	94
LOS ANGELES TIMES MAGAZINE	3976	317	3.9	8.0	184	*114	2.6	2.9	121	*144	2.5	3.6	116	*195	3.3	4.9	153
MADEMOISELLE	4772	380	4.7	8.0	184	*229	5.2	4.8	204	*241	4.2	5.1	163	**95	1.6	2.0	62
MCCALL'S	11874	423	5.3	3.6	82	481	11.0	4.0	172	590	10.0	5.0	160	414	6.9	3.5	98
MEN'S FITNESS	1696	**32	0.4	1.9	44	**20	0.4	1.2	49	**60	1.0	3.5	113	**53	0.9	3.1	98
MONEY	6964	635	7.9	9.1	211	322	7.4	4.6	196	330	5.7	4.7	152	380	6.4	5.5	170
MOTOR TREND	3729	176	2.2	4.7	109	**87	2.0	2.3	99	*160	2.8	4.3	137	*77	1.3	2.1	65
MUSCLE & FITNESS	4485	*253	3.1	5.6	130	*106	2.4	2.4	101	*108	1.9	2.4	99	*142	2.4	3.2	99
NATIONAL ENQUIRER	17481	543	6.8	3.1	72	*255	5.8	1.5	62	325	5.6	1.9	60	484	8.1	2.8	86
NATIONAL EXAMINER	3485	*92	1.1	2.6	61	**102	2.3	2.9	124	*124	2.1	3.6	114	*69	1.2	2.0	61
NATIONAL GEOGRAPHIC	24735	1509	18.8	6.1	141	933	21.3	3.8	160	1146	19.8	4.6	149	1131	19.0	4.6	143
NATIONAL GEOGRAPHIC TRAVELER	1668	*124	1.5	7.5	173	**89	2.0	5.3	227	*106	1.8	6.3	204	**68	1.1	4.1	127
NATURAL HISTORY	1456	*135	1.7	9.3	215	*61	1.4	4.2	177	**92	1.6	6.3	203	**22	0.4	1.5	48
NEWSWEEK	19956	1308	16.3	6.6	152	661	15.1	3.3	141	907	15.7	4.5	146	782	13.1	3.9	122
NEW WOMAN	2987	*195	2.4	6.5	151	**94	2.1	3.1	133	*111	1.9	3.7	119	**74	1.2	2.5	101
NEW YORK	1460	*107	1.3	7.3	170	**56	1.3	3.8	164	**30	0.5	2.1	65	**74	1.2	5.0	157
THE NEW YORKER	2806	263	3.3	9.4	217	*88	2.0	3.1	133	*120	2.1	4.3	138	*165	2.8	5.9	184
THE N.Y. TIMES DAILY	3327	249	3.1	7.5	173	136	3.1	4.1	173	*185	3.2	5.6	179	155	2.6	4.7	145
THE N.Y. TIMES MAGAZINE	3880	304	3.8	7.8	181	*112	2.6	2.9	123	*94	1.6	2.4	78	*149	2.5	3.8	120
OMNI	2495	*137	1.7	5.5	127	*100	2.3	4.0	170	*170	3.0	6.8	219	**168	2.8	6.7	210
ORGANIC GARDENING	2222	*95	1.2	4.3	99	**78	1.8	3.5	148	*174	3.0	7.8	251	**85	1.4	3.8	119
OUTDOOR LIFE	6289	*364	4.5	5.8	134	**80	1.8	1.3	54	*263	4.5	4.2	134	*164	2.6	2.6	81

SIMMONS MARKET RESEARCH BUREAU, INC. 1993

*PROJECTION RELATIVELY UNSTABLE BECAUSE OF SAMPLE BASE-USE WITH CAUTION
**NUMBER OF CASES TOO SMALL FOR RELIABILITY-SHOWN FOR CONSISTENCY ONLY

FIGURE 24.6
Magazine readership cross-tabulated by brand users.
Source: Simmons Market Research Bureau. Reprinted with permission.

viduals who own an Apple Macintosh computer.[21] Media planners and buyers use this information to analyze magazines in terms of reach and concentration with the goal of identifying those magazines that have *both* high reach to the target audience and high concentration of the target audience among the readers of the magazine. A determination of reach and concentration is based on data found in the following report locations (see Figure 24.6):

- Column A estimates the absolute number of individuals in the target audience who read a particular magazine. For example, it is estimated that 100,000 Macintosh owners read *American Baby*.[22]

- Column B translates the raw number of readers into a percentage of the target audience that reads a particular magazine. For example, 1.2 percent of Macintosh owners read *American Baby* while 1.7 percent read *American Health*. This is a measure of the magazine's reach.

- Column C indicates the percentage of a magazine's readership that falls within the target audience. For example, 3.3 percent of the readers of *American Baby* own a Macintosh computer.

- Column D is an index of concentration. This index is interpreted similarly to other Simmons and MRI indices: indices over 115 indicate a significantly higher than expected concentration; indices between 86 and 114 indicate an average concentration; indices of 85 and below indicate a lower than expected concentration. The index is computed by comparing the percentage shown in column C to the overall level of magazine readership exhibited by the target audience.

The information presented in a SMRB or MRI report, when used in conjunction with information on advertising rates, helps the media planner or buyer identify those magazines that have the greatest efficiency, that is, those magazines that reach large segments of the target audience with the lowest CPM. The readership data shown in Figure 24.6 indicates that the consumer magazines *Cosmopolitan, National Geographic,* and *Newsweek* have the potential to efficiently reach the target audience of Macintosh owners because they have higher reach (relative to the other consumer magazines listed) and high concentrations of the target audience (indicated by indices of 115 or above).

NEWSPAPER AUDIENCE MEASUREMENT

Estimates of newspaper audience size are generally expressed in terms of circulation or total audience. Circulation refers to the average number of copies of the newspaper that are in distribution and are available for purchase and reading. The daily circulation of the *New York Times*, for example, is approximately 1,200,000. However, because newspapers are typically read by more than one person, total newspaper audience is calculated by multiplying the average number of readers per copy by the circulation.

---

[21] See Chapter 19, pages 467–471 for a discussion of how to read and interpret the data presented in Columns A–D beneath a specific target group of consumers.

[22] Asterisks placed next to a row indicate that the sample size for that particular piece of data is small and caution should be used when interpreting that data.

For example, if an average of 1.5 people read each issue of the *New York Times*, then the newspaper's total audience is likely to approach 1,800,000. Similar to magazines, newspaper circulation is often audited and verified by the Audit Bureau of Circulation.

The evaluation of a newspaper's cost efficiency is typically made on the basis of its circulation. As with other media, a newspaper's relative cost and value is determined by calculation and examination of its cost per thousand. It is important to point out, however, that using circulation based CPMs to evaluate newspaper efficiency is significantly less meaningful versus similar analyses conducted in electronic media and magazines that evaluate media vehicles in terms of their ability and cost to reach *specific* demographic targets.

OUTDOOR AUDIENCE MEASUREMENT

Outdoor advertising is measured in terms of exposure. One approach to outdoor measurement examines driver recall of driving patterns and behaviors. Within each market, a representative sample of drivers are asked to trace their day's travel on a map, indicating the routes they traveled to each of their specific destinations. Researchers then place plastic overlay sheets with billboard locations on top of each map to determine which billboards were and were not passed. Calculations are then performed to determine the number and types of individuals (in terms of demographic characteristics) passing each billboard.[23]

The Traffic Audit Bureau for Media Measurement (TAB) takes a different approach to measuring exposure. TAB counts the number of people and cars passing an outdoor structure during a specified time period. TAB then coverts their observations into estimates of audience size for a specific outdoor location.

YELLOW PAGES AUDIENCE MEASUREMENT

Circulation and usage are two measures of Yellow Pages audience size.

Circulation

Similar to other print media, Yellow Pages audience size is measured in terms of circulation, which can be operationalized as either the number of households or individuals possessing a particular directory.[24] Circulation data is an important indicator of a directory's potential in a marketplace. After all, it is unlikely that an ad will be seen if a directory is not in an individual's home.

Usage

Over the past several years, local and national Yellow Pages advertisers have increasingly resisted the use of circulation figures for evaluating audience size for the Yellow

---

[23] Jack Z. Sissors and Lincoln Bumba, *Advertising Media Planning, Fourth Edition* (Lincolnwood, IL: NTC Press 1993): 49.

[24] Circulation figures can also be used to calculate directory penetration—the percentage of households in the target geographic area possessing a specific directory.

Pages.[25] They have argued that the presence of a directory in an individual's home demonstrates only the *potential* for an ad to be seen. Given the fact that many individuals have more than one directory in their home, advertisers wanted a method for distinguishing directory usage from directory possession. They wanted to know which directories consumers use so that they could advertise in those directories that are used most often.

In response to Yellow Pages advertisers' need for usage information, the National Yellow Pages Monitor (NYPM), a division of NFO Research, created Yellow Pages directory ratings, which are collected as follows:

> A representative sample of consumers in a market area is sent a diary within which respondents are asked to record one week of their own Yellow Pages usage. Each time a diary-keeper uses the Yellow Pages he or she records the date, name, and code of the directory used, the subject or heading referenced within the directory, where the directory was used, and any actions taken after the directory was used. Data collected from the weekly diaries are accumulated over a calendar year after which circulation and share ratings are calculated and reported.

As the methodology indicates, NYPMs ratings report a directory's share of usage.[26] These ratings are important because they allow Yellow Pages advertisers to distinguish between two directories on more than the basis of gross circulation. The ratings allow an advertiser to target better his or her ads and to understand better the relative cost of different Yellow Pages directories.

Consider the following data:

Directory	Circulation	Full-Page Ad	Cost Per Thousand
A	509,000	$28,000	$55.01
B	505,000	$21,000	$41.58

Two directories, A and B, cover the same geographic area and have comparable circulation. Based on the cost for a full-page advertisement, Directory B appears to be the better value. It has a lower cost per thousand (CPM) versus Directory A when CPM reflects cost-per-thousand *circulation*.

The following table indicates what happens when usage information is considered.

Directory	Total References (000 Per Year)	Share of References	Cost for a Full-Page Ad	Cost Per Thousand References
A	58,400	76.9%	$28,000	$ .48
B	17,500	23.1%	$21,000	$1.20

Based on NYPM's ratings, Directory A appears to be the consumers' choice, that

[25] Melanie Rigney, "Shops Hang Fate on Format, Research," *Advertising Age* (March 16, 1992): S2.

[26] For a more in-depth review of NYPM methodology and industry reactions to Yellow Pages audience research see John P. Cortez, "Researcher NYPM Takes Challenge," *Advertising Age* (March 16,1991): S1.

is, the directory that is used most often. Nearly eight out of every ten references to the Yellow Pages occur in Directory A. Clearly, when CPM is calculated in terms of *usage*, Directory A becomes a better value.

WORLD WIDE WEB

As the discussion in this chapter illustrates, audience measures provide advertisers with information crucial to the media planning process. Audience measures, especially the ratings of specific vehicles within a particular medium, help advertisers make better informed decisions with regard to cost, efficiency, and appropriateness. Thus, it is not surprising that advertisers are requesting methods to evaluate audience size and message delivery in the context of new electronic media, especially advertising placed on the World Wide Web.

Many advertisers have rushed to place advertising on the World Wide Web. They have created stand-alone product and brand "home pages" or have placed their ads on the home pages of electronic magazines, newspapers, and on product-specific pages of search engines such as YAHOO. However, regardless of where on the World Wide Web the advertising appears, advertisers need to know the dynamics of audience exposure. They need to know who is viewing their ad, how often the ad is viewed, and whether the cost to produce and place the advertising is justified given these levels of exposure. Thus, although the development and collection of World Wide Web audience measures and advertising ratings is very complex (both technologically and methodologically), several companies are attempting to develop procedures and software that will collect these measures.

Nielsen Media Research and I/Pro have formed a joint venture to provide subscribers with a range of information about the audience attracted by a specific web site. One product, I/Count, enables a Web site owner to monitor and track the total number of site visits and the geographic and organizational structure of the site visitors. A second product, I/Audit, provides subscribers more detailed information about site visitors and site usage, for example, the time visitors spend reading each "page" and the sections read within each page or document.

The type of information provided by the Nielsen I/Pro venture is only the start. In addition to descriptive measures of site visitation, advertisers also need to know the demographics of site visitors. The Nielsen I/Pro venture, as well as other companies such as NetCount and Web Track, are developing methods to collect demographic and other forms of information demanded by advertisers.

The prior approaches all use the Web site as the unit of analysis, that is, they attempt to measure who is visiting a particular Web site by monitoring the Web site itself. The NPD Group's PC-Meter takes a different approach. The PC-Meter (currently installed in a demographically balanced sample of 1,000 computer-owning households) is a software application that passively monitors user PC activity. The meter identifies and records which Web sites (page by page) are being visited by individuals within the sample households and details the time spent and depth of involvement within each Web site. Thus, similar to the monitoring of television viewing habits, the

PC-Meter monitors the user rather then the Web site itself.

Advertisers and Web site developers continue to debate the relative merits of each approach.

Summary

Advertising agency media planners and buyers have two related tasks. They must place the advertising where the target audience has the greatest potential to see it and they must accomplish this placement with a high degree of cost efficiency.[27] They accomplish these tasks by using information that describes various media vehicles' audience size, characteristics, and cost for advertising placement.

Television and radio program audience measurement is expressed in terms of a share or rating. Ratings are more important to media planners and buyers versus a share because ratings are calculated using a consistent base while shares are not. The A.C. Nielsen Company is the sole provider of television ratings. National ratings are collected using the people meter while local ratings are collected using diaries or a combination of diaries and meters. National radio ratings are collected by RADAR using a telephone interview-recall methodology. Local ratings are collected by Arbitron using a diary methodology.

Television and radio stations use a program's *overall* household and individual ratings to set advertising rates. Media planners and buyers, however, use *target audience* ratings to evaluate a program's efficiency for reaching their specific target audience.

Magazine audiences are evaluated in two ways: (1) circulation information is used to determine the extent to which a particular magazine's circulation base matches an advertiser's target audience and (2) readership information is used to determine target audience incidence and concentration within a magazine's readership. Standard Rate and Data Service collects and publishes relevant information for the former case, Simmons Market Research Bureau and Mediamark Research Inc. provide relevant information for the latter case.

Newspaper and Yellow Pages audience sizes are measured in terms of circulation. Yellow Pages audience size is also evaluated in terms of ratings—a Yellow Pages directory's share of usage.

Outdoor advertising is measured in terms of exposure that represents the number of individuals (either on foot or in cars) passing a particular billboard.

Audience measures and ratings for Internet and World Wide Web advertising is proceeding, but an industry standard has yet to be developed.

---

[27] Sissors and Bumba define this role of media planner as: Planners need to "select one or more vehicles that effectively reach an optimum number of prospects . . . at the lowest cost per thousand prospects reached (called cost efficiency) . . . with a minimum of waste (or nonprospects)." See Sissors and Bumba, *Advertising Media Planning*, p. 10.

Review Questions

1. Define *share*, as used to estimate the size of a television or radio program audience. How is a program share calculated?

2. Define *rating*, as used to estimate the size of a television or radio program audience. How is a program rating calculated?

3. Which measure, share or rating, is more valuable to media planners and buyers? Why?

4. What is the name of the company that provides both national and local television ratings?

5. Describe the procedure by which national television ratings are collected.

6. What problems have been associated with the collection of national television ratings?

7. Describe the procedures by which local television ratings are collected.

8. What is *cost per thousand (CPM)*? How is it calculated?

9. Why is CPM an important component of program evaluation?

10. Describe the process by which media planners use CPM to evaluate the relative cost to advertise in different television or radio programs.

11. What types of television practices are considered to be unethical manipulations of the ratings?

12. How are national radio ratings collected?

13. Describe the two procedures by which local radio ratings are collected.

14. What types of radio programming practices are considered to be unethical manipulations of the ratings?

15. What are two different approaches to magazine audience measurement?

16. What is the Audit Bureau of Circulation? What is its role and how does it satisfy this role?

17. How does information in Standard Rate and Data Service provide insights into magazine audience characteristics?

18. Describe the process by which SRDS information is used to evaluate a magazine's audience characteristics and relative efficiency for reaching a specified target audience.

19. How do SMRB and MRI estimate magazine readership?

20. Describe the procedure by which SMRB and MRI information is used to identify magazines that reach the target audience with greatest media efficiency.

21. How is newspaper audience size estimated?

22. How is outdoor audience size measured?

23. What are the two ways in which Yellow Pages audience size are estimated? Which way do advertisers prefer? Why?

24. How are Yellow Pages ratings collected?

25. How do advertisers use Yellow Pages ratings to evaluate competing Yellow Pages directories?

26. What are the trends in measurement of World Wide Web advertising?

Application Exercises[28]

1. Refer to the Nielsen ratings shown in Figures 24.1 and 24.2 for programs airing between 8:00 P.M. and 9:00 P.M. Use this data to answer each of the following questions. Support your answer with data from the figures.

   a. Which program had the highest overall rating? What was that program's share?

   b. Do more viewers watch the beginning or end of *Cops San Bernadino*? What is the difference in the ratings?

   c. What is the trend in total audience size for *Front Page*?

   d. Which demographic group are most likely to watch *Cops* on Fox? Which groups are least likely to watch *Cops*?

   e. Does the ABC movie attract the same type of audience as *Dr. Quinn*?

2. Examine the Arbitron ratings shown in Figure 24.4. Use the data presented in this figure to answer the following questions. Use data from the figure to support your answers.

   a. Which radio station has the largest total audience size? Which has the smallest total audience?

   b. Which radio station is the strongest among men aged 25–34? Which is strongest among women aged 35–44?

   c. How would you characterize the demographics of individuals who listen to radio station KPSA?

3. You are asked to evaluate the cost efficiency of six television programs with regard to two target audiences: women aged 18–34 and women aged 25–49. The overall rating of each program, its rating among each target audience group, and the cost for a thirty-second advertisement on each program are shown below. Which program or programs would you recommend for each target audience? Do any of the programs reach both target audiences efficiently? Write a memo to your client presenting the results of your analysis and your recommendation as to which of the programs you would select. Be certain to support and justify your recommendations.

Program	Rating (Overall)	Women 18–34 Rating	Women 24–49 Rating	:30 Ad Cost
Matlock	12.6	11.2	13.5	$ 89,000
Frasier	20.7	21.2	19.5	187,000
60 Minutes	13.0	13.2	12.9	119,000
ER	20.0	24.2	26.2	177,000
Melrose Plase	10.7	15.2	8.6	88,000
X Files	14.3	9.9	7.7	123,000

Note: Overall potential viewing audience is 181,000,000 adults aged 18 and older.
   Women 18–34 potential viewing audience is 32,000,000.
   Women 24–49 potential viewing audience is 47,000,000.

4. The target for your client's advertising is senior management in organizations with annual revenues of $100,000,000 or more. Your media department sends you the following table:

---

[28] All application exercises are hypothetical. Names of actual companies and brands are used for illustrative purposes only. All data, unless otherwise indicated, is for illustrative purposes only.

Magazine	Cost for Full-Page B&W Ad	Total Circulation	Target Audience Circulation	Overall CPM
Barrons	$ 5,695	133,000	13,500	$ 42.81
Business Week	42,500	896,000	65,000	47.43
Forbes	37,900	787,782	63,000	48.11
Fortune	43,530	1,077,958	60,000	40.38

The media analyst attaches a note that says: "We recommend *Fortune*. It has the lowest overall cost per thousand of the four magazines analyzed and it reaches about the same number of our people in target audience as do *Business Week* and *Forbes*." Do you agree or disagree with the media analyst's point of view that selects *Fortune* as the most efficient means of reaching the desired target audience? Justify and support your point of view.

5. Prepare a short report of the current status of World Wide Web audience measurement and ratings. Be certain to use articles in *current* trade and consumer magazines.

CHAPTER

25

MEDIA EXPENDITURES: THE ADVERTISING BUDGET AND COMPETITIVE STRATEGIES

The LNA/Mediawatch Multi-Media Service estimates brand, company, and category advertising expenditures for the vast majority of consumer and business-to-business products and services. (As discussed in Chapter 5, LNA is an abbreviation for Leading National Advertisers.) The information reported by LNA plays an important role in the advertising budgeting process and for understanding competitors' media strategies.

Beyond media-specific uses, LNA expenditure data has an additional application to advertising planning. LNA data can provide important insights into marketplace and brand activities by alerting an advertiser to shifts in competitors' brand strategies or the changing dynamics of a product category. This chapter shows you how to interpret, analyze, and apply LNA information to advertising planning.

After reading this chapter, you will be able to

■ Describe the types of information LNA provides and how to interpret this information.

■ Use LNA information for evaluating different advertising budget options.

■ Define a product category and the actions of specific brands within that category using systematic analysis of LNA information.

The LNA/Mediawatch Multi-Media Service estimates advertising expenditures for a broad array of consumer and business-to-business products and services. LNA estimates advertising expenditures by brand, parent company, and product category for ten media: magazines, Sunday magazines, newspapers, outdoor, network television, spot television, syndicated television, cable TV networks, network radio, and national spot radio. Advertising spending is reported quarterly and is summarized for a calendar year in a year-end annual volume. Advertising agencies and others in need of these types of estimates have the option of purchasing LNA information in several formats: interac-

Magazines

LNA compiles all paid advertising space and expenditures in 177 consumer magazines. Monitored publications are supply-marked issues of national editions and current rate cards, as well as tear sheets in regional/demographic editions. Full-run revenues reported are based on current gross one-time rates. Special published rates are used where applicable. Revenues for demographic editions are also based on gross one-time rates; regional rates are supplied by publishers.

Sunday Magazines

LNA measures advertising in the *New York Times Magazine*, the *Los Angeles Times Magazine*, *Parade*, and *USA Weekend*. In addition, LNA measures Sunday magazines distributed with subscribing and proprietary newspapers. These latter expenditures are based on one-time open inch rates and are projected to 125 markets for national categories. Financial and retail advertising expenditures are not projected.

Newspaper

LNA measures advertising space in 88 cities. Display advertising is classified into one of four major categories: retail, general, automotive, or financial. General and automotive are considered national advertising. Advertising expenditures are based on one-time open inch rates and are projected to the top 125 markets for the two national categories. Financial and retail expenditures are not projected. In addition, all available newspaper data collected on a proprietary basis are included.

Outdoor

Outdoor data include poster and paint billboard expenditures in more than 200 plant operator markets. Brand expenditure information is provided by participating plant operators. The market-by-market figures are not projected and represent gross sales volume for participating plant operators only.

Network Television

Mediawatch™, the Arbitron Commercial Monitoring Service, monitors every broadcast minute on the ABC, CBS, NBC, and Fox television networks. All broadcast activity is continuously recorded via magnetic tape. Arbitron estimates brand expenditures by assigning an estimated rate to each network program and then applying this rate to each commercial monitored in the program. Estimated brand expenditures represent the totals of each brand's monitored activity.

Spot Television

Mediawatch™ electronically monitors spot television activity on the major stations in the top seventy-five markets continuously throughout the year. Arbitron collects rate information for each of the monitored stations. Arbitron estimates rates that are a composite of these sources for each day of the week and each minute of the day as required by each station's practices. Each monitored commercial is assigned a rate, which Arbitron accumulates to produce national estimated brand expenditures. In order to be listed for retail/local spot television, a brand must have spent (a) $25,000 or more year to date in retail/local spot television but show advertising activity in other media.

(continued)

FIGURE 25.1

LNA/Mediawatch™ Multi-Media Service methodology.
Source: Competitive Media Reporting.

National Syndicated Television

Mediawatch™ reports on national television activity occurring in satellite-distributed syndicated television. Arbitron gathers program rate information each month from a large cross-section of advertisers and advertising agencies. It uses this information to create representative rates for each program. These rates are then applied to each national commercial in the program.

Cable Television Networks

Mediawatch™ continuously electronically monitors the following cable networks: Cable News Network (CNN), Entertainment and Sports Programming Network (ESPN), The Family Channel (FAM), Lifetime (LIFE), MTV Music Television, Nickelodeon (NICK), TBS Superstation, Turner Network Television (TNT), and USA Network.

Network Radio

Mediawatch™ reports radio activity for fourteen networks offered by the following companies: ABC radio networks, CBS networks, Unistar networks, and Westwood One radio sales networks. Specific program and brand information is obtained by continuous monitoring via audio magnetic tape recordings of these networks satellite broadcasts. Arbitron assigns an estimated rate to each program/time period and then applies this rate to each brand commercial in the program/time period.

Spot Radio

LNA provides national and regional spot radio advertising data from 3,500 stations in more than 200 markets. This information is acquired through major national station representative organizations. Spending estimates are based on station representatives billing figures.

FIGURE 25.1 (continued)

tive on-line, CD, or in bound volumes. Figure 25.1 summarizes the methodology used to collect the data and explains how advertising expenditures in each medium are estimated.[1]

INTERPRETING LNA DATA

A page from the 1993 LNA/Mediawatch Multi-Media Service year-end report is shown in Figure 25.2. This page of the report displays advertising spending by parent company and individual brands within the category of *Consumer Car Rental Services*. The data shown in Figure 25.2 is read and interpreted as follows:

- The LNA source identification is centered at the top of the page along with the time period covered, in this case January to December, 1993.
- The first column of the report, labeled "Class/Company/Brand" presents an alphabetical listing of category advertisers organized by parent company and then by brand within parent company. There are three listings, for example, beneath Chrysler Corporation: Dollar Rent-A-Car, Thrifty Rent-A-Car (both of which are owned by Chrysler),

---

[1] Source: Competitive Media Reporting.

CLASS/BRAND $ LNA/MEDIAWATCH MULTI-MEDIA SERVICE January - December 1993

QUARTERLY AND YEAR-TO-DATE ADVERTISING DOLLARS (000)

CLASS/COMPANY/BRAND	CLASS CODE		10-MEDIA TOTAL	MAGAZINES	SUNDAY MAGAZINES	NEWSPAPERS	OUTDOOR	NETWORK TELEVISION	SPOT TELEVISION	SYNDICATED TELEVISION	CABLE TV NETWORKS	NETWORK RADIO	NATIONAL SPOT RADIO
T414 CONSUMER CAR RENTAL SERVICES								CONTINUED					
AVIS INC (CONTINUED)													
AVIS RENT-A-CAR & AVIS CAR SALES	T414	92 YTD	27.6	--	--	--	27.6	--	--	--	--	--	--
AVIS RENT-A-CAR SYSTEM	T414	Q1	1,077.2	52.6	1.5	1,005.6	12.3	--	5.2	--	--	--	--
		Q2	8,407.9	21.0	1.5	1,670.1	33.6	5,382.1	688.0	77.9	533.7	--	--
		Q3	1,408.5	208.4	0.7	1,144.0	32.4	--	18.7	--	4.3	--	--
		Q4	2,296.8	238.8	1.4	1,830.2	28.5	57.0	138.1	--	--	--	2.8
		93 YTD	13,190.4	520.8	5.1	8,649.9	106.8	5,439.1	850.0	77.9	538.0	--	2.8
		92 YTD	15,925.7	3,654.8	34.7	9,817.6	351.0	25.8	537.0	16.8	120.7	--	1,367.3
COMPANY TOTAL		Q1	1,105.6	52.6	1.5	1,034.0	12.3	--	5.2	--	--	--	--
		Q2	8,431.2	21.0	1.5	1,693.4	33.6	5,382.1	688.0	77.9	533.7	--	--
		Q3	1,472.4	208.4	0.7	1,207.9	32.4	--	18.7	--	4.3	--	--
		Q4	2,333.4	267.1	1.4	1,831.5	35.5	57.0	138.1	--	--	--	2.8
		93 YTD	13,342.6	549.1	5.1	5,766.8	113.8	5,439.1	850.0	77.9	538.0	--	2.8
		92 YTD	16,026.3	3,699.1	34.7	9,846.3	378.6	25.8	537.0	16.8	120.7	--	1,367.3
BEECH HOLDINGS CORP													
BUDGET RENT A CAR & RENT A TRUCK	T414	Q1	2.1	--	--	--	--	--	2.1	--	--	--	--
		Q2	0.3	--	--	--	--	--	0.3	--	--	--	--
		Q3	9.2	--	--	--	--	--	9.2	--	--	--	--
		Q4	11.6	--	--	--	--	--	11.6	--	--	--	--
BUDGET RENT A CAR & WAYNE AUTO CENTER	T414	Q1	1.6	--	--	1.6	--	--	--	--	--	--	--
		Q2	13.5	--	--	13.5	--	--	--	--	--	--	--
		Q3	93.4	--	--	93.4	--	--	--	--	--	--	--
		Q4	14.5	--	--	14.5	--	--	--	--	--	--	--
		93 YTD	123.0	--	--	123.0	--	--	--	--	--	--	--
BUDGET RENT A CAR SYSTEM	T414	Q1	4,436.4	18.2	--	1,776.9	0.6	656.0	211.3	9.4	1,737.8	--	26.2
		Q2	5,664.3	741.9	--	2,326.6	1.2	779.7	171.0	4.2	1,439.7	--	200.0
		Q3	1,980.9	13.8	--	1,035.4	4.8	--	294.2	--	--	614.3	18.4
		Q4	2,292.6	168.0	--	1,614.0	23.5	--	255.9	--	12.8	192.0	26.4
		93 YTD	14,374.2	941.9	--	6,752.9	30.1	1,435.7	932.4	13.6	3,190.3	806.3	271.0
		92 YTD	14,632.7	1,747.5	--	4,918.0	4.5	900.4	1,268.1	173.6	3,377.9	2,237.4	5.3
COMPANY TOTAL		Q1	4,438.0	18.2	--	1,778.5	0.6	656.0	211.3	9.4	1,737.8	--	26.2
		Q2	5,679.9	741.9	--	2,340.1	1.2	779.7	173.1	4.2	1,439.7	--	200.0
		Q3	2,074.6	13.8	--	1,128.8	4.8	--	294.5	--	--	614.3	18.4
		Q4	2,316.3	168.0	--	1,628.5	23.5	--	265.1	--	12.8	192.0	26.4
		93 YTD	14,508.8	941.9	--	6,875.9	30.1	1,435.7	944.0	13.6	3,190.3	806.3	271.0
		92 YTD	14,632.7	1,747.5	--	4,918.0	4.5	900.4	1,268.1	173.6	3,377.9	2,237.4	5.3

----- CONTINUED -----

FIGURE 25.2 Sample page 1 from LNA/Mediawatch™ Multi-Media Service.
Source: Competitive Media Reporting. All rights reserved. Reproduced with permission.

LNA/MEDIAWATCH MULTI-MEDIA SERVICE
January - December 1993

CLASS/BRAND $

CLASS/COMPANY/BRAND	CLASS CODE	10 - MEDIA TOTAL	MAGAZINES	SUNDAY MAGAZINES	NEWSPAPERS	OUTDOOR	NETWORK TELEVISION	SPOT TELEVISION	SYNDICATED TELEVISION	CABLE TV NETWORKS	NETWORK RADIO	NATIONAL SPOT RADIO
T414 CONSUMER CAR RENTAL SERVICES	T414						CONTINUED					
CHRYSLER CORPORATION												
DOLLAR RENT-A-CAR RENTAL SERVICES												
Q1		1,302.0	300.3	--	4.6	10.8	619.8	68.2	--	298.3	--	--
Q2		2,675.3	292.7	--	108.4	10.8	1,202.1	61.0	--	1,000.3	--	--
Q3		903.3	164.3	--	38.9	32.7	324.7	85.1	--	257.6	--	--
Q4		3,069.1	94.6	--	53.7	7.2	1,535.4	255.1	--	1,123.1	--	--
93 YTD		7,949.7	851.9	--	205.6	61.5	3,682.0	469.4	--	2,679.3	--	--
92 YTD		5,588.0	745.6	--	378.0	8.6	1,841.1	432.0	--	2,182.7	--	--
THRIFTY RENT-A-CAR SYSTEMS	T414											
Q1		1,446.3	--	--	168.9	4.2	881.0	21.8	32.4	253.1	--	84.9
Q2		836.1	3.7	--	362.3	52.7	--	62.5	--	188.5	--	166.4
Q3		868.2	35.4	--	115.5	1.2	387.5	42.6	--	286.0	--	--
Q4		3,728.3	35.4	--	124.4	8.8	2,471.6	91.8	--	996.3	--	--
93 YTD		6,878.9	74.5	--	771.1	66.9	3,740.1	218.7	32.4	1,723.9	--	251.3
92 YTD		6,337.8	--	--	1,109.3	49.9	3,728.0	185.2	--	1,265.4	--	--
COMPANY TOTAL												
Q1		2,748.3	300.3	--	173.5	15.0	1,500.8	90.0	32.4	551.4	--	84.9
Q2		3,511.4	296.4	--	470.7	63.5	1,202.1	123.5	--	1,188.8	--	166.4
Q3		1,771.5	199.7	--	154.4	33.9	712.2	127.7	--	543.6	--	--
Q4		6,797.4	130.0	--	178.1	16.0	4,007.0	346.9	--	2,119.4	--	--
93 YTD		14,828.6	926.4	--	976.7	128.4	7,422.1	688.1	32.4	4,403.2	--	251.3
92 YTD		14,699.0	1,686.6	--	3,026.8	80.8	5,620.3	804.0	--	3,480.5	--	--

QUARTERLY AND YEAR-TO-DATE ADVERTISING DOLLARS (000)

FIGURE 25.2 (continued)

and the company total (in this case the sum of Dollar and Thrifty advertising expenditures).

"Q1," "Q2," etc. appear beneath the name of each brand and company total. The rows with these labels represent quarterly spending. Expenditures reported on the row labeled "Q1" represents first quarter spending (January–March), "Q2" represents second quarter spending (April–June), "Q3" represents third quarter spending (July–September), and "Q4" represents fourth quarter spending (October–December).

Total spending is reported after quarterly spending. "93 YTD" reports the total of the current year's spending and corresponds to the time period shown on the top of the report (in this example, calendar year 1993). "92 YTD" represents the total of the prior year's spending for the same time period as 93 YTD.

- The second column lists the LNA category code.
- The third column, labeled "10-Media Total," is the LNA estimate of a brand's or company's total advertising expenditures. The amount shown on the Q1, Q2, Q3, and Q4 lines represent the *total* of each quarter's spending. The total on the YTD lines report the current and prior year's *total* spending. In this example, each row beneath Dollar Rent-A-Car indicates that Dollar's advertising spending is estimated to be

$1,302,000	in first quarter 1993 (Q1).
$2,675,300	in second quarter 1993 (Q2).
$903,300	in third quarter 1993 (Q3).
$3,069,100	in fourth quarter 1993 (Q4).
$7,949,700	for the entire calendar year 1993 (93 YTD) compared to
$5,588,000	for the entire calendar year 1992 (92 YTD).

- The next ten columns list spending in individual tracked media. Dollar Rent-A-Car, for example, is estimated to have spent $851,900 in magazines for the calendar year 1993 compared to $745,600 in 1992. The sum of spending in each individual medium is the figure reported as the "10-Media Total."

Figure 25.3 (page 636) displays the page that contains the end of the *Consumer Car Rental Services* report. Each LNA category report ends with a CLASS TOTAL that computes the sum of all advertising expenditures within that category. The data shown in Figure 25.3 indicates that car rental advertisers are estimated to have spent $134,708,100 in calendar year 1993 compared to $132,377,200 in calendar year 1992.

Care must be taken when using LNA category totals. Category totals provide accurate estimates of category spending *only* when the LNA category is narrowly defined and contains *only* those brands of interest. *Consumer Car Rental Services* is an LNA category of this type because only rental car companies are listed in this category. Other LNA categories are much broader and, consequently, LNA computed category totals in these circumstances overestimate the spending of *specific* product categories. LNA category D121 (*Dental Supplies and Mouthwashes*) for example, contains brands of toothpaste, mouthwash, and toothbrushes. As a result, the category total reports spending for brands in all these categories. Total spending for toothpaste alone would have to be manually calculated by totaling the LNA reported spending of *only* toothpaste brands.

Advertisers capitalize on the ability to understand competitive spending practices in three ways. First, LNA data provides a sound and objective basis for identifying

CLASS/BRAND $

LNA/MEDIAWATCH MULTI-MEDIA SERVICE January - December 1993

QUARTERLY AND YEAR-TO-DATE ADVERTISING DOLLARS (000)

CLASS/COMPANY/BRAND	CLASS CODE	10-MEDIA TOTAL	MAGAZINES	SUNDAY MAGAZINES	NEWSPAPERS	OUTDOOR	NETWORK TELEVISION	SPOT TELEVISION	SYNDICATED TELEVISION	CABLE TV NETWORKS	NETWORK RADIO	NATIONAL SPOT RADIO
T414 CONSUMER CAR RENTAL SERVICES												
local automotive leasing not-itemized												
STANDARD RENT A CAR	T414											
Q1		3.2			3.2							
Q2		3.0			3.0							
Q3		7.7			7.7							
Q4		11.5			11.5							
93 YTD		**25.4**			**25.4**							
CLASS TOTAL												
Q1		37,251.9	1,574.1	1.5	12,134.8	161.4	17,833.6	1,026.7	303.0	2,991.1	--	1,225.7
Q2		41,557.0	2,464.5	34.3	11,989.4	214.9	18,410.9	2,226.8	527.5	4,329.3	--	1,359.4
Q3		19,152.6	1,753.7	0.7	8,953.9	181.6	5,089.0	737.3	331.6	3,450.8	614.3	317.6
Q4		36,746.6	1,817.3	1.4	12,285.7	153.9	17,441.9	807.6	337.1	1,172.9	192.0	258.9
93 YTD		**134,708.1**	**7,609.6**	**37.9**	**45,363.8**	**711.8**	**58,775.4**	**4,798.4**	**1,499.2**	**11,944.1**	**806.3**	**3,161.6**
92 YTD		132,377.2	12,119.6	34.7	55,243.1	618.2	38,109.3	11,390.0	346.5	7,758.3	2,237.4	4,520.1
T419 MISCELLANEOUS PASSENGER TRAVEL												
AMERICAN BUS ASSOCIATION												
AMERICAN BUS ASSOCIATION	T419-9											
Q1		23.6									23.6	
93 YTD		**23.6**									**23.6**	
CAREY INTERNATIONAL CORP.												
CAREY LIMOUSINE SERVICE	T419											
Q1		2.1						2.1				
Q2		2.2				3.0		2.2				
Q3		4.2				3.0		1.2				
Q4		47.1	42.8					1.3				
93 YTD		**55.6**	**42.8**			**6.0**		**6.8**				
GREYHOUND LINES, INC.												
GREYHOUND BUSLINES PASSENGER	T419											
Q1		2,134.3	41.9		8.2			114.2	1,056.7	130.3	695.4	87.6
Q2		4,852.6	75.1		138.9			409.4	2,288.6	621.2	1,077.9	241.5
Q3		261.7			23.7	16.8		32.7	41.8	22.0	85.9	38.8
Q4		3,225.2	119.1				2,084.9	280.3	153.1	242.5		345.3
93 YTD		**10,473.8**	**236.1**		**170.8**	**16.8**	**2,084.9**	**836.6**	**3,540.2**	**1,016.0**	**1,859.2**	**713.2**
92 YTD		12,282.3	38.1		482.0	29.7	32.6	4,198.1	2,068.9	753.8	3,882.9	796.2
TRAILWAYS BUSLINES PASSENGER	T419											
Q1		19.1			19.1							
Q2		42.1			42.1							
Q3		32.8			32.8							
Q4		8.1			8.1							
93 YTD		**102.1**			**102.1**							
COMPANY TOTAL												
Q1		2,153.4	41.9		27.3			114.2	1,056.7	130.3	695.4	87.6
Q2		4,894.7	75.1		181.0			409.4	2,288.6	621.2	1,077.9	241.5
Q3		294.5			56.5	16.8		32.7	41.8	22.0	85.9	38.8
Q4		3,233.3	119.1		8.1		2,084.9	280.3	153.1	242.5		345.3
93 YTD		**10,575.9**	**236.1**		**272.9**	**16.8**	**2,084.9**	**836.6**	**3,540.2**	**1,016.0**	**1,859.2**	**713.2**
92 YTD		12,282.3	38.1		482.0	29.7	32.6	4,198.1	2,068.9	753.8	3,882.9	796.2

FIGURE 25.3 Sample page 2, showing category totals, from LNA/Mediawatch™ Multi-Media Service.

Source: Competitive Media Reporting. All rights reserved. Reproduced with permission.

brand budget requirements. The data permits an advertiser to examine the appropriateness of various budget options in light of levels of competitive spending. Second, LNA spending estimates provide insights into marketplace activities and advertisers' brand strategies and priorities. The data indicate the extent to which advertisers have maintained or shifted support for different products and brands. Third, LNA data provides insights into advertisers' media strategies. LNA data indicates the extent to which advertisers utilize specific media and individual media vehicles to promote and advertise their brands. The remainder of this chapter discusses each of these uses of LNA data.

USE OF LNA FOR EVALUATING BUDGET OPTIONS

At least once a year, advertising managers and their advertising agencies address the question: "How much should we spend on advertising in the upcoming year?" This is a critical question. Allocating too much money to the advertising budget is wasteful and diverts needed resources from other marketing efforts. Allocating too little money reduces the potential for the advertising to be seen and to influence the target consumer.

Several methods are available to help advertisers determine an advertising budget. These methods, in order of their ability to help determine an optimal advertising budget, are: subjective, ratio, objective and task, mathematical modeling, and experimentation.[2] An advertiser may use one method exclusively or may determine the advertising budget based on a combination of methods.[3] LNA data is used with the objective and task approach.

The Objective and Task Method

The objective and task method helps a brand determine its budget by (1) examining the current state of the brand in relation to other brands in the marketplace, (2) identifying

---

[2] An advertiser who uses the *subjective* method primarily relies on his or her intuition when determining the advertising budget. He or she might decide to spend a specific amount on advertising because it "seems right given what I think about the marketplace" or because it is "all we have to spend." The defining characteristics of the subjective approach are the absence of reference to external, objective information and a lack of rational analysis. The subjective approach is the least powerful and most dangerous way to set an advertising budget.

The *ratio* method establishes the advertising budget in terms of a fixed or variable ratio of a predetermined base. The two most common types of ratio methods are *percentage* approaches that set the budget as a percentage of anticipated product sales or total profit and *fixed sum* approaches that build the budget from a prespecified amount taken from each unit of product sold. Additionally, ratios are sometimes applied to the past year's sales or the past year's advertising spending.

Mathematical models use analyses of past advertising-marketplace relationships to create formulas that predict advertising response and impact at various levels of advertising spending. These formulas are very useful when an advertiser wants to explore different "what-if" scenarios to estimate the effects of different overall levels of spending or the effects of manipulating specific components of the budget.

Experimentation is the most powerful (and most costly) method of budget allocation. Here, an advertiser conducts controlled, quantitative field tests to determine the effects of different levels of advertising expenditures on advertising awareness, product perceptions, and product purchase patterns. Experiments of this type are conducted following the guidelines presented in Chapter 7.

[3] Kent M. Lancaster and Judith Stern, "Computer-Based Advertising Budgeting Practices of Leading Consumer Advertisers," *Journal of Advertising* 12 (1984): 4–9; V. J. Blasko and C. H. Patti, "The Advertising Budgeting Practices of Industrial Advertisers," *Journal of Marketing* 48 (Fall 1984): 104–10; S. E. Permut, "How European Managers Set Advertising Budgets," *Journal of Advertising Research* 17 (October 1977): 75–79.

the desired brand position, and then (3) estimating the budget required to achieve the desired brand position. This approach therefore sets the advertising budget in response to explicit objectives and measurable goals that provide a basis for evaluating success or failure. An advertiser may take one of two approaches to identifying his or her brand's budget in this way: *response to competitive spending* and *share of market/share of voice*. Both of these approaches require the use of LNA data.

Response to Competitive Spending The *competitive response* method of budget allocation consists of the following steps:

- identification of the advertiser's competitive set
- identification of competitors' prior year's advertising spending
- adjustment of prior years' spending to estimate current year's spending
- assignment of competitors to high, medium, and low spending groups based on estimates of their current year's advertising spending[4]
- identification of marketing goals
- determination of budget required to meet marketing goals
- budget allocation

Assume that we are asked to recommend a budget for Avis-Rent-A Car. We know that Avis' prior year's budget was estimated to be $16,000,000, a spending level that represents 11.9 percent of the $134,368,500 in estimated total car rental company advertising. We would begin to identify Avis' budget options as follows (see Table 25.1):

- Identify, list, and record the prior year's spending of all competitors.
- Estimate each competitor's current years' spending by adjusting the prior year's budget. Prior years' budgets can be adjusted for overall media inflation or for anticipated

---

[4] Competitors are grouped to avoid inappropriate inferences drawn from analyses of mean levels of advertising. Grouping restricts the range of spending levels within a group, thus making the mean spending level of the group an accurate estimator or the group's spending level. Without groups, given an often wide range of spending levels, the mean becomes less accurate. Consider, for example, a product category in which there are nine advertisers (several major and a number of secondary), with the following spending levels:

Advertiser	Advertising Expenditure
1	27,000,000
2	23,000,000
3	25,000,000
4	3,000,000
5	2,000,000
6	2,500,000
7	400,000
8	300,000
9	400,000

From a decision-making perspective, it would be inappropriate to calculate the overall mean and conclude that the average company spent $9.29 million. It is informative and important to say, however, that three companies averaged $25 million, three companies averaged $2.5 million, and three companies averaged $367,000.

TABLE 25.1 Past- and Current-Year Advertising Expenditures

Car Rental Company	*Past-Year Advertising Expenditures*	*Estimated Current-Year Advertising Expenditures*
Advantage Rent-A-Car	$151,000	$161,570
Airways Rent-A-Car	22,500	24,075
Alamo Rent A Car	30,400,000	32,528,000
Budget Rent A Car	12,200,000	13,054,000
Dollar Rent-A-Car	7,500,000	8,025,000
Enterprise Rent-A-Car	12,000,000	12,840,000
Hertz Rent A Car	38,300,000	40,981,000
Holiday Auto Rent A Car	115,000	123,050
National Car Rental	450,000	481,500
Sav Mor Car Rental	80,000	85,600
Thrifty Car Rental	5,900,000	6,313,000
Avis Rent A Car	16,000,000	to be determined
Other	11,250,000	12,375,000
Total	$134,368,500	

Note: Data are hypothetical and are for illustrative purposes only.

levels of sales (to which the advertiser's prior year's advertising to sales ratio would be applied). In this hypothetical example, we have raised prior years' budgets to account for the anticipated level of media inflation (estimated to be 7 percent).

- Group competitors into high, medium, and low spending categories on the basis of their current year's expenditures. In this example, the grouping process would result in the data shown in Table 25.2.

TABLE 25.2 Advertising Expenditures Grouped By Spending Level

Car Rental Company	*Estimated Current Year's Advertising Expenditures*
High Advertising Expenditures	
Hertz Rent A Car	$40,981,000
Alamo Rent A Car	32,528,000
Moderate Advertising Expenditures	
Budget Rent A Car	$13,054,000
Enterprise Rent-A-Car	12,840,000
Dollar Rent-A-Car	8,025,000
Thrifty Car Rental	6,313,000
Low Advertising Expenditures	
National Car Rental	$481,500
Advantage Rent-A-Car	161,570
Holiday Auto Rental Car	123,050
Sav Mor Car Rental	85,600
Airways Rent-A-Car	24,075

Note: Data are hypothetical and are for illustrative purposes only.

- Evaluate Avis' strategic options in light of their associated budget requirements. In this example, strategic and budget options include the following:

  - Spend at levels comparable to leading advertisers (in this case, Hertz and Alamo). This would require a budget of between $32 and $41 million, a significant increase over the prior year's budget.

  - Spend at levels just above the highest level of moderate advertisers but below that of the highest advertisers. This would require a budget of about $14–$17 million, roughly comparable to the prior year's budget.

  - Spend at levels comparable to the average of the middle group of advertisers. This would require a budget of about $10 million, a level substantially below that of prior year's budget.

  - Spend at levels comparable to the lowest advertisers, a significant reduction versus the prior year's budget.

The enumeration of strategic options (in this case four possible spending levels for Avis) point out the strengths and weaknesses of this approach. The approach is easy to use and defend, and directs attention to competitors' advertising activities. However, the approach still requires a great deal of subjective judgment (for example, in evaluating which of the four options noted previously is the most preferred) and assumes that competitors have used a reasonable basis for setting their advertising budgets.

Share of Market/Share of Voice   The *share of market/share of voice* approach relates desired market share to advertising spending. This approach, in its most basic form, assumes that advertising spending should be roughly equivalent to market share, that is, a brand that accounts for 20 percent of all category sales should also account for about 20 percent of all category advertising spending.[5]

The use of a straight market share/share of voice relationship, however, oversimplifies the marketplace realities faced by different advertisers within the same product category. Research has shown that the market share/share of voice relationship should be modified in the following circumstances:

- New product introductions generally require a higher ratio. It is generally believed that a new product requires a budget that is 150 percent of the targeted end of year two brand share. Thus, for example, if at the end of the second year of sales the brand needs a 12 percent market share, the advertiser must have an 18 percent share of voice (calculated as 1.5 • 12).

- Category leaders, in terms of sales, can spend less than their share of market. Brands that want to increase market share need to spend in excess of their current share of market.

---

[5] For the sake of mathematical simplicity, this example, assumed no growth in category advertising spending or media inflation. Because this assumption may not be true for many product categories, a more accurate budget estimate is often obtained by estimating category advertising spending in light of past growth and then calculating the brand's share of this estimate.

• If economically possible, advertising share of voice in support of brands in fast growing product categories generally should exceed market share.[6]

Thus, it is recommended that when a share of market/share of voice approach is used, the budget level obtained should be evaluated and refined in light of the brand's unique marketplace situation.

LNA DATA AND THE IDENTIFICATION OF MARKETPLACE DYNAMICS AND COMPETITIVE STRATEGIES[7]

The automobile rental category is uncomplicated. There are few brands overall and each parent company supports only one or two brands. Other categories, such as toothpaste and shampoo, are much more complex. These categories contain many brands and parent companies market and support multiple brands. In categories such as these, LNA data can provide important insights into marketplace dynamics and competitors' strategic priorities. This section discusses this application of LNA data.

Organizing LNA Information for Analysis

Insights into marketplace activities and competitors' brand strategies and priorities are facilitated when the raw data provided by LNA is systematically organized. LNA data can be organized in a four-step process:

1. Transfer LNA data from the LNA report to a core spreadsheet.
2. Define subcategories within the category of interest and assign each brand to one subcategory.
3. Create category and subcategory summary tables.
4. Create multibrand spending trend summaries.

Step 1: Transfer LNA Data to Core Spreadsheet   This initial step in data organization creates a spreadsheet on which brand and media expenditures are recorded. The 10-Media Total and spending totals for each brand in each advertising medium are taken directly from the LNA report. The toothpaste category core spreadsheet is shown in Table 25.3 (pages 642–643).

---

[6] The competitive response approach and share of market/share of voice approach use past years spending to estimate required budget levels for the upcoming year. Beyond the fundamental analyses described, additional analyses can be conducted to provide guidance in determining a brand's budget needs. An advertiser of a new product, for example, might want to use LNA information to determine competitive brands' introductory budget levels. This would be accomplished by looking at those brands for which there is past year, but not past two-year expenditures. (For example, when looking at 1995 LNA information sometime in 1996 a new product is likely to be one that shows advertising spending for 1995 but not for 1994.) Relating introductory spending levels to brand share provides an excellent foundation for a better understanding of the advertising investment in a specific product category required to achieve a specific share of sales. An advertiser for an established product might want to examine shifts in competitive spending. That is, when looking at 1995 LNA information (sometime in 1996) an advertiser might want to look at those brands that have significantly increased or decreased their advertising expenditures between 1994 and 1995.

[7] The source for data used in this and the following section is Competitive Media Reporting. The data is used with their kind permission. All rights are reserved.

TABLE 25.3 LNA Core Spreadsheet: Total Brand Expenditures ($ thousands)

Subcategory	Brand	Year	10-Media	Magazines	Sunday Magazines	Newspaper	Outdoor
Regular	Carefree	1993	2.2				
		1992	20.2				
Sensitive	Sensodyne	1993	6,561.7				
		1992	6,450.1	36.0			
Whitening	Pearl Drops	1993	3,811.2	3,811.2			
		1992	2,372.3	2,369.5			
Whitening	Plus White Paste	1993	4,612.4				
		1992	1,414.7				
Whitening	Plus White Gel	1993	277.5				
		1992	2,559.0				
Multiple	Arm & Ham-Tartar	1993	4,279.9				
		1992	8,502.2				
Baking Soda	Arm & Ham-Reg BS	1993	8,465.9				
		1992	5,079.6				
Baking Soda	Colgate Baking Soda	1993	8,118.0	2,715.9			
		1992	8,983.7	1,780.4			
Regular	Colgate Regular	1993	12,078.6	2,609.2	0.0	145.3	
		1992	12,735.8	74.5	1.1	901.5	
Tartar	Colgate Tartar	1993	270.2	270.2			
		1992	5.4				
Regular	Viadent	1993	16.7	16.7			
		1992	0.0	0.0			
Whitening	Rembrandt	1993	2,522.9	260.7			
		1992	2,491.5	2,491.5			
Regular	Check-Up	1993	381.7				
		1992	1,430.9				
Baking Soda	Crest Baking Soda	1993	12,900.6				
		1992	10.7				
Regular	Crest Regular	1993	17,277.8	3,709.6	22.5	436.5	
		1992	23,768.1	2,106.6	712.5	259.3	
Tartar	Crest Tartar	1993	21,359.3	2,135.6	0.0		
		1992	15,638.6	1,207.4	217.0		
Multiple	Crest Tart & Baking	1993	6,018.6				
		1992	0.0				
Sensitive	Crest Sensitive	1993	64.2				
		1992	0.0				
Sensitive	Aqua Fresh Sensitive	1993	8,682.7	18.0			
		1992	2,741.4	0.0			
Tartar	Aqua Fresh Tartar	1993	10,708.4				
		1992	10,602.0				
Regular	Aqua Fresh Regular	1993	4,268.5				
		1992					
Regular	Close Up Regular	1993	7,081.9				
		1992	129.8				
Multiple	Mentadent	1993	13,468.5	865.0			
		1992	2,465.3	550.9			
Sensitive	Plus White Sensitive	1993	32.5				
		1992	0.0				
	Total 1993		153,261.9	16,448.1	22.5	581.8	0
	Total 1992		107,401.3	10,580.8	930.6	1,160.8	0

Net TV	Spot TV	Synd TV	Cable TV	Total TV	Net Radio	Spot Radio	Total Radio
	2.2			2.2			
	20.2			20.2			
3,382.8	1,026.8	798.4	1,317.7	6525.7			
3,809.1	1,171.5	649.1	820.4	6450.1			
	0.0			0.0			
	2.8			2.8			
2,586.1	1,350.4	600.6	75.3	4612.4			
562.5	655.3	157.9	39.0	1414.7			
0.0	277.5	0.0	0.0	277.5			
1,969.2	196.2	385.9	7.7	2559			
2,990.4	215.4	725.3	348.8	4279.9			
7,085.2	550.9	654.8	211.3	8502.2			
6,758.2	628.5	561.9	517.3	8465.9			
4,399.3	227.4	266.8	186.1	5079.6			
3,768.0	1,088.8		540.1	5396.9		5.2	5.2
5,998.9	603.8		600.6	7203.3		0.0	0.0
8,135.6	330.4	123.6	335.0	8924.6	399.5		399.5
10,384.0	442.1	46.0	315.6	11187.7	571.0		571.0
						0.0	0.0
						5.4	5.4
1,829.1	2.7	3.5	426.9	2262.2			
0.0	0.0	0.0	0.0	0.0			
0.0	292.9		88.8	381.7			
1,037.3	16.5		377.1	1430.9			
9,018.9	2,347.5	436.4	844.6	12647.4		253.2	253.2
0.0	10.7	0.0	0.0	10.7		0.0	0.0
7,977.4	2,487.4	1,657.9	978.6	13101.3		7.9	7.9
13,609.2	4,046.1	1,582.7	1,451.7	20689.7		0.0	0.0
10,583.2	4,177.4	3,394.5	1,068.6	19223.7			
9,258.8	1,599.7	2,220.8	1,134.9	14214.2			
4,475.1	999.8	80.5	463.2	6018.6			
0.0	0.0	0.0	0.0	0.0			
	64.2			64.2			
	0.0			0.0			
6,951.5	326.6	567.0	819.6	8664.7			
2,193.9	41.2	320.6	185.7	2741.4			
8,243.1	192.6	1,273.6	999.1	10708.4			
9,317.3	79.5	918.4	286.8	10602			
3,004.0	345.5	688.8	153.6	4191.9		76.6	76.6
0.0	0.0	0.0	0.0	0.0		0.0	0.0
3,570.8	723.7	2,319.9	567.5	7181.9			
0.0	87.5	0.0	42.3	129.8			
10,999.0	1,604.5			12603.5			
	1,914.4			1914.4			
	32.5			32.5			
	0.0			0.0			
94,273.2	18,517.3	13,231.9	9.544.7	135,567.1	399.5	342.9	742.4
69,624.7	11,665.8	7,203.0	5,659.2	94,152.7	571	5.4	576.4

We recommend that in addition to transferring raw LNA information from the LNA report to the spreadsheet, you create your spreadsheet to perform two internal calculations. The spreadsheet shown in Table 25.3 provides two subtotals that are not calculated by LNA. The four television categories are summed into a "Total TV" category and the two radio categories are summed into a "Total Radio" category. These subtotals are easily calculated and permit you to more easily see data trends beyond that indicated by the raw data.

Step 2: Define and Record Subcategories Most multiple brand categories can be divided into smaller subcategories. These subcategories may reflect product pricing, product characteristics, consumer end benefits, or some combination of these and other characteristics. The laundry detergent category, for example, can be divided into subcategories that reflect product form (powder or liquid) and concentration. Products in the shampoo category can be divided on the basis of distribution (mass market or salon), target audience (male or female), and formulation (dandruff, conditioning, treated hair, etc.).

The next step in data organization defines the most meaningful subcategories within the category of interest. Once subcategories are defined each brand is assigned to one (and only one subcategory) and each brand's subcategory assignment is noted on the core spreadsheet (see Table 25.3). In this example, we have determined that subcategories within the toothpaste category do exist and are defined in terms of consumer benefit and product formulation. The subcategories are (1) toothpastes with baking soda, (2) regular toothpastes, (3) sensitive teeth, (4) tartar control toothpastes, (5) special whitening formulas, and (6) toothpastes with multiple characteristics or product benefits.

Step 3: Create Summaries The next set of activities extracts and organizes data from the core spreadsheet. Two sets of tables summarize the *overall trend* in advertising spending. Here, brands are grouped into subcategories and the total current and prior calendar years' spending by brand and subcategory are recorded. Additionally, the dollar change in spending for each brand and subcategory is calculated as well as the percent change for the entire subcategory.[8] This level of data organization is illustrated in Table 25.4. Next, subcategory data is summarized as shown in Table 25.5 (page 646). One type of summary, Table 25.5A transfers subcategory and total spending trends from the prior spreadsheet to their own table. This transfer lets you more easily compare subcategory spending trends in terms of year-to-year dollar and percent changes. A second summary table, Table 25.5B, translates absolute subcategory spending levels into percents. Here the *percent* of total category spending accounted for by each subcategory, as well as each subcategory's year-to-year percentage point change in a share of category spending, is computed and displayed.

---

[8] Care must be taken when using calculations of percent change. Always interpret a percent change within the context of the absolute amount of the base on which the change is calculated. For example, a 300 percent change in total media expenditures has different meanings and implications when the rise is from $1,000 to $3,000 versus $1 million to $3 million.

TABLE 25.4 Subcategory Spending Summary: Year-to-Year Trend ($ thousand)

Brand	Type	1993	1992	Dollar Change	Percent Change
Arm and Hammer Regular	Baking Soda	8,465.9	5,079.6	3,386.3	
Colgate Baking Soda	Baking Soda	8,118.0	8,983.7	−865.7	
Crest Baking Soda	Baking Soda	12,900.6	10.7	12,889.9	
Baking Soda Subtotal		**29,484.5**	**14,074.0**	**15,410.5**	**109.5%**
Colgate Regular	Regular	12,078.6	12,735.8	−657.2	
Viadent	Regular	16.7	0.0	16.7	
Check-Up	Regular	381.7	1,430.9	−1,049.2	
Crest Regular	Regular	17,277.8	23,786.1	−6,490.3	
Aqua Fresh Regular	Regular	4,268.5	0.0	4,268.5	
Close-Up	Regular	7,081.9	129.8	6,952.1	
Carefree	Regular	2.2	20.2	−18.0	
Regular Subtotal		**41,107.4**	**38,084.8**	**3,022.6**	**7.9**
Sensodyne	Sensitive	6,561.7	6,450.1	111.6	
Plus White Sensitive	Sensitive	32.5	0.0	32.5	
Crest Sensitive	Sensitive	64.2	0.0	64.2	
Aqua-Fresh Sensitive	Sensitive	8,682.7	2,741.4	5,941.3	
Sensitive Subtotal		**15,341.1**	**9,191.5**	**6,149.6**	**66.9**
Colgate Tartar Control	Tartar	270.2	5.4	264.8	
Crest Tartar Control	Tartar	21,359.3	15,638.6	5,720.7	
Aqua Fresh Tartar	Tartar	10,708.4	10,602.0	106.4	
Tartar Subtotal		**32,337.9**	**26,246.0**	**6,091.9**	**23.2**
Pearl Drops Regular	Whitening	3,811.2	2,372.3	1,438.9	
Plus White	Whitening	4,612.4	1,414.7	3,197.7	
Plus White Gel	Whitening	277.5	2,559.0	−2,281.5	
Rembrandt	Whitening	2,522.9	2,491.5	31.4	
Whitening Subtotal		**11,224.0**	**8,837.5**	**2,386.5**	**27.0**
Mentadent Baking Soda/Perox	Bak Soda/Peroxide	13,468.5	2,465.3	11,003.2	
Crest Tartar and Baking	Tartar + Baking	6,018.6	0.0	6,018.6	
Arm and Hammer Tartar Ctrl	Tartar + Baking	4,279.9	8,502.2	−4,222.3	
Multiple Characteristics Subtotal		**23,767.0**	**10,967.5**	**17,021.8**	**155.2%**
Total Category		**153,261.9**	**107,401.3**	**45,860.6**	**42.7%**

Source: Competitive Media Reporting. All rights reserved. Reproduced with permission.

Step 4: Create Multibrand Summary   The final step in data organization only takes place when one parent company expends funds on two or more brands. When this occurs, a parent company summary is developed as shown in Table 25.6 (page 647). The grouping of brands within parent company makes it easier to examine corporate spending trends and brand priorities. The organization of data in company-specific tables parallels that of the table shown in Table 25.5.

Identifying Competitive Priorities and Strategies

Once organized, LNA data provides important insights into marketplace activities and advertisers' strategic plans and priorities. Data analysis requires one to

TABLE 25.5 Subcategory Spending Trend Summaries

A.

Subcategory	1993 Spending ($000)	1992 Spending ($000)	Dollar Change ($000)	Percent Change
Baking Soda	29,484.5	14,074.0	15,410.5	109.50%
Regular	41,107.4	38,084.8	3,022.6	7.94
Sensitive	15,341.1	9,191.5	6,149.6	66.91
Tartar	32,337.9	26,246.0	6,091.9	23.21
Whitening	11,224.0	8,837.5	2,386.5	27.00
Multiple Characteristics	23,767.0	10,967.5	12,799.5	155.20

B.

Subcategory	Percent Share of Total 1993	Percent Share of Total 1992	Percentage Point Change
Baking Soda	19.2%	13.1%	6.13%
Regular	26.8	35.5	−8.64
Sensitive	10.0	8.6	1.45
Tartar	21.1	24.4	−3.34
Whitening	7.3	8.2	−0.91
Multiple Characteristics	15.5	10.2	5.30
	100.0	100.0	

Source: Competition Media Reporting. All rights reserved. Reproduced with permission.

- examine the trend in overall category spending,
- determine the consistency between category and subcategory spending trends,
- examine the brand expenditure trends within subcategories,
- examine multibrand advertising spending trends, if appropriate.

As can be seen, each step in the analysis requires that you examine the relevant data, identify important findings and trends, and then infer the meaning of observed findings and trends. Issues, questions, or inferences generated as part of this analytical process can be explored in more rigor or depth with additional secondary or primary research.

Examine Trend in Overall Category Spending   The first step in data analysis compares total category spending to the general rate of media inflation to determine whether the year-to-year trend in total category spending has increased faster than media inflation, remained stable (that is, increased at about the same rate as media inflation), or declined (that is, failed to keep up with media inflation).

The year-to-year category spending trend provides your first insight into category dynamics. Product categories with increasing spending are generally dynamic,

TABLE 25.6 Parent Company Brand Summaries

		1993 Spending ($000)	1992 Spending ($000)	Dollar Change ($000)	Percent Change
Crest Brands					
Crest Baking Soda	Baking Soda	12,900.6	10.7	12,889.9	
Crest Regular	Regular	17,277.8	23,768.1	− 6,490.3	
Crest Sensitive	Sensitive	64.2	0.0	64.2	
Crest Tartar Control	Tartar	21,359.3	15,638.6	5,720.7	
Crest Tartar and Baking	Tartar + Baking	6,018.6	0.0	6,018.6	
Total Crest		**57,620.5**	**39,417.4**	**18,203.1**	**46.2**
Aqua Fresh Brands					
Aqua Fresh Regular	Regular	4268.5	0.0	4,268.5	
Aqua Fresh Sensitive	Sensitive	8682.7	2741.4	5,941.3	
Aqua Fresh Tartar	Tartar	10,708.4	10,602.0	106.4	
Total Aqua Fresh		**23,659.6**	**13,343.4**	**10,316.2**	**77.3**
Arm and Hammer Brands					
Arm & Ham Baking Soda	Baking Soda	8,465.9	5,079.6	3,386.3	
Arm & Ham Tartar Con	Tartar	4,279.9	8,502.2	− 4,222.3	
Total Arm and Hammer		**12,745.8**	**13,581.8**	**− 836.0**	**− 6.2**
Colgate Brands					
Colgate Baking Soda	Baking Soda	8,118.0	8,983.7	− 865.7	
Colgate Regular	Regular	12,078.6	12,735.8	− 657.2	
Colgate Tartar Control	Tartar	270.2	5.4	264.8	
Total Colgate		**20,466.8**	**21,724.9**	**− 1,258.1**	**− 5.8**

Source: Competitive Media Reporting. All rights reserved. Reproduced with permission.

that is, existing brands are being aggressively supported and/or product line extensions and new products are being introduced into the marketplace. Stable spending generally indicates a less dynamic and less active category while categories with a spending decline tend to be the least dynamic. In this example, as seen in the last row of Table 25.4, total 1993 toothpaste spending of about $153 million represents a 42.7 percent increase over 1992, significantly greater than the estimated 6 percent media inflation that occurred during this period. The substantial increase in category spending might lead us to infer that the toothpaste category is highly dynamic and competitive. A category in which advertisers acknowledge the need to commit funds to support brand development and growth. Finally, the large increase in spending alerts us to the high potential for line extension and new product activity.

Determine Consistency Between Category and Subcategory Spending Trends
The second step in data analysis provides additional insights into category dynamics by comparing the total category spending trend to trends in subcategory spending. If

the spending pattern for the total category is consistent among the subcategories then it is likely that corporate priorities have remained constant. Stable spending indicates that advertisers are continuing to support subcategories of products in the same way from year to year. On the other hand, subcategory spending trends that run counter to the overall category trend tend to indicate a dynamic product category in which there is a high likelihood of changing advertiser strategies and priorities. Here, advertisers are moving support from some subcategories of products to others.

The extent to which advertiser spending strategies have changed or remained constant can be determined by using LNA data to answer the following three groups of related questions:

1. Which subcategories (if any) show spending trends consistent with the overall category? Why are these subcategories following the overall category spending trend? What are the characteristics of these subcategories versus those subcategories (if any) with counter category spending trends?

2. Which subcategories (if any) show spending trends counter to the overall category? What are the characteristics of these subcategories versus those subcategories (if any) with category consistent spending trends? Why are these subcategories not following the overall category spending trend? How are funds from declining subcategories being used? Are they being saved or reallocated? Where are funds from growing subcategories coming from? Are they coming from new allocations or from other subcategories?

3. What insights into advertiser strategies and marketplace dynamics can be drawn from answers to the prior two sets of questions?

Table 25.5 provides the information required to answer the prior questions. The data in the table indicates that subgroup spending in the toothpaste category does not follow the pattern of overall category spending. Table 25.5A shows the absolute amount of funds allocated to each product subcategory. The third and fourth columns ("Dollar Change" and "Percent Change") provide important insights. Table 25.5B provides a different perspective on spending trends. Here, each subcategory's share of total spending is presented. The third column in this table, "Percentage Point Change," notes changes each subcategory's percentage point change in the share of spending between the two years.

An examination of these tables indicates that subcategory spending trends do not follow that of the overall category. First, the percent increases in spending for each subcategory are out of line with the approximately 43 percent overall category spending increase. Second, in terms of absolute dollars, two subcategories show dramatic spending increases while other subcategories show far less increases. In terms of subcategories' *share* of overall spending, two subcategories show a marked increase in the share of spending, two subcategories are relatively constant, and two show a marked decline. This pattern of absolute dollar allocation and share of allocation, when interpreted in response to the three questions raised earlier, may indicate a change in marketers' strategies and priorities within the toothpaste category. We might infer from the data that

regular and tartar control toothpastes remain important core product categories. In terms of absolute spending levels, these subcategories continue to receive the greatest amount of advertising support. However, the *share* of total spending accounted for by regular and tartar control brands shows significant declines while the share of spending for baking

soda and multiple characteristic brands shows a significant increase. These share trends, when placed in the context of absolute levels of spending, indicate that advertisers are investing additional dollars (rather than shifting existing dollars) in support of these latter types of toothpastes. We might speculate that this pattern of subcategory spending reflects advertisers' belief that these specialized, multiple ingredient-multibenefit brands are the "brands of the future."

Examine Brand Expenditure Trends within Subcategories Next, individual brand spending trends within each subcategory are examined. Similar to the prior step, brand spending within each subcategory is examined for consistency with its subcategory spending trend. This step provides additional, deeper insights into advertisers' strategies. A consistent trend within a subcategory generally indicates that advertisers of similar types of products are following the same strategy. Inconsistencies within a subcategory generally indicate that advertisers have adopted different marketing and advertising strategies than their direct competitors. As in the prior step, advertiser brand strategies are inferred from following answers to the three related questions:

1. Which individual brands (if any) show spending trends consistent with their subcategory?
2. Which individual brands (if any) show spending trends counter to their subcategory?
3. What insights into advertiser strategies and marketplace dynamics can be drawn from answers to the prior two sets of questions?

In this example, an examination of individual brand spending within each toothpaste subcategory reveals a high level of inconsistency. As shown in Table 25.4, each subcategory contains brands with different spending trends. The prior questions would, for the regular toothpaste subcategory, be answered as follows:

> There are seven brands in the regular toothpaste subcategory. Expenditures in this subcategory have risen by about $3 million (or about 8%) between 1992 and 1993. The rise in subcategory expenditures is due to increases in two brands: Aqua Fresh and Close-Up. Other brands in the regular subcategory show different spending patterns. Spending for Colgate and Viadent is relatively stable while spending for Check-Up and Crest show significant declines. This spending pattern may imply that advertisers' have reordered their brand priorities for this subcategory of toothpaste.

Examine Multibrand Advertising Spending Trends The final step provides insights into individual advertiser strategies by examining the spending pattern of multibrand advertisers. This examination provides insights into how advertisers are leading or responding to changes in category and subcategory structure and how corporate brand strategies may be changing. In this example, multibrand advertisers are Crest, Aqua-Fresh, Arm and Hammer, and Colgate. The spending patterns of these advertisers, as shown in Table 25.6, reveal different spending patterns and may reflect different marketing strategies and corporate priorities as follows:

- Advertising support for all Crest brands has increased by about 46 percent between 1992 and 1993, demonstrating the manufacturer's commitment to continued support of

this product line. The allocation of the budget among the various Crest brands appears to indicate that although the regular brand is still important (the prior year's spending was $17 million), this brand is becoming *relatively* less important than more specialized Crest brands. Significant increased support is seen for the baking soda, tartar control, and tartar control with baking soda brands. Additionally, the absence of 1992 expenditures for Crest sensitive, coupled with low 1993 spending, may indicate that Crest is test marketing a sensitive formula toothpaste. The test marketing of a sensitive toothpaste would be in keeping with what appears to be Crest's increasing emphasis on specialized formulations.

- Aqua Fresh also appears to have strong commitment to its brands. Advertising spending nearly doubled between 1992 and 1993. Aqua Fresh may have adopted a strategy that directly responds to Crest's strategy. Aqua Fresh is spending heavily in support of a sensitive toothpaste (perhaps wanting to establish itself before Crest fully enters the segment) and in support of its regular toothpaste (a segment for which Crest is decreasing support). Finally, Aqua Fresh spending for tartar control remains strong, protecting itself from increased competitive spending in this subcategory.

- Arm and Hammer shows a small spending decline and a significant shift in spending priorities. While year to year spending is down slightly, individual brand support has changed. Arm and Hammer shows increased support for its baking soda brand and decreased support for its tartar control brand.

- Colgate appears to have adopted a conservative position. Colgate's overall spending is down slightly between 1992 and 1993. The pattern of spending on individual brand during this period is relatively unchanged.

Summary: Analysis of Marketplace Activities

This section presented one approach to the examination of LNA information. LNA information provided the basis for drawing inferences about category trends, changing category structure, and specific advertiser's priorities and strategies. It is important to remember, however, that all of the conclusions drawn from the data were *inferred* from observations of the data. Your own analysis of LNA data must take a similar perspective, specifically, that inferences drawn from LNA data are interesting, insightful, and provide a basis for better understanding a product category. But, the inferences are unproven. Consequently, you must treat the insights drawn from LNA data as directional and as areas that might beneficially be explored with additional secondary or primary research.

USING LNA DATA TO IDENTIFY COMPETITIVE MEDIA STRATEGIES

LNA information can also provide an understanding of category and brand media strategies. As such, it makes an important contribution to a specific brand's media plan by helping to determine advertising media that will be the most and least difficult to break through competitive clutter. The analysis provides these insights by determining

- which advertising media account for the greatest share of expenditures (and thus are the most cluttered in terms of competitive messages);
- the extent to which a subcategory of products and individual brands follow similar me-

dia strategies, providing insights into the consistency of media strategies among advertisers and types of products.

This analysis is parallel to that presented in the prior section. However, here the focus is on advertising expenditures by advertising medium. As a result, three sets of tables are developed that summarize the trend in spending *within each of the ten tracked advertising media*. These tables, similar in format to the prior tables, report the *percent* of the total budget allocated to each medium. Table 25.7 (pages 652–653) shows the percent of each advertiser's expenditures by medium for the current and past year. Table 25.8 (pages 654–655) shows the organization of brands by subcategory and the most recent year's allocations for each brand and subcategory, while Table 25.9 (pages 656–657) is a summary of subcategory allocations to each advertising medium.

The first three steps in the analysis of media expenditures are similar to the first three steps in the prior analysis. Now, however, the focus is on advertising media rather than total advertising expenditures. The three steps are as follows:

1. Examine the trend in overall category media expenditures.
2. Determine consistency between category and subcategory spending trends.
3. Examine the pattern of media allocation for brands within subcategories.

Examine Overall Category Media Expenditures

The first step in the analysis of media expenditures examines two aspects of advertisers' dollar allocation among different media. First, to determine advertisers' current media preferences and strategies, the percent of total expenditures allocated to each individual medium is examined. The data for this part of the analysis are shown in Table 25.7. The data shown on the bottom of the table indicate that for the category overall there has been little change in media allocations over the past two years. Second, the media allocations of individual advertisers are visually examined to determine if any advertisers have altered their specific strategy of media allocation. An examination of Figure 25.7 indicates that advertisers have been quite consistent in their year-to-year allocation of funds among advertising media.

Determine Consistency Between Category and Subcategory Spending Trends

The second step in media analysis determines the extent to which the pattern of media allocation for the total category is or is not consistent among the subcategories. This is accomplished by comparing subcategory to overall category trends in media allocation. Consistency among the subcategories generally indicates that advertisers are following the same media strategy for all brands in the category. Inconsistency between subcategory and category media allocation generally indicates that advertisers are using specialized media strategies for each product subcategory. As in the prior analysis, this step of the analysis requires that you address the following questions:

1. Which subcategories (if any) show patterns of media allocation consistent with the overall category? Why are these subcategories following the overall trend in media allocation? What are the characteristics of these subcategories versus those subcategories (if any) with counter category media allocation?

TABLE 25.7 LNA Care Spreadsheet: Percent Brand Expenditure by Medium

Subcategory	Brand	Year	10-Media	Magazines (%)	Sunday Magazines (%)	Newspaper (%)	Outdoor (%)
Regular	Carefree	1993	2.2				
		1992	20.2				
Sensitive	Sensodyne	1993	6,561.7	0.5			
		1992	6,450.1	0.0			
Whitening	Pearl Drops	1993	3,811.2	100.0			
		1992	2,372.3	99.9			
Whitening	Plus White Paste	1993	4,612.4				
		1992	1,414.7				
Whitening	Plus White Gel	1993	277.5				
		1992	2,559.0				
Multiple	Arm & Hammer-Tartar	1993	4,279.9				
		1992	8,502.2				
Baking Soda	Arm & Hammer-Reg BS	1993	8,465.9				
		1992	5,079.6				
Baking Soda	Colgate Baking Soda	1993	8,118.0	33.2			
		1992	8,983.7	19.8			
Regular	Colgate Regular	1993	12,078.6	21.6		1.2	
		1992	12,735.8	0.6		7.1	
Tartar	Colgate Tartar	1993	270.2	100.0			
		1992	5.4	0.0			
Regular	Viadent	1993	16.7	100.0			
		1992	0	0.0			
Whitening	Rembrandt	1993	2,522.9	10.3			
		1992	2,491.5	100.0			
Regular	Check-Up	1993	381.7	0.0			
		1992	1,430.9	0.0			
Baking Soda	Crest Baking Soda	1993	12,900.6	0.0			
		1992	10.7	0.0			
Regular	Crest Regular	1993	17,277.8	21.5	0.1	2.5	
		1992	23,768.1	8.9	3.0	1.1	
Tartar	Crest Tartar	1993	21,359.3	10.0	0.0		
		1992	15,638.6	7.7	1.4		
Multiple	Crest Tartar and Baking	1993	6,018.6				
		1992	0.0				
Sensitive	Crest Sensitive	1993	64.2				
		1992	0.0				
Sensitive	Aqua Fresh Sensitive	1993	8,682.7	0.2			
		1992	2,741.4	0.0			
Tartar	Aqua Fresh Tartar	1993	10,708.4				
		1992	10,602.0				
Regular	Aqua Fresh Regular	1993	4,268.5				
		1992	0.0				
Regular	Close Up Regular	1993	7,081.9				
		1992	129.8				
Multiple	Mentadent	1993	13,468.5	6.4			
		1992	2,465.3	22.3			
Sensitive	Plus White Sensitive	1993	32.5				
		1992	0.0				
	Percent 1993			10.7	0.0	0.4	0.0
	Percent 1992			9.9	0.9	1.1	0.0

Net TV (%)	Spot TV (%)	Synd TV (%)	Cable TV (%)	Total TV (%)	Net Radio (%)	Spot Radio (%)	Total Radio (%)
	100.0			100.0			
	100.0			100.0			
0.5	0.2	12.2	20.1	99.5			
59.1	18.2	10.1	12.7	100.0			
	0.0						
	0.1						
56.1	29.3	13.0	1.6	100.0			
39.8	46.3	11.2	2.8	100.0			
0.0	100.0	0.0	0.0	100.0			
77.0	7.7	15.1	0.3	100.0			
69.9	5.0	16.9	8.1	100.0			
83.3	6.5	7.7	2.5	100.0			
79.8	7.4	6.6	6.1	100.0			
86.6	4.5	5.3	3.7	100.0			
46.0	13.3		6.6	65.9		0.1	0.1
66.8	6.7		6.7	80.2		0.0	0.0
67.4	2.7	1.0	2.8	73.9	3.3		3.3
81.5	3.5	0.4	2.5	87.8	4.5		4.5
						0.0	0.0
						100.0	100.0
72.5	0.1	0.1	16.9	89.7			
0.0	0.0	0.0	0.0	0.0			
0.0	76.7		23.3	100.0			
72.5	1.2		26.4	100.0			
69.9	18.2	3.4	6.5	98.0		2.0	2.0
0.0	100.0	0.0	0.0	100.0		0.0	0.0
46.2	14.4	9.6	5.7	75.8			
57.3	17.0	6.7	6.1	87.0			
49.5	19.6	15.9	5.0	90.0			
59.2	10.2	14.2	7.3	90.9			
74.4	16.6	1.3	7.7	100.0			
0.0	0.0	0.0	0.0	0.0			
	100.0			100.0			
	0.0			0.0			
80.1	3.8	6.5	9.4	99.8			
80.0	1.5	11.7	6.8	100.0			
77.0	1.8	11.9	9.3	100.0			
87.9	0.7	8.7	2.7	100.0			
70.4	8.1	16.1	3.6	98.2		1.8	1.8
0.0	0.0	0.0	0.0	0.0		0.0	0.0
49.0	10.2	32.8	8.0	100.0			
0.0	67.4	0.0	32.6	100.0			
81.7	11.9			93.6			
	77.7			77.7			
	100.0			100.0			
	0.0			0.0			
61.5	12.1	8.6	6.2	88.5	0.3	0.2	0.5
64.8	10.9	6.7	5.3	87.7	0.5	0.0	0.5

TABLE 25.8   Brand Detail Within Subcategory Spreadsheet: Percent Media Expenditures

Subcategory	Brand	Year	10-Media	Magazines (%)	Sunday Magazines (%)	Newspaper (%)	Outdoor (%)
Baking Soda	Arm & Hammer-Reg BS	1993	8,465.9				
Baking Soda	Colgate Baking Soda	1993	8,118.0	33.2			
Baking Soda	Crest Baking Soda	1993	12,900.6	0.0			
Baking soda subcategory			**29,484.5**	**9.2**			
Regular	Colgate Regular	1993	12,078.6	21.6		1.2	
Regular	Viadent	1993	16.7	100.0			
Regular	Check-Up	1993	381.7	0.0			
Regular	Crest Regular	1993	17,277.8	21.5	0.1	2.5	
Regular	Aqua Fresh Regular	1993	4,268.5				
Regular	Close Up Regular	1993	7,081.9				
Regular	Carefree	1993	2.2				
Regular subcategory			**41,107.4**	**15.4**	**0.1**	**1.4**	
Sensitive	Sensodyne	1993	6,561.7	0.5			
Sensitive	Plus White Sensitive	1993	32.5				
Sensitive	Crest Sensitive	1993	64.2				
Sensitive	Aqua Fresh Sensitive	1993	8,682.7	0.2			
Sensitive subcategory			**15,341.1**	**0.4**	**0.0**	**0.0**	**0.0**
Tartar	Colgate Tartar	1993	270.2	100.0			
Tartar	Crest Tartar	1993	21,359.3	10.0			
Tartar	Aqua Fresh Tartar	1993	10,708.4				
Tartar subcategory			**32,337.9**	**7.4**			
Whitening	Pearl Drops	1993	3,811.2	100.0			
Whitening	Plus White Paste	1993	4,612.4				
Whitening	Plus White Gel	1993	277.5				
Whitening	Rembrandt	1993	2,522.9	10.3			
Whitening subcategory			**11,224.0**	**36.3**			
Multiple	Mentadent	1993	13,468.5	6.4			
Multiple	Crest Tartar and Baking	1993	6,018.6				
Mutliple	Arm and Hammer-Tartar	1993	4,279.9				
Mutliple subcategory			**23,767.0**	**3.6**			

Source: Competitive Media Reporting. All rights reserved. Reproduced with permission.

2. Which subcategories (if any) show patterns of media allocation counter to the overall category? What are the characteristics of these subcategories versus those subcategories (if any) with category consistent spending trends? Why are these subcategories not following the overall category trend in media allocation? Why do the brands and products in these subcategories require different patterns of media allocation?

3. What insights into advertiser media strategies can be drawn from answers to the prior two sets of questions?

Net TV (%)	Spot TV (%)	Synd TV (%)	Cable TV (%)	Total TV (%)	Net Radio (%)	Spot Radio (%)	Total Radio (%)
79.8	7.4	6.6	6.1	100.0			
46.0	13.3		6.6	65.9		0.1	0.1
69.9	18.2	3.4	6.5	98.0		2.0	2.0
66.3	**13.8**	**3.4**	**6.5**	**89.9**		**0.9**	**0.9**
67.4	2.7	1.0	2.8	73.9	3.3		3.3
	76.7		23.3	100.0			
46.2	14.4	9.6	5.7	75.8			
70.4	8.1	16.1	3.6	98.2		1.8	1.8
49.0	10.2	32.8	8.0	100.0			
0.0	100.0			100.0			
55.2	**10.2**	**11.7**	**5.2**	**82.2**	**1.0**	**0.2**	**1.2**
0.5	0.2	12.2	20.1	99.5			
	100.0			100.0			
	100.0			100.0			
80.1	3.8	6.5	9.4	99.8			
67.4	**9.5**	**8.9**	**13.9**	**99.6**			
49.5	19.6	15.9	5.0	90.0			
77.0	1.8	11.9	9.3	100.0			
58.2	**13.5**	**14.4**	**6.4**	**92.6**			
56.1	29.3	13.0	1.6	100.0			
	100.0			100.0			
72.5	0.1	0.1	16.9	89.7			
39.3	**14.5**	**5.4**	**4.5**	**63.7**			
81.7	11.9			93.6			
74.4	16.6	1.3	7.7	100.0			
69.9	5.0	16.9	8.1	100.0			
77.7	**11.9**	**3.4**	**3.4**	**96.4**			

    Table 25.9 presents the information required to answer these questions. The data indicate that there is little variation among the subcategories. The pattern of media allocation in each product subcategory is consistent with the total category's pattern of media allocation. Thus, it appears that advertisers have not customized or modified media strategies for specific subgroups of products. All types of toothpaste are heavily advertised in the same medium—television.

TABLE 25.9 Subcategory Summary: Percent Media Expenditures

	10-Media	Magazines	Sunday Magazines	Newspaper	Outdoor	Net TV
Totals Baking Soda	29,484.5	2,715.9	0.0	0.0	0.0	19,545.1
Totals Regular	41,107.4	6,335.5	22.5	581.8	0.0	22,687.8
Totals Sensitive	15,341.1	54.0	0.0	0.0	0.0	10,334.3
Totals Tartar	32,337.9	2,405.8	0.0	0.0	0.0	18,826.3
Totals Whitening	11,224.0	4,071.9	0.0	0.0	0.0	4,415.2
Totals Multiple	23,767.0	865.0	0.0	0.0	0.0	18,464.5
Totals Baking Soda	29,484.5	9.2%				66.3%
Totals Regular	41,107.4	15.4%	0.1%	1.4%		55.2%
Totals Sensitive	15,341.1	0.4%				67.4%
Totals Tartar	32,337.9	7.4%				58.2%
Totals Whitening	11,224.0	36.3%				39.3%
Totals Multiple	23,767.0	3.6%				77.7%

Source: Competitive Media Reporting. All rights reserved. Reproduced with permission.

Examine the Pattern of Media Allocation for Brands Within Subcategories

The final step in the analysis examines individual brand media allocations within a subcategory. This step in the analysis helps to determine if any specific advertiser has adopted a media plan that allocates funds counter to similar products. Advertisers who follow the subcategory trend are those whose pattern of media allocation reflects that of the total subcategory. Advertisers who have adopted a counter strategy to media usage are those whose pattern of media allocation is significantly different from that of the total subcategory.

The data required for this step in the analysis is shown in Table 25.8. As can be seen, there is little deviation within a subcategory. All brands in a subcategory follow the same pattern of media allocation.

Summary: Media Expenditures

The analysis in this section of the chapter provided insights into advertisers' media priorities and strategies. This type of analysis of LNA information is useful when attempting to determine the extent of competitive clutter in various media and the appropriateness of advertising in media not heavily utilized by the category or subcategory as a whole. The analysis clearly demonstrated consistency in media usage in all brands in the product category. Television is the dominant, and most cluttered, advertising medium. Other media are far less heavily utilized and may provide an opportunity to present the message without a great deal of competitive clutter.

The analysis of media utilization can be taken one step further when a visual inspection of the data suggests that a more detailed analysis might prove useful. Here, the

Spot TV	Synd TV	Cable TV	Total TV	Net Radio	Spot Radio	Total Radio
4,064.8	998.3	1,902.0	26,510.2	0.0	258.4	258.4
4,182.1	4,790.2	2,123.5	33,783.6	399.5	84.5	484.0
1,450.1	1,365.4	2,137.3	15,287.1	0.0	0.0	0.0
4,370.0	4,668.1	2,067.7	29,932.1	0.0	0.0	0.0
1,630.6	604.1	502.2	7,152.1	0.0	0.0	0.0
2,819.7	805.8	812.0	22,902.0	0.0	0.0	0.0
13.8%	3.4%	6.5%	89.9%		0.9%	0.9%
10.2%	11.7%	5.2%	82.2%	1.0%	0.2%	
9.5%	8.9%	13.9%	99.6%			
13.5%	14.4%	6.4%	92.6%			
14.5%	5.4%	4.5%	63.7%			
11.9%	3.4%	3.4%	96.4%			

prior analysis can be conducted for each quarter of the year rather than for the year as a whole. This more detailed analysis might indicate seasonality in spending and opportunities for advertising when competitive clutter is low (that is, in those quarters of the year when competitors are spending a lower percentage of their budget.)

Summary

The LNA/Mediawatch Multi-Media Service estimates brand, company, and category advertising expenditures for a broad range of consumer and business-to-business products and services in ten advertising media: magazines, Sunday magazines, newspapers, outdoor, network television, spot television, syndicated television, cable TV networks, network radio, and national spot radio. Advertising spending is reported quarterly and is summarized for a calendar year in a year-end annual volume.

LNA data helps to inform an advertiser's judgment in three areas. First, LNA data provides a sound and objective basis for identifying brand budget requirements. The data permits an advertiser to examine the appropriateness of various budget options in light of levels of competitive spending. Second, LNA spending estimates provide insights into marketplace activities and advertisers' brand strategies and priorities. The data indicates the extent to which advertisers have maintained or shifted support for different products and brands. Third, LNA data provides insights into advertisers' media strategies. LNA data indicates the extent to which advertisers utilize specific media and individual media vehicles to promote and advertise their brands.

Finally, with regard to the latter two uses of LNA data, it is important to remember that all inferences drawn from the analysis of LNA data are unproven. Consequently, you must treat the insights drawn from LNA data as directional and as areas that might beneficially be explored with additional secondary or primary research.

Review Questions

1. What is the LNA/Mediawatch Multi-Media Service?

2. What types of information are provided by the LNA/Mediawatch Multi-Media Service?

3. What is the *objective and task* method of identifying advertising budget options?

4. What are the steps underlying the objective and task approach?

5. How does the *response to competitive spending* approach differ from the *share of market/share of voice* approach?

6. What do the "Category Totals" at the end of an LNA category report represent? Can these totals always be used without modification? Why or why not?

7. What are the steps that guide the organization of LNA information when the goal is to understand competitive brand priorities and strategies? Describe the types of tables and analyses that are created at each step.

8. What are the steps by which LNA information can be used to develop an understanding of advertisers' media strategies? Summarize the types of analyses conducted at each step.

Application Exercises

1. You are the agency media planner assigned to the Crest toothpaste account. The account team has asked for your budget recommendation for the 1994 Crest brand that contains both tartar control and baking soda. Write a memo to the account team that focuses on budget determination and (1) presents and analysis of competitive spending, (2) places the brand's spending in the context of competitive spending, (3) discusses budget options, and (4) presents a budget recommendation for the upcoming year. Be certain to support your discussion and recommendations with appropriate data.

2. LNA estimates media expenditures for each of the product categories that follow. Using the most recent LNA volumes in your school library, report the PIB classification in which the data can be found for each product category and explain whether or not (and why) the category totals reported by LNA are an appropriate summary for the product category.

   - Lip makeup
   - Toilet soaps
   - Coffee, tea, cocoa, and derivatives
   - Ice cream, frozen novelties, and sherbet
   - Cheese products
   - Exercise equipment
   - Golf equipment
   - Jewelry

3. LNA estimates media expenditures for each of the product categories listed next. Each category's PIB code is noted. Refer to the latest LNA volumes in your school library and examine the brands and products within each category. If you feel that a category does not contain any subcategories explain why. If you feel that there are subcategories within a category, then provide a description of and rational for the subcategories of products you feel comprise that category.

D118–Women's scents and fragrances
D127–Diapers (including infant and adult)
F125–Pasta products and pasta product dinners
F163–Cookies and crackers
F224–Bottled waters
G424–Toys
T141–Car and truck tires and tubes
T151–Car batteries

4. The Denorex shampoo account has been placed in review. Your agency has been invited to pitch the account. Several members of the research team begin a review of secondary information, paying particular attention to materials published in trade magazines. Other members of the research team begin a content analysis of advertising within the shampoo category. You have been asked to use LNA information to discern category, advertiser, and specific brand trends.

Go to your library and obtain the most recent LNA data for the shampoo category. Examine, organize, and analyze this information and then prepare an internal agency memo that describes

- the structure of the shampoo category,
- the current importance of product subcategories and shifts (if any) in their importance,
- multibrand advertisers' strategies for existing product support and new product introduction,
- trends in media allocation,
- opportunities in media selection.

Be certain to support your conclusions with clear, appropriate tables and charts. (The tables and charts that you develop for data analysis may not be the best format for communicating your insights and conclusions.)

APPENDIX

A

GUIDE TO COMPUTER-ASSISTED DATA ANALYSIS*

This appendix discusses computer-assisted data analysis. The material in this appendix will help you in two ways: it provides a clear, easy to follow introduction to using computers for data analysis and it takes you through the procedures required for one of the most widely used statistical analysis programs—SPSS, the Statistical Package for the Social Sciences. When you have finished reading this appendix, you will have a better understanding of how SPSS works and how it can facilitate data analysis. (More detailed information on SPSS can be obtained through SPSS manuals.) Second, and perhaps more important, this appendix uses SPSS as a framework for showing you the steps underlying the process of data preparation and analysis. The appendix makes explicit the sequence of events a researcher might follow and the types of analyses a researcher might conduct. Thus, when you have completed the appendix, you should better understand how a researcher approaches the task of finding meaning in data.

INTRODUCING SPSS

SPSS is a computer program that allows academic researchers, students, and practitioners to quickly and easily analyze quantitative data. SPSS is a valuable tool in understanding research data and real-world phenomena. When used appropriately, SPSS facilitates the discovery of relationships that exist in samples of people and helps determine if these relationships are true for the populations from which samples are drawn. SPSS enables a researcher to evaluate data once (1) a research project has been structured, (2) a survey has been developed, (3) a sample has been selected, and (4) data has been collected.

We will use SPSS to conduct data analysis within the context of an advertising research study.

THE RESEARCH STUDY

Imagine that the State of California has asked our advertising agency to develop a television campaign designed to keep at-risk teenagers in school. Preliminary discussions identify three different appeals, which the agency labels "Fear," "Now," and "Future:"

---

*Appendix A was written by Colleen Sheehan.

- "Fear" uses scare tactics.
- "Now" uses a neutral tone and focuses on the immediate advantages of staying in school.
- "Future" uses a neutral tone and focuses on the long-term advantages of staying in school.

In terms of creative approach, the agency is unsure whether they should use a movie star, a sports star, or a "real" person as a spokesperson in the ad.

Given the range of options, nine rough commercials are developed. Each commercial represents a unique combination of appeal and spokesperson, as follows:

Commercial 1: "Fear" appeal with a movie star spokesperson
Commercial 2: "Fear" appeal with a sports star spokesperson
Commercial 3: "Fear" appeal with a "real" spokesperson
Commercial 4: "Now" appeal with a movie star spokesperson
Commercial 5: "Now" appeal with a sports star spokesperson
Commercial 6: "Now" appeal with a "real" spokesperson
Commercial 7: "Future" appeal with a movie star spokesperson
Commercial 8: "Future" appeal with a sports star spokesperson
Commercial 9: "Future" appeal with a "real" spokesperson

The agency conducted research after the rough commercials were developed. Extensive interviews with target individuals were conducted. Each individual was interviewed after seeing *one and only one* of the commercials.

We will examine the most important data collected by the research, specifically, the data obtained by the following questions:

Question 3: Self-report of likelihood to drop out. Obtained before seeing a commercial.

Questions 4–6: Respondents' *reactions to the advertising*. Each question used a nine-point scale. Question 4 used the end points "strongly liked/strongly disliked." Question 5 used the end points "extremely enjoyable/extremely unenjoyable." Question 6 used the end points "fun to watch/not fun to watch."

Questions 7–9: Respondents' *reactions to the message*. Each question used a nine-point scale. Question 7 used the end points "very believable/not at all believable." Question 8 used the end points "very honest/not at all honest." Question 9 used the end points "very truthful/not at all truthful."

Questions 10–11: Respondents' *intent to stay in school*. Each question used a nine point scale. Question 10 used the end points "very likely to stay in school/not at all likely to stay in school." Question 11 used the end points "very likely to graduate/not at all likely to graduate."

NOTE: Questions 4–11 were asked after a respondent viewed a commercial.

BEGINNING DATA ANALYSIS: HAVE A PLAN BEFORE YOU START

When conducting data analysis, the best place to start is to have a clear idea of what you want to find out. If you thoroughly understand your research question, then SPSS can be very helpful when it comes to manipulating large amounts of data, finding patterns, and testing hypotheses. SPSS can help you (1) summarize your data, (2) create

appropriate tables and graphs, (3) examine relationships among your variables, and (4) perform tests of statistical significance on your hypotheses.

The best place to start is with a formal statement of what you want to learn. Once this statement has been explicitly stated, you can develop a plan of the events that needs to take place in order to explore and focus on what you want to learn. In this research, the research questions are as follows:

- Does the type of appeal affect attitudes toward the ad, attitudes toward the message, and intent to stay in school?
- Does the type of spokesperson affect attitudes toward the ad, attitudes toward the message, and intent to stay in school?
- Is there any sort of combined (or interactive) effect of appeal and type of spokesperson on attitudes toward the ad, attitudes toward the message, and intent to stay in school?

Identification of the key research questions tells us what we need to learn. With these questions in mind, we then have to make explicit the steps that will permit us to conduct the analyses that will answer these questions. In this research study, similar to other research, we will need to take the following steps:

Step 1: Tell SPSS About Our Data

Step 2: Conduct a Reality Check for Accuracy

Step 3: Perform Necessary Data Manipulations

Step 4: Check Accuracy of Data Manipulations

Step 5: Conduct Required Analyses and Answer Research Questions

Step 6: Conduct Additional Analyses for Additional Insights

The remainder of this appendix discusses each of these steps.

STEP 1: TELL SPSS ABOUT OUR DATA

SPSS is not fussy. It will examine any data that we ask it to examine whether or not the data is correct. As a result, it is important that we accurately identify our measures.

We tell SPSS about our data by using commands. (In fact, all of our communications with SPSS are by commands.) Four commands are needed to prepare SPSS for our data:

DATA LIST—commands that tell SPSS where to find each variable.

VARIABLE LABEL—commands that tell SPSS the name of each variable.

VALUE LABEL—commands that tell SPSS the name of each response option.

DATA—commands that tell SPSS where to find your data.

Each of these commands is discussed in this section.

Telling SPSS Where the Data is Located

A DATA LIST command comes first. This command tells SPSS where to find each variable in our data statements. The DATA LIST command takes the following form:

```
DATA LIST variable name, variable location
```

where DATA LIST indicates the name of the command, the variable name is our short-hand name for the variable and the variable location tells SPSS where to find each variable as reflected in the column codes in our questionnaire (see text page 309). In our research example, the DATA LIST command takes the following form:

```
DATA LIST ID 1-3 Stayin 4 Appeal 5 Spokes 6 Q4 7 Q5 8 Q6 9 Q7 10 Q8 11 Q9 12
Q10 13 Q11 14 Sex 15.
```

This command tells SPSS that a respondent's identification number can be found in columns 1 through 3, the code for the commercial's appeal can be found in column 5, the code for type of spokesperson can be found in column 6, the ratings for Question 4 can be found in column 7, the respondent's gender can be found in column 15, etc.

Telling SPSS Variable Names

The DATA LIST command tells SPSS where to find each variable and provides a shorthand label for that variable. Data is easier to work with, however, when each variable is clearly identified with a descriptive label. We tell SPSS the name of each variable with a VARIABLE LABELS ID command. The VARIABLE LABELS ID command takes the following form:

```
VARIABLE LABELS ID variable shorthand 'variable long description'
```

where VARIABLE LABELS ID indicates the name of the command, the variable short-hand is the variable name specified in the DATA LIST command and the 'variable long description' is the descriptive name you want SPSS to use whenever it refers to that variable. In our research example, the VARIABLE LABELS ID command would be

```
VARIABLE LABELS ID, 'Identification number'/
    Stayin 'Precommercial likelihood to stay in school'/
    Appeal, 'Type of Commercial Appeal'/
    Spokes, 'Type of Commercial Spokesperson'/
    Q4, 'Question 4, Ad liking'/
    Q5, 'Question 5, Ad enjoyment'/
    Q6, 'Question 6, Ad fun to watch'/
    Q7, 'Question 7, Ad believable'/
    Q8, 'Question 8, Ad honest'/
    Q9, 'Question 6, Ad truthful'/
    Q10, 'Question 10, Intent to stay in school'/
    Q11, 'Question 11, Likelihood to graduate'/
    Sex, 'Respondent gender'.
```

These commands provide a longer descriptive name for each variable. We have, for example, told SPSS that the variable "Stayin" should be referred to as "Precommercial likelihood to stay in school," while "Q4" should be identified and referred to as "Q4, Ad liking."

Telling SPSS About Individual Responses

So far we have used the DATA LIST command to tell SPSS where to find each variable and what shorthand name to use to refer to that variable. We have used the VARI-ABLE LABELS command to provide a more complete description of each variable.

Now it is necessary to specify the meaning of the response options used in each question on the questionnaire. We accomplish this with a VALUE LABELS command.

You will recall that a question's response categories are translated into numbers or values so that they can be entered into the computer. SPSS needs a way to let us know what those numbers or values mean when output is generated. VALUE LABELS (a maximum of 20 characters) are used to explain what the numerical values represent. When numbers represent themselves in "counts and amounts," such as age, income, etc., value labels are not needed to explain the number's meaning. When the number represents a category (e.g., Protestant, Catholic, Jewish), a value label is needed for each number. Note that if more than one variable has the same set of values, the VALUE LABELS can be specified once for the entire set.

The VALUE LABELS command takes the following format:

```
VALUE LABELS variable shorthand response 1 `response 1 meaning' etc.
```

where VALUE LABELS indicates the name of the command. The variable shorthand is the variable name specified in the DATA LIST command. Each variable shorthand is followed by that variable's response options and the meaning of each option. In our research study, the VALUE LABELS command would be

```
VALUE LABELS Stayin 1 'Will stay in' 2 'Won't stay in'/
    Spokes 1 'Movie' 2 'Sports' 3 'Real'/
    Appeal 1 'Fear' 2 'Now' 3 'Future'/
    Q4 to Q11 1 'Extremely positive' 2 'Very positive' 3 'Positive' 4
    'Slightly positive' 5 'Neutral' 6 'Slightly negative' 7 'Negative' 8
    'Very negative' 9 'Extremely negative'/ Sex 1 'Male' 2 'Female'.
```

These commands tell SPSS, for example, that a value of '1' for commercial appeal means that the respondent saw a commercial with the "Fear" appeal, a value of '2' means that they saw a commercial with the "Now" appeal and a value of '3' means they saw a commercial with the "Future" appeal. Since Questions 4–11 all used the same type of scale (although the end points varied) the values for these scales are coded together. In all scales a value of '1' is interpreted to mean 'Extremely positive' (for example, 'extremely believable' or 'extremely honest') while a value of '9' is interpreted to mean 'Extremely negative' (for example, 'not at all believable' or 'not at all honest'). Of course, each of the scales in question 4 to question 11 could have been coded individually.

Telling SPSS to Read the Data
The final step before the start of data analysis tells SPSS to read our data. The command begins with a BEGIN DATA command and ends with an END DATA command. The data appears between the two commands as follows:

```
BEGIN DATA.
001113564398751
002221837393842
(Data continues)
END DATA.
```

Each line of data represents an individual respondent and, in our study, would be interpreted as follows:

Variable	Column	Value	Meaning
ID	1–3	001	Respondent number 1
Stayin	4	1	Respondent says will stay in school
Appeal	5	1	Respondent saw "Fear" appeal
Spokes	6	3	Respondent saw "real" person
Q4	7	5	Rating for ad liking is 5
Q5	8	6	Rating for ad enjoyment is 6
Q6	9	4	Rating for ad fun to watch is 4
Q7	10	3	Rating for ad believability is 3
Q8	11	9	Rating for ad honesty is 9
Q9	12	8	Rating for ad truthfulness is 8
Q10	13	7	Rating for stay in school is 7
Q11	14	5	Rating for likely to graduate is 5
Sex	15	1	Respondent is male

Putting It All Together

All of the prior commands are combined to form the beginning of our SPSS instructions. As a result, our initial set of SPSS commands would be

```
DATA LIST ID 1-3 Stayin 4 Appeal 5 Spokes 6 Q4 7 Q5 8 Q6 9 Q7 10 Q8 11 Q9 12
Q10 13 Q11 14 Sex 15,
VARIABLE LABELS ID, 'Identification number'/Stayin 'Precommercial likelihood
     to stay in school'/
     Appeal, 'Type of Commercial Appeal'/
     Spokes, 'Type of Commercial Spokesperson'/
     Q4, 'Question 4, Ad liking'/
     Q5, 'Question 5, Ad enjoyment'/
     Q6, 'Question 6, Ad fun to watch'/
     Q7, 'Question 7, Ad believable'/
     Q8, 'Question 8, Ad honest'/
     Q9, 'Question 6, Ad truthful'/
     Q10, 'Question 10, Intent to stay in school'/
     Q11, 'Question 11, Likelihood to graduate'/
     Sex, 'Respondent gender'.
VALUE LABELS Stayin 1 'Will stay in' 2 'Won't stay in'/
     Appeal 1 'Fear' 2 'Now' 3 'Future'/
     Spokes 1 'Movie' 2 'Sports' 3 'Real'/
     Q4 to Q11 1 'Extremely positive' 2 'Very positive' 3 'Positive' 4
     'Slightly positive' 5 'Neutral' 6 'Slightly negative' 7 'Negative' 8
     'Very negative' 9 'Extremely negative'/
     Sex 1 'Male' 2 'Female'.
BEGIN DATA.
001113564398751
002221837393842
(Data continues)
END DATA.
```

STEP 2: CONDUCT A REALITY CHECK FOR ACCURACY

At the start of data analysis, we hope that we have provided SPSS with all the proper instructions and have typed our data accurately between the BEGIN DATA and END

DATA commands. However, it is always a good idea to confirm that this is the case before beginning data analysis.

We check the integrity of our data by asking SPSS to construct a frequency table for each of our variables. As discussed in the text (see pages 328–329), a frequency distribution is a description of the number of times that various attributes of a variable are observed in a sample. The distribution summarizes how many times each response category was reported. Looking at the frequency of responses to a question allows us to get a feel for what is going on in the sample and tells us if the data is valid and ready for further analyses.

A request for frequency data takes the form of the command:

```
FREQUENCIES variables = variable name(s).
```

where FREQUENCIES is the name of the command and variables = variable name(s) specifies the names of the variables for which you want to run a frequency distribution. Either of the following commands, in this example, result in a set of frequency distributions for all variables:

```
FREQUENCIES variables = all.
FREQUENCIES variables = ID to Q11.
```

The first command asks for a frequency distribution of all variables. The second command asks for a frequency distribution starting at variable ID and ending at variable Q11 (in effect, all variables).

Table Q4, the frequency distribution for responses to Q4 "Ad Liking" is one of the tables that results from this SPSS command.

```
Q4  Q4 Ad Liking
```

Value Label	Value	Frequency	Percent	Valid Percent	Cum Percent
Extremely positive	1.00	74	33.2	33.4	33.4
Very positive	2.00	34	15.3	15.4	48.8
Positive	3.00	20	9.0	9.0	57.8
Slightly positive	4.00	12	5.4	5.4	63.2
Neutral	5.00	27	12.2	12.3	75.5
Slightly negative	6.00	14	6.3	6.3	81.8
Negative	7.00	34	15.3	15.4	97.2
Very negative	8.00	5	2.3	2.3	99.5
Extremely negative	9.00	1	.5	.5	100.0
. . .		1	.5	Missing	
	Total	222	100.0	100.0	

Notice how SPSS uses the VARIABLE LABELS and VALUE LABELS to label the table. The data in the table would be interpreted as follows:

This table shows that the sample of 222 people responded to Question 4, which asked each respondent to rate his or her liking of the ad. We know this by looking at the Total row of the Frequency column. We can also see that 74 people provided an "Extremely positive" rating and 34 people provided a "Very positive" rating from looking at the numbers in the Frequency column.

Each level of agreement is assigned a numeric code that appears in the Value column, for example, "Extremely positive" = 1 and "Very positive" = 2. These numbers were assigned to these responses in the questionnaire and were defined by the VALUE LABELS command. Once the computer knows that a number defines a response category, it is able to group the data into the proper categories and tally the frequencies.

The Percent column tells you the percentage of people who chose each response, including the percentage of missing responses. For example, 33.2 percent of all respondents selected the most positive rating (a value of '1,' "Extremely positive").

The Valid Percent column calculates percentages based on only those people who answered the question. Missing responses are *excluded*; the computer automatically removes anyone who did not answer before calculating the valid percentages. By looking at the Valid Percent, we see that 33.4 percent of all respondents who answered the question selected the most positive rating.

The last column in a SPSS frequency table is Cum Percent (cumulative percent). The cumulative percent is the sum of the valid percentages as each response category is added. For example, we can see that 63.2 percent of the people who responded to this question were *at least* slightly positive. This column is very important for finding trends in the data.

The table that reports the results of Q4 looks reasonable. There is only one missing response and all responses fall into the proper range.

Now consider the frequency distribution shown in Table Q5, responses to the "Ad Enjoyment" question:

```
Q5  Q5 Ad Enjoyment
                                                  Valid       Cum
Value Label          Value  Frequency   Percent  Percent    Percent
                     0.00        79       35.6     47.0       47.0
Extremely positive   1.00        54       24.3     32.1       79.1
Very positive        2.00        34       15.3     20.2       99.3
Positive             3.00         0        0.0      0.0       99.3
Slightly positive    4.00         0        0.0      0.0       99.3
Neutral              5.00         0        0.0      0.0       99.3
Slightly negative    6.00         0        0.0      0.0       99.3
Negative             7.00         0        0.0      0.0       99.3
Very negative        8.00         0        0.0      0.0       99.3
Extremely negative   9.00         1         .5       .7      100.0
                      . . .      54       24.3   Missing
                                ----      -----   -------
             Total              222      100.0    100.0
```

Something appears to be wrong with the data for this question. There are many missing responses, about one-third of the sample is reported to have provided a rating of "0" (which is not permitted given the rating scale used) and many of the scale options have not been selected. The data for this question would need to be examined and the data input fixed before additional data analysis.

STEP 3: PERFORM NECESSARY DATA MANIPULATIONS

Some analyses focus only on the variables collected. The variables are not combined or altered in any way. In these cases, this step can be skipped. Other studies, such as ours, require the manipulation of variables before further analysis.

Our study used three questions to probe reactions to the advertising, three questions to probe reactions to the message, and two questions to probe intent to stay in school. Multiple questions were used to increase the reliability of the measures in each area. Assuming that each set of questions does measure the same thing, we can combine the individual scale questions to obtain one overall measure for commercial liking, one overall measure for message reaction, and one overall measure for intent to stay in school. This can be done if each set of scale's coefficient alpha is .8 or greater. (For a review of coefficient alpha see page 347.)

The first step in calculating a coefficient alpha is to obtain the intercorrelations of the measures in each set of scales. We ask SPSS to generate a correlation matrix using the command

```
CORRELATION variables = variable name(s).
```

where CORRELATION is the name of the command and variables = variable name(s) specifies the names of the variables that we want to correlate. We would, for example, obtain a correlation matrix for the three measures of "ad liking" by using the command

```
CORRELATION variables = Q4 Q5 Q6.
```

in other words, correlate variables Q4, Q5, and Q6. The result of this command is the correlation matrix shown in the following table:

```
Correlation Variables Q4, Q5, Q6
                      Q4                Q5                Q6
Q4          1.0000           .8462**           .7125**
Q5           .8462**         1.0000            .8046**
Q6           .7125**          .8046**         1.0000

*-Signif. LE .05     **-Signif. LE .01     (2-tailed)
```

The data in this matrix is interpreted as follows: The correlation between variable Q4 and Q5 is .8462, the correlation between variable Q4 and Q6 is .7125, and the correlation between variable Q5 and Q6 is .8046. All correlations are significant at a probability level of .01. (See text pages 375–377 for a discussion of the correlation coefficient.)

A correlation matrix for the remaining two sets of measures would be requested as follows:

```
CORRELATION variables = Q7 Q8 Q9.
CORRELATION variables = Q10 Q11.
```

resulting in the following tables:

```
Correlation Variables Q7, Q8, Q9
                 Q7                Q8                Q9
Q7         1.0000           .8289**           .7102**
Q8          .8289**         1.0000            .8308**
Q9          .7102**          .8308**         1.0000

*-Signif. LE .05     **-Signif. LE .01     (2-tailed)
Correlation Variables Q10, Q11
                 Q10               Q11
Q10        1.0000           .9437**
Q11         .9437**         1.0000

*-Signif. LE .05     **-Signif. LE .01     (2-tailed)
```

The information presented in the correlation matrices can be used to calculate the coefficient alpha. A manual calculation of the coefficient alpha for the first two sets of scales obtains the following coefficient alphas: Liking = .924, Message = .919. Since each alpha exceeds the cutoff value of .8 we can feel confident in combining the three individual attitudes toward the ad scales (Questions 4, 5, and 6) into a single measure of ad reaction. Likewise, we can feel confident in combining the three individual attitudes toward the message scales (Questions 7, 8, and 9) into a single measure of message reaction. The high correlation between the two intent to stay in school scales provides similar confidence for combining these two measures into a single measure.

We ask SPSS to combine the individual scales into a single measure with a COMPUTE command. This command takes the form:

```
COMPUTE name of new variable = calculation.
```

where COMPUTE is the name of the command, the name of the new variable appears on the left of the equal sign, and the computation needed to form the new variable is specified on the right of the equal sign.

The first variable we wish to compute is an overall advertising reaction score, which will be defined as the *average* of the three rating scales that measured reactions to the advertising. We use the following command to calculate this new variable (which we will call "AdReact") for each respondent using the command:

```
COMPUTE AdReact = (Q4+Q5+Q6)/3.
```

Similarly, we ask SPSS to compute our new variables "MesReact" (reaction to the message) and "Intent" (intention to stay in school) using the commands:

```
COMPUTE MesReact = (Q7+Q8+Q9)/3.
COMPUTE Intent = (Q10+Q11)/3.
```

At this time, these are all the new variables that we will need to compute.

STEP 4: CHECK ACCURACY OF DATA MANIPULATIONS

The creation of three new variables (AdReact, MesReact, and Intent) seems straightforward. However, because good decisions rely on good data, we need to check the accuracy of our COMPUTE commands before beginning data analysis. We check the results of our manipulations similar to the way we check the integrity of the original data set. The data is examined in frequency tables.

We request frequency tables for the new variables the same way we requested the tables for the original variables. The command is of the form:

```
FREQUENCIES variables = variable name(s).
```

where FREQUENCIES is the name of the command and variables = variable name(s) specifies the names of the variables for which we want to run a frequency distribution.

In this case, our command would specify the names of our three new variables, as follows:

```
FREQUENCIES variables = AdReact MesReact Intent.
```

The frequency distribution for the AdReact variable is shown in the AdReact table:

AdReact

Value Label	Value	Frequency	Percent	Valid Percent	Cum Percent
	1.00	55	24.8	25.7	25.7
	1.50	11	5.0	5.1	30.8
	2.00	23	10.4	10.7	41.6
	2.50	9	4.1	4.2	45.8
	3.00	16	7.2	7.5	53.3
	3.50	10	4.5	4.7	57.9
	4.00	21	9.5	9.8	67.8
	4.50	10	4.5	4.7	72.4
	5.00	13	5.9	6.1	78.5
	5.50	1	.5	.5	79.0
	6.00	3	1.4	1.4	80.4
	6.50	4	1.8	1.9	82.2
	7.00	8	3.6	3.7	86.0
	7.50	3	1.4	1.4	87.4
	8.00	10	4.5	4.7	92.1
	8.50	4	1.8	1.9	93.9
	9.00	13	5.9	6.1	100.0
	.	8	3.6	Missing	
	Total	222	100.0	100.0	

The distribution in this table would be compared to the frequency distributions of the three measures comprising the AdReact measure (i.e., Q4, Q5, and Q6). Similarly, the frequency distribution of the MesReact and Intent measures would be examined and compared to the distributions of their component variables. If the frequency distributions of all computed variables appear reasonable, we can begin data analysis. (Finally, note that in the AdReact table there are no VALUE LABELS. This is because no value labels were specified for the new computed variable. VALUE LABELS, as well as VARIABLE LABELS, can be specified for computed variables in the same way that they are specified for original variables. These commands typically follow the COMPUTE statement that forms the variable.)

STEP 5: CONDUCT REQUIRED ANALYSES AND ANSWER RESEARCH QUESTIONS

The first step in data analysis typically calculates descriptive statistics for each interval or ratio level variable. There are several ways to accomplish this. We can request descriptive statistics using a DESCRIPTIVES command or we can request means with

the MEANS command. Both commands take the same form as the FREQUENCIES command:

```
DESCRIPTIVES variables = variable name(s).
MEANS variables = variable name(s).
```

where DESCRIPTIVES and MEANS are the command name followed by the names of the variables to be examined. While either option provides information on variable means, the DESCRIPTIVES command is often preferred over the MEANS command because it provides more information. A example of a DESCRIPTIVES table for variable Q8 is shown in the following table:

```
Number of valid observations (listwise) = 212.00
Variable Q8                Q8 Ad honest
Mean          2.534        S.E. Mean     .094
Std Dev       1.384        Variance     1.917
Kurtosis     -.033         S.E. Kurt     .327
Skewness      .819         S.E. Skew     .164
Range         6.000        Minimum      1.00
Maximum       7.00         Sum        555.000
Valid observations-219     Missing observations-3
```

A third way to obtain descriptive information is to add a request for descriptive statistics to the FREQUENCY command. This new command takes the form

```
FREQUENCIES variables = variable name(s) / statistics = names of
statistic(s).
```

where FREQUENCIES is the name of the command, variable name(s) specifies the names of the variables for which you want to run a frequency distribution and names of statistic(s) specifies the requested descriptive statistic(s). Our data would use the two commands:

```
FREQUENCIES variables = Sex Stayin.
FREQUENCIES variables = Q4 to Intent / statistics = all.
```

The first command requests a frequency distribution for the variables Sex and Stayin. No further statistics are requested because these are nominal measures. The second command requests a frequency distribution for all variables from Q4 to Intent (our last calculated variable). All descriptive statistics have been requested for these variables. The following table is one outcome of this command:

```
MesReact
```

Value Label	Value	Frequency	Percent	Valid Percent	Cum Percent
	1.00	54	24.3	24.7	24.7
	1.33	5	2.3	2.3	26.9
	1.67	13	5.9	5.9	32.9
	2.00	34	15.3	15.5	48.4
	2.33	24	10.8	11.0	59.4

2.67	11	5.0	5.0	64.4
3.00	20	9.0	9.1	73.5
3.33	5	2.3	2.3	75.8
3.67	10	4.5	4.6	80.4
4.00	12	5.4	5.5	85.8
4.33	7	3.2	3.2	89.0
4.67	4	1.8	1.8	90.9
5.00	9	4.1	4.1	95.0
5.33	4	1.8	1.8	96.8
5.67	1	.5	.5	97.3
6.00	5	2.3	2.3	99.5
7.00	1	.5	.5	100.0
.	3	1.4	Missing	
Total	222	100.0	100.0	

Mean	2.534	Stderr	.094	Median	2.333
Mode	1.000	Std dev	1.384	Variance	1.917
Kurtosis	-.033	S E Kurt	.327	Skewness	.819
S E Skew	.164	Range	6.000	Minimum	1.000
Maximum	7.000	Sum	555.000		
Valid cases	219	Missing cases	3		

Once descriptive statistics have been collected and examined, the analyses relevant to the key research questions can be conducted.

The research design is a factorial (see text pages 151–153), and as a result, the research questions need to be examined using analysis of variance (ANOVA). In this case, the SPSS command for analysis of variance takes the form:

```
ANOVA variables = variables name(s) by factor 1 (range of factor 1) factor
2/ statistics = name of requested statistics.
```

where ANOVA is the SPSS command that requests analysis of variance, variables = variable names(s) indicates the names of the dependent variables. Factor 1 is the first dimension on which we will examine the data, and range of Factor 1 specifies the value of the beginning and ending level of this factor. Factor 2 is the second dimension on which we will examine the data, and range of Factor 2 specifies the value of the beginning and ending level of this second factor. Statistics specify the names of the various statistical procedures requested. The SPSS command for our data is

```
ANOVA AdReact MesReact Intent by Appeal (1,3) Spokes (1,3) / statistics =
all.
```

that tells SPSS to conduct an analysis of variance in which one factor is Appeal and the second factor is Spokes. Respondents are coded so that Appeal and Spokes each ranges from 1 to 3. We want the analysis conducted for three variables: AdReact, MesReact, and Intent. Finally, we are requesting all available statistics.

Two types of tables are printed for each requested variable. Let us examine the set of tables printed for AdReact. First, SPSS calculates mean values, as follows:

```
                    * * * C E L L   M E A N S * * *
               AdReact
         BY Appeal      Type of Commercial Appeal
            Spokes      Type of Commercial Spokesperson


TOTAL POPULATION
   2.43
   (210)


Appeal Type of Commercial Appeal
1 (Fear)   2 (Now)   3 (Future)
   2.53      2.34       2.20
   (67)      (74)       (69)


Spokes Type of Commercial Spokesperson
1 (Movie)   2 (Sports)   3 (Real)
   1.77        2.48        2.84
   (71)        (73)        (66)


Appeal
               1 (Fear)      2 (Now)      3 (Future)
Spokes
(Movie)    1      2.15          1.98          1.15
               (24)          (24)          (23)
(Sports)   2      2.88          2.33          2.27
               (23)          (24)          (26)
(Real)     3      2.58          2.68          3.33
               (20)          (26)          (20)
```

The presentation of means in the prior output moves from the most to the least general level of analysis.

- The data reported under TOTAL POPULATION, represents the *overall* sample mean for the AdReact measure. The overall sample mean (based on the responses of 210 people) was 2.43, indicating that the overall average on the AdReact measure for all nine commercials was quite positive.

- The next portions of the Cell Means output present means by research condition. The data beneath "Appeal Type of Commercial Appeal" represents the means for the three types of commercial appeals averaged across type of spokesperson. While reactions to all three types of commercial appeals were positive, reactions to the "Future" appeal seem to be the most positive. The data beneath "Spokes Type of Commercial Spokesperson" represents the means for the three types of commercial spokespeople averaged across type of appeal. Again, while reactions to all three types of commercial spokespeople were positive, reactions to the movie spokesperson appear to be the most positive.

- The data on the bottom of the Cell Means output is the most important. This data represents the mean AdReact score for each commercial. The score in the upper left corner, for example, indicates that the average AdReact score for the commercial that used the "Fear" appeal and movie celebrity spokesperson was 2.15. Similarly, the score in the lower right-hand corner notes that the average AdReact score for the commercial that used the "Future" appeal and "real" spokesperson was 3.33. Note the interesting

trends in the data as you examine the AdReact scores for each individual type of spokesperson. For example, the most positive AdReact score was in response to the movie spokesperson within the "Future" appeal. The least positive response was to the "real" person within the "Future" appeal.

Next, SPSS generates an analysis of variance table. The table takes the following format:

```
Analysis of Variance
   AdReact
BY Appeal      Type of Commercial Appeal
   Spokes      Type of Commercial Spokesperson
```

Source of Variation	Sum of Squares	DF	Mean Square	F	Sig of F
Main Effects	68.598	4	17.149	469.527	.000
Appeal	11.713	2	5.857	160.346	.000
Spokes	9.338	2	4.669	127.825	.000
2-Way Interactions	.816	4	.204	5.583	.000
Appeal Spokes	.816	4	.204	5.583	.000
Explained	69.414	8	8.677	237.555	.000
Residual	5.150	202	.037		
Total	74.564	210	.500		

```
210 cases were processed.
0 cases (0.0%) were missing.
```

An examination of the significance column indicates that both main effects are significant at a probability level of less than .001. In terms of reactions to the advertising (i.e., the AdReact measure), we can conclude that

- type of appeal influenced reactions to the commercial. An examination of the means shows that the most positive reactions were for the "Future" appeal.
- type of spokesperson affected reactions to the commercial. An examination of the means shows that the most positive reactions were for the commercial with the movie celebrity spokesperson.

However, the Analysis of Variance table also indicates that there is a statistically significant interaction between type of appeal and type of spokesperson. The combination of the two factors affects "liking" in a way that is different from the independent influence of each factor. An examination of the individual commercial means indicates that the most positive reactions to the commercial were in response to the movie spokesperson coupled with a "Future" appeal.

Having determined how AdReact varies as a function of appeal and spokesperson, we would next examine the mean and ANOVA tables for the remaining two variables, MesReact and Intent. The ANOVA table for MesReact (reactions to the message) is

```
Analysis of Variance

    MesReact
BY Appeal      Type of Commercial Appeal
   Spokes      Type of Commercial Spokesperson
```

Source of Variation	Sum of Squares	DF	Mean Square	F	Sig of F
Main Effects	28.054	4	7.013	4.438	.002
Appeal	13.414	2	6.707	4.244	.016
Spokes	1.747	2	.874	.553	.577
2-Way Interactions	3.164	4	.791	.501	.735
Appeal Spokes	3.164	4	.791	.501	.735
Explained	31.218	8	3.902	2.469	.016
Residual	222.809	202	1.580		
Total	254.027	210	1.705		

```
210 cases were processed.
0 cases (0.0%) were missing.
```

This table indicates that only one main effect, Appeal, is significant. Neither the effect of spokesperson or the interaction is significant. An examination of the means (not shown) indicates that the "Future" appeal is responded to the most positively.

```
Analysis of Variance

    Intent
BY Appeal Type of Commercial Appeal
   Spokes Type of Commercial Spokesperson
```

Source of Variation	Sum of Squares	DF	Mean Square	F	Sig of F
Main Effects	104.272	4	26.068	4.217	.003
Appeal	68.980	2	34.490	5.580	.005
Spokes	38.511	2	19.255	3.115	.047
2-Way Interactions	26.212	4	6.553	1.060	.379
Appeal Spokes	26.212	4	6.553	1.060	.379
Explained	130.484	8	16.311	2.639	.010
Residual	871.589	202	6.181		
Total	1002.073	210	6.725		

```
210 cases were processed.
0 cases (0.0%) were missing.
```

This table indicates that both main effects, Appeal and Spokesperson, have a significant effect on the target's intent to stay in school. An examination of the means (not

shown) indicates that the "Future" appeal generates the most positive intent to stay in school regardless of the spokesperson and that the movie spokesperson generates the most positive intent to stay in school regardless of appeal. There is no interaction between appeal and type of spokesperson on an individual's intent to stay in school.

Draw Conclusions

The research provides clear direction for commercial selection. In terms of each key measure:

- "Liking" is affected independently by type of appeal and by type of spokesperson. It is also affected by the interaction of these two manipulations. The best liked commercial is the one that joins a "Future" appeal with a movie spokesperson.
- Message reactions are only affected by the type of appeal. The message in the "Future" appeal is responded to the most positively. The type of spokesperson used in the ad does not affect reactions to the message.
- Intent to stay in school is affected independently by type of appeal and type of spokesperson. Intent to stay in school is the highest after seeing the "Future" appeal (regardless of spokesperson) and after seeing the commercials with movie spokespeople (regardless of appeal).

Given these findings, it appears that the commercial that combines the "Future" appeal with a "real" spokesperson shows the greatest potential.

STEP 6: CONDUCT ADDITIONAL ANALYSES FOR ADDITIONAL INSIGHTS

The analyses presented in the prior step answered the key research questions and helped us to identify the combination of appeal and spokesperson that had the greatest positive impact on the target audience in terms of three key measures: AdReact (reactions to the advertising), MesReact (reactions to the message), and Intent (intention to stay in school). The data indicated that the commercial that joins the "Future" appeal with a "real" spokesperson shows the greatest potential.

While our analysis could stop here, we always try to conduct supplemental analyses to help us maximize our understanding of what caused the results. We would, for example, perform the following analyses:

- *t* tests of AdReact, MesReact, and Intent, examining the differences (if any) in reactions to commercials between men and women.
- *t* tests of individual scale measures (Questions 4–11) among those showing positive and negative intent to stay in school after seeing the commercials to isolate those aspects of the commercials that differed between these two groups.
- *t* tests of AdReact, MesReact, and Intent, examining the differences (if any) in reactions to commercials among those whose intention to stay in school was either more or less positive after seeing the commercials.
- chi-square tests of intent to stay in school before viewing commercials among appeal groups to make certain that all groups were equivalent before seeing the commercials.
- chi-square tests of intent to stay in school before viewing commercials among spokesperson groups to make certain that all groups were equivalent before seeing the commercials.

CONCLUSION

Computers can significantly reduce the amount of time required for data analysis. However, computers are also good at quickly providing a mountain of extraneous and incorrect data. The application of computers to data analysis therefore requires patience, accuracy, verification, and a data analysis plan. When these elements are present, data analysis flows smoothly, insights into the meaning of the data are obtained, and better decisions are made.

APPENDIX

B

STATISTICAL TABLES

TABLE B1. Table of Random Numbers

159	268	549	326	459	595	025	309	573	391	291	649	206	219	605
306	597	780	216	250	211	298	862	003	598	355	100	264	559	506
135	339	583	551	119	365	207	987	562	483	295	108	369	055	530
698	145	803	669	871	035	698	025	159	365	478	980	478	536	057
102	015	668	023	687	995	103	570	157	456	320	142	025	107	309
289	106	279	856	320	219	687	510	698	408	059	209	209	419	250
068	597	894	658	981	209	320	548	774	459	982	015	369	658	015
514	028	219	354	201	256	684	753	205	367	450	219	057	304	531
368	719	025	699	642	118	479	305	692	159	356	458	852	651	025
983	302	488	665	102	362	543	655	483	025	367	495	029	321	112
259	320	589	158	025	022	368	698	459	026	308	459	652	102	325
594	668	102	259	656	362	262	459	987	859	510	269	354	102	985
110	236	987	589	620	126	320	410	259	296	036	321	259	871	219
026	039	658	620	129	981	259	307	108	873	569	584	103	608	690
891	259	875	309	658	108	657	598	874	930	092	210	264	409	395
216	029	359	259	321	029	950	548	991	029	354	856	039	549	056
036	298	852	354	569	206	348	875	595	689	258	652	250	369	208
025	698	546	250	364	210	069	540	269	358	957	720	195	036	259
563	323	339	548	795	874	159	350	059	369	584	055	479	028	024
579	320	259	656	348	971	112	205	943	622	359	549	201	268	598
489	365	269	641	025	775	452	369	651	449	236	335	025	359	157
975	026	605	248	980	365	259	651	159	358	157	581	257	268	856
156	219	324	102	029	665	123	335	778	106	982	429	563	995	872
105	326	020	574	496	982	546	459	168	697	506	250	622	059	266

Value of z	*If the value of Z is positive, then the percent of . . .* *the area below +z is* *If the value of Z is negative, then the percent of . . .* *the area above −z is*	*the area above +z is* *the area below −z is*
0.00	.5000	.5000
0.01	.5040	.4960
0.02	.5080	.4920
0.03	.5120	.4880
0.04	.5160	.4840
0.05	.5199	.4801
0.06	.5239	.4761
0.07	.5279	.4721
0.08	.5319	.4681
0.09	.5359	.4641
0.10	.5398	.4602
0.11	.5438	.4602
0.12	.5478	.4522
0.13	.5517	.4483
0.14	.5557	.4443
0.15	.5596	.4403
0.16	.5636	.4364
0.17	.5675	.4325
0.18	.5714	.4286
0.19	.5753	.4247
0.20	.5793	.4207
0.21	.5832	.1768
0.22	.5871	.4129
0.23	.5910	.4090
0.24	.5948	.4052
0.25	.5987	.4013
0.26	.6026	.3974
0.27	.6064	.3936
0.28	.6103	.3897
0.29	.6141	.3859
0.30	.6179	.3821
0.31	.6217	.3873
0.32	.6255	.3745
0.33	.6293	.3707
0.34	.6331	.3669
0.35	.6368	.3632
0.36	.6406	.3594
0.37	.6443	.3557
0.38	.6480	.3520
0.39	.6517	.3483
0.40	.6554	.3446

(continued)

Value of z	If the value of Z is positive, then the percent of... the area below +z is / If the value of Z is negative, then the percent of... the area above −z is	If the value of Z is positive, then the percent of... the area above +z is / If the value of Z is negative, then the percent of... the area below −z is
0.41	.6591	.3409
0.42	.6628	.3372
0.43	.6664	.3336
0.44	.6700	.3300
0.45	.6736	.3264
0.46	.6772	.3228
0.47	.6808	.3192
0.48	.6844	.3156
0.49	.6879	.3121
0.50	.6195	.3085
0.51	.6950	.3050
0.52	.6985	.3015
0.53	.7019	.2981
0.54	.7054	.2946
0.55	.7088	.2912
0.56	.7123	.2877
0.57	.7157	.2843
0.58	.7190	.2810
0.59	.7224	.2776
0.60	.7257	.2743
0.61	.7291	.2709
0.62	.7324	.2676
0.63	.7357	.2643
0.64	.7389	.2611
0.65	.7244	.2578
0.66	.7454	.2546
0.67	.7486	.2514
0.68	.7517	.2483
0.69	.7549	.2451
0.70	.7580	.2420
0.71	.7611	.2389
0.72	.7642	.2358
0.73	.7673	.2327
0.74	.7704	.2296
0.75	.7734	.2266
0.76	.7764	.2236
0.77	.7794	.2206
0.78	.7823	.2177
0.79	.7852	.2148
0.80	.7881	.2119
0.81	.7910	.2090

(continued)

	If the value of Z is positive, then the percent of . . .	
	the area below $+z$ is	the area above $+z$ is
	If the value of Z is negative, then the percent of . . .	
Value of z	the area above $-z$ is	the area below $-z$ is
0.82	.7939	.2061
0.83	.7697	.2033
0.84	.7995	.2005
0.85	.8023	.1977
0.86	.8051	.1949
0.87	.8078	.1922
0.88	.8106	.1894
0.89	.8133	.1867
0.90	.8159	.1841
0.91	.8186	.1814
0.92	.8212	.1788
0.93	.8238	.1762
0.94	.8264	.1736
0.95	.8289	.1711
0.96	.8315	.1685
0.97	.8340	.1660
0.98	.8365	.1635
0.99	.8389	.1611
1.00	.8413	.1587
1.01	.8438	.1562
1.02	.8461	.1539
1.03	.8485	.1515
1.04	.8508	.1492
1.05	.8531	.1469
1.06	.8554	.1446
1.07	.8577	.1423
1.08	.8599	.1401
1.09	.8621	.1379
1.10	.8643	.1357
1.11	.8665	.1335
1.12	.8686	.1314
1.13	.8708	.1392
1.14	.8729	.1271
1.15	.8749	.1251
1.16	.8770	.1230
1.17	.8790	.1210
1.18	.8810	.1190
1.19	.8830	.1170
1.20	.8849	.1151
1.21	.8869	.1131
1.22	.8888	.1112

(continued)

Value of z	*If the value of Z is positive, then the percent of . . .* the area below $+z$ is *If the value of Z is negative, then the percent of . . .* the area above $-z$ is	*the area above $+z$ is* *the area below $-z$ is*
1.23	.8907	.1093
1.24	.8925	.1075
1.25	.8944	.1056
1.26	.8962	.1038
1.27	.8980	.1020
1.28	.8997	.1003
1.29	.9018	.0985
1.30	.9032	.0968
1.31	.9049	.0951
1.32	.9066	.0934
1.33	.9082	.0918
1.34	.9099	.0901
1.35	.9115	.0885
1.36	.9131	.0869
1.37	.9147	.0853
1.38	.9162	.0838
1.39	.9177	.0823
1.40	.9192	.0808
1.41	.9207	.0793
1.42	.9222	.0778
1.43	.9236	.0764
1.44	.9251	.0749
1.45	.9265	.0735
1.46	.9279	.0721
1.47	.9292	.0708
1.48	.9306	.0694
1.49	.9319	.0681
1.50	.9332	.0668
1.51	.9345	.0655
1.52	.9357	.0643
1.53	.9370	.0630
1.54	.9382	.0618
1.55	.9394	.0606
1.56	.9406	.0594
1.57	.9418	.0582
1.58	.9429	.0571
1.59	.9441	.0559
1.60	.9452	.0548
1.61	.9463	.0537
1.62	.9474	.0526

(continued)

	If the value of Z is positive, then the percent of . . .	
	the area below +z is	the area above +z is
Value of z	If the value of Z is negative, then the percent of . . .	
	the area above −z is	the area below −z is
1.63	.9484	.0516
1.64	.9495	.0505
1.65	.9505	.0495
1.66	.9515	.0485
1.67	.9525	.0475
1.68	.9535	.0465
1.69	.9545	.0455
1.70	.9554	.0446
1.71	.9564	.0436
1.72	.9573	.0427
1.73	.9582	.0418
1.74	.9591	.0409
1.75	.9599	.0401
1.76	.9608	.0392
1.77	.9616	.0384
1.78	.9625	.0375
1.79	.9633	.0367
1.80	.9641	.0359
1.81	.9649	.0351
1.82	.9656	.0344
1.83	.9664	.0336
1.84	.9671	.0329
1.85	.9678	.0322
1.86	.9686	.0314
1.87	.9693	.0307
1.88	.9699	.0301
1.89	.9706	.0294
1.90	.9713	.0287
1.91	.9719	.0281
1.92	.9719	.0281
1.93	.9732	.0268
1.94	.9738	.0262
1.95	.9744	.0256
1.96	.9750	.0250
1.97	.9756	.0244
1.98	.9761	.0239
1.99	.9767	.0233
2.00	.9772	.0228
2.01	.9778	.0222
2.02	.9783	.0217

(continued)

Value of z	**If the value of Z is positive, then the percent of . . .** the area below +z is / **If the value of Z is negative, then the percent of . . .** the area above −z is	**If the value of Z is positive, then the percent of . . .** the area above +z is / **If the value of Z is negative, then the percent of . . .** the area below −z is
2.03	.9788	.0212
2.04	.9793	.0207
2.05	.9798	.0202
2.06	.9803	.0197
2.07	.9808	.0192
2.08	.9812	.0188
2.09	.9817	.0183
2.10	.9821	.0179
2.11	.9826	.0174
2.12	.9830	.0170
2.13	.9834	.0166
2.14	.9838	.0162
2.15	.9842	.0158
2.16	.9846	.0154
2.17	.9850	.0150
2.18	.9854	.0146
2.19	.9857	.0143
2.20	.9861	.0139
2.21	.9864	.0136
2.22	.9868	.0132
2.23	.9871	.0129
2.24	.9875	.0125
2.25	.9878	.0122
2.26	.9881	.0119
2.27	.9884	.0116
2.28	.9887	.0113
2.29	.9890	.0110
2.30	.9893	.0107
2.31	.9896	.0104
2.32	.9898	.0102
2.33	.9901	.0099
2.34	.9904	.0096
2.35	.9906	.0094
2.36	.9909	.0091
2.37	.9911	.0089
2.38	.9913	.0087
2.39	.9916	.0084
2.40	.9918	.0082
2.41	.9920	.0080
2.42	.9922	.0078

(continued)

Value of z	If the value of Z is positive, then the percent of... the area below +z is / If the value of Z is negative, then the percent of... the area above −z is	If the value of Z is positive, then the percent of... the area above +z is / If the value of Z is negative, then the percent of... the area below −z is
2.43	.9925	.0075
2.44	.9927	.0073
2.45	.9929	.0071
2.46	.9931	.0069
2.47	.9932	.0068
2.48	.9934	.0066
2.49	.9936	.0064
2.50	.9938	.0062
2.51	.9940	.0060
2.52	.9941	.0059
2.53	.9943	.0057
2.54	.9945	.0055
2.55	.9946	.0054
2.56	.9948	.0052
2.57	.9949	.0051
2.58	.9951	.0049
2.59	.9952	.0048
2.60	.9953	.0047
2.61	.9955	.0045
2.62	.9956	.0044
2.63	.9957	.0043
2.64	.9959	.0041
2.65	.9960	.0040
2.66	.9961	.0039
2.67	.9962	.0038
2.68	.9963	.0037
2.69	.9964	.0036
2.70	.9965	.0035
2.71	.9966	.0034
2.72	.9967	.0033
2.73	.9968	.0032
2.74	.9969	.0031
2.75	.9970	.0030
2.76	.9971	.0029
2.77	.9972	.0028
2.78	.9973	.0027
2.79	.9974	.0026
2.80	.9974	.0026
2.81	.9975	.0025
2.82	.9976	.0024

(continued)

TABLE B2. *(continued)*

Value of z	*If the value of Z is positive, then the percent of . . .* the area below +z is *If the value of Z is negative, then the percent of . . .* the area above −z is	*the area above +z is* *the area below −z is*
2.83	.9977	.0023
2.84	.9977	.0023
2.85	.9978	.0022
2.86	.9979	.0021
2.87	.9979	.0021
2.88	.9980	.0020
2.89	.9981	.0019
2.90	.9981	.0019
2.91	.9982	.0018
2.92	.9982	.0018
2.93	.9983	.0017
2.94	.9984	.0016
2.95	.9984	.0016
2.96	.9985	.0015
2.97	.9985	.0015
2.98	.9986	.0014
2.99	.9986	.0014
3.00	.9987	.0013
3.05	.9989	.0011
3.10	.9990	.0010
3.15	.9992	.0008
3.20	.9993	.0007
3.25	.9994	.0006
3.30	.9995	.0005
3.35	.9996	.0004
3.40	.9997	.0003
3.45	.9997	.0003
3.50	.9998	.0002

TABLE B3. Critical Values of the t Distribution

Degrees of Freedom	One-Tail Test: Probability (Alpha =)			
	.05	.025	.005	.0005
	Two-Tail Test: Probability (Alpha =)			
	.10	.05	.01	.001
1	6.314	12.706	63.657	636.620
2	2.920	4.303	9.925	31.598
3	2.353	3.187	5.841	12.924
4	2.132	2.776	4.604	8.610
5	2.015	2.571	4.032	6.869
6	1.943	2.447	3.707	5.959
7	1.895	2.365	3.499	5.408
8	1.860	2.306	3.355	5.041
9	1.833	2.262	3.250	4.781
10	1.812	2.228	3.169	4.537
11	1.796	2.201	3.106	4.437
12	1.782	2.179	3.055	4.318
13	1.771	2.160	3.012	4.221
14	1.761	2.145	2.977	4.140
15	1.753	2.131	2.947	4.073
16	1.746	2.120	2.921	4.015
17	1.740	2.110	2.898	3.965
18	1.734	2.101	2.878	3.922
19	1.729	2.093	2.861	3.883
20	1.725	2.086	2.845	3.850
21	1.721	2.080	2.831	3.186
22	1.717	2.074	2.819	3.792
23	1.714	2.069	2.807	3.767
24	1.711	2.064	2.797	3.745
25	1.708	2.060	2.787	3.725
26	1.706	2.056	2.779	3.707
27	1.703	2.052	2.771	3.690
28	1.701	2.048	2.763	3.674
29	1.699	2.045	2.756	3.659
30	1.697	2.042	2.750	3.646
40	1.684	2.021	2.704	3.551
60	1.671	2.000	2.660	3.460
120	1.658	1.980	2.617	3.373
∞	1.645	1.960	2.576	3.291

TABLE B4. Critical Values of the Chi-Square Distribution

Degrees of Freedom	*Chi-square Value Required to Obtain a Probability Level (Alpha =)*			
	.10	*.05*	*.01*	*.001*
1	2.71	3.84	6.64	10.83
2	4.61	5.99	9.21	13.81
3	6.25	7.82	11.34	16.27
4	7.78	9.49	13.28	18.47
5	9.24	11.07	15.09	20.52
6	10.65	12.59	16.81	22.46
7	12.02	14.07	18.48	24.32
8	13.36	15.51	20.09	26.13
9	14.68	16.62	21.67	27.88
10	15.99	19.31	23.21	29.59
11	17.28	19.68	24.72	31.26
12	18.55	21.03	26.22	32.91
13	19.81	22.36	27.69	34.53
14	21.06	23.69	29.14	36.12
15	22.31	25.00	30.58	37.70
16	23.54	26.30	32.00	39.25
17	24.77	27.59	33.41	40.79
18	25.99	28.87	34.81	42.31
19	27.20	30.14	36.19	43.82
20	28.41	31.41	37.57	45.32
21	29.62	32.67	38.93	46.80
22	30.81	33.92	40.29	48.27
23	32.01	35.17	41.64	49.73
24	33.20	36.42	42.98	51.18
25	34.38	37.65	44.31	52.62
26	35.56	38.89	45.64	54.05
27	36.74	40.11	46.96	55.48
28	37.92	41.38	48.28	56.89
29	39.09	42.56	49.59	58.30
30	40.26	43.77	50.89	59.70
40	51.81	55.76	63.69	73.40
50	63.17	67.51	76.15	86.66
60	74.40	79.08	88.38	99.61
70	85.53	90.53	100.43	112.32
80	96.58	101.88	112.33	124.84
90	107.57	113.14	124.12	137.21
100	118.50	124.34	135.81	149.44

TABLE B5. Critical Values of the Pearson Correlation Coefficient

Degrees of Freedom	One-Tail Test: Probability (Alpha =) .025	One-Tail Test: Probability (Alpha =) .005
	Two-Tail Test: Probability (Alpha =) .05	Two-Tail Test: Probability (Alpha =) .01
1	.997	1.000
2	.950	.990
3	.878	.959
4	.811	.917
5	.754	.874
6	.707	.834
7	.666	.798
8	.632	.765
9	.602	.735
10	.576	.708
11	.553	.684
12	.532	.661
13	.514	.641
14	.497	.623
15	.482	.606
16	.468	.590
17	.456	.575
18	.444	.561
19	.433	.549
20	.432	.537
21	.413	.526
22	.404	.515
23	.396	.505
24	.388	.496
25	.381	.487
26	.374	.479
27	.367	.471
28	.361	.463
29	.355	.486
30	.349	.449
40	.304	.393
50	.273	.354
60	.250	.325
70	.232	.303
80	.217	.283
90	.205	.267
100	.195	.254

Index